George Coulson Workman

The Text of Jeremiah

Or, a critical investigation of the Greek and Hebrew: with the variations in the LXX

retranslated into the original and explained

George Coulson Workman

The Text of Jeremiah
Or, a critical investigation of the Greek and Hebrew: with the variations in the LXX retranslated into the original and explained

ISBN/EAN: 9783337419400

Printed in Europe, USA, Canada, Australia, Japan

Cover: Foto ©Lupo / pixelio.de

More available books at **www.hansebooks.com**

THE TEXT OF JEREMIAH;

OR,

A CRITICAL INVESTIGATION OF THE GREEK AND HEBREW,
WITH THE VARIATIONS IN THE LXX. RETRANSLATED
INTO THE ORIGINAL AND EXPLAINED.

BY THE

Rev. GEORGE COULSON WORKMAN, M.A.,

PROFESSOR OF OLD TESTAMENT EXEGESIS AND LITERATURE IN
VICTORIA UNIVERSITY, COBOURG, ONT., CANADA.

WITH

An Introductory Notice

BY

Professor FRANZ DELITZSCH, D.D.

EDINBURGH:
T. & T. CLARK, 38 GEORGE STREET.
1889.

TO

MY VENERABLE AND VALUED FRIEND,

PROFESSOR FRANZ DELITZSCH, D.D.

OF THE

UNIVERSITY OF LEIPZIG,

IN ADMIRATION OF

HIS DEEP PIETY AND PROFOUND SCHOLARSHIP,

THIS BOOK IS DEDICATED

AS A TOKEN OF

GRATITUDE AND AFFECTION.

CONTENTS.

	PAGE
PREFACE, ...	ix
INTRODUCTORY NOTICE, ...	xv
PRELIMINARY OBSERVATIONS, . . .	xxiii

CHAPTER I.
THE RELATION OF THE VERSION, ... 1

CHAPTER II.
THE VARIATIONS—OMISSIONS, ... 18

CHAPTER III.
THE VARIATIONS—ADDITIONS, . 70

CHAPTER IV.
THE VARIATIONS—TRANSPOSITIONS, . . . 95

CHAPTER V.
THE VARIATIONS—ALTERATIONS, . 135

CHAPTER VI.
THE VARIATIONS—SUBSTITUTIONS, . . 155

CHAPTER VII.

THE ORIGIN OF THE VARIATIONS, . . . 182

CHAPTER VIII.

THE CHARACTER OF THE TRANSLATION, . . . 210

CHAPTER IX.

THE RESULTS OF THE INVESTIGATION, . 229

CHAPTER X.

THE CONSPECTUS OF THE VARIATIONS, . . . 283

CORRECTION.

Omit "bride" and "bridegroom," chap. vii. 34, on page 129, lines 15, 16 from the top.

PREFACE.

As intimated on the title-page, the present volume is an earnest attempt to solve the difficult problem of the variations between the Greek and Hebrew texts of Jeremiah. Besides discussing the condition and relation of the texts, and explaining the nature and origin of the divergences between them, I have endeavoured to deduce the fundamental principles of deviation, by the application of which the Septuagint translation reveals important matter, as well for the Hebrew grammar and the Hebrew lexicon, as for the history, the interpretation, the correction, and the reconstruction of the present Massoretic text.

Although the latter portion of the work has been prepared exclusively for scholars, the former and by far the larger portion of it has been prepared, as well for general as for special students of the Old Testament. It is intended to be used by all who have an interest in the critical condition of the Scripture text. For this reason, the entire discussion has been written in such a style that any one, whether acquainted with Greek and Hebrew or not, may read it easily and intelligently. Having aimed throughout at plainness and perspicuity, I have purposely avoided, so far as practicable, the use of purely technical language, and have everywhere explained the terms and translated the words and expressions, which an ordinary English reader might not reasonably be expected to understand.

In trying to recover the original of the Septuagint by the process of retranslation, I have been encouraged by many competent judges to believe that the method I have adopted for exhibiting the deviations to the best advantage will be regarded as both convenient and important, inasmuch as it not only presents concisely a general view of the divergences in this book, but also indicates clearly how the same kind of service may be performed for the other books of Jewish Scripture. A very small amount of work has hitherto been done in this department. Without a guide, therefore, in a comparatively untrodden field, I have striven to beat out a path which other investigators may tread more confidently than I have dared, and more successfully, perhaps, than I have hoped, to tread myself.

Owing to the extent of this prophetic book, comprising, as it does, almost a twelfth part of the whole Old Testament, the work has naturally cost a great expenditure of time and toil. After nearly three years and a half of patient and painstaking study, in connection with other absorbing and exacting duties, having been engaged at this inquiry since the summer of 1885, I am aware that it is still, in some respects, deficient as well as incomplete. Much more time might have been devoted advantageously to the investigation. A longer study would have enabled me more thoroughly to weigh difficult and doubtful words, more fully to discuss personal and proper names, and more copiously to illustrate generic and specific kinds of deviation.

Many important features of the Septuagint, moreover, have been briefly indicated in a paragraph or two that might have been abundantly exemplified by striking and convincing illustrations; but the want of time and the fear of making too large a volume have deterred me from multiplying examples. I have spared no pains, however, to make the work as thorough as its compass would permit. The results of my researches, therefore, are modestly submitted to Biblical scholars and students for careful and unprejudiced consideration, with the consciousness that, had more time and study been allowed, they might have been much more complete, but also with the conviction that, inexhaustive as they are, they will be found to be a serviceable contribution to the science of Old Testament text-criticism.

Several distinguished scholars have desired to see the Septuagint text of Jeremiah entirely re-translated into Hebrew. Having often been advised by persons of experience to publish a complete and accurate retranslation of the book, as soon as an opportunity for investigating the Greek manuscripts may be afforded, I shall esteem it a great favour if practised critics, after an examination of the work, will have the kindness to give me any suggestions that may occur to them, particularly in the way of indicating imperfections, or of pointing out improvements.

While personally responsible for the views advanced, the positions maintained, and the conclusions reached throughout the whole discussion, I desire, in this place, to express my deep gratitude to all who have assisted me in any respect with the investigation. My grateful acknowledgments are especially due for kind advice and constant interest during the preparation of the work to Professor Franz Delitzsch, D.D., the eminent Old Testament commentator; for useful suggestions and valuable services in the process of retranslation to Dr. S. Mandelkern, the excellent Hebrew specialist; for careful and conscientious help in comparing the

Targum of Jonathan with the Septuagint translation, and in revising the manuscript of the variations for the press, to Dr. M. Chamizer, the able Literary Manager of the famous Oriental printing-house of W. Drugulin, Leipzig, where the last chapter of the work was composed and stereotyped.

Although the terms of notation or abbreviation employed throughout the last chapter are few and simple, yet it may be worth while giving, in this connection, a brief explanation of them. In the text, "Deest" indicates the absence from the Septuagint of the word or words standing opposite to it, and "Desunt," the absence from the same of the words or verses opposite to which it stands. In the footnotes, "Cf." refers to a similar reading, and "ut" to an identical reading, in the Hebrew; "Vid." refers to a similar or like rendering in the Greek; "Inc." denotes a different verse-division in the version; "Targ." stands for the Targum of Jonathan; "Alex." for the Alexandrian Codex, and "Aram." for Aramaic.

The volume is now given to the world with the hope that it may prove an interest-awakening and a science-furthering investigation. In so far as this discussion of one of the most complicated questions of Old Testament interpretation shall stimulate the spirit of Scriptural inquiry or help the progress of Biblical criticism, and thus promote the cause of sacred truth of which the prophet Jeremiah was a powerful and uncompromising preacher, my reverent researches will be rewarded, and my earnest wishes realized.

G. C. WORKMAN.

LEIPZIG, *January* 1889.

INTRODUCTORY NOTICE

BY

PROFESSOR DELITZSCH.

There is no prophetic life and no prophetic book, of which so many details are known to us, as the life of Jeremiah and the collection of his prophecies. We know that this prophet twice dictated his prophecies to his amanuensis, Baruch, as Paul the Epistle to the Romans to Tertius; that king Jehoiakim burned one roll, and that Jeremiah then prepared a new and, according to chap. xxxvi. 32, a greatly enlarged edition, which, perhaps, was left unfinished, to be gradually completed. It was possibly concluded in Egypt either by the prophet himself or by his secretary, Baruch; but that we do not know. This, however, is certain, that the collection of prophecies, as it now stands before us, has not the form which it finally received from Jeremiah, or from his faithful servant. The original arrangement must have been another and a different one, because the present order of the component parts of the book amongst themselves gives the impression of an arbitrary and a confused disarrangement. Besides, this later redaction or revision shows itself to be such by insertions from the book of the Kings. But even the form which the later redactor gave the collection is not perfectly preserved. Chap. xxvi. 17 was evidently not written by the redactor of the collection. It betrays itself at once as a later and a very misleading insertion. In chap. xl. 1, a divine revelation to Jeremiah is announced, but no such communication follows. It seems that here chaps. xxx., xxxi. have got out of their right place. The expression וְיָעֵפוּ ("and they shall be weary"), in chap. li. 64, is manifestly repeated from ver. 58. The historical piece, vers. 59–64, therefore, may originally have occupied another position in this prophetic book.

From what standpoint the prophet's last edition was arranged we do not know, but the singular disarrangement, by which the later redactor has destroyed the original arrangement, nevertheless, cannot be purely arbitrary or absolutely thoughtless. The considerations by which he was governed, or the principles by which he was guided, must certainly be penetrable. But, so far as I can survey the literature of the interpretation and explanation of the book, no one, as yet, has been successful in finding out the point of view from which the later redactor has torn to pieces things which chronologically and essentially belong to each other, and has placed them together, as they now appear. J. J. Staehelin in his discussion of the arrangement of Jeremiah's prophecies divides the book into seven parts,[1] and Anton Scholz in his monograph on the relation between the Greek and Hebrew texts of Jeremiah divides it into six decades;[2] but neither in Staehelin's seven nor in Scholz's six divisions is a planned unity of contents perceptible. As for me, I flatter myself with the opinion, that I may have succeeded in discovering the views which influenced the redactor.

The collection of Jeremiah's prophecies, as it now lies before us, according to my opinion, falls into nine groups or books of which each three, in a certain sense, form a trilogy, and that, indeed, in the following manner:— **1.** The book of the time of Josiah, or of the calling and first preaching of the prophet, chaps. i.-vi. **2.** The book of the time of Jehoiakim, or the preaching at the gate of the Temple, in the cities of Judah (Anathoth), and in the streets of Jerusalem, especially concerning the idolatry of the people, chaps. vii. - xii. **3.** The book of the irrevocable curse, belonging to the

---

[1] *Zeitschrift der deutschen Morgenländischen Gesellschaft*, t. iii., 1849, p. 216.
[2] *Der masorethische Text und die LXX - Uebersetzung des Buches Jeremias*, 1875.

time of Jeconiah, chaps. xiii. – xx. Hereupon follow the three middle groups. **4.** The book against the shepherds of the people, without chronological arrangement, chaps. xxi. – xxv. **5.** The book of the conflict of Jeremiah with the false prophets, belonging partly to the time of Jehoiakim and partly to the first years of Zedekiah, chaps. xxvi. – xxix. Here along with Jeremiah, as true prophets, are mentioned the elder Micah and the contemporary Uriah; and, as false prophets, Hananiah, Ahab, Zedekiah, and Shemaiah, the warning against false prophets in chap. xxvii. constituting a keynote. **6.** The book of the restoration of Israel, without chronological arrangement, chaps. xxx.–xxxiii. The remaining three groups form the conclusion of the collection. **7.** The book of the accounts of the unbelief and scepticism of the kings and of the people of Israel. accounts belonging to the time of Jehoiakim, and encompassed by incidents of the time of Zedekiah, chaps. xxxiv.–xxxviii. **8.** The book of the destinies of the people after the destruction of Jerusalem, chaps. xxxix.–xlv., with the supplementary notice respecting Baruch, chap. xlv., standing in un-chronological position. **9.** The book of the prophecies concerning the nations, a decade of oracles, beginning with Egypt and ending with Babylon, chaps. xlvi. – li., belonging partly to the time of

Jehoiakim, chaps. xl.–xlix. 33, and partly to the time of Zedekiah, chaps. xlix. 34–39; l.–li.

This is, as I think, the distribution aimed at by the redactor of our Hebrew text of Jeremiah. Such seem to me to have been the motives which impelled him to destroy the ancient order of the general contents of the book, and to substitute the present singular arrangement. I dare venture to hope that my results will bear examination. All kind of questions respecting the incorrect position, which many sections of the book appear to occupy, admit of a solution in this way. The outpouring of the intoxicating cup, chap. xxv., which is properly the exordium to book **9**, stands in book **4**, because the doom therein pronounced embraces all the shepherds (rulers) of the nations. The scourging of idolatry, chap. x. 1–16, stands in book **2**, because in that book the prophet's preaching is preëminently directed against the idol-worship of the people, chaps. vii. 18, 31; viii. 2. The section, which relates the conspiracy to take the prophet's life, because of his preaching against the Temple and the City, in the beginning of Jehoiakim's reign, chap. xxvi., although it belongs to the history of the prophetic discourse in chaps. vii.–xii., stands in book **5**, because it relates a part of Jeremiah's struggle with the priests, the prophets, and the princes. The history of the burning recension. I also regard the version as of very great importance for the history and the criticism of the Old Testament text.

The present investigation transports the question respecting the nature and origin of the variations in the prophecy of Jeremiah to an entirely new stage, inasmuch, especially, as it presents a complete and comprehensive view of the differences between the Greek and Hebrew texts in a way in which it hitherto has never been presented. The author thereby contributes to the science of Biblical criticism a work of valuable and lasting service. This production of my friend is the fruit of several years of indefatigable labour; and, if he sometimes thinks too favourably of the Septuagint translator, this is only the result of the loving devotion with which he has absorbed himself in the study of the Alexandrian text.

FRANZ DELITZSCH.

LEIPZIG, *December* 1888.

PRELIMINARY OBSERVATIONS.

A CRITICAL investigation of any Old Testament writing involves particularly a fourfold inquiry. It embraces a thorough discussion of the character and condition of the present Hebrew or Massoretic text, and a careful consideration of the nature and importance of the other textual authorities. Of the latter there are principally four, namely, the Aramaic, the Syriac, the Latin, and the Greek translations. Each of these possesses some significance, and furnishes some materials for the lower or textual criticism of the Hebrew Scriptures; but the Greek translation, commonly called the Septuagint, or the Alexandrian version, is universally regarded as by far the most important of them all. Because of its age and influence, scholars in general are agreed that the Septuagint translation constitutes the principal aid for the Biblical critic in the textual work of the Old Testament. Hence the need of determining, as nearly as possible, its true nature and its real worth.

In undertaking to investigate the text of Jeremiah by the help of the Septuagint, one is confronted at the outset with the character of the deviations in the version. The differences between the Greek and Hebrew are so numerous and so striking, that the question of their origin challenges immediate attention. The first thing necessary, therefore, in commencing a comparative study of the two texts, is an honest endeavour to solve the problem of the divergences between them. Not till this has been accomplished, can the Septuagint be safely or intelligently employed in the textual criticism of this prophetic book. Before attempting a solution of the problem, it will be expedient to explain the plan proposed in the present inquiry for this purpose.

In order the more completely to exhibit the character of the version, as well as the more clearly to account for its deviations, the method here adopted is that of retranslation; that is, of translating the Greek back again into Hebrew. By this means it can be shown, substantially at least, just what sort of text the original Hebrew manuscript of the Alexandrian version must have been. By this means, too, the nature and origin of the variations, it is believed, can be most readily demonstrated, the differences between the Greek and Hebrew most easily appreciated, and the importance of the Septuagint for purposes of text-criticism most accurately estimated.

In the complete Conspectus of the variations at the end of the work, the divergences are arranged in parallel columns, the divergent words, or letters only, so far as practicable, being punctuated. In this way the differences between the two texts become manifest at once. The right-hand column contains the deviations from the Greek in the Hebrew; the left-hand column contains the deviations from the Hebrew in the Greek, retranslated into Hebrew. If the words in the latter be systematically substituted for those in the former, and carefully inserted where they logically belong in the present Massoretic text, the original of the version may be promptly and approximately obtained. This method has the advantage of giving a concise and comprehensive view of the variations without repeating subject-matter common to each text alike, except in so far as such a repetition is necessary in order to display the variations clearly and conspicuously.

An important rule observed in retranslating, it should be stated, is that of endeavouring to explain the minor variations by means of similar Hebrew letters. Wherever there seemed to be the slightest reason for believing that the original of the one text was substantially, if not identically, the same as the original of the other, an effort has been made to find a resembling substitute. The constant observance of this rule has been most advantageous in discovering the various principles of divergency deduced and illustrated in the accompanying discussion. But for its systematic application, several fundamental illustrations could scarcely have been ascertained. As the arrangement of the Greek words follows almost slavishly the Hebrew order, even to the reproduction of the smallest particles and the most peculiar idioms, the intensely literal character of the Septuagint translation has helped materially in applying this simple but extremely essential rule.

Notwithstanding the extreme literalness of the translation, however, it is often difficult to tell whether an apparent deviation in the version represents a real deviation in the original manuscript. For this reason, many doubtful words in Greek are indicated in connection with the Conspectus of the variations. Sometimes, too, it is difficult to determine whether or not a peculiar Greek expression represents a variant Hebrew reading; and, if it does, it is practically impossible to tell how it should be retranslated. One example out of several that might be given is found in chap. xlix. 16, where the combination ἡ παιγνία σου ἐνεχείρησέ σοι, stands for תִּפְלַצְתְּךָ הִשִּׁיא אֹתָךְ ("thy terribleness hath deceived thee"). The Hebrew word translated "terribleness" does not elsewhere occur throughout the Bible, and its exact signification here is exceedingly obscure. In all such cases of obscurity, Hebrew scholars will be able to appreciate the great perplexity experienced very frequently in the work of retranslation.

As in the English, so also in the Alexandrian, version, the same expression, even in a similar connection, is not uniformly translated. This want of uniformity greatly increases the difficulty of retranslation, because the same word, or the same combination of words, is differently rendered by different translators in different books, as well as in different parts of the same book. Although in general this book is characterized by great consistency in the use of many specific terms, yet sufficient irregularity appears in certain portions of it to justify the supposition that several persons were employed in making the Greek version. For these reasons, as doubt was frequently inevitable and certainty sometimes impracticable, the retranslation of very many words and phrases must be regarded as tentative, and not in any sense as final. In all such instances of uncertainty, other investigators might give another and, perhaps, a happier rendering of the Greek.

Even in passages where a special textual arrangement in the version is unquestionable, it is by no means easy always to determine which expression should be used in retranslating from the Greek, since one must choose between two and three and sometimes four synonymous Hebrew words. As the choice requires the exercise of both taste and skill, alternatives have often been presented for the consideration of those experienced in this kind of criticism. In the case of a word of rare or single occurrence, it is practically, if not absolutely, impossible to decide with certainty. A simple example of perplexity occurs in the opening sentence of the book, which, in the Septuagint, reads, Τὸ ῥῆμα τοῦ Θεοῦ ὃ ἐγένετο ἐπὶ Ἰερεμίαν. In this superscription, which forms a common introduction to the prophetic books, as may be seen by reference to Hosea, Joel, Micah, Zephaniah, and which reproduces an original Hebrew text, as every competent critic will perceive, it is quite uncertain whether the expression Τὸ ῥῆμα τοῦ Θεοῦ should be rendered דְּבַר־יְהֹוָה (the word of Jehovah) or דְּבַר־אֱלֹהִים (the word of God). Inasmuch as the latter, so far as has been ascertained, nowhere else occurs in such a superscription, the former has been given in the Conspectus of the variations. The Alexandrian introduction, though, may be translated, "The word of God (or, the word Jehovah) which was to Jeremiah."

When quoting from the English Bible, it will be seen, the Revised Version, except in a few cases of verbal translation, has always been used; but, when translating from the Septuagint, it will be observed, a literal rendering of the Greek text has invariably been given. The Greek word κύριος, which generally represents the Hebrew word יְהֹוָה, has been regularly translated by the English word "Jehovah." The term in Hebrew is not a divine title, but a divine name, and, therefore, should be literally reproduced. Not only is "Jehovah" a tolerably accurate, though very debatable, reproduction in English of the present Hebrew word, but also it is an euphonious word which has long become naturalized in the language. This pronunciation of this name of the Deity, moreover, has been in circulation, more or less extensively, since the sixteenth century, at least. For these reasons, it seems to be quite expedient to retain the common form of the old English word.

By way of distinguishing the Hebrew phrase אָמַר יְהוָה ("says Jehovah") from נְאֻם־יְהוָה ("a declaration of Jehovah"), which throughout this book is usually represented by the Greek λέγει κύριος or εἶπε κύριος, the latter Hebrew phrase has been regularly translated by "declares Jehovah." The word נְאֻם, which is a passive participle in the construct state used as a substantive, is so uniformly rendered in the Septuagint as a verb that it may, perhaps, have been so considered by the Greek translators, who render it as though it was formerly pronounced נָאַם, and employed as an emphatic synonym for אָמַר. Whether probable or not, the supposition is here suggested as being possible, at least. The words in Hebrew are not identical, as the rendering of them in the English versions might seem to ordinary readers to imply, and there appears to be a great propriety in observing the true distinction between them, when giving an exact translation of them.

The Greek text used throughout the present work is that of Tischendorf, this having been esteemed the best edition of the Septuagint available at the time that the investigation was commenced. The Hebrew text employed is Hahn's edition of van der Hooght. When citing Hebrew words, the Massoretic pointing has generally been reproduced, wherever a point of punctuation or of accentuation might be regarded as really essential; but wherever such a point might be regarded as purely euphonic, its reproduction has not always been observed. This remark, of course, applies to the use of the signs for aspirate-letters and tone-syllables. It should be noted further that in exhibiting the different kinds or classes of variation, several examples have been once or twice repeated, because the same example sometimes illustrates two and three different species of divergency.

The last chapter of the work, which comprises the Conspectus of the variations, is so arranged as to constitute a kind of critical apparatus, by means of which Biblical critics may examine the full results of the investigation in detail, and by the use of which they may apply the different principles of variation to the textual criticism of the other Hebrew Scriptures. The footnotes in this chapter contain references to parallel passages and analogous constructions, both in this book and in other books of the Old Testament; citations from the Targum, when it either agrees with or corresponds to the Septuagint translation; doubtful and peculiar words and phrases in the Greek, which seem to possess a special interest; a few readings from the Alexandrian manuscript, which appear to be of some importance; and an occasional Aramaic word, which suggests the possible origin of a deviation in the version.

In discussing the character and condition of the present Hebrew text, an endeavour has been made, first to ascertain the facts, and then to let these speak for themselves. Indeed, throughout the whole investigation the scientific or comparative method has been employed. This method has already been successfully applied to physical and to philological science, and it may be as properly, if not as fruitfully, applied to Biblical as to any other science. All true theories must be formed from facts, tested with facts, and established by facts. Sweeping generalizations from insufficient data, or from superficial knowledge of them, are utterly valueless. Only by collecting all the evidence available can sound principles be deduced or safe inferences drawn.

From copious internal evidence it must with disappointment be admitted that the character of the Massoretic text of Jeremiah is deplorably unsatisfactory. This text is both imperfect and defective. Its imperfections have long been recognized by most impartial critics, and its defects are now acknowledged by every competent scholar. The question of its absolute integrity or infallibility is no longer a matter of debate. Difficulties and obscurities abound all through the book. As the Hebrew stands at present, it is often hard either to give a tolerable translation of it, or to obtain an intelligible meaning from it. Of many passages more than one rendering is fairly possible; and of many other passages an adequate rendering or interpretation is practically impossible.

From ample external evidence, moreover, the condition of the Hebrew text is also exceedingly unsatisfactory. It can be proved conclusively to have suffered not only from corruption, but also from alteration. In many ways and at different times it has unquestionably undergone considerable change. Apart from manifest alterations, transpositions, interpolations and revisions, the independent testimony of each ancient version, especially of the Septuagint translation, establishes this fact beyond a doubt. A critical comparison of the Greek and Hebrew shows clearly that the latter text has been extensively and systematically modified. Such a comparison further shows that the ancient manuscript, from which the original of the Massoretic text was taken, differed essentially from that now known to us, as well as materially from that known to the makers of the Alexandrian version.

It has been commonly supposed that the chief sources of textual divergency between the Greek and Hebrew were either the caprice and ignorance of translators, or the carelessness and indifference of copyists. For this reason, the variations have been hitherto attributed, partly to accident but principally to design. The supposition seems both unreasonable and incredible. Such surprising deviations as occur throughout the version must have had a worthy origin. If the Alexandrian translators were authoritatively employed to make a version of the Hebrew Scriptures, as has been generally held, it is natural to suppose that they were properly qualified for their duties, as well as reasonable to believe that they honestly performed their work. Assuming in this investigation the efficiency and integrity of the Greek translators, the facts collected and the principles deduced demonstrate the hypothesis of a special text, or text-recension, as it is technically termed, from which the Septuagint translation was originally made. No other explanation of the divergences, it can be shown, is either adequate or admissible.

Since, in several other Old Testament books, the Greek text differs greatly from the Hebrew text, it may be asked, as Graf, for instance, asks, Why should the hypothesis of a special text-recension be assumed simply for this book, and not for those other books in which divergences abound? In reply, it may be stated that the variations in the present book are exceptionally numerous and significant, and that their number, as well as their nature, establishes the truth of the hypothesis respecting their origin. The same hypothesis, though, it may be added, seems to be just as probable in reference to Daniel, Esther, Job, and Proverbs, as in reference to Jeremiah. Only on this assumption can the variations in each of these books be satisfactorily explained. Indeed, the same hypothesis possibly may, and probably does, apply to each book of the Old Testament.

The theory of different text-recensions of the

ancient Jewish Scriptures is rapidly and rationally finding favour. In their Preface to the Revised Version of the Hebrew Bible, the English translators openly acknowledge its reasonableness and probability. "The Received or, as it is commonly called, the Massoretic text of the Old Testament Scriptures," they say, "has come down to us in manuscripts which are of no very great antiquity, and which all belong to the same family or recension. That other recensions were at one time in existence is probable from the variations in the Ancient Versions, the oldest of which, namely the Greek or Septuagint, was made, at least in part, some two centuries before the Christian era."

This assertion of the Revisers is exceedingly important, inasmuch as an unreasonable prejudice against such an assumption has hitherto prevailed. There has been a great reluctance, on the part of Christian scholars in the past, to acknowledge that the Septuagint translators could have used a Hebrew text different from that which the Massorites employed. The proofs, though, are so overwhelming that the conclusion is inevitable. That there were certainly two recensions of the book of Jeremiah, at the time of its translation into Greek, when all the facts are considered, and when all the evidence is weighed, cannot be reasonably doubted. That this was possibly the case respecting many, if not all, of the other books of the Old Testament may be just as reasonably believed. The ancient circumstances of the Jewish people and the early condition of their sacred writings render the supposition not simply possible but probable.

During the present investigation, the thought has often been suggested that, instead of two, there may have once been several recensions of certain books, at least. Just how many it is useless to conjecture. There appear to have been Scripture rolls for public services, for official purposes, and for private use. Different distinguished individuals, as well as families, may have possessed a copy. The probability of this suggestion, which partially explains how variations might gradually and naturally arise, is strengthened by the statement of a recent writer in an able article on the Revised Version of the Old Testament. Speaking of the ancient documents and rolls, of which the existing Hebrew manuscripts present a later revision of the sacred text, which has restored to it the greater purity in which it now appears in contrast to the versions, he asserts, "We are expressly informed that there were standard copies kept in the Temple, perhaps also in some synagogues. This would not exclude, rather it seems to imply, the existence of diverging readings in manuscripts belonging to families or individuals."[1]

In considering the nature of the Septuagint, the purpose has been, so far as possible, to let the translation tell its own story. An unprejudiced examination of the Greek text shows the groundlessness of the charge of arbitrariness generally

[1] *Edinburgh Review*, October, 1885, p. 460.

brought against the Alexandrian translators, and the inadequacy of the opinion popularly entertained respecting the character of their work. That they sometimes made mistakes, considering the circumstances of their time, was natural. With all their practised skill, the Massorites have also made mistakes. That they sometimes translated conjecturally, considering the condition of their manuscript, was inevitable. Rather than change the sacred text, modern translators have also done the same. In rendering obscurely written parchment rolls no other course could be pursued. The very mistakes and imperfections of the version, most of which can be with almost scientific certainty explained, attest the genuine integrity of the Greek translators and the exceeding conscientiousness with which their arduous labours were performed.

When indicating the importance of the Septuagint, no undue excellence has been intentionally claimed for it. If a preference for its general textual arrangement has been emphatically expressed, this has been because it really appears to possess the preference in this respect. Only a few of its more striking features of superiority have been pointed out. Beautiful illustrations of superior reading might have been many times increased, but space forbade the multiplying of examples. A sufficient number has been given, though, to indicate that the critical value of the version can scarcely be too highly estimated. An impartial consideration of its character proves that for the emendation of the Massoretic text, an entire reconstruction of which the English Revisers have suggested but have not attempted, the Septuagint translation claims the foremost place as the chief corrective instrument in the textual criticism of this prophetic book.

The absence of a critical edition of the Septuagint has been urged as an excuse for not attempting by its help to reconstruct the present Hebrew text. Some scholars, believing that the Greek text is in a very different state from that in which it left the hands of the Alexandrian translators, propose to postpone the use of it altogether as a critical aid till after it has been restored, so far as possible, to its original form. Just how much reason there may be for holding that the Septuagint has suffered seriously by transmission is a question that must be left for settlement to those who have the time and opportunity to investigate it. It is evident, of course, that before the full value of the version can be clearly evinced, the Greek text itself must first be thoroughly investigated. Only when this has been accomplished can perfectly satisfactory work with it be performed. Sometimes one of the other manuscripts, it has been noticed in the process of retranslation, presents a more probable reading than that presented by the Vatican manuscript used by Tischendorf. But, notwithstanding the uncritical condition of the Septuagint, this investigation shows that even in its present state it furnishes valuable textual materials, and reveals important critical results.

Inasmuch as this book has existed in a twofold form for upwards of two thousand years, at least, and inasmuch as its ancient form has been considerably modified, it is now impossible to ascertain with certainty the exact shape which it may have received either from the prophet Jeremiah or from his secretary, Baruch. That is, its absolutely original form can never be discovered, because of the manifold textual changes that were made in it during the centuries that intervened between the period of its composition and the time of its establishment by the Massorites. In so far, however, as the present Greek text can be relied upon, as representing a trustworthy text of the date of its translation, it brings us many centuries nearer to the materials with which to work in reconstructing the sacred text. In endeavouring to recover the original of the version by the method of re-translation, the relation between the Greek and Hebrew will be made more manifest, and the relative age and purity of each text will become more clear.

The ancient Hebrew or Aramaic manuscript from which the Septuagint was translated belonged to the third century before Christ, whereas the oldest Hebrew manuscript of which the age is definitely known belongs to the tenth century after Christ. If, therefore, the original of the Greek text was a good one, as it most probably was, and, if the work of translation was well done, as it most certainly seems to have been, then, so far as the original text of the Septuagint can be regained, we have a text of Jeremiah in a recension four or five hundred years older than the text attested and established by the Massorites, and twelve or thirteen hundred years older than the earliest Hebrew manuscript at present in existence. The original of the Septuagint unquestionably represented much more nearly the original form of the book than the existing Hebrew represents it. For this reason, its careful reproduction, so far as practicable, becomes a matter of the utmost possible importance.

Up to the present time, the Massoretic text has generally been taken by modern translators as the groundwork of Old Testament criticism, because it has been commonly supposed to furnish the best attested text of the Jewish Scriptures. In some respects, it is undoubtedly entitled to special consideration; but it possesses no such exceptional claim to authority as to entitle it to infallibility. On the contrary, it is now known and acknowledged to be fallible and imperfect in many places and in many ways. Since the publication of the Revised Version especially, the question of its absolute trustworthiness has come into prominence as never before. The judgment, though, of Christian scholars differs greatly as to how far the supremacy should be given to it. While the English Revisers have made the Massoretic text the basis of their work, they have frequently departed from it, having quite often, in an instance of extreme difficulty, adopted a reading on the authority of the ancient versions, which is always inserted in the margin, but never incorporated with the text. The American Revisers, on the other hand, have refused even this reference to secondary sources, as they regard the versions, and have suggested the omission from the margin of all renderings from the Septuagint and other textual authorities.

Although the Hebrew has ever been the received text in the Protestant Church, yet a portion of Christendom has always adhered to the authority of the Greek; and, "for a long period, the Septuagint was the Old Testament of the far larger part of the Christian Church."[1] Hence both its age and history entitle it to the profoundest consideration. The opinion, there is a reason to believe, is gradually gaining ground that hitherto enough importance has not generally been attached to this ancient version, and that due attention has not generally been given to its testimony. Whatever may be shown to be its value in reference to the other books, its value for the textual criticism of this book is inestimable. Its critical significance for the text of Jeremiah points to the conclusion, not only that it should be constantly consulted, but also that it should be carefully compared, in investigating the text of every Old Testament writing. In comparing the Hebrew with the Greek throughout each book certain inquiries

---

[1] Smith's *Dictionary of the Bible*, vol. iii., p. 1204.

should be made. Firstly, do the two texts agree?
Secondly, if they disagree, were their originals
similar or different? Thirdly, if similar, by what
principle can the variations be explained? Fourthly,
if different, which text exhibits the more primitive
or more probable rendering? The answers to these
questions, it is thought, can be most easily obtained
by turning the Greek back into Hebrew again.

Because, as has been mentioned, the present
Massoretic text rests upon documents of no very
great antiquity, documents which are supposed to
represent a single prototype of the time of the
Emperor Hadrian, several distinguished scholars,
like Lagarde and his disciples, find in the Alexandrian version the leading or controlling factor
for the restoration of the Old Testament text to
its original purity. The textual supremacy of the
Septuagint is vigorously maintained and, perhaps,
justly claimed by this school of critics, on the
ground of the significantly greater age of its
Hebrew or Aramaic original. Thus far, this principle of giving the precedence to the Septuagint has
only been partially applied by Wellhausen to the
books of Samuel, and thoroughly applied by Cornill
to the book of Ezekiel, the latter scholar having,
by this method, entirely and even radically reconstructed the Ezekiel text. If the Greek translation
of Jeremiah really bears the relation which it seems
to bear to the original form of this book, then it
should not simply be consulted in correcting and
emending the present Hebrew, but, when its text

has been restored, it should itself be made the basis of reconstruction.

Thus a critical and impartial consideration of the character and condition of the Massoretic text of Jeremiah, and also of the nature and importance of the Septuagint translation of it, will prove conclusively, it is believed, that the popular notions that prevail respecting each text are entirely incorrect. In the past, too much dependence has been placed upon Massoretic teaching and tradition. The more carefully the true relation between the Greek and Hebrew is investigated, the more clearly it will appear that most of the traditional views of this, as well as of every other, book of Jewish Scripture have been the outcome both of prejudice and of prepossession. Whether they have been more largely due to the one than to the other cause, or whether they have been equally due to each, it is useless to discuss, because it is impossible to determine. At all events, they have resulted from an exercise of criticism which only a predilection for a preconceived opinion could produce.

Earnest Christian scholars are now labouring to find a better text of the Old Testament. In their inquiries and discussions, the central and essential question is the comparative worth or excellence of the Greek and Hebrew texts. On whichever side the final verdict may fall, after the fullest and deepest researches have been made, the proved results of Biblical criticism must neither be discarded nor discredited. Both on philological and theological grounds, Biblical science requires a prudent application to all the books of Scripture of the most improved as well as of the most approved methods of textual criticism. A perfect text of the Old Testament is unattainable at present, and may not be attainable in future; but a more perfect one than we now possess may easily be attained. Towards its attainment the interests of truth demand the employment of every aid available and the use of every means accessible. "For," as Canon Cheyne says, "the true spiritual meaning of the Scriptures can only be reached through the door of the letter; and the nearer we approach to a correct reading of the text, the more vivid will be our apprehension of the sacred truths which it conveys."[1]

It is not now denied, and it should no longer be concealed, that the received text of the Old Testament is both faulty and defective. There is no use of saying respecting it, "Peace, peace; when there is no peace." It is worse than useless to make claims for Scripture, or for Scripture text, that cannot be maintained. What is needed is a sober knowledge of the true state of the case. By all efforts, we should seek to ascertain the facts; and, at all hazards, we should strive to let the facts be known. The truth must be sought at any cost, and it must not be sold at any price. The truth, moreover, has nothing to fear, but everything to hope, from critical investigation. "We can do

[1] *The Prophecies of Isaiah*, vol. ii., third edition, p. 240.

nothing," Paul declares, "against the truth, but for the truth." Reverent textual criticism, however keen or searching, can only lead to the adoption of sounder principles, and to the employment of correcter methods, in the discovery and elucidation of the truth. Every judicious Christian teacher, therefore, should proclaim, as the venerable Delitzsch, in the Introduction to his new and valuable commentary on the book of Genesis, with weighty words of golden worth, significantly proclaims, " God is the God of truth ; love of truth, yielding to the constraint of truth, giving up the traditional views, which cannot stand the test of truth, is a sacred duty, a part of the fear of God.'

THE TEXT OF JEREMIAH.

CHAPTER I.

THE RELATION OF THE VERSION.

THE relation of the Septuagint translation of the Old Testament to the present Hebrew text is an interesting subject of investigation which has been too little regarded in the past. For this reason, the true value of the Alexandrian version for purposes of text-criticism has been either greatly underestimated or largely overlooked. Although, of late years, considerable discussion amongst distinguished scholars has taken place upon the nature and significance of this ancient textual authority, the question is only just beginning to receive that measure of attention which its importance properly deserves. Very divergent views have been advanced, and very opposite opinions still prevail, respecting its real critical worth for the interpretation and correction of the so-called Massoretic text of the Old Testament.

In general, the Greek and Hebrew renderings of the Jewish Scriptures pretty closely correspond. There are, however, notable exceptions to this rule. The Books of Jeremiah, Proverbs, Job, Esther, and Daniel exhibit remarkable irregularities. In the first-named book especially, the dissimilarity of the readings is prodigious. A casual comparison of the texts in question discovers singular discrepancies, such as changes in the position of the chapters, in the order of the prophecies, and in the arrangement of the general contents of the book. A closer investigation reveals divergences of a much more serious sort, such as modifications of statements and expressions, and transpositions of words and verses. A minute examination discloses the absence from the Greek of an enormous amount of matter belonging to the Hebrew, the presence in the former of very many words and phrases wanting in the latter, and the existence in both Greek and Hebrew of a great variety of minor differences of more or less significance. So numerous altogether are the variations, and so startling in many places is their character, that it has sometimes been a question in the minds of earnest critics which of these texts is the more authoritative, or which one ought to be adopted in translating this ancient book of prophecy into a modern tongue.

From authentic sources, these divergences are

proved to have existed at a very early date. Reference was made to them by Origen and Jerome, each of whom commented on the character of the Alexandrian version in his day. The former, after referring to the numerous variations in the Book of Job, describes the relation of the Greek and Hebrew to each other in the present book as follows:—"We have observed many such things also in Jeremiah, in which we found much transposition and alteration of the reading in the prophecies."[1] The latter, in discussing the differences between the two texts, scarcely more than mentions the general character of the deviations in the Greek. Neither of these early Christian Fathers attempted seriously to explain them, although the latter was disposed to attribute them chiefly to the carelessness of copyists.

Not simply are the divergences thus proved to be very old, but their extreme age indicates that most of them quite probably belonged to the Septuagint translation at the time that it was made. Hence many Hebrew scholars have concluded that the Greek translators used a much conciser copy of this book than that now represented by the Massoretic text. As Jeremiah spent

---

[1] πολλὰ δὲ τοιαῦτα καὶ ἐν τῷ Ἱερεμίᾳ κατενοήσαμεν, ἐν ᾧ καὶ πολλὴν μετάθεσιν καὶ ἐναλλαγὴν τῆς λέξεως τῶν προφητευομένων εὕρομεν. *Epistola ad Africanum*, tomus xvii., p. 25; Lommatzsch edition.

the evening of his life in Northern Egypt, and as he may have ended there, as well his prophecies as his career, it has been naturally suggested that an earlier and a more authentic edition of the prophet's writings was in use amongst the Jews of Alexandria than amongst the Jews of Palestine and Babylonia. The likelihood of this suggestion, which does not appear to be unreasonable, has been much disputed, and the subject still remains a matter of debate. In this investigation, the question will be carefully considered in the clear light of the only hypothesis that consistently accounts for all the variations in this prophetic book.

In modern times three general opinions have prevailed respecting the comparative excellence of the Greek and the Hebrew text of this particular book. Some scholars have thought the former quite superior to the latter; others, while giving precedence to the latter, have placed both texts, in general, upon pretty nearly the same level; others again have thought the latter not merely preferable to the former, but alone authoritative in presenting Jeremiah's words. Of those who have claimed superiority for the Greek, the principal are J. D. Michaelis, Movers and de Wette, Hitzig, Bleek and Scholz. Of those who have regarded the Hebrew as exhibiting, on the whole, the better readings, but the Greek, in spite of many supposed errors of translation, as approaching much more nearly that which one might reasonably expect the original Hebrew to have been, Ewald, Schrader, and Kuenen are the most distinguished. Of those who have considered the Hebrew incomparably superior to the Greek, the most prominent are Eichhorn, Rosenmüller and Spohn, Kueper, Hävernick and Wichelhaus, Nägelsbach and Hengstenberg, Keil, Graf and Orelli. These are particularly decided in pronouncing for the integrity of the Massoretic text. They one and all attribute only inferiority and uncertainty to the Septuagint translation. Indeed, the most interpreters in Europe and America, especially since the labours of Graf, have looked upon the Alexandrian version as totally untrustworthy, and as critically valueless.

Not only do modern opinions greatly differ as to the respective values of the texts in question, but also they widely differ as to the true origin of the manifold divergences between them. Several reasons for the variations have been assigned. They have been ascribed to carelessness, to ignorance, to haste, to design, and to different text-recensions. Some of these theories are the outcome of an almost superstitious veneration for the Massoretic text. They have arisen from a powerful and prevalent persuasion that the Hebrew text alone represented the ancient and original form of the book, and that no other version or recension could, by any possibility, be correct. Without such a prejudice or prepossession, it is practically inconceivable either why or how the first four theories should have ever been suggested. Hitherto almost any explanation of the variations has been commonly considered more credible than the supposition that the Hebrew was not absolutely worthy of implicit confidence. In this connection these hypotheses require to be more fully stated. Each one of them does not call for an extended treatment, but each one claims, at least, a brief discussion and consideration.

The first hypothesis was proposed about the beginning of the fifth century of our era, by Jerome, and was adopted in the present century by Grabe. These have both attributed the variations to the carelessness of copyists. Divergences were, doubtless, sometimes due to such a cause; but errors by transcribers have not been restricted to the Septuagint. They belong as truly and, perhaps, as frequently to the Hebrew as to the Greek. Guilty, though, as copyists often are in this respect, it is impossible to account for many, much less for most, of the discrepancies on this hypothesis. Though some words had been overlooked, or added to the text, or even wrongly copied, by a transcriber, such mistakes, at least the great majority of them, must have been discovered and corrected on revision. In such a standard copy of the Jewish Scriptures as the Septuagint was for many centuries, as it is, indeed, and always has been, in the Eastern Catholic Church, it is incredible that a prodigious number of transcriber's errors (the divergences amount to many thousand in this book alone) should have escaped detection and correction.

The second hypothesis has been adopted at different times by a few interpreters, who have held that very many of the variations were due to want of understanding on the part of the translator. Even Hitzig, Graf, and Umbreit have endeavoured to account for a considerable number of so-called abridgments and omissions by ascribing them to ignorance. This hypothesis is both unworthy and inadequate. It neither comports with the probabilities nor explains the great majority of the divergences. The translator must have had the fullest qualifications for his arduous undertaking. Without the necessary scholarship he would surely not have been selected for his sacred and important task. From the nature of his office and the character of his work, he must have been considered altogether competent by those responsible for his dignified appointment. A devout and cultured Jew, living at the height of Alexandrian learning, trained in all the wisdom of the schools of that distinguished age, he, doubtless, was an efficient scholar, both in Hebrew and in Greek. Of his competency his translation, where his Hebrew text was not corrupt, or in some respect imperfect, affords the clearest and the most convincing proof, as will later on be fully shown, it is believed.

The third hypothesis has been suggested by Dean R. Payne Smith.[1] He supposes that the discrepancy between the texts was chiefly due to haste in the transcription of the Hebrew original of the Septuagint. During the period of his captivity in Egypt, either before or after Jeremiah's death, the prophet's secretary, Baruch, it is thought, may have employed a number of persons to prepare, as speedily as possible, perhaps on separate parchment rolls, a copy of this book of prophecy, which he desired to take back with him into Palestine. Were it only probable, a number of omissions might be easily explained on this hypothesis. It does not appear, however, to possess the slightest probability. As many of Jeremiah's prophecies had been delivered before the prophet left his native land, and had been for some time in his secretary's possession, Baruch had no need to have a special copy of them made. Moreover, apart from a large

---

[1] *Speaker's Commentary*, vol. v., pp. 324, 325.

proportion of the omissions for which it absolutely fails to account, the hypothesis altogether overlooks the numerous additions to the Septuagint, as well as the other kinds of deviation which continually occur throughout the book. This conjecture, therefore, must be looked upon as worthless, so far as furnishing a solution of the problem is concerned.

The fourth hypothesis has been maintained by Kueper and Hävernick, Spohn and Nägelsbach, Wichelhaus, Keil and Graf. These scholars, together with the great majority of recent expositors, ascribe the variations almost entirely to design. By them the Alexandrian version is considered a corrupt translation of the present Hebrew text. According to their hypothesis, the differences of rendering arose, partly from the arbitrariness and fickleness of the translator, and partly from the caprice and negligence of the transcribers, especially the later copyists. An unprejudiced consideration of the phenomena presented by a careful investigation of the two texts shows this hypothesis to be untrue. The variations are of such extent and character that they cannot have proceeded from either of the causes indicated, or from both of them combined. The very nature of the Septuagint itself disproves the theory. The Greek translation of this book in general, and of large portions of it in particular, reproduces the Hebrew text, where there is reason to believe that the original of each text was formerly the same, with such literalness and fidelity, that it is utterly incredible that a translator or transcriber should have made such arbitrary and prodigious changes, as more or less abound in nearly every section of the work. It is only reasonable to assume that the Alexandrian version must have essentially agreed with the ancient Hebrew manuscript from which it was translated.

The fifth hypothesis was first proposed by Eichhorn. He suggested that the translator of the Septuagint used a Hebrew text which differed, as the variations indicate, from the traditional Massoretic text. He also believed that Jeremiah himself authorized various versions of his prophecies during his own lifetime. As the book is extant in a twofold form, both in respect to matter and arrangement, the hypothesis of different text-recensions, two at least, has been adopted and defended by Bertholdt, Michaelis, Movers, and Bleek. A Palestinean recension is supposed to have formed the original of the present Hebrew text, and an Alexandrian recension the original of the Septuagint translation. These two recensions, it is thought, must have been in circulation, the one in Asia, the other in Egypt, from some remote but unknown period in the past. Whether, from the time this book became incorporated with the other prophetic books by Ezra or Nehemiah, it always had in Palestine and Babylonia the form in which it now appears in Hebrew, as Movers and Bleek believe, is questionable, but that the original manuscript from which the Septuagint was translated was not the same as the existing Hebrew text is unquestionable. The truth of this assertion can be fully demonstrated.

The general character of the variations has often been discussed by modern scholars, their approximate number indicated, and their distinctive features more or less completely pointed out. They have received, perhaps, the fullest treatment from the pen of Dr. Anton Scholz.[1] He has given a tolerably complete and systematic classification of their more important kinds. A full and sufficient explanation of them, though, has never yet been given. The problem, notwithstanding, must certainly admit of a solution. There must have been a worthy cause for such remarkable divergences. They are too numerous to have been accidental, too significant to have been intentional. Although thus far no satisfactory account of them has been put forth, the need of a new and thorough investigation

---

[1] *Der masoretische Text und die LXX - Uebersetzung des Buches Jeremias*, Regensburg, 1875.

of them has often been expressed, and has much more frequently been felt. In view of the importance of the problem, it appears a little singular that some of those who have maintained the existence of a twofold text-recension have not endeavoured to present a complete and scientific proof of their hypothesis. Even the conservative critic, Keil, significantly says, "None of the advocates of a special text-recension, which lay at the basis of the Alexandrian version, has given himself the trouble more accurately to investigate the nature of the translation."[1]

A fresh and full discussion is thus considered desirable, as well by some of those who commonly depreciate the value of the Septuagint, as by all of those who look upon it as a most important textual authority. The question of the variations is too momentous to remain unanswered, at least, to rest without an earnest effort being made to answer it. Its solution must affect the true interpretation of many portions of this old prophetic book. A minute examination is, moreover, necessary, in order, if possible, to determine which of these two ancient authorities

---

[1] "Keiner von den Verteidigern der Hypothese einer der alexandrinischen Uebersetzung zu Grunde liegenden besondern Textrecension hat sich der Mühe unterzogen, die Beschaffenheit dieser Uebersetzung genauer zu untersuchen." *Biblischer Commentar über den Propheten Jeremia*, etc., p. 24.

is the more correct, or which more nearly represents the original form of the book as it existed in the prophet's day. Only by close and careful investigation can the comparative excellence of each text be estimated. The inquiry has a further importance still. It concerns the critical relation of the Greek and Hebrew texts for all the ancient Jewish Scriptures. As Scholz has well observed, "The solution of the question is not alone important for the Book of Jeremiah, but decisive for the criticism of the entire Old Testament. Should the decision fall in favour of the Septuagint, then the opinion of the almost absolute trustworthiness of the Hebrew text must be not immaterially modified."[1]

After discussing briefly the chief features of the Septuagint translation of Jeremiah, in the Introduction to his critical commentary on this book, Graf emphatically asserts, "With the innumerable evidences of the arbitrariness and capriciousness of the Alexandrian translator, it is quite impossible to give his work—for one can scarcely call it a translation —any critical authority, or infer from it a different form of his Hebrew text from that which has been

---

[1] "Die Lösung der Frage ist nicht allein für das Buch Jeremias von Wichtigkeit, sondern entscheidend für die Beurtheilung des ganzen alten Testamentes. Fällt nämlich die Entscheidung zu Gunsten der LXX., so muss die Ansicht von der fast absoluten Zuverlässigkeit des hebräischen Textes nicht unwesentlich modifizirt werden." *Der masoret. Text und die LXX-Uebersetzung*, etc., pp. 4, 5.

handed down to us."¹ This judgment is unjust, and can be proved to be untrue. The Alexandrian version cannot, indeed, be properly called a translation of the present Hebrew text. In this sense, and in this sense only, Graf's statement is unquestionably true. There must have been a special text from which the version has been made. On no other hypothesis can the divergences between the Greek and Hebrew be explained. That the Septuagint does not reproduce the Hebrew text as known to us is very obvious; that it does represent another and a very different text is quite demonstrable. The peculiar arrangement of many portions of the book, especially of the prophetic parts, furnishes a probable indication that it once existed in another form from that in which we have it in our Hebrew Bibles; but the nature, as well as the number, of the variations furnishes conclusive evidence that such a supposition is correct.

Before proceeding to adduce the arguments for the existence of a special text-recension, which formed the original of the Alexandrian version of Jeremiah, it may be advisable to present in brief

---

[1] "Bei den unzähligen Beweisen der Eigenmächtigkeit und Willkürlichkeit des alexandrinischen Uebersetzers ist es ganz unmöglich seiner Bearbeitung — denn Uebersetzung kann man es kaum nennen — irgend eine kritische Auctorität zuzuerkennen und daraus auf eine von der uns überlieferten verschiedene Gestalt seines hebräischen Textes zu schliessen." *Der Prophet Jeremia*, Einleitung, p. lvi.

an outline of the plan proposed for the proving of this hypothesis. Either the omissions from the Greek, which amount to a few thousand words, or the additions to the Greek, which number several hundred words, are sufficiently significant of themselves for such a purpose; but these two classes of variation together render the evidence cumulative. A great variety of minor differences also gives the combined arguments additional strength. Each line of proof will be developed by itself. Afterwards the sum-total of the evidence will be taken as establishing the hypothesis beyond a doubt. The chief divergent features between the two texts may be grouped conveniently in five general classes, namely, (1) Omissions of letters, words, phrases, verses, and paragraphs; (2) Additions of letters, words, phrases, and sentences; (3) Transpositions of letters, words, verses, and chapters; (4) Alterations of mood, tense, gender, person, number, and case; (5) Substitutions of parts of speech, rhetorical expressions, syntactical forms, proper names, etc. This order will be followed throughout the investigation, and the evidence afforded by each class of variation will be indicated in its proper place.

It should be noted here that these five terms have been adopted simply for convenience' sake, some of them having always been employed by critics in discussing the character of the Septuagint translation of this particular book. Certain variations have so long been characterized as Omissions, and certain others as Additions, by those who have attributed all the divergences between the Greek and Hebrew texts exclusively to design that it is expedient to retain these terms, but only with a meaning modified to suit the present hypothesis of a special text-recension. In this discussion, the variations are not in any sense, or, indeed, in any instance, regarded as intentional. They are regarded simply as textual characteristics, or as recensional peculiarities. This theory assumes that the translator, in every case, endeavoured to reproduce the text before him, as literally and as faithfully as the genius of his language would justly allow.

With this view of the translation, the hypothesis implies that these words must be understood as being used only in an accommodated sense. Taking the Massoretic text as the accepted standard, and making it the basis of the investigation, by Omissions are meant forms and expressions in the Hebrew that are wanting in the Greek; by Additions are meant forms and expressions in the Greek that are wanting in the Hebrew; by Transpositions, Alterations and Substitutions are meant peculiarities of reading which these terms naturally express, but peculiarities that belonged in general to the individual manuscript that formed the original of the Alexandrian version. An occasional instance of each class of variation may have arisen from oversight, on the part of the translator or transcriber, but not properly from intention. A variation, moreover, may have been due sometimes to accident, but never to design. With this explanation of the sense in which these terms are used in this investigation, it will be in order now to exhibit the proof, furnished by each species of divergence, of a special text-recension from which the Septuagint translation has been made.

CHAPTER II.

THE VARIATIONS—OMISSIONS.

BECAUSE of their number and significance, the Omissions claim consideration first. In pointing out and dealing with their several species, an endeavour will be made to give a reasonable explanation of each kind, and also to show the folly and unfairness of ascribing them to carelessness, to ignorance, to haste, or to design. The inadequacy of the first three theories has already been evinced. The fourth hypothesis, because of its general acceptance by leading scholars, demands a special examination. By way of testing it thoroughly, it will be necessary to consider carefully the causes of omission which its chief defenders have supposed are everywhere manifest throughout this book.

It is assumed by Graf and others that the translator must have been responsible for the omissions, because of the improbability of any later writer having added such a quantity of matter to the Massoretic text. This is a most remarkable assumption. It is not fair to suppose either that the omissions were made capriciously by the translator, or that they were inserted arbitrarily by a later hand. The alternative suggested is as unnecessary as the method of reasoning is unjust. It is simply begging the question to assume that all such variations arose from one or other of these two causes, or, indeed, from both of them put together. Many of the omissions, as some of the ablest critics have admitted, appear to have been due directly to interpolation at a date subsequent to the time of the Septuagint, although, doubtless, some of them may have existed in the Palestinean recension long before the work of translation was commenced.

Granting with Graf that it is improbable that a later writer should have added the omissions, it is still more improbable that the translator should have left them out. This supposition practically implies on his part personal dishonesty—dishonesty, too, of a very serious sort, inasmuch as he has nowhere given an intimation of any such design. Such a charge has never been substantiated against the translator of any ancient classic work. The Septuagint translators were appointed to prepare for general circulation a Greek version of the Hebrew Bible, and the Scriptures must have seemed to them as holy as they seemed to any other learned Jews. That any one of these men should have capriciously abridged his text appears to one unprejudiced incredible and inconceivable. The sacred character of his text, and the solemn nature of his task, alike forbid the supposition that many, much less most, of the omissions were due to arbitrary purpose on his part. He must have been an honest man, who did his duty conscientiously and in good faith.

The unreasonableness of the alternatives assumed by Graf appears so evident as scarcely to require to be more fully pointed out. As, however, he repeatedly refers to them, it seems important, in this connection, to quote Bleek's observations in regard to them. His judgment is deliberate and just. After speaking of the extreme literalness and fidelity of extensive portions of the Septuagint translation of this book, he says, "It is, therefore, altogether improbable that the translator elsewhere, and in so many places, should have allowed himself such arbitrary alterations, and especially omissions, as must have been the case, if all the changes which his text furnishes against the Hebrew-Massoretic text had proceeded from him. Even so little is it at all probable that these changes in general should be placed to the account of later transcribers of the Septuagint. For there would occur in the manuscripts of the Septuagint even greater deviations from the Hebrew text, and, in part, greater coincidences with it, than is the case, or than already was the case at the time of Origen."[1]

Notwithstanding the evident unreasonableness of Graf's hypothesis, he alleges further, not only that the translator deliberately omitted difficult and, to him, unknown and unnecessary expressions, but also that he, in his constant striving after brevity, systematically abridged his text. This system of abridgment, Graf believes, is very manifest. He professes to discover traces of it throughout the entire book. Believing that the translator started out with the intention of being concise, Graf accuses him of having utterly disregarded the prophet's style, and of having left out terms at pleasure whenever he failed to understand, or happened to mistranslate, a word or phrase. Unrighteous as this accusation seems, even Hitzig, who is often favourable in his judgments of the

[1] "Es ist schon deshalb durchaus unwahrscheinlich, dass der oder die Uebersetzer selbst sich anderswo und an so vielen Stellen solche willkürliche Aenderungen und besonders Auslassungen sollten erlaubt haben, als der Fall müsste gewesen sein, wenn von ihnen alle die Aenderungen herrührten, welche ihr Text gegen den hebräisch-masorethischen darbietet. Ebenso wenig ist irgend wahrscheinlich, dass dieselben im Allgemeinen auf Rechnung späterer Abschreiber der Sept. kommen sollten. Denn da würden in den Handschriften der Sept. selbst grössere Abweichungen und theilweise grösseres Zusammentreffen mit dem hebräischen Texte stattfinden, als der Fall ist und als schon zu Origenes Zeit der Fall war." *Einleitung in das Alte Testament*, Fünfte Auflage, pp. 320, 321.

Septuagint, admits a frequent tendency on the part of the translator to curtail his text, and also to omit important matter from a verse or passage, if the remainder only seemed to furnish a tolerably complete sense. The admission of the one critic is as unworthy as the allegation of the other.

The constant and unimportant repetitions that characterize the writings of Jeremiah have given a certain measure of plausibility to this hypothesis, because they are so much more numerous in the Hebrew than in the Greek; but the theory is no more reasonable or satisfactory on that account. If the translator had a system of omission, he certainly did not adhere to it, for he frequently leaves in his text the very class of words he is accused of systematically leaving out of it. Quite often, too, this is the case, even when the equivalent expression is wanting in the Massoretic text. Such inconsistencies are incompatible with the supposition of a system. The omissions really indicate neither system nor design. The charge of systematic abridgment, moreover, implies stupidity, as well as dishonesty, on the part of the translator, and can be easily refuted. It is only reasonable to believe that he endeavoured in every case to give, so far as possible, an accurate rendering of the original which he used.

As Graf is the ablest and most distinguished

advocate of the theory of design, and as his defence of it is both the fullest and the strongest that exists, there appears to be a great propriety, as well as a great advantage, in making his discussion the basis, in a general sense of the term, of the present investigation of the different kinds of variation. If the falsity of his view can be demonstrated, then the truth of the hypothesis of a special text-recension, which formed the Hebrew original of the Alexandrian version, must follow as a necessary and inevitable conclusion.

It is not easy accurately to classify the great variety of divergences which Graf discusses somewhat unmethodically in the Introduction to his commentary, but at least nine species of omission may be indicated as characterizing the system of abridgment which he believes the Greek translator adopted and observed. Each class requires a special examination, and will be considered in the order most convenient for discussion. An effort will be made to answer Graf's objections respecting each and every class.

1. The translator has omitted certain set phrases and fixed forms, which are peculiar to Jeremiah, and which are repeated with exceeding frequency in the Massoretic text, because he considered them unimportant and unnecessary. For instance, for the constantly recurring formulæ, "Jehovah

Sabáoth," and "Jehovah Sabáoth the God of Israel," "Jehovah" only, as a rule, occurs in the Septuagint, and the word "Sabáoth," according to Graf's estimate, is wanting fifty-six times. The phrase, "thus says Jehovah," fails equally often with this latter term, and the form, "declares Jehovah," is omitted sixty-four times in the Greek.

The continual repetition of these formulæ in the Hebrew, though a remarkable peculiarity of the prophet's style, is entirely unnecessary. In not a single case where they are absent from the Greek is their presence needed by the context. The sense is always good, and the style is generally better, without them. Sometimes one of them, perhaps, would be appropriate where it is wanting in the Septuagint, but such instances are very rare. Hitzig, for example, thinks that "declares Jehovah," in chap. xxv. 7, improves the construction of the sentence; but he cannot claim that the phrase is really essential. Its presence or absence is chiefly, if not entirely, a matter of taste. Scholz's explanation of the constant recurrence of these words in Hebrew is worth considering. He says, "Not fewer than one hundred and seventy-seven times is the phrase, N'um Adonai, repeated, and, indeed, in numerous places where it can only have the meaning that it is repeated, in order to insure that the thing said is certainly true, because it is the word of God, somewhat as a preacher appeals to Bible passages as to the word of God." [1]

Had it been the purpose of the translator arbitrarily to abridge his text by omitting every unimportant or unnecessary expression, he might have much more frequently omitted such formulæ. He surely would have omitted them, too, in harmony with some rule. Instead of this being the case, these forms are found in many places where, according to Graf, they should not appear, if systematic omission had been the translator's aim. This species of omission is further proved to have been unintentional on his part by the important fact, apparently overlooked by Graf, that the Greek often has some one or other of these forms where the Hebrew has them not. Without noticing the numerous instances in which a similar formula occurs in each text, it may be sufficient here to give some illustrations of the foregoing statement.

It should be mentioned, before pointing out the passages, that they are not confined to any particular part of the translation, but are widely

[1] "Nicht weniger als hundertsiebenundsiebzigmal wird im masorethischen Texte die Phrase Ne'um Adunai wiederholt, und zwar in zahlreichen Stellen, wo sie fast nur den Sinn haben kann wiederholt zu versichern, dass das Gesagte gewiss wahr sei, weil Gottes Wort, etwa wie ein Prediger sich auf Bibelstellen als auf Gottes Wort beruft." *Der masoret. Text und die LXX-Uebersetzung*, etc., p. 101.

scattered throughout the whole work. In chap. ii. 2, "says Jehovah;" in chap. v. 1, "declares Jehovah;" in chap. xvi. 2, "says Jehovah the God of Israel;" in chap. xxxii. 28, "the God of Israel;" in chap. xlix. 18, "Sabáoth;" in chap. l. 21, "declares Jehovah," are present only in the Septuagint. In chap. xxiii. 29, "declares Jehovah" occurs twice in the Greek, but only once in the Hebrew; and in chap. xxiii. 30, for "declares Jehovah" in the Hebrew, "declares the Lord God" is given in the Greek. In vers. 37, 38 of this latter chapter, instead of "says Jehovah," the Septuagint has, in each verse, "says Jehovah our God." In chap. li. 62 the Greek also presents the two words "Lord Jehovah" for the single word "Jehovah." Even the phrase, "thus says Jehovah," which often serves to introduce a new or sudden turn of thought, is not in this sense uniformly found in either text. It, too, is wanting in Hebrew once, at least, namely, chap. ii. 31, where it appears in Greek.

2. The translator has omitted synonymous words and pleonastic expressions, which seem to have been used in Hebrew, either to strengthen a clause or to intensify a thought, because he considered all such terms superfluous. When several terms of this kind came together he is supposed to have regarded one or two of them,

at most, as quite enough, and, for this reason, to have purposely determined not to reproduce them all in his translation.

This supposition might possess some plausibility, at least, if such omissions could be regularly or systematically traced, though even then it would be most improbable. No regularity, however, can be discovered. In the Hebrew text, for instance, chap. i. 10, there are four verbs of destruction, while in the Septuagint there are only three. In each text the verbs of destruction are followed by two verbs of restoration. If the variation had been due to design, the translator would undoubtedly have omitted two words instead of one. The parallelism then would have been perfect; while, as the verse now stands, it is imperfect. It should be observed, moreover, that the combination here in Greek is identical with that in Hebrew, chap. xviii. 7. In this latter place, though, the Septuagint has only two of the foregoing verbs. It should be noted further that in chap. xxxi. 28, where five verbs of destruction appear in Hebrew, only the first and the last appear in Greek. Had these omissions been the outcome of a system, such irregularities could not have occurred.

Again, in Hebrew, chaps. vii. 4; xxii. 29, for the sake of emphasis, it is supposed, there is a threefold occurrence of the phrase, "the temple of Jehovah," in the first passage, and also of the word "earth" in the second passage; while, in Greek, there is but a twofold occurrence of the corresponding term in each particular verse. For the reason indicated, the increased emphasis, the Hebrew is regarded as superior to the Greek. As an analogy in favour of the former, "Holy, holy, holy," Isa. vi. 3, has been cited. The cases, though, are scarcely parallel, and the analogy suggested is not by any means conclusive, either for the Hebrew or against the Greek. There is no good ground for holding that sufficient force is not expressed in each of these two passages in the Septuagint, nor is there any reason to believe that the absent words were left out by design. If desire for brevity had been the cause of these divergences, no repetition needed to have been made at all. A single use of each term would have been enough.

Another example of a similar sort is found in chap. xlvi. 20, where the verb "come" occurs twice in the Hebrew and only once in the Greek. But, in this latter verse, as Hitzig rightly holds, the Septuagint gives a vastly better meaning than that which the Hebrew gives; and the reading, "comes upon her," which the Greek presents, is not only the one supported by many ancient authorities, but also is the one acknowledged by Graf to be the simpler of the two. The reading of the Septuagint is evidently correct. Although superfluous expressions are not so frequent in the Greek as in the Hebrew, yet more or less unnecessary words and phrases are sometimes found in the former when they are wanting in the latter, as, for example, "land," chap. i. 15; "from all the countries," chap. iii. 18, etc. In every instance of this species of divergence there must have been a corresponding deviation in the ancient manuscripts. At all events the Greek translator, doubtless, reproduced the reading which he found before him in his text.

3. The translator has omitted short sentences and half-verses which are not necessary to the meaning of a verse, but which are essential to the parallelism of its members, because he regarded them as redundant. In this way, by his constant striving after brevity, he not only has impaired the prophet's composition, but also has ignored a prominent peculiarity of Hebrew style, especially in poetry.

In this, as well as in the foregoing, species of omission, Graf argues that the variations must have arisen from the arbitrariness of the translator, because of the incredibility of any reviser or any editor having supplemented them, when the style of Jeremiah was already too diffuse. Having, in a previous section, shown the unfairness and unreasonableness of this argument, it is sufficient here to add that it is more conceivable that an editor should have inserted harmless terms occasionally for the sake of balancing a sentence, or of perfecting a parallelism, than that the translator should have mutilated the prophet's style by capriciously abridging his Hebrew text. It is not necessary, however, to assume either of these alternatives in order to explain the deviations, except in certain passages which really bear traces of revision, and which will be indicated in the proper place. By whom or when revised, of course, is quite unknown. The passages thus expanded and interpolated appear in their revised form in the Massoretic text.

In the majority of instances in Greek where variations of this kind occur, the parallelism is not at all disturbed, much less destroyed, by the omission. Even in those cases where the Hebrew parallelism is thought to be superior to the Greek, the sense in Greek is almost invariably unimpaired by the divergence. The form of chap. xii. 3 is more pregnant and, it may be, more poetical in Hebrew than in Greek, but it cannot be justly claimed that the style of the Septuagint is imperfect, or that the text is incomplete. In some of

Graf's examples, as, for instance, chaps. xx. 5; xxi. 4; xxix. 12; xlvi. 14, not only is the parallelism of the Septuagint unaffected by the various divergences, but also the symmetry of the verse-members is excellent in every case. Could it be shown that the parallelism of the Greek was frequently inferior to that of the Hebrew, it would afford no proof of arbitrary omission on the part of the translator. It would simply indicate the character of the manuscript he used.

In many places, perhaps, it may be admitted that the parallelism of the Hebrew is somewhat better than that of the Septuagint, but this is far from being universally, or even commonly, the case. Quite frequently the two texts agree; but, when they disagree, the one is often practically as symmetrical as the other. In a number of important passages, though, the parallelism is decidedly improved by the reading given in the Greek. Examples of this kind are found in chaps. ii. 20, 24; iv. 15, 19; v. 20; xviii. 7; xxv. 9; xxxix. 17. So far as this species of omission is concerned, unless it can be believed that the translator sometimes changed a reading with reference to the parallelism, and at other times without reference to it, it must be naturally assumed that he always tried to give a true translation of the text he had. This charge of overlooking a marked peculiarity of Hebrew style cannot be sustained. In view of all the circumstances of the case, it seems surprising that it should ever have been seriously made.

4. The translator has omitted minor explanations and detailed descriptions, where he could not leave out entire verses, because he looked upon them as irrelevant. By so doing, he has destroyed the rhythm of the sentences. Omissions of this kind, it is maintained, abound throughout the Septuagint, particularly in the narrative portions of the book.

This charge implies that the translator mutilated his ancient text, because he had not a proper acquaintance with one of the most conspicuous features of the Hebrew language. Like the foregoing charge, it really carries its own refutation with it. Without being influenced by a powerful prejudice, it is impossible for a moment to suppose that the rhythm was either disregarded or overlooked. A cultured Alexandrian scholar, who was born and bred, perhaps, in Judaism, as well as taught and trained in classic literature, cannot have been deficient in linguistic feeling, or wanting in literary appreciation of the peculiar genius of the ancient Jewish tongue. The English and German translators of the Old Testament did not overlook such manifest peculiarities of style as the Hebrew idiom presents, some sixteen or seventeen centuries later, when, as critics all acknowledge, the grammatical niceties of the language were most imperfectly understood. Want of rhythmical perception or appreciation would not have led the Septuagint translator to mutilate his sacred text. The charge implies the grossest ignorance, as well as the greatest inconsistency and dishonesty.

Some of Graf's examples in support of his assertion are exceedingly unfortunate, to say the least. Chap. xxii. 30 has been selected as a specimen of a mutilated sentence, but the missing member, "he shall not prosper in his days," is not really required. The rhythm of the verse in Greek is good, and the meaning given is complete. Indeed, the sense in which the additional words in Hebrew should be understood can only be determined by the latter portion of the verse, which is also differently rendered in each text. Chap. xxv. 3 has been adduced as another illustration of a dismembered verse, but the lacking clause, "the word of Jehovah was to me," was not left out by design. If the conjunction καὶ, as Graf asserts, shows that the absent words must have been present in the original of the Septuagint, it does not prove that the translator omitted them. They may have been overlooked by a subsequent transcriber. The translator surely would not leave out words essential to the construction of the verse in Greek. He must, at least, have understood the genius of his mother tongue.

In discussing this species of omission, Graf again resorts to his favourite practice of maintaining that, in one passage after another, the sentences and clauses wanting must have been omitted by the translator, because there was not the least occasion for a later writer to insert them. The first sentence of chap. xxiii. 10, "For the land is full of adulterers," was left out, he says, because of its apparent inappropriateness. Its nature quite excludes the supposition of its subsequent insertion, he believes. The words appear to be most inappropriate, it is true, but their absence is in favour of the Septuagint, to the original of which they certainly did not belong. Several of Graf's illustrations argue nothing for or against either of the texts. They simply indicate that the original of the one was shorter than that of the other. The text of the one is generally just as good as the text of the other, though the Greek is much conciser in chaps. xxxiv. 10, 11; xxxv. 8; xxxvi. 17, 32; xxxviii. 12; xlii. 20, 21; xliv. 29. In chap. xxxvi. 6 the sentence, "which thou hast written from my mouth, the words of Jehovah," is probably a gloss taken from ver. 4, as Hitzig thinks; and in chap. xl. 4 the whole second half of the verse is possibly an interpolation, as Movers and Hitzig both believe.

That the rhythm of the Hebrew is sometimes superior to the rhythm of the Greek is, doubtless, true; but this fact furnishes no fair reason to assert that the difference was due to the caprice of the translator, or to his ignorance of style. To be convinced of the injustice of this allegation, it is only necessary to observe the accuracy and fidelity with which he everywhere has done his work, having reproduced the original Hebrew with a literalness which extends, wherever practicable, to the order of the words as they must have stood in his ancient Hebrew manuscript. Respecting this class of variations also, it is more reasonable to suppose that certain clauses, here and there, were, at some time, inserted in the Massoretic text by Jewish sticklers for style, who were too regardful of the rhythm, than that they were omitted from the Septuagint by the Greek translator, who, according to Graf's theory, was quite regardless of it. The latter both observed it and preserved it with the utmost care. If the Greek text is less rhythmical than the Hebrew, and to some extent, perhaps, it is, he cannot be held responsible for the deficiency. It is possible that an occasional word or clause may have been overlooked in the translation or in the transcription, but this, as well as the foregoing, species of omission can only be explained by the hypothesis of a special text-recension.

5. The translator has omitted proper names and personal or official titles, which appear with frequency, and with some degree of regularity, in the historical parts particularly of the Massoretic text, because he thought them entirely unnecessary.

Wichelhaus attaches great importance to the annexing of the father's name to the names of persons, and indicates the rule by which, in Hebrew, he supposes they occur. He says, "If, therefore, in any passage, the name receives a special stress, if, as it were, the whole personality appears on the scene, the surnames are annexed according to the same law, by which it is, at one time, uttered with a lighter, at another time, expressed with a heavier, emphasis."[1] These titles, though, are not nearly so important as he believes, nor does their repetition in Hebrew seem to have been governed by any regular rule. Although Graf apparently adopts the extreme view of Wichelhaus, he grants that these appended names and titles are not essential to a right understanding

[1] "Quare si quo loco vis quædam inest nomini, si tota quasi persona in scenam prodit, apponuntur cognomina eadem lege, qua modo leviore pronuntiatur sono, modo altiore voce effertur." *De Jeremiæ Versione Alexandrina*, pp. 70, 71.

of the context, and that their presence or absence is a matter of indifference, so far as they concern the subject-matter of the book.

Graf's assumption, that these admittedly unimportant appendages must have been intentionally omitted by the translator, because it is incredible that a later editor should have given himself the superfluous trouble of introducing such a number of unnecessary names and titles, had they not stood originally in the Massoretic text, is again gratuitous and unreasonable. While some of these variations possibly indicate recensional divergences, others of them very probably were made by a ater hand. Hitzig admits this probability in chap. xl. 9, in reference to "the son of Ahikam, the son of Shaphan," which is in apposition to the name of Gedaliah. At the first mention of Gedaliah in the preceding chapter, ver. 14, and also in the present chapter, ver. 5, as well in the Greek as in the Hebrew, the full form of the name is given, and its repetition here is entirely superfluous. Whether many of these differences were due to subsequent insertion or not, some of them very likely were; and it is unreasonable to suppose that they were the outcome of purpose or caprice on the part of the translator.

Some of this species of omission appear to indicate the primitive character of the Hebrew manuscript which formed the original of the Septuagint translation. In ancient times such formulæ seem not to have been repeated with so much frequency as they were in modern times. The name "Pashhur," in chap. xx. 6, which Graf suggests could very well be spared after the pronoun "thou," may not have stood in the earliest Hebrew texts, and surely did not stand in the original of the Greek. In chap. xl. and following chapters, the addition to the Hebrew of "the son of Nethaniah" after the name of Ishmael, of "the son of Kareah" after the name of Johanan, and of "the son of Ahikam," or "the son of Ahikam the son of Shaphan," after the name of Gedaliah, is almost invariably unnecessary, wherever it is wanting in the Septuagint. Indeed, after an individual has once, in any given paragraph or chapter, been definitely indicated or described, the repetition of the full form of the name in that particular paragraph or chapter becomes practically superfluous in every case. At the beginning of an entirely new section, there is an appropriateness in expressing a person's name in full, with the surname attached. This is the rule apparently adopted in the other Hebrew books, as Movers very properly has observed.[1]

---

[1] "Regula enim de cognominibus vel titulis cum nominibus coniunctis hæc est, ut in oratione vulgari historica nomen cum

The frequent recurrence, moreover, of the titles, "the priest" and "the prophet," which characterizes the Massoretic text, is also a species of redundancy. These titles are altogether unnecessary wherever they are wanting in the Septuagint, and their absence is in favour of the originality of the version. In every instance, too, the meaning is just as explicit in the Greek as in the Hebrew. Although, as Graf has stated, the name "Nebuchadnezzar" is wanting twenty-three times in the Septuagint, in no case is the omission necessary to the sense. The context always makes clear who is meant. Instead of being a defect, its absence is a great improvement. For Jeremiah's time the repetition of this name was entirely superfluous. For a later time it may have seemed desirable to a teacher or transcriber. For this reason, Movers rightly regards these repetitions as later glosses. After the death of Jeremiah, he supposes, when Nebuchadnezzar had successors with whom he might possibly be confused, his name was frequently appended.

The charge of systematic omission is perfectly disproved again by the important fact that sometimes such appendages do not appear in Hebrew

cognomine vel titulo tantum initio novæ narrationis coniungi soleat, narratione autem progrediente, nisi maior orationi vis concilianda est, solum nomen admittatur." *De utriusque recensionis vaticiniorum Jeremiæ*, etc., p. 4.

where they do appear in Greek. This fact has been observed by Scholz. He says, "That it did not lie in the purpose of the Alexandrian translator, or in his manuscript, to abridge such names or surnames follows with evidence in abundance from this, that the Septuagint itself in certain passages has such appendages where they are wanting in the Massoretic text."[1] A few examples are sufficient for the purpose; for instance, "the son of Hananiah," chap. xxxv. 4; "the son of Neriah," chap. xxxvi. 14. There are also other appositional repetitions in Greek where there are none in Hebrew, such as "king of Judah," chaps. xxi. 3; xxxvi. 2; "king," chap. xxxvi. 9; "king of Babylon," chap. xxxii. 1; and also "Jeremiah," chap. xxxvi. 18.

6. The translator has omitted sometimes one and sometimes two from the group of words, "sword and famine and pestilence," which quite frequently occurs in Hebrew, because he did not carefully regard the context in which these words were found.

In chap. xxviii. 8, where two of them are want-

[1] "Dass es nicht in der Absicht des alexandrinischen Uebersetzers und seiner Vorlage gelegen ist, solche Namen oder Beinamen abzukürzen, geht zum Ueberflusse noch daraus mit Evidenz hervor, dass LXX. selbst an einigen Stellen solche Zusätze haben, wo sie im masorethischen Texte fehlen." *Der masoreth. Text und die LXX-Uebersetzung*, etc., p. 100.

ing in the Septuagint, Graf thinks that the latter
text seems to be mutilated by the omission, because
this portion of the verse is disproportionate in
length to the preceding part; but the single term
expressed in Greek is amply sufficient, both for the
sense and for the rhythm, if the meaning of the
passage be observed. The introductory word in
this place is not "sword" but "war;" and the
Greek is really superior to the Hebrew, since there
is a special contrast in vers. 8, 9 between war and
peace. Although the union of the three words
now under consideration is common in the Hebrew,
their combination is by no means uniform. They
vary both in respect to number, and also in respect
to order of combination, in different portions of
the book. A few illustrations of this variety of
number and order may be given.

In chaps. xiv. 12; xxi. 9; xxiv. 10; xxvii.
8, 13; xxix. 17, 18; xxxii. 24, 36; xxxviii. 2;
xlii. 17, 22; xliv. 13, the order of the words in
Hebrew is "sword, famine and pestilence." Their
number and order in Greek are just the same in
chaps. xiv. 12; xxxii. 36. This order is changed
in both texts in chap. xxxiv. 17, where the
arrangement is "sword, pestilence and famine,"
and also in chap. xxiv. 10, in the Greek, where the
arrangement is "famine, pestilence and sword."
In chap. xxi. 7 again, the Hebrew has "pestilence,

sword and famine," while the Greek has "pestilence, famine and sword." In the first half of xiv. 15, where only two of these terms occur, both texts are in complete agreement. In chap. xiv. 16, where two of these words also appear in each text, the general order in the Hebrew is reversed, while in the Greek it is retained. Thus the latter has the advantage of arrangement, if it were of any particular significance.

The difference between the Hebrew and the Greek respecting this group of words is thus seen to be only occasional. As examples of irregular arrangement appear in each text, and as two instead of three words also sometimes occur in each, no real importance can be attached either to their order or to their number, and no certain conclusion can be drawn as to which form is the more original or correct. When both of the texts agree, no question of superiority can be raised, and when they disagree, no argument in favour of the one or of the other can be established. In this particular, the one text is practically as good as the other. A diversity existed, doubtless, in the ancient manuscripts. In view of the foregoing facts, it is manifestly foolish and unfair to suppose that the translator sometimes omitted one of the three words because he saw that only two occurred occasionally in his Hebrew text. Everything indicates that he tried to give a true translation of the text he had.

7. The translator has omitted names and dates and specifications of various kinds, which abound in Hebrew, because he considered them meaningless or useless.

As Graf believes it impossible to regard such variations in the Hebrew text as glosses, or as in any sense the additions of a later hand, he asserts again that all such terms, when wanting in the Septuagint, must have been capriciously left out. This alternative also is unnecessary and unfair. His illustrations, too, do not support his charge. He instances, first, the omissions, of which there are several, in chap. xxviii. 3, 4; but the Septuagint here contains all that is essential to the sense, and really presents a more concise and finished reading than the Hebrew furnishes, as Hitzig honestly admits. The latter also points out very properly that the second half of ver. 3 in Hebrew, on account of the date in ver. 1, was quite superfluous for the readers of Jeremiah's time, and that the long repetition in ver. 4 was rendered desirable solely by reason of the additions to the Massoretic text.

In the remaining examples of this sort adduced by Graf, there is no more evidence of design in the omissions than in the passage just considered.

The reading of the Septuagint in chap. xxi. 7 is the usual one throughout this book, and closely corresponds to that of both the texts in chaps. xix. 7, 9; xxxiv. 21; xliv. 30. Had the absent words, "into the hand of Nebuchadrezzar, king of Babylon," been present in his text, the translator would undoubtedly have reproduced it. The variation in chap. xxxvi. 9, instead of indicating wilful omission and abridgment, as Graf and Hitzig claim, rather affords a clear proof of a twofold reading of this passage in the ancient manuscripts. For the sentence, "all the people that came from the cities of Judah unto Jerusalem," in the Hebrew, there is only the clause, "the house of Judah," in the Greek. But the one word "Judah" is common to both the texts, so that they cannot have been originally alike. The supposition is absurd. The same may be asserted also of the supposed omissions in chaps. xlii. 9; xliv. 24. The Septuagint translation of these passages is terse and good, and must have been made from a manuscript which was different from the present Hebrew text in manifold respects.

Again, the illustrations Graf has given of design in the absence from the Septuagint of detailed information respecting individuals, as in chap. xxvi. 22, or in the absence of one from a succession of well-known names, as in chap. xxxvi. 25

26, or in the absence of definite chronological data in some of the superscriptions, as in chaps. xxv. 1; xlvii. 1, are really no more fortunate or satisfactory. In not a single example is there any apparent or probable, much less certain, evidence of intentional omission. The text of the Greek is shorter than that of the Hebrew, but in every instance it is excellent, so far as this class of variation is concerned. The Septuagint appears to represent as accurately as the process of translation and transmission rendered possible the Hebrew text which the translator used.

8. The translator has omitted difficult words, uncommon terms, and unfamiliar phrases, whose meaning was, perhaps, obscure, or possibly unknown, because he thought such terms unsuited to the context in which they stood.

The expression "plundered," in chap. iv. 30, is supposed to be an illustration of this kind; but the word is quite unnecessary, as well as difficult with certainty to construe. Some critics consider it in apposition with the preceding pronoun "thou;" but Hitzig, with whom Graf agrees, holds that it is in apposition with the subject of the succeeding verb. Although the form of the word is admittedly irregular in its present position, it cannot have been omitted through ignorance, because it frequently occurs elsewhere in Jeremiah, or by intention, because the translator could have rendered it then as readily as we are able to render it now.

The first half of chap. l. 36, "A sword is upon the boasters, and they shall become foolish," cannot have been omitted because the words were either difficult or unknown, as Graf seems to suggest by citing it in this connection, inasmuch as they are all simple words and easy to translate. The same is also true of the phrase, "and all the kings of Zimri," in chap. xxv. 25. The proper name is a familiar one, but it is nowhere else in Scripture used of a distinct body of people, and its application here in that sense is somewhat difficult to explain. At least, it is not known what particular tribe is meant, as the race referred to cannot be certainly identified. The translator had no greater reason to omit the words than we have, on account of the uncertainty of the reference in this obscure clause.

There is nothing either inappropriate or offensive in the use of the expression for "eunuch" in chap. xxxviii. 7 that should have led to its intentional omission, as Graf seems also to suggest. On the contrary, by the first mention of a person, as in the present case, the description is exceedingly appropriate. Even though the term had seemed unsuitable, which is incredible, that would have formed no justification for omitting it, had it stood in the original text. The term "fatness" again in chap. xxxi. 14 was not omitted for either of the reasons indicated, because it was a familiar word, and is several times translated in other parts of the Old Testament. A further proof of this assertion is afforded by the circumstance that, instead of this term, the expression, "the sons of Levi," appears in the Septuagint. The translator would not have ventured to omit one word and to insert two words in its place. The original of the Greek was evidently different from that of the Hebrew, and the reading of the former in this verse is similar to the reading of the latter in chap. xxxiii. 18.

The last word in chap. xxxvi. 18, Graf thinks, was omitted because it was unknown to the translator. Hitzig also thinks that he skipped over it on account of its obscurity. The Greek, though, had a verb, which was very similar in form and signification to the root of the noun here rendered "ink." This fact must have been generally known, as well as the fact that fluids of various colours were used for writing by the ancient Jews. Moreover, had the word appeared in the Alexandrian recension, its meaning would have been at once apparent from the connection, even though to the translator its derivation had appeared obscure, which seems entirely improbable. Some interpreters regard the word in this place as superfluous, because the meaning of the sentence is self-evident without it. On this account, they claim, it must have been omitted; but it is much more reasonable to suppose that it was wanting in the original of the Septuagint. The word was altogether unnecessary for the people of the prophet's time; and for the princes, to whom it is addressed, the information it contains was absolutely useless. As Scholz observes, "They knew as well as Baruch that the utterances were written 'with ink,' because they had just had them read to them from the roll. Thus the author of this remark has not understood the point in question."[1]

On close investigation, there seems to be no evidence in the book that the translator ever left out words because they were either difficult or unknown. If the derivation of a word was doubtful, or if its meaning was obscure, he transcribed it literally, as, for instance, $ἀσιδα$ in chap. viii. 7; $χανῶνας$ in chaps. vii. 18; xliv. 19. Modern translators, it should be observed, have often done the same thing. A similar transcription of the

---

[1] "Dass die Aussprüche 'mit Tinte' geschrieben waren, wussten sie so gut wie Baruch, denn sie hatten sich ja aus der Rolle vorlesen lassen. Der Urheber dieser Bemerkung hat also den Fragepunkt nicht verstanden." *Der masoreth. Text und die LXX-Uebersetzung*, etc., pp. 103, 104.

first word, it may be pointed out, is found in the Alexandrian version of Job xxxix. 13, and of the second word, in the English version of Amos v. 26. Nothing could have justified a translator in leaving out or passing over words because they were obscure or difficult. He was bound either to translate them or to reproduce them. Scholz's remark on this point is very reasonable. He says, "A translator cannot simply pass over unknown words. The words, as they stand, should and must be translated. In cases, therefore, where the ordinary means for finding the meaning of a word fail, there remains nothing but either to seek to divine the meaning, or to apply for advice to the kindred Semitic languages, or finally to give the Hebrew word untranslated back again with Greek letters. Our translator has pursued all these ways. This observation is of high importance for the characteristic of his work. It evidences the groundlessness of the assertion that he has left untranslated words and passages, because they seemed to him particularly difficult."[1]

9. The translator has omitted lengthy passages,

[1] "Ein Uebersetzer kann nicht über unbekannte Wörter einfach hinweggehen. Die Wörter, die dastehen, sollen und müssen übersetzt werden. Es erübrigt also in Fällen, wo die gewöhnlichen Mittel, die Bedeutung eines Wortes zu finden, versagen, nichts, als entweder den Sinn zu errathen suchen, oder bei den verwandten semitischen Sprachen sich Raths zu erholen, oder endlich das hebräische Wort unübersetzt mit griechischen Buchstaben wie-

which are substantially the same as those occurring in earlier chapters of the book, because he thought their repetition undesirable, and thus endeavoured to avoid it.

Repetition, both on a large and small scale, is peculiarly characteristic of the writings of Jeremiah, particularly in the prophetic portions of his work. Quite frequently whole paragraphs, some of them significantly long, from the earlier prophecies, are nearly word for word repeated in the later ones. In many instances, they seem to suit the context in the second place almost as well as in the first. Not always, though, by any means, can this be said to be the case. Sometimes the repetition is manifestly inappropriate. Many of these repeated passages appear to be interpolations. Some of them should possibly be so regarded even when they are found in both the texts. When they occur in Hebrew only, their want of genuineness is scarcely at all questionable.

Approximately thirty-seven of these longer passages are repeated in the Hebrew Bible. Thirty of them, or thereabouts, are correspondingly re-

derzugeben. Alle diese Wege hat unser Uebersetzer betreten. Diese Beobachtung ist von hoher Bedeutung für die Charakteristik seiner Arbeit: sie zeigt zur Evidenz die Grundlosigkeit der Behauptung, dass er Wörter und Stellen, weil sie ihm besonders schwierig vorkamen, unübersetzt gelassen habe." *Der masoreth. Text und die LXX-Uebersetzung*, etc., p. 24.

peated in the Alexandrian version. The seven passages that are wanting in the Septuagint are apparently, in every instance, in the Hebrew out of place. Their insertion in the latter cannot be accounted for with certainty. Whether they were incorporated in some Hebrew manuscripts, at a very ancient date, or were added to the Massoretic text, at a period later than the Septuagint, are questions to which no positive answer can be given. They probably belong, however, to more modern times. Kühl's suggestion is worthy of consideration. He supposes that these additions came into the Massoretic text at a later time, and that they did not belong to the original of the Greek translator, or, if they did, that they simply appeared in the margin of his text as glosses which he naturally did not adopt.[1] In any case, they seem to be interpolations for reasons that will now be fully pointed out.

Taking these seven omitted passages in the order in which they are repeated in the Hebrew, it will be observed, first, that chap. viii. 10–12 is almost identical with chap. vi. 12–15. The idea in each is just the same, and the language is very slightly different. The repetition is not merely superfluous, but, as Hitzig indicates, it is disturbing to the sense. Ver. 13, which is united in thought to the

[1] *Das Verhältniss der Massora zur Septuaginta*, p. 56.

clause, "their fields to them that shall possess them," in that part of ver. 10 which is common to both texts, begins badly and awkwardly, as it stands in Hebrew, having no natural connection with what immediately precedes. In chap. vi. 12-15, on the other hand, the passage is appropriate and in place. There no valid objection to it can be urged. Its absence from the Septuagint in this chapter is significant. Even Graf acknowledges that its presence does not suit the context in the latter so well as in the former place. Whether it be a gloss or not, it certainly lies under the suspicion, pointed out and emphasized by Hitzig, of having been sometime supplementarily interpolated in the Hebrew text.

With the exception of the last few words, "but they did them not," chap. xi. 7, 8 is wanting in the Septuagint. The omitted verses somewhat correspond to chap. vii. 24-26. The first part of ver. 8 in the former chapter is almost exactly the same as ver. 24 in the latter chapter. Since Graf refers to it in this connection, the passage claims attention for that reason. In the first place, it should be observed that the passages, though similar, are not sufficiently alike to have suggested the omission of one of them in order to avoid the repetition, even though it were probable that the translator ever left out words and verses on that ground. In the second place, the three words expressed in the Greek do not prove, as Graf asserts, the presence in the original of the Septuagint of the omitted portions of the passage. According to the Hebrew text, these three words are to be understood as referring to the forefathers mentioned in ver. 7; but there is also a logical connection between them and ver. 6, to which they directly refer in the Greek, and to which they may also properly refer in both the Hebrew and the Greek. The repetition here is quite unnecessary, and Hitzig is in error when he says that without it vers. 9, 10 would be ungrounded and unintelligible. In the third place, the repeated passage may have been, as Movers is inclined to view it, a simple gloss taken from chap. vii. 24-26.

A similar explanation must be given of chap. xvii. 3, 4, which coincides in Hebrew pretty nearly with chap. xv. 13, 14. The modifications in the two passages are slight, or, at least, unimportant. Both Graf and Hitzig regard the passage in the former place as the original of the passage in the latter place. Both also regard the two verses as destroying all connection where they stand in chap. xvii. 3, 4. Their reasoning, though, in each respect, is altogether inconclusive. To believe with them respecting the origin of chap. xv. 13, 14, is to suppose that a portion of an earlier chapter was taken from a later one, and was inserted where it would disturb the sense. The supposition is utterly unreasonable. It is also inconsistent with the principle of omitting parallel passages which Graf unworthily ascribes to the translator. Ver. 10 of this latter chapter is evidently connected in sense with ver. 15, but the continuation of thought does not require the leaving out of vers. 11-14, as Graf gratuitously asserts. Whether the passage in question is more appropriate in chap. xvii. than in chap. xv., as the critics mentioned claim, is open to discussion. The fact that it appears in chap. xv., both in Hebrew and in Greek, affords conclusive evidence of its great age, if not of its absolute genuineness; and the fact that it does not appear in chap. xvii. of the Septuagint renders its repetition there suspicious, to say the least. Besides, chap. xvii. 1-4 is all omitted in the Greek, and the whole paragraph may be dropped out without any detriment whatever to the context. For this reason, in addition to the reasons that have been already indicated, it is practically certain that the first part of this chapter did not belong to the translator's manuscript.

An examination of chap. xxx. 10, 11 leads to a very similar result. The passage occurs in substance in chap. xlvi. 27, 28, and is, in the one place or the other, undoubtedly a gloss. Perhaps, in each place, it should be regarded as an interpolation. If so, it must be very old, since, in this latter chapter, it is found in both the texts. De Wette, Hitzig, Movers, on account of some divergences from the prophet's usual style, which seem to characterize them, consider these two verses spurious, and ascribe them to the so-called Deutero-Isaiah. With the exception of the phrase, "my servant Jacob," which is frequent in the second part of Isaiah, Graf answers their objections as to authorship with considerable success. While there is nothing in the language absolutely incompatible with Jeremiah's style, there is something peculiar in a few of the expressions used. Graf and Hitzig, however, both consider the passage more appropriate in chap. xxx. 10, 11 than in chap. xlvi. 27, 28, and they suppose it was omitted from the former chapter by the translator, because it succeeds the latter chapter in the Septuagint. Whether the passage suits the one place better than the other, or whether it is genuine in either place, where it is omitted in the Greek, it was, doubtless, wanting in the original of the Septuagint, a possible alternative which even Hitzig honestly suggests.

The long paragraph, chap. xxxiii. 14-26, is a very significant omission, the partial occasion for which, Graf believes, was the consideration that it was composed, for the most part, of literal or substantial repetitions of preceding passages. Vers. 15, 16 almost coincide with chap. xxiii. 5, 6; vers. 17, 18 sound a little like xxxv. 19; vers. 20, 22, 25, 26 somewhat resemble chap. xxxi. 35–37. The chief occasion, though, he thinks, was the non-fulfilment of the prophecy concerning David, and respecting the promised increase of the Levites and of the Davidic dynasty. He also attributes somewhat to the translator's supposed constant habit of abridgment. But the genuineness of this paragraph is held in doubt by Michaelis, Jahn, and Hitzig, the latter of whom regards the whole section as a succession of single sentences taken from various sources. Bleek, de Wette, and Movers share substantially the same doubt. From the style, as well as from the subject-matter of the prophecy, a strong argument for the spuriousness of the passage has been presented by the last four critics. The question of its genuineness, however, does not really concern this brief discussion. The special purpose of the present investigation is to show the great injustice of asserting that it was intentionally omitted by the Greek translator. It is much more easy, as Bleek has justly said, to conceive how a later writer might have added the whole prophecy than to imagine why any person should have left it out. It may possibly have belonged to the original of the Massoretic text, but certainly did not belong to the original of the Septuagint translation.

A still more positive result is obtained by the examination of chap. xxxix. 4–13. The narrative coincides in general, though not in detail, with the historic account in chap. lii., and also in 2 Kings xxv. The genuineness of the greater portion of this chapter has long been questioned by interpreters. The absent passage, whether spurious in this place or not, can with no more propriety be ascribed to Jeremiah than can the fifty-second chapter of this book, or the corresponding passage of the Second Book of Kings. The verses wanting do not properly belong in this connection. They not only interrupt the narrative, but also they disturb the order of the thought. The account which they contain, too, does not agree with that in chap. lii. In that chapter, the ninth day of the fourth month is mentioned as that on which provisions in the city failed; in this chapter, it is mentioned as the day on which the city was taken by storm. The connection, moreover, between ver. 3 and ver. 14, as in the Septuagint, is easy and natural; whereas ver. 13, which is a repetition of ver. 3, seems to have been inserted in the Hebrew for the purpose of uniting ver. 12 to ver. 14. By omitting vers. 4-13, the narration from chap. xxxviii. 28 proceeds logically and connectedly to the end. This fact, though, furnishes no reason to suppose with Graf that the whole passage was omitted, because it seemed unnecessary to the translator. He did not find it in his text. Its absence from the Septuagint affords important evidence of the critical value of this ancient version. Its testimony respecting this very dubious paragraph is weighty, and also worthy of the fullest consideration.

The remaining passage, chap. xlviii. 40, 41, which is substantially the same as chap. xlix. 22, admits of treatment similar to that which the foregoing passages have received. It is entirely unnecessary, where it is absent from the Greek, and any plausible reason for its repetition has never yet been given. Graf supposes that this passage was omitted from the Septuagint, because chap. xlviii. 40, 41 in the Hebrew comes after chap. xlix. 22 in the Greek. But it cannot have been omitted on that ground, as Hitzig properly contends. Both he and Movers consider it an extraneous, if not a spurious, addition. Owing to the divergences between the two passages in the Hebrew, the adding of a predicate and the changing of a preposition, the former critic holds that Jeremiah hardly would himself have used, and in the later passage, chap. xlix. 22, have corrected, his own words. No intentional omission on the ground of repetition can in fairness be supposed. The absent verses did not belong to the original of the Septuagint translation, or else they would have been carefully reproduced.

Each of these seven passages, where wanting in the Septuagint, is, when critically and impartially considered, apparently out of place. That they were in every instance glosses by a later hand, as some interpreters suppose, seems altogether probable; but that they were not present in the translator's manuscript seems absolutely certain. It is incredible that the translator should have found these passages in his text, and then have left them out, because he thought them spurious or inappropriate. It is also inconceivable that he should have wilfully omitted them, because he tried, as much as possible, to avoid unnecessary repetitions, inasmuch as thirty times or more he has repeated passages quite as unnecessary to the context as these appear to be. If he found the whole thirty-seven before him, why did he omit just these seven passages? Why should they, and they alone, have been left out and all the others have been left in? The only reasonable answer to this question seems to be that they did not belong to his original, and that they are, in every case, interpolations by a later hand. It is significant that each of these omitted passages, apart from its inappropriateness where it is absent from the

Greek, is of doubtful origin and of suspicious character.

If one supposes that these passages really did belong to his original, one must believe that the translator left them out because of their apparent spuriousness or inappropriateness. He cannot have omitted them without first considering whether they were genuine or not. If, after consideration, he decided not to reproduce them, as Graf supposes, then very little value can be attached to his translation. It is merely an arbitrary and untrustworthy piece of literary work without any critical worth whatever. After showing the mechanical and unreliable character of the translation, if such an unworthy opinion of the translator be entertained, Kühl pertinently says, "Why then did he do it only in these seven passages and not in every place, where—sometimes at no very great intervals—repetitions occur? and wherefore did he, in spite of his former lack of critical acumen, in his omissions which, by this supposition, would still be a product of his arbitrariness, hit upon exactly the seven passages, whose originality, indeed, is doubtful in the very highest degree? With that view, these questions ever remain unanswered, and they elicit from every impartial observer the acknowledgment that here, and if here, then, of course, in other passages as well, the Septuagint is wholly in the right. At all events, though, too depreciative is the judgment of Graf, who will attribute to it no authority whatever." [1]

Graf's theory respecting the seven passages just considered apparently rests on the assumption that they are always wanting in the Septuagint where, according to the order of the prophecies in that version, they, if repeated, would appear a second time. This supposition, though, is incorrect. One exception to this rule exists, and that is quite sufficient for the purpose of disproof. Chap. xxxix. 4–13 is absent from the Greek, while it is present in chap. lii., notwithstanding the fact that the latter chapter ends the book in both the Hebrew and the Greek. Although each of these seven repeated passages appears to be of very dubious character, and, although each one, if not entirely inappropriate where it is wanting in the Septuagint, might be, at least, omitted without at all disturb-

---

[1] "Warum that er es denn blos an diesen sieben Stellen und nicht überall, wo (manchmal in nicht allzugrossen Zwischenräumen) Wiederholungen stattfinden? und weshalb trifft er bei seinen Auslassungen (trotz seines sonstigen Mangels an scharfsinniger Kritik), die bei dieser Annahme doch ein Produkt seiner Willkür wären, gerade die sieben Stellen, deren Ursprünglichkeit in der That im höchsten Grade zweifelhaft ist? Diese Fragen bleiben bei jener Ansicht immer unbeantwortet, und sie nöthigen jedem unparteiischen Beobachter das Zugeständniss ab, dass hier, und wenn hier, dann jedenfalls auch an anderen Stellen, die LXX. in vollem Recht ist, jedenfalls aber das Urtheil Grafs zu abschätzig ist, der ihr gar keine Autorität zuschreiben will." *Das Verhältniss der Massora zur Septuaginta*, p. 60.

ing the connection or injuring the sense, it is remarkable that Graf attributes the omission in each case to the self-same arbitrary practice by which he persistently endeavours to account for the various species of omission that have already been discussed. When it suits his purpose, he accuses the translator of the grossest ignorance, and, when such a supposition is clearly contradicted by the facts, he accuses him of the greatest arbitrariness. This kind of reasoning is inconsistent and confutes itself. His theory is altogether too accommodating. It maintains that the translator systematically abridged his text, and then it holds him responsible for numberless omissions which no sort of system can explain.

It should be also noted here that many other passages are repeated in the Septuagint, not where they occur the first time in the Hebrew, but where they occur the second time. This is a most significant fact, and it affords additional disproof of Graf's unjustifiable and unjust assumption. Scholz has an important observation on this point. "If, however," he says, "there was need of a still further proof, the supposition of intentional omission is excluded by this, that the Greek translation, in a number of passages, does not express repeating and like-meaning verses, while it has them in a second place. How would that be conceivable with a translator who translates without consideration?"[1] Such a supposition is both unreasonable and absurd. The translator had neither reason nor desire to abridge his text. Had the repetition of unnecessary matter been his aim, he might have left out many times as much as he has been accused of leaving out. An unprejudiced investigator, who carefully considers all the facts, must grant at once the unreasonableness of Graf's accusation. He must also admit with Kühl, not only respecting the seven long repeated passages in particular, but also respecting the numberless unnecessary omissions in general, that the ground of their omission was not a subjective but an objective one; that is, it lay not in the arbitrary procedure of the translator, but in the peculiar form of his original.[2]

It is still more remarkable, if possible, that in each of the other cases in which a parallel passage is repeated in the Septuagint of this book, Graf

---

[1] "Völlig aber ausgeschlossen ist, wenn es noch eines weiteren Beweises bedürfte, die Annahme von dem absichtlichen Auslassen dadurch, dass die griechische Uebersetzung in einer Anzahl von Stellen sich wiederholende, gleichlautende Verse das erste Mal nicht ausdrückt, während sie dieselbe an zweiter Stelle hat. Wie wäre das bei einem Uebersetzer, der leichtfertig übersetzt, denkbar?" *Der masoreth. Text und die LXX-Uebersetzung*, etc., p. 26.

[2] "Der Grund der Auslassung ist kein subjektiver, d. h. er liegt nicht in dem eigenmächtigen Verfahren des Uebersetzers, sondern ein objektiver (äusserer), d. h. er liegt in der Gestaltung seines Originals." *Das Verhältniss der Massora zur Septuaginta*, p. 56.

supposes that the translator had forgotten that he had once already rendered it. Otherwise, he seems to think, all such passages would have been omitted. In his opinion, the translator must have been not only incompetent and inconsistent, but also endowed with a very treacherous memory, which frequently forgot to apply the principles of his own most imperfect scheme. Such ingenuity of explanation in a Biblical scholar is exceedingly unusual, to say the least, and certainly was worthy of a better cause. How such a monstrous supposition could have been deliberately suggested seems itself almost inexplicable. The assumption that the translator had a system, and then forgot to apply it in some thirty out of thirty-seven lengthy passages, is so ridiculous that it scarcely claims a formal answer; and yet, since Graf has made the accusation, it must not be passed by without some attention, notwithstanding its absurdity.

Apart from the utter improbability that a definite rule of translation could be forgotten four times, at least, as often as it was remembered by one who is supposed to have made it specially for his personal guidance, it seems sufficient further to observe that some of the passages repeated in the Septuagint stand so near to each other as to render the idea of forgetfulness wholly inconceivable to a person who takes into account all the facts of the case. Scholz has answered Graf's suggestion on this point aptly and completely. He says, "If it is a principle of the translator to pass over passages and expressions, which repeat themselves, as superfluous in a second place, how could he so neglect this his own principle that he applied it in only a comparatively small number of cases, whereas, in by far the great majority of places, he likewise translates the recurring passages, and, indeed, not merely in cases where an oversight was possible,— although that from the first is improbable in the highest degree, as certainly not the next best into whose hands the book fell devoted himself to the translation. We have rather, with the greatest likelihood, to suppose that it is the work of a 'Teacher in Israel,' who by frequent reading had made himself familiar with the book in all of its details."[1]

[1] "Wenn es Grundsatz des Uebersetzers ist, Stellen und Aussprüche, die sich wiederholen, als überflüssig an zweiter Stelle zu übergehen, wie konnte er diesen seinen Grundsatz so ausser Acht lassen, dass er ihn nur in einer verhältnissmässig kleinen Anzahl von Fällen anwandte, in den weitaus meisten Stellen dagegen die wiederkehrenden Stellen ebenfalls übersetzt, und zwar nicht blos in Fällen, wo ein Vergessen möglich war — obgleich das von vorneherein im höchsten Grade unwahrscheinlich ist, da sicherlich nicht der Nächstbeste, dem das Buch in die Hand fiel, sich an die Uebersetzung machte. Wir haben vielmehr mit höchster Wahrscheinlichkeit anzunehmen, dass es die Arbeit eines 'Lehrers in Israel' ist, der mit dem Buche in allen seinen Einzelnheiten durch vielmaliges Lesen sich vertraut gemacht hat." *Der masoreth. Text und die LXX-Uebersetzung*, etc., p. 26.

The examination of a great variety of minor omissions, which Graf does not attempt to classify, as well as a considerable number of longer ones, which have, as yet, not been discussed in this investigation, affords still further proof that the translator used another and a different text from that transmitted to us by the Massorites. Both their nature and their number are too significant to be overlooked. Not simply do they supply important evidence for the hypothesis of a special text-recension, but they furnish useful material for the history of the whole Old Testament Scriptures. They also shed a flood of light upon the present character and condition of the Massoretic text. On the ground of being either unnecessary, or superfluous, or inappropriate, or interpolated, some of them have been rejected by Graf himself. On the same ground many of them have been rejected by Hitzig or by Movers, or by both. On a similar ground, moreover, others of them must be regarded either as spurious or as suspicious, to say the very least.

The great majority of the omissions may be characterized generally as unnecessary; that is, neither are they requisite for the complete grammatical construction of the text, nor are they essential for a proper understanding of it. This is true especially of all or nearly all of those belonging to each of the nine species of omission that have already been investigated. It is also just as true of all or nearly all of those remaining undiscussed. Their presence or absence is practically immaterial, although, in several instances, the reading in the Hebrew may be considered preferable to the reading in the Greek. By characterizing the omissions in general as unnecessary, it is not meant that they are generally spurious, although unquestionably they sometimes are; nor is it meant that many of them did not belong to the original of the Massoretic text, although undoubtedly some of them did not. They are thus characterized principally against Graf and others who assert that the omissions from the Septuagint indicate a mutilated text.

A considerable number of omissions may be characterized appropriately as superfluous. They are not only unnecessary, but also redundant. This redundancy, in many places, doubtless, points to textual divergences. These may have generally belonged to the Palestinean recension. Whether this can always be claimed to be the case, however, is very questionable. The question, too, is one that cannot easily be answered. Such omissions are described in this connection as superfluous, some of them on his own admission, especially again against Graf and his arbitrary theory of intentional omission on the part of the translator.

A significant number of omissions must be characterized properly as inappropriate. They are not only unnecessary and superfluous, but also out of place. In many passages, they either interrupt the progress of the narrative, or disturb the harmony of the thought. For various and manifest reasons they do not properly belong where they are wanting in the Greek. It is not always easy to account for their existence, although a possible explanation may, in some instances, be pretty safely suggested. Their origin was, doubtless, due to a variety of causes, which extended over a long period of time.

A still more significant number of omissions can only be characterized correctly as interpolated. They cannot be truthfully described by any other term. They are not only unnecessary and superfluous and inappropriate, but also spurious as well. They cannot have been uttered by the prophet, nor can they have belonged to any authorized edition of his writings. That some of them are ancient appears probable; but how old, of course, it is impossible to tell. That many, if not most, of them arose after the making of the Septuagint translation seems practically certain; but when or by whom they arose can never be determined. It may be possible, however, to account for some of them conjecturally.

THE VARIATIONS—OMISSIONS. 69

The omissions of letters, of which there are several, are also worthy of some consideration here. This species of omission is of special interest, because it shows how a number of important variations may be naturally explained. Some of these divergences may have been recensional; others of them may have been transcriptional. Except in so far as the context pronounces the one form or the other to be preferable, it is difficult to decide which reading is the more primitive. By placing the examples together, their comparative excellence may the more easily be estimated. The instances are as follows:—

בְּעָרְבִי—, i. 14; בְּבַפֶּיךָ—בְּכְנָפֶיךָ, ii. 34; תֵּפַח—תִּפָתַח
כְּעֶרֶב, iii. 2; רַבִּים—רְבָבִים (?) וַיָּמִינוּ—וַיַּמְרָעוּ, iii. 3;
כְּלָה—, vi. 2; (?) וּמְנָעָה—וְהַמִגְאָנָה, iv. 1; מִפִּיו—מִפְּנֵי
כָּל, vi. 6; מְשׁוּבָתָם—מַחְשְׁבוֹתָם, vi. 14; וְאָן—וְאֵין,
יָשִׁיתָה—יָשִׁיתָה, vi. 19; אֵשׁ—אִישׁ, vi. 23; l. 42;
מְשִׁבוֹתֵינוּ—מַחְשְׁבוֹתֵינוּ, xi. 19; כַּלֶם—וַאֲכָלֵם, xv. 16;
עִינַי—לַעֲנָה, xviii. 12; זֵרֶם—זָרִים, xviii. 14; xxiii. 15;
בַּעֲלוֹת—בָּהֵעָלוֹת, xxxvii. 11; אֵלֵינוּ—אֶל־הֵינוּ, xliii. 2;
קוֹלֵד—קָלוֹנֵךְ, xlvi. 2; בְּכַרְמִישׁ—בְּכַרְכְּמִישׁ, xlvi. 12;
דְלָתַיִם—דִבְלָתַיִם, xlviii. 6; עָרוֹד—בַּעֲרוֹעֵר, xlviii. 22;
וּבָאיִים—וּבָאֵימִים, xlix. 9; הֵשִׁיתוֹ—הִשְׁחִיתוּ, l. 38;
מְנָחָה—מְנוּחָה, li. 27; וְאָבְנוֹ or וְאַבְנַיִם—וְאַשְׁפְּנוּ,
li. 59.

CHAPTER III.

THE VARIATIONS—ADDITIONS.

Convincing as is the evidence obtainable from the Omissions of a twofold text-recension of this book, the evidence derivable from the Additions is, if possible, more conclusive still. Their number, as well as their importance, has not as yet been properly appreciated. Even Bleek, who is a great admirer of the Alexandrian version and a vigorous advocate of different text-recensions, has failed to point out their significance. He says, "The Septuagint only seldom has additions, and these consisting simply of single words or members."[1] This statement, however, is scarcely accurate. Though small compared with that of the omissions, it is true, their number, notwithstanding, is considerable. They really amount to several hundred words. Significant as their number is, their nature is much more significant. Instead of being confined exclusively to "single words

[1] "Nur selten hat die Septuaginta Zusätze, und nur in einzelnen Worten oder Gliedern bestehende." *Einleitung in das Alte Testament*, p. 318.

or members," as he says, they are composed occasionally of sentences, and frequently of groups of words, which sometimes modify the meaning of a passage, at other times explain a difficulty in the Massoretic text, at other times again exhibit a reading, not only different from but also superior to the one which the Hebrew gives.

Respecting the additions, Graf is almost as unreasonable and inconsistent in his allegations as he is in reference to the omissions. He says, for instance, "Of the additions to the Massoretic text, which, on the other side, occur in the Septuagint, only a few are to be found which can prompt the supposition that they exhibit genuine text, that might have been omitted from the present Hebrew through the fault of copyists."[1] This bare assertion, of course, is true; but the implication is false. There is no ground whatever to suppose that variations of this kind were often due to oversight or omission on the part of those who anciently transcribed the Massoretic text, although it may not be improbable that here and there a word or two may have been overlooked. The additions are too numerous and significant to be explained on any rational

[1] "Unter den Zusätzen zu dem masoretischen Texte, die andrerseits in LXX. vorkommen, finden sich nur wenige, die zu der Annahme veranlassen können, dass sie ächten Text darstellen, der in dem jetzigen hebräischen durch Schuld der Abschreiber weggefallen wäre." *Der Prophet Jeremia*, Einleitung, p. xlix.

hypothesis other than the one suggested and illustrated by the examples of omission that have already been discussed. They afford conclusive evidence of a special text-recension. They represent, undoubtedly, a very ancient text, and bear invaluable testimony to its general excellence throughout.

The theories of explanation held by Graf are not merely incorrect but contradictory. He claims that the translator systematically abridged his text, and contends that the omissions from the Septuagint were due to his persistent striving after brevity, because of the impossibility of believing that they were left out by a later writer or transcriber from the Hebrew text. He then suggests that everywhere a later hand is recognizable in the additions as well as in the omissions of the Septuagint. If it is incredible, when discussing the omissions, to suppose that such variations were due to a later hand, it is certainly just as incredible when discussing the additions. According to this hypothesis, to be consistent, he should attribute all the variations to the Greek translator. When it suits his convenience, though, he ascribes them to the translator, and when it does not, he ascribes them to a later editor or reviser. Graf seems to be driven to this desperate alternative respecting the origin of the additions by perceiving that, although he believes that the translator systematically abridged his text, no one could believe that he abridged it and enlarged it at the same time.

As the omissions prove the improbability of Graf's hypothesis, so also the additions prove its impossibility. They demonstrate not only the unfairness of asserting that the translator was always striving after brevity, but also the unreasonableness of supposing that he either added to or took away from the ancient Hebrew text which he employed. It is useless to suppose that he neglected his own principle of systematic omission, or that he forgot in all such cases to apply it. Even Graf himself sees the preposterousness of such a supposition. Hence he regards the additions, in almost every case, as spurious, and endeavours to account for them by alleging that they belong to a later time. Having given a brief discussion of their character, he says, "After the explanation, there can be no longer a doubt that the text-form presented by the Greek translator is a mutilated and corrupted one, that arose, in a much later time, out of the Hebrew text which has been preserved to us."[1] How far this state-

[1] "Nach dem Dargelegten kann es keinem Zweifel mehr unterworfen sein, dass die von dem griechischen Uebersetzer dargebotene Textgestalt eine aus dem uns hebräisch erhaltenen Texte in viel späterer Zeit entstandene verstümmelte und verderbte ist." Einleitung, p. li.

ment is from harmonizing with the facts will be evinced by carefully examining the additions. That they were not taken from the air, to render literally a German phrase, is very evident; and that they were due neither to translator nor transcriber can be very clearly shown. As a rule, they bear the marks of age and genuineness upon them, and thus proclaim their own originality or primitive character. As Graf ascribes them now to one cause and then to another, it is by no means easy to arrange his objections to their genuineness systematically. It seems better, though, so far as practicable, to attempt to classify them. For convenience' sake, they may be generally grouped in five distinct classes.

1. Many additions prove themselves to be spurious, because they violate the sense of the verses or the parallelism of the verse-members. This is a somewhat serious accusation. Graf indicates only a few instances of this kind, and none of those are really to the point.

In chap. iv. 29, for example, where the Hebrew has "they go into the thickets," the Greek has "they go into the caves and hide themselves in the thickets." It is unfair to say that the parallelism of the verse in Greek is violated. There may just as properly be three predicates as two. If one supposes with Schleusner that the Hebrew word translated "thicket" was repeated in the Septuagint, one has still to account for the additional verb "to hide." The latter clearly indicates an ancient reading, a similar form of which occurs in other parts of the Old Testament, as, for instance, in 1 Kings xviii. 13. The two texts in the present verse seem never to have been the same. Besides the additions in the Greek the minor variations are important, and in favour of the Septuagint. Instead of going up "into the rocks," the Greek has going up "upon the rocks;" instead of "the whole city," it has "the whole country." This latter reading is superior to the one in Hebrew, inasmuch as "country" forms a natural contrast to "city" in the following member of the verse, as Hitzig freely admits. In this same member the absence of the article from the word for "city" is also favourable to the Septuagint. The people would naturally flee from every city in the whole land, and not merely from the whole city of Jerusalem.

The added words, "and your olive-yards," in chap. v. 17, cannot be fairly said to violate the parallelism. There may as well be three as two particulars. The fact that a similar addition is found in the Septuagint translation of Ps. iv. 8 affords a further proof that the text employed by the translator presented in each passage a reading different from the Massoretic text. If the parallelism of the Greek were inferior to that of the Hebrew, which is not really the case, it would not disprove the genuineness of the Septuagint, nor would it prove that the words were added either by the translator or by a later hand. It would rather indicate their originality, because, to an impartial mind, it is incredible that any person should have intentionally injured the Hebrew style by adding to the text of Scripture. The words in Greek are surely genuine.

In chap. xxxii. 19, the peculiar clause, "the great God Sabáoth, and Jehovah of great name," was neither added by a later hand, as Graf assumes, nor arbitrarily inserted in its present place, as Hitzig says. The variation seems to have been due, partly to an accidental repetition, and partly to an imperfect condition of the original Hebrew text. The words, "the great God," were apparently repeated by mistake, either in transcribing the Hebrew original or the Greek translation. The remaining words evidently arose from imperfection in the ancient manuscript, as they contain exactly the letters, but in a different order, of the last three words of the 18th and the first word of the 19th verse. In the Massoretic text, we have גדל ׃ צבאות שמו ׃ יהוה ; in

the Septuagint, we have צבאות שם וגדל יהוה or
צבאות וגדל שם יהוה. Thus, by means of the Hebrew
letters, the variation may be explained. The explanation is rendered the more probable, inasmuch
as the last three words of ver. 18 are wanting in
the Septuagint, but are found, as indicated, in the
19th verse. The case affords an illustration either
of textual imperfection, or of transcriptional carelessness, or, perhaps, of both.

In chap. xiv. 15, for the words, "by the sword,"
in Hebrew, the Greek has "of grievous death they
shall die." This cannot have been an arbitrary
variation, as Graf suggests. The translator would
not, and a later writer could not, consistently
with reason, so have changed the sacred text.
The words in the Hebrew are very simple, and
evidently belonged to the Palestinean recension.
The sentence in the Septuagint is most unusual,
and must have belonged to the Alexandrian recension. It occurs but once in the Hebrew Bible,
and that is in chap. xvi. 4 of this book; whereas
it occurs twice in the Greek translation, once in
this latter chapter, and once in the passage under
consideration. The expression, therefore, is peculiar
to the prophet Jeremiah. In each passage of the
Septuagint the words in Greek are identical; and
they are just as appropriate in the one as in the
other. The very peculiarity of the language is a

proof of its genuineness, or, at least, of recensional differences in the ancient Hebrew manuscripts.

There may be, now and then, a passage in the Greek where, owing to the presence of an additional word or clause, the parallelism is less perfect than in the Hebrew, but such instances, if such there be, are really very rare. In the great majority of cases the additions either affect the parallelism favourably, or they affect it not at all. In none of these places, though, is there the slightest reason to suppose that the improvement is due either to translator or reviser. Examples of superior parallelism due to the additions in the Septuagint may be found by comparing the Hebrew with the Greek in chap. i. 17, where the latter has "fear not before them and be not dismayed before them" instead of "be not dismayed at them, lest I dismay thee before them;" v. 20, where it has "the house of Judah" instead of "Judah;" ix. 25, where it has "the sons of Moab" instead of "Moab."

2. Many additions, inconsistently with the former system of abridgment, are taken from other passages, and inserted where they do not properly belong, or where they are altogether out of place. This assertion can be shown to be entirely incorrect by carefully examining the passages which Graf has cited by way of illustration.

The added phrase, "because they shall not profit you at all," chap. vii. 4, Graf says, is taken from ver. 8. But the form of the expression in the latter verse is not the same as that which is given here. The one is not a repetition of the other, nor can the one be fairly claimed to have been taken from the other. The language in each verse is different, and the number of words used also varies. Even had the phrases been identical, no reason for supposing that the one was repeated from the other would have been apparent. At all events, as they are now found, each one is most appropriate in the form, as well as in the place, in which it stands.

In like manner, the added clause, "to your own hurt," chap. vii. 9, Graf considers, is taken from ver. 6. His supposition here again is just as incorrect as in the preceding case. The Septuagint renders the clause in ver. 6 literally, and, moreover, exactly as it also stands in Hebrew, chap. xxv. 7. In this latter passage, on the other hand, the words are wanting in the Septuagint. Why should a translator be accused, for no conceivable reason whatever, of omitting words because they were unnecessary in one place, and of inserting them in another place where they were quite as unnecessary? Only a foolish theory would admit such an absurdity. The words were neither arbitrarily added in chap. vii. 9 nor arbitrarily omitted in chap. xxv. 7. The first two verses of this present chapter are wanting in the Greek; there are also several other omissions, of more or less importance, in other parts of the chapter. The significant additions which likewise characterize it, as well as the omissions, point to a special text-recension.

The addition, "and those who are going in at these gates," chap. xix. 3, Graf regards as a repetition from chap. xvii. 20. The suggestion, though, is quite gratuitous. The words are just as appropriate in the one place as in the other. The combination is a somewhat common one. It occurs in chaps. xvii. 20; xxii. 2, of both the Hebrew and the Greek, and also in chap. vii. 2, of the Hebrew. In this latter verse, however, it is wanting in the Greek. It is unreasonable to suppose that the words were purposely omitted in chap. vii. 2 and purposely added in chap. xix. 3. The long additional expression, "and I wrote the deed and sealed it and called witnesses," chap. xxxii. 25, Graf says, is taken from ver. 10. As the transaction was important, and as its bearing on the future of the nation was likely to be permanent, it is natural that the prophet should have spoken as the passage reads in the Septuagint. The translator surely had no reason to repeat the sentence in the present

verse, if he did not find it in his manuscript.
A further proof that the original of each text was
different is furnished by the important fact that,
while the two sentences in question are added to
the Greek in this member, the sentence, "and call
witnesses," is omitted from it in the preceding
member, of the verse.

Graf also supposes that the addition, "more
than their fathers," chap. xvii. 23, is taken from
chap. vii. 26, to which it bears a close resemblance.
Hitzig considers the whole verse wanting in
originality, as well as in appropriateness. Whether
right or not, his supposition is much more plausible
than that of Graf. It is far more likely that the
whole verse was interpolated at some time, than
that the additional clause in Greek was inserted by
the translator. If chap. xvii. 23 be an interpolation, it must have been added prior to the existence of the Alexandrian version. In any case, the
rendering of the verse in Greek points to recensional differences, and indicates that the translator
reproduced the text he had before him.

3. Other additions are inserted in a manner
that is altogether improper and inappropriate.
An examination of the instances cited by Graf
will show this allegation also to be false.

The sentence, "great is the distress upon thee,"
chap. xi. 16, cannot have been intentionally added

F

by any one at any time. Even if the hypothesis of arbitrary insertion on the part of the translator were probable, which is not the case, he would not have ventured to insert words inappropriately, or in a way to render the construction difficult. The presence of the sentence here is certainly not easy to explain. Either it was found in the translator's manuscript, as the Greek text is very plain, and gives a tolerable sense; or it was accidentally added by an ancient copyist, as the variation may be partially explained by means of the Hebrew letters. This latter alternative seems not unreasonable or improbable, inasmuch as the word for "great" occurs in one part of the verse in Hebrew and in another part of it in Greek. Possibly, therefore, it was overlooked at first, and afterwards inserted with the other words which may have been repeated by mistake. The words in Greek might easily have been derived from the words in Hebrew, especially if the original text were indistinct, in the following manner :—גדלה הצרה אשר־ עליך (יש) for גדלה הצית אש עליה. There is a similarity in the sound, as well as in the form, of the Hebrew words in each case.

The added words, "to their meeting," chap. xxvii. 3, did not arise from arbitrary insertion, as Graf assumes; nor did they arise from careless repetition of similar consonants, as Hitzig asserts.

There is no real resemblance between ירושלם and לקראתם, as the latter critic claims. The words make excellent sense in the connection in which they stand. There is nothing improper or inappropriate about them. The phrase is quite uncommon in Jeremiah, but the idea expressed is good. It unquestionably belonged to the Alexandrian recension at the time that the Septuagint translation was made. The addition of the word, "waters," at the beginning of chap. xlvi. 8, was also not due to intention. As the same word ends the preceding verse in Greek, it may have been repeated by accident. It is, perhaps, more probable, however, that it belonged to the translator's text. The reference here is to the troops of soldiers sweeping over the country like the rushing billows of an overflowing river. The repetition of the word, moreover, makes the reading correspond exactly to the figure used for an army in Isa. viii. 7. The waters symbolize the advancing host of the Egyptians, whose mighty army is likened to the annual inundation of the Nile, just as in this latter chapter the Assyrian army is likened to the periodical floods of the Euphrates. The added word is not unfavourable to the Septuagint.

The clause, "and of all the land," chap. li. 28, was also not added to the Septuagint, as Graf suggests. It simply occupies another place in the same sentence. In Greek it stands in the first half, in Hebrew it stands in the second half, of the verse. Although the order of the words in the former is different from the order in the latter, the rhythm of the verse-members in the Septuagint is excellent. The rendering of the verse in Greek is, in several respects, superior to that of the verse in Hebrew, it also should be pointed out. The singular "king" is better than the plural "kings," which appears to be incorrect. All the pronouns in the Septuagint, moreover, refer consistently and properly to the monarch, "the king," whereas in the Hebrew two of them refer to the people, "the Medes," and only one refers to the ruler of the country. It is significant that this one has the same form that each one has in Greek. This fact indicates that the reading, "king of the Medes," is more accurate than "kings of the Medes." It also seems to show that the words, "of his dominion," which are wanting in the Septuagint, may have been added by a later hand to the Massoretic text.

The ejaculation, "so may it be, O Jehovah," chap. iii. 19, is not inappropriate where it stands in Greek, nor can one fairly claim that it did not belong to the translator's text. The words were naturally interjected by the prophet, and they correspond with a similar form of expression in chap. xi. 5. As the appended words, "falsehoods falsely," chap. xxvii. 15, are simply regarded by Graf as "very useless at least," it may be quite sufficient to reply that this objection does not prove them to be spurious, nor does it prove them to have been intentionally inserted by any one. The same objection merely is urged against the reading, "the sword of Jehovah," instead of "sword," chap. xlvi. 10. In neither of these two cases is the addition absolutely useless. On the contrary, it increases the significance of the statement in each verse. In the latter example, moreover, the definite form in Greek is a classical one, as may be seen at once by a reference to 1 Chron. xxi. 12.

4. Other additions again are explanatory glosses or circumlocutions, which are frequently incorrect. This charge can be as easily refuted as the foregoing ones by studying the examples which Graf adduces in support of his assertion.

The exclamation, "O Jerusalem!" chap. xiii. 20, cannot be shown to be a gloss. It probably represents the only true reading in this place. It belongs as naturally and as properly here as in ver. 27, where it appears in both the Hebrew and the Greek. Even the form of the verse in the Massoretic text indicates that some such word was understood, and possibly, at some time, was expressed. The Hebrew verb is feminine and singular, while the possessive pronoun which qualifies its subject is plural. "This shows," as Streane has observed, "that the subject is a noun of multitude, viz., Jerusalem personified as the daughter of Zion. This thought harmonizes with the words, 'the flock that was given thee,' the inhabitants of the land in general."[1]

Neither can the additional clause, "a letter to the settlement (captivity) at Babylon," chap. xxix. 1, be proved to be a gloss. The addition does not really interrupt the connection of thought in the sentence, as Hitzig asserts. It rather properly explains exactly what seems to have taken place. Consistently with the rest of the verse, the relative pronoun "which," in the Septuagint, is plural, and refers to "*the words* of the writing" that was sent by Jeremiah as a letter from Jerusalem to Babylon. The whole verse, which is quite as complete in the Greek as in the Hebrew, indicates the existence of a special text-recension. In the first member of the verse in Greek there are two short omissions, "the prophet" and "the residue;" and in the second member there is the important addition just discussed, and there is also a long omission, "whom Nebuchadnezzar had carried away captive from Jerusalem to Babylon." Hitzig

[1] *The Cambridge Bible for Schools and Colleges*, Jeremiah and Lamentations, p. 107.

admits that this latter sentence is rightly wanting in the Septuagint, inasmuch as it is rendered superfluous by the succeeding verse.

The added clause, "upon him," chap. xvii. 5, is not an explanatory note. The sentence is an exceedingly easy one. No explanation whatever was needed to make its meaning plain. Instead of simplifying the verse, the addition renders it, if anything, somewhat more difficult. Neither a translator nor a later writer would have attempted after this fashion to explain the sacred text. In Hebrew the verse reads, "Cursed is the man that trusteth in man, and maketh flesh his arm;" in Greek the latter sentence reads, "and places the flesh of his arm upon him." The language in the original of each text was just the same, with the exception of the two additional words, "upon him." The pronoun evidently refers to the second word for man, in the first of the two sentences, as its antecedent. The reading in the Septuagint, though peculiar, is perfectly intelligible, and appears to reproduce an ancient form of the Hebrew text which the translator used.

The added sentence, "and they have concealed their cause of stumbling (punishment) from me," chap. xviii. 20, is neither a paraphrase nor a gloss. It is rather a genuine piece of ancient text. It affords a most convincing proof of the hypothesis of a special text-recension which formed the original of the Alexandrian version. There is no reason whatever to regard it as a gloss with Graf, nor to consider it with Hitzig an excess or a redundance in one verse. Instead of appearing to be an interpolation, it rather bears the appearance of genuineness; and instead of injuring the parallelism of the verse-members, it rather gives them a rhythmical balance. Thus both objections to it are unjust, and the latter, that the words should be rejected because they overload the verse, is really absurd. Hitzig also foolishly supposes that the translator wrongly inserted the sentence after the analogy of ver. 22, because of having incorrectly interpreted it. The sentence is most appropriate where it stands, and gives an increased significance to the verse. There seems to be a happy contrast in the Septuagint between ver. 20 and ver. 23. In the former, addressing Jehovah, the prophet says, "they have concealed their cause of stumbling from me;" in the latter, he says, "let their cause of stumbling be before thee."

The addition in chap. xxii. 17 is also neither a paraphrase nor a gloss. It is another certain proof of a twofold reading in the ancient Hebrew manuscripts. Moreover, the rendering of the Septuagint is capital. In the Hebrew, the first half of the verse reads, "But thine eyes and thine heart are not but for thy covetousness;" in the Greek it reads, "Behold, neither are thine eyes nor is thy heart good, but for thy covetousness." Instead of "But," the Septuagint has "Behold;" instead of one copula with a negative, it has two negatives of the verb *to be*; and, instead of no adjective qualifying either noun, it has the adjective, "good," qualifying each of the substantives, the very term the verse requires to make the sense complete. The differences between the two texts in this verse are so peculiar and important that they must have been recensional. They cannot have been the outcome of intention on the part of the translator, or on the part of any writer of a later time. There is no unfitness in any of the added words. The variations in the Greek are all appropriate, and represent a classic form of Hebrew text.

5. Some additions are due to ignorance, or to want of understanding, in translating the original Hebrew text. The charge that the translator omitted portions of his manuscript through ignorance appears entirely improbable, but the charge that he or a transcriber added to the text through ignorance seems utterly unreasonable. In not a single instance does Graf establish the probability of this charge.

The addition at the end of chap. i. 17, "because I am with thee to deliver thee, declares Jehovah," does not rest upon an erroneous understanding of the text, as Graf asserts, nor did it arise from a false interpretation of the preceding clause, as Hitzig says. It affords another striking evidence of a special text-recension. It, moreover, harmonizes perfectly with the context in the Septuagint, which contains encouragement and comfort for the prophet. Neither is the addition taken from ver. 8, as Graf believes. This assurance of the divine presence and deliverance occurs in the Hebrew of this chapter twice, namely, vers. 8, 19; whereas, in the Greek, it occurs thrice, namely, vers. 8, 17, 19. It belongs as naturally and as appropriately in the present place in Greek as in either of the other places in both the Hebrew and the Greek. The Septuagint rendering of the latter half of the verse is almost wholly different from the Massoretic rendering, but it is entirely consistent with itself, as well as with the context.

The added clause, "and concerning this man," chap. xxii. 18, was not inserted, because the translator misunderstood the meaning of vers. 14–17 of this chapter. Between the two texts, throughout these latter five verses, there are minor variations of different kinds and of considerable significance in every verse. The discrepancies, indeed, point clearly to a special manuscript in each case. The present addition is another example of recensional divergences. In Tischendorf's edition of the

Septuagint, the clause is printed as if it were in apposition to "Jehoiakim" in the preceding clause. This construction seems not to be correct. The added words appear more properly to refer to "Shallum the son of Josiah," whose fate the prophet has described in vers. 11, 12. In perfect consistency with this supposition, as Hitzig grants, a plural verb, "they shall be buried," follows in ver. 19 of the Septuagint. The plural verbs in Greek, moreover, in ver. 15 and also in ver. 16, fully confirm this supposition.

The added word "earth," chap. xxxiii. 2, does not seem to have arisen either from intentional insertion or from imperfect understanding. Neither does it necessarily appear so incorrect as Graf assumes. It rather appears exceedingly appropriate where it stands, and seems unquestionably to have belonged to the translator's text. It also gives a necessary completeness to the verse. Properly speaking, it is really another word, and not an additional word in the sentence, inasmuch as it simply takes the place of the second word, "Jehovah," which is wanting in the Septuagint. The repetition of this latter term in Hebrew is somewhat peculiar, if not, indeed, altogether superfluous; whereas, the rendering of the verse in Greek is admirable, Graf's objection to the contrary notwithstanding. To an unprejudiced critic it seems to be superior, for the reason that it makes much more natural sense, and corresponds much more nearly with the parallel passage, Isa. xlv. 18, which it very closely resembles. The order of the words is slightly different, but the language is almost identical.

The addition of "Jehovah" at the end of chap. xxxviii. 27, Graf characterizes as "quite thoughtless" or unmeaning, but it is by no means certain that his criticism is correct. The verse has a very significant meaning in the Septuagint, and the closing words are quite consistent with the context in the Greek. In ver. 20 of this latter text, instead of urging Zedekiah to obey "the *voice* of Jehovah," Jeremiah is described as urging him to obey "the *word* of Jehovah." In the three succeeding verses in the Hebrew, with some slight verbal variations, the prophet is represented as declaring to the king "the word" which Jehovah had shown him. In the next two verses, the king is represented as requesting the prophet to "let no man know of these words," and to mention but one of the subjects of their conversation, if "the princes" should hear of their private meeting, and should inquire of him the nature of their conference. Shortly afterwards, as seems to have been expected, "the princes" came to Jeremiah, and interviewed him, when he answered them according to the commandment of the king. "Then," continues the record in the Septuagint, "they (the princes) left off speaking, because the word of Jehovah was not reported." Instead of being meaningless, the reading in the Greek seems to be the ancient and correct one, and it seems also to explain how the reading in the Hebrew should be understood, inasmuch as in its present form it is somewhat incomplete.

Thus a close examination of the various species of addition, as classified for this investigation, shows how unfounded and unfair are Graf's objections to their genuineness. In not a single instance is his allegation strictly true. In some cases, it is difficult to account with certainty for the additional word or words, but these are very few indeed. They probably were due in part, if not in whole, to the imperfect condition of the ancient manuscripts. The great majority of them, however, were due to recensional divergences. Instead of belonging to a later date than the time of the Septuagint translation, they belong to a much earlier date. Instead of having arisen out of the received Hebrew text, they arose out of a widely different text. Instead of being generally spurious, they are generally, if not always, genuine. If they do not, in every case, exhibit the original text, they do, at least, exhibit a very ancient form of it—a much more ancient form, perhaps, than that exhibited by the Massoretic text. In numerous passages Graf, as well as Hitzig and Movers, recognizes the superiority of the Septuagint reading, and also the probable primitive character of the additions. In the remaining passages, as a rule, if the Greek does not represent a more primitive reading than the Hebrew, it represents, at all events, the reading of a different recension—the Alexandrian recension.

The additions of letters, of which there are a few, are interesting, inasmuch as they explain the origin of a number of variations. Like the omissions of letters, it is difficult to determine which of them were recensional and which transcriptional, as some of them were evidently due to one cause and some of them to another. The following are the chief examples:—

תִּשָּׁא—תִּשָּׁאֵל (?) vii. 16; xi. 14; נַאֲצָלֵנוּ—נִצָּלֵנוּ, vii. 10; דִּמְיוֹן—דֹּמֶן, viii. 2; שָׁפָתַיִם—שְׁפַיִם, iii. 21; vii. 29; אֲשֶׁר—אֵשׁ (?) xi. 16; וְהֲאַגְּרֵם—וְהִגַּרְתִּים, ix. 21; xvi. 4; וּבְקַעְתִּי—וּבְקִיתִי (?) xix. 7; נֶאֱנַחְתִּי—נֶחָנְתָּ, xviii. 21; יְלַהֲכוּ—יֵלְכוּ (?) xxx. 16; אֲבֵלָה—אֵלֶּה, xxii. 23; —וּדְלָיָהוּ, xxxii. 12; הָעֹמְדִים—הָעֵדִים, xxxi. 21; בְּנַבְרוּת—בִּגְרוּת, xli. 17; —וּגְדַלְיָהוּ, xxxvi. 25; —בְּעָרֵי, גִּלְעָד—גָּד, xlix. 1; צִירִים—צַיִּים, l. 39; בְּשַׂעֲרֵי, xliv. 6; יִתְעַלָּף—יִתְעַל (?) li. 3.

CHAPTER IV.

THE VARIATIONS—TRANSPOSITIONS.

THE character of the Transpositions in the Septuagint is remarkable, and the evidence they furnish of recensional divergences is significant. They comprise letters, words, verses and chapters. Of these four species, some one or other kind occurs in nearly every chapter of the book. The transposition of chapters, being the most manifest and striking, has always attracted much attention. On account of its interest and importance, this species of transposition should be considered first.

From about the middle of chap. xxv. to the beginning of chap. lii. the numbering of the chapters is entirely different. This difference is chiefly due to the position occupied by the nine prophecies against foreign nations. In each text, this group of prophecies stands together; but, in the Greek, it is found near the middle, in the Hebrew, near the end, of the book. In the former, it follows immediately after chap. xxv. 13; in the latter, it begins with chap. xlvi. Not only does the general arrangement of these prophecies differ widely, but also their particular order of sequence amongst themselves differs considerably. Their order in the Greek is Elam, Egypt, Babylon, Philistia, Edom, Ammon, Kedar, Damascus, Moab; their order in the Hebrew is Egypt, Philistia, Moab, Ammon, Edom, Damascus, Kedar, Elam, Babylon.

Although it is not the special purpose of this investigation to discuss exhaustively either the arrangement or the order of these prophecies, being chiefly concerned with the arguments for a different text-recension, yet the subject is too interesting in itself to be entirely left alone, and too important for the present hypothesis to be very slightly touched. It, therefore, claims a fair and full consideration. The discussion involves two questions—the position and the grouping of these nine prophecies. Respecting each it can be shown that the Alexandrian version exhibits the more ancient as well as the more natural form of this prophetic book.

The first question is of particularly great importance, because of the logical relation between the different parts of the book. It admits, moreover, of a thoroughly critical treatment and of a tolerably certain settlement. The second question is of comparatively small importance, because the grouping of the individual prophecies is practically immaterial, so long as the subject-matter in each case is substantially the same. This question, further, does not admit of a decisive answer. At least, while the one may seem more original than the other, it, perhaps, can never be determined with absolute certainty which grouping is the more correct. Much may be said, as much already has been said, in favour of the combination in each text. It may, however, be pretty positively settled which one the translator had before him in the manuscript he used.

Taking these questions in the order of their importance, it is necessary to consider, first, the correctness, and, secondly, the originality, of the position of the prophecies in each case. Their position, it should be observed, must be considered independently of the position of similar prophecies in any other book of Scripture. In some of the other books, the prophecies against the heathen do not stand at the end of the work, but occupy a position analogous to that here occupied by the present group in Greek. The analogy, though interesting and significant, is in no way conclusive. The indirect evidence it furnishes, while favourable to the Septuagint, is not sufficient of itself to decide the matter with perfect certainty. The position of this group has nothing whatever to do with that of either of the other groups. The question, therefore, must be considered simply on its own merits; and it must be determined, if at all, by the relation of these nine prophecies to the general contents of the book. In endeavouring to determine it, reference must be made particularly to the relation between the two parts into which chap. xxv. is divided by their insertion immediately after ver. 13 in the Septuagint, or rather by their removal to the beginning of chap. xlvi. in the Massoretic text.

A careful reading of chap. xxv. in the Hebrew will show that there is really something wanting after ver. 13 to connect it logically with the section which begins with ver. 15. In this latter section there is an enumeration of the nations to which the prophet is said to have been directed by Jehovah to offer, figuratively, of course, the wine-cup of the divine fury; or, in other words, to foreshadow the ruin of those nations whose overthrow should be involved in the general destruction which is described in ver. 11. In the main, the names of these nations correspond with the names of those against whom the nine prophecies in question were proclaimed. For this reason, one would naturally expect them to appear in close connection with the enumeration mentioned. This expectation is realized in the Septuagint.

Here the group of prophecies begins directly after ver. 13, and the section commencing with ver. 15 follows at once as chap. xxxii. In this position, the prophecies stand connected with kindred matter; whereas, in the position which they occupy in the Hebrew, they stand unconnected with any thing whatever of a kindred character. Having, therefore, in this latter text no logical connection with the preceding chapters, they are manifestly out of place.

Moreover, as chap. xxv. 13 in the Hebrew reads, it has no legitimate connection either with that which goes before or with that which follows. In its present form it is altogether inappropriate, "because," as Bleek observes, "in the foregoing part of the book there are no threatening discourses whatever against heathen nations."[1] In the Septuagint, on the other hand, ver. 13 ends with the clause, "in this book." This term here, as elsewhere in Jeremiah, seems to be equivalent to a volume, or a collection of prophetic writings, of which the prophet wrote, or rather dictated, several; and it refers both to what immediately precedes and to what immediately succeeds. It is to be understood of the "book," or roll, which

---

[1] "Da im vorhergehenden Theile des Buches sich noch gar keine Drohreden wider fremde Völker finden." *Einleitung in das Alte Testament*, p. 326.

contained the prophecies against the "nations" mentioned in the section already discussed. In the Massoretic text, these prophecies are not included in this "book," but in another "book," or, perhaps, in what might have been a separate roll or volume.

Again, the section beginning with ver. 15 indicates that the prophecies properly belong where they stand in Greek. They form the natural connection between the two parts of this chapter, vers. 8-13 constituting a suitable introduction, and vers. 15-30 a suitable supplement. Their presence, too, is required here, not only by the general enumeration given in this latter section, but also by the special description it contains, that is, of the wine-cup of the divine fury. In the prophecy respecting Edom, chap. xlix. 12, where this same term occurs, the words are not an "echo" from ver. 28 of this section, as Hitzig suggests; but, with the prophecies in their right position, they form a faint outline in the former verse of a picture which in the latter verse appears in full. In the one case the figure is partially, in the other case completely, developed. From these considerations, it is evident that, in the Septuagint, these prophecies occupy their proper place.

Not only is this earlier position the one which, from their relation to the context, they would naturally occupy, but also it is the one which they must have originally occupied in each text. That is, this is where they evidently stood in the originals of both the Hebrew and the Greek. That their position in the former was once the same as their position in the latter, is rendered practically certain by a critical comparison of the two texts. These prophecies at one time must have stood in the middle of the book, following immediately after chap. xxv. 13, because the sentence, "which Jeremiah hath prophesied against all the nations," occupies the same place in each text. In the Hebrew, though, it stands as the conclusion of ver. 13, while, in the Greek, it stands as the introduction to these nine prophecies. The sentence is not an appositional expression, as the Hebrew implies, but an introductory title, and has no direct relation to ver. 13. It simply connects the two parts of this "book," or roll. It should, moreover, be translated, "What (the things which) Jeremiah prophesied against the nations," and should be placed as a superscription to the prophecies, as it is found in the Septuagint translation. It, of course, as critics all agree, was not inserted here by Jeremiah, but by his secretary Baruch, or by an early editor, just as many, if not all, of the other superscriptions to chapters and paragraphs and prophecies were inserted.

This opinion receives the strongest possible support from Bleek, who regards the sentence in question as undoubtedly intended for a superscription in each text, and considers it appropriate where it stands only when, as in the Septuagint, it is followed by a series of utterances concerning foreign nations. After showing its unsuitableness as a title to the list of nations given in vers. 15–38, he says, "The maker of the Massoretic recension, however, who transplanted those other oracles against individual nations from here to the end of the book, has, as Movers also properly observes, misunderstandingly drawn the doubtful words to the context of the prophecy, together with the insertion of כל, and then also, for the purpose of connecting it with the foregoing, has placed at the beginning of ver. 14 a כי, which likewise did not originally stand there, and which the Septuagint does not express."[1] This explanation, though good so far as it goes, does not go far enough. As the whole of ver. 14 is wanting in the Septuagint, it, too, may have been inserted by

[1] "Der Urheber der masorethischen Recension aber, der jene anderen Orakel wider einzelne Völker von hier an den Schluss des Buches verpflanzte, hat (wie richtig auch Movers bemerkt) die fraglichen Worte missverständlich mit zum Contexte der Weissagung gezogen—mit Einschaltung von כל und dann auch v. 14 (am Anfange) zur Anknüpfung an das Vorhergehende ein כי gesetzt, was ursprünglich ebenfalls nicht dastand, und was die Septuaginta auch nicht ausdrückt." *Einleitung in das Alte Testament*, p. 326.

an ancient copyist or editor, in order to connect ver. 13 with ver. 15, after the prophecies, which the words in question originally introduced, had been removed. At any rate, the fact that the introductory sentence occupies exactly the same place in each text seems to prove that it is an ancient title, and not a "gloss," as Orelli[1] surprisingly asserts; and the additions mentioned by Bleek appear to indicate that ver. 13 in Hebrew was changed, and ver. 14 inserted, not through misunderstanding, but through intelligent design.

A further comparison of the two texts corroborates the probability of this conjecture. The omissions from the Septuagint in vers. 8–14 indicate that this section was once substantially the same in each text. The absence of "all," in the first member of ver. 9, Hitzig admits to be a better reading because of the singular, "that nation," in ver. 12, and "that land," in ver. 13. The clause, "and unto Nebuchadnezzar, the king of Babylon, my servant," in ver. 9, Graf himself regards as the addition of a later hand, as well as the clauses, "the king of Babylon . . . and the land of the Chaldeans," in ver. 12. The absence of the whole of ver. 14, which is unsuited to the context, is also in favour of the reading in the Septuagint. It appears unquestionably to have been either a gloss

[1] *Kurzgefasster Kommentar*, etc., Vierte Abteilung, p. 217.

or a marginal note. A literal rendering of vers. 11-13, as they now stand in the Greek, and as they once seem to have stood in the Hebrew, will illustrate the superiority of the Septuagint translation of the section under consideration. It will also show how appropriately this passage introduces the prophecies in question, and how admirably the reading of the version corresponds with the probabilities, so far as they can be estimated, and also with the facts, so far as they can be ascertained. The verses read, "And all the land (Judah) shall be a desolation, and they (the Jews) shall serve amongst the nations seventy years; and when the seventy years are accomplished (compare chap. xxix. 10), I will punish that nation (Babylonia), and I will make them (the Babylonians) a perpetual desolation; and I will bring upon that land (Babylonia) all my words which I have pronounced against it, even all that is written in this book."

Having shown that the position of these prophecies in the Septuagint is not only the proper one, but also the original one, even in the Massoretic text itself, it is worth observing that this position corresponds to that of similar prophecies in other Old Testament books. The analogy, as has already been admitted, possesses no special argumentative importance, but it is interesting, to say the least. Concerning the different positions and the respective claims of each to originality, Kühl significantly says, " In the other great prophets, Ezekiel and Isaiah, the prophecies against the heathen stand in the middle, between penal and expostulatory discourses to the particular people and Messianic predictions of the future. In like manner, we could, with perfect right, expect them here also in the middle. Now we even actually find in chap. xxv. an enumeration of the nations, to whom the prophet, at the command of Jehovah, should reach forth the wine-cup of the divine fury; and the number and names of these nations substantially correspond with the nations against which the prophecies in chaps. xlvi.-xlix. (li.) are directed. If one reads chap. xxv., there really remains something missing; one seeks even here the presentation of the prophecies, such as chaps. xlvi.-xlix. (li.)." [1]

[1] " In den andern grossen Propheten, Ezechiel und Jesaja, stehen die Weissagungen gegen die Heiden in der Mitte zwischen Straf- und Mahnreden an das eigene Volk und messianischen Zukunftsweissagungen. Wir könnten sie also mit Fug und Recht hier auch in der Mitte erwarten. Nun finden wir auch wirklich in Kap. xxv. eine Aufzählung der Völker, denen der Prophet auf Jahwes Geheiss den Becher des Gotteszornes reichen soll; und die Anzahl und Namen dieser Völker stimmen im Wesentlichen überein mit den Völkern, gegen die sich die Weissagungen in Kap. xlvi.-xlix. (li.) richten. Liest man Kap. xxv., so bleibt wirklich etwas fehlen; man sucht die Ausführung der Weissagungen, also Kap. xlvi.-xlix. (li.), schon hier." *Das Verhältniss der Massora zur Septuaginta*, p. 15.

As this collection of prophecies forms in each text a connected whole, it is evident that the entire group has been, at some time, we know not when, by some one, we know not who, for some reason, we know not why, bodily transferred from one part to another part of the book. Their removal, moreover, was clearly intentional, and not accidental. The reason may have been to give precedence to the prophecies respecting the Jews, and thus to keep them separate, deeming "the end of the book the fitting place for them," as Streane suggests, "and by this position leaving the prophecies which had to do with the Jews themselves distinct and preceding them."[1] At all events, their arbitrary transposition was not the work of the Alexandrian translator, inasmuch as both the Hebrew and the Greek prove that, in the Septuagint, these prophecies occupy their proper and original place. The change was evidently made by a later editor or copyist in the Massoretic recension or text itself.

On this point, Scholz, in discussing the difference of arrangement which he with Bleek attributes to a subsequent reviser, forcefully observes, "That the alterations do not proceed from the translator appears from the character of his translation incon-

---

[1] *The Cambridge Bible for Schools and Colleges*, Jeremiah and Lamentations, Introduction, p. xxxvi.

testable. It is unthinkable that he should have made such great changes, while he not merely, with tolerable accuracy, translates from word to word, but even renders sentences in which he can find no sense, writes Hebrew words, whose meaning he does not know, with Greek letters, without translating them, and so forth. The words, 'And I will bring upon that land all my words which I have pronounced against it, even all that is written in *this book*,' ver. 13, also speak decidedly for this, that the prophecies against the nations formerly stood here, and, indeed, so much the more, as the words, 'and the king of Sheshach shall drink after them,' etc., ver. 26, are certainly spurious; so that, thus, in the prophecy, xxv. 14–38, respecting the land concerning which, according to ver. 13, the discourse must chiefly be, not a syllable stood in '*this book.*' Hence it follows that the arrangement of the book in six great divisions (Dekaden) is in the Septuagint alone correct."[1]

[1] "Dass die Aenderungen nicht vom Uebersetzer herrühren, geht aus dem Charakter seiner Uebersetzung umwidersprechlich hervor. Es ist undenkbar, dass derselbe, während er nicht nur mit ziemlicher Genauigkeit von Wort zu Wort übersetzt, selbst Sätze, in denen er keinen Sinn finden kann, widergibt, hebräische Wörter, deren Bedeutung er nicht kennt, mit griechischen Buchstaben, ohne sie zu übersetzen, schreibt u. s. w., so grosse Aenderungen sollte gemacht haben. Auch sprechen die Worte, v. 13, 'Et adducam super terram illam omnia verba mea, quae locutus sum contra eam, omne, quod scriptum est in *libro isto*,' entschieden dafür, dass die Weissagungen gegen die Völker ehemals hier standen, und zwar um so

Notwithstanding the convincing character of the evidence respecting the ancient position of these prophecies, it is remarkable that in the latest commentary on this book of any critical importance, Orelli asserts, not only that the place they occupy in the Septuagint is not the more correct, but also that it is not their primitive position. He considers that their insertion after chap. xxv. 13 awkwardly cuts this chapter into two pieces. He admits, though, that their position in the Massoretic text is not the original one. "In the earliest editions of the book," he says, "most of the declarations respecting foreigners, which now stand at the end of it, must have stood in the immediate neighbourhood of chap. xxv."[1] He is disposed to believe that they formerly followed immediately after this chapter. Kuenen, who has long advocated this latter position, also admits that "with chap. xxv., particularly with vers. 15–26, the first group of prophecies against the heathen is certainly

mehr, als die Worte, v. 26, 'et rex Sesach bibet post eos,' u. s. w. sicher unächt sind, so dass also in der Weissagung, xxv. 14–38, von dem Lande, von dem nach v. 13 hauptsächlich die Rede sein müsste, in dem *libro isto* keine Sylbe stünde. Hiezu kommt, dass die Einrichtung des Buches in 6 Dekaden nur bei LXX. richtig ist." *Der masoreth. Text und die LXX-Uebersetzung*, etc., p. 156.

[1] "In den frühesten Ausgaben des Buches die meisten jetzt an seinem Schluss befindlichen Sprüche über die Auswärtigen sich in unmittelbarer Nähe von c. 25 befunden haben müssen." *Kurzgefasster Kommentar*, etc., Vierte Abteilung, p. 217.

connected."[1] Ewald and Kühl, it is worth noting further in this connection, both make the same admission respecting their position in the Hebrew, but the former supposes that they stood originally just before chap. xxv., because he thinks the words, "these nations," ver. 9, indicate this place, while the latter supposes that they once stood just after ver. 29, because he thinks the rest of the chapter constitutes a kind of recapitulation of the entire group.

In answer to Kühl, it should be pointed out that vers. 30-38 form a natural conclusion to chap. xxv., as it now stands, but that they would not follow naturally after the group of prophecies, as he suggests. It would be neither natural nor appropriate to say, "Therefore prophesy thou against them all these words," etc., just after the prophecies had already been delivered. In answer to Ewald, it should be remarked that the two words, "these nations," imply no such position of these prophecies as he proposes, even though they both were genuine. The pronoun, "these," however, is not only superfluous, as Hitzig says, but is also wanting in the Septuagint, in which the reading, " all the nations round about it," is, as Hitzig likewise says, indisputably preferable.

[1] "Met H. xxv., bepaaldelijk met vs. 15-26, hangt de eerste groep der profetiën tegen de heidenen stellig zamen." *Historisch-Kritisch Onderzoek*, etc., Tweede Deel, 1863, p. 218.

In reply to all of these four critics, each of whom suggests for these nine prophecies a position other than that which they now occupy in either of the texts, it is sufficient to observe that, whereas the prophecies might stand tolerably well, perhaps, just after chap. xxv., as Ewald and Orelli both believe, there are only two positions legitimately under consideration in the discussion of this subject. We are concerned at present with two, and only two, textual authorities. The question is, Which one of these preserves the original position in the ancient text-recensions by means of which they have been individually handed down to us? From this investigation, it is manifest that the position in the Septuagint is the earlier and the more original of the two; that is, it is the most original of which there is at present any record. There is not a vestige of evidence to show that the prophecies ever occupied other than one of two positions in either the Palestinean or the Alexandrian recension; and the form of chap. xxv., and of ver. 13 especially, clearly indicates that they now should stand in the middle of that chapter, and that they once did stand there in each recension. If the position in the Septuagint, therefore, does not represent the prophet's own arrangement, it certainly indicates the form in which his writings were originally arranged.

Coming now to the discussion of the second question, it is also necessary to consider the correctness and the originality of the order of sequence of these prophecies amongst themselves. Judging the matter from circumstantial considerations, Graf maintains that the order in the Hebrew text is the more natural. He says, " The succession in which these nations are mentioned is such as most naturally follows from the situation and the circumstances. Egypt appears first, because from the defeat of her forces, described in chap. xlvi. 3-12, the disaster, indeed, proceeded to the other nations; then comes Philistia, which bordered alike on Egypt and on Judah; and the three countries which lay immediately on the other side, Moab and Ammon, the ever-united kindred nations, and Edom, the kindred nation of Judah; then Syria, which bordered on Israel, and which once stood in such manifold relations to it; finally, the Arabian tribes which dwelt away as far as the Euphrates." [1]

[1] "Die Reihenfolge, in welcher diese Völker aufgeführt werden, ist so wie sie sich aus Lage und Umständen am natürlichsten ergab : Aegypten erscheint zuerst, denn von der xlvi. 3-12 geschilderten Niederlage seiner Kriegsmacht ging ja das Unglück über die andern Völker aus, dann kommt Philistäa, welches zugleich an Aegypten und an Juda grenzte, und die drei Länder, welche auf der andern Seite zunächst lagen, Moab und Ammon, die stets verbundenen Brudervölker, und Edom, das Brudervolk Juda's, dann das an Israel grenzende und mit diesem einst in so vielfachen Beziehungen stehende Syrien, endlich die bis nach dem Euphrat hin wohnenden arabischen Stämme." *Der Prophet Jeremia*, p. 506.

There is something interesting, it must be admitted, in the order of these prophecies in the Hebrew, proceeding, as it does, to some extent, from the countries near to Palestine to those which are more distant from it; but this principle is not, by any means, consistently observed. A certain geographical arrangement, too, is traceable, though it is not very definite or distinct. In general, its course is from the south toward the north and east, but this direction is not followed with sufficient accuracy to possess any very great significance. Indeed, the principle which underlies the grouping in either text is far from obvious, and cannot be with certainty determined. When Graf asserts, however, that the order in the Hebrew follows most naturally from all the circumstances, his assertion is too sweeping by a good deal. After the prophecies had been fulfilled, the order might be regarded as more natural, perhaps; but, from chap. xxv. 13, one might most naturally expect the prophecy against Babylon to come first. It does not occupy this position, though, in either of the texts. In the Greek, it stands in the third place of the group, coming immediately after the prophecy against Egypt; in the Hebrew, it stands at the very end of the group. Streane considers that it is more natural to begin with Egypt, because this was "the nation whose overthrow by Nebuchadnezzar would be the signal to the rest of a similar fate."[1] This prophecy, however, would not necessarily be so understood until after the events predicted had transpired.

Graf also considers that the order of these prophecies in Hebrew is suited both to their subject-matter and to their time of composition.[2] The first assertion is possibly correct; the second assertion is probably incorrect. While the order in chaps. xlvi.-li. agrees in general with the enumeration which is given in chap. xxv. 15-26, the succession of the prophecies against Moab, Ammon and Edom in this latter chapter is inverted. This enumeration of nations, however, does not in each text exactly correspond. The Septuagint, besides omitting "and all the kings of the land of Uz," ver. 20; "the isle," ver. 22; "and all the kings of Arabia," ver. 24; "and all the kings of Zimri," ver. 25; "and the king of Sheshach shall drink after them," ver. 26, reads "Roz" for "Buz," ver. 23; "Persians" for "Medes," and "all the kings of the East" for "all the kings of the North," ver. 26. Thus, while the Hebrew order fairly suits the subject-matter in the Massoretic text, it does not specially suit the subject-matter in

---

[1] *The Cambridge Bible for Schools and Colleges*, Jeremiah and Lamentations, p. 284.
[2] *Der Prophet Jeremia*, Einleitung, p. li.

the Alexandrian text. That this order agrees with the time of the composition of these prophecies is neither certain nor probable. It is not certain, inasmuch as there are no historic data available for purposes of proof; it is not probable, inasmuch as the prophecy against Babylon can hardly have been spoken at a later period than any of the rest. Instead of having been composed last, one would naturally expect from chap. xxv. 8-12 that it would have been composed first. The exact time, however, of the composition of the respective prophecies cannot be absolutely shown.

The prophecies in the Greek, Graf further says, have been quite arbitrarily transposed by an application to them of later circumstances. This assertion is even more groundless than either of the two preceding ones. There is not the slightest reason for supposing that the ancient order in the Greek was ever intentionally changed. That a prophecy may have been accidentally misplaced is possible, perhaps, although there is no conclusive evidence that this is really the case. In the Hebrew, on the other hand, not only is there considerable reason for supposing that the order has been changed, but also there is substantial evidence of such a change. The Hebrew order has the appearance of having been altered, partly with reference to the enumeration of nations in chap. xxv.

15-26, and partly with reference to the supposed order of fulfilment of the prophecies. The position of the prophecy against Babylon is an indication that it must have been inserted purposely in this place by some one after the events predicted had already taken place. Further evidence of this assertion is furnished by the fact that the statement, "and the king of Sheshach shall drink after them," chap. xxv. 26, is unquestionably spurious. It is plainly an interpolation having no legitimate connection where it stands. It seems, as Bleek believes, and as Graf himself admits, to have been added by a later hand with reference to the position of the prophecy respecting Babylon, which appears in Hebrew as chaps. l., li. The whole sentence is wanting in the Septuagint, as well as the word "Sheshach" also in chap. li. 41. This latter term, moreover, cannot have proceeded from Jeremiah, as Hitzig says, because, as he justly adds, the prophet had no reason whatever to employ such a form of cabalistic writing.

While there is no probability that the order in the Greek has been "arbitrarily transposed," as Graf asserts, and while there is great probability that the order in the Hebrew has been purposely arranged according to a principle, partly geographical, partly chronological, the absolute correctness of the one or of the other is difficult, if not impossible, to determine. Inasmuch as the Hebrew has been evidently altered, there is good reason to regard the order in the Greek as the more correct. What the principle underlying the order in the Septuagint may have been, however, is by no means clear. Scholz, though, offers a suggestion which, if not convincing, is at least ingenious. He says, "Why does the short utterance respecting Elam, which certainly had long since ceased to play an important part, stand at the very beginning? Possibly, because the first exploit of the ancestor of Israel was performed against an Elamite (Gen. xiv.). The second World-wide Power with which Israel came into hostile relations is Egypt, and the third is Babylon—the last as the inheritress of Nineveh. Thus were the utterances respecting the three great nations first brought into chronological order."[1]

The question of the priority of the order of sequence in each text is also difficult to decide with certainty. As the succession in the Septua-

---

[1] "Warum steht der kleine Ausspruch über Aelam, das zudem längst aufgehört hatte, eine entscheidende Rolle zu spielen, voran? Etwa, weil die erste That des Stammvaters Israels gegen einen Alamiten gerichtet ist Gen. xiv.? Die zweite Weltmacht, mit der Israel feindlich zusammentraf, ist Aegypten, die dritte Babel, letzteres zugleich als Erbin Ninive's. So wurden zuerst die Aussprüche über die grossen Völker in chronologischer Ordnung gebracht." *Der masoreth. Text und die LXX- Uebersetzung*, etc., p. 157.

gint appears to be the more correct, so also, with greater reason, it appears to be the more primitive. Whether this arrangement indicates the order of the composition of each particular prophecy or not, it seems to indicate the original order of its publication in manuscript form. The exact period of the composition of each, however, is not definitely known and cannot be definitely determined. The small amount of accurate historical information which we possess respecting these ancient times renders the determination of the date of many, if not most, of them absolutely impossible. According to the list of nations, chap. xxv. 15-26, one would naturally expect, if the order in this section had any real significance, that the prophecy against Egypt should stand first in the collection, and that against Elam last. Instead of this being the case, Elam begins the group. Hence it is evident that the arrangement in the Greek was not determined with reference to this enumeration. It is reasonable, therefore, to believe that this was its original place in the collection. The translator gave, one must assume, the order which obtained in the ancient manuscript which he used. Had he found the succession in chap. xxv. 15-26 reproduced, he surely would have followed it. The great age of the Septuagint, and the circumstances under which the translation was made, all point to the conclusion that it presents, as nearly as can be known, the primitive order of sequence of these prophecies amongst themselves.

It is significant, though, that at the end of the prophecy against Elam and at the commencement of chap. xxvi. in the Septuagint, it is stated that this prophecy was composed in the beginning of the reign of Zedekiah. This statement shows that the order of the prophecies in the Alexandrian version was not made to harmonize with the time of their respective composition, inasmuch as one of them, at least, must have been composed earlier than the reign of Zedekiah, if the date of the prophecy against Egypt be correct. As both the Hebrew and the Greek agree in reference to this date, there is reason to regard it as authentic. This latter prophecy was probably read to king Jehoiakim, and was certainly delivered before the time of Pharaoh-Necho's disastrous overthrow at Carchemish. Disregarding this date, Scholz, who defends the Alexandrian order, supposes that the prophecy against Elam was "composed earlier than any other;" and Kühl, who defends the Massoretic order, asserts that it was "written later than the rest." The record of the first date seems to be an explanatory note which formerly stood in the margin of the ancient manuscripts. In that case it was probably, at a time prior to the translation of the Septuagint, inserted in the text as a chronological subscription, because of the unexpected place which this prophecy occupied in the ancient collection.

If this supposition be correct, the marginal note, or the chronological subscription, whichever it may be, affords important evidence of the originality of the order in the Septuagint. However the historic statement may be explained, it apparently indicates the primitive position of this particular prophecy. Scholz's discussion of this question is worthy of consideration. "That the prophecy against Elam stands in the original place appears, in the highest degree, probable," he says, "through this, that the Greek text here displays an indubitably primitive peculiarity. The prophecy against Elam has in connection with it, and, indeed, *alone in the whole book, a subscription:* 'In the beginning of the reigning of king Zedekiah was this word concerning Elam.' It is quite incredible that a reviser of the present Massoretic text, for instance, should have hit upon the thought of converting here for the only time, against the usage of the entire book, as well as against his own custom, a superscription into a subscription; while, on the contrary, it is perfectly explicable how a reviser may have held it in order to remove this peculiarity by placing the subscription at the beginning of a section."[1]

Moreover, as the name of Babylon does not appear in the list of nations given in chap. xxv. 15-26, being rightly wanting, as has been pointed out, the transposition of three of the prophecies, namely, those respecting Elam, Moab and Damascus, leaving the prophecy respecting Babylon where it stands in Greek, would make the order of sequence of the prophecies amongst themselves harmonize in general with the above-mentioned enumeration. The change might have been made easily and with very little trouble, if the translator had been disposed to tamper with his text. For the reason that he did not make this change, it is quite improbable that the divergent order of the prophecies was due, in any sense, to intention on his part. The originality of the arrangement in the Septuagint is further indicated by the fact

[1] "Dass die Weissagung gegen Aelam bei LXX. an ursprünglicher Stelle steht, wird höchst wahrscheinlich dadurch, dass der griechische Text hier eine unzweifelhaft ursprüngliche Eigenthümlichkeit zeigt. Die Weissagung gegen Aelam hat bei ihnen und zwar *allein im ganzen Buche eine Unterschrift:* Ἐν ἀρχῇ βασιλεύοντος Σεδεκίου βασιλέως ἐγένετο ὁ λόγος οὗτος περὶ Αἰλάμ. Es ist ganz unglaublich, dass z. B. ein Bearbeiter des jetzigen masorethischen Textes auf den Einfall sollte gekommen sein, gegen den Gebrauch des ganzen Buches und seinen eigenen hier das einzige Mal eine Ueberschrift in eine Unterschrift zu verwandeln, während es umgekehrt vollkommen erklärlich ist, wie ein Diaskeuast es für in Ordnung gehalten habe, diese Unregelmässigkeit dadurch zu beseitigen, dass er die Unterschrift an den Anfang des Stückes stellte." *Der masoreth. Text und die LXX-Uebersetzung,* etc., p. 157.

that it is entirely independent of any principle either of geographical position or of prophetical fulfilment. On this point Scholz again significantly observes, "Finally, there speaks directly for the Septuagint the circumstance, that the regulating principle in the Massoretic text, which is plainly conformable to chap. xxv. 14 *seq.*, is manifest, while in the Septuagint it is, at least, obscure. But now how could it happen that any one should set aside what was clear and also, on superficial reading, easy to understand, and put in its place what even to himself was unintelligible?! So much the more, as to put the separate pieces in another place, instead of following the simple copy, could not be done without trouble. Whereas, how easily, especially if the translator had been 'inconsiderate and superficial,' could, in some way, a short prophecy, for instance, against Damascus have fallen out! Likewise, moreover, do preponderating reasons also speak for the originality of the order of the prophecies in the Septuagint."[1]

Thus the investigation of the position, and also

[1] "Endlich spricht für LXX. gerade der Umstand, dass das ordnende Princip bei dem masorethischen Texte sichtlich dem cap. xxv. 14 ff. conform, klar, bei LXX. aber mindestens unklar ist. Wie käme nun aber Jemand dazu, Klares und auch bei oberflächlichem Lesen leicht Erkennbares bei Seite zu legen, und ihm selbst Unverständliches an die Stelle zu setzen?! Um so mehr, als es nicht mühelos sein konnte, statt der einfachen Abschrift die einzelnen Stücke an anderer Stelle unterzubringen. Wie leicht konnte da,

of the order of the prophecies, leads to a similar conclusion. In each respect the Septuagint translation possesses the superiority. Of the correctness and originality of the position in the version, there can be no reasonable doubt; and, if the order in the latter be not the absolutely correct and original one, it is apparently and with great probability, the earlier one of the two. The order, moreover, is most likely the one which the Greek translator found before him in the manuscript he used. The justice of this conclusion appears to be unquestionable. Its reasonableness, it is believed, will be admitted by every unprejudiced investigator. Kuenen even, though he is generally against the Septuagint, honestly acknowledges the probability that the position in the Hebrew has been intentionally changed, as well as the improbability that either the position or the order in the Greek was changed by the translator. While believing that neither text exhibits the primitive form of the book in respect to these nine prophecies, he frankly says, " It does not follow from this that they have always stood, as in the Massoretic text, at the end of the entire collection;"

zumal wenn der Uebersetzer 'leichtfertig und oberflächlich' gewesen wäre, etwa eine kleine Weissagung z. B. gegen Damaskus ausfallen! So sprechen also auch überwiegende Gründe für die Ursprünglichkeit der Reihenfolge der Weissagungen bei LXX." *Der masoreth. Text und die LXX-Uebersetzung,* etc., p. 158.

and he justly adds, "neither has it been proved that the Greek translator took the liberty of transposing and transplanting these prophecies."[1]

There is the clearest evidence that both the ancient position and the ancient order in the Massoretic text have been, at some time, arbitrarily changed. The transposition in each case was evidently made by a later editor or reviser after the events predicted had transpired. An impartial consideration of all the circumstances renders this conclusion practically certain. The reason for the change in each respect has been so clearly and forcibly stated by Bleek, that it is important in concluding this discussion to quote in full his very reasonable explanation. "Were the Massoretic recension," he says, "the more original, then it would be absolutely impossible to conceive how a later Alexandrian redactor, even if he gave the oracles in the book in general a position other than that in which he found them, should have happened also so to transpose the individual ones against each other, as they present themselves in the Septuagint, that he placed as the very first the oracle respecting Elam (which in the Massoretic text is the last but

---

[1] "Daaruit volgt echter nog niet, dat zij altijd, gelijk in de Masora, aan het einde der gansche verzameling hebben gestaan ; . . . ook is het onbewezen, dat de Grieksche vertaler zich veroorloofd heeft, die godspraken om te zetten en te verplaatsen." *Historisch-Kritisch Onderzoek*, etc., Tweede Deel, p. 240.

one), and as the third the one respecting Babylon (which in the Massoretic text is the last of all), and so forth. Much sooner, on the contrary, can one imagine, if these oracles formerly had the position and the order which they have in the Septuagint, how the later redactor, who transferred them from that place to the end of the whole collection, could happen also to change their order of sequence amongst themselves. For as, a little while before, the immigration of the Jews with the prophet into Egypt was related, together with the prophecies respecting the destruction which would meet them there, such as those referring to the conquest of the country by Nebuchadnezzar and the fall of Pharaoh-Hophra, he (the redactor) might easily feel occasioned to place at the head of the group of prophecies respecting the individual heathen nations the two respecting Egypt, which at first stood after the one respecting Elam; and likewise he might find it suitable to place quite at the end the great oracle concerning the chief adversary of the covenant-people, namely, the Chaldeans, which followed immediately after those concerning Egypt. By this means, though, no doubt, the displacement of the position of the whole of these prophecies was naturally and easily brought about."[1]

---

[1] "Wäre die masorethische Recension die ursprünglichere, so würde sich durchaus nicht begreifen lassen, wie ein späterer Alexan-

The transposition of chapters, which was owing to the bodily removal of the prophecies against the heathen nations from the middle to the end of the book, as shown by the foregoing investigation, furnishes no real evidence of different text-recensions. The transposition of verses, owing to the arbitrary rearrangement of these prophecies amongst themselves, also affords no certain evidence of a special text-recension. The two texts, so far as the general position and arrangement of these prophecies are concerned, were probably at one time substantially, if not identically, the same. There are, how-

drinischer Redactor, wenn er auch diesen Orakeln im Allgemeinen im Buche eine andere Stellung gab, als worin er sie vorfand, sollte dazu gekommen sein, auch die einzelnen gegen einander so umzustellen, wie sie in der Sept. sich finden, dass er das Orakel über Elam (im masorethischen Texte das vorletzte) zuvörderst stellte, das über Babel (im masorethischen Texte das letzte) als das dritte, u. s. w. Weit eher kann man sich dagegen denken, wenn diese Orakel früher die Stellung und Reihenfolge wie in der Sept. hatten, wie der spätere Redactor, der sie von dort an das Ende der ganzen Sammlung stellte, dazu kommen konnte, auch ihre Aufeinanderfolge zu ändern. Denn da kurz vorher die Einwanderung der Juden mit dem Propheten in Aegypten erzählt war, mit Weissagungen über das Verderben, welches sie dort treffen werde, sowie über die Eroberung des Landes durch Nebukadnezar und den Untergang des Pharao Hophra, so konnte er leicht veranlasst werden, von der Sammlung der Orakel über die einzelnen fremden Völker die beiden über Aegypten, welche erst hinter dem über Elam standen, an die Spitze zu stellen; und ebenso konnte er es angemessen finden, das grosse Orakel über den Hauptwidersacher des Bundesvolkes, über die Chaldäer, welches unmittelbar auf die über Aegypten folgte, ganz an den Schluss zu stellen. Dadurch schon aber wurde von selbst und leicht eine Verrückung der Stellung dieser sämmtlichen Orakel herbeigeführt." *Einleitung in das Alte Testament,* p. 325.

ever, a few instances of verse-transposition, namely, chaps. x. 5-9; xxiii. 7, 8; xxxi. 35-37, which apparently indicate recensional divergences. In the latter example, the order of the verses is 37, 35, 36. The transposition, though unimportant in itself, appears to be recensional, because of a number of minor but significant variations in these verses. In each of the former examples, the transposition is so important that it requires a more complete discussion.

In the Alexandrian version, chap. x., ver. 5 follows ver. 9, which, vers. 6, 7, 8 being omitted from the Greek, comes immediately after ver. 4. Ver. 9 has really no legitimate connection with ver. 8, but is grammatically connected with ver. 4, being manifestly the continuation from this latter verse of the detailed description of an idol, begun in ver. 3 and completed in ver. 5. A close comparison of the two texts shows that, in this passage, the construction of the Greek is much more natural than that of the Hebrew, which seems to have been considerably glossed, vers. 6, 7, 8 being probably interpolations. A careful study of the section also shows that the description in vers. 3, 4 is violently interrupted by the insertion of the interpolated verses; that ver. 9 should stand directly after ver. 4, and that ver. 5 should follow ver. 9, because it forms a logical conclusion to the whole account.

Its position in the Septuagint is not simply the preferable one, it is the only proper one. The transposition of this verse, if not actually due to textual divergency, was likely due either to interpolation or to displacement in the Massoretic text.

In chap. xxiii. again, vers. 7, 8 stand in the Septuagint at the very end of it, immediately after ver. 40. These verses are a substantial repetition of chap. xvi. 14, 15; and it will be observed that in this latter place in each text they follow words of threatening or warning, just as they follow such words in the present place in Greek. It was customary with the prophet, in delivering his solemn messages, to mingle encouragement with reproof, as may be seen by referring to chaps. iv. 27; v. 10, 18; xxvii. 22. For this reason, their later position here in Greek is perfectly appropriate. Their earlier position here in Hebrew may have been due to their arbitrary insertion by some one in order to connect the promise of a national restoration with that of a national deliverer, and thereby to foster Messianic hopes and expectations. Either these verses were removed from the end of the chapter, and inserted after ver. 6, as suggested, or the difference of arrangement was recensional. In any case, as Graf and Hitzig both admit, because of the peculiar connection between ver. 6 and ver. 9 in Greek, their changed position was not due to the translator. He did not find them where they now appear in Hebrew in his manuscript.

The transposition of words, on the other hand, of which there are examples scattered throughout the entire book, evidently indicates a twofold text-recension. Transpositions of this kind occur in nearly every chapter, from one to four and five examples in a single chapter being sometimes found. Their nature, as well as their number, shows that they belonged to the translator's text. The most, if not the whole, of them must have been recensional. They cannot have been either accidental or intentional. In some cases, the frequency, in other cases, the nature, of the transpositions is a proof of their recensional character. Such instances are, "saith the Lord," chaps. i. 19; iii. 16; v. 11; xiii. 14; xix. 12; xxxi. 37; xlviii. 38; "from the Lord," chaps. xi. 1; xviii. 1; xxi. 1; xxxii. 1; xl. 1; "the priest" and "the prophet," chaps. vi. 13; xiv. 18; xxiii. 11, 33; "sword," chaps. xiv. 16; xxi. 7; xxiv. 10; "the priests," chaps. xxvii. 16; xxviii. 5; "evil," chaps. vi. 19; xix. 3; "behold," chaps. vii. 11; xxiii. 30; "the beasts of the earth," chaps. xv. 3; xvi. 4; "gladness" and "mirth," chaps. xvi. 9; xxv. 10; "the Lord," chap. li. 12, 56; "to a stock," chap. ii. 27; "I have purposed it," chap. iv. 28; "murder," "commit adultery" and "steal," chap. vii. 9; "the herbs," chap. xii. 4; "I will cause them to know," chap. xvi. 21; "far" and "near," chap. xxv. 26.

There are many cases in which it is impossible to tell which order of the words transposed is the earlier or the more original. The one is practically as good as the other, and the one is just as likely as the other to be correct: as, for instance, "backsliding" and "wickedness," chap. ii. 19; "seed," chap. ii. 21; "saying," chap. ii. 27; "if," chap. ii. 28; "no more," chap. ii. 31; "bride" and "maid," chap. ii. 32; "stocks" and "stones," chap. iii. 9; "the prophets," chap. iv. 9; "not at all," chap. vi. 15; "bride" and "bridegroom," chap. vii. 34; "they shall be," chap. viii. 2; "summer" and "harvest," chap. viii. 20; "hammers," chap. x. 4; "any more," chap. x. 20; "day," chap. xiv. 17; "O Lord," chap. xiv. 22; "this people," chap. xv. 1; "brazen," chap. xv. 20; "out of the womb," chap. xx. 18; "unto them," chap. xxi. 3; "great," chap. xxii. 8; "well with *thee*," chap. xxii. 15; "the smiths," chap. xxix. 2; "peace," chap. xxix. 7; "words," chap. xxix. 23; "that maketh himself a prophet" and "is mad," chap. xxix. 26; "the Lord," chap. xxxi. 3; "flock," chap. xxxi. 12; "to Babylon," chap. xxxii. 5; "that is in Anathoth," chap.

xxxii. 8; "fields," chap. xxxii. 15; "way" and "heart," chap. xxxii. 39; "honey," chap. xli. 8; "unto Jeremiah the prophet," chap. xlii. 2; "to deliver" and "to save," chap. xlii. 11; "there," chap. xlii. 15; "an astonishment and a curse," chap. xliv. 12; "daughter," chap. xlviii. 18; "the snare," chap. xlviii. 43; "a fear," chap. xlix. 5; "evil tidings," chap. xlix. 23; "in the land," chap. l. 22; "and thou art also taken," chap. l. 24; "habitation," chap. l. 45; "the trumpet," chap. li. 27; "and all the land," chap. li. 28; "Nebuchadnezzar the king of Babylon," chap. li. 34; "Babylon," chap. li. 41; "five cubits," chap. lii. 22; "continually," chap. lii. 33.

It is unreasonable to suppose that all these transpositions of words, amounting to nearly ninety cases, were arbitrarily made by the translator. They were most likely textual peculiarities. This likelihood amounts to a certainty where several examples of the same sort occur. The one order of words belonged to the original of the Greek, the other to the original of the Hebrew. An occasional example may, of course, in each text have been accidental. The position, though, of "saith the Lord," chap. i. 19, in the Septuagint is the proper one, and is the same as that in the Hebrew, chap. xv. 20, and also as that in both the Hebrew and the Greek, chap. i. 8. The order of the transposed words in the Greek, chaps. ii. 27 ; xii. 4, is more poetical than the order in the Hebrew. While the words "priest" and "prophet" are transposed in several passages, the order "prophet" and "priest" occurs in Greek, chap. xxiii. 34. The parellelism is improved by the transposition in the Septuagint, chaps. iv. 28 ; xvi. 21.

The Greek order, it will be seen, of "murder," "commit adultery," and "steal," chap. vii. 9, corresponds with the order of the commandments in the Decalogue, Exod. xx. 13, 14, 15 ; Deut. v. 17, 18, 19. The Greek position of "the priests," chaps. xxvii. 16 ; xxviii. 5, is evidently recensional, as the two passages are so similar and stand so near to each other. The Greek order of "the beasts of the earth," chaps. xv. 3 ; xvi. 4, is shown to be recensional, partly for the same reason, and partly for the reason that the Greek and the Hebrew order of these words, chap. vii. 33, is just the same. The Greek order of the transposed words, chap. xxv. 26, is exactly like the Hebrew order, chap. xlviii. 24. The frequent occurrence of "from the Lord," always in a superscription, and also of "the priest" and "the prophet," always in a similar construction, proves these transpositions to have been recensional. Certain verbal combinations, though common, are not uniform in either text, as has been shown by the discussion of the group of words, "sword, famine, and pestilence."

The transpositions of letters are also worthy of consideration. Some of them are significant, as possibly indicating recensional divergences; others of them are important, as probably representing superior readings in the Septuagint; all of them are interesting, as plainly showing the origin of a considerable number of variations. While this species of transposition cannot be employed to prove the present hypothesis, it is not at all improbable that some examples were due to different text-recensions, although, of course, it is impossible to point out instances with certainty. Some of these divergences apparently arose from transcription, others of them from dictation. As the transposition may as easily and as likely have taken place in copying or dictating the original of the Hebrew as in copying or dictating the original of the Greek, it cannot be determined now in which recension the variation first occurred, except in so far as the context proves the reading in the one case or the other to be right.

In certain cases, it ought to be observed, the transposition does not seriously affect the sense, the rendering in each text being equally admissible; in many cases, the reading in the Hebrew is superior; in other cases, the reading in the Greek is not simply preferable but correct. Such examples in the Septuagint are "destroyed" for "burned up," chap. ii. 15, which better suits the context; "burned" for "broken down," chap. iv. 26, which corresponds with chaps. xlix. 2; li. 58; "be consumed" for "shall die," chaps. xi. 22; xlii. 17, 22, which corresponds with chaps. xiv. 15; xliv. 12; "in his forest" for "in his cities," chap. l. 32, which agrees with chap. xxi. 14, and which, as Hitzig says, is required by the sense.

As their number is considerable, it is unnecessary to examine each of them in detail. Scholars can make the examination for themselves. Their chief significance consists, partly in showing how many divergences arose, and partly in showing how the Septuagint translation may be used for purposes of text-criticism. The following examples occur:—

נִצְּתָה—נִתְּצוּ, ii. 15; לְמוֹקֵשׁ—מַלְקוֹשׁ, iii. 3; נִצְּתוּ—נוֹאֲלוּ, iv. 26; נִלְאוּ—נוֹאֲלוּ, v. 4; הָיְתָה—הַגַּיְא, vi. 2; מָשְׁחָתִים—מַשְׁחִיתִם, vi. 28; צוּרָף—עָרוֹף, vi. 29; אַחֲרוֹן—אָרְחִים, ix. 1; נִתְּצוּ—נִצְּתוּ, ix. 9; יוּבָא—אָרְחוֹתֵינוּ—אַחֲרִיתֵנוּ, x. 9; יִתַּמּוּ—יָמֻתוּ, xi. 22; מְנַאֲצַי—נִמְצָאוּ, xii. 4; עֵמֶק—עָקֹב, xv. 16; וְהִשְׁכֵּל—וּבָשְׁלוּ, xvii. 9; וְהָרְחָם—וְרַחְמָה, xx. 11; עֹשְׁקוֹ—עָשׁוּק, xx. 17; עֹשְׁקִי—עוֹשֵׁק, xxi. 12; שׁוּב—שָׁבוּ, xxii. 3; נֶאֱנַחְתְּ—נֶחֱנָתְ, xxii. 23; הוֹי— xxiii. 14;

(?)יֹאבְלוּ—יֵלֵכוּ, xxx. 7; נִשָּׂאתִי—אָנוּשׁ, xxx. 12; הָיָה,
xxx. 16; וְיֶחֱזָקוּ—(?) יָרְמוּ—יֵמַדּוּ, xxxi. 37;
(הָ)אָרֶץ—הָאוֹצָר, xxxviii. 11; וְכָסְדוּ—יִדָּרְפוּ,
xxxiv. 5; הִתַּמּוּ—תְּמוּתוּ, xlii. 22; יִתַּמּוּ—יָמוּתוּ, xlii. 17;
לְהָרַע—לְרָעָה, xliii. 2; מַעֲשֵׂיָה—הוֹשַׁעְיָה, xliv. 27;
עִירָהּ—עָרֶיהָ, xlvi. 12; קוֹלָהּ—קָלוֹנָהּ, xlviii. 15;
חָשַׁבְתִּי—, xlviii. 32; יָדַם—דָּם, xlix. 9; בְּצָרֶיךָ—בְּיָרֵךְ
נִשָּׂאֵם—נָאָשָׁם (?), l. 7; סְחַבְתִּי or שָׁחַטְתִּי, xlix. 10;
הוֹי—הָיוּ, l. 32; בְּיֶעָרוֹ—בְּעָרָיו, l. 26; מְעָרָה—עָרִים,
li. 2; בְּעֵבֶר—בָּעֲרָבוֹת, lii. 8.

CHAPTER V.

THE VARIATIONS—ALTERATIONS.

The nature of the Alterations, which are very numerous, is of the greatest possible importance. The evidence they furnish is really sufficient of itself to establish the present hypothesis. No other kind of evidence can be more significant for proving the existence of special text-recensions. This class of variation cannot have been due either to accident or to design. It is more reasonable to suppose that the translator arbitrarily abridged his text by leaving out unnecessary and unimportant matter, although this latter supposition is foundationless, than to suppose that he arbitrarily altered the grammatical forms he found before him, and that to an extent which, more or less, in multitudes of cases, affects the understanding of the text. A certain license of translation he undoubtedly possessed. When the construction of the Greek required, or properly permitted, a slight change of form that would not affect the meaning of a passage, then a change, of course, would be quite justifiable; but when the genius of the language in no way called for such a change, then it would be altogether unjustifiable.

In nearly every case, however, the alterations that occur are entirely unnecessary on linguistic grounds. The translator could just as easily have reproduced the form in Hebrew as he could give the form in Greek. Besides, the rendering in the Greek in general is good, and represents an excellent Hebrew text. This would not have been the case had the translator been dishonest or incompetent. The supposed arbitrary character of this class of variation has not even the amount of plausibility that so many scholars seem to think belongs to the divergences that have already been discussed. For most of the alterations, which appear in all parts of the book, there was not the least necessity on any ground; and, consequently, for making them there was not the slightest excuse. The charge of arbitrariness respecting them, therefore, is as unreasonable as the practice of it would have been inexcusable.

Incredible as the supposition seems, it is remarkable, notwithstanding, that Graf attributes the alterations to the same unworthy cause as that to which he ascribes the omissions, the additions, and the transpositions. He deliberately asserts, "Of the arbitrariness of the translator, nearly every verse bears witness; it is sufficient, therefore, to cite only some of the most striking examples of the different ways in which it manifests itself. Without regard to the grammatical forms of the text, and often quite contrary to sense and connection, person or number is changed."[1] He then indicates a number of illustrations, as he believes, of the translator's arbitrariness in each of these respects. Before presenting a complete classification of the different species of alteration that occur, it will be interesting to examine some of his examples.

Beginning with the instances he gives of change of person, it should be observed that the third person instead of the first in the second member of chap. ii. 25 does not at all affect the meaning of the verse. The Greek expresses the sense as accurately as the Hebrew expresses it; and, if both readings are not equally good, both, at least, are equally admissible. The second person instead of the third in the second sentence of ver. 30 of this same chapter is really required by the sense, inasmuch as the smiting of the children was designed, in the opinion of the prophet, to teach the parents

---

[1] "Von der Willkür des Uebersetzers legt fast jeder Vers Zeugniss ab, es genügt daher von den verschiedenen Weisen, in welchen sich dieselbe zeigt, nur einige der schlagendsten Beispiele anzuführen. Ohne Rücksicht auf die grammatischen Formen des Textes und oft ganz gegen Sinn und Zusammenhang wird Person oder Numerus geändert." Einleitung, p. lii.

wisdom. The second person of the pronouns in the succeeding sentence harmonizes with the second person of the verb in this sentence. A translation of it shows that the whole verse, as it stands in Greek, is admirable. The latter reads, "In vain have I smitten your children; *ye have not received instruction: the sword hath devoured your prophets, like a destroying lion, and ye have feared not.*" The added sentence, the change of person, and the omission of "your" before "sword," all afford convincing proof that the translator had another and a special text before him.

The second person instead of the first in the opening sentence of chap. viii. 6 is perfectly consistent with the context, as will appear from a literal translation of the first half of the verse in Greek. It should be rendered, "Hearken ye, now, and hear; not thus do (will) they speak, there is not a man repenting him of his wickedness, saying, What have I done?" The meaning given here is good, and the addition of the word "now," as well as the change of person and number, proves that the original of the Greek in this verse, too, was different from the original of the Hebrew. The second person instead of the first in the first member of chap. xxii. 14 is perfectly in harmony with the context in the Septuagint. In the latter, the words, "that saith," are wanting; and the verse commences with a direct reference to Jehoiakim, the subject of the passage, "*Thou* hast built for *thyself* a wide (symmetrical) house," etc. The second person, moreover, as in Greek, agrees exactly with the beginning of the next verse in both Greek and Hebrew, which reads, "Shalt thou reign?" etc. The whole section, vers. 13–23, presents a number of divergences that point clearly to a special text-recension. The third person instead of the first in the last member of chap. xvi. 13 is not contrary to the meaning of the verse as it stands in Greek, the latter half of which may be correctly rendered, "and there shall ye serve other gods, *which* shall show you no favour." The adverbial clause, "day and night," is wanting in the Septuagint, but the sense expressed in Greek is excellent. This difference of reading is undoubtedly recensional.

Besides these alleged examples of wilful change of person, Graf gives some illustrations of what he believes to be a special kind of arbitrary alteration of person. In the Massoretic text, Jeremiah sometimes represents himself as suffering with the people concerning whom he prophesies, or as mourning in the person of that people. In the Alexandrian text, these personal lamentations, as a rule, do not appear. An examination of a number of such passages will prove that they did not appear in the translator's manuscript. The second person instead of the first in both members of chap. x. 19 is shown to be a recensional divergence by the omission of "me" from this verse, by the continuation of the second person through the first member of ver. 20, by the addition of "it is destroyed" to the same member, and by the resumption of the first person in the second member of this latter verse. The similar changes of person in chaps. xiii. 17; xiv. 17; xlviii. 31, are all evidences of the same fact. In each of these three examples the rendering in the Septuagint suits the context. In the second example, the formula with which the verse begins properly introduces a divine address, and not a human lamentation, as is well illustrated by chap. xiii. 12. The Greek is thus superior to the Hebrew. That the two texts in chaps. xiv. 17; xlviii. 31, were originally different is further shown by the additions and omissions that occur in each of these two passages.

Graf's charges of wilful change of number on the part of the translator are no more reasonable than are those of wilful change of person. When his examples are subjected to a critical investigation, they illustrate the existence of another text in nearly every case. The plural for the singular in the second half of chap. iii. 6 is neither incorrect nor contrary to the sense. Although "Israel" is spoken of in the singular in the first member of this verse, the collective plural is perfectly admissible in speaking of the conduct of the people individually. The word for "she" here is wanting in the Septuagint, and the word "backsliding," having been derived from another Hebrew root, is rendered "colony." In the Greek the verse reads, "Hast thou seen what the *colony* of Israel hath done *to me? they are* gone up upon every high mountain and under every green tree, and there *have* played the harlot." The sense expressed in Greek is quite as good as that expressed in Hebrew, but the original texts were slightly different. It is incredible that the translator should have added the words " to me," and have omitted the pronoun "she," and have changed the number of two principal verbs in a single member of one verse.

Neither is the singular for the plural in the first half of chap. xxii. 7 incorrect or contrary to the sense. The construction of the Greek is just as allowable as that of the Hebrew. The reading, "I will bring against thee *a destroying man* and his *weapon,*" harmonizes perfectly with the context. The substitution of "bring" for "prepare," as well as the change of number, proves the existence of another text. The singular for the plural in the middle of ver. 26 of this same chapter is not merely not improper, but is even superior to the form in Hebrew. The verse in Greek reads, "And I will cast thee out, and thy mother that bare thee, into a country, where *thou wast* not born, and there shall ye (thou and thy mother) die." The meaning expressed is preferable in the Septuagint, and the translator, doubtless, reproduced the text he had before him. He would not gratuitously have changed the number of a principal verb, and have omitted the word "another," which is possibly, as Hitzig thinks, a gloss, and which, at all events, is quite unnecessary.

The plural for the singular in the first half of chap. xxvi. 19 is quite as correct, and quite as consistent with the context, as the form in the Hebrew is. Indeed, the plural might most naturally be expected in this place. The reference is not confined to " Hezekiah " alone, but to the " king of Judah and all Judah," as the rendering of the Septuagint shows. The latter reads, " Did Hezekiah king of Judah and all Judah put him at all to death? did *they* not fear the Lord?" etc. The singular for the plural in the first half of chap. xxxii. 36 is perfectly appropriate. The reference in the Septuagint here is to the prophet, and the form, " whereof *thou sayest*," is just the same as that in the corresponding part of ver. 43 in Greek. A further evidence that these divergences are recensional is furnished by the fact that, in a similar account, chap. xxxiii. 10, the plural form, "whereof ye say," is found in both the Hebrew and the Greek.

The singular for the plural in the first half of chap. l. 42 is another illustration of recensional divergency. Instead of the verb "hold" here, the Septuagint has the participle "having;" and the reference in the sentences criticized by Graf is very properly to "nation" in the preceding verse. Consistently with this explanation, vers. 41, 42 in Greek read, "Behold, a people cometh from the north; and a great nation and many kings shall be stirred up from the uttermost parts of the earth, *having* bow and spear: *it is* cruel, and *has* no mercy." Not only is the text of the Septuagint different from that of the Hebrew, but also it makes excellent sense. The singular for the plural in the first half of chap. li. 28 is altogether the preferable reading. Indeed, it seems to be the only reading that harmonizes with the context. The plural "kings" in Hebrew is probably incorrect, as indicated by the singular pronoun "his" in the last sentence of the verse.

Thus a fair consideration of Graf's principal examples shows that there is not a particle of evidence of arbitrary alteration on the part of the translator. The charge, therefore, of wilful change of person and number is not only not sustained, but also shown to be foundationless. In none of the foregoing examples is either the sense or the connection injured by the alteration, as Graf asserts. In some passages, the reading in the Hebrew is preferable to the reading in the Greek; but from this it does not follow that the translator was in any way to blame for the inferiority of the Alexandrian rendering. He was not responsible for the nature or condition of the ancient manuscript he used. It may have been, and, doubtless, was quite frequently imperfect. The Hebrew, too, in many places may have been, and, doubtless, was improved by later hands. Moreover, the original of the Hebrew was probably, in some instances, superior to that of the Greek, just as the original of the Greek was certainly, in other instances, superior to that of the Hebrew. There was not the least occasion for the translator to make the alterations that occur, and there is not the slightest reason to suppose that he did make them.

In his brief and partial discussion of the alterations, which occur almost as frequently as he asserts, but which do not testify as he alleges, Graf neither pretends to treat them thoroughly, nor attempts to classify them systematically. He simply gives a few examples of the two kinds just considered. They comprise, though, changes of species or conjugation (voice and mood), tense, gender, person, number, and case. Of certain kinds of alteration, there are numerous examples; of others, there are not so many ; of some, there is only one or two. As they all appear together in the Conspectus of the variations elsewhere, a few examples of each kind will be sufficient for the purposes of systematic classification. In some instances, the form in Hebrew is superior ; in other instances, the form in Greek is preferable. The comparative merit of each reading will be left to the judicial consideration of each critic. Some of these alterations, it will be observed, were due to difference of punctuation ; but none of them were due to arbitrariness on the part of the translator.

Except in cases where the letters were originally the same, the alterations indicate a special text-recension in nearly every instance. An exception, of course, must be made in the case of divergences which were required by the genius of the language in which the work of translation was done. An active for a passive, or a singular for a plural, and *vice versa*, are examples of this kind. Even then, as is frequently the case, where the form in Greek represents an excellent form in Hebrew, the original texts were probably different.

The instances of change of number, it should be observed, are very numerous. The plural for the singular in a great many passages, while, doubtless, sometimes due to different punctuation,

K

at other times to textual divergency, may have been due in general to the well-known fact that the plural is often used in Greek where the singular is used in Hebrew. The singular for the plural, on the other hand, seems almost always to indicate a textual difference. As both the singular and the plural occur occasionally in a single verse, it is possible that these forms were not so definitely fixed at one time as they are to-day, and as they have been since the Massoretic system became established.

The following classification furnishes illustrations of the chief kinds of alteration that occur:—

Species or Conjugation.

Kal for Niphal.—יֹאמֵר–יֹאמְרוּ ("it shall be said"—"they shall say"), chaps. iv. 11; vii. 32; xvi. 14; נִבְחַר–בָּחֲרוּ ("it shall be chosen"—"they shall choose"), chap. viii. 3.

Kal for Piel.—לְשַׁנּוֹת–לִשְׁנוֹת ("to change"—"to repeat"), chap. ii. 36.

Kal for Hiphil.—הִרְאִיתַנִי–רָאִיתִי ("thou shewedst me"—"I saw"), chap. xi. 18; תְּבִאֵהוּ–יָבוֹא ("cause it to come"—"it may or shall come"), chap. xiii. 1; אַשְׁמִיעֲךָ–תִּשְׁמַע ("I will cause thee to hear"—"thou shalt hear"), chap.

xviii. 2 ; וְיִכָשְׁלוּ—וַיַכְשִׁלוּם ("they have caused them to stumble"—"they shall stumble"), chap. xviii. 15; וְיִשְׁמָעוּ—וַיַשְׁמִיעוּ ("they had caused to hear"—"they had heard"), chap. xxiii. 22.

Kal for Hophal.—וְיִקָחוּ—וְלָקַח ("shall be taken up"—"they shall take up"), chap. xxix. 22.

Niphal for Kal.—יִשָׁבֵר—יִשְׁבֹּר ("breaketh"—"is broken"), chap. xix. 11; נִקְרֵאת—קָרְאוּ לָךְ ("they have called thee"—"thou hast been called"), chap. xxx. 17; תִּשָּׂרֵף—תִּשְׂרֹף ("thou shalt burn"—"shall be burned"), chap. xxxviii. 23.

Niphal for Hiphil.—יִשָּׁמַע—מַשְׁמִיעַ ("publisheth"—"is heard"), chap. iv. 15; יִשָּׁמַע—הַשְׁמִיעוּ ("publish ye"—"let it be published"), chaps. iv. 5 ; v. 20.

Hiphil for Kal.—יַעַבְרוּ—יַעֲבֹרוּ ("is passed away"—"have taken away"), chap. xi. 15.

Hiphil for Hophal.—הֻקָם—הֵקִימוּ ("is performed"—"have performed"), chap. xxxv. 14.

Hophal for Kal.—יוֹשָׁב—יוֹשֵׁב ("inhabiting"—"being inhabited"), chap. ix. 10.

Hophal for Hiphil.—מָשְׁחִיתָם—מַשְׁחִיתִים ("they deal corruptly"—"they are corrupted"), chap. vi. 28 ; הִדִּיחָם—הִדִּחוּ ("he had driven them"—"they had been driven"), chap. xvi. 15.

Tense.

Perfect for Imperfect.—הָיוּ—יִהְיוּ ("shall become"—"were"), chap. v. 13; הָיָה—יִהְיֶה ("shall be"—"was"), chap. xxxv. 9.

Imperfect for Perfect.—תִּשְׁמָעוּ—שָׁמָעְנוּ ("we have heard"—"ye shall hear"), chap. xxx. 5.

Perfect for Infinitive.—עָשְׂתָה—עֲשׂוֹתָהּ ("to do"—"has done"), chap. xi. 15; וָאֶכְרֹת—לִהַכְרִית ("to cut off"—"I will cut off"), chap. xlvii. 4.

Infinitive for Perfect.—בְּבָחֳנִי—וּבָחַנְתָּ ("mayest try"—"to try"), chap. vi. 27; עֲשֹׂה—עָשָׂה ("did do"—"to do"), chap. xxii. 15.

Imperative for Perfect.—וָאֶשְׁמָע—הִקְשַׁבְתִּי הַקְשִׁיבוּ־נָא וּשְׁמָעוּ ("I hearkened and heard"—"hearken now and hear"), chap. viii. 6; זִרְעוּ, קִצְרוּ—זָרְעוּ, קָצָרוּ ("they have sown, they have reaped"—"sow, reap"), chap. xii. 13.

Imperative for Imperfect.—עוֹלְלוּ—וְעוֹלְלוּ ("they shall glean"—"glean"), chap. vi. 9.

Imperfect for Infinitive.—הֲגָנֹב רָצֹחַ וְנָאֹף וְהִשָּׁבֵעַ וַתִּרְצְחוּ וַתִּנְאֲפוּ וַתִּגְנְבוּ וַתִּשָּׁבְעוּ ("to steal, to murder, and to commit adultery, and to swear," etc.—"ye murder, and commit adultery, and steal, and swear," etc.), chap. vii. 9; וַיִּסְכוּ—וְהַסֵּךְ ("to pour out"—"they pour out"), chap. vii. 18.

THE VARIATIONS—ALTERATIONS. 149

Perfect for Participle. — נָתַתִּי‎—נֹתֵן‎ ("giving" —"I have given"), chap. v. 14; יָלַד‎—יֵלֵד‎ ("travailing"—"hath travailed"), chap. xxx. 6.

Participle for Infinitive.—אֹמְרִים‎—לֵאמֹר‎ ("to say"—"saying"), chaps. vi. 14; vii. 4; xi. 21; דִּבֶּר‎—לְדַבֵּר‎ ("to speak"—"speaking"), chap. xxxviii. 4.

Imperfect for Participle.—יֵלֵךְ‎—הֹלֵךְ‎ ("walking"—"shall walk"), chap. x. 23.

GENDER.

Masculine for Feminine.—נַפְשׁוֹ‎—נַפְשָׁהּ‎ ("herself"—"himself"), chap. iii. 11.

Feminine for Masculine. — הָשׁוֹב‎—הֲיָשׁוּב אֵלֶיהָ‎ תָּשׁוּב אֵלָיו‎ ("shall he return unto her?"—"shall she *verily* return unto him?"), chap. iii. 1.

PERSON.

First for Second. — נַפְשִׁי‎—נַפְשֶׁךָ‎ ("thy life"—"my life"), chap. xi. 21; עָשִׂיתִי‎—עָשִׂיתָ‎ ("thou shalt make"—"I will make"), chap. xxviii. 13.

First for Third.—נָתַתִּי‎—נָתַן יְהוָֹה‎ ("the Lord hath given"—"I have given"), chap. xxv. 5.

Second for First.—שָׁבַרְתִּי‎, נִתַּקְתִּי‎—שָׁבַרְתָּ‎—נִתַּקְתָּ‎ ("I have broken, I have burst"—"thou hast broken, thou hast burst"), chap. ii. 20; לְבָבֶם—לִבִּי ("my heart"—"your heart"), chap. viii. 18; עֲלֵיכֶם, עֵינֵיכֶם—עָלֵינוּ, עֵינֵינוּ ("for us, our eyes"—"for you, your eyes"), chap. ix. 17; שִׁבְרִי, מַכָּתִי—שִׁבְרֵךְ, מַכָּתֵךְ ("my hurt, my wound"—"thy hurt, thy wound"), chap. x. 19; נַפְשִׁי, עֵינִי—נַפְשְׁכֶם, עֵינֵיכֶם ("my soul, my eye"—"your soul, your eyes"), chap. xiii. 17.

Second for Third.—לָקָחוּ—לְקַחְתֶּם ("they received"—"ye received"), chap. ii. 30; מָרָתָה—מָרִית ("she hath been rebellious"—"thou hast been rebellious"), chap. iv. 17; בִּרְחֹבֹתֶיהָ—בִּרְחֹבֹתַיִךְ ("in her streets"—"in thy streets"), chap. xlix. 26.

Third for First.—עַל־פָּנַי—עַל־פָּנֶיהָ ("before me"—"before her"), chap. vi. 7; מַרְעִיתִי—מַרְעִיתָם ("my pasture"—"their pasture"), chap. xxiii. 1; הִדִּיחָם—הִדַּחְתִּים ("I had driven them"—"he had driven them"), chap. xxiii. 8; וְיָשַׂמְתִּי—וְיָשֵׂם ("I will set"—"he shall set"), chap. xliii. 10; וְהִצַּתִּי—וְהִצִּית ("I will kindle"—"he shall kindle"), chap. xliii. 12.

Third for Second.—אֲבוֹתֵיכֶם—אֲבוֹתֵיהֶם ("your fathers"—"their fathers"), chaps. iii. 18; vii. 25; xliv. 10; בָּגְדָה—בְּגַדְתֶּם ("ye have dealt treacherously"—"she has dealt treacherously"), chap.

iii. 20; צַוָּארָם – צַוָּארֶךָ ("thy neck" — "their neck"), chap. xxx. 8; שָׁמְעוּ–שְׁמַעְתֶּם ("ye have obeyed"—"they have obeyed"), chap. xxxv. 18; אוֹתָם–אֶתְכֶם ("you"—"them"), chap. xxxviii. 5; קִנּוֹ – קִנֶּךָ ("thy nest" — "his nest"), chap. xlix. 16.

NUMBER.

Singular for Plural (Noun).—מִשְׁפָּחַת–מִשְׁפָּחוֹת ("families"—"family"), chap. ii. 4; הַבְּעָלִים– הַבַּעַל ("Baalim"—"Baal"), chap. ii. 23; בְּמִבְטָחַיִךְ, בְּמִבְטַחֵךְ, לוֹ–לָהֶם ("thy confidences, in them"— "thy confidence, in it"), chap. ii. 37; כַּעֲנָנִים– כְּעָנָן ("as clouds"—"as a cloud"), chap. iv. 13; מֶרְחָק–מֶרְחַקִּים ("distances" — "distance"), chap. viii. 19.

Singular for Plural (Verb).—שָׁמַעַתְּ–שְׁמַעְתֶּם ("ye have obeyed"—"thou hast obeyed"), chap. iii. 13; בָּגַד–בָּגְדוּ ("have dealt treacherously"— "has dealt treacherously"), chap. v. 11; וְיִשְׁמְעוּ– וְיִשְׁמַע ("they may hear"—"he may hear"), chap. vi. 10; דִּבַּרְתָּ–דִּבַּרְתֶּם ("speak ye" — "speak thou"), chap. xi. 2; עָשִׂיתָ–עָשׂוּ ("they have done"—"thou hast done"), chap. xxxviii. 9.

Singular for Plural (Adjective).—נִלְחָמִים–

נִלְחָם ("fighting"—"fighting"), chap. xxxiv. 7;
הַנִּשְׁאָר—הַנִּשְׁאָרִים ("left"—"left"), chap. xl. 6;
מְבַקֵּשׁ — מְבַקְשֵׁי ("seeking" — "seeking"), chap.
xliv. 30.

Singular for Plural (Pronoun). — קוֹלוֹ—קוֹלָם
("their voice" — "his voice"), chap. vi. 23;
שְׁבוּתוֹ—שְׁבוּתָם ("their captivity" — "his captivity"), chap. xxxi. 23; וּנְתַתּוֹ—וּנְתַתָּם ("put them"—"put it"), chap. xxxii. 14; אַתֶּם אֹמְרִים—
אַתָּה אֹמֵר ("ye are saying"—"thou art saying"),
chap. xxxii. 36, 43; עָלָיו—עֲלֵיהֶם ("upon them"—
"upon him"), chap. xxxvi. 31; עָלֶיהָ—עֲלֵיהֶם
("to them"—"to it"), chap. xxxvi. 32.

Plural for Singular (Noun). — נָהָר — נְהָרוֹת
("river"—"rivers"), chap. ii. 18; דְּרָכַיִךְ—דַּרְכֵּךְ
("thy way"—"thy ways"), chaps. ii. 33; iv. 18;
גּוֹיִם—גּוֹי ("nation" — "nations"), chaps. ii. 11;
vi. 22; רָעֹתַיִךְ—רָעָתֵךְ ("thy wickedness"—"thy
wickednesses"), chap. iii. 2; דְּבָרַי—דְּבַר ("word"—
"words"), chap. xxxi. 10.

Plural for Singular (Verb).—הַהֵימִירוּ—הַהֵימִיר
("hath changed"—"have changed"), chap. ii. 11;
הָלְכוּ—הָלְכָה ("she has gone"—"they have gone"),
chap. iii. 6; יִפְקְדוּ—יִפְקֹד ("he shall set"—"they
shall set"), chap. xiii. 21; עָשׂוּ—עָשָׂה ("it does"—

THE VARIATIONS—ALTERATIONS.

"they do"), chap. xviii. 10; גְעַרְתָּ—גְעַרְתֶּם ("thou hast rebuked"—"ye have rebuked"), chap. xxix. 27; וְהָיְתָה—וְהָיוּ ("it shall become"—"they shall become"), chap. xlix. 2.

Plural for Singular (Adjective).—הַיּוֹצֵא—הַיּוֹצְאִים ("going out"—"going out"), chap. v. 6; צֶדֶק—צְדָקוֹת ("righteous"—"righteous"), chap. xi. 20.

Plural for Singular (Pronoun).—לַעֲשֹׂתוֹ—לַעֲשֹׂתָם ("to perform it"—"to perform them"), chap. i. 12; קְצִירְךָ, לַחְמֶךָ—קְצִירְכֶם, לַחְמֵיכֶם ("thy harvest, thy bread"—"your harvest, your bread"), chap. v. 17; שָׁמְעוֹ—שָׁמְעָם ("its fame"—"their fame"), chap. vi. 24; לִבּוֹ—לִבְּכֶם ("his heart"—"your heart"), chap. xvi. 12; אֹתוֹ—אֹתָם ("it"—"them"), chap. xxv. 12; קוֹלָהּ—קוֹלָם ("her sound"—"their sound"), chap. xlvi. 22.

Plural for Dual.—הָאֲבָנִים—הָאֲבָנַיִם ("the two stones"—"the stones"), chap. xviii. 3.

CASE.

Nominative for Objective.—הִטּוּ אֶת־אָזְנָם—הִקְשִׁיבָה אָזְנָם ("they inclined their ear"—"their ear hearkened"), chap. vii. 24, 26; תֵּרַדְנָה עֵינַי דִּמְעָה—הוֹרִידוּ עַל־עֵינֵיכֶם דְּמָעוֹת ("let mine eyes run down with tears"—"let tears run down from your eyes"), chap. xiv. 17.

Objective for Nominative.—הֲיָשׁוּב אֵלֶיהָ עוֹד הֲשׁוֹב תָּשׁוּב אֵלָיו עוֹד ("shall he return unto her again?"—"shall she *verily* return unto him again?"), chap. iii. 1.

CHAPTER VI.

THE VARIATIONS—SUBSTITUTIONS.

The Substitutions also are very numerous and noteworthy. They present, moreover, a great variety of species. Taken together with the other kinds of variation, they greatly increase the evidence for the existence of special text-recensions. While they are all equally interesting, they are not all equally important in support of this hypothesis, for the reason that some of them were due to difference of punctuation. Many of them, however, bear the clearest witness to the existence of recensional divergences.

Not only is their number great, but also their nature is significant. They are, indeed, of such a character that they could not possibly have been due to wilful change on the part of the translator or transcriber. As the same general arguments, in answer to Graf's charge of arbitrariness, that were applied to the preceding class are also applicable to the present class of variations, it is superfluous to repeat them here. It is scarcely more than necessary to indicate their nature and significance. Before proceeding to classify them for this purpose, though, it will be proper to examine some of the examples of supposed arbitrariness that he adduces, by way of once more showing his unfairness and unreasonableness.

Graf refers particularly to but one species of substitution, namely, that of pronouns for substantives. Of this species, he gives only a few examples; but each one helps to establish the hypothesis to which he is so bitterly and so uncompromisingly opposed. The substitution of "toward them" for "toward this people" in the first member of chap. xv. 1 exhibits an admirable reading. In the Septuagint, the latter words, "this people," appear in the second member of the verse, and the words "of my sight" are absent altogether. The verse in Greek reads, "Then said Jehovah unto me, Though Moses and Samuel stood before me, yet my mind could not be *toward them:* cast *this people* out, and let them go forth." The variations in this verse afford an interesting illustration of recensional divergences. The original of the Alexandrian was evidently different from that of the Massoretic text.

The substitution of "you" for "this people," and of "to you" for "to my people," in the middle of chap. xxix. 32, together with the other variations in this verse, also affords a beautiful illustration of textual differences. A translation of the verse in Greek will fully demonstrate this statement, as well as advantageously exhibit the divergences. It reads, "Therefore, thus saith Jehovah, Behold, I will punish Shemaiah and his seed; *and they* shall not have a man among *you to behold* the good that I will do unto *you; they shall not see it."* Here is conclusive evidence of a special text-recension. The verse in Greek has a peculiarly rhetorical Hebrew ending. The supposition that in one verse the translator arbitrarily made two substitutions, changed an indicative into an infinitive and a singular into a plural, added a conjunction and a sentence, and omitted an adjective and two sentences, is really too absurd to merit any further discussion. It is merely worth remarking, in this connection, that the simple assemblage of words, "because he hath spoken rebellion against the Lord," which occurs twice in the Hebrew text, here and in ver. 16 of the preceding chapter, does not occur at all in the Septuagint translation of this book. Hitzig supposes properly that in each of these two passages it is a gloss.

The substitution of "them" for "Elam," in the first member of chap. xlix. 37, is another excellent illustration of recensional divergency. The one word was as easy to reproduce in the translation as the other was. No conceivable reason can be suggested for the substitution, unless it be that the pronoun was the more natural reading. The reference here is to "the outcasts of Elam," in the concluding sentence of the preceding verse. Instead of repeating the proper name, it is really preferable to supply a plural pronoun, as in the Septuagint. Not only is the Greek construction more natural, but also more in harmony with the other plural pronouns that occur throughout the verse. The Greek reads, "And I will cause *them* (the outcasts) to be dismayed before their enemies that seek their life: and I will bring upon them *according* to the heat of my anger; and I will send *my* sword after them *to their destruction.*" One has only to compare the two texts to perceive that several other variations (one of them, "to their destruction," being idiomatic) prove a different original to have been the certain cause of such divergences.

As Graf has given only these few illustrations of this kind of substitution, it is unnecessary to examine any others in detail. His charge of arbitrariness is just as unsuccessful respecting this class of variations as respecting the preceding class. In every instance it is shown to be without foundation. Each one of his examples not only proves his allegation to be false, but also proves the hypothesis of a special text-recension to be true. A multitude of other instances might be indicated that furnish evidence just as conclusive as those considered furnish. Their general nature and importance will appear in classifying and illustrating their several species. The different kinds may be arranged in five distinctive groups,—parts of speech, rhetorical expressions, syntactical forms, proper names, and letters.

Before exemplifying each class, it should be stated that, in the case of synonyms, where an article occurs for a noun, as "the princes" for "the princes of Judah," chap. xxiv. 1; or a noun for a pronoun, as "after the Holy One of Israel" for "after me," chap. ii. 2; or one proper noun for another, as "Jehovah the God of Israel" for "Jehovah," chap. xxxii. 28; or one common noun for another, as "inhabitants" for "men," chap. xi. 23; "land" for "men," chap. xxxvi. 31; "the city" for "the people," chap. xxxvii. 4; "in the land" for "in the cities," chap. xl. 5, etc., there is no reason whatever to suspect the translator of having made the changes. The character of his translation proves the suspicion to be groundless. He had no need to make such alterations, and without necessity he certainly would not have made them.

While, in the great majority of cases, the synonymous words and expressions are practically equivalent, as well for the subject-matter as for the sense, there are places where the Greek presents the more difficult, and, for this reason, the preferable reading; for example, "the inhabitants of Chaldea" for "the land of the Chaldeans," chap. l. 45, to which Scholz has directed attention. "In the Greek text," as he rightly says, "according to Hebrew custom, the name of the people is placed as the name of the country; and the words must be translated 'the inhabitants of Chaldea.' It is absolutely inconceivable that the translator, if his Hebrew text had had 'land,' should have abandoned this perfectly proper and corresponding designation, and should have made the useless difficulty for his Greek readers."[1]

Parts of Speech.

Substitutions belonging to this class, it will be seen at once, were often due to punctuation, or rather to the utter absence of punctuation. In cases where the consonants were alike, the varia-

---

[1] "Im griechischen Texte ist der Völkername nach hebräischer Weise als Ländername gesetzt; und die Worte müssen übersetzt werden: 'Bewohner Chaldäa's.' Es ist geradezu undenkbar, dass der Uebersetzer, wenn sein hebräischer Text 'terra' gehabt hätte, diese ganz richtige und entsprechende Bezeichnung verlassen, und seinen griechischen Lesern die unnütze Schwierigkeit sollte gemacht haben." *Der masoreth. Text und die LXX-Uebersetzung,* etc., pp. 107, 108.

tion naturally explains itself; but in cases where the consonants were not alike, the original manuscripts were evidently different. Such cases certainly indicate recensional divergences, and possibly indicate archaic readings in the ancient Hebrew texts. The following examples of the principal species may be given :—

Noun for Adjective. — אָנוּשׁ — אֱנוֹשׁ ("sick" — "man"), chap. xvii. 9; אֱנוֹשׁ—אָנוּשׁ ("woeful" — "man"), chap. xvii. 16; פֶּסַח—פָּסֵחַ ("lame" — "passover"), chap. xxxi. 8.

Adjective for Noun. — נֵס—נָס ("standard" — "fleeing"), chap. iv. 21; רֵעָה—(רֵעִים) דֵּעָה ("knowledge"—"feeding"), chap. iii. 15.

Noun for Article. — הַדָּבָר — יְהוָה דְּבַר ("the word"—"word of Jehovah"), chap. v. 13.

Article for Noun.—יְהוּדָה שָׂרֵי—הַשָּׂרִים ("the princes of Judah"—"the princes"), chap. xxiv. 1.

Noun for Adverb.—שֵׁם—שָׁם ("there"—"name"), chap. xlvi. 17.

Adverb for Noun.—אַמַּת—אֱמֶת ("measure"— "truly"), chap. li. 13.

Noun for Preposition.—אֵל—אַל ("against" — "God"), chap. l. 29.

Preposition for Noun. — עַם—עִם ("people" — "with"), chap. xxxi. 2.

L

Noun for Pronoun.—אַחֲרֵי—אַחֲרֵי קְדוֹשׁ יִשְׂרָאֵל ("after me"—"after the Holy One of Israel"), chap. ii. 2; אֵלֶּה—אֵלָה ("these"—"oak"), chap. ii. 34; אֲלֵיהֶם—אֶל־הָעָם הַזֶּה ("upon them"—"upon this people"), chap. xi. 11; מַלְכֶיהָ—מַלְכֵי יְהוּדָה ("her kings"—"kings of Judah"), chap. xxv. 18; בְּיוֹם יְהוָה—בַּיּוֹם הַהוּא ("at that day"—"at the day of Jehovah"), chap. xxv. 33; עָרֶיהָ—עָרֵי יְהוּדָה ("her cities"—"the cities of Judah"), chap. xxxiv. 1.

Pronoun for Noun.—חֲמָתִי—חֲמַת יְהוָה ("the fury of the Lord"—"my fury"), chap. vi. 11; לוֹ—לַיהוָה ("to Jehovah"—"to him"), chaps. viii. 14; xl. 3; לְמַעַן שְׁמֶךָ—לְמַעֲנֶךָ ("for thy name's sake"—"for thine own sake"), chap. xiv. 7; לִי—לְרַגְלִי ("for my feet"—"for me"), chap. xviii. 22; אֵלֶה—אָלָה ("swearing"—"these"), chap. xxiii. 10; נָתַתִּי—נָתַן יְהוָה ("the Lord hath given"—"I have given"), chap. xxv. 5; אוֹתוֹ, אֶת־אוּרִיָּהוּ—אֶת־נִבְלָתוֹ ("Uriah, his dead body"—"him, him"), chap. xxvi. 23; עֵינֵי—עֵינָיו—מֶלֶךְ־בָּבֶל ("the eyes of the king of Babylon"—"his eyes"), chap. xxxiv. 3; אוֹתוֹ—אֶת־יִרְמְיָהוּ ("Jeremiah"—"him"), chap. xxxviii. 6, 13.

Noun for Verb.—דְּבַר—דִּבֶּר ("hath spoken"—

"word"), chaps. ix. 11; xxiii. 17; חֶפְצִי—חָפַצְתִּי
("I delight" — "my delight"), chap. ix. 23;
חֶרֶב—חָרֹב ("slay" — "sword"), chap. l. 21;
פְּקַדְתִּיהָ—פְּקֻדָּתָהּ ("I will visit thee"—"thy visitation"), chap. l. 31.

Verb for Noun.—יֵבוֹשׁוּ—בֹּשֶׁת ("confusion"—"may be confused"), chap. vii. 19; וְעָשִׂיתִי—עֲטֶרֶת ("abundance"—"I will execute"), chap. xxxiii. 6; וְרָם—רָם ("haughtiness"—"is lifted up"), chap. xlviii. 29; כְּמַהְפֵּכַת—כַּהֲפוֹךְ ("as the overthrowing"—"as he overthrew"), chap. l. 40; נָסְכּוֹ—נָסַכוּ ("his molten image"—"they melt"), chap. li. 17.

Verb for Adjective.—שָׁדַד—שָׁדוּד ("laying waste"—"hath laid waste"), chap. xxv. 36; יָלַד—יֶלֶד ("travailing"—"hath travailed"), chap. xxx. 6; בָּא וְיָצָא—בָּא וְיָצָא ("coming in and going out"—"came in and went out"), chap. xxxvii. 4; אֹמֵר—אָמֹר ("saying"—"to say"), chap. xliv. 26; גֵּאָה—גֵּאָה ("proud"—"has exalted"), chap. xlviii. 29.

Adjective for Verb.—נָטָה—נֹטֶה ("turneth aside"—"turning aside"), chap. xiv. 8; עָמַד—עֹמֵד ("stood"—"standing"), chap. lii. 12.

Verb for Adverb.—מָלֵא—מָלְאוּ ("aloud"—"were collected"), chap. xii. 6; יַחְדָּו—יֶחֱדוּ ("together"—"shall be glad"), chap. xxxi. 13.

Adverb for Verb.—שָׂמָה – שָׁמָּה ("make it"—"there"), chap. xiii. 16; מֵאֲנָה–מֵאַיִן ("refuseth"—"whence"), chap. xv. 18; שֵׁב–שָׁב ("sit down"—"again"), chap. xxxvi. 15.

Verb for Interjection.—הָיָה – הוֹי ("alas!"—"is"), chap. xxx. 7.

Interjection for Verb.—הוֹי–הָיוּ ("shall be"—"alas!"), chap. li. 2.

Verb for Pronoun.—כָּלָה–כֻּלֹּה ("every one"—"ceased"), chaps. viii. 6; xv. 10; xx. 7.

Pronoun with Preposition for Verb.—בָּה–בָּא ("it is come"—"upon her"), chap. xlvi. 20.

Pronoun for Article.—נַפְשָׁם–הַנֶּפֶשׁ ("the soul"—"their soul"), chap. iv. 10; דְּרָכַי–הַדֶּרֶךְ ("the way"—"my ways"), chap. vii. 23; עַמִּי–הָעָם ("the people"—"my people"), chap. viii. 5; עַמּוֹ–הָעָם ("the people"—"his people"), chaps. xxvi. 23; xl. 6; מִלְחַמְתֵּךְ–הַמִּלְחָמָה ("the war"—"thy war"), chap. xlix. 26.

Article for Pronoun.—עָרֶיךָ, אַרְצֵךְ–הֶעָרִים, הָאָרֶץ ("thy land, thy cities"—"the land, the cities"), chap. iv. 7; הֶעָרִים – עָרָיו ("its cities"—"the cities"), chap. iv. 26; שְׁכֵנַי–הַשְּׁכֵנִים ("my neighbours"—"the neighbours"), chap. xii. 14; רַחְמָה–הָרֶחֶם ("her womb"—"the womb"), chap. xx. 17.

Conjunction for Article.—הַשָּׁמַיִם—כַּשָּׁמַיִם ("the heaven"—"as heaven"), chap. li. 53.

Conjunction for Pronoun.—קַשְׁתָּם—כְּקֶשֶׁת ("their bow"—"as a bow"), chap. ix. 2; כִּי—אֲשֶׁר ("which"—"because"), chap. xi. 17; כַּאֲשֶׁר—אֲשֶׁר ("what"—"as"), chap. xxxii. 24.

Conjunction for Preposition.—לְהַר—כְּהַר ("to a mountain"—"as a mountain"), chap. li. 25; לְנָשִׁים—כְּנָשִׁים ("to women"—"as women"), chap. li. 30.

Conjunction for Interjection.—הִנֵּה—כִּי־אִם ("behold"—"but if"), chap. vii. 8.

Interjection for Pronoun.—הֵמָּה—הִנֵּה ("these"—"behold"), chap. v. 5.

Adverb for Pronoun with Preposition.—בָּהּ—שָׁם ("in it"—"there"), chap. xlix. 18, 33.

Pronoun with Preposition for Adverb.—שָׁם— עָלֶיהָ (בָּהּ) ("there"—"in it"), chap. xxxv. 7.

Adverb for Noun with Preposition.—בִּירוּשָׁלָ͏ם—שָׁם ("at Jerusalem"—"there"), chap. xxxv. 11.

Rhetorical Expressions.

This species of substitution is very frequent. It occurs in nearly every chapter of the book. In some instances, the variations probably arose from similarity between the forms of the words; in other instances, they certainly arose from textual differences in the ancient manuscripts. In by far the greater number of instances, this latter will be found on close examination to be the case. They are all exceedingly interesting, but the following examples of the more important of them will suffice to show their nature and significance :—

Similar Text.—בְּהָדְשָׁהּ—בְּחָדְשָׁהּ ("in her month"—"in her humiliation"), chap. ii. 24; רֹעִים—רֵעִים ("lovers"—"shepherds"), chap. iii. 2; כָּעֹרֵב—כַּעֲרָבִי ("as an Arabian"—"as a raven"), chap. iii. 2; צָרִים (צָרִים)—נֹצְרִים ("watchers"—"companies"), chap. iv. 16; כְּאִישׁ—כְּאֵשׁ ("as a man"—"as fire"), chap. vi. 23; גַּלִּים—גָּלִים ("heaps"—"captivity"), chap. ix. 10; הַמּוּלָה—הַמִּילָה ("tumult"—"her circumcision"), chap. xi. 16; מִצָּפוֹן—מָצֻפוֹן ("from the north"—"overlaid"), chap. xv. 12; וַהֲשִׁבֹתִים—וְהֹשַׁבְתִּים ("I will bring them again"—"I will cause them to dwell"), chap. xvi. 15; מָגוֹר—מָגוּר ("a terror"—"a settlement"), chap. xx. 4; חֵן—חֹם ("grace"—"heat"), chap. xxxi. 2; פֶּסַח—פִּסֵּחַ ("lame"—"passover"), chap. xxxi. 8; הַיּוֹנָה—הַיְּוָנָה (הַיְוָנִית) ("oppressing"—"Grecian"), chaps. xlvi. 16; l. 16; כִּקְוֵה—כְּקוֹרֵא ("the hope"—"the collector"), chap. l. 7; פָּרֶיהָ—פָּרְיָה ("her bullocks"—"her fruit"), chap. l. 27; וַיֵּבֹשׁוּ—וְיָבֵשׁוּ ("they shall be dried up"—"they shall be ashamed"), chap. l. 38; מֵחָרֶב—(מֵאֶרֶץ) מֵחֶרֶב ("from the sword"—"from the land"), chap. li. 50.

Different Text.—הָאָרֶץ—הָאִשָּׁה ("the land"—"the woman"), chap. iii. 1; שְׁרִרוּת—מוֹעֵצוֹת ("stubbornness"—"devices"), chap. iii. 17; שְׁבָרֵיכֶם—מְשׁוּבֹתֵיכֶם ("your backslidings"—"your wounds"), chap. iii. 22; קְנֵה הַטּוֹב—קִנָּמוֹן ("sweet cane"—"cinnamon"), chap. vi. 20; דְּבָקוּ־בָם—דְּרָשׁוּם ("whom they have sought"—"to whom they have cleaved"), chap. viii. 2; תַּאֲוַת—שְׁרִרוּת ("stubbornness"—"desire"), chaps. ix. 13; xvi. 12; xviii. 12; וְתָבוֹאנָה—וְתַעֲנֶינָה ("they may come"—"they may speak"), chap. ix. 16; אוֹר—רוּחַ ("wind"—"light"), chaps. x. 13; li. 16; תַּנִּים—יְעֵנִים ("jackals"—"ostriches"), chap. x. 22; יוֹשְׁבֵי—אַנְשֵׁי ("men"—"inhabitants"), chap. xi. 23; יֵלְכוּ—יִלְדוּ ("they grow"—"they bring forth"), chap. xii. 2; אַחֲרִיתֵנוּ—אָרְחֹתֵינוּ ("our latter end"—"our ways"), chap. xii. 4; עַיִט—מְעָרָה ("bird of prey"—"cave"), chap. xii. 9; נִשְׁבָּה—נִשְׁבַּר ("is taken captive"—"is destroyed"), chap. xiii. 17; הָאֲגָרֵם—הַגְּרֵם ("give them over"—"collect them"), chap.

xviii. 21; תַּעֲשׂוּ–תִּשְׁמָעוּ ("ye will hear"—"ye will do"), chap. xxii. 5; הֲדַר כְּבוֹדוֹ–דִּבְרֵי קָדְשׁוֹ ("his holy words"—"his glorious majesty"), chap. xxiii. 9; שִׂנְאָה–שְׁנִיָּה ("a taunt"—"a hatred"), chap. xxiv. 9; רֵיחַ מוֹר–קוֹל רֵחַיִם ("the sound of the millstones"—"the perfume of myrrh"), chap. xxv. 10; הָאָרֶץ–הָעִיר ("the city"—"the country"), chap. xxix. 7; כְּעֵץ פְּרִי–כְּגַן רָוֶה ("a watered garden"—"a fruitful tree"), chap. xxxi. 12; רְעֵבָה–דְּאָבָה ("sorrowful"—"hungry"), chap. xxxi. 25; אֶרֶץ–אִישׁ ("men"—"land"), chap. xxxvi. 31; הָעִיר–הָעָם ("the people"—"the city"), chap. xxxvii. 4; בַּבּוֹר–בַּחֲבָלִים ("with cords"—"into the pit"), chap. xxxviii. 6; יוֹם–עֵת ("the day"—"the time"), chap. xxxviii. 28; בָּאָרֶץ–בְּעָרֵי ("in the cities"—"in the land"), chap. xl. 5; בְּיַעֲרוֹ–בְּעָרָיו ("in his cities"—"in his forest"), chap. l. 32.

Syntactical Forms.

This class of substitution, of which there are many examples, possesses a remarkable significance. Its number, too, is nearly as important as its nature. Comprising idiomatic expressions, which are peculiar to the Hebrew language, the cases prove conclusively recensional divergences. The only variety necessary to note in this connection is that kind of Hebraism which consists in the joining of an infinite absolute to the finite form of a verb to give emphasis or intensity to the idea expressed. The following are illustrations of such hebraisms :—

Emphatic for Unemphatic Form.—תָּשׁוּב–יָשׁוּב שׁוּב ("return"—"verily return"), chap. iii. 1 ; הָיוֹ יִהְיֶה–יִהְיֶה ("were"—"really were"), chap. xxii. 24 ; נָתוֹן אֶתֵּן–נָתַתִּי ("I will put"—"verily I will put"), chap. xxxi. 33 ; וְנָסַב סָבִיב–וְנָסַב ("shall turn about"—"shall verily turn about"), chap. xxxi. 39 ; הִנָּתֵן תִּנָּתֵן–הִנְנִי נֹתֵן ("behold, I will give"—"verily it shall be given"), chaps. xxxii. 28 ; xxxiv. 2 ; וְשַׁכֵּר יַשְׁכִּיר–וְהִשְׁכַּרְתִּי ("I will make drunk"—"I will verily make drunk"), chap. li. 57.

Unemphatic for Emphatic Form. — וָאֲדַבֵּר וָאֲדַבֵּר אֲלֵיכֶם–אֲלֵיכֶם הַשְׁכֵּם וְדַבֵּר ("I spake unto you, rising up early and speaking"—"I spake unto you"), chap. vii. 13.

Proper Names.

Of this class of substitution there are several varieties, such as one proper noun for another, a proper noun for a common noun, and *vice versa*. In some cases, the original texts were just the same; in other cases, they were different. The following examples of each variety may be given by way of illustration :—

Proper Noun for Proper Noun.—אָמוֹן–אָמוֹץ ("Amon"—"Amoz"), chaps. i. 2; xxv. 3; יְהֹוָה צְבָאוֹת–אֱלֹהַיִךְ ("Lord of hosts"—"thy God"), chap. ii. 19; קְדוֹשׁ יִשְׂרָאֵל–יְהוָה ("the Lord"—"the Holy One of Israel"), chap. iii. 16; אֱלֹהֵיהֶם–אֱלֹהֵי קְדוֹשִׁים ("their God"—"their Holy God"), chap. iii. 21; לֵאלֹהֵיכֶם–לַיהוָה ("to the Lord"—"to your God"), chap. iv. 4; יְהוָֹה–אֲדֹנָי יְהוָה ("the Lord God"—"the Lord"), chaps. vii. 20; xiv. 13; xxxii. 17; יְהוָה–יְהוָה צְבָאוֹת ("Lord of hosts"—"Lord"), chaps. vi. 9; ix. 16; xi. 20; xx. 12; xlix. 26; l. 33; li. 58; הָאֱלֹהִים–יְהוָה אֱלֹהֵינוּ ("Lord our God"—"God"), chap. viii. 14; יְהוּדָה–אֲדוֹמִים ("Judah"—"Idumea"), chap. ix. 25; מֵאוּפָז–אוּפָז ("Uphaz"—"Mophaz"), chap. x. 9; הָאֱלֹהִים–יְהוָה ("Lord"—"God"), chaps. xiv. 10; l. 15; יְהוָה–יְהוָה אֱלֹהֵינוּ ("Lord our God"—"Lord"), chap. xiv. 22; יְהוָה–יְהוָה אֱלֹהֵי צְבָאוֹת צְבָאוֹת ("Lord God of hosts"—"Lord of hosts"), chap. xv. 16; יְכָנְיָהוּ–כָּנְיָהוּ ("Coniah"—"Jeconiah"), chap. xxii. 24, 28; יְהֹוָה—יְהֹוָה אֱלֹהֵינוּ ("Lord"—"Lord our God"), chap. xxiii. 38; בּוּז—רוֹז ("Buz"—"Roz"), chap. xxv. 23; פָּרַס—מָדַי ("Medes"—"Persians"), chap. xxv. 25; יְהֹוָה—יְהֹוָה אֱלֹהֵי יִשְׂרָאֵל ("Lord"—"Lord God of Israel"), chap. xxxii. 28; וְכָנְיָה—יַאֲזַנְיָה ("Jaazaniah"—"Jeconiah"), chap. xxxv. 3; אַשּׁוּר—אֲרָם ("Syrians"—"Assyrians"), chap. xxxv. 11; יִשְׂרָאֵל—יְרוּשָׁלַם ("Israel"—"Jerusalem"), chap. xxxvi. 2; שְׁלֶמְיָהוּ וִיהוֹנָתָן—שְׁמַעְיָהוּ וְאֶלְנָתָן ("Shemaiah and Elnathan"—"Shelemiah and Jonathan"), chap. xxxvi. 12; בָּרוּךְ—יִרְמְיָהוּ ("Jeremiah"—"Baruch"), chap. xxxvi. 32; שְׂרָיָה—יִרְאִיָּה ("Irijah"—"Seraiah"), chap. xxxvii. 13, 14; אֱלִישָׁע—אֱלִישָׁמָע ("Elishama"—"Elisha"), chap. xli. 1; יְזַנְיָה עֲזַרְיָה בֶּן־מַעֲשֵׂיָה—בֶּן־הוֹשַׁעְיָה ("Jezaniah the son of Hoshaiah"—"Azariah the son of Maaseiah"), chap. xlii. 1; יְהֹוָה—יְהֹוָה אֱלֹהִים ("Lord"—"Lord God"), chaps. xlii. 4; li. 62; יְהֹוָה—יְהֹוָה אֱלֹהֶיךָ ("Lord thy God"—"Lord"), chap. xlii. 5; יְהֹוָה—יְהֹוָה אֱלֹהֵינוּ ("Lord our God"—"Lord"), chap. xlii. 20; מַעֲשֵׂיָה—הוֹשַׁעְיָה ("Hoshaiah"—"Maaseiah"), chap. xliii. 2; יְהֹוָה—אֲדֹנָי יְהֹוָה צְבָאוֹת אֱלֹהֵינוּ ("Lord, the Lord of hosts"—"Lord our

God "), chap. xlvi. 10 ; אֵיתָם—אֶלְעָלֵה (" Elealeh "
—" Etham "), chap. xlviii. 34 ; נִבְרִים — נִמְרִים
(" Nimrim "—" Nivrim "), chap. xlviii. 34 ; יְהוָֹה
— יְהוָֹה צְבָאוֹת (" Lord " — " Lord of hosts "),
chap. xlix. 18 ; יְהוֹיָקִים — יְהוֹיָכִין (" Jehoiachin "—
" Jehoiakim "), chap. lii. 31.

Proper Noun for Common Noun. — צוּר — צוּר
(" rock " — " Zor "), chap. xxi. 13 ; אָחָז — אֶרֶז
(" cedar "—" Ahaz "), chap. xxii. 15 ; צִיּוֹן — צִיֻּנִים
(" waymarks "—" Zion "), chap. xxxi. 21 ; הַמִּשְׂגָּב —
חֲמָת (" the citadel "—" Hamath "), chap. xlviii. 1 ;
צוֹעֲרָה — צְעוּרֶיהָ (" her little ones " — " Zoar "),
chap. xlviii. 4 ; (לְ) מִלְכֹּם — מַלְכָּם (" their king "—
" Milcom "), chap. xlix. 1, 3.

Proper Noun for Adjective. — הַשְּׁלִישִׁי — הַשְּׁלִישׁוּל
(" third "—" Salathiel "), chap. xxxviii. 14 ; אֵיתָן—
אֵיתָם (" strong " — " Etham "), chap. xlix. 19 ;
גֵּיא אֵיתָן — אֵיתָן (" strong " — " Gaithan "), chap.
l. 44.

Proper Noun for Verb. — הֶעֱבִיר — (ת)הִשְׁבִּי
(" pass by "—" Hishbi "), chap. xlvi. 17 ; הֻתָּה —
חֲגַת(גַּת) (" broken down " — " Hagath "), chap.
xlviii. 1.

Common Noun for Proper Noun. — עַד־יַהַץ —

עָרֵיהֶם ("unto Jahaz"—"their cities"), chap. xlviii. 34.

Common Noun for Common Noun.—אוֹר—רוּחַ ("wind"—"light"), chaps. x. 13; li. 16; אִישׁ—אֶרֶץ ("men"—"land"), xxxvi. 31.

Verb for Proper Noun.—עָשָׂו—(ה)עָשׂוּ ("Esau"—"have done"), chap. xlix. 8; פְּקוֹד ("Pekod"—"punish"), chap. l. 21.

Adverb for Proper Noun.—מְרִירוּת—מְרָתַיִם ("Merathaim"—"sharply"), chap. l. 21.

Letters.

The number of substitutions of letters is very large. Some of them were, doubtless, due to imperfection or corruption in the ancient manuscripts; others of them evidently arose from similarity of consonants in the early Hebrew and Aramaic alphabets. The resemblance between many of the letters in the earlier alphabets was much greater than it is now in our Hebrew Bibles. A comparison of the old Semitic characters will show at once how easy it must have been to be misled in transcribing them, especially if they happened to be written indistinctly. In the transitional stages from the primitive cursive form to the present rectangular form of writing, it is quite natural that such substitutions should have often taken place. It is not always possible in retranslating to determine with certainty the nature of each substitution. For this reason, while most of the examples collected should be regarded as tolerably probable, a few of them must be regarded as purely conjectural but reasonably possible.

In some passages, it will be readily observed, the Hebrew, in other passages, the Greek exhibits the primitive as well as the superior form of text. Both their number and their nature are so interesting that the whole list of substitutions of letters is here appended for the critical examination and consideration of Hebrew scholars, each of whom may compare the merits of each reading for himself. For this reason, it is not necessary to direct attention in this connection to examples of superior reading in either text. Owing to the possible confusion of so many letters in the ancient alphabets, because of the irregularity and indistinctness of the characters, it has been thought advisable to submit the complete collection for the inspection especially of those particularly interested and skilled in Semitic palæography. The more doubtful instances of supposed substitution, it will be seen, are indicated by an interrogation point. The following is the list:—

THE VARIATIONS—SUBSTITUTIONS.

א = ב (וְסֹבְרִי—וּשְׂאֵרִי ב) (?), li. 35). ד = הַנְאָלָה—הַפְּרֻלָּה, xxxii. 8). ה = ח (אֵלֶךְ—הָלְכָה, ii. 25; בָּא—בָּה, xlvi. 20; בְּנָה—בְּנֹא, xlvi. 25; אֱלִיל—הֵילִלוּ, הוֹרִידֵם—אוֹרִידֵם, xlviii. 31; הוֹשַׁיקוּ—אֶזְעַק, li. 40). ח = (?)(נוֹאֲלוּ—נוֹחֲלוּ), v. 4; סָתְמָה—שָׁאֲפָה, ii. 24; פָּרְשָׂה—פָּרְחָה, ii. 24; הַחֹרֶב—הָאֹרְבִים, li. 12). ע = (וַתַּפְצִעֲנָה—וְתָבוֹאֶינָה, ix. 16; לְרֵעָה—לְדֵעָה, xxxi. 12; וְהַעֲבַרְתִּי—וְהַאֲבַדְתִּי, xlix. 38). ת = (תֵּצֵא—תֵּצֵת, xxi. 12; נָבֹא תֵצֵא—נָצֹת תֻצַּת(ת), xlviii. 9; עֵת—אֵיד, xlviii. 16).

ב = ג (בְּעָלְתִּי—בָּעַלְתִּי) (?), xxxi. 32). ו = (בְּעֲבוּר—וַעֲבֹד(ת), xiv. 4; בְּצוּרֵי—בַּעֲבָרֵי, xlviii. 28). כ = (עָבוּר—עֲבָרוֹ)(?), xxiii. 9; סְבָבְךָ—סְבִיבֶךָ, xlvi. 14; וְלַבֹּשֶׁת—וּבַבַּשָׁן)(?), li. 11). ל = (חָבְרוּ—הֻבָּרוּ, xxii. 20). מ = (בִּדְבָרִים—בַּדְּבָרִים, xxxviii. 24; בְּאֶרֶץ—מֵאֶרֶץ, xlvi. 10). נ = (הָרַבִּים—הָרַבִּים)(?), xi. 15). ס = (מִתְפָּאַרְתְּכֶם—בְּתַבוּאֹתֵכֶם)(?), xii. 13; לָסוּחַ—וּלְהֶרְפַת—וּלְחָרָבוֹת, xxv. 9; וּכְזוּ—לְשֹׁרֵק, xv. 3; וּפְרָרוּ(?), l. 37). צ = (עֲצוּר—עֲבָרוֹ)(?), xxiii. 9). ק = (בַּחוּרִים—בַּעֲבָדִים, iv. 29; עָמֹק—עֵמֶק, xvii. 9). ר = (עֲבָדִים)(?), xxx. 16; בְּצָרָה—בְּשֶׁבִי, xlviii. 32).

ג = צ (יָצַעְתִּי—יָגַעְתִּי)(?), xlv. 3).

ד = י (לָמֶּה—לְמִי, ii. 24). ל = עַד—עַל, xxv. 31). ר = פְּחַדְתִּי—וַיִּצַק or (?)(וּמוּצָק—בַּמַּעֲצָד, x. 3). ק = יָבוּר—תָּנוּד, רָעָה—דֵּעָה, iii. 15; וְתַגְוּרָדוֹ—יִתְגּוֹרָדוּ, בָּחַרְתִּי, ii. 19; הָרָקָה—דָּמִיתִי, v. 7; וְתִגְוּרָדוּ—יִתְגּוֹרָדוּ, vi. 2; וְנִדְנָה—הַפְקֵד, וְרֹעִי—וּדְעִי, vi. 18; הַשֹּׁקֵר—הָפְקַד, vi. 6;

בְּרֵךְ—מִבַּיִךְ, viii. 14; הִרְבָּנוּ—הֲדַמָּנוּ, וְנִרְמָה xiii.
25; מְרִי—בְּדִי, xx. 8; וְרִדָם—הָדָם, xiv. 9; אָהַד—
הָאָבָה, xxxi. 12; לְנֶחָבָה—לְדַאֲבָה, xxiv. 2; הָאַהֵר—
בְּיָד—רְחָבָה, xxxi. 25; אַהֵר—אֶהָד (bis), xxxii. 39;
יָדְמִי—נָרְמָתָה—דָמְתָה, xlvii. 5; xli. 9; בּוֹר—
וְרָמִי, xlvii. 6; יְעִרָה—יְעָדָה, xlvii. 7; עַד—עִיר, xlviii.
32; וַיַרְאָה—יָדְאָה, xlviii. 34; עָרִיהָם—עַדְיַחֵץ, xlix.
22; יְרִבּוּ—יְדַמּוּ, xlix. 26; l. 30; הֲדַר—הָדָד, xlix.
27, תֵּרְבּוּ—תַּדַּמוּ—וְהַעֲבַרְתִּי—וְהַאֲבַדְתִּי, xlix. 38;
li. 6; בְּרֹאשׁ—בְּרִי־אשׁ, li. 14; הַיְלֵד—הֵידָד, li. 58).
ת = (בְּעֵד—בְּעֵת, xi. 14; עֵת—אֵיד, xlviii. 16).
א = ח (אֲקִים—הָקִים), xi. 5; אֶרְפָּא—הֶרְפָּא, xv. 18;
וְאַאֲיִד—וְהַעֵר, xxxii. 25; וְאָשִׁיב—וְהָשִׁיב, xlii. 12;
(?) , בְּעָרְב—בִּקְרָה) ב = . — , וְאֶכְרִית—לְהַכְרִית, xlvii. 4;
ii. 23; בַּגּוֹיִם—הַגּוֹיִם, xxv. 11; בַּיָּם—הַיָּם, xxxi.
35; וּבַגִּלְעָד—וְהַגִּלְעָד; בְּבַרְזֶל—הַבַּרְזֶל, l. 19). ד =
(הָוָה—הַתַּוָה) ו = , ix. 4; וְרִדָם—הָדָם, xiv. 9).
טָבוּחוּ—טָבְחָה, xxxi. 7). ח = (לָהֶם—לָחֶם), xvi. 7;
אַתֶּם—אַתָּה, v. 17; (אַתָּה—=) ם = הַמַּרְצָה—הַמְּרוּצָה, xxii. 17);
בָּעֲדָם—בַּעֲדָה, xxix. 7; וְלַעֲבָדִים—וְלַעֲבָדָיה, xiii. 18;
קוֹלָם—קוֹלָה, xlvi. 22). ס = (וְרֹבִיס—וְרֹבִיהָ, iv. 29).
= ע ר = (צָרָה—עֶדְרָם, תְּעָלַת—תִּהֲלַת, xlviii. 2).
vi. 18; וְשִׁבָּר—וְשַׁבָּה, xiii. 17; הַקָּבֹר—הַרֲכָה, xxv.
15). ת = (אֲחֹה—אַתָּה), i. 6; xiv. 13; xxxii. 17;
זֶה; בִּלְאַת—מְרֵעָה (?), xvii. 16; תִּיָקְרִי—הִזְקָרִי, vi. 8;
נָוֹת—, xxxiii. 12).
ו = ד (ב = בַּהַשְׁפֵּל—וְהַשְׁפִּיל, iii. 15). ד = (צִדְקָם—צִיּוֹן,
עָבְרָה—עָבְרוּ, ii. 12; הִרְבָּה—הָרְבּוּ, xxx. 17). ח =

THE VARIATIONS—SUBSTITUTIONS.

ix. 2; הָפְכָה—לְמָדוּ, ix. 4; וּפָּתַח—חָפְשָׁה, xxxi. 8; עַד־בַּיִת—עֲרָבוֹת, v. 6; יֲ = (?) עָשָׂה—עֵשָׂו (?), xlix. 8). בְּבֹוֹ—הַנֵּה—נָתְנָה, vi. 2; מוּנְאֲצֵי—נִבְצָאוּ, xv. 16; וְהָיָה—בְּמִי, xv. 18; טִיחָה—שׁוּחָה, xviii. 20, 22; וְרָשׁוּם—יְרֵשׁוּם, xxiii. 4; וְרָחֳצָה—וְשָׁבִיעַ—יָשְׁבִיעַ, xx. 16; וְיָשְׁבוּ—וְיָשְׁבֵי, xxxi. 24). ד = (לוֹ—לָךְ, xxii. 15). ל = (וְנָפַל—לִפֹּל, xxi. 9; וְסַגַּר—לְסַגֵּר, xxiii. 19; לְוִרְשָׁה—לְוֵצָה (?), ר = (לִנְקוָה—וּמִקְוֵה, l. 7). xxxiv. 17).

צְמָץ—אָמוֹן, ע = (בַּדְרָךְ—בְּדֵירוֹן, xii. 13). ף = ן i. 2; xxv. 3).

ז = ר (אוֹ—אָז, xi. 15). צ = (אֲבְחַק—אֶזְעַק(?), xx. 8). or וּבָזָרוּ—וּבָזְהוּ, ר = (אֶרֶץ—אֵזְלוּ, xv. 17). ז = ש וּפִזְּרוּ, l. 37). (אֶשְׁחַק—אֶזְעַק(?), xx. 8).

ח = ד (יָדִיד—יָחִיד(?), vi. 26). ה = ח חָרְבֹוּ—חָרְבוּ, ii. 12; נֶחֱרַת or הֶחֳרַת—דָּרַת, ii. 24; בְּחַרְשָׁה—בְּחָרְשָׁה, viii. 16; בִּקְהַל—בְּמָחוֹל, xxxi. 4, 13; וְהָלְלוּ—וְחָלְלוּ, xxxi. 5). כ = (נְכִרְסוּ—חֶרְסוּ(?), xiii. 22; וַיְשַׁלְּחֵם—וַיְשַׁלְּכֵם, xxxviii. 11). ך = שַׁלַּח—שָׁלֹךְ, xvii. 8). מ = (פֻּךְ(?)—פָּכָה—שׂוּחָה(?), ii. 6; וְשׂוּחָה—פָּסַק, xlvi. 15). ע = (מִיַּעֲרָם—בִּיַּעַר(?), ii. 25). ר = (לִסְחֹב—לִסְחֹף(?), xv. 3).

ב = כ (שְׁפַנְיָה—שׁוּפַטְיָה or צְפַנְיָה, xxxviii. 1).

י = ב (אֲדָם—אָדָם, xviii. 17). ר = (וְאָבְלוּ—יָאָבְלוּ, v. 17; יִרְכְּבוּ—יִרְכְּבוּ, vi. 9; עוֹלְלוּ—עוֹלֵל יְעוֹלְלוּ, vi. 23; וּבְקַעִים—וְצֹאנִי—יְצֹאנִי(?), ix. 10; לָגָלוּת—לַגֹּלִים, x. 20; תַּמְעֲשֵׂנִי—תַּנְעִשֵׁנִי; יִפְּרוּ—יְסָרְנוּ, x. 24; שָׁבְרוּ—טֹרְיוּ, xx. 10; שְׁלַבֵּי—שָׁלְבוֹ—רֹדַּי

M

וְרָדְפוּ ;וְצָלְלוּ—וְהִצְטַל, xx. 11; יָמַתִי—וּמַתִי, xxi. 6;
לִי ;xxvii. 6, לְעָבְדוֹ—עַבְדוֹ, xxxi. 2; שָׂדוּדֵי—שָׂרִידֵי
,בּוֹר—בְּיַד ;xxxi. 3, לוֹ— תִּשְׁעוּ—תִּשְׁתָּעוּ, xxxi. 5;
xli. 9; דְּרָכוֹ—דַּרְכּוֹ, xlvi. 9; בְּחוֹל—בַּחַיִל, xlvi. 22).
בְּרָעִיתָם—מֵרֵעִיתִי, פְּלוֹתָם—פַּלֹּתִי, ix. 15; ס =
xxiii. 1; בְּשָׂרָם—בִּשְׁבִי, xxx. 16). ש = (יִרְאִיָּה—
שִׁדְיָה, xxxvii. 13, 14). ת = (יְרָעָתָם—וְרָעִים, vi. 29;
קְבָרֵי—קִבְרַת, xxvi. 23).

ע = ד (עֵת—יוֹם(?), xxxviii. 28).

ק = ד (בִּיקָבְךָ—בִּיקָבִים, xlviii. 33).

א = ין (לִשְׁאָה—לִשְׁנָה, xxiv. 9).

ב = כ (בַּאֲשֶׁר—כַּאֲשֶׁר, v. 19; שָׁבוּר—שָׁפוּר, xxiii. 9;
בַּחֲלַקְלָקוֹת—כַּחֲלַקְלָקוֹת, xxiii. 12). ד = ו (יֵלְכוּ—יֵלְדוּ,
xii. 2). מ = ב (פָּלִיל—בָּלִיל (?), xx. 9). מ = בְ (חָמָה—
בְחֵמָה, xxxvi. 32). צ = ל (אוֹלֵיהֶם—אוֹלֵיכֶם, xxxi. 9).
ק = ע (בְּרָכָה—בְּקָרָה, ii. 23). ק = ב (בֹּקֶר—בְּקָרָה(?),
מְשָׁרֶקֶת—מְשָׂרֶקֶת, ii. 23; קָרָאי—קָרִי, xviii. 20).

ו = ד (עַמּוֹ—עַמְּךָ, xxxi. 7). ל = ד (יְלֵל—יָלַךְ, xlvi. 22).
ם = ד (יוֹם—יֶרַח, xxxi. 19). ם = ד (עֲנָקִים—עִנְקָה,
xlix. 4). ן = ד (אָיִן—אָיֵךְ or אַיֵּךְ, xxxvi. 17).

ב = כ (בָּהֶם—לָהֶם, viii. 9; בָּכֶם—לָכֶם, xiv. 13; לְכֹל
—בְּכֹל, xix. 13; xxix. 22; לַנְּבִיאִים—בַּנְּבִיאִים, xxiii. 9;
לִיִשְׂרָאֵל—בְּךָ, xlvi. 11; בְּבוֹא—לָבוֹא, xlvi. 13; בְּךָ—לְךָ,
אַבְדּוֹן—בְּיִשְׂרָאֵל, xlix. 1). ד = אֲבֵדָה—אַבְדָלָה
xii. 11; עַל—עַד—אַבְחוֹד—אֲהָבוֹד, xiii. 14; xxxi. 39).
ו = צִוָּה—יִצְלָח, וָאֲכָרִית—לְהַכְרִית, xlvii. 4). מ =
xxii. 30; לְשֵׁמִים—לְשָׁלֵל, xlix. 32). ן = ד (בַּרְזֶן—בַּרְזֶל,

THE VARIATIONS—SUBSTITUTIONS. 179

דְּבָרַי—כְּדָלִי, xv. 17; וָאֶרֶץ—וְאֵלָיו (?) ר = .(xxxix. 3
אָחָד—אֵלָיו, ii. 19). ת = .(xxv. 34

ב = מ) בְּצִיּוֹן—מִצִּיּוֹן, ix. 18; בְּרָחֵם—מֵרָחֵם, xx. 17;
בִּשְׁלֹשׁ—מִשָּׁלֹשׁ = בִּן־שָׁלֹשׁ, xxi. 1; בַּעֲטָרָה—מַעֲטָרָה,
xxv. 3; בִּקְרְיָה—מִיקְרָאָם, xlvi. 25; בְּנֻהָּ—מָנֹא, xlviii.
33; נְמֵרִים—בְּרִים, xlviii. 34; כַּבִּיר—סָבִיר(?), li. 27;
בִּגְבָעוֹת ח = .(li. 54 ,בְּאֶרֶץ—בְּאָרֶץ; בְּבָבֶל—מְבָבֶל
—הַגְּבָעוֹת, iii. 23; כִּבְיָהּ—כְּבִידָם, xli. 17). ב =
(לְטַמֵּא—לְמַדְתִּי(?), ii. 33). כ = בְּדָם—מִמֶּנּוּ, iv. 8;
בְּדַבֵּר—בְּבַרִי, xlviii. 32). ל = בִּלְבַּל—בַּלָּהָם, xlix.
1). נ = ב) נָתָן—בְּיָתָן or נָתָן, xxxviii. 1; עֲנָקִים—בְּנָקָם,
xlvii. 5; עֲנָקִים—עַבְּנֶךָ, xlix. 4). צ = ק) דָּקְרִימוֹ
דָּקַרְצוּ, li. 12). ק = ח) בִּקְהַל—בִּדְחוֹל, xxxi. 4, 13).
ר = ת) תָּגוּר—בָּגוֹר, vi. 25; וָרָת—זָמֶת(?), xiii. 27). ת =
25; אֵת—יוֹם, xxxviii. 28).

ד = ר) דָּעִיר—רָעָם, xxvi. 19). יר = ם) עָשִׂינוּ—עֹשִׂים,
xxxvii. 4). ת = ם) לְנָעֲלוֹת—לְנָעֲלִים(?), ix. 10).

ג = נ) בִּהֲרַת—גְּהֶרֶת(?), viii. תָּגוּר—תָּנוּד, iv. 1). ד = ר
16). ח = כ) תֶּהֳבַּל—תִּנָּבֵל, xiv. 21). כ = נְהַר—
בָּחַד(?), vi. 29). מ = ב) בְּרֶגֶן—גְּרֶגֶל, xxxix. 3; —נֹם
מֹם, xlvi. 14; וּבְמָתֶיהָ—וּבְנָתֶיהָ, xlix. 2). ר = ד
(דָּהֳרֵת—דָּהְנָיוֹת, xxxvii. 16).

נו = ם) בָּדָם—בָּמָּנוּ, iv. 8; אֵינָם—אֵינֵנוּ, xxxi. 15;
אֲרִיצֵם—אֲרִיצוּ, xlix. 19).

ן = ח) וָאֶהֱיֶה—וְאֶרֶץ(?), vi. 14). ם = חֵן) חֹם—חֵן, xxxi. 2).

ס = ט) לִשְׂרֹד—לִסְחֹב(?), xv. 3). כ = כַּבִּיר—סָבִיר(?),
li. 27). מ = שׂ) לְבַד—לִי סוּרֵי, ii. 21). שׁ = חֲסִירוּ—

180   THE TEXT OF JEREMIAH.

הִשְׁאִירוּ(?), v. 10). = שׂ (וְנָסְעוּ—וְנָשְׂאוּ, xxxi. 24).
= ת (הָסִירוּ—הוֹתִירוּ(?), v. 10).
ע = א (וְנָסְעוּ—וְנָשְׂאוּ, xxxi. 24; בָּלְעָה—בָּלָּה, xlviii.
5). = ז (רֹגֶז—רֹגַע(?), xxxi. 35). = ח (בְּעָבִים—
בַּחֻרִים, iv. 29; אֶצְחַק—אֶצְעַק or אֶשְׂחַק, xx. 8; בָּעַלְתִּי
—בָּחַלְתִּי(?), xxxi. 32). = י (עָצָר—יָקָר(?), xx. 9).
= כ (מַרְפֵּה—בְּלֶכֶת(?), xvii. 16). = פ —צִעִירֵי
צְעִירֵי, l. 45). = צ (בְּעָבְרִי—בְּצוּרִי(?), xlviii. 28).
= שׂ (רֵעַ—רֵשׁ(?), xxxi. 35).
ס = ב (פָּחַדְתִּי—בָּחַרְתִּי, ii. 19). = כ (יִפָּלֵא—יִפָּלֵא,
xxxii. 17, 27). = שׂ (הֻפְקַד—הָשְׁקֵד, vi. 6).
ף = ך (וְסָתַם—נָס(בְּ)מָךְ(?), xlvi. 15).
צ = ג (וְגַלְבִיעוֹת—וּגְבָרִים, ii. 6). = ח (וְגָבַר—וְצָבַר,
vi. 27). = מ (בְּצֶקֶךָ—בְּמֵישָׁךְ, li. 13). = ס (הִצִּיעֻנִי
—הִסִּיעֻנִי(?), li. 34). = ק (עָצָר—יָקָר(?), xx. 9). = שׂ
(הִצִּיעֻנִי—הִשִּׁיעֻנִי(?), li. 34).
ד = ם (עָרֵי־חָץ—עָרֵיהֶם, xlviii. 34). = ן (בְּאָרֶץ—
בְּאֹזֶן, xliii. 13). = ן (בְּצִיד—בִּיוּן, xlviii. 9).
ק = ג (הַמִּזְרָקוֹת—הַמִּזְלָגוֹת, lii. 18). = ד (סָפַקְתִּי—
סָפַדְתִּי, xxxi. 19). = ח (הִתְקַלְקְלוּ—הִתְהַלְּחֲלוּ, iv. 24).
= כ (וְתֹקֶף—וְתֹכָה, vi. 29). = מ (עָמֹק—עָקֹב, xvii. 9).
= צ (קֹלֵל—צוֹלֵל, x. 18). = ר (הַצִּנֹּק—הַצִּנּוֹר,
xxix. 26).
ר = ד (רְשׁוּךְ—דָּשׁוּךְ(?), ii. 16; עֲרָבוֹת—עַד־בַּיִת, v. 6;
בְּהַד—בְּהַר(?), vi. 29; עֲבָדֻהוּ—עֲבָדֻהוּ or עָבָרָתוֹ, vii.
29; הָעֲבוֹד(ת)—בַּעֲבוּר, ix. 20; בְּאַרְמְנוֹתֵינוּ—בְּאַרְמְתָם,
xiv. 4; תַּרְבִּית—תַּרְבִּית(?), xiv. 14; xxiii. 26; הֲיַרְעַ
—הֲיָדַע, xv. 12; וְהִשְׁבַּרְתִּי—וְהִשְׁבַּדְתִּי, xv. 14; קָרִים

THE VARIATIONS—SUBSTITUTIONS. 181

—בַּסְעָרֵי, קָדִים—, xviii. 14; יָקָד (?)—עָצַר, xx. 9; בְּמֹדֶךָ—, בַּעֲרוּגַר, xxxi. 8; יִשְׂרְפוּ—כְּסָפָּדוּ, xxxiv. 5; עֶבְרָתוֹ—, בְּעֶרְוַת, xlviii. 6; יָרִיקוּ—יָדִיקוּ, xlviii. 12; עֲבָתוֹ—, xlviii. 30; קִיר־חָרָשׂ—קִיר־חֶרֶשׂ, xlviii. 31, 36; וּשְׁאֵרִי—, דֵּק—רֵיק, li. 2; זֵדִים וָדֹוּדָה—זָרִים וְזָרָה, li. 34; וְטֹדִי(?)—, li. 35; רְבָלָתָה—רְבְלָתָה, lii. 9, 10, 26).

= ו (יָחֵן—יוֹם, xxxi. 19; בְּאָרֶץ—בָּאוֹן, xliii. 13).

= ח (אֲרָזוֹ—בְּאָרָיוֹ, xxii. 15). = י אִיְּבוֹ—אִיְּבָתוֹ or הָאֵיבָה, ix. 7). = יְ חָבָרִי—חֲבָרִימוּ(?), li. 11). = כ מֶלֶכֶת—בְּרֹחָה(?), לְזָרוֹת—לְזִפּוֹת(?), iv. 11). = כ נְבוּכַדְרֶאצַר—, הַמְּזֻרְקוֹת—הַמִּזְרָקוֹת, lii. 18). = נ אָמַר—אָבֵן (= ן, xv. 11). = ת סָמָר—סָבְעַת, xxxix. 3).

שׂ = שׁ (שָׁאַפָּה—שָׂהֲפָה = שָׂהֲבָה, ii. 24; וָאֶשְׂבַּע—, שָׂבַעַת—שִׁבְעַת, v. 24; שׂוּחָה—שִׂיחָה, v. 7; נָשָׂא—נָשָׁא, xviii. 20, 22; וְהִשָּׁאֵל—יָפָאֲלוּ, xx. 11; נְשָׂאתִי—אֲנוֹשׁ, xxiii. 39; לְשֹׂאֲה—לְשִׁיאָה, xxiv. 9; וְשִׁיאֲכֶם—קָשִׁיר, xxx. 12; תִּשָּׂאוּ—תָּשֵׁא, xxxvii. 9; xliv. 9.

שׂ = שׁ (מְשָׂרֶקֶת—מְשַׂרְקָת, ii. 23; תִּשָּׁא—תִּשְׂאַל(?), vii. 16; xi. 14; וְשָׂמָה—וְשָׁמָּה, xiii. 16; שָׂדַי—שָׁדַיִם, xviii. 14; שְׂדוּדִי—שָׁדוּדִי, xxxi. 2; קִיר־חָרָשׁ—קִיר־חָרָשׂ, xlviii. 31, 36). = שׂ שַׂבְחָה—זָבְחָה, xlviii. 32).

ת = א (לְמִדְתִּי—צַלְבָּיְתָ, ii. 33). = ד לְטַמֵא—, ii. 6). = ח וְיֹחַלְתִּ—וְיָלְדָה, xxxi. 8). = ט יִפָּתֵשׁ—, רֶנֶשֶׁת, xxxi. 40). = י גָּאוֹד—גָּגוֹד, iv. 1; רָעָתֶךָ—רָעָתְךָ, xxii. 22; תְּבוּנוּנוּ—תְּבוּנֵנוּ, xxiii. 20). = ע תָּנִים—וְעֵינַיִם, x. 22; xlix. 33). = נ מֵעַתָּה—מָלְאָה, iii. 4).

CHAPTER VII.

THE ORIGIN OF THE VARIATIONS.

Having accounted in general for the variations, it next becomes expedient fully to explain them in detail. Important as it is to know their nature, to understand their origin is still more important. Had they all a similar origin? Were they all due to the same cause? If they were due to different causes, why and how was this the case? So far as practicable, it is particularly desirable to obtain a definite answer to these questions, not only for the sake of solving the problem of their origin, but also for the sake of understanding how to deal with the divergences in comparing the Hebrew with the Greek. When the variations have received an adequate explanation, then we shall be in position to see what conclusions the deviations of the version warrant respecting the contemporary Hebrew of the Bible. Not till this has been accomplished shall we be able rightly to estimate the valuable help the Septuagint is adapted to afford, as well in reconstructing as in correcting the present Massoretic text.

Several causes of divergency have been already indicated. In order to ascertain them all, it will be necessary to analyze somewhat more closely the enormous mass of simple and complex variations that occur. In this way only can one properly expect to discover the fundamental principles that underlie them. The method here adopted of translating the Greek back into the Hebrew enables one to deduce these primary principles to the best possible advantage. Before a deviation has been retranslated, it often seems arbitrary and capricious. It is partly, if not wholly, because of this fact that the charge of arbitrariness against the Greek translator has been received with favour in such unexpected quarters and by such divergent schools. By the method of literal retranslation, which is purely philological and not by any means mechanical, a large number of remarkable divergences, which otherwise would appear inexplicable, can be readily and reasonably explained. By this method, moreover, the underlying principles can be traced with almost mathematical precision and with almost scientific certainty. The process of accounting for the variations thus becomes a matter, not of theory but of principle, not of hypothesis but of proof.

Such a scientific explanation has a further purpose. A complete account of the causes of textual variation will help us to determine the laws of textual transmission. By showing how the divergences arose in this prophetic book, we may also show how they arose in the other prophetic books. Indeed, the principles of explanation which apply to the variations in Jeremiah apply, to a greater or a lesser extent, to those in all the Jewish Scriptures. An illustration of some one or other of them appears in every Hebrew writing of the Bible. It may not be, perhaps, too much to say that in most, if not all, of the books of the Old Testament, illustrations, on a larger or a smaller scale, of every principle deducible from this investigation may be somewhere found. The question of the origin of the variations, therefore, is of paramount importance, and demands a thorough and impartial consideration.

The origin of the variations cannot, of course, in every case, be certainly explained. Each text has had its own particular history. Each, too, has shared a very different fate. The fortunes and misfortunes of ancient manuscripts, like those of nations and of individuals, are very varied and very difficult to determine. Much of their history always has been, and ever will be, wrapped in complete obscurity. In the nature of things, without miraculous intervention such as the Scripture writings neither claim nor warrant, it could not possibly be otherwise. This fact is too well known to need discussion, as well as too irrelevant to the present subject to call for further treatment here. Although it is impossible to account for every single variation with absolute certainty, yet the most of them may be explained with tolerable probability.

Before attempting to explain the origin of the variations, and to point out the principles to be applied in systematically accounting for them, it will be proper to observe that the question is a complicated one. The divergences had not a common origin. Some were due to one cause, some to another cause, and some to a combination of causes. The principles deduced and demonstrated in the subsequent discussion, though, will show that there was a worthy reason for the deviation of the version in almost every instance, as well as indicate a possible explanation of the variation in nearly every case. They will also prove that the translator of the Septuagint, as unworthily insinuated, was not a dishonest and ignorant pretender, who arbitrarily tampered with the sacred text; but an honest and efficient scholar, who faithfully reproduced the original Hebrew, so far as the imperfect and corrupt condition of his manuscript allowed.

The first cause of variation was *text-recension*.

This was the fundamental ground of the deviations. In the foregoing investigation, it has been shown that a prodigious number of them was due directly to recensional divergences in the ancient Hebrew manuscripts. The originals, however, of the Greek and Hebrew texts respectively were not entirely unlike. Though different, they were not altogether different. At one time, too, they were a great deal more alike than they are now. Their agreement at the present time, moreover, is much more complete than has been commonly supposed. That is, the divergences in the ancient text-recensions were not so frequent as the deviations in the Alexandrian version seem to indicate. In many places, where the divergences appear considerable, when scientifically analyzed, they point to a very similar original. In many other places, where the divergences appear remarkable, when literally retranslated, they exhibit an identical Hebrew text. In addition to the examples given in the preceding chapters of this work, others will be given in illustration of other principles of deviation still to be discussed.

A second cause of variation was *interpolation*. This was a very fruitful source of deviation. As has been pointed out repeatedly in discussing the omissions, there is abundant evidence, admitted, not merely by Movers and Hitzig, but even by

Graf himself, that the Massoretic text has been materially amplified by glosses. The hand of an interpolator is often manifest, especially in certain portions of the book. The number of probable interpolations is very large. A considerable proportion of the omissions appear to owe their origin exclusively to this cause. Such glosses may have been due, partly to the introduction of kindred matter from other books of Scripture, and partly to the transference of explanatory matter from the margin to the body of the text. Many examples of interpolation have been already indicated. Hence, it is unnecessary to repeat them or to multiply them here.

A third cause of variation was *revision*. This was, perhaps, a more prolific source of deviation than that of simple interpolation, inasmuch as it seems to have been systematically practised by editors or redactors appointed for the purpose. Graf finds it convenient, for the most part, to pass over this manifest peculiarity of the Hebrew. Other scholars, though, like Movers, Hitzig, Bleek, and Kühl, have justly indicated its significance. Scholz, too, has collected and discussed a number of important passages which furnish striking illustrations of revisional divergences. One of the most remarkable is chap. x. 2-16. As some features of the variations in this section have already been described, it is sufficient here to add that the absent verses in this section were easy both to translate and to interpret; and that, therefore, there is, not only the less reason to believe that they were intentionally omitted, but also the more reason to believe that they were arbitrarily inserted. Other interesting passages, particularly pointed out by Scholz, are chaps. xxvii. 16-22; xxix. 11; xxxi. 17; xl. 4. He supposes very plausibly that at first and for a time the apparent insertions in these passages possessed the form of marginal observations or remarks. "By degrees," he says, "these observations, here and there, swelled to such a multitude that it became necessary to put order into these additions which had been arranged amongst themselves in rows; that is, these passages underwent a revision. This was evidently not performed by one who was unacquainted with the sacred Scripture, but by a teacher, and certainly, too, by one of the most illustrious of teachers."[1]

A fourth cause of variation was *transcription*. It is probable that a number of divergences were

---

[1] "Nach und nach schwollen diese Bemerkungen stellenweise zu solcher Menge an, dass es nothwendig wurde, Ordnung in diese an einander gereihten Zusätze zu bringen, d. h. diese Stellen erfuhren eine Ueberarbeitung. Diese ist selbstverständlich nicht von einem der heiligen Schrift Unkundigen ausgegangen, sondern von einem Lehrer und auch unter diesen gewiss von einem der angesehensten." *Der masoreth. Text und die LXX-Uebersetzung*, etc., p. 104.

due to this cause. Errors on the part of copyists occur, to a greater or a lesser extent, in nearly every ancient manuscript. It is also probable that mistakes of this kind in some degree belong to both the texts. A few examples of variation which seem to have been owing to so-called Homœoteleuton, or like-ending clauses, are, perhaps, most easily and naturally explained in this way. Graf and Hitzig both endeavour to account for some of the omissions on this ground. The latter, for example, needlessly suggests that the sentence, "the man and the beast that are upon the face of the earth," chap. xxvii. 5, has fallen out of the Septuagint, as indicated, through oversight. He also unnecessarily supposes that the omissions from the middle of ver. 12 to the end of ver. 14 of the same chapter, were due to a similar cause; but the supposition has very little probability. The eye of a transcriber would hardly overlook so many words at once; and besides, as Hitzig himself admits, ver. 13 interrupts the connection between admonition and dissuasion in this passage, and was most likely wanting in the original of the Greek. It seems probable that additions rather than omissions arose from Homœoteleuton, and that, when the one or the other was due to this cause, only a few words at most would be added or omitted at a time. In transcribing letters and words of like form, or letters and words of similar sound, a copyist might easily make a mistake. Indeed, an occasional error of this sort was almost inevitable. For this reason, therefore, some of the additions, omissions, transpositions, alterations, and substitutions of letters may have been, and, doubtless, were due to this cause. As sometimes the one and sometimes the other exhibits the better reading, it is often impossible to tell in which recension the error of transcription arose. This can only be conjecturally determined by the sense required by the context in each case.

A fifth cause of variation was *corruption*. Many deviations unquestionably arose because of an imperfect text. There is conclusive evidence that the originals, both of the Hebrew and the Greek, were more or less corrupt. Old writings cannot be transmitted free from imperfection. From various causes, and in many ways, they suffer from corruption, owing to the wear and tear of time. This corruption may be due partly to great age, partly to careless penmanship, and partly to imperfect preservation. Besides, illegible, indistinct, or mutilated parchment rolls have been occasionally rendered more imperfect, it is supposed, by efforts to restore them. Thus difficulties of translation are materially increased by the uncertainty often experienced in deciphering obscurely written, badly worn, or poorly preserved manuscripts. Where a variation was most likely due to corruption arising from transmission, it is often difficult to decide with certainty which recension was the more imperfect. In some places, the imperfection was manifestly in the Massoretic recension, as, for instance, chaps. iv. 1; xi. 15; xxxi. 2; xl. 5. In other places, the fault was clearly in the Alexandrian recension, as, for instance, chaps. xxvii. 18-22; xxxi. 22. In a few places, there may have been corruptions in each text, as, for example, chaps. ii. 23, 24, 31; iii. 3, where the two texts seem originally to have been substantially the same.

A sixth cause of variation was *abbreviation*. Although there are not many examples of divergent readings that have arisen from this cause, yet there appear to be a few. It has often been conjectured that discrepancies of numbers in different parts of the Old Testament may be explained by assuming the existence at one time of a system of symbolical notation. But, inasmuch as no such symbols of notation occur in the present text of the Hebrew Bible, this conjecture has been regarded as ingenious but improbable. The modern Jews, though, made frequent use of abbreviations, and the numerical employment of letters was once common alike to the Hebrews and the Greeks. Hence, it is highly probable that similar signs of number, and similar symbols of abbreviation, may have been employed either by the original authors of Scripture, or by the later copyists and scribes. In several cases of difference of dates in this book, abbreviation seems to be the most natural as well as the most probable explanation, and it may possibly explain numerical divergences in other books. The "eighth" instead of the "fifth" year of Jehoiakim, chap. xxxvi. 9, is an example of this kind. The symbol for the number 5 = ה might be easily mistaken for that of the number 8 = ח, a species of substitution that very frequently occurs, as the list of resembling letters in the preceding chapter indicates. Movers and Hitzig suppose אֵיךְ, chap. iii. 19, is an abbreviation for אָמֵן יְהֹוָה כִּי. The example is interesting, and the explanation is possible. Again, according to Movers, אִישׁ, chap. v. 1, which is wanting in the Septuagint, has come into the Hebrew text, partly through abbreviation, and partly through repetition of the similar consonants אִם־יֵשׁ. Whether probable or not, the suggestion is worthy of consideration. "My fury," for "the fury of the Lord," chap. vi. 11, may have possibly arisen from the translator regarding י, the abbreviation for יְהֹוָה, as a suffix of the first person singular. "My anger," for "the anger of the Lord," chap. xxv. 37, Hitzig and Movers think, arose from his reading this letter again as a pronominal suffix. An example of an exactly opposite kind occurs in Jonah i. 9, where the letter was read as an abbreviation for יְהוָה. "An Hebrew" (עִבְרִי) in the Massoretic text, is rendered "a servant of Jehovah" in the Alexandrian version. Here, besides the abbreviation, the letter ר was also read by the Greek translator for the letter ד. In this way the variation is easily and naturally explained. Moreover, "the *four* and twentieth day" for "the *five* and twentieth day," in chap. lii. 31, may most likely have arisen from the confusion of ד with ה, the numerical signs for four and five respectively, as Hitzig also has suggested.

A seventh cause of variation was *punctuation*. The number of deviations due directly to this cause is very great. In this book alone it amounts to a few hundred. Examples, moreover, occur in every book of the Old Testament. The reason, of course, suggests itself at once. In its original form the Hebrew, as is well known, had no vowel-points, the consonants only having been written in the ancient manuscripts. Thus the mode of writing greatly increased the difficulties of translation. As the language had long ceased to be a living one, and as the version was made from an unpointed or unpunctuated text, it was inevitable that variations should occasionally occur. Without the help of punctuation, it was impossible to decide with certainty the meaning of a word in every case. Ambiguity would necessarily arise, not only from the double signification of individual words, but also from their doubtful relation to each other. As the context often admitted of more than one rendering, the translator, without a definite notation of vowel-points, was perfectly excusable for making many divergences. The Massoretic system of punctuation, which is additional to the letters, and auxiliary both to the proper pronunciation and to the true interpretation of the language, almost wholly obviates the ancient difficulties of translation, by removing the cause of ambiguity. But even the Massorites, with all their trained acquaintance with the language, and with all their practised skill in punctuation, did not entirely avoid mistakes. A careful examination of the appended list will prove the correctness of this statement. Sometimes the one, sometimes the other, reading is superior; sometimes each one is alike good, as scholars will observe from the following examples:—

אַחֲרֵי—אַחֲרַי, i. 3; דְּבָרַי—דְּבָרָי, i. 12; גָּלוּת—גָּלוּת
—נְתַקְתִּי; שָׁבַרְתִּי—שָׁבַרְתִּי, ii. 13; יָכְלוּ—יָכְלוּ, ii. 2;
—אֶת־הָרָעוֹת, ii. 23; קָלָה—קָלָּה, ii. 20; נְתַקְתִּי,
—אֵלֶּה; בַּמַּחְתֶּרֶת—בַּמַּחְתָּרֹת, ii. 33; אֵת הָרָעוֹת
תָּזְלִי, לִשְׁגוֹת—תֵּזְלִי, לִשְׁנוֹת, ii. 34; אֵלֶּה, ii. 36;

THE ORIGIN OF THE VARIATIONS. 195

—וַתְבַקְּשֵׁנוּ, רֵעִים—רֵעִים, iii. 1; מַקֵּל—מַקֵּל, iii. 9;
נָס—נֵס, וַתְּבַקְּשֵׁנוּ, iii. 25; עֲרָלוּת—עֲרָלוֹת, iv. 4;
iv. 21; רַבּוּ—רַבּוּ, v. 6; לַהֲרֻגִים—לְהֹרְגִים, iv. 31;
בְּשָׂרוֹתֶיהָ—בְּשָׂרוֹתֶיהָ, v. 7; וָאֶשָּׁבַע—וָאַשְׁבִּיעַ
הֶעָזוּ, v. 24; שִׁבְעַת—שֶׁבַע, v. 19; בָּאָרֶץ—בָּאָרֶץ
הֵעֹזוּ, vi. 1; עֵצָה—עֵצָה, vi. 6; בְּעַמִּי—בְּעַמִּי, vi. 27;
כָּלָה—, vii. 7; בָּאָרֶץ—בָּאָרֶץ, vi. 30; קֹרְאוּ—קָרְאוּ
אֲסִיפָם — אֲסִיפֵם, viii. 6; xv. 10; xx. 7; כָּלָה,
; לְגַלִּים — לְגַלִים, ix. 7; שׁוֹחֵט — שָׁחַט, viii. 13;
יוֹשֵׁב—יוֹשֵׁב, ix. 10; דָּבָר—דָּבָר, ix. 11; xxiii. 17;
יַעַבְרוּ — יַעַבְרוּ, ix. 21; נִבְלַת — נִבְלַת, xi. 15;
— הוֹדִיעַנִי, הַמּוֹלָה — הַמּוֹלָה, xi. 16; יָפֶה — יָפֶה
; חַיּוֹת — חַיַּת, xi. 21; וְלֹא — וְלֹא, xi. 18; הוֹדִיעַנִי
— שָׁמֵמָה; שָׁמָה — שָׁמָה, xii. 9; לְאָכְלָה — לְאָכְלָה
שָׁמְעוּ, xii. 11; זַרְעוּ קָצְרוּ—קָצְרוּ, xii. 13; שְׁמָמָה,
—שָׁמְעוּ, xiii. 11; וְשָׁמָה—וְשָׁפָה, xiii. 16; כָּלָה—כָּלָה;
—אַחֲרֵי, xiii. 19; הַגְלַת—הָגְלָת, xiii. 23; הָרַע—הָרַע
אַחֲרֵי, xiii. 27; נָטָה—נָטָה, xiv. 8; מִצָּפוֹן—מִצָּפוֹן,
xv. 12; וַיְהִי—וַיְהִי, xv. 16; מֵאֲנָה—מֵאֲנָה, xv. 18;
—וַהֲשִׁבוֹתִים, xvi. 12; xviii. 12; שְׁרִרוּת—שְׁרִרוּת
—בָּשָׂר, xvi. 18; בְּנִבְלַת—בְּנִבְלָת, xvi. 15; וַהֲשִׁבוֹתִים
וַאֲנַשׁ — וְאָנֻשׁ, xvii. 5; יָרֵא — יִרְאֶה, xvii. 8; בָּשָׂר,
הָאֲבָנִים—הָאֲבָנִים, xvii. 16; אֱנוֹשׁ—אָנוֹשׁ, xvii. 9;
אֶרְאֶם — אֶרְאֵם, xviii. 6; בְּיָדַי — בְּיָדִי, xviii. 3;

יוֹצֵר – יוֹצֵר, xviii. 18; בְּלָשׁוֹן – בַּלָּשׁוֹן, xviii. 17;
– בְּמָצוֹר וּבְמָצוֹק, xix. 8; מַצָּתָה – מַצֻּתְהָ, xix. 1;
לָמָגוֹר, xix. 11; יְשַׁבֵּר – יִשָּׁבֵר, xix. 9; בַּמָּצוֹר וּבְמָצוֹק –
יְגִיעָה, xx. 4; וְהִפַּס – וְהַפַּם; וְהִגְלָם – וְהִגְלָם; לְמָגוֹר –
– יְגִיעָה, xx. 5; לַעַג – לֹעֵג, xx. 7; רִיבִי – רִיבִי, xx. 12;
צוּר – צוּר, xxi. 7; וְהִפַּם – וְהִפַּם, xx. 15; שָׁבִיחַ – טַפֵּחַ,
בַּמָּקוֹם – בִּמְקוֹם (?), xxii. 7; וְכֵלָיו – וְכֵלָיו, xxi. 13;
וְהָשְׁלַךְ – וְהָשְׁלַךְ, xxii. 15; עָשֹׂה – עָשָׂה, xxii. 12;
– לִמְנַאֲצֵי דְּבַר, xxiii. 10; אֵלֶּה – אָלָה, xxii. 19;
וּבְפַחֲזוּתָם – וּבְפַחֲזוּתָם, xxiii. 17; לִמְנַאֲצֵי דְבַר,
שָׁדַד – שֹׁדֵד, xxiii. 36; לָאִישׁ – לָאִישׁ, xxiii. 32;
– הֲכִתָּהוּ, xxvi. 4; בְּתוֹרָתִי – בְּתוֹרָתִי, xxv. 36;
וַיַּעַבְדוּ = וַיַּעַבְדָה – וַיַּעֲבָדָה, xxvi. 19; הֲכִתָּהוּ, xxvii. 11;
נְטָעוּ – נָטָעוּ, xxxi. 2; עָם – עָם, xxx. 6; יָלַד – יֶלֶד,
xxxi. 5; פֶּקַח – פְּקַח, xxxi. 8; יַחְדּוּ – יַחְדָּיו, xxxi. 13;
דְּבָרַי – דִּבְרֵי, xxxi. 20; תּוֹרָתִי – תּוֹרָתִי, xxxi. 33;
וְנָבוֹא, xxxiii. 2; עָשֹׂה – עָשָׂה, xxxii. 32; רָעַת – רָעַת
– וַיָּצָא – וַיֵּצֵא, xxxvi. 15; שָׁב – שָׁב, xxxv. 11; וְנָבוֹא
תִּשָּׂאוּ – תִּשָּׂאוּ, xxxvii. 5; וַיַּעֲלוּ – וַיַּעֲלוּ, xxxvii. 4;
עֵינַי – עֵינַי, xxxviii. 23; תִּשָּׂרֵף – תִּשָּׂרֵף, xxxvii. 9;
– לַעֲבֹר; וַיֵּשֶׁב – וַיֵּשֶׁב, xl. 5; מַשָּׂאת – מַשֵּׂאת, xl. 4;
לַעֲבֹר, xli. 10; גְּבָרִים – גְּבָרִים, xli. 16; xliii. 6;
xliv. 20; יֵצֵא – יָצָא, xliv. 17; אָמֹר – אָמֵר, xliv. 26;
תִּפְשֵׂי – תִּפְשֵׂי, xlvi. 9; הַיּוֹנָה – הַיּוֹנָה, xlvi. 16; l. 16;

THE ORIGIN OF THE VARIATIONS.   197

לְמִשְׁפָּט — לַמִּשְׁפָּט, xlvi. 17; קָרְאוּ שֵׁם — קָרְאוּ שָׁם
xlvi. 28; מְהֵרָה — מִהֲרָה, xlviii. 9; מֵאַיִן — מֵאָיִן,
xlviii. 16; וְשִׂכְנוּ — שִׁכְנוּ; עָזְבוּ — עִזְבוּ, xlviii. 28;
(?), בַּדָּיו — בַּדָּיו, xlviii. 29; וָרָם — וָרָם; גָּאָה — גֵּאָה
xlviii. 30; מַלְכָּם — מִלְכֹּם, xlix. 3; עֲשׂוּ — עֲשׂוֹ, xlix. 8;
הֵדִיחוּ —, בָּצְרָה — בָּצְרָה, xlix. 22; מִקְוֵה — מִקְוֶה, l. 7;
l. 17, הֵדִיחוּ, l. 21; חֶרֶב — חָרֵב, l. 26; בָּאוּ — בֹּאוּ,
אֶל־קָדוֹשׁ — (?); פְּלֵיטָה — פְּלֵטָה, l. 27; פְּרִיָה — פֶּרְיָהּ,
יִתְהַלָּלוּ — יִתְהֹלָלוּ; וִיבֹשׁוּ — וְיֵבֹשׁוּ, l. 29; אֶל קָדוֹשׁ,
l. 38; אֶמֶת — אַמַּת, li. 13; נָסְכּוּ — נִסְכּוּ, li. 17;
מֵחָרֵב —, li. 38; יֵעָרוּ — נֵעוֹרוּ, li. 34; מַעֲדָנַי — מֵעֲדָנַי
הָרְחָבָה — הָרְחָבָה, li. 50; נָתַן — נִתַּן, li. 55; מֵחֹרֵב,
li. 58; עֹמֵד — עָמַד, lii. 12.

An eighth cause of variation was *dictation*. A considerable number of divergences appears to have arisen from this cause. That dictation was anciently practised in making or in transcribing manuscripts is well known. Indeed, the prophet Jeremiah practised it himself. In the beginning of chap. xxxvi., he is described as dictating his prophecies to his secretary, Baruch, who wrote them upon "a roll of a book." In like manner, it is probable that, in multiplying copies of the Scriptures, one person dictated, while another, perhaps, while several others, transcribed the language after him. In consequence of imperfect hearing, or of indistinct pronunciation, or possibly of both, divergences would naturally occur. In the articulation of gutturals and sibilants and liquids mistakes might easily arise. Moreover, as Jeremiah's prophecies were delivered to a number of different communities, and attracted much attention at the time, many of them may have been learned by heart and afterwards orally transmitted. Recensional differences, not only of words, but also of phrases, may have arisen in this latter way. Certain classical and idiomatic expressions seem to point to oral transmission as their probable cause; for instance, such divergences as "Holy One of Israel" for "Lord," "Lord God of Hosts" for "Lord God," etc. The number of verbal variations that may be explained by dictation or by oral transmission is pretty large. In some cases, dictation seems to be the possible, in other cases, the probable, in other cases again, the unquestionable, explanation of the deviations in the version. The following examples are submitted for careful consideration :—

אֶל—עַל, i. 7, etc.; הָרְבֵּה—חָרְבוּ, ii. 12; נָצְתָה—
נְתָצוּ, ii. 15; ix. 9; מַשְׁרֶקֶת—מְשָׂרֶכֶת, ii. 23; אֶל—
עַל, ii. 27, etc.; מֵאֵין תִּכָּלְמִי—מֵאֲנָת הִכָּלֵם, iii. 3;
נָצְתוּ—נִתְּצוּ, iv. 24; הִתְחַלְחָלוּ — הִתְקַלְקָלוּ, iv. 26;

THE ORIGIN OF THE VARIATIONS. 199

הִשְׁאִירוּ or הוֹתִירוּ — הֵסִירוּ, v. 4; נוֹחֲלוּ — נוֹאֲלוּ, נִתְקוּ — נְתָקָה, vi. 19; מְשֻׁבָתָם — מַחְשְׁבֹתָם, v. 10; שָׁב: תֹּד — שָׁבְתָּה, vii. 10; נֶאֱצָלְנוּ — נִצַּלְנוּ, vi. 29; תַּעֲלוּזִי — בְּעֵת — בְּעֵד, xi. 14; אָקִים — הָקִים, ix. 5; תָּלוּי (?), xi. 15; נָשִׁיתָה — נַשִּׁיתָה, xi. 19; נִדְהָם — וְהוֹשַׁבְתִּים — וַהֲשִׁיבֹתִים, xii. 15; xvi. 15; נָשְׁבָּה — נָרְדָם — מֵאֲנָה אַרְפֵּא — מֵאֲנָה הֵרָפֵא, xv. 18; נִשְׁבַּר — נִכְמְסוּ — נֶחְמְסוּ (?), xiii. 22; xiii. 17; קָרְאוּ — כָּרוּ, xviii. 14; יִנָּטְשׁוּ — יִנָּתְשׁוּ, xvii. 8; יְשַׁלַּח — מִשְׁבוּתֵינוּ — מַחְשְׁבֹתֵינוּ, וּבָקָתִי — וְהַאֲגֵרֵם — וְהַגְּרֵם, xviii. 21; xviii. 20; xviii. 12; וּבָקַעְתִּי (?), xix. 7; אֶזְעָק — אֶצְעָק or אֶצְחָק, xx. 8; וְלֶחֳרָבוֹת — וַיָּנוּבוּ נוּם — וַיִּנְאֲמוּ נְאֻם, xxiii. 31; הַבִּנְיָה — הוֹי בנֹה, xxii. 13; בָּאָחֵז — בָּאָרֶץ, xxii. 15; שָׁמוֹעַ — וְהִלְלוּ — וְחִלְּלוּ, xxxi. 5; וְהָמוֹן, xxx. 18; וְאַרְמוֹן, xxv. 15; הַחָמָר — הַחֵמָה, xxv. 9; וּלְחֶרְפַּת — בַּחֲלֹתִי — בָּעַלְתִּי, xxxi. 32; וְנִשָּׂאוּ, xxxi. 24; וְנָסְעוּ, xxxi. 19; כְּפָדְתִּי — סָפַקְתִּי, שְׁמוּעָה, xxxi. 18; וַיִּשְׁלָחֵם — וַיִּשְׁלְחֵם (?), xxxvi. 24; פָּקְדוּ — פָּחֲדוּ, xxxvi. 22; וְאֵשׁ — וְאֵת, חֲנַמְאֵל — חֲנַנְאֵל, xxxi. 38; וְעָדָה — וְעָטָה, xliii. 10; (?), וְנָטַל — וְנָטָה, xliii. 2; אֵלֵינוּ — אֱלֹהֵינוּ, xxxviii. 11; וְאָשִׁיב — וְהֵשִׁיב, xlii. 12; תְּהִלַּת — בָּהּ — בָּא, xlvi. 20; יַעֲדָה — יַעֲטָה, xliii. 12; בִּמְעֲטֵיךְ — xlviii. 2; מָלְאָה — מַעֲלָה, xlviii. 5; תַּעֲלַת

בְּמָעֲוָד — וּבְנֹתֶיהָ, xlviii. 7; עֵת — אֵיד, xlviii. 16; וּבְנֹתֶיהָ
— וּבָמֹתֶיהָ, xlix. 2; נָסַע — נָסוּ or נִשָּׂא, xlix. 8;
— תְּפוּשִׂי — תָּפוֹז, l. 11; הוֹי — הָיוּ, li. 2; מִזְרָקוֹת
מְזַלְגוֹת, lii. 19.

A ninth cause of variation was *derivation*. Numerous striking divergences are readily explained in this way. The combination of consonants often permitted or rendered possible a twofold etymology of a word. The Massorites derived it from one root; the translator derived it from another. Without the vowel-points, the proper root could not be known with certainty, except in so far as the context determined the sense required to be expressed. The connection, though, sometimes left room for ambiguity. Hence deviations would naturally arise for which the Greek translator was not justly responsible. Whether he was well or ill acquainted with the classic Hebrew, there is reason to believe that he was well acquainted with the kindred Aramaic. With this latter he may have been almost as familiar as with his mother tongue. That the derivation of Hebrew words at the time of the translation of the Septuagint was more doubtful than during the days of the Massorites is questionable; that it was more difficult before the punctuation was fixed by the insertion of the diacritic points than afterwards is unquestionable. This latter fact should be borne in mind, not so much to palliate the translator's errors, as to extenuate the faults of his translation, by showing that he was neither culpably nor carelessly to blame for them. Not only was his derivation in every case permissible, but also it was in several cases preferable. From the following list it will be seen that, in a few instances, a variation arose from a substitution of letters in connection with a different derivation of a word :—

נפח—פתח, i. 14; יבל—כול, ii. 13; אישש—יאש, ii. 25; xviii. 12; זלל—אזל, ii. 36; ישב—שבב, iii. 6; viii. 12; קלל—קול, iii. 9; נוס—נסס, iv. 6, 21; צרר—נצר, iv. 16; זון—זון or זנה, v. 8; עזז—עוז, vi. 1; בלה—כול, vi. 11; אצל—נצל, vii. 10; ספה or אסף—יסף, vii. 21; דמה—דמן, viii. 2; ix. 21; xvi. 4; שבב—שוב, viii. 4; בלה—בלל, viii. 6; xv. 10; xx. 7; גלה—גלל, ix. 10; מול—המל, xi. 16; נחל—חלה, xii. 13; ישב—שוב, xii. 15; xvi. 15; xxiii. 3; פרץ—נפץ, xiii. 14; li. 20 seq.; אנה—מאן, xv. 18; חוס—חסה, xvii. 17; שיח—שוח, xviii. 20, 22; נחת—נגד or גוד, xx. 10; יצת—יצא, xxi. 12; שוב—ישב, חתת, xxi. 13; רעה—רעע, xxii. 22; נום—נאם, xxiii. 8; נשא—נשה, xxiii. 31; xxiii. 39; חדה—יחד, יעל—עלה, xxx. 13; עוד—יעד, xxx. 20; נוח—נחם, xxxi. 13; xxxi. 15; xlii. 10; ראה—ירא,

xxxii. 21 ; נשא-נשא, xxxvii. 9; שוב-שבה, xli. 10; עור-נער, l. 38 ; בוש-יביש, xlviii. 2 ; דמם-דמין, li. 38 ; מנח-נוח, li. 59.

A tenth cause of variation was *word-division*. The illustrations of this kind of deviation are exceedingly interesting. Here again the discrepancy was partly due to absence of punctuation. It was also partly due to the ancient custom of writing Hebrew words without any divisions between them, either in the form of spaces or of points. Had the consonants been punctuated, or had the words been separated, variations of this sort might have been avoided; but, as the letters were unpunctuated, and written close together without any marks or signs to separate between them, it is only natural that divergences should have arisen from this cause. It is no wonder, therefore, that the translator, with nothing to guide him but the connection in which they stood, should have divided some words differently from the way in which they were divided by the Massorites. Even the latter have not always hit upon the best division which the construction of a passage properly and logically required. It seems very probable that, in every endeavour to translate an ancient unpointed manuscript, some divergences would inevitably arise ; so that, after the Hebrew ceased to be a spoken language, no two renderings of an entire book would be in all respects alike. Some of the variations due to word-division in this book afford excellent sense. In certain instances, as the following list will show, the reading in the Greek is better than the reading in the Hebrew:—

— הַדּוֹר אַתֶּם — אֶת צֵעָה — אֶצְטָעָה=אֶתְצָעָה, ii. 20; — רְבָבִים, ii. 33; לֹא־כֵן — לָכֵן, ii. 31; וְלֹא יְרָאתָם — מֵאֵין תִּפְלָמִי — מֵאַנְתְּ הִכָּלֵם; רֹעִים רַבִּים, iii. 3; (?), מִבְּלִי־גֵהָה — מַבְלִיגִיתִי; עַד־בַּיִת — עֲרָבוֹת, v. 6; — מֶחֱרוֹן אַף, יָשֵׁב; תֹּךְ — שָׁבְתְּךָ, ix. 5; viii. 18; מֵחֶרֶף, xii. 13; עָשִׁירוֹ לֹא — עֹשֶׁר וְלֹא, xvii. 11; הַבֵּנֵה — הוֹי בֵנֶה (?), xx. 2; בְּנָן מְמֻנֶּה — בִּנְיָמִן, הָאֱלֹהֵי מִקָּרֹב; מֵעֲבָרִים—מֵעֲבָרִים, xxii. 20; xxii. 13; אַתֶּם הַמַּשָּׂא—אֶת־מַה־מַּשָּׂא, xxiii. 23; אֱלֹהִים קָרֹב— —בָּם עוֵּר, xxxi. 2; וְלֹא הָרְגוּ—לְהַרְגִּיעוֹ, xxiii. 33; בְּמוֹעֵד, xxxi. 8; גָּדֹל הוּא (הָיָה)—גְּדַלְיָהוּ, xli. 9; עָרֵי מָעוֹזוּ — עַד יָם יָעוּז, xlvi. 15; נָ(ס)(מְ)קְמָה — נָסַחַף — בָּדֵי־אֵשׁ, xlviii. 32; עֲרֵיהֶם — עֲדִי־יָהֵן, xlviii. 34; בְּרֹאשׁ, li. 58.

An eleventh cause of variation was *word-composition*. A surprising number of deviations may be explained by difference of spelling. The vowel-letters י and ו, which, before the Massoretic system of notation was invented, to some extent supplied the place of the vowels *i* and *ē*, *ō* and *ū*, were not employed so frequently in ancient as in modern times. The truth of this statement is illustrated by the marked tendency to their more frequent employment, which is manifest in the later books of the Old Testament. Even in the earlier books, the usage is by no means uniform. The writing of some words was almost invariable; the writing of others was very variable. In the same book, too, the usage fluctuates. Had these letters been always written in the translator's manuscript where they are now written in the Hebrew text, many significant deviations could not have occurred. The absence of the one or the other of these letters, and sometimes of both of them, as in chaps. xlix. 20; l. 13, explains such variations perfectly. An examination of each list of illustrations given will show that the Greek again, in many places, presents the preferable reading.

The following passages are submitted as examples of cases where *Waw* was wanting in the ancient manuscripts :—

ו. וּלְחֹמוֹת = וּלְחֹמִת–וּלְחֹמַיִת, i. 18; יָכְלוּ–יָכְלוּ =
בַּמַּחְתֶּרֶת, ii. 23; קוֹלָה = קֹלָה–קֹלָה, ii. 13; יוּכְלוּ
– בַּמַּחְתֶּרֶת = בַּמַּחְתָּרוֹת, ii. 34; עֲרָלוֹת = עֲרָלֹת–
עֲרָלַת, iv. 4; נָסוּ–בֶס = נוּסוּ, iv. 6; חֻקּוֹת = חֻקֹּת
חֻקַּת, v. 24; בָּמוֹת = בָּיִת–בָּמַת, vii. 31;

THE ORIGIN OF THE VARIATIONS. 205

נְבָלַת — נִבְלַת, ix. 5; שׁוּב, תּוֹךְ = שָׁב: תֹּךְ—שָׁבְתָה
= נְבָלוֹת, xi. 15; עָשְׂתָה—עֲשׂוֹתָה = עֲשׂוֹתָהּ, ix. 21; =
בַּצָּרוֹת = חַיּוֹת = חַיָּה, xii. 9; xxvii. 6; — חַיַּת
= אַיֶּלֶת — אַיָּלֶת, xiv. 1; בַּצֹּרֶת or בַּצֹּרֶת—בַּצָּרַת
אַיָּלוֹת, xiv. 5; כְּאוֹרַח (ז"ח) — כְּאוֹרֵחַ = כְּאֹרַח
—וְהִגְלָם, xiv. 9; כְּגִבֹּר—כְּגִבֵּר = כְּגִבּוֹר, xiv. 8;
וְהִגְלָם = וְהִגְלוּם; וְהִגְלָם — וְהִגְלָם = וְהִגְלוּם, xx. 4;
מִשְׁפָּחוֹת = מִזְמוֹת — מִזְמַת = מִזְמוֹת, xxiii. 20; =
לְשִׂמְחוֹת = מִשְׁפַּחַת—מִשְׁפָּחֹת, xxv. 9; xxx. 25; =
בְּתוּרֹתַי—בְּתוֹרָתִי, xxv. 12; לְשִׂמְחַת—לְשִׂמְחֹת =
בְּתוֹרוֹתַי, xxvi. 4; מַחְשָׁבוֹת = מַחְשָׁבֶת—מַחְשֶׁבֶת,
xxix. 11; li. 29; תְּעָלָה—תְּעָלָה = תְּעָלָה, xxx. 13;
תּוֹרָתִי—בְּקֹהָל—בְּמָהָל = בְּמָחוֹל (?), xxxi. 4, 13; —
xxxi. עַד — עָד = עוֹד; xxxi. 33, תּוֹרוֹתַי = תּוֹרָתִי
—וּבְמֹרָא = וּבְמוֹרָא, xxxii. 5; יֵלֵךְ—יֵלֵךְ = יוֹלֵךְ; 39
וּבְמֹרָאִים, xxxii. 21; רָעוֹת—רָעַת = רָעוֹת, xxxii. 32;
הָאֹצָר = הָאוֹצָר, xxxvi. 15; שׁוּב = שָׁב — שֵׁב
מַשֹּׁאוֹת = מַשֹּׂאת—מַשֹּׁאת, xxxviii. 11; הָאָרֶץ (∞)
תָּמָתוּ=תָּמוּתוּ, xlii. 17; יִתַּמּוּ (∞) יָקִיתוּ=יָמוּתוּ, xl. 5;
שֻׁדַּד—שֻׁדַּד = שׁוֹדֵד, xlviii. 18; xlii. 22, יִתַּמּוּ (∞)—
וּמַחְשְׁבוֹתָיו, xlix. 14; שָׁלַח — שָׁלַח = שָׁלוּחַ
— חָצֵר = חָצוֹר, xlix. 20; וּמַחְשֵׁבָתוֹ — וּמַחְשַׁבְתּוֹ
חָצֵר, xlix. 28, 30, 33; (∞)—תָּפְשׂוּ = תָּפְשׂוּ, תָּפֻזוּ
זֶרַע = זוֹרֵעַ, l. 13; מַפָּתָהּ—מַפָּתָהּ = מַבּוּחֶיהָ, l. 11;

206   THE TEXT OF JEREMIAH.

חָמוֹת = ,li. 38 ; נְעוּרוּ = נְעוּרוּ—נָעֲרוּ, l. 16 ; זֶרַע—
חֲמָת—חֹמֹת, li. 58 ; מִנְחָה = מְנֻחָה—מִנְחָה, li. 59.

The following are examples of cases where *Yod*
was absent from the ancient manuscripts :—

שָׁפָם—שְׁפָם = שְׁפָיִם, iii. 2 ; פָּעֹרֶב—כָּעֶרֶב = בְּעַרְבִי,
vi. 14 ; וְאָן—וְאֵן = וְאֵין, iii. 21 ; vii. 29 ; (שְׁפָתַיִם)—
כְּאִשׁ = כְּאֵשׁ, vi. 15 ; בְּנָפָלִם—בַּנֹּפְלִים = בַּנֹּפְלִים—
מַשְׁחָתִים—מַשְׁחִתִים = מַשְׁחִיתִים, vi. 23 ; l. 42 ; כְּאֵשׁ,
vi. 28 ; רְבִיבִים, viii. 7 ; מוֹעֲדָה—מוֹעֲדָה = מוֹעֲדֶיהָ
xvi. 19 ; אֵךְ = אַךְ—אַךְ, xiv. 22 ; רְבִיבָם—רְבִיבִם =
—מְכְשָׁלָם = מִכְשָׁלִים, xviii. 14 ; זֶרֶם—זָרֶם = זָרִים
מִכְשֹׁלָם, xviii. 23 ; יְגִיעָה—יְגִיעָה = יְגִיעֶיהָ, xx. 5 ;
דְּבָרָה—דְּבָרֵהּ = דְּבָרָיו, xx. 12 ; צֶדֶק—צֶדֶק = צַדִּיק,
xxviii. 6 ; אַדִּרוֹ — אַדִּירָיו = אַדִּירָיו, xxx. 21 ;
וּבְיָדוּ — וּבְיָדוֹ = כְּדַרְכּוֹ—כְּדַרְכָּו = כִּדְרָכָיו, xxxii. 19 ;
וּבְיָדָיו, xxxiv. 3 ; אָן—(דֻּ׳׳ן) אַךְ = אֵיךְ, xxxvi. 17 ;
—אִיבוֹ = אֹיְבָיו, xliv. 7 ; הַוְּתֵר — הוֹתֵר = הוֹתִיר
אִיבוֹ, xliv. 30 ; מְהִירָה = מָהֳרָה—מְהֵרָה, xlviii. 16 ;
יִתֹמֶה = יְתֹמָיו, xlviii. 44 ; אֵלֶה—אֵלֶה = אֵלֶיהָ;
וּמַחְשַׁבְתּוֹ—וּמַחְשְׁבָתוֹ = וּמַחְשְׁבוֹתָיו, xlix. 11 ; יְתֹמָה
—שׁוֹבְבָם = שׁוֹבְבִים, xlix. 20 ; יֵשֵׁם — יַשֵּׁם = יַשִּׁים
שׁוֹבְבָם, l. 6 ; מַפְתֵּהּ — מַפְתֵּהּ = מַפְתְּחֶיהָ, l. 13 ;
כְּפָעֳלָה—כְּפָעֳלָה = עֲצָבָיו — עֲצָבָיו, l. 17 ; עֲצָבוֹ

פְּקֻדָּתוֹ = פְּקַדְתִּיהּ — פְּקַדְתֵּהּ, כְּפָעֳלָיהּ, l. 29; מֵיפִיץ = מֵיפִיץ—מָפֵיץ, li. 20. (or פְּקֻדָּתֵהּ), l. 31;

A twelfth cause of variation was *word-signification*. There are many passages that furnish apparent evidence of this kind. Several words or expressions, whose ordinary meaning the translator must have known, seem once to have possessed a signification that has disappeared; or, at least, that has not been retained in translating the Massoretic text. It is not unreasonable to suppose that many words had meanings formerly which do not appear in modern Hebrew lexicons. It is also not improbable that the translators of the Septuagint may have been acquainted with ancient significations with which the Massorites were unacquainted. Some indications also occur of Aramaic influence. As Knobel[1] has discussed the Chaldaisms or Aramaisms in the Massoretic text, it is unnecessary to refer to them in this discussion. It should be observed, however, that a still greater Aramaic colouring is apparent in the Alexandrian text. In chap. xv. 18, for instance, where the verb נָצַח is rendered "overcome" in Greek, the meaning expressed is rather Aramaic than Hebrew. In chap. l. 42, where the verb חָזַק is translated "having" in the Septuagint, either the texts were

[1] *Jeremias Chaldaizans*, MDCCCXXXI.

different, or this verb was then given its ordinary Aramaic meaning of having or possessing. A few other instances naturally suggest either Aramaic meanings, or meanings of words in earlier times that in later times were either overlooked or lost. The following may be given as examples of possible Aramaic significations :—

(הֵן — אִם (הֵן), iii. 1; יָרְדוּ—יִמְחָאוּ (יֵרְדוּ), v. 31; (אֲוִר), אוֹר—רוּחַ (עֲבַדְתִּי), vii. 29; עֲבָדְהוּ—עֶבְרָתוֹ x. 13; li. 16; עֲבוֹד—עֲבוּר (עָבוּד), xiv. 4; אֵלָה—אֲבֵלָה (אֵלָיהָ), xxxi. 21; שָׁב—יֵשֵׁב (תּוּב), xxxvi. 15.

A thirteenth cause of variation was *Greek-transmission.* Some deviations were undoubtedly due to errors in copying the Greek manuscripts. Examples of such mistakes in copying the ancient Hebrew manuscripts have been already noted. Although this is a similar cause of variation, the principle has a particular application, and, therefore, claims a separate consideration. In order to determine accurately how much the manuscripts of the Septuagint have suffered by transmission in this way, in addition to examining them carefully, it is necessary to compare the ancient and modern characters in which they have been written. Such an undertaking involves a special investigation of itself, and does not belong directly to the present discussion. In the work of retranslation, though, a number of instances have been met that prove that many variations may be adequately explained by applying this principle, as well to the Greek as to the Hebrew manuscripts. An application of the principle to all the books of the Old Testament would be interesting; and, if not fruitful, the results, at least, would be important. A few of the more probable examples occurring in this book, some of which were long ago suggested by Schleusner in his *Thesaurus*, may be given here. The following possible cases will be sufficient for the present purpose:—

ἀναστροφῆς for ἀποστροφῆς, vi. 19; κατευθηνόντων for κατευθυνόντων, xv. 11; μαναά for μάννα, xvii. 26; μήτηρ for μήτρη, xx. 17; ναός for λαός, xxx. 18; ἐπὶ μεροῦ for ἐφ' ἡμέρας, xxxi. 19; οἴμους for ὤμους, xxxi. 21; ὦ ἀδών for ἕως ᾅδου, xxxiv. 5; χενέθ for χερέθ, xxxvii. 16; γῆς for τῆς, xlvi. 27; ἡ πτοητός for ἡ ἀπτόητος, l. 2; ἐν σοί for ἐκ σοῦ, li. 20; σκεῦος for σκότος, li. 34.

CHAPTER VIII.

THE CHARACTER OF THE TRANSLATION.

It has been frequently asserted, and is at present commonly believed, that the Alexandrian version of the Old Testament has been very unequally translated. The translation of the Pentateuch and of the historic books has been considered tolerably accurate and trustworthy, but the translation of the poetic and prophetic books has been considered utterly inaccurate and untrustworthy. Owing to the number and the nature of the deviations, in these latter books particularly, the translators of them are believed to have allowed themselves to take all sorts of liberties with their text. They are supposed, as has been shown, to have abridged it, amplified it, modified it, and, in many ways and places, falsified it. In short, by implication, they have been accredited with having done everything but honest work, and with having been anything but honourable men.

Because of its alleged inaccuracy and incorrectness, a poor opinion of the Septuagint has hitherto prevailed. It still prevails, too, as a deeply-rooted prejudice. This prejudice is chiefly, if not wholly, due to the acceptance of a false hypothesis respecting the character and the causes of the manifold divergences. It has been almost universally believed that both the Greek and Hebrew must and could be traced back to the same original manuscripts. This fact affords the reason why so many and such inconsistent theories have been suggested for the purpose of accounting for the enormous number of deviations in this book. On no other supposition, could the charge of arbitrariness have been received with so much favour in such numerous and unexpected quarters. Had the true nature and origin of the variations been adequately understood, the unworthy views, so widely prevalent, would long ago have been rejected. Indeed, they would never have been seriously entertained.

The general character of the translation of this particular book has been already noticed in dealing with the various classes of divergency that everywhere abound. Some of its chief features also have been briefly indicated. These, however, need to be more thoroughly discussed. It is particularly necessary to ascertain, as accurately as possible, the exact character of the translation, for the sake of showing its real importance for purposes of text-criticism. We have nothing to do at present with the condition of the Alexandrian text itself. That is a separate subject of investigation. Apart from the condition of this text, the critical value of the Septuagint depends essentially upon two things— the nature of the Greek translation, and the nature of the Hebrew manuscript from which it has been made. If the translation bears indications of fidelity and care, and if the manuscript shows evidences of purity and age, the testimony of the version is entitled to the greatest possible regard.

The first important feature of the translation is its *literalness*. This feature applies in general to the whole work. The narrative portions, though, it will be found, have been more accurately rendered than have the poetic portions, of the book. The difference, which is very perceptible, is significant. It admits, however, of a rational explanation. While partly due to imperfection or corruption in the ancient manuscripts, it was largely, if not chiefly, due to the greater perplexity that was experienced in translating poetry than was experienced in translating prose, from an unpointed text. The absence of punctuation would naturally render the work of reproducing the striking figures peculiar to the Hebrew particularly difficult. Competent critics will readily appreciate this statement. Unprejudiced observers, too, on carefully examining the

Hebrew text itself, will find that the same difficulty was also experienced by the Massorites.

Whatever may be thought or shown by scholars to be the case with reference to the other prophetic books, this book has been translated with the utmost carefulness. As a rule, wherever the originals of the two texts were the same, the Greek exactly reproduces the present Hebrew text; and wherever the original of the one was different from that of the other, the Greek accurately represents a classic Hebrew text. The whole book indicates that this text originally was very carefully translated. So far as the condition of the ancient manuscript admitted, the work was unquestionably well done. Not merely is the translation literal, but the literalness extends to the order of the words, often of the smallest particles, in the sentences. Of page after page, and chapter after chapter, this is true. The most peculiar constructions, moreover, are scrupulously reproduced. No modern English or German version of the book, it is not too much to say, is nearly so literal in all respects as is the Alexandrian version.

Indeed, so slavishly literal is the translation, and so accurately does it represent the Hebrew idiom, that the Greek, when retranslated into the original, takes at once the Hebrew form. Even the legitimate license of translation has been most sparingly employed. The translator very often did not use it when the genius of his language warranted its use. In short, the work is Hebraized, the Greek style having been sacrificed to the Hebrew style. Were it necessary, innumerable examples might be given. One needs, however, only to examine the translation to observe that it frequently adheres too closely to the original to be tolerable Greek. The almost exact correspondence of the Greek to the Hebrew form may be proved by practical experiment. The greater portion of the version can be literally translated back into classic Hebrew, with scarcely any change whatever in the present order of the words. From these considerations, one may say with Scholz, "A translation which follows the original from word to word, even where the language in which it is translated is opposed, must be regarded as a translation in the strictest sense of the term."[1]

The second feature of the translation is its *faithfulness*. This characteristic is specially illustrated in the case of Hebraisms, a few examples of which have been given in another place. An instance now and then occurs in which an idiom of this kind

---

[1] "Eine Uebersetzung, die von Wort zu Wort, selbst wo die Sprache, in welche übersetzt wird, widerstrebt, dem Originale nachgeht, muss als eine Uebersetzung im strengsten Sinne des Wortes angesehen werden." *Der masoreth. Text und die LXX-Uebersetzung*, etc., p. 22.

is wanting in the Septuagint. Whenever this is the case, then either the original manuscript did not contain it, or it has accidentally disappeared in the process of transmission. The translator was in no respect responsible for the omission,—firstly, because of the simplicity of the construction; secondly, because of the fact that such idioms are frequently translated by him; and, thirdly, because of the still more significant fact, that such idioms are sometimes present in the Alexandrian, where they are absent from the Massoretic, text. For these reasons it is evident, not only that he understood such peculiarly idiomatic Hebrew forms, but also that he faithfully reproduced them whenever he found them.

In his acute but incomplete discussion of the relation between the Greek and Hebrew of this book, Movers long since directed attention to this feature of the translation. Although he has made some observations upon its significance, he has pointed out but one passage where a Hebraism of this kind occurs only in the Septuagint. As has been shown, however, it occurs in several passages. A single instance, perhaps, would not be thought sufficient to establish with certainty the character of such a variation. Were there not more than one example, it might with reason be suggested that the idiom had accidentally disappeared from the

Massoretic text. The number, though, renders the suggestion worthless. In nearly every case, moreover, the examples occur along with other deviations which indicate their nature past all peradventure. They can be nothing other than recensional divergences. It is inconceivable that the translator invented them, or that he at any time introduced expressions foreign to the Greek language, where his original gave him no occasion for it. These Hebraisms in themselves furnish incontrovertible proof of a special text-recension. In no other way is it possible adequately to account for them. In addition to the direct testimony they bear in support of this hypothesis, they also prove conclusively the great fidelity with which the translator did his work.

Besides the repeated occurrence of this special kind of idiom in the Alexandrian, where it is wanting in the Massoretic, text, other idiomatic expressions peculiar to the Hebrew also frequently occur. One of the most remarkable idioms of the Jewish language is the employment of a Waw Conversive or Consecutive to modify the meaning of a primary tense. Notwithstanding the apparently arbitrary character of this idiom, which was not only foreign to the Greek, but also incapable of being adequately transferred to that or to any other language, it, nevertheless, was reproduced with almost painful accuracy. So faithfully was the work performed, that this idiom appears in many places only in the Septuagint. The version often has it where the Hebrew has it not. But one explanation can be given of this fact. The idiom belonged to the translator's manuscript, and was conscientiously retained. On this point, again, Scholz's observation is pertinent and important. After showing fully how the Greek sentences generally bear unmistakably the type of the Hebrew language, he says, "To this it may be added, that a number of short words which stand only in the Greek text are Hebraisms. On Greek ground these cannot have come into the text. On the contrary, a translator, whose only aim was to make his readers acquainted with the contents of the book, would have had every reason to omit, for instance, the ו as sign of the apodosis or consequent clause. That he does not do it, is to us a further proof of the scrupulous exactness of his work."[1]

The third feature of the translation is its *purity*. This feature refers to the original of the Greek.

[1] "Hiezu kommt noch, dass eine Anzahl der im griechischen Texte mehr stehenden Wörtchen Hebraismen sind. Auf hellenistischem Boden können diese nicht in den Text gekommen sein. Im Gegentheil hätte ein Uebersetzer, dem es nur darum zu thun war, seine Leser mit dem Inhalte des Buches bekannt zu machen, allen Grund gehabt, z. B. ו als Zeichen des Nachsatzes wegzulassen. Dass er es nicht thut, ist uns ein weiterer Beweis der scrupulösen Genauigkeit seines Werkes." *Der masoreth. Text und die LXX-Uebersetzung*, etc., p. 109.

As elsewhere indicated, there are frequent traces in the Massoretic text of a systematic revision of this book. In certain parts, the indications are not simply striking but decisive, the original text seeming to have been extensively enlarged or amplified. As illustrations of this influence have been given in another place, it is superfluous either to repeat them or to multiply them. Bleek's judgment on this point, though, is so important and so just, that it deserves to be quoted here in full. "When we impartially consider the individual variations of both texts," he says, "it can be determined from internal grounds, in many cases, with the greatest degree of probability, that, in these cases, the Alexandrian recension gives us still the original text, the Massoretic recension one somewhat revised. This is primarily the case respecting rather longer passages which the Massoretic text has, but which the Septuagint has not, where, throughout, it is much more likely that the same are later additions, than that, belonging originally to the text, they should have been omitted by later transcribers or compilers."[1]

[1] "Wenn wir die einzelnen Abweichungen beider Texte unbefangen betrachten, so lässt sich nach inneren Gründen in vielen Fällen mit dem grössten Grade von Wahrscheinlichkeit urtheilen, dass hier die Alexandrinische Recension uns noch den ursprünglichen Text liefert, die masorethische einen etwas überarbeiteten. Dies gilt zuvörderst in Bezug auf etwas grössere Stellen, welche der masorethische Text hat, nicht aber die Sept., wo überall viel wahrscheinlicher ist, dass

As the custom of text-revision was long and widely practised, this book may have been repeatedly revised. For such a custom there is ample authority, and for such a probability there is abundant evidence. The habit of re-editing and recasting Scripture, which may have begun, perhaps, with Ezra or Nehemiah, appears to have survived till tolerably modern times. Referring to this practice of revising ancient Hebrew writings, which, whenever it commenced, prevailed for many centuries amongst Jewish scholars or literati, Dr. Edersheim observes, "There are scarcely any ancient Rabbinical documents which have not been interpolated by later writers, or, as we might euphemistically call it, been recast and re-edited." [1] The activity and influence of these later Scripture revisers are becoming more universally acknowledged every year. Even Ryssel, in his recent able but conservative work on the text of Micah, admits the remarkable progress of this opinion amongst impartial critics, particularly since the time of Hitzig.[2] Moreover, he quotes, with apparent approbation, the words of Cheyne in his valuable commentary

dieselben spätere Zusätze sind, als dass sie, dem Text ursprünglich angehörend, sollten durch spätere Abschreiber oder Sammler ausgelassen sein." *Einleitung in das Alte Testament*, p. 321.

[1] *Sketches of Jewish Social Life*, p. 131. (Quoted from Cheyne on Isaiah.)

[2] *Untersuchungen über die Textgestalt und die Echtheit des Buches Micha*, p. 223.

on the book of Isaiah, where the latter of the Massoretic text significantly asserts, "It is becoming more and more certain that the present form, especially of the prophetic Scriptures, is due to a literary class (the so-called Soferim, 'scribes' or 'scripturists'), whose principal function was collecting and supplementing the scattered records of prophetic revelation."[1]

The fourth feature of the translation is its *priority*. This feature, like the preceding one, applies particularly to the manuscript from which the version was translated. By the priority of the translation, therefore, is meant the priority of the text from which it was made, as compared with the present Massoretic text. In general, the Greek presents the earlier and the more original form of the book. Paragraph after paragraph might be indicated in support of this assertion. The priority of many passages is admitted by Hitzig; the originality of a few is admitted even by Graf himself. While it is not advisable to multiply examples, there is one group of chapters, namely, xxvii.-xxix., which claims, in this connection, some consideration. The differences between the two texts in these chapters are remarkable, as well as manifold. Graf evidently either did not see, or did not want to see, that, in these chapters, the devia-

---

[1] *The Prophecies of Isaiah*, vol. ii., third edition, p. 228.

tions are, in some respects, more striking than they are in any other portion of the book. The peculiarities appear, not only in the frequency, but also in the form of the divergences. Movers, Bleek, and Hitzig have so thoroughly discussed them, that it is scarcely more than necessary here to indicate some of the more singular of them. The style is manifestly more than usually diffuse, even for Jeremiah, and differs very considerably from the prophet's ordinary mode of speech.

On examination, it will be observed that the title, "the prophet," occurs continually in connection with the name of the person of that office mentioned, and is in nearly every place superfluous. The spelling also, as well as the language, is peculiar. This is the case especially with proper names, compounded with Jehovah, which have both a longer and a shorter ending. As a rule, throughout this book the longer form prevails; in this group of chapters, though, the shorter form generally occurs. With only four exceptions, chaps. xxviii. 12; xxix. 27, 29, 30, the name of "Jeremiah" here has the shorter ending, whereas it elsewhere always has the longer ending. The same exceptional ending also here appears in other proper names; as, for instance, "Zedekiah," chaps. xxvii. 12; xxviii. 1; xxix. 3; "Jeconiah," chaps.

xxvii. 20; xxviii. 4; xxix. 2; "Hananiah," chap. xxviii. 1, 5, 10, 11, 12, 13, 15, 17. A striking difference, too, appears in the spelling of the name of "Nebuchadnezzar." In the book of Jeremiah, it is generally written with the letter *r;* but, in these three chapters, it is frequently written with the letter *n.* Such peculiar features, taken together with the numerous unnecessary additions to the Hebrew, consisting of words, phrases, half-verses, whole verses, and an entire paragraph, naturally point to only one conclusion — a conclusion which Kühl has the candour to admit. His admission is the more significant, inasmuch as he, in general, has adopted and defended Graf's hypothesis. After pointing out the chief peculiarities here, which clearly indicate a later redaction or revision, he observes, "The text of the Septuagint, in these chapters, is, if not exactly like the original text, yet much more nearly like it than the Massoretic text is."[1]

The fifth feature of the translation is its *superiority.* This feature again applies, of course, to the original of the version. The Septuagint presents not only a purer and an earlier, but also a superior, form of the book. The Greek generally

[1] "Der Text der LXX. steht also dem ursprünglichen Texte in diesen Kapiteln, wenn auch nicht ganz gleich, so doch bedeutend näher als der massoretische Text." *Das Verhältniss der Massora zur Septuaginta,* etc., p. 63.

exhibits a shorter and, in many respects, a better text than the Hebrew exhibits. The original of the version was tolerably, if not entirely, free from glosses. Hitzig believes that it was a text, as yet, not amplified or glossed at all. Whether, as he supposes, the process of interpolation had not commenced at the time of the translation has not been definitely determined. One thing, at least, is certain, the interpolations in the Hebrew are vastly greater than they are in the Greek. The Massoretic text, moreover, as has been frequently and fully evinced, abounds in superfluities, redundances, and useless or unnecessary repetitions of various kinds. The text which the Septuagint represents, on the other hand, is concise and admirable. In contrast to the former, which is remarkably verbose and pleonastic, the latter is exceedingly brief and terse. These differences were unquestionably recensional. While it is improper to suppose, with some, that all that the Massoretic text has more than the Alexandrian is pure interpolation, it is proper to suppose that much of it is. The characteristic brevity and conciseness of the Septuagint are so manifestly textual, and so clearly indicative of age and originality, that their significance in these respects can scarcely be overestimated. "The translator," as another has said, "has had before him a more concise and excellent text, and, therefore, in all difficult critical questions of dispute, one must take the final verdict of the Septuagint." [1] Should this last statement seem too strong, it is safe, at least, to say that the Greek should everywhere be consulted in translating the Hebrew of this prophetic book.

Besides these excellences of the Septuagint in respect to style, its superiority of text in many passages has been admitted by several distinguished critics. Even Graf sometimes makes such an admission. Movers, Michaelis, and de Wette, though, give a decided preference to the Alexandrian version. Hitzig also frequently acknowledges the originality or superiority of the reading in the Septuagint. In some cases, the Greek exhibits a more complete, in some cases, a more classic, in some cases, a more suitable reading than the Hebrew. In other cases, the form in Greek is preferable to the form in Hebrew, because it is the more natural. In other cases, again, the superiority of the former to the latter is proved by parallel passages. By a critical comparison, the reason for the preference in each case, it is thought, will be at once apparent. A

---

[1] "Der Uebersetzer habe einen kürzern, vortrefflicheren Text vor sich gehabt, und man müsse demnach in allen schwierigen kritischen Streitfragen den letzten Entscheid von der Septuaginta holen." (Quoted from Kühl's Monograph.)

few interesting and striking examples of superior text, which all impartial scholars must admit, may now be pointed out. These are taken simply from the first few chapters. As the complete list with references and parallel passages appears in the Conspectus at the end of the book, the following only need be given here :—"The word of Jehovah which was to Jeremiah" for "The words of Jeremiah," chap. i. 1 ; "fear not before them and be not dismayed at them, for I am with thee to deliver thee, declares Jehovah," for "be not dismayed at them, lest I dismay thee before them," chap. i. 17 ; "thou hast broken thy yoke, and burst thy bands," for "I have broken thy yoke, and burst thy bands," chap. ii. 20 ; "wherefore do ye speak to me?" for "wherefore will ye plead with me?" chap. ii. 29 ; "thou hast not obeyed" for "ye have not obeyed," chap. iii. 13 ; "the ark of the covenant of the Holy One of Israel" for "the ark of the covenant of the Lord," chap. iii. 16 ; "from the north country and from all the countries" for "from the land of the north," chap. iii. 18 ; "if he will put away his abominations from his mouth" for "if thou wilt put away thine abominations out of my sight," chap. iv. 1 ; "in him shall they praise God at Jerusalem" for "in him shall they glory," chap. iv. 2 ; "behold, they are coming" for "behold," chap. iv. 16 ; "the cities were burned with fire" for "the cities thereof were broken down," chap. iv. 26; "leave under her foundations, because they are Jehovah's" for "take away her branches, for they are not the Lord's," chap. v. 10, etc.

Thus, in these five respects, the translation is shown to possess the highest possible merit. Each feature indicated is favourable to the Septuagint, or rather to the Alexandrian recension from which it was translated. A further proof of its excellence is furnished by the evidence of other translations of the book, namely, the Latin, the Syriac, and the Aramaic versions. This evidence is so important that it must not be neglected, although it is not expedient to discuss it fully, because the subject does not belong to this investigation. In a considerable number of passages, both the Latin and the Syriac versions, or the Vulgate and the Peshitto, as they are called respectively, agree with the Septuagint against the Massoretic text. As Scholz has pointed out these passages, it is unnecessary to indicate them here. The testimony of the Vulgate is most significant, because, as it is supposed, with the exception of the book of Psalms, it was translated independently of the Septuagint from a Hebrew text. The testimony of the Peshitto is very interesting, because, as it is believed, it was translated partly from the Hebrew and partly from the Greek. Whenever the Syriac agrees with the Greek and Latin against the Hebrew, the translator must have thought the reading of these versions better than the reading of the Hebrew text.

The superiority of the Septuagint is still further shown by the evidence afforded by the Aramaic version. Although this version is a Targum, or a free interpretation, and not a literal translation, yet its testimony indicates how very many divergent passages were understood at the time that it was made. As in the case of the other versions, a full consideration of the evidence does not belong to this discussion. In comparing the Greek and Hebrew, though, it has been thought important also to compare both of them with the Aramaic; and, as the results are very valuable, to indicate them in the Conspectus of the variations at the end of the work. On examining the results of the comparison, the examples will show that, in some passages, by the words given, in other passages, by the sense expressed, the Aramaic agrees with the Greek against the Hebrew. By comparing these results, moreover, with those of Scholz, or by comparing the individual texts themselves, it will be seen that sometimes one, sometimes two, and sometimes three of these ancient versions agree with the Greek, and disagree with the Hebrew.

This fact speaks for itself. Where the Latin, the Greek, the Syriac, and the Aramaic correspond, their combined testimony becomes practically indisputable, and furnishes an overwhelming argument in favour of the Septuagint.

CHAPTER IX.

THE RESULTS OF THE INVESTIGATION.

AFTER having discussed the nature and origin of the variations, and after having considered the character of the Greek translation, it is necessary now to indicate the practical results of the investigation. These are not only of the greatest interest, but also of the highest value. In addition to their grammatical and lexical significance, they will be found important, some for the history, some for the interpretation, some for the correction, and some for the reconstruction of the present Massoretic text. Before indicating them, it will be proper to point out a further inconsistency which characterizes the arguments of a conservative critic, such as Graf, in dealing with the Alexandrian version.

In his extraordinary allegation, as was shown in the early part of this discussion, Graf attributes to the Septuagint nothing but caprice and imperfection. The foregoing investigation proves the charges that he brings against the translator to be unjust, and the arguments that he adduces in support of them to be untrue. His opinion of the version is biassed and one-sided, and his treatment of the divergences is based upon a false hypothesis. It is no wonder, therefore, that some of his conclusions should be strangely inconsistent. Proceeding on a wrong assumption, he utterly misrepresents the character of the translation, and practically contradicts himself in discussing its nature and importance.

Graf first asserts, for instance, that the work (he refuses to call it a translation) possesses no critical authority whatever, and afterwards admits that his sweeping assertion is not strictly true. "When we, therefore, deny to the Alexandrian version any critical value," he says, "it must not by this be understood that in it the traces of a better reading than that of the Massoretic text may not here and there have been retained."[1] In making this admission he partially corrects himself, as well as wholly negatives his former statement. If the Greek preserves some readings that are better than the corresponding readings in the Hebrew, it must be taken into account in every case of textual comparison ; and, if any superiority should be conceded to the Septuagint, it must, at least, possess some critical authority. That it is an authority

[1] "Wenn wir sonach der alexandrinischen Uebersetzung jeden kritischen Werth absprechen, so soll damit nicht gesagt sein, dass sich nicht darin hie und da die Spuren einer bessern Lesart als der masorethischen erhalten haben können." Einleitung, p. lvii.

of the first rank can be proved by rational and convincing evidence. Had Graf devoted more attention to ascertaining the true nature of the variations, he must inevitably have modified, as well his later as his earlier judgment.

Firstly, the results are important for the history of the Old Testament text. This investigation proves conclusively that the Septuagint was translated from a special manuscript. This manuscript, though differing widely from the original of the existing Hebrew manuscripts, was not, as has been shown, entirely different. In certain parts, the manuscripts were identical; in other parts, they were substantially alike; in other parts again, they were exceedingly unlike, though not so much unlike, for the reasons already indicated, as would at first appear. The narrative and historic portions, as a rule, are very similar; yet even here the differences, though often slight, are manifestly textual. The poetic and prophetic portions, though, are so divergent that, after the fullest allowance has been made for glosses and for imperfections, nothing but the hypothesis of a special manuscript can explain the differences. After all the other probable causes of variation are pointed out, there still remains the fundamental cause of different text-recensions.

Owing to the absence of definite information on

the subject, it is difficult to treat the history of the text of the Old Testament thoroughly or scientifically. For the present purpose, however, it may be roughly but conveniently divided into three general periods. For the history of the Hebrew text alone four periods might appropriately be made, but for the history of the Greek and Hebrew texts combined three only appear to be sufficient. The interval between the official composition and the official collection of the books of ancient Scripture may constitute the first period; the interval between the formation of the canon and the translation of the Septuagint may constitute the second period; the interval between the time of the translation and the present time may constitute the third period. The practical advantage of this division, it is thought, will be promptly admitted and appreciated.

Of the first period, extending to the time of Ezra and Nehemiah, very little now is known with certainty. The nature and condition of the ancient text are wrapt in much obscurity. So far as has been ascertained, various durable materials appear to have been used for manuscripts, and archaic Hebrew characters, akin to the old Phœnician alphabet, appear to have been employed in writing. In the well-known Siloam inscription the words are separated by dots; but this custom was rather exceptional, perhaps, than universal. Commonly, it is supposed, the characters were written close together, without any marks of division between the words, and without any vowel signs to indicate their true pronunciation or interpretation. Hence errors in translating, as well as in transcribing, Hebrew manuscripts would easily arise, partly because of the irregularity of the characters, and partly because of the practice of writing them. From one or other of these causes, too, divergences would naturally creep into the Scripture text.

Of the second period, extending to the time of the Septuagint translation, somewhat more is known. During this period the different recensions, or families of manuscripts, may possibly have arisen. But, perhaps, the most important information furnished respecting the history of the text throughout this period concerns the Hebrew alphabet. Apparently, there was a gradual change from the archaic to the cursive, and from the cursive to the Aramaic or rectangular form of writing. This investigation, it is believed, will throw some light upon the kind of characters from which the Greek translation of this book was made. The frequent and unexpected substitution of letters, quite similar in the earlier, but quite dissimilar in the later, alphabets, seems to indicate that the Alexandrian recension was written in the Aramaic-

Egyptian or Palmyrian characters. In many places, where the ancient manuscripts were evidently alike, the variations may be most reasonably explained by reference to the one or the other of these irregular alphabets. This investigation also shows that the translation of this book was made from a totally unpointed text; that is, a text in which there were neither signs of separation nor points of punctuation. The nature of the divergences proves conclusively that this must have been the case. Owing to the similarity of letters, to the absence of word-signs, and to the non-existence of vowel-points, more or less confusion was inevitable. Had the characters been distinct, or the words divided, or the vowels indicated, such deviations as frequently appear could not possibly have occurred.

Of the third period, extending to the present time, the information respecting the Old Testament text is tolerably full and definite. We are now concerned, however, only with such data as belong alike to both the Hebrew and the Greek. Since the time of the translation, each text has had its own distinctive history. While the manuscripts of each have suffered somewhat by transmission, the text of the Greek may have remained substantially the same. With the Hebrew, on the other hand, the reverse of this has been the case. Whether or not the process of Scripture interpolation began before the time of the Septuagint, it seems afterwards, as has been shown, to have been practised extensively in the Hebrew manuscripts until the days of the Massorites. The relation of the two texts practically establishes beyond a doubt that, during this period, the Palestinean recension suffered considerably by revision and interpolation, liberties having been taken, not only with the language, but also with the subject-matter, of the text. The extraordinary care of the Jews for the protection of their Scriptures from corruption can be traced back only for a certain distance in the past. It merely extends to the time when the Massoretic system was invented or completed, in the early centuries of the Christian era. While this system, therefore, guarantees the purity of the Hebrew since the time that it was adopted, it affords no guarantee whatever for its uncorrupted preservation at a period previous to that date. "The popular notion as to the absolutely sacred guardianship of the Hebrew text by the Jews is only partially founded on fact. It is true as regards the post-Massoretic, not the pre-Massoretic, text."[1] The truth of this observation is undeniable. It is also significant as showing that the process of fixing the Hebrew text was gradual, and may have extended over many centuries. In all probability,

[1] *Edinburgh Review*, October, 1885, p. 457.

it was fixed at first for public and official purposes. Afterwards, fixedness would be required both for safety and for uniformity.

The preceding paragraph assumes with students of the Septuagint generally that, apart from occasional imperfections and corruptions arising from transmission, the Greek text actually reproduces the Hebrew original employed by the Alexandrian translator. Cornill, for instance, in the exhaustive Prolegomena to his new and scholarly discussion of Ezekiel, asserts emphatically that, "in the Septuagint, we have reason to welcome a perfectly trustworthy witness to the Hebrew text of Ezekiel, as used at Alexandria in the third century before Christ."[1] This position may appear, perhaps, extreme, if not untenable. It may be held by some that the version, as it now exists, simply represents the form in which it circulated amongst the Jews previous to the days of Origen, or the shape it had assumed in the centuries intervening between the time of the translation and the date of the earliest Greek manuscripts. This question must, of course, be settled before the absolute critical value of the version can be definitely determined. It will, undoubtedly, be admitted by all scholars that, in the Septuagint, we have an authoritative version of a Hebrew

[1] *Das Buch des Propheten Ezechiel*, p. 102.

manuscript belonging to the third century before Christ, only when there are good grounds for believing that the oldest and best Greek manuscript that we possess substantially preserves the original translation.

Secondly, the results are important for the interpretation of the Old Testament text. A number of examples might be given where the Greek either helps to explain a difficult passage, or serves to show how a doubtful or disputed expression should be understood. For instance, in the Revised Version, the word רַדְנוּ, in the latter half of chap. ii. 31, is rendered "We are broken loose;" whereas, in the Authorized Version, it is rendered "We are lords." The Septuagint translation proves that the latter rendering is correct. The figure is not that of an animal having broken loose, but of a person having become master, or of one having obtained power to carry out one's own will. In the last part of ver. 34 also, the former version puts in the text, "I have not found it at the place of breaking in," and in the margin, "thou didst not find them," etc.; while the latter version translates, "I have not found it by secret search." The Septuagint indicates that the sentence should be rendered, "I did not find them breaking in (at house - breaking)." The words translated "breaking in" mean literally digging through or under, for the purpose of entering or undermining a house; and the same forms occur in Exod. xxii. 2, in both the Hebrew and the Greek.

Again, in the Revised Version, the first half of chap. v. 12 is rendered, "They have denied the Lord, and said, It is not he;" and, in the Authorized Version, it is rendered, "They have belied the Lord, and said," etc. The words in the original translated "It is not he" are commonly interpreted, It is not God who speaks, as if the prophet were proclaiming his own inventions; or, God is not, as if the people were speaking after the analogy of the impious man described in Ps. xiv. 1. But the Hebrew words לוֹא־הוּא are translated in the Septuagint by the phrase Οὐκ ἔστι ταῦτα, which in classic Greek often has the meaning, "it is not so," or, "these things are not true." Demosthenes repeatedly uses the expression in this sense. The parallelism of the verse-members, as well as the nature of the context, proves that the Alexandrian rendering is right. The people rejected the prophet's message of warning, and refused to believe that his prophecy was true. Hence the Hebrew should be translated, "They have denied the Lord, and said, *that is not so.*" In this way, the Septuagint shows how the verse was understood at the time of the translation, and also how it should be understood to-day. Hitherto, in modern times, this passage has been mistranslated, and its meaning has been misconceived.

For the interpretation or explanation of certain expressions peculiar to this book, the Septuagint is particularly important. One unusual expression refers to Messianic prophecy. In the Hebrew, there are two passages whose prophetic character has always possessed a special interest, namely, chaps. xxiii. 6; xxxiii. 16. In the Greek, the latter verse, together with the whole latter half of the chapter, is entirely wanting; while the former verse, with the exception of one word, is literally reproduced. Instead of צִדְקֵנוּ ("our righteousness"), the Greek has יְהוֹצָדָק ("Jah or Jehovah is righteous"), the term being a proper name, which occurs in both texts, Hag. i. 1; Ezra iii. 2, and elsewhere. As the corresponding words in Hebrew may also be regarded as a proper name, and as the order of the words in each text is identical, the Septuagint shows, not only how the verse was once interpreted, but also how it should be now translated. In the Authorized Version, the second member of the verse is rendered, "and this is his name whereby he shall be called, THE LORD OUR RIGHTEOUSNESS;" in the Revised Version, on the other hand, the latter words are rendered, "The Lord is our righteousness." In the one version, the Messianic testimony is emphasized by typographical expedients; in the other version, the passage properly appears in ordinary type. In neither version, though, is the rendering quite correct. The word translated "shall be called" is not a passive but an active verb, which is followed by a pronominal suffix in the objective case. In the translation, this pronoun is improperly omitted. The Hebrew, therefore, may be literally translated, "and this is his name which *one* shall call *him*, The Lord is our righteousness;" or, regarding the latter words in the original as a proper name, after the analogy of "Jehovah-Jireh," Gen. xxii. 14; "Jehovah-Nissi," Exod. xvii. 15; "Jehovah-Shammah," Ezek. xlviii. 35, it may be better translated, "and this is his name which *one* shall call *him*, Jehovah-Tsidkenu."

The Septuagint shows that this latter rendering is preferable. It shows more. It also indicates the proper subject of the verb "shall call." In the Alexandrian version, the passage reads, "and this is his name which *Jehovah* shall call *him*, Jehozadak." The order of the words in both texts is exactly alike, the only difference in the readings being צִדְקֵנוּ ("Tsidkenu"), in the one text, for יְהוֹצָדָק ("Jehozadak"), in the other text. As "Jehovah" is the subject of the verb in Greek, so also it may be in Hebrew. Indeed, the construction of the Hebrew implies as much. Grammatically, "Jehovah" may be taken as the subject of the verb, instead of being taken as in apposition with its object; and the passage may be naturally and properly translated, "and this is his name which *Jehovah* shall call *him*, Tsidkenu." But for the Messianic reference, it would probably have been so translated by scholars from the first. Even the Massoretic accentuation seems to show clearly that "Jehovah" belongs to the word preceding and not to the word succeeding it, and, therefore, should be construed, as just indicated.

As the word for Jehovah occurs twice in this passage in Greek, once as the subject of the verb and once as a portion of the proper name, it is evident that the verse was understood, as thus explained, at the time of the translation. It is also evident that at that time there was no thought in the minds of the readers of the Alexandrian recension of characterizing the person mentioned in this passage as other than a human being. Interpreters of prophecy have commonly endeavoured to find here a belief, on the part of the ancient Jews, in the divinity of the promised Messiah; or, at least, an expectation, on the part of the Hebrew prophet, that the coming king whom he foretold should be a divine individual. The Septuagint translation of this book plainly indicates that no such notion was entertained by the translator, and

Q

that he never for a moment supposed that the future ruler he both promised and described was to be a Divine Being.

Moreover, the omission from the Septuagint of the parallel passage, chap. xxxiii. 16, where the term "Jehovah-Tsidkenu" appears in the Hebrew as the name of the restored Jerusalem, is also very significant. The absence of the passage there, as well as the form of the passage here, in the Greek, is exceedingly important for the subject of Messianic prophecy, the character of which differs in different prophetic books. In Jeremiah, as compared with Isa. ix. 2-7, for instance, where the idea first appears, it is supposed by W. Robertson Smith,[1] there is a perceptibly diminished emphasis on the advent of a personal Messiah. The expectation of a national deliverer, who should introduce a reign of peace, is simply but emphatically expressed. This deliverer, however, is spoken of as a temporal prince. Nothing in the book, when studied in connection with the Septuagint, or when interpreted by the help of that translation, points to an eternal "Prince of Peace." Thus the Alexandrian version sheds some light upon the gradual growth and modification of the Messianic idea in the Church, and upon the historic development of the Messianic doctrine in the Scripture. The idea of the expected

[1] *The Prophets of Israel*, p. 277.

Messiah grew and changed in each successive century; and in no other age, it is believed, was its expression so minute and circumstantial, as in the period extending from the close of the Old to the opening of the New Testament.

Another unusual expression, peculiar to the Massoretic text, has reference to the term, "the servant of Jehovah," which is frequently found and variously applied in Scripture. Properly speaking, a servant of Jehovah was one who voluntarily gave himself to the service of God, and earnestly endeavoured to do his divine will. Spontaneity and fidelity are two essential elements in the idea of the term. With this signification, " the servant of Jehovah" was a distinguished title of honour under the old covenant. In this sense, it is applied to Moses, in Deut. xxxiv. 5; to Joshua, in Judg. ii. 8; to David, in Ps. xviii. 1. In the Hebrew, chaps. xxv. 9; xxvii. 6; xliii. 10, the words "my servant" are applied to Nebuchadnezzar. In each of these three chapters, though, the expression is significantly wanting in the Septuagint. This fact renders the character of the words in Hebrew suspicious, and their application questionable. Elsewhere throughout the whole Old Testament, they are applied only to a person or to a people of righteous purpose. In this sense, they are used of Abraham, in Gen. xxvi. 24; of Israel, as Jehovah's people, in Isa. xli. 8; of Jacob, as a synonym for Israel, in Isa. xliv. 1, 2; xlv. 4; also in this book, chaps. xxx. 10; xlvi. 27 of the Hebrew, and in the latter chapter only of the Greek.

From these considerations, the words "my servant," in the Hebrew, can scarcely have originated from Jeremiah. He would hardly have applied them to a person like Nebuchadnezzar. The king of Babylon was not a servant of Jehovah in the ordinary acceptation of the term, nor can it be appropriately used of him. After the Babylonian captivity, however, some one, who regarded him as a predetermined instrument of Jehovah for executing the divine purposes respecting his covenant people, may have inserted the words where they appear in the Massoretic text. This suggestion seems the more probable, inasmuch as in Ezek. xxix. 20, Nebuchadnezzar is said to have received Egypt as the wages for himself and his army in serving against Tyre, "because they wrought for me, saith the Lord God." It is also worthy of note in this connection, that the distinguished Jewish commentator, Rashi, in his annotations on chap. xxv. 9, says nothing whatever about the phrase "my servant," as though he did not find it in his text; whereas, in chap. xxvii. 6, he explains the words to mean that Nebuchadnezzar was a servant of Jehovah only in the sense of being a scourge.

His comment on the expression reads, "he should do my pleasure to recompense my enemies."[1]

There is still another unusual species of expression, peculiar to the Hebrew text of Jeremiah, on the nature of which the Septuagint also gives some information. In the Hebrew, chaps. xxv. 26; li. 41, the term "Sheshach" occurs as a synonym, it is supposed, either for Babylon or for Babylonia, according to a secret or cabalistic system of writing, technically called Atbash, which was practised amongst the ancient Jews, and which consisted in substituting the last letter of the Hebrew alphabet for the first, the last but one for the second, and so on through the whole series. On this principle of transposition, as the consonants only were formerly written in Hebrew, the letters Sh Sh Ch which compose the word *Sheshach* would correspond to the letters B B L of which the word *Babel* (Babylon) is composed. This term is wanting altogether in the Septuagint, being found there in neither passage; but its mystic meaning seems to be confirmed by the latter passage, chap. li. 41, where Sheshach and Babylon occur in the parallel members of the Hebrew verse. In chap. li. 1, however, where another instance of this kind of cabalistic writing occurs, the Septuagint shows how the mystical name should be translated. The expres-

[1] ישעיה רצוני ליפרע כישׂבאי.

sion " Leb-kamai," which stands in the text of the
Revised Version, and is rendered in the margin,
"The heart of them that rise up against me,"
becomes, when transmuted according to the figure
of Atbash, Ca S D I M, which is equivalent to
Chaldea or the Chaldeans. As this is the actual
rendering of the Greek in this verse, the singular
term is proved to be a Jewish cipher, and its
significance is made very plain. Properly, therefore, the word Chaldea or Chaldeans should take
the place of "Leb-kamai" in the text.

Although a love for fancifully playing upon
words, and a liking for artificially dealing with
letters, were always characteristic of the Hebrew
writers, it has been doubted whether this peculiar
practice of writing words by substituting consonants according to their position in the alphabet
is as old as Jeremiah. Let that be as it may, the
system dates from an unknown antiquity, and may
be older than the prophet's time. The important
question is, Did Jeremiah himself invent or
authorize such ciphers? Most probably he did
not. They seem to have belonged only to the
Palestinean recension, having possibly been adopted
by the Jews during the period of the Babylonian
captivity. During the exile, there may have been
a purpose in their adopting such mystical names to
designate Babylonia or Chaldea, because of their

captive condition in that country. For the Jews
of Jeremiah's day, however, both in Palestine and
in Egypt, there was no need whatever either to
adopt or to employ such terms. For this reason,
as well as for the reason that the word "Sheshach,"
chap. li. 41, and the sentence, "and the king of
Sheshach shall drink after them," chap. xxv. 26,
are wanting in the Septuagint, they seem not to
have belonged to the Alexandrian recension.

Thirdly, the results are important for the correction of the Old Testament text. The number of places where the Greek corrects the Hebrew is somewhat large. It is not necessary, however, to furnish a complete list of such passages. A few of the more interesting or more important will suffice. In chap. i. 17, for instance, God is represented in the Hebrew as sending the prophet on his mission of remonstrance to the people, with the menacing words, " be not dismayed at them, lest I dismay thee before them." The reading is apparently incorrect, and may have arisen from some imperfection in the ancient manuscript. Such a menace seems entirely out of place, as well as altogether out of harmony with the character of God. The context here leads one to expect words of encouragement not threatening, of comfort not intimidation. On account of his youth, the prophet would naturally be timid in undertaking the duties of the prophetic office, under the peculiar circumstances of his time, and surely a degree of fear that was inevitable would not cause him to forfeit his rightful claim to God's protecting care. The Septuagint renders the latter half of this verse, "Fear not before them, and be not dismayed at them; because I am with thee to deliver thee, declares Jehovah." The reading, which here corrects the Hebrew, is a classic one, occurring several times in this book, as well as many times in the other books of the Old Testament. The addition also improves the parallelism of the verse, closely corresponds with the idea in vers. 8, 19, and admirably harmonizes with the context.

Again, the latter part of chap. ii. 34 in the Hebrew reads, "upon all these." In the margin of the Revised Version, though, it is stated that some ancient authorities have "every oak." This is the rendering of the Septuagint, with which, moreover, the Syriac closely corresponds. The words, as they are found in Hebrew, are exceedingly obscure and difficult to explain. The variant reading in the version was due merely to a slight difference of punctuation, the consonants having been exactly alike; but the pointing of the Septuagint appears to be correct. There is a contrast here expressed between slaying a person who was caught in the act of breaking into a house, which was permitted by the ancient Mosaic law, and slaying a person who was caught, not in committing but in exposing and denouncing crime, which was both cruel and detestable. According to this passage, the victims whom Israel slew were not criminals but innocents, not persons guilty of house-breaking, but persons guilty only of reproving her for her idolatry. She had shed innocent blood under the trees, or in the groves, where she had practised her idolatrous worship, and where for which her victims had reproved her. Thus the construction in the Greek is clear, and shows how the Hebrew should be read. The whole latter half of this verse may be rightly rendered, "I did not find them breaking in (at house-breaking), but upon every oak."

In chap. vi. 6, for the word "trees," which stands in the text, the Revised Version has in the margin "her trees." This is the rendering, not only of the Greek, but also of the Latin and the Syriac versions. The difference of reading, again, was due to the insertion of a single dot or point. The last letter of the word translated "trees" should contain a small dot (Mappik), as in Deut. xx. 19, and should be construed as a suffix of the third person singular. Although, in besieging a city, the Jews were commanded to spare, so far as possible, the fruit-trees, partly because of their innocence and partly because of their usefulness, yet they were permitted to use the wood of other trees for the purpose of carrying on a siege. The foreign army mentioned in this passage would probably cut down trees, both for building their bulwarks against the city and for clearing away all obstacles to their approach. Another example of a similar kind, where the variation was due to the insertion of the same point, occurs also in chap. xii. 9. Instead of the reading, "to devour," the Greek has "to devour her." This latter seems to be the better reading of the two, and to represent the proper punctuation.

In chap. xii. 2, the word translated "they grow" means literally in Hebrew they go or proceed. In the Septuagint, the word used means they bear or produce; and, apparently, may be just as properly applied to trees as to men. The latter reading is required by the parallelism of the verse, this clause of which, according to the Greek, being translated, "they produce, yea, they bring forth fruit." The variation arose from the substitution of a single letter, the Massorites having read ילך, and the Greek translator ילד. As the former verb in Hebrew does not mean "to grow," and is nowhere else used in this sense, it is evidently incorrect. Even Hitzig gives no reason why the latter verb may not be used, as indicated. In chaps. xi. 23; xxiii. 12, for "even the year of their visitation," one should read "in the year," etc., as suggested in the margin of the Revised Version. In each verse, this is the rendering of the Greek, and the Hebrew should be rendered accordingly. The reference is to a period of calamity during which the judgment here foretold should be fulfilled.

Another place in which the Greek corrects the Hebrew occurs in chap. xv. 14, where the latter is rendered in the text of the Revised Version, "I will make them to pass with thine enemies," etc., and in the margin, "I will make thine enemies to pass," etc. According to some ancient authorities, the Revisers further state, the clause is rendered, "I will make (cause) thee to serve thine enemies," etc. These authorities are specially the Alexandrian, Syriac, and Aramaic versions. Other manuscripts also exhibit the same reading, which is unquestionably the correct one, as even Graf, along with many other critics, honestly admits. This rendering, moreover, agrees exactly with the parallel passage in chap. xvii. 4, where the same form is found in Hebrew, that is found here in Greek. The variation between the two verbs in this sentence arose from the simple substitution of a ר for a ד in the ancient texts.

In chap. xxiii. 17, instead of the rendering, "that despise me, the Lord hath said," the Revisers place in the margin, "that despise the word of the

Lord." This is the reading, not only of the Greek, but also of the Syriac, version. The variation was due again to punctuation, which in the versions is evidently right. An utterance of Jehovah in the broken form in which it here appears in Hebrew nowhere else occurs, as Graf has pointed out. In ver. 33 of this same chapter, instead of the exclamatory question, "What burden!" the Septuagint and Vulgate have, as the Revisers indicate, "Ye are the burden." This latter reading, which arose simply from a different division of the words in the Hebrew, gives a vastly better meaning, and undoubtedly expresses what the prophet meant to say. The case affords a beautiful example of a superior word-division on the part of the Greek translator. In ver. 39 also, instead of "I will utterly forget you" the Latin, Greek, and Syriac versions have, "I will lift you up." This reading is required by the parallelism of the verse, which, as it stands in Hebrew, makes no appropriate sense. The figure is one of lifting up a burden, and of casting it away. Punctuation here again explains the variation.

Fourthly, the results are important for the reconstruction of the Old Testament text. The instances of correction just discussed furnish interesting illustrations. In every case, apparently, the Greek reading should take the place of the Hebrew reading. In every case, too, notwithstanding the great difficulty of translating an unpointed and unpunctuated text, the superiority of the Septuagint was due to the translator having either divided or punctuated the consonants more correctly than did the Massorites. Such examples not only bear witness to the fidelity with which, under the most disadvantageous circumstances, the Alexandrian version was made, but also to its importance for purposes of text-criticism. Some other examples of superior readings, whose value for reconstructing the present Massoretic text will be readily acknowledged by scholars, it is believed, may now be given. These may be arranged in several classes, as the passages are numerous.

The first class comprises whole verses. In certain places, the Hebrew is so imperfect that it is practically impossible to render it intelligibly. Chap. xi. 15, for instance, is so obscure that, as it stands, no clear or consistent meaning can be obtained from it. The ancient manuscript was evidently corrupt or indistinct. On the other hand, the reading in the Greek is good, and makes excellent and appropriate sense. The people, having by their idolatry forsaken Jehovah, and having by their hypocrisy forfeited all claims upon him or his house, are here rebuked for their deceitful service by the prophet, who asks if they suppose that prayers and sacrifices can rescue them or atone for them. The entire verse is rendered in the Septuagint, "Why has the beloved wrought abomination in my house? Shall vows and holy flesh remove from thee thy wickednesses, or by these shalt thou escape?"

Another verse of doubtful rendering in the Hebrew occurs in chap. xvii. 11. In the Authorized Version, the partridge is represented as sitting on eggs and hatching them not. Both verbs are here translated incorrectly. The Revised Version gives a more adequate rendering of them, as well as of the remaining portions of the verse; but, by its marginal readings, it leaves the reader still in doubt about the true translation of the verse, which, in the Greek is very plain, and may be rendered, "As the partridge *calleth* (and) gathereth *what* she hath not brought forth, so is he that getteth *his* riches not by right; in the midst of his days they shall leave him, and in his end (latter time) he shall be a fool." The Greek shows that the subject of the verb "shall leave" is the noun "riches," and not the pronoun "he." The idea is not that the rich man should suddenly die and leave his wealth, but that his wealth should speedily leave him, ere he had lived out half his days; so that, during the rest of his life, he should be regarded as an example of wicked folly. The point of the prophet's illustration thus appears to be that, as the partridge was popularly supposed to call together the young of other birds which would forsake her when they heard the cry of their true parent, so ill-gotten gains would prove but a short-lived possession to the dishonest man. The Septuagint also shows that originally the two texts in this verse, though very similar, were not identical. As they now appear respectively, one variation between them was due to a different division of the Hebrew consonants; the other variations between them were due to different readings in the ancient manuscripts.

Still another imperfect verse in Hebrew occurs in chap. xxxi. 25, the construction of the words of which is very simple, but the form of one of which, at least, is very questionable. The verse in Greek, on the contrary, is admirably rendered, and reproduces a superior text. It reads, "For I have satiated *every* thirsty soul, and every hungry soul have I replenished." This rendering is much more symmetrical than that in our English Bibles, and presents a perfect contrast between the thirsty and the hungry souls of whom the prophet speaks. That the original of each text was slightly different, is demonstrated by the presence of the additional pronoun "every," as well as suggested by the form of the words in Hebrew, respectively translated "weary" and "sorrowful." Literally, the former word means weak or faint, the latter languishing or pining. If the words in each original were alike, the one must have meant faint with thirst, the other pining with hunger; so that both should be translated as they are in the Septuagint, the rendering of which is corroborated by the connection of thought in this with that in the preceding verse. While it is barely possible that the former word was written differently in each ancient manuscript, it is very probable that the latter was. Instead of דְּאָבָה, the translator apparently read, with Schleusner, רְעֵבָה. In ver. 12 of this chapter also, where the same root occurs, and where a similar idea is expressed in the Greek, the rendering of the Alexandrian version is superior to that of the English translation. The Septuagint renders the last member of this verse, "and their soul shall be as a *fruitful tree*, and they shall not *hunger* any more."

The second class comprises verse-members. A number of examples might be given, but a few will be sufficient. For the sake of conciseness, the words in Greek, which show how the Hebrew may be reconstructed, will be indicated by italics. In the second member of chap. ii. 19, the reading of the Septuagint, "and *I have* not *been pleased with* thee," gives a superior rendering of this portion of the verse, and seems to show that the construction in the Hebrew is not simply peculiar but imperfect. In the first member of ver. 34 of this same chapter, too, the Septuagint reading, "Also in thy *hands* is found the *blood* (plu.) of the souls of the innocents," is preferable in each case. The word "hands" instead of "skirts" is much more appropriate in this place, and was evidently the original reading in the early manuscripts. The variation possibly arose from the Massorites having mistaken the meaning of the Hebrew word for wing or skirt, which may have been written anciently without the letter כ, and may have had the same form as the word for hand. It is significant that the Syriac version also agrees here with the Alexandrian version.

In the middle of chap. xi. 19, the Greek rendering, "*come* and let us *put* wood into his food (bread)," which is supported by the Aramaic version, shows how the passage may be intelligibly translated. As the sentence stands in English, it does not accurately represent the original Hebrew. The word translated "fruit" means literally bread or food. It is nowhere in the Old Testament used of vegetable fruit, and to give it such a peculiar meaning here is to violate the usage of the language. Neither can the word be properly applied to Jeremiah. His fruit could not reasonably mean

R

either his activity, or his posterity, or his words of prophecy, all of which have been suggested by way of exposition. Neither can the whole expression be appropriately applied to the prophet with the force of a proverb, because of the reasons just indicated. The Septuagint shows how the sentence should be rationally translated, as well as how it was unquestionably understood at the time of the translation. It is significant that Jerome seems to cite the rendering of the Septuagint with approval. It is still more significant that the Aramaic translator also uses a verb meaning to put or to place, and, instead of the word "wood," renders "deadly poison." The idea intended to be expressed was that of destroying the prophet by poisoning him; that is, by putting pulverized poisonous wood into his food. The superior rendering of the version was recensional, and was due to the presence of the verb "come," and to the absence of the letter ה, in the original Hebrew manuscript. This latter variation, it should be observed, may have arisen from dictation.

In the second member of chap. xiii. 18, the Greek reading, "for the crown of your glory (your glorious crown) has been taken down *from your head*," again shows how the sentence should be rendered. The Hebrew word, translated "principalities," in the Authorized Version, and "head-tires," in the Revised Version, is not a noun in apposition with crown, as indicated by the Massoretic punctuation, but a noun and preposition, as shown by the Septuagint translation. The singular verb in Hebrew, as well as the general construction of the sentence, shows that the rendering of the Alexandrian version is correct. On account of their changed circumstances, the youthful monarch and his royal mother were to sit in humiliation, not because their head-dresses were come down, but because their regal glory was gone.

Again, the first part of chap. xv. 16 is rendered in the Septuagint, "*from those despising* thy words; *destroy* them." This reading, which arose from a slightly different combination of letters in the original, seems to suit the context better than the reading in the Hebrew, which is certainly peculiar, and, in the present connection, apparently inappropriate. The feeble figure of eating words is scarcely analogous to the bold figure of eating a parchment roll in Ezek. iii. 1–3. In ver. 15 of each text, the prophet asks Jehovah to avenge him of his persecutors; in ver. 16 of the Greek, he prays for their destruction. Thus the parallelism in the Greek is more complete than in the Hebrew. The superiority of the Septuagint in this passage will appear more clearly by translating, together with the variant reading, the immediately preceding and the immediately succeeding sentence. The passage reads, "Know that for thy sake I have suffered reproach from those despising thy words; destroy them, and let thy word be unto me for the joy and rejoicing of my heart."

Once more, the first part of chap. xvi. 7 is rendered in the Septuagint, "neither shall *bread* be broken at (in) *their* mourning," etc. This reading shows how the Hebrew should be reconstructed. The variation was due to the simple substitution or alteration of a single letter, and is supported by other ancient manuscripts. In the Revised Version, the words "for them" should be translated "bread," and the word "*bread*," which is printed in italics, should be expunged. The verb "break" here in the Hebrew does not of itself necessarily mean to break bread. It only has this signification when the word for bread, as in Isa. lviii. 7, is expressed as its object. Moreover, the words "for them" are further shown to have arisen erroneously from the word "bread," because, as Graf admits, they do not harmonize with the singular Hebrew suffix after the verb "to comfort," which is improperly translated as a plural pronoun in the English Bible.

Further, the second member of chap. xviii. 14 should be reconstructed by the help of the Septuagint. While the general sense of the Hebrew words is clear, the combination of adjectives is peculiar, and difficult to understand. The Revised Version does not give an adequate translation of them either in the margin or in the text. The reading in the Greek, which arose from a text similar to that of the Hebrew, but more complete than the latter is, gives an excellent rendering of the sentence. Before translating the Septuagint here, it should be observed that the form of the first member in Hebrew is somewhat unusual; and that its form in Greek, which represents a very similar text, is so interesting as to be worthy of careful consideration. A translation, therefore, of the whole Greek verse, because of its possible correctness, if not probable superiority, may advantageously be given. It reads, " Shall *protuberances* depart from rocks, or the snow from Lebanon? or, shall waters *borne violently by the wind* turn aside?"

Lastly, in the middle of chap. xli. 9, the Septuagint reading, "*the same is the great pit,*" appears undoubtedly to be the true one. In the Authorized Version, the rendering, "because of Gedaliah," is absolutely false, as Graf affirms; and, in the Revised Version, the rendering, "by the side of Gedaliah," is essentially wrong, as he also asserts. The words in the original do not properly admit of either rendering, and cannot, as they stand, be grammatically construed. The Hebrew reading here is utterly indefensible, and was evidently due to textual imperfection, or to erroneous transcription, or, perhaps, to both. The originals of the present Greek and Hebrew texts are very similar; and the one, as scholars know, was easily derivable from the other by a slight confusion of the letters. The excellence of the construction in the Greek is worth indicating by a translation of the context. The whole verse reads, "Now the pit wherein Ishmael cast all those whom he had slain (*the same is the great pit* which Asa the king had made for fear of Baasha, king of Israel), this Ishmael filled with them that were slain."

The third class comprises single words. A very large number of places might be pointed out where a suffix, or a verbal form, or a particle of some kind represents a manifestly superior reading in the Septuagint. As many such instances have been already noticed by Movers and Hitzig, as well as by Graf himself, and as many others will be at once observed by those who take the trouble critically to compare the Hebrew with the Greek throughout, brevity forbids the multiplying of examples. For reasons that will plainly appear to scholars, a small number of such places in the Hebrew, which should be reconstructed by the Greek, may here be briefly indicated. These are, "shall blaze forth" for "shall break forth," chap. i. 14; "wall" for "walls," chap. i. 18; "destroyed" for "burned up," chap. ii. 15; "stained" for "marked," chap. ii. 22; "burned" for "broken down," chap. iv. 26; "a refiner" for "refining," chap. vi. 29; "shall be consumed" for "shall die," chaps. xi. 22; xlii. 17, 22; "drought" for "droughts," chap. xiv. 1; "tamarisk" for "heath," chap. xvii. 6; "deep" for "deceitful," chap. xvii. 9; "shall be inhabited" for "shall remain," chap. xvii. 25; "moulded" for "potter," chap. xix. 1; "Ahaz" for "cedar," chap. xxii. 15; "these" for "swearing," chap. xxiii. 10; "reproach" for "desolations," chap. xxv. 9; "multitude" for "mounts," chap. xxxii. 24; "earth" for "Jehovah," chap. xxxiii. 2; "your princes" for "his wives," chap. xliv. 9; "voice" for "shame," chap. xlvi. 12; "the name" for "there," chap. xlvi. 17; "upon her" for "it is come," chap. xlvi. 20; "wild ass" for "heath," chap. xlviii. 6; "altars" for "daughters," chap. xlix. 2; "in her forest" for "in his cities," chap. l. 32; "around" for "hollow," chap. lii. 21.

The fourth class comprises proper names. In chap. xxxviii. 1, where the name "Shephatiah" appears in Hebrew, the Septuagint has "Zephaniah." The former word, as Graf remarks, nowhere else occurs. For this reason, as the latter word occurs in chaps. xxix. 25; xxxvii. 3, of both the Hebrew and the Greek, it may be correct. In chap. xlii. 1, instead of "Jezaniah the son of Hoshaiah," the Greek reads, "Azariah the son of Maaseiah." As the name Azariah occurs in chap. xliii. 2 of both texts, and as the name Maaseiah also occurs with it in this latter chapter, the reading of the Septuagint seems to be the proper one. In other places again, such as "Gihon" for "Shihor," chap. ii. 18; "Assyrians" for "Syrians," chap. xxxv. 11; "On" for "land of Egypt," chap. xliii. 13; "Gilead" for "Gad," chap. xlix. 1, the version preserves not only the more correct, but also the more primitive reading, as Hitzig acknowledges respecting the first three of these examples. In each case, the name in Greek gives a more definite designation of the place described.

In chap. xli. 5, "Salem" for "Shiloh" affords another preferable reading. The former is supposed to have been situated nearer to Shechem than the latter was; and, for this reason, Hitzig again admits that the narrative in Greek furnishes the more natural order of the neighbouring cities mentioned in this passage. From the account given in Gen. xxxiii. 18, where the word is rightly rendered as a proper name in the Authorized Version, Salem was evidently a city in the land of Canaan, and is probably identical with the present *Sâlim*, a little village lying somewhat east of *Nâblus*, the modern name of the ancient Shechem.[1] The latter seems formerly to have been the designation of a town, as well as of a tract of country. The occurrence of Salem here in the Greek version of Jeremiah corroborates the testimony of the Septuagint reading in Gen. xxxiii. 18, according to which the word is in apposition with the expression, "city of Shechem," which immediately follows. The Hebrew word שָׁלֵם seems not to be an adjective, as commonly assumed by modern scholars, but a proper name, occurring elsewhere only in Gen. xiv. 18. Having the same form in each verse, it should be translated and spelled each time in the same way, and not in a different way, as in the English version.

The Septuagint seems, moreover, to present an older and a superior form of the personal name in chap. xlix. 27. Instead of "Ben-hadad," the Greek here has υἱοῦ Ἄδερ, as in 1 Kings xv. 18, 20; xx. 1; 2 Kings xiii. 3, 24; Amos i. 4. The latter for the former term occurs so frequently and so uniformly in the version that the recensional character of the reading is unquestionable. The regularity of the spelling indicates that the original of the Greek expression was either בֶּן־הֲדַר, or more probably, perhaps, בֶּן־אֲדַר. This latter name or title denotes "the son of Adar," which was apparently the

---
[1] Smith's *Dictionary of the Bible*, vol. iii., p. 1222.

designation of an ancient Syrian divinity, akin if not equivalent to the old Assyrian deity, an appellation of which appears in the word Adrammelech, as found in 2 Kings xvii. 31 ; xix. 37. The method of spelling the word "Nebuchadnezzar," in the Septuagint, also indicates a more primitive pronunciation of the name, and one in all probability more like the Assyrian original, which, Schrader says, is written *Na-bi-uv-ku-du-ur-ri-u-ṣu-ur* in the cuneiform inscriptions, but was pronounced *Nabû-kudurri-uṣur* by the native Babylonians.[1] Throughout this book, the word in Greek is almost regularly written Ναβουχοδονόσορ, corresponding to נְבוּכַדְנֶאצַּר in Hebrew. It is significant and noteworthy that the Vulgate adopts the spelling of the Septuagint, and writes the word "Nabuchodonosor," which is an exact transliteration of the Greek.

There are also a few places where the Septuagint shows a proper name in the Hebrew to be either wrongly formed or wrongly punctuated. In chap. xxxix. 3, for instance, the name "Samgar-Nebo" is apparently incorrect. Such a form does not elsewhere occur in the Bible, and Schrader says that it has not yet been found in the cuneiform inscriptions.[2] According to all analogy, in the Scripture spelling of Assyrian proper nouns compounded with

---

[1] *Die Keilinschriften und das Alte Testament*, Zweite Auflage, p. 361.
[2] *Ibid.* p. 416.

"Nebo," the latter term should begin the name, as in Nebuchadnezzar, Nebuzaradan, and Nebushazban. The fact that the corresponding word in Greek is Σαμαγώθ, and that the two succeeding words, each of which begins with "Nebo," are Ναβουσάχαρ and Ναβουσαρείς, seems to confirm this supposition. In chap. xlix. 1, 3, again, the Revised Version has in the text "Malcam," and in the margin "their king." The word in Hebrew is incorrectly pointed. As it stands, it should be translated as a common noun with suffix, and not as a proper noun. With its present punctuation, therefore, the rendering of the margin is alone correct. The context shows, however, that the word in each verse is a proper name, and should be punctuated according to the Septuagint "Milcom." This was the name of the god of Ammon, and it seems never to have been properly pointed otherwise.

A careful comparison of the proper names of this book, as they occur respectively in each text, possesses a still further significance. It proves conclusively that the mode of spelling and pronouncing them, observed by the translator, was very often not the same as that adopted by the Massorites. It also seems to indicate that the ancient pronunciation of proper names differed greatly from that expressed at present in our Hebrew Bibles. In translating into Greek, the laws of euphony, doubtless, would sometimes forbid the precise reproduction of a peculiarly Semitic sound, especially in the case of consonants. In the case of vowels, little or no difficulty would be felt. Whenever an exact equivalent of a consonant, therefore, was wanting in his language, the translator would be obliged, of course, to employ the letter or the combination of letters, which most nearly represented the Hebrew original. This course, it will be seen, he has consistently pursued. After making the fullest allowance, though, for such euphonic or linguistic peculiarities, which occur with almost systematic regularity, there still remains a number of remarkable divergences that can be explained only on the supposition that many names were once spelled and pronounced differently from the way in which they are to-day. The information furnished by the Septuagint respecting the ancient mode of spelling and pronouncing Hebrew proper names, it will be found, is of the greatest possible importance.

As the principal deviations of the version are manifest to scholars, it is not necessary to give many illustrations here. A few examples of the divergent method of expressing vowel sounds should be given, though, to show that the vowel notation of the Massorites is not the same as was that of the Alexandrian translator. When the latter, for instance, writes an *ă* for an *ĭ*, as Γαλαάδ for גִּלְעָד (Gilead); an *ĕ* for an *ĭ*, as Ἐμμήρ for אִמֵּר (Immer); an *ŏ* for an *ă*, as Γοδολίας for גְּדַלְיָהוּ (Gedaliah); an *ō* for an *ū*, as Ἀζώρ for עַזּוּר (Azzur), and Πασχώρ for פַּשְׁחוּר (Pashhur); an *ĕ* for an *ă* and an *ē* for an *ū*, as Σελλήμ for שַׁלֻּם (Shallum), it is unreasonable to suppose that the change of vowel in each case was due to arbitrariness on his part. Every time he could as easily have given the one sound as he gave the other. In corresponding cases, it will be found, he has reproduced such vowels with scrupulous fidelity, as an *ī* in Δαυίδ for דָּוִד (David), and *ă* in Γαμαρίος for גְּמַרְיָה (Gemariah), an *ā* in Ῥαχάβ for רֵכָב (Rechab), an *ē* in Ῥαχήλ for רָחֵל (Rachel), and an *ū* in Σαμουήλ for שְׁמוּאֵל (Samuel). When, in other books, moreover, the Septuagint writes an *ă* and an *ō* in Σαμψών for שִׁמְשׁוֹן (Samson), the rational conclusion is that the name was so pronounced at the time that the translation was made. It is not just to assume that the pronunciation, represented in the Septuagint, was simply that which prevailed amongst the Jews of Egypt, and, therefore, would naturally be less pure than that which prevailed amongst the Jews of Palestine, as some scholars have assumed. Nor is it fair to assert with some, for reasons that need not be now discussed, that the Massoretic pronunciation of proper names is absolutely correct, or that it infallibly represents the sound of every name as it was originally pronounced. Both from its age and character, it is quite reasonable to suppose that the version generally reproduces the earlier pronunciation. It is here sufficient, further, to observe that there are good grounds for believing that changes were at some time arbitrarily made in the form of certain Hebrew proper names. "Many," as Nestle says, "seem to have first arisen after the origin of the Septuagint."[1]

The investigation also furnishes some new and important suggestions for the Hebrew grammar. In chap. ii. 20, the rendering of which in Greek is excellent, by a different division of the letters, the Septuagint translates the two words אַתְּ צִעָה, as though they were a verb of the Hithpael species, אֶתְצָעָה. According to the Massoretic system, this latter form is not now properly permissible, the law of euphony requiring אֶצְטָעָה. As the translator evidently had before him the same consonants that the Hebrew has, and as he surely must have been acquainted with all the grammatical forms of the Hebrew language, he could hardly have regarded the combination as he did, had the

---

[1] "Manche scheinen erst nach der Entstehung der LXX. entstanden zu sein." *Die Israelitischen Eigennamen*, etc., p. 125.

form not been legitimate. It is highly improbable that he should have made such a mistake. The case is especially interesting, because it suggests the possibility, either that the present law of euphony in such verbal forms was not then strictly observed, or that it was not fully established when his Hebrew manuscript was made. In ver. 33 of this same chapter, there occurs a group of words, לֹאִיכֶן כִּי גַם (not only, but also), which is peculiar in Hebrew at the present time, but which at one time may possibly have existed in the language.

In chap. iv. 5, the verb מָלְאוּ, which is translated "aloud" in the Revised Version, is rendered in the Septuagint by the adverb מָלֵא, as though the latter were formerly a synonym for מְאֹד. In chap. v. 12, the expression לוֹא־הוּא being rendered by Οὐκ ἔστι ταῦτα (these things are not so), indicates that the word הוּא, which is now used, sometimes as a pronoun and sometimes as a verb, was then used also as an adverb. This word is supposed to have been originally a demonstrative; and, besides its frequent occurrence as a personal pronoun and as a copula, it occasionally occurs as a demonstrative adjective to indicate an object already mentioned as well known, somewhat after the manner of our remote demonstrative *that*. The present passage shows that it was likewise once employed as a demonstrative adverb.

In chaps. iii. 21; vii. 29, the Septuagint has "lips" for "bare heights." In each passage, the rendering in Greek is tolerably appropriate; but, in the latter passage especially, it suits the context exceedingly well. It is unlikely that the translator had before him שְׂפָתַיִם, the ordinary Hebrew word for lips. He evidently found in his manuscript a combination of letters similar to that in the Massoretic text; and instead of שְׁפָיִם, undoubtedly read שָׂפָם. Hence this latter word seems clearly to be an ancient dual form for the mouth or the lips, as it is rendered in both the English and Alexandrian versions of Ezek. xxiv. 17, 22.

In chap. xi. 21, the two words וְלֹא are rendered by the Septuagint εἰ δὲ μή. The translation is interesting, inasmuch as it seems to indicate that the ancient punctuation may have been וְלֻא, a form that is equivalent to וְאִם־לֹא, which occurs in 1 Sam. ii. 16, and which is substantially translated there in Greek as the words under consideration are translated here. Another interesting combination in Greek is found in chap. xiii. 27, where, for the present Hebrew expression מָתַי עוֹד, the Septuagint has עַד־מָתַי עֹד.

In a large number of passages, moreover, one

preposition in the Greek stands for another preposition in the Hebrew. Sometimes each species of this sort of substitution is favourable to the Septuagint. Indeed, the form in Greek often corrects the form in Hebrew, as in chap. iii. 20, for instance, where the preposition מ (from) is rendered in the Septuagint ב (to). The variation evidently arose from the similarity of these two letters in the ancient alphabet, but the Greek preserves the proper reading. In Hebrew lexicons, it is stated that the verb בָּגַד rarely occurs with the preposition מ (from), and the present passage is cited as an example. Besides being the only instance, this verb appears not to have been rightly used with מ (from). The verse, therefore, should be rendered, "Surely as a wife proves faithless to her husband, so ye have proved faithless to me, O house of Israel, declares Jehovah." This case furnishes but one example out of very many that might be given of the way in which the Septuagint corrects peculiar or exceptional uses of prepositions in the present Hebrew text.

The testimony of the Septuagint is especially significant respecting the use of "in" or "into" and "on" or "upon," both of which in Hebrew are very often incorrectly used. Example after example might be given where the Greek presents, not only the preferable, but also the proper, form of one or

s

other of these words. In the Hebrew, the prepositions אֶל and עַל, which are rightly rendered in the version by εἰς and ἐπί respectively, are constantly and inconsistently interchanged, as though they were substantially synonymous. Very often this is the case where the sense, as well as the grammar, requires a distinction to be made. In the Greek, on the other hand, a distinction in harmony with the most classic Hebrew usage almost uniformly occurs. The version frequently has an אֶל for an עַל and *vice versa*, where the one or the other wrongly stands in the Hebrew. The translator's use of these two prepositions is so admirable, and so agreeable to the genius of the Jewish language, that apparently, in his manuscript, the true distinction between them was more carefully observed than it is in the present Massoretic text. The difference between the texts in this respect, while probably in part recensional, may possibly have been in part transcriptional. The difference, too, is decidedly in favour of the Septuagint.

For other unusual grammatical expressions, particularly for the so-called ἅπαξ λεγόμενα, or words that occur but once throughout the Hebrew Bible, the Septuagint will also be found to be of the greatest value. Many such terms, in this book especially, are of very doubtful significance, and of very questionable correctness. In chap. xiv. 9, for example, the word translated "astonied" is both obscure and inappropriate. The corresponding word in the version, on the other hand, affords an excellent sense. The first member of this verse in Greek is rendered, "Why shouldst thou be as a man *asleep*, as a *man* that cannot save?" The parallelism here is perfect, and the meaning expressed is superior to that in the Hebrew. In the former case, the divergency was due to the substitution of a ד for a ר and of a ה for a ד; in the latter case, it was due to the absence of the letter ו. Each of these kinds of variation occurs with frequency. In this way, the version shows not only how variations arose, but also how they may be proved and estimated. The Hebrew of Jeremiah, as is well known, is remarkable for its numerous textual peculiarities. It displays a great many words and forms which cannot have belonged to the language in its purer state, but which may be corrected or emended by the aid of the Septuagint translation.

In addition to the examples given in the preceding paragraphs of the important results obtained from this investigation for the grammar and the lexicon, it might be much more fully shown, did space permit, how the Septuagint helps to throw light upon Hebrew forms of rare or single occurrence, as well as serves to furnish valuable suggestions and corrections for future grammars and lexicons. One more example may be given by way of further illustration. In the last German edition of Gesenius's Dictionary, it is stated that the verb "to send," שָׁלַח, which is naturally followed by the accusative of the person or the thing sent, is followed by the accusative of the person sent with the letter ל only in 2 Chron. xvii. 7. The Septuagint shows that the same construction also occurs in chap. xvi. 16 of this book. This verse is rendered in the English Bible, as though the noun following the verb "send" in each member was in the dative, because of the preposition ל (for) that stands with it in each case; whereas, the preposition here appears to be as certainly the sign of the accusative, as it is in the passage mentioned in Chronicles, where the nouns following it are correctly construed in the English version as accusatives. According to the Greek rendering of each passage under consideration, therefore, the present verse should be translated, "Behold, I will send many fishers, declares Jehovah, and they shall fish them; and, afterward, I will send many hunters, and they shall hunt them from every mountain, and from every hill, and out of the holes of the rocks."

There still remains to be considered another textual peculiarity of some grammatical importance. The use of the pronoun by the Septuagint, in many passages, is exceedingly interesting, to say the least. There are a few places where its absence is significant, as "father" for "my father," chap. iii. 19; "mother" for "my mother," chap. xv. 10; "brother" for "my brother," chap. xxii. 18. The simplicity of the expression in each instance seems to indicate its antiquity. At all events, the form in Greek points to a peculiarity of the translator's text. The simpler reading is undoubtedly recensional, and it is apparently ancient.

There are also a good many places where the substitution of a pronoun for an article, or an article for a pronoun, is significant. It is barely possible that occasionally, owing to the genius of his language, the translator may have substituted an article for a pronoun, especially because a few divergences of this kind may be conjecturally explained in this way. It is hardly probable, however, that this was often if, indeed, ever the case. The recensional character of this species of substitution is well illustrated by an instance that occurs in chap. xxvii. 3, where the Greek has a pronoun, but the Massoretic text has neither a pronoun nor an article with the noun "messengers." The construction of the Hebrew, though, absolutely requires either the one or the other, as the accompanying adjective with article indicates; and, since the noun with article would have been a natural reading, which could have been easily and legitimately reproduced, had it appeared in the original of the Alexandrian text, the presence of the pronoun here in Greek warrants the conclusion that it belonged to the translator's manuscript. The following are the chief examples that occur of the substitution of an article for a pronoun :—

הָאֹהֶל—אֹהָלַי, iv. 7 ; הָאָרֶץ—אַרְצֵךְ ; הֶעָרִים—עָרַיִךְ, iv. 20 ; הַמַּרְעִית—מַרְעִיתָם, iv. 26 ; הֶעָרִים—עָרָיו, x. 21 ; הֵמָּה אֹמְרִים —הַשְּׁכֵנִים—שְׁכֵנַי, xii. 14 ; הַבַּחוּרִים—בַּחוּרֵיהֶם, xviii. 21 ; הָאֹמְרִים, xiv. 15 ; וְהָרֶחָם—וְרַחֲמָה, xx. 17 ; הָאֹמְרִים—הֵם אֹמְרִים xxvii. 9.

The substitution of a pronoun for an article in the Septuagint is much more frequent than that of an article for a pronoun. As the Greek was an article-loving as well as a participial-loving language, the greater frequency of the pronoun in the version proves this peculiarity to be unquestionably recensional. Wherever a pronoun in the Greek stands for an article in the Hebrew, as a rule, there is reason to believe that the translator found the form before him in the text he used. The fact, moreover, of its greater frequency in the Hebrew original of the Greek translation suggests the supposition that the pronoun was much more common in earlier times than was the article, the more frequent use of which may probably have belonged to a later development of the language. If this supposition be correct, it indicates, not only the primitive nature of the Hebrew pronoun, but also the archaic character of the Alexandrian recension. In any case, the textual peculiarity is significant, and worthy of the carefullest consideration. Of this kind of substitution the following instances occur:—

הַנֶּפֶשׁ — נַפְשָׁם, iv. 10; הַבַּיִת הַזֶּה — בֵּיתִי, vii. 11; — הַנָּשִׁים; וַאֲבוֹתֵיהֶם — וְהָאָבוֹת; בְּנֵיהֶם — הַבָּנִים — הַדֶּרֶךְ, וּנְשֵׁיהֶם, vii. 18; שָׂדֵיהֶם — הַשָּׂדֶה, vii. 20; דְּרָכַי, vii. 23; עַמִּי — הָעָם; בַּתַּרְמִית — בְּתַרְמִיתָם, — הַבַּחוּרִים; שְׁבוּעָתִי — הַשְּׁבוּעָה, xi. 5; viii. 5; הַמְּלָכִים, בְּנַחֲלָתִי — בְּנַחֲלָה, xii. 14; בַּחוּרֵיהֶם, xi. 22; וַאֲבוֹתֵיהֶם — וְהָאָבוֹת וְהַבָּנִים; מַלְכֵיהֶם —, xiii. 13; בָּרֶכֶב, נְבִיאֵיהֶם — הַנְּבִיאִים, xiv. 13; וּבְנֵיהֶם, xiii. 14; יוֹמִי — הַיּוֹם, בְּרִכְבֵיהֶם וּבְסוּסֵיהֶם — וּבַסּוּסִים, xvii. 25; — וְהַנְּבִיאִים; עַמּוֹ — הָעָם, xxvi. 23; xl. 6; וּנְבִיאֵיכֶם, xxvii. 15; קָדְשׁוֹ — הַקֹּדֶשׁ, xxxi. 23; סְרִינוֹתֵיכֶם — הַסְּרִינוֹת, תּוֹעֲבֹתֵיכֶם — הַתּוֹעֵבָה, xliv. 22; xlvi. 4; מִלְחַמְתְּךָ — הַמִּלְחָמָה, xlix. 26.

Having indicated briefly a very few of the more

important practical results obtained from the investigation, it seems advisable, before presenting the complete Conspectus of the variations, to sum up concisely the general conclusions that have been reached by the present inquiry. Partly by way of recapitulation, therefore, and partly by way of amplification, it will be seen, the following final results are now submitted for careful consideration :—

1. The book of Jeremiah, from the time of its completion and publication, or shortly afterwards, appears to have existed in a twofold form.

2. One edition of his prophecies was possibly authorized in Egypt by the prophet himself, and, therefore, may be called the Egyptian or Alexandrian recension; another edition was probably sanctioned in Babylonia or Palestine by the Jewish Synagogue, and, therefore, may be called the Babylonian or Palestinean recension.

3. The Alexandrian recension represented the shape of the book as it was circulated in Egypt, and as it may have been published by Jeremiah or by Baruch; the Palestinean recension represented the shape of the book as it was circulated in Asia, and as it may have been altered and expanded, during the centuries intervening between the date of the prophet's death and the time of the Septuagint translation, by Jewish copyists or scribes.

4. The version reproduces in substance the Alexandrian recension, and presents, as nearly as can be determined, the norm, or the original form, of the book, as it may have left the hands of the prophet or of his secretary; the Massoretic text reproduces in modified form the Palestinean recension, and presents the shape which that recension had received by glosses and interpolations from the times of Jeremiah to the days of the Massorites.

5. The Septuagint was translated as faithfully as the condition of the ancient Hebrew manuscript would permit, and as literally as the genius of the flexible Greek language would allow, the translator or translators having in no way arbitrarily changed the original Hebrew text, and having in no instance been influenced either by personal scruple, theological bias, or religious tendency.

6. From striking evidence furnished by numerous passages, sometimes because of the different derivation of the same word, and sometimes because of the peculiar use of a similar term, the version seems to have been made by several persons, two or three, at least, apparently having taken part in the work of translation.

7. Although each text contains mistakes, as has repeatedly been shown, yet the Greek translators made mistakes more frequently than did the

Massorites, owing chiefly to the difficulty of translating a badly worn or an indistinctly written manuscript from an unpunctuated or an unpointed text.

8. While both texts have suffered somewhat from the process of transmission, the original of each having, undoubtedly, been more or less corrupt, the Hebrew text in general is in a better condition at present than is the Greek text, owing principally to careful and, perhaps, repeated redaction or revision.

9. By applying the general principles of variation deduced and demonstrated in the foregoing discussion, corruptions and imperfections in both texts may be discovered and explained, the one text helping to correct the errors or to rectify the mistakes in the other text.

10. After making due allowance for the various causes of divergence, some of which are true of all the books, and all of which are true of some of the books, of the Old Testament, the Septuagint translation will be found to be of the utmost value for the purposes of text-criticism.

CHAPTER X.

THE CONSPECTUS OF THE VARIATIONS.

CAPUT L.

1 דִּבְרֵי ירמיהו	דְּבַר־יְהֹוָה אֲשֶׁר הָיָה אֶל־ירמיהוּ[a]
אשר בענתות	אֲשֶׁר יָשַׁב[b] בענתות
2 אשר	כַּאֲשֶׁר (אשר)
אמון	אָמֵץ (אמוץ)
3 עד־תֹּם	עד
עד־גְּלוֹת	עד־יְגלוּת[c]
4 אֵלַי לֵאמֹר	אֵלָיו
6 אֲהָהּ	אַתָּה (הֲוַה אַתָּה)[d]
7 עַל־כָּל	אֶל־כָּל
וְאֵת כל	וּבְכָל
9 אֹתִידוּ	אֹתִידוּ אֵלַי[e]
10 היום הַזֶּה	היוֹם[f]
על־הגוים ועל־הממלכוֹת	על־גוים ועל־ממלכוֹת
וְלַהֲרוֹס[g]	
11 יִרְמְיָהוּ	Desunt
אֲנִי רֹאֶה[h]	
12 על־דברי לעשתוֹ	על־דִּבְרִי[i] לעשתם
13 אֵלַי שֵׁנִית	שֵׁנִית אֵלַי
אֲנִי רֹאֶה[k]	Deest

---

[a] ut Hos. 1:1; Joel 1:1; Micah 1:1; Zeph. 1:1. [b] Targ. דְּקַבֵּל אַחְסָנְתֵּהּ. [c] ut Ezek. 1:2. [d] Cf. 4:10; 14:13; 32:17. [e] ut Ezek. 2:9. [f] ut vs. 18. [g] ut 18:7. [h] ut 24:3. [i] Targ. פִּתְגָּמֵי. [k] ut 24:3.

14 תִּפָּתַח	תֵּפָתַח
15 לְכָל־מִשְׁפְּחוֹת מַמְלְכוֹת צָפוֹנָה	לְכָל־מַמְלְכוֹת הָאָרֶץ[a] מִצָּפוֹן
וְעַל כָּל־חוֹמֹתֶיהָ סָבִיב	וְעַל כָּל הַחוֹמוֹת סְבִיבֶיהָ
17 אֲלֵיהֶם	Deest
אַל־תֵּחַת מִפְּנֵיהֶם פֶּן־אֲחִתְּךָ	אַל־תִּירָא מִפְּנֵיהֶם וְאַל־תֵּחַת[b]
לִפְנֵיהֶם	מִפְּנֵיהֶם כִּי אִתְּךָ אֲנִי לְהַצִּילֶךָ
	נְאֻם־יְהוָה[c]
18 וַאֲנִי	Deest
הַיּוֹם	הַיּוֹם הַזֶּה[d]
וּלְעַמּוּד בַּרְזֶל וּלְחֹמוֹת נְחֹשֶׁת	וּלְחֹמַת[e] נְחֹשֶׁת בְּצוּרָה[f] לְכָל־מַלְכֵי
עַל־כָּל־הָאָרֶץ לְמַלְכֵי יְהוּדָה	יְהוּדָה
לְכֹהֲנֶיהָ	Deest
19 נְאֻם־יהוה לְהַצִּילֶךָ	לְהַצִּילֶךָ אָמַר יהוה

CAPUT II.

1 וַיְהִי דְבַר־יְהוָה אֵלַי לֵאמֹר	Desunt
2 הָלֹךְ וְקָרָאתָ בְאָזְנֵי יְרוּשָׁלִַם	
לֵאמֹר	וַיֹּאמֶר
זָכַרְתִּי לָךְ	זָכַרְתִּי
לֶכְתֵּךְ אַחֲרַי בַּמִּדְבָּר בְּאֶרֶץ לֹא	לֶכְתֵּךְ אַחֲרֵי קְדוֹשׁ יִשְׂרָאֵל אָמַר
זְרוּעָה	יְהוָה
3 רָעָה תָּבוֹא אֲלֵיהֶם	רָעָה תָּבוֹא עֲלֵיהֶם[g]
נְאֻם־יהוה	אָמַר[h] יהוה
4 וְכָל־מִשְׁפְּחוֹת	וְכָל־מִשְׁפָּחַת[i]
6 וּבְשׁוּחָה בְּאֶרֶץ צִיָּה וְצַלְמָוֶת	וְשָׁפָה בְּאֶרֶץ צִיָּה וְגַלְמוּד
7 אֶרֶץ הַכַּרְמֶל	הַכַּרְמֶל
9 נְאֻם־יְהוָה[k]	Deest
11 הַהֵימִיר גּוֹי אֱלֹהִים	הֶחֱמִירוּ גּוֹיִם[l] אֱלֹהֵיהֶם

[a] ut 15:4; 24:9 etc. [b] Cf. 23:4; 30:10; 46:27; Deut. 1:21 etc. [c] ut vss. 8, 19. [d] ut vs. 10.—Targ. יוֹמָא דֵין. [e] Targ. וּבְשׁוּר. [f] Cf. 15:20. [g] Targ. עֲלֵיהוֹן. [h] Targ. אֲמַר. [i] Targ. וְיָרְעִית. [k] Alex. ἀμαρ יהוה. [l] Targ. קַדְמָיָא לָא שְׁבָקוּ.

2:12-23] THE CONSPECTUS OF THE VARIATIONS. 285

12 הָרְבּוּ מְאֹד	הַרְבֵּה מְאֹדᵃ
13 לַחְצֹב לָהֶם בֹּארוֹת בֹּארֹת	וַיַּחְצְבוּ לָהֶם בְּאֵרוֹת
לֹא־יָכְלוּ הַמָּיִם	לֹא־יָכְלוּ לְהָכִיל הַמָּיִםᵇ
15 נָהַר	וְיִתְנוּ
עָרָיו נִצְּתָה	וְעָרָיו נִתְצוּᵈ
16 יְרִעֵךְ קָדְקֹד	וְדָשׁוּד וַיִּבְהֲקוּ לֹהּᵉ (וַיַּנְדְּפוּךְ)
17 עָזְבֵךְ אֶת־יהוה אֱלֹהַיִךְ בְּעֵת	עָזַבְךְ אֹתִי נְאֻם־יהוה אֱלֹהָיִךְ
מוֹלִיכֵךְ בַּדָּרֶךְ	
18 לְדֶרֶךְ מִצְרַיִם	וּלְדֶרֶךְ מִצְרַיִם
מֵי שִׁחוֹר	מֵי גִיחוֹן
לְדֶרֶךְ אַשּׁוּר	וּלְדֶרֶךְ אַשּׁוּר
מֵי נָהָר	מֵי נְהָרוֹתᶠ
19 תְּיַסְּרֵךְ רָעָתֵךְ וּמְשֻׁבוֹתַיִךְ תּוֹכִחֻךְ	תִּיסְרֵךְ מְשֻׁבוֹתַיִךְ וְרָעָתֵךְ תּוֹכַחְתֵּךְ
כִּי־רַע וָמָר עָזְבֵךְ אֶת־יהוה אֱלֹהָיִךְ	כִּי מַר עָזְבֵךְ אֹתִי נְאֻם־יהוה אֱלֹהָיִךְ
וְלֹא פַחְדָּתִי אֵלָיִךְ	וְלֹא בְּחַרְתִּי בָךְ (אֹתָךְ)
יְהוָה צְבָאוֹת	אֱלֹהָיִךְ
20 שָׁבַרְתִּי ... נִתַּקְתִּי	שְׁבַרְתִּי ... נִתַּקְתִּי
לֹא אֶעֱבוֹד	לֹא אֶעֱבוֹד לָךְ
כִּי עַל־כָּל	כִּי אֶרֶךְ עַל־כָּל
כָּל־עֵץ רַעֲנָן	כָּל־עֵץ עָבֹתᵍ
אַתְּ צֹעָה זֹנָה	שָׁם אֶתְצְעָה (= אֶצְטַעֲא) זֹנָה (אֶשְׁפֵּךְ בְּתַאֲוָתִי)ʰ
21 שׂוֹרֵק כֻּלֹּה זֶרַע אֱמֶת	שׂוֹרֵק זֶרַע (גֶּפֶן פּוֹרִיָּה) כֻּלֹּה אֱמֶת
לִי סוּרֵי	לְמַר (לְמְרִי?)
22 נִכְתָּם עֲוֹנֵךְ	נִכְתָּמְתְּ בַּעֲוֹנוֹתַיִךְ
אֲדֹנָי יְהוִה	יְהוָה
23 הַבְּעָלִים	הַבַּעַלⁱ
דַּרְכֵּךְ	וְדִרְכֵּיִךְ
דְּעִי	וּדְעִי

ᵃ ut Gen. 15:1; 41:49 etc. ᵇ ut II. Chron. 7:7.—Targ. דְּלָא יָכְלִין לְקַיָּמָא.
בֵּיָא. ᶜ Targ. יְרִיבוּן. ᵈ Targ. צָדְיָן. ᵉ Targ. וְיִבְזוּן נִכְסָךְ. ᶠ Cf. Ps. 137:1.
ᵍ ut Ezek. 20:28 (Gk. & Heb.). ʰ Cf. Ezek. 16:15. ⁱ Targ. טָעֲוַת.

בְּעֶרֶב קָלֹה מְשָׂרֶקֶת׃ דרכיה[a]	בִּבְרָה קָלֹה מְשָׂרֶקֶת דרכיה׃
פֶּרֶא (פָּתֶא = פָּתָה) לְמֵי־מִדְבָּר	24 פֶּרֶה לָמֻּד מִדְבָּר
סְחָפָה רוּחַ (סְחָפַה בְרוּחַ)	שֹׁאֲפָה רוּחַ
נְתָנָהּ	תַּאֲוָתָהּ
בְּהָדְשָׁהּ (בהדשה)	בְּחָדְשָׁהּ
(מִיַּעַן?) מִדְרָךְ מוֹקֵשׁ[b]	25 מִיחָף
וַתֹּאמֶר אֶתְאוֹשֵׁשׁ (נוֹאַשׁ לִי)	וַתֹּאמְרִי נוֹאָשׁ לוֹא
אַהֲבָה	אֲהַבְתִּי
הָלְכָה	אֵלֵךְ
בְּנֵי יִשְׂרָאֵל	26 בֵּית יִשְׂרָאֵל
וּמַלְכֵיהֶם וְשָׂרֵיהֶם	מַלְכֵיהֶם שָׂרֵיהֶם
לָעֵץ אָמְרִיב כִּי אָבִי אַתָּה	27 אֹמְרִים לָעֵץ אָבִי אַתָּה
יְלָדְתָּנִי	יְלִדְתָּנוּ[c]
פְּנֵי עָלַי	פָּנוּ אֵלַי
פְּנֵיהֶם[c]	פָּנִים
אִם־יָקוּמוּ וְיוֹשִׁיעוּ	28 יָקוּמוּ אִם־יוֹשִׁיעוּךָ
כִּי מִסְפַּר עָרֶיךָ הָיוּ אֱלֹהֶיךָ יְהוּדָה	כִּי מִסְפַּר עָרֶיךָ הָיוּ אֱלֹהֶיךָ יְהוּדָה
וּמִסְפַּר חֻצּוֹת יְרוּשָׁלַם קִטְּרוּ לַבַּעַל[d]	
תְּדַבְּרוּ (תְּדוֹבֵבוּ?)	29 תָּרִיבוּ
כֻּלְּכֶם פְּשַׁעְתֶּם וְכֻלְּכֶם בְּגַדְתֶּם בִּי	כֻּלְּכֶם פְּשַׁעְתֶּם בִּי
לְקַחְתֶּם	30 לָקְחוּ
אָכְלָה חֶרֶב	אָכְלָה חַרְבְּכֶם
כְּאַרְיֵה מַשְׁחִית וְלֹא יְרָאתֶם׃	כְּאַרְיֵה מַשְׁחִית׃
שִׁמְעוּ[e] דִּבְרֵי־יְהוָה כֹּה אָמַר יְהוָה	31 הַדּוֹר אַתֶּם רְאוּ דְבַר־יְהוָה
הֲלֹא רִדְנוּ וְלוֹא־נָבוֹא אֵלֶיךָ עוֹד	הֲרִדְנוּ לוֹא־נָבוֹא עוֹד אֵלֶיךָ
32 הֲתִשְׁכַּח בְּתוּלָה עֶדְיָהּ כַּלָּה קִשֻּׁרֶיהָ	הֲתִשְׁכַּח כַּלָּה עֶדְיָהּ בְּתוּלָה קִשֻּׁרֶיהָ
מַה־עוֹד תֵּיטִבִי דְרָכַיִךְ (בִּדְרָכֵךְ[f])	33 מַה־תֵּיטִבִי דַּרְכֵּךְ
לָאֵכֵן גַּם אֶת־הָרָעוֹת לִמַּדְתִּי אֵת־	לָכֵן גַּם אֶת־הָרָעוֹת לִמַּדְתְּ אֶת־דְּרָכָיִךְ
דְּרָכָיִךְ	

---

[a] Inc. vs. 24. [b] Targ. בְּאָחֳרָהַבְרָיא לְנֶכְסַיָּא. [c] Targ. אַפֵּיהוֹן. [d] Cf. 11:13. [e] Inc. vs. 31.—Targ. סַבְרִלוּ. [f] Targ. בְּאוֹרְחָתָךְ.

[2:34-3:6] THE CONSPECTUS OF THE VARIATIONS.   287

בְּכַפַּיִךְ	34 בִּכְנָפַיִךְ
דְּמֵיa	דַּם
Deest	אֶבְיוֹנִים
לֹא־בְמַחְתֶּרֶת	לֹא־בְמַחְתֶּרֶת
עַל־כָּל־אֵלֶּה	עַל־כָּל־אֵלֶּה
כִּי תָזֹלִי מְאֹד לִשְׁנוֹת	36 מַה־תֵּזְלִי מְאֹד לִשְׁנּוֹת
פִּי גַם מֵאֵת זֶה	37 גַּם מֵאֵת זֶה
במבטחךb	במבטחיך
תצליחי לו	תצליחי להם

CAPUT III.

אִם (הֵן)	1 לֵאמֹר הֵן
הֲשׁוֹב תָּשׁוּב אֵלָיו עוֹד	הֲיָשׁוּב אֵלֶיהָ עוֹד
הָאִשָּׁה הַהִיא	הָאָרֶץ הַהִיא
רֵעִים רַבִּים	רֵעִים רַבִּים
וַתָּשׁוּבִי (וְתָשׁוּבִי)	וְשׁוֹב
אֶל־שֹׁפִי	2 עַל־שְׁפָיִם
עַל־הַדְּרָכִים	עַל־דְּרָכִים
כְּעָרָב (בַּ)מדברc	כַּעֲרָבִי בַּמִּדְבָּר
וּבְרָעָתֵךְ	וּבְרָעָתֵךְ
וַיִּמָּנְעוּ רְבִבִים וּמַלְקוֹשׁ לוֹא הָיָה וימנו (ויהיו) רעים רבים למוקש לךd	3 וַיִּמָּנְעוּ רְבִבִים וּמַלְקוֹשׁ לוֹא הָיָה
פְּנֵי (מצח) אשה זונה	וּמֵצַח אִשָּׁה זוֹנָה
מֵאַיִן תִּכָּלְמִי מִפְּנֵי (בִּפְנֵי)־כֹל	מֵאַנְתְּ הִכָּלֵם
הֲלוֹא מֵעַתָּה קָרָאת לִי אָבִי וְאַלּ־י־	4 הֲלוֹא מֵעַתָּה קָרָאתְ לִי אָבִי
נְעוּרָיִךְ (נְעִירוֹתַיִךְ, נְעִירוֹתָיִךְ)	אַלּוּף נְעוּרַי אָתָּה
הָרָעוֹת הָאֵלֶּה	5 הֲרֵעֹתִי
עשתה לי	6 עשתה
יָשְׁבָהe (מוֹשָׁבָה)	מְשֻׁבָה
הָלְכוּf	הֹלְכָה הִיא

a Cf. Gen. 4:10, 11; I. Kings 2:5.   b Targ. רוּחְצָנֵיךְ.   c Cf. Ps. 102:7.
d Cf. 23:1 seq.   e Vid. vss. 8, 12.   f Targ. אָזְלִין אִנּוּן.

וַתִּזְנִינָה־שָׁם	וַתִּזְנִי־שָׁם
הַזְנוֹתָהּ	7 עָשָׂתָה
תָּשׁוּבִי (שׁוּבִי)	תָּשׁוּב
וַתֵּרֶא בְּגִדָה בְּמִדָּה יְהוּדָה	וַתֵּרֶא בָּגוֹדָה אֲחוֹתָהּ יְהוּדָה
עַל־כָּל־אֹדוֹת אֲשֶׁר־חָפְשָׂה בְּאֵר נֹאֲפָה יֹשָׁבֶת יִשְׂרָאֵל	8 עַל־כָּל־אֹדוֹת אֲשֶׁר נִאֲפָה מְשֻׁבָה יִשְׂרָאֵל
וְשִׁלַּחְתִּיהָ	שִׁלַּחְתִּיהָ
וָאֶתֵּן לָהּ סֵפֶר כְּרִיתֻת בְּיָדֶיהָ	וָאֶתֵּן אֶת־סֵפֶר כְּרִיתֻתֶיהָ אֵלֶיהָ
Deest	אֲחוֹתָהּ
וַתְּהִי מִקַּל זְנוּתָהּ	9 וְהָיָה מִקֹּל זְנוּתָהּ
וַתִּנְאַף אֶת־הָעֵץ וְאֶת־הָאֶבֶן	וַתֶּחֱנַף אֶת־הָאָרֶץ וַתִּנְאַף אֶת־הָאֶבֶן וְאֶת־הָעֵץ
וּבְכָל־זֹאת	10 וְגַם־בְּכָל־זֹאת
Desunt	אֲחוֹתָהּ
	נְאֻם־יְהוָה
צִדֵּק נַפְשׁוֹ יִשְׂרָאֵל	11 צִדְּקָה נַפְשָׁהּ מְשֻׁבָה יִשְׂרָאֵל
שׁוּבָה אֵלַי יֹשֶׁבֶת יִשְׂרָאֵל	12 שׁוּבָה מְשֻׁבָה יִשְׂרָאֵל
וְלֹא אָשׂוּם פָּנַי עֲלֵיכֶם	לוֹא־אַפִּיל פָּנַי בָּכֶם
וְלֹא אֶטּוֹר לָכֶם	לֹא אֶטּוֹר
לֹא־שְׁמַעַתְּ	13 לֹא־שְׁמַעְתֶּם
אֶל־צִיּוֹן	14 צִיּוֹן
רָעָה (רֹעִים) בְּהַשְׂכִּיל	15 דֵּעָה וְהַשְׂכִּיל
עַל־הָאָרֶץ נְאֻם־יְהוָה בַּיָּמִים הָהֵמָּה	16 בָּאָרֶץ בַּיָּמִים הָהֵמָּה נְאֻם־יְהוָה
בְּרִית קְדוֹשׁ יִשְׂרָאֵל	בְּרִית יְהוָה
וְלֹא יַעֲלֶה עַל־לֵב לֹא יַעֲלֶה עַל־לֵב לֹא יִזָּכֵר וְלֹא יִפָּקֵד	וְלֹא יַעֲלֶה עַל־לֵב וְלֹא יִזְכְּרוּ־בוֹ וְלֹא יִפְקֹדוּ
בַּיָּמִים הָהֵם וּבָעֵת הַהִיא	17 בָּעֵת הַהִיא
וְנִקְווּ כָל־הַגּוֹיִם אֵלֶיהָ	וְנִקְווּ אֵלֶיהָ כָל־הַגּוֹיִם
Deest	לְשֵׁם יְהוָה לִירוּשָׁלִָם

---

[a] Targ. וּפְלָחֵין. [b] ut Lev. 19 : 29; II. Chron. 21 : 13. [c] Vid. vss. 6, 12.
[d] Targ. אִגֶּרֶת גֵּט פִּטּוּרִין. [e] ut Deut. 24 : 1. [f] Targ. בְּדִקְנָלֵילָא. [g] Vid. vss. 6, 8. [h] ut II. Kings 8 : 11. [i] Cf. Nahum 1 : 2. [k] Targ. לְצִיּוֹן. [l] ut 33 : 15; 50 : 4, 20.

שְׁרֵרוּת	מוֹעֵצוֹת
18 מארץ צפון	מארץ צפון וּמִכֹּל הָאֲרָצוֹת[a]
אבותיכם	אבותיהם[b]
19 אֵיךְ	אָמֵן יְהוָֹה כִּי[c]
נחלת צְבִי	נחלת אֱלֹהִים[d]
אָבִי תִקְרְאוּ־לִי	אב תקראו־לי (תִקְרְאוּנִי)
תשובו	תשובו
20 אָכֵן בגדה אשה מֵרֵעָה	אַךְ כְּמוֹ בגדה אשה בְּרֵיעָהּ[e]
בִּגְדֵהֶם	בִּגְדָהּ
21 עַל־שְׁפָיִים	מָשְׁפָּם
תחנוני	וְתַחֲנוּנֵי[f]
דרכם	דרכיהם
אלהיהם	אלהי קָדְשָׁם[g]
22 ארפה מְשׁוּבֹתֵיכֶם	וְאַרְפָּה שְׁבָרֶיכֶם[h]
אָתָנוּ לָךְ	עֲבָדִים (נְתוּנִים) לָךְ[i]
23 מִגְּבָעוֹת	הַגְּבָעוֹת
הָמוֹן	וְהָמוֹן
24 אֶת־בְּנֵיהֶם	וְאֶת־בְּנֵיהֶם[k]
25 וּתְכַסֵּנוּ	נְתְכַסֵּנוּ

CAPUT IV.

1 תָּשׁוּב . . . תָּשׁוּב	יָשׁוּב . . . יָשׁוּב
וְאִם תָּסִיר שִׁקּוּצֶיךָ מִפָּנַי	וְאִם־יָסִיר שִׁקּוּצָיו מִפִּיו[l]
וְלֹא תָנוּד	וּמִפָּנַי יָגוּר
2 וְנִשְׁבַּעְתָּ	ונשבע
יִתְהַלָּלוּ	יהללו אֶת־אֱלֹהִים בִּירוּשָׁלָם
3 לְאִישׁ יהודה וְלִירוּשָׁלַם	לְאַנְשֵׁי יהודה וּלְיֹשְׁבֵי ירושלם[m]
אֶל־קֹצִים	עַל־קֹצִים

---

[a] ut 16:15; 23:8 etc. [b] Targ. אֲבָהָתְהוֹן. [c] Cf. 11:5. [d] ut II. Sam. 20:19; 21:3. [e] Targ. בְּנָא דְרַשְׁקְרָא אִתְּתָא בִּבְעֲלָהּ. [f] Targ. וּבְיאֲנָחָן. [g] Cf. Hab. 1:12. [h] ut 6:14; 8:11; Zech. 11:16; Ps. 60:4; 147:3. [i] חַכְנָא לְפוּלְחָנָךְ. [k] Targ. יָת בְּנֵיהוֹן. [l] Cf. Zech. 9:7. [m] ut 11:2, 9.—Targ. וּלְיָתְבֵי יְרוּשְׁלֵם.

4 לַיהוָֹה	לֵאלֹהֵיכֶם
עָרְלוֹת	עָרְלַת (עָרְלוּת, קָשִׁי*)
אִישׁ יְהוּדָה	אַנְשֵׁי יְהוּדָה
5 וּבִירוּשָׁלַם הַשְׁמִיעוּ	וְיִשָּׁמַע בִּירוּשָׁלָם
וְאָמְרוּ	אמרו
וְתִקְעוּ שׁוֹפָר בָּאָרֶץ	תקעו עַל־הָאָרֶץ (בָּאָרֶץ) שׁוֹפָר
מַלְאוּ	מָלֵאᵇ (מְאֹד)
וְאָמְרוּ	אמרו
6 שְׂאוּ נֵס	הִנָּשְׂאוּᶜ(?) (שְׂאוּ) וְנֵסוּ
7 נָסַע יָצָא	נסע וְיָצָא (וַיֵּצֵא)
אַרְצֵךְ	הָאָרֶץ
עָרַיִךְ	וְהֶעָרִים
מֵאֵין יוֹשֵׁב	מֵאֵין יוֹשֵׁב בָּהֵן
8 עַל־זֹאת	עַל־אֵלֶּה
סִפְדוּ	וְסִפְדוּ
חֲרוֹן	Deest
מִמֶּנּוּ	מִכֶּם
9 וְנָשַׁמּוּ הַכֹּהֲנִים	וְהַכֹּהֲנִים יִשְׁמָּרוּ
10 אֲהָהּ	אַתָּהᵈ
לָכֶם	Deest
וְנָגְעָה	וְהִגָּהᵉ נָגְעָה
עַד־הַנָּפֶשׁ	עַד־נַפְשָׁם
11 יֵאָמֵר	יֹאמְרוּ
רוּחַ צַח שְׁפָיִם	רוּחַ תּוֹעָה (סִיעָה)
לוֹא לִזְרוֹת	לוֹא לְזַכּוֹת
12 מֵאֵלֶּה	Deest
מִשְׁפָּטִים	מִשְׁפָּטַיᶠ
13 כַּעֲנָנִים	כְּעָנָןᵍ
15 מַדָּן	מִדָּן יָבוֹא
וּמַשְׁמִיעַ	וְיַשְׁמַע
מֵהַר	מְהֵרָי

ᵃ Targ. רֶשַׁע.   ᵇ ut 12:6.   ᶜ ἀναλαβόντες.   ᵈ Cf. 1:6; 14:13; 32:17.
ᵉ Targ. וּבָעֵר.   ᶠ Targ. פּוּרְקָנוּת דִּינַי.   ᵍ ut Ezek. 38:9, 16. Targ. כַּעֲנָנָא.

16 הִנֵּה	הִנֵּה בָאוּ (בָאִים)
עַל־יְרוּשָׁלִַם	בִּירוּשָׁלִַם
נֹצְרִים	צֹרְרִים (צָרִים)
מֵאֶרֶץ הַמֶּרְחָק	מֵאֶרֶץ מֶרְחָק[a]
17 מְרָתָה	מְרִיתָ[b]
18 דַּרְכֵּךְ	דְּרָכָיִךְ
19 קִירוֹת לִבִּי הוֹמֶה־לִי לִבִּי	וְקִירוֹת לִבִּי הוֹמָה נַפְשִׁי יָרְגַז (וַיִּגְעַשׁ, יִתְגָּעֵשׁ) לִבִּי
שָׁמַעְתִּי[c]	שִׁמְעָה (שָׁמַעַת)[c]
20 שֶׁבֶר עַל־שֶׁבֶר נִקְרָא	וָשֹׁד שֶׁבֶר נִקְרָא
שֻׁדְּדוּ אֹהָלַי רֶגַע יְרִיעֹתַי	שֻׁדַּד הָאֹהֶל (אָהֳלִי) רָגְעוּ (רָגְזוּ) יְרִיעֹתַי
21 אֶרְאֶה־נֵּס	אֶרְאֶה־נָס (נָסִים)
אֶשְׁמְעָה קוֹל שׁוֹפָר	שׁוֹמֵעַ קוֹל שׁוֹפָרוֹת (שׁוֹפָר)
22 כִּי אֱוִיל עַמִּי	כִּי אֱוִילֵי[d] (אוּלַי) עַמִּי
וְלֹא נְבוֹנִים הֵמָּה	וְלֹא נְבוֹנִים
23 רָאִיתִי אֶת־הָאָרֶץ וְהִנֵּה־תֹהוּ	רָאִיתִי עַל־הָאָרֶץ וְהִנֵּה אֵינֶנָּה (אַיִן)
וָבֹהוּ	
24 וְהִנֵּה רְעָשִׁים	וְהָמָה רְעָשִׁים
הִתְקַלְקָלוּ	(הִתְחַלְחָלוּ) מִתְחַלְחָלִים
25 אֵין הָאָדָם	אֵין אָדָם
26 הַמִּדְבָּר	מִדְבָּר[e]
וְכָל־עָרָיו נִתְּצוּ	וְכָל־הֶעָרִים נִצְּתוּ בָאֵשׁ[f]
מִפְּנֵי חֲרוֹן אַפּוֹ	וּמִפְּנֵי חֲרוֹן אַפּוֹ אָבְדוּ (כָּלוּ)
27 כִּי־כֹה אָמַר	כֹּה אָמַר
28 כִּי־דִבַּרְתִּי זַמֹּתִי וְלֹא נִחַמְתִּי	כִּי־דִבַּרְתִּי וְלֹא נִחַמְתִּי זַמֹּתִי וְלֹא־
וְלֹא־אָשׁוּב מִמֶּנָּה	אָשׁוּב מִמֶּנָּה
29 וְרֹמֵה קֶשֶׁת בֹּרַחַת כָּל־הָעִיר	וּקֶשֶׁת דְּרוּכָה בְּרֹחַת כָּל־הָאָרֶץ[g]
בָּאוּ בֶּעָבִים וּבַכֵּפִים	בָּאוּ בַּחֹרִים (בִּמְעָרוֹת) וּבַיְעָרִים
	(וּבֶעָבִים) נֶחְבָּאוּ[h] וְעַל־כֵּפִים
כָּל־הָעִיר עֲזוּבָה	כָּל־עִיר עֲזוּבָה

[a] ut 6:20.—Targ. בְּאַרְעָא רְחִיקָא. [b] Targ. כְּרַבְתְּ. [c] Targ. שְׁמָעַת. [d] Cf. II Kings 24:15. [e] Targ. כְּבַדְבָּרָא. [f] ut 49:2; 51:58. [g] Targ. כָּל יָתְבֵי אַרְעָא. [h] Targ. לְאִטַּמְּרָא.

אֵין־יוֹשֵׁב	וְאֵין־יוֹשֵׁב
Deest	שָׁדוּד 30
וְתַעֲדִי	כִּי־תַעֲדִי
יָפְיֵךְ	תִּתְיַפִּי
עֲגָבִיךְ[a]	עֲגָבִים
צְעָקָתֵךְ	צָרָה 31
ותפרש כפיה[b]	תפרש כפיה
לַהָרְגִים (עַל־הַהֹרְגִים)	לְהֹרְגִים

CAPUT V.

וראו	וְרֹאוּ 1
אס־תמצאו אם־איש (אֹש = אם־איש)	אם־תמצאו אִישׁ אם־איש
וּמְבַקֵּשׁ	מבקש
ואסלח להם[c] (אָמַר) נְאָם־יְהֹוָה	ואסלח לה
Deest	וְאִם 2
לֹא (לְ)שֶׁקֶר	לַשֶּׁקֶר
Deest	הֲלוֹא 3
וּמָאֲנוּ (וַיְמָאֲנוּ) (bis)	מאנו (bis)
כִּי לֹא־יָכְלוּ (נִלְאוּ, נוֹחֲלוּ)[d]	נוֹאֲלוּ 4
וּמִשְׁפַּט אֱלֹהִים[c]	משפט אלהיהם
וּמִשְׁפַּט אֱלֹהִים וְהִנֵּה	משפט אלהיהם אַךְ הֵמָּה 5
אריה מֵהַיַּעַר וּזְאֵב עַד־בַּיִת	אריה מיער זאב עֲרָבוֹת 6
וְנָמֵר שֹׁקֵד	נמר שקד
כל־היוצאים מהנה יטרפו	כל־היוצא מהנה יטרף
כי רבו[f]	כי רבו
בְּמַשְׁבּוּתֵיהֶם	משבותיהם
וָאַשְׂבִּעַ[h] אוֹתָם	ואשבע אותם 7
וּבְבָתֵּי זוֹנוֹת יתגוררו (יתלוננו)	ובית זונה יתגודדו
סוסים זונים[i] (מוזנים, מַזְנִים) היו	סוסים מְיֻזָּנִים מַשְׁכִּים הָיוּ 8

[a] Targ. רַהֲבָךְ. [b] Targ. וּפֶרֶשָׂא יְדָהָא. [c] Targ. לְהוֹן. [d] Cf. Ezek. 19:5.
[e] Targ. אוֹרְחָן דְּתַקְנָן קֳדָם יְיָ. [f] Vid. vs. 4. [g] ut Ps. 44:13. [h] Targ. שַׂבַּעֲרֵית.
[i] Targ. אִגִּירוֹסִין.

THE CONSPECTUS OF THE VARIATIONS. [5:10-22

אֶל־אִשָּׁת	עַל־אִשָּׁת[a]
10 עָלוּ בְשָׁרוֹתֶיהָ כִּי לוֹא לַיהוָה הֵמָּה	עָלוּ עַל־שָׂרוֹתֶיהָ
חָסִירוּ נְטִישׁוֹתֶיהָ	הַשְׁאִירוּ (הוֹתִירוּ) יְסֹדוֹתֶיהָ (אֲשִׁיוֹתֶיהָ)[b] כִּי לַיהוָה הֵמָּה
11 בָּגוֹד בָּגְדוּ בִּי בֵּית יִשְׂרָאֵל וּבֵית יְהוּדָה נְאֻם־יְהוָה	בָּגוֹד בִּגְדָה בִּי נְאֻם־יְהוָה בֵּית יִשְׂרָאֵל וּבֵית יְהוּדָה
12 כִּחֲשׁוּ בַּיהוָֹה	כִּחֵשׁ בַּאדֹנָיו
13 וְהַנְּבִיאִים יִהְיוּ לְרוּחַ וְהַדִּבֵּר	נְבִיאֵינוּ הָיוּ לְרוּחַ וּדְבַר יְהוָֹה
כֹּה יֵעָשֶׂה לָהֶם	Desunt
14 אֱלֹהֵי	
דַּבֶּרְכֶם	דְּבֶּרְתָּם
הִנְנִי נֹתֵן	הִנֵּה נָתַתִּי
לְאֵשׁ	אֵשׁ
15 גּוֹי אֵיתָן הוּא גּוֹי מֵעוֹלָם הוּא	Deest
גּוֹי לֹא תֵדַע לְשֹׁנוֹ וְלֹא תִשְׁמַע מַה־יְדַבֵּר	גּוֹי אֲשֶׁר לֹא תִשְׁמַע קוֹל לְשׁוֹנוֹ[c] (שְׂפָתוֹ)
16 אַשְׁפָּתוֹ כְּקֶבֶר פָּתוּחַ	Deest
17 וְאָכַל קְצִירְךָ וְלַחְמֶךָ יֹאכְלוּ בָּנֶיךָ וּבְנוֹתֶיךָ יֹאכַל צֹאנְךָ וּבְקָרֶךָ יֹאכַל גַּפְנְךָ וּתְאֵנָתֶךָ יְרֹשֵׁשׁ עָרֵי מִבְצָרֶיךָ אֲשֶׁר אַתָּה בֹּטֵחַ בָּהֵנָּה בֶּחָרֶב	וְאָכְלוּ קְצִירְכֶם וְלַחְמֵיכֶם וְאָכְלוּ בְּנֵיכֶם וּבְנוֹתֵיכֶם וְאָכְלוּ צֹאנְאֲכֶם וּבְקָרֵיכֶם וְאָכְלוּ (גַּפְנֵיכֶם) כַּרְמֵיכֶם וּתְאֵנֵיכֶם וְזֵיתֵיכֶם וְרִשְּׁשׁוּ (וְיָרְשׁוּ) עָרֵי מִבְצָרֵיכֶם אֲשֶׁר אַתֶּם בֹּטְחִים (בְּטַחְתֶּם) בָּהֵנָּה בֶּחָרֶב
18 וְגַם בַּיָּמִים הָהֵמָּה נְאֻם־יְהוָה לֹא־אֶעֱשֶׂה אִתְּכֶם כָּלָה	וְהָיָה בַּיָּמִים הָהֵמָּה נְאֻם־יְהוָה אֱלֹהֶיךָ לֹא־אֶעֱשֶׂה אֶתְכֶם לְכָלָה[d]
19 כַּאֲשֶׁר עֲזַבְתֶּם אוֹתִי וַתַּעַבְדוּ בְּאֶרֶץ	בַּאֲשֶׁר עֲבַדְתָּם בָּאָרֶץ
20 בְּבֵית יַעֲקֹב	אֶל־בֵּית יַעֲקֹב
וְהַשְׁמִיעוּהָ בִיהוּדָה לֵאמֹר	וְיִשָּׁמַע בְּבֵית־יְהוּדָה[e]
22 אֲשֶׁר־שַׂמְתִּי	אֲשֶׁר שָׂם (הֲשָׁם)

[a] Targ. כַּל אִתַּת. [b] ut 50:15. [c] Cf. Deut. 28:49. [d] ut Ezek. 13:13; II. Chron. 12:12. [e] Targ. בְּדְבֵית יְהוּדָה.

וַיִּתְגָּעֲשׁוּ וְלֹא יוּכָלוּ	וַיִּתְגָּעֲשׁוּ וְלֹא יוּכָלוּ
וַיָּסֻרוּ	23 סָרוּ
הֲנֵתַן לָנוּ	24 הַנֹּתֵן
יוֹרֶה	וְיוֹרֶה
בְּעִתּוֹ שְׁבֻעֹת חֻקּוֹת קְצִיר יִשְׁמָר־לָנוּ	בְּעֵת שְׁבֻעַת[a] חֻקַּת קָצִיר וְיִשְׁמָר־לָנוּ
כְּשַׁךְּ יְקוֹשִׁים הֵצִיבוּ (וּמוֹקְשִׁים יַצִּיבוּ) לְהַשְׁחִית[b] אֲנָשִׁים וַיִּלְכְּדוּ	26 יָשׁוּר יְקוֹשִׁים הֵצִיבוּ מַשְׁחִית אֲנָשִׁים יִלְכֹּדוּ
כְּפַח נִצָּב (בְּרֶשֶׁת פְּרוּשָׂה)	27 כִּכְלוּב
שָׁמְנוּ עָשְׁתוּ גַּם עָבְרוּ דִבְרֵי־רָע וַיַּעֲבְרוּ דִין[c]	28 שָׁמְנוּ עָשְׁתוּ גַּם עָבְרוּ דִבְרֵי־רָע דִּין
Deest	וְיַצְלִיחוּ
אַלְמָנָה	אֲבִיוֹנִים
עַל־הָאָרֶץ	30 בָּאָרֶץ
נְבוּאוּ שֶׁקֶר[d]	31 נִבְּאוּ בַשֶּׁקֶר
יְמַחֲאוּ יְדֵיהֶם (יָרְדוּ בִּידֵיהֶם)	יִרְדּוּ עַל־יְדֵיהֶם
אָהֵב	אָהֲבוּ
לְאַחֲרִית[e]	לְאַחֲרִיתָהּ

CAPUT VI.

הָעֹזּוּ	1 הָעִזוּ
הַנָּוָה וְהַמְעֻנָּגָה דָּמִיתִי בַּת־נְוָה הָרָמָה (רָמָתִי) בְּתַדִּצִיּוֹן (וְעָבְרָה רָמָתֵךְ)	2 בַּת־צִיּוֹן
וְתִקְעוּ	3 תִּקְעוּ
וְרֵעוּ[g] (וְיִרְעוּ) אִישׁ בְּיָדוֹ	רָעוּ אִישׁ אֶת־יָדוֹ
הִתְקַדְּשׁוּ עָלֶיהָ לְמִלְחָמָה	4 קַדְּשׁוּ עָלֶיהָ מִלְחָמָה
וְנַעֲלֶה עָלֶיהָ[h]	וְנַעֲלֶה
כִּי־יִנָּטוּ צִלְלֵי־יוֹם	כִּי־יִנָּטוּ צִלְלֵי־עָרֶב
וְנַעֲלֶה עָלֶיהָ[i]	5 וְנַעֲלֶה

[a] Cf. Ezek. 16:49. [b] Targ. לְחַבָּלָא. [c] Targ. אוֹרָיְתָא עָבְרוּ עַל־סָהֲדֵי. [d] Targ. כִּתְבַהּוֹן שְׁקַר. [e] Targ. לְסוֹפָא. [f] τὸ ὕψος. [g] Targ. וְיִסְדְּרוּן. [h] Vid. vs. 5. [i] Vid. vs. 4.

THE CONSPECTUS OF THE VARIATIONS.   [6:6-16

אַרְמְנוֹתֶיהָ	יְסוֹדוֹתֶיהָ (מוֹסְדוֹתֶיהָ)
6 צְבָאוֹת	Deest
כִּרְתוּ עֵצָה וְשִׁפְכוּ עַל־יְרוּשָׁלַ͏ִם	כָּרַת עֵצָה שָׁפַךְ עַל־יְרוּשָׁלַ͏ִם הַיִל
סֹלְלָה הִיא הָעִיר הָפְקָד	(הַיִל) הוֹי עִיר הַשֶּׁקֶר כָּל־עשֶׁק
כֻּלָּהּ עשֶׁק בְּקִרְבָּהּ	בְּקִרְבָּהּ
7 כְּהָקִיר בּוֹר מֵימֶיהָ	כְּהָקִיר בּוֹר מַיִם
עַל־פָּנַי	עַל־פָּנֶיהָ
חֳלִי וּמַכָּה	בָּחֳלִי וּבְמַכָּה
8 הִוָּסְרִי יְרוּשָׁלָ͏ִם	תּוּסַר יְרוּשָׁלָ͏ִם
9 כֹּה־אָמַר יְהוָה צְבָאוֹת	כִּי כֹה־אָמַר יְהוָה
עוֹלֵל יְעוֹלְלוּ	עוֹלְלוּ עוֹלְלוּ
הָשֵׁב יָדְךָ	הָשִׁיבוּ
עַל־סַלְסִלּוֹת	עַל־סַלְסִלּוּ (= סַלּוּ)
10 עַל־מִי אֲדַבְּרָה	אֶל־מִי אֲדַבְּרָה
וְיִשְׁמָעוּ	וְיִשְׁמַע
11 חֲמַת יְהוָה מָלֵאתִי נִלְאֵיתִי הָכִיל	חֲמָתִי מִלֵּאתִי וְאֶחְאַפֵּק וְכִלִּיתִים
שְׁפֹךְ עַל־עוֹלָל	אֶשְׁפֹּךְ עַל־עוֹלָל
כִּי־גַם־אִישׁ עִם־אִשָּׁה	כִּי־אִישׁ וְאִשָּׁה
מְלֵא יָמִים	מְלֵאֵי יָמִים
12 שָׂדוֹת וְנָשִׁים יַחְדָּו	שְׂדוֹתֵיהֶם וּנְשׁוֹתֵיהֶם יַחַד
עַל־ישְׁבֵי הָאָרֶץ	עַל־ישְׁבֵי הָאָרֶץ הַזֹּאת
13 כִּי מִקְּטַנָּם וְעַד־גְּדוֹלָם כֻּלּוֹ	כִּי מִקְּטַנָּם וְעַד־גָּדוֹל[b] כָּל־צְבִי
בּוֹצֵעַ בָּצַע וּמִנָּבִיא וְעַד־כֹּהֵן	בֶּצַע מִכֹּהֵן וְעַד־נָבִיא (נָבִיא
כֻּלּוֹ עֹשֶׂה שָּׁקֶר	הַשֶּׁקֶר)[c] כֻּלָּם עֹשִׂים שֶׁקֶר
14 בַּת־עַמִּי עַל־נְקַלָּה לֵאמֹר	עַמִּי מַקְלִים וְאֹטְרִים[d]
שָׁלוֹם וְאֵין שָׁלוֹם	וְאַיֵּה (וְאָן) שָׁלוֹם
15 תּוֹעֵבָה עָשׂוּ	כָּלוּ (אָבְדוּ)
גַּם־בּוֹשׁ לֹא־יֵבוֹשׁוּ גַּם־הַכְלֵים	וְלֹא כְבוּשִׁים יֵבֹשׁוּ גַּם־כְּלִמָּתָם
לֹא יָדְעוּ לָכֵן יִפְּלוּ בַּנֹּפְלִים	(הַכְּלִמָּה) לֹא יָדְעוּ לָכֵן יִפֹּל:
בְּעֵת־פְּקַדְתִּים יִכָּשְׁלוּ	בְּנָפְלָם וּבְעֵת־סְקִדָה[e] יֹאבֵדוּ
16 לִנְתִיבוֹת עוֹלָם	לִנְתִבוֹת יְהוָה עוֹלָם[f] וּרְאוּ
דֶּרֶךְ הַטּוֹב	הַדֶּרֶךְ הַטּוֹב

---

[a] ut 8:10. [b] Targ. בְּגוּלְהוֹן. [c] Targ. בְּגוּלְהוֹן עָבְדֵי שְׁקַר. [d] Vid. 7:4.
[e] Alex. בֵּית־סְקֻדְתָם. [f] Cf. Gen. 21:33.

כֹּפֶרa לְנַפְשׁוֹתֵיכֶם	מַרְגּוֹעַ לְנַפְשְׁכֶם
הִקְשִׁיבוּ לְקוֹל הַשּׁוֹפָר	17 הַקְשִׁיבוּ לְקוֹל שׁוֹפָר
שִׁמְעוּ הַגּוֹיִם וְרֹעֵי עֶדְרָם	18 שִׁמְעוּ הַגּוֹיִם וּדְעִי עֵדָה אֶת־אֲשֶׁר־בָּם
שִׁמְעִי אָרֶץb	19 שִׁמְעִי הָאָרֶץ
פְּרִי מְשׁוּבָתָםd	אָנֹכִי מֵבִיא רָעָה אֶל־הָעָם הַזֶּה אָנֹכִי מֵבִיא עַל־הָעָם הַזֶּה רָעָה פְּרִי מַחְשְׁבֹתָם
מָאָס	וַיִּמְאָסוּ־בָהּ
20 לְבוֹנָה מִשְּׁבָא תָבוֹא וְקָנֶה הַטּוֹב לִבוֹנָה מִשְּׁבָא תָּבִיאִי וְקִנְּמוֹן
הִנְנִי נֹתֵן אֶל־הָעָם הַזֶּה מִכְשֹׁלִים וְכָשְׁלוּ בָם	21 הִנְנִי נָתַן עַל־הָעָם הַזֶּה מִכְשֹׁל וְכָשְׁלוּ
יֹאבֵדוּ	וְאָבָדוּ
מִצָּפוֹןc	22 מֵאֶרֶץ צָפוֹן
וְגוֹיִםf יֵעוֹרוּf מִקְצֵה אָרֶץ	וְגוֹי גָּדוֹל יֵעוֹר מִיַּרְכְּתֵי־אָרֶץ
וְלֹא יְרַחֵמוּ קוֹלוֹ כַיָּם יֶהֱמֶה עַל־סוּסִים וְרָכַב יַעֲרֹךְ כְּאֵשׁ לַמִּלְחָמָה עָלַיִךְ	23 קוֹלָם כַּיָּם יֶהֱמֶה וְעַל־סוּסִים יִרְכָּבוּ עָרוּךְ כְּאִישׁ לַמִּלְחָמָה עָלַיִךְ
אֶת־שָׁמְעָםg חֲבָלִיםi	24 אֶת־שָׁמְעוֹ חִיל
אַל־תֵּצְאוּ בַשָּׂדֶה (אֶל־הַשָּׂדֶה) וּבִדְרָכִים אַל־תֵּלְכוּ כִּי חֶרֶב לְאֹיְבִים תָּגוּר מִסָּבִיב	25 אַל־תֵּצְאִיh הַשָּׂדֶה וּבַדֶּרֶךְ אַל־תֵּלֵכִי כִּי חֶרֶב לָאֹיֵב מָגוֹר מִסָּבִיב
אֵבֶל יָחִיד יָבֹא שֹׁד עֲלֵיכֶם	26 אֵבֶל יָחִיד יָבֹא הַשֹּׁדֵד עָלֵינוּ
וְתֵדַע נְתַתִּיךָ בְּעַמַּי מִבְחָן (מִבְצָר) וְתֵדַע אֲנִי בְּבָחֳנִי	27 נְתַתִּיךָ בְעַמִּי מִבְצָר וְתֵדַע וּבָחַנְתָּ
Deest	28 סָרֵי
תֵּלְכֵי מַעֲקַשִּׁים כֻּלָּם מָשְׁחָתִים	הֹלְכֵי רָכִיל כֻּלָּם מַשְׁחִיתִם
נָהָר מֻפַּח מֵאִשָּׁם עֹפֶרֶת כָּהָד (נָכֹחַ)	29 נָחַר מַפֻּחַ מֵאֵשׁ תַּם עֹפֶרֶת

---

a Cf. Job 33:24. b ut Isa. 1:2. c Targ. כָּל. d Targ. בּוֹעֲרֵיהוֹן. e ut 4:6; 6:1; 46:20; 50:3, 41.—Targ. בְּצַמָּנָא. f Targ. וְעַבְדִין. g Targ. יִרְהֲגוּן. h Targ. שַׁעְבְּדוּן. i Targ. חֶבְלִין.

לשוא צרף צרוף ורעים לא נתקו לשוא צרף צוֹרֵף וּרֵעָתָם[a] לֹא נִתָּקוּ
30 כסף נמאס קראו להם כי מאס כסף נמאס קראו להם כי מאס
יהוה בהם   בהם יהוה

CAPUT VII.

1 הַדָּבָר אֲשֶׁר־הָיָה אֶל־יִרְמְיָהוּ
   מֵאֵת יְהוָֹה לֵאמֹר

2 עֲמֹד בְּשַׁעַר בֵּית יְהוָֹה וְקָרָאתָ
Desunt { שָׁם אֶת־הַדָּבָר הַזֶּה וְאָמַרְתָּ
   הַבָּאִים בַּשְּׁעָרִים הָאֵלֶּה
   לְהִשְׁתַּחֲוֹת לַיהוָֹה

3 צְבָאוֹת

4 אַל־תבטחו לכם אֶל־דברי אל־תבטחו לכם על[b]־דברי השקר
   השקר   כִּי מְאוּמָה לֹא יוֹעִילוּ לָכֶם
   לאמר   אֹמְרִים[c]
   היכל יהוה היכל יהוה היכל הֵיכַל יהוה הֵיכַל יהוה

5 אם־עשׂר תעשׂו   וְעָשׂוֹר תַּעֲשׂוּ

6 גר־יתום   וְגֵר וְיָתוֹם

7 בָּאָרֶץ   בְּאֶרֶץ

8 הִנֵּה   כִּרְאֹם

   לבלתי הועיל   אֲשֶׁר לֹא יוֹעִילוּ

9 הֲגָנֹב רָצֹחַ וְנָאֹף וְהִשָּׁבֵעַ לשקר   וַתִּרְצָחוּ וַתִּנְאֲפוּ וַתִּגְנְבוּ וַתִּשָּׁבְעוּ
   וקטר לבעל והלך   לשקר וַתְּקַטְּרוּ לבעל וַתֵּלְכוּ[d]
   לא־ידעתם   לא־ידעתם: לְרַע[e] לָכֶם

10 הַזֶּה   Deest
   נצלנו למען עשׂות   נִצַּלְנוּ לְבִלְתִּי עֲשׂוֹת

11 הָיָה הַבַּיִת הַזֶּה אֲשֶׁר נִקְרָא   בֵּיתִי אֲשֶׁר נִקְרָא שְׁמִי שָׁם לִפְנֵיכֶם
   שְׁמִי־עָלָיו בְּעֵינֵיכֶם גַּם אָנֹכִי   וְהִנֵּה אָנֹכִי רָאִיתִי
   הִנֵּה רָאִיתִי

---

[a] Targ. וְעוֹבָדֵיהוֹן בִּישַׁיָּא. [b] Targ. כָּל. [c] Vid. 6:14.—Targ. דְּאָמְרִין.
[d] Cf. Exod. 20:13, 14, 15; Deut. 5:17, 18, 19. [e] Inc. vs. 10. [f] ut 7:6;
25:7.

[7:12-27

12 כִּי לְכוּ־נָא	כִּי לְכוּ
13 נְאֻם־יְהוָה	Deest
הַשְׁכֵּם וְדַבֵּר וְלֹא שמעתם	וְלֹא שְׁמַעְתֶּם אֵלָי
14 וְעָשִׂיתִי	לָכֵן גַּם־אֲנִי אֶעֱשֶׂה
16 וְאַל־תִּשָּׂא בַעֲדָם רִנָּה וּתְפִלָּה וְאַל־תִּפְגַּע־בִּי כִּי אֵינֶנִּי שֹׁמֵעַ אֹתָךְ	וְאַל תְּחַשְּׁבָם לָהֶן אֹתָםᵃ(?) וְאַל־תִּתְפַּלֵּל וְאַל־תִּתְפַּגַּע־בִּי בַעֲדָם כִּי לֹא אֶשְׁמָע
18 הַבָּנִים... וְהָאָבוֹת... וְהַנָּשִׁים לְמְלֶכֶת הַשָּׁמַיִם וְהַסֵּךְ נְסָכִים	בְּנֵיהֶם... וַאֲבוֹתֵיהֶם... וּנְשֵׁיהֶם לִצְבָא הַשָּׁמַיִם וַיַּסְכוּ נְסָכִים
19 בֹּשֶׁת פְּנֵיהֶם	יֵבוֹשׁוּᵇ פְּנֵיהֶם
20 אֲדֹנָי יְהֹוִה	יְהוָה
וַחֲמָתִי נִתֶּכֶת אֶל־הַמָּקוֹם הַזֶּה עַל־הָאָדָם	וַחֲמָתִי נִתֶּכֶת עַל־הַמָּקוֹם הַזֶּה וְעַל־הָאָדָם
וְעַל עֵץ הַשָּׂדֶה	וְעַל־כָּל־עֵץ שְׂדֵיהֶם
21 צְבָאוֹת אֱלֹהֵי יִשְׂרָאֵל	Deest
סְפוּ עַל־זִבְחֵיכֶם	אִסְפוּ עִם־זִבְחֵיכֶם
22 אֶת־אֲבוֹתֵיכֶם	אֶל־אֲבוֹתֵיכֶם
בְּיוֹם הוֹצִיאִᵃ	בְּיוֹם הַעֲלוֹתִי
עַל־דִּבְרֵי עוֹלָה	עַל־דִּבְרֵי עוֹלוֹתᶜ
23 בְּכָל־הַדֶּרֶךְ	בְּכָל־דְּרָכֶי
24 וְלֹא שָׁמְעוּ וְלֹא־הִטּוּ אֶת־אָזְנָם בִּשְׁרִרוּת	וְלֹא שָׁמְעוּ אֵלַי וְלֹא הִקְשִׁיבָה אָזְנָםᵈ
25 אֲבוֹתֵיכֶם	Deest
עַד הַיּוֹם הַזֶּה	אֲבוֹתֵיהֶם
הַשְׁכֵּם וְשָׁלֹחַ	וְעַד הַיּוֹם הַזֶּה
	וְהַשְׁכֵּם וָאֶשְׁלַח
26 וְלֹא הִטּוּ אֶת־אָזְנָם וַיַּקְשׁוּ אֶת־עָרְפָּם	לֹא הִקְשִׁיבָה אָזְנָםᵉ וַיַּקְשׁוּ אֶת־צַוָּארָם
הֵרֵעוּ	
27 וְדִבַּרְתָּ אֲלֵיהֶם אֶת־כָּל־הַדְּבָרִים הָאֵלֶּה וְלֹא יִשְׁמְעוּ אֵלֶיךָ וְקָרָאתָ אֲלֵיהֶם וְלֹא יַעֲנוּכָה	Desunt

---

ᵃ Vid. 11:14. ᵇ Targ. הִרְבְּהָתוּן. ᶜ Targ. עֲלָוָן. ᵈ ut Ps. 10:17.
ᵉ ut Ps. 10:17.

7:28-8:4] THE CONSPECTUS OF THE VARIATIONS. 299

ואמרת אליהם את־הדָּבָר הַזֶּה	28 ואמרת אליהם
אשר לוא־שמע	אשר לוא־שָׁמְשׁוּ
Deest	אֱלֹהָיו
ולא לקח	ולא לקחוּ
Deest	וְנִכְרְתָה
ושאי על־שָׂפָם	29 ושאי על־שְׂפָתִים
את־הדור אֲשֶׁר עָשָׂה אֵלֶּה[c]	את־הדור עֶבְרָתוֹ
ובנו במת[d] התפת	31 ובנו במות החפת
אשר לא צויתי אתם (צויתים)	אשר לא צויתי
ולא־יאמרו עוד בָּמַת[d] התפת	32 ולא־יָאָמֶר עוד החפת
גיא ההרְגִים[e]	גיא ההרֵנָה
קול ששׂים וקול שְׂמֵחִים	34 קול ששון וקול שָׂמְחָה
לחרבה תהיה כָּל־הארץ	לחרבה תהיה הארץ

CAPUT VIII.

ויציאו	1 ויוציאוּ
נביאים	הַנְּבִיאִים
היושבים בירושלם	יושבי־יְרוּשָׁלָם
ולירח ולכל־הכוכבים	2 ולירח
ואשר דָּבְקוּ בָם[f]	ואשר דְּרָשׁוּב
לא יֵסָפְדוּ[a]	לא יֵאָסֵפוּ
והיו לדמיון[h] על־פני האדמה	לדמן על־פני האדמה יהיו
כי בחרו במות[i] מחיים[g] ולכל השארית	3 וְנִבְחַר מות מחיים לכל השארית
Deest	הרעה
בכל־המקום	בכל־המקומות הנשארים
Deest	נאם יהוה צבאות
ואמרת אליהם כי כה אמר יהוה	4 ואמרת אֲלֵיהֶם כה אמר יהוה
היפלו ולא יקומו אם־ישָׁוּב ולא חזאיפל לא יקום חַשּׁוֹבַב לא ישוב	

---

[a] Aram.=עֲבַדְתֻהוּ=לְבָדְהוּ. [b] Targ. בְּבַת. [c] Vid. vs. 32. [d] Vid. vs. 31.
[e] Targ. קְטִילַיָּא. [f] Cf. Deut. 10:20; 30:20. [g] ut 16:4. [h] Vid. 9:21;
16:4. [i] Targ. וְיִתְרְצוּן בְּמוֹתָא. [k] Cf. Deut. 30:19.

5 הָעָם הַזֶּה יְרוּשָׁלִַם	עַמִּי הַזֶּה (זה)
הֶחֱזִיקוּ בַּתַּרְמִית מֵאֲנוּ	וְהֶחֱזִיקוּ בְּתַרְמִיתָם וּמֵאֲנוּ
לָשׁוּב	(וַיְמָאֲנוּ) לָשׁוּב
6 הִקְשַׁבְתִּי וָאֶשְׁמָע	הַקְשִׁיבוּ־נָא וּשְׁמָעוּ
כֻּלֹּה שָׁב בִּמְרֻצוֹתָם	כֻּלֹּה גָּס (שָׁט^a) מִמְּרוּצָתוֹ
בַּמִּלְחָמָה	בִּמְצֻהֲלָתוֹ (בִּמְצַהֲלָה)
7 גַּם חֲסִידָה בַשָּׁמַיִם יָדְעָה מוֹעֲדֶיהָ	גַּם־הַחֲסִידָה בַשָּׁמַיִם יָדְעָה מוֹעֲדָהּ
וְתוֹר וְסוּס וְעָגוּר שָׁמְרוּ אֶת־	תוֹר וְסוּס שָׂדַי^b עָגוּר שָׁמְרוּ
עֵת בֹּאָנָה וְעַמִּי לֹא יָדְעוּ אֵת	אֶת־עִתּוֹתָם בָּאָן וְעַמִּי הַזֶּה (זה)
מִשְׁפַּט יְהוָה	לֹא יָדְעוּ אֵת מִשְׁפְּטֵי יְהוָה
8 חֲכָמִים אֲנַחְנוּ	כִּי חֲכָמִים אֲנַחְנוּ
אָכֵן הִנֵּה	Deest
לַשֶּׁקֶר עָשָׂה עֵט שֶׁקֶר סֹפְרִים	לַשֶּׁקֶר הָיָה עֵט שֶׁקֶר לַסֹּפְרִים
9 חָתוּ וַיִּלָּכְדוּ הִנֵּה בִדְבַר־יְהוָה	חָתוּ וַיִּלָּכְדוּ כִּי תוֹרַת יְהוָה מָאָסוּ^{c}
מָאָסוּ וְחָכְמַת־מֶה לָהֶם	וְחָכְמַת־מָה בָּהֶם^d
10 שְׂדוֹתֵיהֶם	וּשְׂדוֹתֵיהֶם
כִּי מִקָּטֹן וְעַד־גָּדוֹל כֻּלֹּה בֹּצֵעַ בָּצַע מִנָּבִיא וְעַד־כֹּהֵן כֻּלֹּה	
11 עֹשֶׂה שָּׁקֶר׃ וַיְרַפּוּ אֶת־שֶׁבֶר בַּת־עַמִּי עַל־נְקַלָּה לֵאמֹר שָׁלוֹם	
12 שָׁלוֹם וְאֵין שָׁלוֹם׃ הֹבִישׁוּ כִּי תוֹעֵבָה עָשׂוּ גַּם־בּוֹשׁ לֹא־	Desunt
יֵבוֹשׁוּ וְהִכָּלֵם לֹא יָדָעוּ לָכֵן יִפְּלוּ בַנֹּפְלִים בְּעֵת פְּקֻדָּתָם	
יִכָּשְׁלוּ אָמַר יְהוָה׃	
13 אָסֹף אֲסִיפֵם	וְאָסְפוּ אֲסִיפָם
אֵין עֲנָבִים בַּגֶּפֶן וְאֵין תְּאֵנִים	אֵין עֵנָב בַּכְּרָמִים וְאֵין תְּאֵנִים
בַּתְּאֵנָה וְהֶעָלֶה נָבֵל	בַּתְּאֵנִים וְהֶעָלִים נוֹבְלִים (נָבְלוּ)
וָאֶתֵּן לָהֶם יַעַבְרוּם	Deest
14 עַל־מָה אֲנַחְנוּ יֹשְׁבִים הֵאָסְפוּ וְנָבוֹא אֶל־עָרֵי הַמִּבְצָר וְנִדְּמָה־שָּׁם כִּי יְהוָה אֱלֹהֵינוּ הֲדִמָּנוּ	וְנָדַמָּה־שָּׁם כִּי הָאֱלֹהִים הִשְׁלִיכָנוּ (הִרְמָנוּ)
כִּי חָטָאנוּ לַיהוָה	כִּי חָטָאנוּ לוֹ

---

^{a} Aram. שָׁט. ^{b} Cf. Ps. 50:11. ^{c} ut Amos 2:4. ^{d} Cf. I. Kings 3:28.

8:15-9:4]   THE CONSPECTUS OF THE VARIATIONS.   301

קַוִּינוּ[a] לְשָׁלוֹם וְהִנֵּה בֶהָלָה[b]	15 קַוֵּה לְשָׁלוֹם וְהִנֵּה בְעָתָה
קוֹל דַּהֲרַת (נַהֲרַת?) סוּסָיו מִקּוֹל מִצְהֲלַת רֶכֶב סוּסָיו (אַבִּירָיו)	16 נַחֲרַת סוּסָיו מִקּוֹל מִצְהֲלוֹת אַבִּירָיו
וְיָבוֹא וְיֹאכֵל	וַיָּבוֹאוּ וַיֹּאכֵלוּ
נְחָשִׁים מְמִיתִים Deest	17 נְחָשִׁים צִפְעֹנִים נְאֻם־יְהוָֹה
18 מִבְּלִיגִית (מִבְּלִי־נָהָה?) עֲלֵי יָגוֹן לִבְּכֶם דָּוִי	18 מַבְלִיגִיתִי עֲלֵי יָגוֹן עָלַי לִבִּי דַוָּי
מֵאֶרֶץ מֶרְחָק[c] אִם־מַלְכָּהּ[d] אֵין שָׁם כִּי הִכְעִסוּנִי וּבְהַבְלֵי נֵכָר	19 מֵאֶרֶץ מַרְחַקִּים אִם־מַלְכָּהּ אֵין בָּהּ מַדּוּעַ הִכְעִסוּנִי בְהַבְלֵי נֵכָר
עָבַר קַיִץ כָּלָה קָצִיר Deest	20 עָבַר קָצִיר כָּלָה קָיִץ 21 הָשְׁבַּרְתִּי
בְּשָׁמָּה הֶחֱזִקַתְנִי צִירִים (חֲבָלִים) כַּיּוֹלֵדָה[e]	שָׁמָּה הֶחֱזִקָתְנִי
וְהַצֳּרִי אֵין בַּגִּלְעָד מַדּוּעַ	22 הֲצֳרִי אֵין בַּגִּלְעָד כִּי מַדּוּעַ
23 מֵרֵיתָן רָאשֵׁי[f] לְרָאשִׁי מַיִם וּלְעֵינַי[g] מְקוֹר דְּמָעוֹת וְאֶבְכֶּה אֶת־עַמִּי הַזֶּה[h]	23 מִי־יִתֵּן רֹאשִׁי מַיִם וְעֵינִי מְקוֹר דִּמְעָה וְאֶבְכֶּה

CAPUT IX.

מְלוֹן אַחֲרוֹן (רָחוֹק)	1 מְלוֹן אֹרְחִים
וַיִּדְרְכוּ אֶת־לְשׁוֹנָם כְּקֶשֶׁת[i] שֶׁקֶר וְלֹא אֱמוּנָה גְבָרָה (גָבַר) עַל־הָאָרֶץ אָמַר יהוה	2 וַיִּדְרְכוּ אֶת־לְשׁוֹנָם קַשְׁתָּם שֶׁקֶר וְלֹא לֶאֱמוּנָה גָּבְרוּ בָאָרֶץ נְאֻם־יְהוָֹה
וְעַל־אֲחֵיהֶם	3 וְעַל־כָּל־אָח
יָהֵתֵלּוּ וֶאֱמֶת לֹא יְדַבֵּרוּ לָמְדָה לְשׁוֹנָם	4 יְהָתֵלּוּ וֶאֱמֶת לֹא יְדַבֵּרוּ לִמְּדוּ לְשׁוֹנָם

---

[a] Vid. 14:19.—Targ. כְּבַרְנָא. [b] Cf. 15:8. [c] Targ. רְחִיקָא. [d] Targ.
בַּלָּא. [e] Cf. 49:24. [f] Inc.cap.IX. [g] Targ. וְעֵינַי. [h] Cf. II. Chron. 1:10.
[i] Targ. כְּנִשְׁתָּא.

הֶחֱוּוּ* וְלֹא נלאו שָׁב (שׁוּב):		הָחֲוָה נלאו:
תֹּךְ בתוך מרמה במרמה	5	שִׁבְתְּךָ בתוך מרמה במרמה
אָמַר יהוה		נְאֻם־יהוה
Deest	6	צְבָאוֹת
כי אעשה מפני רָעַת* בת־עמי		כי־אֵיךְ אעשה מפני בת־עמי
חֵץ שׁוֹחֵט* לשונם מרמוֹת* דִּבְרֵי	7	חץ שָׁוחֻט לשונם מרמה דבר
פִּיהֶם* את־רעהו ידבר שלום		בפיו שלום את־רעהו ידבר
ובקרבו יסים הָאיבָה (רַב אֵיבָתוֹ)		ובקרבו ישים ארבו
לֹא־אֶפְקֹד*	8	לא־אפקד־בָּם
שָׂאוּ נהי	9	אֶשָּׂא בכי וָנֶהִי
כי נִתְּצוּ (כָּלוּ) מבלי־איש לא		כי נצתו מבלי־איש עובר ולא
שמעו		שמעו
לְגַלִּים (לִגְלוֹת) ולמעון תנים	10	לגלים מעון תנים
מי־האיש הַנָבוֹן	11	מי־האיש החכם
דְּבַר פִּי־יהוה אליו יֻגַּד לָהֶם (וַיֻגְּדֵם)		דבר פי־יהוה אליו וְיַגִּדָהּ
מבלי עבר בָּהּ		מבלי עבר
ויאמר יהוה אֵלַי	12	ויאמר יהוה
Deest		ולֹא־הָלְכוּ בָהּ
תַּאֲוַת לבם חָיָל*	13	שְׁרִרוּת לבם
Deest	14	צְבָאוֹת
מאכילם עֳנִי (עָקָה)		מאכילם את־העם הזה לַעֲנָה
ושלחתי אַחֲרֵיהֶם עליהם את־החרב עד	15	ושלחתי אחריהם את־החרב עד
כְּלוֹתָם בָּהּ		עד כלותי אותם
כה אמר יהוה כה אמר יהוה קראו	16	כה אמר יהוה צבאות התבוננוּ
		וקראו
ותבֹּאנָה		ותבואנה
וּתְמַהֵרְנָה ותשׂאנה (וְתָבֹאֶינָה)	17	ותשאנה עלינו נֶהִי ותרדנה
ותרדנה עיניני דִמְעָה		עינינו דמעה
ועפעפיכם דְּמָעוֹת' ועפעפיכם יזלו־		ועפעפינו יזלו־מים
מים		
נשמע בציון	18	נשמע מציון

---

a Targ. אִיעָשֶׂה. b Cf. Ps. 55:12.—Inc. vs. 5. c Targ. . . . בִּדְקֳדָם חוֹבֵי
—Cf. Hos. 10:15. d Targ. בְּנִירֵי דִי בְחָרֵב. e Targ. נְבִלִין. f Targ. בִּצְבְחוֹן.
g ut 5:9, 29. h ut 7:24. i Vid. 23:15.—Targ. עָקָא. k ut Ps. 119:171.
l Targ. דְּבִדֵן.

9:19-10:4] THE CONSPECTUS OF THE VARIATIONS. 303

כִּי־עֲזָבְנוּ אֶרֶץ כִּי הִשְׁלִיכוּ מִשְׁכְּנוֹתֵינוּ	כִּי־עֲזָבְנוּ הָאָרֶץ וְהִשְׁלַכְנוּ מִשְׁכְּנוֹתֵינוּ	19 כִּי־שְׁמַעְנָה נָשִׁים דְּבַר־יהוה וְתִקַּח אָזְנְכֶם דְּבַר־פִּיו	שְׁמַעְנָה נָשִׁים דְּבַר־יְהוָה וְתִקַּח אָזְנֵיכֶם[a] דִּבְרֵי־פִּיו
20 כִּי־עָלָה מָוֶת בְּחַלּוֹנֵינוּ בָּא בְּאַרְמְנוֹתֵינוּ לְהַכְרִית עוֹלָל מִחוּץ בַּחוּרִים מֵרְחֹבוֹת	כִּי־עָלָה מָוֶת בְּחַלּוֹנֵיכֶם בָּא בְּאַרְמְנֹתָם לְהַכְרִית עוֹלָלִים[c] מִחוּץ וּבַחוּרִים מֵרְחֹבוֹת
21 דַּבֵּר כֹּה נְאֻם־יְהוָה וְנָפְלָה נִבְלַת הָאָדָם כְּדֹמֶן עַל־ פְּנֵי הַשָּׂדֶה וּכְעָמִיר	Deest וְהָיוּ נִבְלֹת הָאֲנָשִׁים לְדִמְיוֹן[d] עַל־פְּנֵי שָׂדֵה אַרְצָם (אַדְמָתָם) כֶּחָצִיר (כְּעֵשֶׂב)
22 אַל־יִתְהַלֵּל עָשִׁיר	וְאַל־יִתְהַלֵּל עָשִׁיר
23 הַשְׂכֵּל וְיָדֹעַ אוֹתִי עֹשֶׂה חֶסֶד מִשְׁפָּט וּצְדָקָה בָּאָרֶץ כִּי־בְאֵלֶּה חָפַצְתִּי	הַשְׂכֵּל וִידוֹעַ עֹשֵׂה חֶסֶד וּמִשְׁפָּט וּצְדָקָה עַל־הָאָרֶץ כִּי־בָאֵלֶּה חֶפְצִי
24 עַל־כָּל־מוּל בְּעָרְלָה	עַל־כָּל־מוּלֵי עָרְלָתָם וְעַל־אֲדוֹמִים[e]
25 וְעַל־יְהוּדָה וְעַל־מוֹאָב וְעַל כָּל־קְצוּצֵי פֵאָה עֲרֵלִים עַרְלֵי־לֵב	וְעַל־בְּנֵי מוֹאָב[f] וְעַל כָּל־קְבוּץ הַזָּאת עַרְלֵי־בָשָׂר[g] עַרְלֵי־לְבָבָם (הַלֵּב)

CAPUT X.

1 הַדָּבָר אֲשֶׁר דְּבַר יהוה	דְּבַר יהוה אֲשֶׁר דִּבֶּר
2 אֶל־דֶּרֶךְ הַגּוֹיִם כִּי־יֵחַתּוּ הַגּוֹיִם מֵהֵמָּה	אֶל־דַּרְכֵי הַגּוֹיִם כִּי־יֵחַתּוּ הֵמָּה מִפְּנֵיהֶם (לִפְנֵיהֶם)
3 כִּי־עֵץ מִיַּעַר כְּרָתוֹ מַעֲשֵׂה	עֵץ הוּא מִיַּעַר כָּרַת מַעֲשֵׂה חָרָשׁ
4 יְדֵי־חָרָשׁ בַּמַּעֲצָד: בְּכֶסֶף וּבְזָהָב יְיַפֵּהוּ בְּמַסְמְרוֹת וּבְמַקָּבוֹת יְחַזְּקוּם וְלֹא יָפִיק	יְדֵי־חָרָשׁ עֵץ הוּא מִיַּעַר כָּרַת מַעֲשֵׂה חָרָשׁ בְּמַעֲצָד: בְּכֶסֶף וּבְזָהָב וּמָצַק (וּמַסֵּכָה): בְּמַסְמְרוֹת וּבְמַקָּבוֹת מְיַפִּים (יְיַפּוּ) יְחַזְּקוּם:יַצִּיגוּם[h] וְלֹא יְפִיקוּ(יָמוּטוּ[i])

[a] Targ. אוּדְנֵיכוֹן. [b] Targ. לִבְנֵי. [c] Targ. יָנְקִין. [d] Vid. 8:2; 16:4. [e] Targ. [f] Targ. בּוֹאֲבָאֵי. אֲדוֹמָאֵי. [g] Targ. עַרְלִין בְּבִשְׂרְהוֹן. [h] Inc. vs. 5. [i] Cf. Isa. 41:7.

5 כְּתֹ֫מֶר מִקְשָׁה הֵ֫מָּה וְלֹא יְדַבֵּ֑רוּ	Deest
אֲל־תִּֽירְא֥וּ מֵהֶ֖ם	אל־תיראו אותם
וְגַם־הֵיטֵ֖יב אֵ֥ין אוֹתָֽם	וטוב אין בהם
6 מֵאֵ֥ין כָּמ֖וֹךָ יְהוָ֑ה גָּד֥וֹל אַתָּ֖ה	
7 וְגָד֥וֹל שִׁמְךָ֖ בִּגְבוּרָֽה׃ מִ֣י	
לֹ֤א יִֽרָאֲךָ֙ מֶ֣לֶךְ הַגּוֹיִ֔ם כִּ֥י לְךָ֖	Desunt
יָאָ֑תָה כִּ֣י בְכָל־חַכְמֵ֧י הַגּוֹיִ֛ם	
וּבְכָל־מַלְכוּתָ֖ם מֵאֵ֥ין כָּמֽוֹךָ׃	
8 וּבְאַחַ֖ת יִבְעֲר֣וּ וְיִכְסָ֑לוּ מוּסַ֥ר	
הֲבָלִ֖ים עֵ֥ץ הֽוּא׃	
9 כֶּסֶף מְרֻקָּע מִתַּרְשִׁישׁ יוּבָא	כֶּסֶף מִקְשָׁה הוּא לֹא יְהַגּוּ כֶּסֶף
וְזָהָב מֵאוּפָז מַעֲשֵׂה חָרָשׁ	מְרֻקָּע הוּא מִתַּרְשִׁישׁ יָבוֹא
וִידֵי צוֹרֵף תְּכֵלֶת וְאַרְגָּמָן	זָהָב מֵאוּפָז (מוּפָז[a]) וִידֵי צוֹרְפִים
לְבוּשָׁם מַעֲשֵׂה חֲכָמִים	מַעֲשֵׂי חָרָשִׁים כֻּלָּם תְּכֵלֶת
כֻּלָּם	וְאַרְגָּמָן לְבוּשָׁם
10 וַיהוָה אֱלֹהִים אֱמֶת הוּא־אֱלֹהִים	
חַיִּים וּמֶלֶךְ עוֹלָם מִקִּצְפּוֹ	Desunt
תִּרְעַשׁ הָאָרֶץ וְלֹא־יָכִלוּ גוֹיִם	
זַעְמוֹ	
12 עֹשֵׂה אֶרֶץ בְּכֹחוֹ מֵכִין תֵּבֵל	יְהוָה עָשָׂה הָאָרֶץ בכחו[b] הַמֵּכִין
בְּחָכְמָתוֹ וּבִתְבוּנָתוֹ נָטָה	תֵּבֵל בְּחָכְמָתוֹ וּבִתְבוּנָתוֹ נָטַד
שָׁמָיִם	הַשָּׁמָיִם
13 לְקוֹל תִּתּוֹ הֲמוֹן מַיִם	וַהֲמוֹן מַיִם
מִקְצֵה ׳אָרֶץ	מִקְצֵה הָאָרֶץ
וַיּוֹצֵא רוּחַ	וַיּוֹצֵא אוֹר[c]
14 הֹבִישׁ כָּל־צוֹרֵף מִפָּסֶל כִּי שֶׁקֶר	הֹבִישׁ כָּל־צוּרָה עַל־פְּסִילָיו כִּי שֶׁקֶר
נִסְכּוֹ וְלֹא־רוּחַ בָּם	נָסַךְ לֹא־רוּחַ בָּם
15 הֶבֶל הֵמָּה מַעֲשֵׂה תַּעְתֻּעִים	הֲבָלִים הֵמָּה מַעֲשֵׂי מְתַעְתְּעִים
	(מְתַעְתְּעִים)
16 וְיִשְׂרָאֵל שֵׁבֶט	
צְבָאוֹת	Desunt

---

[a] Μωφάζ. [b] Cf. 51:15. [c] Vid. 51:16.

[10:17-11:7] THE CONSPECTUS OF THE VARIATIONS. 305

17 אִסְפִּי מֵאֶרֶץ כִּנְעָתֵךְ יוֹשֶׁבְתִּי אָסֶה מָחוּץ כנעתך (קִנְיָנֵךְ) יוֹשְׁבִים בְּמִבְחָר בַּמָּצוֹר	
18 הִנְנִי קוֹלֵעַ	הִנְנִי צוֹלֵעַ (מַצְלִיעַ) Deest
בַּפַּעַם	
וַהֲצֵרֹתִי לָהֶם	בְּצָרָה
לְמַעַן יִמְצָאוּ	לְמַעַן תִּמָּצֵא מַפָּתֵךְ[b]
19 אוֹי־לִי עַל־שִׁבְרִי נַחְלָה מַכָּתִי	אוֹי עַל־שִׁבְרֵךְ נַחְלָה מַכָּתֵךְ
אַךְ זֶה חֳלִי וְאֶשָּׂאֶנּוּ	אַךְ זֶה חָלְיֵךְ וַיִּשָּׂאֵהוּ
20 אֹהָלִי שֻׁדָּד וְכָל־מֵיתָרַי נִתָּקוּ	אָהֳלֵךְ שֻׁדַּד וְכָל־יְרִיעוֹתַיִךְ אָבַד
בָּנַי יְצָאֻנִי וְאֵינָם אֵין נֹטֶה	נִתְּקוּ בְנֵי וְצֹאנֵךְ אֵינָם אֵין עוֹד
עוֹד אָהֳלִי וּמֵקִים יְרִיעוֹתִי	מָקוֹם (נָוֶה) אָהֳלֵי מָקוֹם יְרִיעוֹתִי
21 כִּי נִבְעֲרוּ הָרֹעִים	כִּי הָרֹעִים נִבְעָרוּ
לֹא הִשְׂכִּילוּ וְכָל־מַרְעִיתָם נָפוֹצָה	לֹא הִשְׂכִּילָה כָּל־הַצֹּאן מַרְעִית וְנָפוֹצוּ
22 שְׁמָמָה מְעוֹן תַּנִּים	לִשְׁמָמָה[c] וּמְעוֹן רְעֵנִים
23 לֹא לָאִישׁ הֹלֵךְ וְהָכִין	וְלֹא־אִישׁ יֵלֵךְ וְיָכִין
24 יַסְּרֵנִי יְהוָה	יַסְּרֵנוּ יהוה
אַל־בְּאַפְּךָ פֶּן־תַּמְעִטֵנִי[d]	וְאַל־בְּאַף פֶּן־תַּמְעִיטֵנוּ
25 וַאֲכָלֻהוּ	Deest

CAPUT XI.

1 אֲשֶׁר־יִרְמְיָהוּ מֵאֵת יְהוָה	מֵאֵת יהוה אֶל־יִרְמְיָהוּ
2 וְדִבַּרְתָּם אֶל־אִישׁ יְהוּדָה וְעַל־יֹשְׁבֵי יְרוּשָׁלִָם	וְדִבַּרְתָּ אֶל־אַנְשֵׁי יְהוּדָה וְאֶל־הַיֹּשְׁבִים בִּירוּשָׁלִָם[e]
4 הוֹצִיאִי־אוֹתָם	הַעֲלוֹתִי (אֲשֶׁר הֶעֱלֵיתִי) אוֹתָם
וַעֲשִׂיתֶם אוֹתָם כְּכֹל	וַעֲשִׂיתֶם כֹּל
5 הָקִים אֶת־הַשְּׁבוּעָה	אָקִים שְׁבוּעָתִי
6 אֶת־כָּל־הַדְּבָרִים הָאֵלֶּה	אֶת־הַדְּבָרִים הָאֵלֶּה
וּבְחֻצוֹת יְרוּשָׁלִָם	וּמִחוּץ לִירוּשָׁלִָם
7 כִּי הָעֵד הַעִדֹתִי בַּאֲבוֹתֵיכֶם בְּיוֹם הַעֲלוֹתִי אוֹתָם מֵאֶרֶץ	Desunt

[a] σκολ. [b] Targ. פּוּרְעֲנוּת חוֹבַיְכוֹן. [c] Targ. לְצָדוּ. [d] Cf. Ps. 79:7.
[e] Vid. vs. 9; 4:3.

מִצְרַיִם עַד־הַיּוֹם הַזֶּה הַשְׁכֵּם וְהָעֵד לֵאמֹר שִׁמְעוּ בְּקוֹלִי:	
8 וְלֹא שָׁמְעוּ וְלֹא־הִטּוּ אֶת־אָזְנָם וַיֵּלְכוּ אִישׁ בִּשְׁרִירוּת לִבָּם הָרָע וָאָבִיא עֲלֵיהֶם אֶת־כָּל־ דִּבְרֵי הַבְּרִית־הַזֹּאת אֲשֶׁר צִוִּיתִי לַעֲשׂוֹת	Desunt
9 בְּאִישׁ יהודה ובישבי ירושלם	בְּאַנְשֵׁי יהודה וּבְיֹשְׁבִים בִּירוּשָׁלִָם[a]
10 הָלְכוּ הָמָה הֵפֵרוּ	וְהִנֵּה הֵמָּה הֹלְכִים וְהֵפֵרוּ (וַיָּפֵרוּ)
אֲשֶׁר כָּרַתִּי אֶת־אֲבוֹתָם	אֲשֶׁר נָתַתִּי לַאֲבוֹתָם
11 הִנְנִי מֵבִיא אֲלֵיהֶם רָעָה	הִנְנִי מֵבִיא עַל־הָעָם הַזֶּה רָעוֹת[b]
12 וְהוֹשֵׁעַ לֹא־יוֹשִׁיעוּ	אֲשֶׁר לֹא־יוֹשִׁיעוּ
13 מִזְבְּחוֹת לַבֹּשֶׁת	Deest
14 וְאַל־תִּשָּׂא בַעֲדָם וְרִנָּה וּתְפִלָּה בְּעַד רָעָתָם	וְאַל־תִּתְחַנֵּן בַּעֲדָם [לָבוֹא] בְּעַד הִנֵּה ובתפלה[d] בְּעֵת רָעָתָם[e]
15 מֶה לִידִידִי בְּבֵיתִי עֲשׂוֹתָהּ הַמְזִמָּתָה הָרַבִּים וּבְשַׂר־קֹדֶשׁ יַעַבְרוּ מֵעָלָיִךְ כִּי רָעָתֵכִי אָז תַּעֲלֹזִי	לָמָּה הַיְדִידָה (וִידִידְתִי) בְּבֵיתִי עֲשׂתָה (מ)זמתה תִּרְגָּנִים (הָרְגָנִים, הַגְּדָרִים) וּבְשַׂר־קֹדֶשׁ יַעֲבְרוּ מֵעָלַיִךְ רָעָתֵכִי אוֹ (אִם) תֶּחֶלְצִי בָהֶם
16 זַיִת רַעֲנָן יְפֵה פְרִי־תֹאַר לְקוֹל הֲמוּלָּה גְדֹלָה הִצִּית אֵשׁ עָלֶיהָ וְרָעוּ דָּלִיּוֹתָיו	זַיִת יָפֶה רַעֲנָן בְּתֹאַר לְקוֹל הֲמוּלָּה הוּצַת אֵשׁ עָלֶיהָ גְּדֹלָה הַצָּרָה עָלַיִךְ[f] רֵעוּ דָּלִיּוֹתֶיהָ
17 צְבָאוֹת	Deest
אֲשֶׁר עָשׂוּ לָהֶם לְקַטֵּר לַבָּעַל	כִּי עָשׂוּ לָהֶם בְּקַטְּרָם לַבָּעַל
18 וַיהוה הוֹדִיעַנִי הִרְאִיתָנִי	יהוה הוֹדִיעֵנִי רָאִיתִי (אֶרְאֶה)
19 כְּכֶבֶשׂ אַלּוּף	כְּכֶבֶשׂ תָּמִים
וְלֹא יָדַעְתִּי כִּי־עָלַי מַחֲשָׁבוֹת נָשְׁחִיתָה	חָשְׁבוּ לֹא יָדַעְתִּי עָלַי חָשְׁבוּ מַחֲשָׁבָה רָעָה[g] לֵאמֹר לְכוּ וְנַשְׁחִיתָה (וְנַשְׁלִיכָה[h])

[a] Vid. vs. 2; 4:3.   [b] Targ. עֲלֵיכוֹן.   [c] Cf. 3:5.   [d] Vid. 7:16.   [e] Targ. בְּעִדָּן בְּרִישְׁתְּהוֹן.   [f] Targ. עֲלָךְ.   [g] Targ. עֵצָתִין בִּישָׁן.   [h] Targ. וְנִרְמֵי.

[11:20-12:11] THE CONSPECTUS OF THE VARIATIONS.   307

20 וַיהוָה צְבָאוֹת שֹׁפֵט צֶדֶק
וָלֵב
  יהוה שפט צדקות
  וְלִבּוֹת (וּלְבָבוֹת)

21 הַמְבַקְשִׁים אֶת־נַפְשְׁךָ לֵאמֹר
בְּשֵׁם יהוה
וְלֹא תָמוּת בְּיָדֵינוּ
  המבקשים את־נפשי האמרים[c]
  על־שם יהוה
  וְלֹא (וְאִם־לֹא[b]) תמות בידינו

22 לָכֵן כֹּה־אָמַר יְהוָה צְבָאוֹת הִנְנִי
פֹקֵד עֲלֵיהֶם הַבַּחוּרִים יָמֻתוּ
בַחֶרֶב בְּנֵיהֶם וּבְנֹתֵיהֶם יָמֻתוּ
בָּרָעָב
  הִנֵּה אֶפְקֹד עליהם בחוריהם[c]
  בחרב ימותו ובניהם ובנתיהם
  יתמו ברעב[d]

23 אֶל־אַנְשֵׁי עֲנָתוֹת שְׁנַת פְּקֻדָּתָם
  עַל־הַיּוֹשְׁבִים בַּעֲנָתוֹת בִּשְׁנַת[e] פקדתם

CAPUT XII.

2 ילכו   ילדו

3 תִּרְאֵנִי וּבָחַנְתָּ לִבִּי אִתָּךְ הַתִּקֵם
כְּצֹאן לְטִבְחָה וְהַקְדִּשֵׁם לְיוֹם
הֲרֵגָה
  וּבְחִנַת לבי אתך הקדשם ליום
  הרגתם (ההרגה[f])

4 וְעֵשֶׂב כָּל־הַשָּׂדֶה
לֹא יִרְאֶה אֶת־אַחֲרִיתֵנוּ
  וכל־עשב השדה
  לא יראה האלהים את־ארחתינו

5 כִּי אֶת־רַגְלִים רַצְתָּה וַיִּלְאוּךָ
וְאֵיךְ תְּתַחֲרֶה
וּבְאֶרֶץ שָׁלוֹם
וְאֵיךְ תַּעֲשֶׂה
  אַתָּה רגליך ירוצו וילאוך ואיך
  תתחרץ
  ובארץ שלומך (השלום)
  איד תעשה

6 קָרְאוּ אַחֲרֶיךָ מָלֵא
  קראו מאחריך מלאו (התמלאו)

8 נָתְנָה עָלַי בְּקוֹלָה
  נתנה עלי קולה[g]

9 הַעַיִט צָבוּעַ
הָעַיִט סָבִיב עָלֶיהָ
כָּל־חַיַּת הַשָּׂדֶה הֵתָיוּ לְאָכְלָה
  הַמְעָרַת צבוע
  המערה מסביב לה
  כל־חית השדה ויאתיו לאכלה[h]

11 שָׂמָהּ לִשְׁמָמָה אָבְלָה עָלַי שְׁמֵמָה
שְׁמֵמָה
  שָׂמָה (הוּשָׂמָה) לשממה אָבְדָהּ
  (אֲבָדָהּ) עלי שממה

---
[a] Targ. דְאַנְדְּרִין. [b] Cf. I. Sam. 2:16. [c] Targ. מִצַּדְרֵהוֹן. [d] ut 14:15; 44:12. [e] Vid. 23:12. [f] ut 7:32; 19:6. [g] Targ. אַתְרְגוּשְׁתָּהּ. [h] Targ. לְנִבְזָה.

מִקְצֵה הָאָרֶץ עַד־קְצֵה הָאָרֶץ	12 מִקְצֵה אָרֶץ וְעַד־קְצֵה הָאָרֶץ
זָרְעוּ חִטִּים וְקֹצִים קָצְרוּ נֶחֱלוּ חֲלוֹחֵיהֶם	13 זָרְעוּ חִטִּים וְקֹצִים קָצָרוּ נֶחְלוּ
לֹא יוֹעִלוּ לָהֶם בֹּשׁוּ מִתְּבוּאֹתָם	לֹא יוֹעִלוּ וּבֹשׁוּ מִתְּבוּאֹתֵיכֶם
מֵחֲרוֹן לִפְנֵי יהוה	מֵחֲרוֹן אַף־יהוה
כִּי כֹה אָמַר יהוה	14 כֹּה אָמַר יהוה
הַשְּׁכֵנִים ͣ	שְׁכֵנַי
הַנֹּגְעִים בְּנַחֲלָתִי	הַנֹּגְעִים בַּנַּחֲלָה
וְאֶת־יְהוּדָה	וְאֶת־בֵּית יְהוּדָה
וְהוֹשַׁבְתִּים (וְהוֹשַׁבְתִּים)	15 וַהֲשִׁיבֹתִים
אֶת־דַּרְכֵּךְ ͤ עַמִּי	16 אֶת־דַּרְכֵי עַמִּי
וּבְנֹה	וְנִבְנוּ
וְאִם לֹא יָשׁוּבוּ	17 וְאִם לֹא יִשְׁמָעוּ
Deest	נְאֻם־יהוה

CAPUT XIII.

Deest	1 אֵלַי
וּבַמַּיִם לֹא יָבוֹא	וּבַמַּיִם לֹא תְבִאֵהוּ
Desunt {	3 שֵׁנִית
	4 אֲשֶׁר קָנִיתָ
וְלֵךְ פְּרָתָה	לֵךְ פְּרָתָה
כַּאֲשֶׁר צִוָּה אוֹתִי יהוה	5 כַּאֲשֶׁר צִוָּה יהוה אוֹתִי
לְטָמְרְשָׁם	6 לְטָמְנוֹ־שָׁם
וָאֵלֵךְ פְּרָתָה הַנָּהָר	7 וָאֵלֵךְ פְּרָתָה
וְהִנֵּה נִשְׁחַת הָאֵזוֹר לֹא יִצְלַח לְכֹל אֲשֶׁר לֹא־יִצְלַח לְבֵ־	וְהִנֵּה נִשְׁחַת הָאֵזוֹר לֹא יִצְלַח לַכֹּל
וְאֶת־גְּאוֹן יְרוּשָׁלָיִם:	9 וְאֶת־גְּאוֹן יְרוּשָׁלַם הָרָב:
הָרַב ͩ הַגָּאוֹן הַזֶּה	10 הָעָם הַזֶּה הָרָע
הַהֹלְכִים בִּשְׁרִרוּת לִבָּם וְהֹלְכִים אַחֲרֵי אֱלֹהִים ͤ אֲחֵרִים	אַחֲרֵי אֱלֹהִים אֲחֵרִים
וְהָיוּ ͨ	וַיְהִי
עָלַי מְתַנִי אִישׁ	11 אֶל־מָתְנֵי אִישׁ

ͣ Targ. בָּעַרְיָא. ͪ Targ. כְּאֹרַח. ͨ ut vs. 10. ͩ Inc. vs. 10. ͤ Targ. וִיהוֹן.

אֶת־בֵּית יִשְׂרָאֵל	אֶת־עַל־בֵּית יִשְׂרָאֵל
Deest	נְאֻם־יְהוָֹה
לְעַם וּלְתִפְאֶרֶת וְלִתְהִלָּה וְלֹא שָׁמְעוּ אֵלָי	לְעַם וּלְשֵׁם וּלְתְהִלָּה וּלְתִפְאָרֶת וְלֹא שָׁמֵעוּ
וְאָמַרְתָּ אֲלֵיהֶעַם הַזֶּה	12 וְאָמַרְתָּ אֲלֵיהֶם
Desunt {	אֶת־הַדָּבָר הַזֶּה כֹּה־אָמַר יְהוָֹה אֱלֹהֵי יִשְׂרָאֵל
וְהָיָה כִּי־יֹאמְרוּ[c] אֵלֶיךָ	וְאָמְרוּ אֵלֶיךָ
אֶת־יוֹשְׁבֵי הָאָרֶץ	13 אֶת־עַל־יוֹשְׁבֵי הָאָרֶץ
וְאֶת־הַמְּלָכִים הַיֹּשְׁבִים בָּנִים לְדָוִד עַל־כִּסְאוֹתָב[b]	וְאֶת־הַמְּלָכִים הַיֹּשְׁבִים לְדָוִד עַל־כִּסְאוֹ
וְאֶת־הַנְּבִיאִים וְאֶת־יְהוּדָה וְאֶת־כָּל־הַיֹּשְׁבִים בִּירוּשָׁלַם שֵׁכָּר	וְאֶת כָּל־יֹשְׁבֵי יְרוּשָׁלָם שִׁכָּרוֹן
וְהַפִּצוֹתִים אִישׁ אֶל אָחִיו וַאֲבוֹתֵיהֶם וּבְנֵיהֶם יַחַד לֹא־אֶחְמוֹל אֲשֶׁר יְהוָֹה (נְאֻם־יְהוָֹה)	14 וְנִפַּצְתִּים אִישׁ אֶל־אָחִיו וְהָאָבוֹת וְהַבָּנִים יַחְדָּו נְאֻם־יְהוָֹה לֹא־אֶחְמוֹל
וְאַל־תִּגְבָּהוּ	15 אַל־תִּגְבָּהוּ
וְשָׂמָה צַלְמָוֶת וְשָׁתוּ לַעֲרָפֶל	16 וְשָׂמָה לְצַלְמָוֶת יָשִׁית לַעֲרָפֶל
וְאִם לֹא תִשְׁמָעוּ תִּבְכֶּה נַפְשְׁכֶם	17 וְאִם לֹא תִשְׁמָעוּהָ תִּבְכֶּה נַפְשִׁי
Deest	וְדָמֹעַ תִּדְמַע
וְתֵרַדְנָה עֵינֵיכֶם דְּמָעוֹת כִּי נִשְׁבַּר עֵדֶר יְהוָֹה	וְתֵרַד עֵינִי דִּמְעָה כִּי נִשְׁבָּה עֵדֶר יְהוָֹה
אֱמֹר לַמֶּלֶךְ וְלַגְּבִירִים (וְלַגִּבּוֹרִים) הַשְׁפִּילוּ וְשֵׁבוּ כִּי הוּרַד מֵרָאשָׁבֶם	18 אֱמֹר לַמֶּלֶךְ וְלַגְּבִירָה הַשְׁפִּילוּ שֵׁבוּ כִּי יָרַד מַרְאֲשׁוֹתֵיכֶם
	19 כֻּלָּה הָגְלָת שְׁלוֹמִים
	20 שְׂאִי[a] עֵינֵיכֶם וּרְאִי[a]
	21 כִּי־יִפְקֹד עָלַיִךְ
נֶחְשָׁפוּ (נִכְמְסוּ, נִרְאוּ, דָּמוּ[d]) עֲקֵבַיִךְ	22 נֶחְמְסוּ עֲקֵבָיִךְ
לִמּוּדִים הָרַע (הָרָעוֹת)	23 לִמֻּדֵי הָרֵעַ
כְּקַשׁ עוֹבֵר מֵרוּחַ לַמִּדְבָּר[f]	24 כְּקַשׁ עוֹבֵר לְרוּחַ מִדְבָּר

[a] ut 15:2; Exod. 12:26. [b] Cf. Ps. 122:5. [c] Targ. .... וִיהִי. [d] Targ. דְּכָרְיָן. [e] παραδειγματισθήναι.—Targ. אִתְחֲזִי. [f] Targ. בְּקַשָּׁא דְּבַר דָּן הֲוָה רוּחָא לְבִדְבְּרָא.

25 מְנָת־מִדַּיִךְ מֵאִתִּי   וּמְנָת־מָדַיִךְ מֵאִתִּי
27 נִאֻפַיִךְ וּמִצְהֲלוֹתַיִךְ זִמַּת זְנוּתֵךְ   נִאֻפַיִךְ וּמִצְהֲלֹתַיִךְ וְזָרַתᵇ (וְנֵזֶר)
   עַל־גְּבָעוֹת בַּשָּׂדֶה   זְנוּתֵךְ עַל־הַגְּבָעוֹת וּבַשָּׂדוֹת
   לֹא תִטְהֲרִי אַחֲרֵי מָתַי עֹד   כִּי לֹא תִטְהֲרִי אַחֲרַי עַד־מָתַי עֹד

CAPUT XIV.

1 אֲשֶׁר הָיָה דְבַר־יהוה   וַיְהִי דְבַר־יהוה
  עַל־דִּבְרֵי הַבַּצָּרוֹת   עַל־הַבַּצֹּרֶת (הַבַּצָּרֹתᵃ)
2 קָדְרוּ לָאָרֶץ   וְקָדְרוּ עַל־הָאָרֶץ
3 וְאַדִּירֵיהֶם   וְאַדִּירֶיהָ
  לֹא־מָצְאוּ מַיִם   וְלֹא־מָצְאוּ מַיִםᵈ
  שָׁבוּ   וְשָׁבוּ
  בֹּשׁוּ וְהָכְלְמוּ וְחָפוּ רֹאשָׁם   Deest
4 בַּעֲבוּר הָאֲדָמָה חַתָּה   נַעֲבוֹדᵉ(ת) הָאֲדָמָה חָדַל
  בָאָרֶץ   Deest
5 כִּי גַם־אַיֶּלֶת בַּשָּׂדֶה יָלְדָה וְעָזוֹב   גַּם־אַיָּלוֹת בַּשָּׂדֶה יַלְדוּ וְיַעַזְבוּ
6 וּפְרָאִים   פְּרָאִים
   שָׁאֲפוּ רוּחַ כַּתַּנִּים   וְשָׁאֲפוּ רוּחַ
   כִּי־אֵין עֵשֶׂב   כִּי־לֹא הָיָהᶠ עֵשֶׂב
7 אִם־עֲוֹנֵינוּ עָנוּ בָנוּ יהוה עֲשֵׂה   עֲוֹנֵינוּ קָמוּ בָנוּ יהוה עֲשֵׂה לָנוּ
  לְמַעַן שְׁמֶךָ כִּי־רַבּוּ מְשׁוּבֹתֵינוּ   לְמַעֲנֶךָ כִּי־רַבּוּ עֲוֹנֵינוּ לְפָנֶיךָ
  לְךָ חָטָאנוּ   (לְנֶגְדְּךָ) כִּי לְךָ חָטָאנוּ
8 מִקְוֵה יִשְׂרָאֵל מוֹשִׁיעוֹ בְּעֵת צָרָה   מִקְוֵה יִשְׂרָאֵל יהוהᵍ וְתוֹשִׁיעַ בְּעֵת
  לָמָּה תִהְיֶה כְגֵר בָּאָרֶץ וּכְאֹרֵחַ   רָעָהʰ לָמָּה תִהְיֶה כְגֵר עַל־הָאָרֶץ
  נָטָה לָלוּן   וּכְאֶזְרָח נֹטֶה לְמָלוֹןⁱ
9 כְּאִישׁ נִדְהָם כְּגִבּוֹר   כְּאִישׁ נִרְדָּם אוֹ כְגֶבֶר (וּכְגֶבֶר)
  וְאַתָּה בְקִרְבֵּנוּ   וְאַתָּה בָּנוּ
  וְשִׁמְךָ עָלֵינוּ נִקְרָא אַל־תַּנִּחֵנוּ   וְשִׁמְךָ נִקְרָא אַל־תִּשְׁכָּחֵנוּ

ᵃ Targ. בְּמַשְׁחִיתָךְ וּבְשִׁטוּתָיךְ.   ᵇ ἀπαλλοτρίωσις.   ᶜ Cf. 17:8.   ᵈ Targ.
יַעְבֹּד.   ᵉ Aram. וְלָא אֲשָׁכְּחוּ כְיָא.   ᶠ ut vs.5.—Targ. לָא הֲוֹו.   ᵍ ut 17:13.
ʰ Cf. 15:11.   ⁱ Targ. דְּסָטָא לְבָבָא.

14:10-19] THE CONSPECTUS OF THE VARIATIONS. 311

כֵּן אהבו לָנוּעַ רגליהם לא חשכו אהבו לנִיעַ (=לְהָנִיעַ) רגליהם ולא חשכו הָאֱלֹהִים לא יְאַשְּׁרָם‎ᵃ	10 כֵּן אהבו לָנוּעַ רגליהם לא חשכו וַיהוָה לא רָצָם וְיִפְקֹד הַטֹּאתָם
Deest	
כי אם יצמו אל-תִּפְלָתָם‎ᵇ אנכי אכלה אותם	12 כי יצמו אל-רִנָּתָם אנכי מְכַלֶּה אותם
אַתָּה יְהוָה‎ᶜ נביאיהם מנבאים‎ᵈ ואמרים ורעב לא-יהיה בָכֶם כי אמת וְשָׁלוֹם‎ᵉ אמת אתן על-הָאָרֶץ וּבַמָּקוֹם הזה	13 אֲהָהּ אֲדֹנָי יֱהוִה הנביאים אמרים להם ורעב לא-יהיה לכם כי שלום אמת אתן לכם במקום הזה
כי חֲזִיוֹנוֹת שקר וקסמים וְנַחֲשׁ וְתַרְמִית‎ᶠ לבם	14 חזון שקר וקסם וֶאֱלוּל וְתַרְמֻת לבם
הנבאים בשמי שֶׁקֶר האמרים לא יהיה עַל-הָאָרֶץ הזאת מְמוֹתֵי תַחֲלָאִים יָמֻתוּ‎ᵍ (בְּמוֹת חֳלִי) הנביאים	15 הנבאים בשמי וְהֵמָּה אמרים לא יהיה בָּאָרֶץ הזאת בַּחֶרֶב הנביאים הָהֵמָּה
ויהיו משלכים מפני החרב והרעב‎ʰ ואין מקבר אוֹתָם וּנְשֵׁיהֶם	16 יהיו משלכים מפני הרעב והחרב ואין מקבר לָהֵמָּה הֵמָּה נשיהם
תֵּרַדְנָה עיני דִּמְעָה לילה הוֹרִידוּ על-עֵינֵיכֶם דְּמָעוֹת יומם וָלָיְלָה	17 תֵּרַדְנָה עיני דמעה לילה ויומם
כי שבר גדול נשברה בת-חֵילַת בת-עמי מכה נחלה מאד	כי שבר נשברה בת-עמי וּמַכָּה נחלה מאד
כי כהן גם-נביא אֲשֶׁר לא ידעו	18 כי גם-נביא גם-כהן ולא ידעו
וּמִצִּיּוֹן תֵּקַע נפשך‎ⁱ קַוִּינוּ‎ᵏ לשלום לעת מרפא	19 אִם-בְּצִיּוֹן גָּעֲלָה נפשך קַוֵּה לשלום וּלְעֵת מרפא

ᵃ Alex. לֹא רָצָם. ᵇ Targ. צְלוֹתְהוֹן. ᶜ Vid. 1:6; 4:10; 32:17. ᵈ Targ. דִּמְתְנַבָּן. ᵉ Cf. 33:6; Isa. 39:8. ᶠ Vid. 23:26. ᵍ ut 16:4. ʰ ut 16:4. ⁱ Cf. 6:8; Ezek. 23:17. ᵏ Vid. 8:15.—Targ. סַבַּרְנָא.

20 יָדַעְנוּ יהוה רִשְׁעֵנוּ עֲוֺן אֲבוֹתֵינוּ   יְדַעְנוּ יהוה רִשְׁעוֹתֵינוּ עֲוֺנוֹת[a]
כִּי חָטָאנוּ לָךְ   אֲבוֹתֵינוּ כִּי חָטָאנוּ לְפָנֶיךָ[b]
21 אַל־תִּנְאַץ   הֲרֵף (אַל־תִּנְאַץ?)
אַל־תְּנַבֵּל   אַל־תְּחַבֵּל (תְּאַבֵּד)
אַל־תָּפֵר בְּרִיתְךָ אִתָּנוּ   אַל תָּפֵר בְּרִיתְךָ אֲשֶׁר אִתָּנוּ
22 בְּהַבְלֵי הַגּוֹיִם מַגְשִׁמִים   בֶּאֱלִילֵי (בִּפְסִילֵי) הַגּוֹיִם מַגְשִׁמִים
יִתְּנוּ רְבִיבִים   יִתְּנוּ רְבִיבָם (רָבַם, רְוָיָתָם)
יהוה אֱלֹהֵינוּ וּנְקַוֶּה־לָּךְ   וּנְקַוֶּה־לָךְ יהוה

CAPUT XV.

1 אֵין נַפְשִׁי אֶל־הָעָם הַזֶּה שַׁלַּח   אֵין נַפְשִׁי אֲלֵיהֶם שַׁלַּח אֹתָם הָעַם הַזֶּה
מֵעַל־פָּנָי
3 וְאֶת־הַכְּלָבִים לִסְחֹב וְאֶת־עוֹף   וְאֶת־הַכְּלָבִים לִטְרֹף וְאֶת־חַיַּת הָאָרֶץ
הַשָּׁמַיִם וְאֶת־בֶּהֱמַת הָאָרֶץ   וְאֶת־עוֹף הַשָּׁמַיִם
4 לְזַעֲוָה   לִזְוָעוֹת(?)[c]
עַל־אֲשֶׁר־עָשָׂה   עַל־כָּל־אֲשֶׁר־עָשָׂה
5 כִּי מִי־יַחְמֹל עָלַיִךְ יְרוּשָׁלִַם   מִי־יַחְמֹל עָלַיִךְ יְרוּשָׁלִַם וּמִי יָירָא
וּמִי יָנוּד לָךְ   (יִפְחַד) מִמֵּךְ
לִשְׁאֹל
6 עָלָיִךְ   } Desunt
נִלְאֵיתִי הִנָּחֵם
7 בְּשַׁעֲרֵי הָאָרֶץ שִׁכַּלְתִּי אִבַּדְתִּי   וְלֹא אֲנִיחֵם עוֹד
אֶת־עַמִּי מִדַּרְכֵיהֶם לוֹא שָׁבוּ   בְּשַׁעֲרֵי עַמִּי סִכְּלוּ אִבְּדוּ אֶת־עַמִּי
מִפְּנֵי רָעָתָם
8 עָצְמוּ־לִי אַלְמְנוֹתָו   עָצְמוּ אַלְמְנוֹתֵיהֶם[d]
הֵבֵאתִי לָהֶם עַל־אֵם בָּחוּר שֹׁדֵד   הֵבֵאתִי עַל־אֵם בַּחוּרִים[e] שֹׁדֵד
בַּצָּהֳרָיִם   בַּצָּהֳרָיִם
עִיר וּבֶהָלוֹת   עִיר וּבֶהָלָה
9 יֹלֶדֶת הַשִּׁבְעָה   יָלְדָה שִׁבְעָה
בָּאָה שִׁמְשָׁהּ בְּעֹד יוֹמָם   בָּאָה הַשֶּׁמֶשׁ לָהּ בְּעוֹד חֲצִי הַיּוֹם
יְשָׁאֲרִיתָם   שְׁאֵרִיתָם

---

[a] Targ. וְחוֹבֵי. [b] Targ. קֳדָמָךְ. [c] ἀνάγκας. [d] Targ. אַרְמְלָתְהוֹן. [e] Targ. עוּלֵימֵיהוֹן.

נְאֻם־יְהוָה	Deest
10 אֽוֹי־לִ֣י אִמִּ֔י כִּ֣י יְלִדְתִּ֔נִי אִ֥ישׁ רִ֖יב וְאִ֣ישׁ מָד֑וֹן	אוי־לי אם ילדתני איש ריב ומדון כאיש ריב
לֹֽא־נָשִׁ֥יתִי וְלֹא־נָֽשׁוּ־בִ֖י כֻּלֹּ֥ה מְקַלְלַֽוְנִי׃	ולא־נשה־בי איש כ'חי כלה במקללוני
11 אָמַ֣ר יְהוָ֔ה אִם־לֹ֥א שֵֽׁרוֹתִ֖ךָ לְט֑וֹב	אמן אדני לישרים בהםᵃ (למישרים לכת) (?)
בְּעֵ֣ת רָעָ֔ה וּבְעֵ֥ת צָרָ֛ה אֶת־הָאֹיֵֽב׃	בעת רעותיהם ובעת צרתם לטוב אל־האיב
12 הֲיָרֹ֥עַ בַּרְזֶ֖ל בַּרְזֶ֣ל מִצָּפ֑וֹן וּנְחֹֽשֶׁת׃	הירע (הֲיָדַע) ברזל (וְצָפֹּוי) נחשת ברזל ומצפון
13 חֵילְךָ֧ וְאוֹצְרוֹתֶ֛יךָ לָבַ֖ז אֶתֵּ֑ן לֹ֣א בִמְחִ֔יר וּבְכָל־חַטֹּאותֶֽיךָ׃	חילךְ: ואוצרתידᵇ לבז אתן במחיר בכל־חטאותיך
14 וְהַֽעֲבַרְתִּי֙ אֶת־אֹ֣יְבֶ֔יךָ בְּאֶ֖רֶץ לֹ֥א יָדָ֑עְתָּ	והעבדתיךᶜ סביב לאיבידְ בארץ אֲשֶׁר לאᵈ ידעת
15 אַתָּ֣ה יָדַ֔עְתָּ	Deest
יְהוָה֙ זָכְרֵ֣נִי וּפָקְדֵ֔נִי	וְנַקֵּנִי
אַל־לְאֶ֥רֶךְ אַפְּךָ֖ תִּקָּחֵ֑נִי	אל־לארדְ אף
דַּ֕ע שְׂאֵתִ֥י עָלֶ֖יךָ חֶרְפָּֽה׃	כי נשאתיᵉ עליך חרפה
16 נִמְצְא֤וּ דְבָרֶ֙יךָ֙ וָאֹכְלֵ֔ם וַיְהִ֤י דְבָֽרְךָ֙ לִ֔י	נמצאו מפאצי דבריך כלם ויהי דברךᶠ לי
יְהוָ֥ה אֱלֹהֵ֖י צְבָא֑וֹת	יהוה צבאות
17 וָאֶעְלֹ֔ז	וְאֶעֱרָץ
כִּי־זַ֖עַם מִלֵּאתָֽנִי׃	כי־זעם מלאתי
18 לָ֤מָּה הָיָה֙ כְאֵבִ֣י נֶ֔צַח מַכָּתִ֥י אֲנוּשָׁ֖ה	למה מכאיבי ינצחוני מאנה ארפא
כְּמ֥וֹ אַכְזָ֖ב מַ֥יִם לֹ֥א נֶאֱמָֽנוּ׃	כמי אכזב לא נאמנים
19 לְפָנַ֣י תַּעֲמֹ֑ד	ולפני תעמד
יָשֻׁ֥בוּ הֵ֖מָּה	וישבו המה
20 וְהִצַּלְתִּ֖יךָ נְאֻם־יְהוָֽה׃	Deest
21 וְהִצַּלְתִּ֕יךָ	ולהצילך
מִכַּ֖ף עָרִצִֽים׃	מכף תחלואים

ᵃ ατευδωνοντασ αυτων. ᵇ Inc. vs. 13. ᶜ Cf. 17:4.—Targ. וְהָשֵׁיתִךְ עֲבָדוּן. ᵈ Targ. דְּלָא. ᵉ Targ. דְקַבֵּלִית. ᶠ Targ. בְּדָרֱךְ. לְבַעֲלֵי דְבָבֵיכוֹן

CAPUT XVI.

Deest	1 וַיְהִי דְבַר־יְהֹוָה אֵלַי לֵאמֹר
2 לֹא־תִקַּח לְךָ אִשָּׁה וְלֹא־יִהְיוּ לְךָ וְאַתָּה לֹא־תִקַּח לְךָ וְלֹא־יִהְיוּ לְךָ בָּנִים וּבָנוֹת אָשָּׁה אָמַר יְהוָה אֱלֹהֵי יִשְׂרָאֵל וְלֹא־יִהְיוּ לְךָ בֵן וּבַת	
4 לְדֹמֶן עַל־פְּנֵי הָאֲדָמָה וּבַחֶרֶב וּבָרָעָב יִכְלוּ וְהָיְתָה נִבְלָתָם לְמַאֲכָל לְעוֹף הַשָּׁמַיִם וּלְבֶהֱמַת הָאָרֶץ	לְדָמְיוֹן עַל־פְּנֵי הָאֲדָמָה וּלְבֶהֱמַת הָאָרֶץ יִהְיוּ וְלַעוֹף הַשָּׁמַיִם בַּחֶרֶב יִפְּלוּ וּבָרָעָב יִכְלוּ
5 כִּי־כֹה אָמַר יְהוָה בֵּית מַרְזֵחַ	כֹּה אָמַר יְהוָה בְּמַרְזְחָם (הַמַּרְזֵחַ)
נְאֻם־יְהֹוָה אֶת־הַחֶסֶד וְאֶת־הָרַחֲמִים	Desunt
6 וּמֵתוּ גְדֹלִים וּקְטַנִּים בָּאָרֶץ הַזֹּאת לֹא יִקָּבֵרוּ וְלֹא־יִסְפְּדוּ לָהֶם וְלֹא יִתְגֹּדַד וְלֹא יִקָּרֵחַ לָהֶם	לֹא־יִסְפְּדוּ לָהֶם וְלֹא יִתְגּוֹדְדוּ וְלֹא יִקָּרְחוּ
7 וְלֹא־יִפְרְסוּ לָהֶם עַל־אֵבֶל לְנַחֲמוֹ עַל־מֵת וְלֹא־יַשְׁקוּ אוֹתָם	וְלֹא־יִפְרְסוּ לָהֶם לֶחֶם בְּאֶבְלָם לְנַחֵם עַל־מֵת וְלֹא־יַשְׁקוּ אוֹתוֹ
8 וּבֵית־מִשְׁתֶּה לֹא־תָבוֹא	בֵּית־מִשְׁתֶּה לֹא־תָבוֹא אַתָּה
9 צְבָאוֹת	Deest
קוֹל שָׂשׂוֹן וְקוֹל שִׂמְחָה	קוֹל שִׂמְחָה וְקוֹל שָׂשׂוֹן
10 אֵת כָּל־הָרָעָה הַגְּדוֹלָה הַזֹּאת וּמֶה עֲוֹנֵנוּ	אֵת כָּל־הָרָעוֹת הָאֵלֶּה מֶה עֲוֹנֵנוּ
11 עַל אֲשֶׁר־עָזְבוּ אֲבוֹתֵיכֶם אוֹתִי	עַל אֲשֶׁר־עָזְבוּ אוֹתִי וַאֲבוֹתֵיכֶם
12 לַעֲשׂוֹת	Deest
שְׁרִרוּת לִבּוֹ־הָרָע	תַּאֲוַת לִבְּכֶם־הָרָע
13 עַל־הָאָרֶץ	אֶל־הָאָרֶץ
יוֹמָם וָלָיְלָה	Deest
לֹא־אֶתֵּן	לֹא־יִתֵּנוּ
14 וְלֹא־יֵאָמֵר עוֹד חַי־יְהוָה אֲשֶׁר הֶעֱלָה אֶת־בְּנֵי יִשְׂרָאֵל	וְלֹא־יֹאמְרוּ עוֹד חַי־יְהוָה הַמַּעֲלֶה אֶת־בְּנֵי יִשְׂרָאֵל

[a] Vid. 8:2; 9:21.   [b] Inc. vs. 6.   [c] τῶν ἀρεστῶν.   [d] Targ. לְאַרְעָא.
[e] Targ. וְלָא יָהוֹן בִּשְׁבִיתָא עוֹד.

[16:15–17:5] THE CONSPECTUS OF THE VARIATIONS. 315

15 אֶת־בְּנֵי יִשְׂרָאֵל	אֶת־בֵּית יִשְׂרָאֵל
אֲשֶׁר הֱדִיחָם שָׁמָּה וַהֲשִׁבוֹתִים	אֲשֶׁר הִדְּחוּ שָׁמָּה וְהֲשִׁבוֹתִים אֶל־
עַל־אַדְמָתָם	אַדְמָתָם[a]
17 לֹא נִסְתְּרוּ מִלְּפָנָי	Deest
וְלֹא־נִצְפַּן עֲוֹנָם	וְלֹא־נִצְפְּנוּ עֲוֹנוֹתֵיהֶם[b]
18 וְשִׁלַּמְתִּי רִאשׁוֹנָה מִשְׁנֵה עֲוֹנָם	וְשִׁלַּמְתִּי מִשְׁנֵה רָעָתֵיהֶם וְחַטֹּאתֵיהֶם
וְחַטָּאתָם עַל־חַלְלָם	עַל־אֲשֶׁר חִלְּלוּ
בְּנַבְלַת	בְּנַבְלַת
וְתוֹעֲבוֹתֵיהֶם מִלְּאוּ	וְעֵרְוֹתֵיהֶם אֲשֶׁר מִלְאוּ בָּהֶם
19 עֻזִּי וּמָעֻזִּי	אַתָּה עֻזִּי וְעֹזְרִי (עֲזַרְתִּי)
בְּיוֹם צָרָה	בִּימֵי רָעָה
מֵאַפְסֵי־אָרֶץ	מִקְצֵה הָאָרֶץ
אַךְ־שֶׁקֶר נָחֲלוּ אֲבוֹתֵינוּ הָבֶל	אֵיךְ שֶׁקֶר נָחֲלוּ אֲבוֹתֵינוּ הֲבָלִים
21 הִנְנִי מוֹדִיעָם בַּפַּעַם הַזֹּאת	הִנְנִי מוֹדִיעָם בְּפַעַם (פַּעַת) הַזֹּאת
אוֹדִיעָם אֶת־יָדִי וְאֶת־גְּבוּרָתִי	אֶת־יָדִי וְאוֹדִיעָם אֶת גְּבוּרָתִי

CAPUT XVII.

Desunt	1 חַטַּאת יְהוּדָה כְּתוּבָה בְּעֵט בַּרְזֶל בְּצִפֹּרֶן שָׁמִיר חֲרוּשָׁה עַל־לוּחַ לִבָּם וּלְקַרְנוֹת מִזְבְּחוֹתֵיכֶם׃ 2 כִּזְכֹּר בְּנֵיהֶם מִזְבְּחוֹתָם וַאֲשֵׁרֵיהֶם עַל־עֵץ רַעֲנָן עַל גְּבָעוֹת הַגְּבֹהוֹת׃ 3 הֲרָרִי בַּשָּׂדֶה חֵילְךָ כָל־אוֹצְרוֹתֶיךָ לָבַז אֶתֵּן בָּמֹתֶיךָ בְּחַטָּאת בְּכָל־גְּבוּלֶיךָ׃ 4 וְשָׁמַטְתָּה וּבְךָ מִנַּחֲלָתְךָ אֲשֶׁר נָתַתִּי לָךְ וְהַעֲבַדְתִּיךָ אֶת־אֹיְבֶיךָ בָּאָרֶץ אֲשֶׁר לֹא־יָדָעְתָּ כִּי־אֵשׁ קְדַחְתֶּם בְּאַפִּי עַד־עוֹלָם תּוּקָד׃ 5 כֹּה אָמַר יְהוָה

---

[a] Targ. לְאַרְעֲהוֹן. [b] Targ. חוֹבֵיהוֹן ... וְלָא מְסַדְּרָן חוֹבֵיהוֹן. [c] Vid. 18:23; 31:34; 36:6.—Targ. יַחֲסְרוֹן עַל דְּחָלֵי.

אֲשֶׁר יִבְטַח בָּאָדָם וְשָׂם בָּשָׂר	אֲשֶׁר מָבְטָחוֹ בָּאָדָם וְשָׂם בָּשָׂר
זְרֹעוֹ עָלָיו	זְרֹעוֹ
6 וְשָׁכַן חֲרָרִים בַּמִּדְבָּר אֶרֶץ מְלֵחָה	וְשָׁכַן מְלֵחִים וּבַמִּדְבָּר וּבְאֶרֶץ מִלֵחָה
וְלֹא תֵשֵׁב	אֲשֶׁר לֹא[a] תֵּשֵׁב
7 בָּרוּךְ הַגֶּבֶר	וּבָרוּךְ הַגֶּבֶר
8 כְּעֵץ	כְּעֵץ פּוֹרֵחַ
יְשַׁלַּח שָׁרָשָׁיו וְלֹא יִרְאֶ[b]	יַשְׁלִיךְ שָׁרְשׁוֹ לֹא יֵרֶא (= יִירָא)
וְהָיָה עָלֵהוּ רַעֲנָן וּבִשְׁנַת בַּצֹּרֶת	וְהָיָה עָלֵהוּ (עָלָיו) עָלֶה רַעֲנָן בִּשְׁנַת
לֹא יִדְאָג	בַּצֹּרֶת לֹא יִפְחָד (יִירָא)?
9 עָקֹב הַלֵּב מִכֹּל וְאָנֻשׁ הוּא מִי	עָקֹב הַלֵּב מִכֹּל מִכֹּל וְאָנֻשׁ[c] הוּא וּמִי
יֵדָעֶנּוּ	יֵדָעֶנּוּ
10 אֲנִי יְהוָה חֹקֵר לֵב בֹּחֵן כְּלָיוֹת וְלָתֵת לָאִישׁ כִּדְרָכוֹ	וּבֹחֵן כְּלָיוֹת וְלָתֵת לָאִישׁ כִּדְרָכָיו
כִּפְרִי מַעֲלָלָיו	וּכְפִי מַעֲלָלָיו
11 קֹרֵא דָגַר וְלֹא יָלָד עֹשֶׂה עֹשֶׁר	קֹרֵא קָרָא דָגַר (אָגַר) אֲשֶׁר לֹא יָלַד
וְלֹא בְמִשְׁפָּט	עָשָׂה עָשְׂרוֹ לֹא בְמִשְׁפָּט
12 מֵרִאשׁוֹן	Desunt
מְקוֹם	
13 וְסוּרַי בָּאָרֶץ יִכָּתֵבוּ	סוּרַי (סָרַי) עַל־הָאָרֶץ יִכָּתְבוּ
מְקוֹר מַיִם־חַיִּים	מְקוֹר חַיִּים[d]
15 יָבוֹא נָא	יָבוֹא
16 לֹא־אַצְתִּי מֵרֹעֶה אַחֲרֶיךָ וְיוֹם	וְלֹא נִלְאֵיתִי[e] מָלֶכֶת אַחֲרֶיךָ וְיוֹם
אָנוּשׁ	אֱנוֹשׁ[f]
מוֹצָא שְׂפָתַי נֹכַח פָּנֶיךָ	מוֹצָאֵי שְׂפָתַי לְפָנֶיךָ
17 אַל־תִּהְיֶה־לִי לִמְחִתָּה	אַל־תִּהְיֶה־לִי לְנֵכֶר (לְזָר)[g]
אָתָּה	Deest
18 וּמִשְׁנֵה שִׁבָּרוֹן	מִשְׁנֵה שִׁבָּרוֹן
19 אֵלַי	Deest
בְּשַׁעַר בְּנֵי־עָם	בְּשַׁעֲרֵי בְּנֵי עַמֶּךָ
בּוֹ (bis)	בָּהֶם (bis)
20 יֹשְׁבֵי	Deest
21 הִשָּׁמְרוּ בְּנַפְשׁוֹתֵיכֶם	שִׁמְרוּ נַפְשׁוֹתֵיכֶם
וַהֲבֵאתֶם בְּשַׁעֲרֵי יְרוּשָׁלִָם	וְאַל־תֵּצְאוּ מִשַּׁעֲרֵי יְרוּשָׁלִָם

[a] Targ. דְּלָא.   [b] ut Ps. 64:7 (Gk. & Heb.).   [c] Vid. vs. 16.   [d] ut Ps. 36:10; Prov. 16:22.   [e] Targ. לָא עַכְבֵּית.   [f] Vid. vs. 9.   [g] εἰς ἀλλοτρίωσιν.

17.22–18.8] THE CONSPECTUS OF THE VARIATIONS.

22 וְקִדַּשְׁתֶּם	קַדֵּשׁוּ
23 וַיַּקְשׁוּ אֶת־עָרְפָּם	לְבִלְתִּי וַיְקַשּׁוּ אֶת־עָרְפָּם מֵאֲבוֹתֵיהֶם לְבִלְתִּי שְׁמֹעַ אֵלַי
24 אִם־שָׁמֹעַ תִּשְׁמְעוּן בֹּה	אִם־תִּשְׁמְעוּן Deest
25 רֹכְבִים בָּרֶכֶב וּבַסּוּסִים אִישׁ יְהוּדָה וְיֹשְׁבֵי יְרוּשָׁלִָם וְיָשְׁבָה הָעִיר הַזֹּאת	וְרֹכְבִים עַל־רִכְבֵּיהֶם וְסוּסֵיהֶם אַנְשֵׁי יְהוּדָה וְהַיּוֹשְׁבִים בִּירוּשָׁלִָם וְתוּשָׁב (וְנוֹשְׁבָה) הָעִיר הַזֹּאת
26 וּמִסְּבִיבוֹת יְרוּשָׁלִַם וּמִן־הַשְּׁפֵלָה וּמִן־הַנֶּגֶב עֹלָה וְזֶבַח וּמִנְחָה וּלְבוֹנָה וּמְבִאֵי תוֹדָה בֵּית יְהוָה	וּמִסָּבִיב יְרוּשָׁלִַם וּמֵאֶרֶץ הַשְּׁפֵלָה וּמִן־אֲשֶׁר לַנֶּגֶב עֹלוֹת וּזְבָחִים וּקְטֹרֶת וּמִנְחָה(?) וּלְבוֹנָה הַמְבִאִית תוֹדָה אֶל־בֵּית יְהוָה
27 וְאִם־לֹא וּלְבִלְתִּי שְׂאֵת מַשָּׂא וּבֹא בְשַׁעֲרֵי יְרוּשָׁלִַם אַרְמְנוֹת יְרוּשָׁלִָם	וְהָיָה אִם־לֹא לְבִלְתִּי שְׂאֵת מַשָּׂא וּלְבִלְתִּי בֹא בְשַׁעֲרֵי יְרוּשָׁלִַם חוּצוֹת[c] יְרוּשָׁלִָם

CAPUT XVIII.

1 אֶל־יִרְמְיָהוּ מֵאֵת יְהוָה	מֵאֵת יְהוָה אֶל־יִרְמְיָהוּ
2 אַשְׁמִיעֲךָ אֶת־דְּבָרִי	תִּשְׁמַע אֶת־דְּבָרַי
3 עַל־הָאָבְנָיִם	עַל־הָאֲבָנִים
4 בַּחֹמֶר בְּיַד הַיּוֹצֵר כַּאֲשֶׁר יָשָׁר בְּעֵינֵי הַיּוֹצֵר	בְּיָדָיו כַּאֲשֶׁר יָשָׁר בְּעֵינָיו
6 הֲכַיּוֹצֵר הַזֶּה כַּחֹמֶר בְּיַד הַיּוֹצֵר כֵּן אַתֶּם בְּיָדִי בֵּית יִשְׂרָאֵל	Deest כַּחֹמֶר הַיּוֹצֵר אַתֶּם בְּיָדִי
7 וְעַל־מַמְלָכָה לִנְתוֹשׁ וְלִנְתוֹץ	אוֹ עַל־מַמְלָכָה לְנָתְשָׁם
8 מֵרָעָתוֹ אֲשֶׁר דִּבַּרְתִּי עָלָיו אֲשֶׁר חָשַׁבְתִּי לַעֲשׂוֹת לוֹ	מֵעַל־רָעוֹתֵיהֶם אֲשֶׁר חָשַׁבְתִּי לַעֲשׂוֹת לָהֶם

---

[a] Targ. עֲלָוָן. [b] Targ. לְבֵית. [c] ἄμφοδα.

9 וְעַל־מַמְלָכָה לִבְנוֹת וְלִנְטוֹעַ וּמַמְלָכָה לְהַבְנוֹת וּלְהִנָּטֵעַ
10 וְעָשָׂה הָרָעָה בְּעֵינַי וְעָשׂוּ הָרָעָה לְפָנַי[a]
   לְהֵיטִיב אוֹתוֹ לַעֲשׂוֹת לָהֶם
11 אֱמָר־נָא אֶל־אִישׁ יְהוּדָה וְעַל־ אֱמֹר אֶל־אַנְשֵׁי יְהוּדָה וְאֶל־יוֹשְׁבֵי
   יוֹשְׁבֵי יְרוּשָׁלִַם יְרוּשָׁלִַם
   לֵאמֹר כֹּה אָמַר יְהֹוָה Deest
   שׁוּבוּ נָא יָשׁוּב נָא
   וְהֵיטִיבוּ דַרְכֵיכֶם וּמַעַלְלֵיכֶם וְהֵיטִיבוּ מַעַלְלֵיכֶם
12 וְאָמְרוּ נוֹאָשׁ וַיֹּאמְרוּ נִתְאוֹשַׁשׁ
   מַחְשְׁבוֹתֵינוּ מַחְשְׁבוֹתֵינוּ
   שְׁרִרוּת תַּאֲוַת[b]
14 הֲיַעֲזֹב מִצּוּר שָׂדַי שֶׁלֶג לְבָנוֹן הֲיֹעָזְבוּ מִצּוּר שָׂדִים אַם־שַׁלְגּ (וְשֶׁלֶג)
   אִם־יִנָּתְשׁוּ מַיִם זָרִים קָרִים מִלְּבָנוֹן אִם־יִנָּשְׁפוּ מַיִם זָרִים קָדִים
   נוֹזְלִים נוֹזְלִים
15 וַיִּכָּשְׁלוּם וְיִכָּשְׁלוּ
   דֶּרֶךְ לֹא סְלוּלָה אֵין לָהֶם דֶּרֶךְ לַעֲבֹר
16 שְׁרֵקוֹת עוֹלָם וּשְׁרוֹקַת עוֹלָם
   כֹּל עוֹבֵר עָלֶיהָ וְיָנִיד יִשֹּׁם וְיָנִיד כָּל הָעוֹבְרִים עָלֶיהָ יִשֹּׁמּוּ וְיָנִידוּ
   בְּרֹאשׁוֹ בְּרֹאשָׁם
17 אֲפִיצֵם לִפְנֵי אוֹיֵב עֹרֶף וְלֹא־פָנִים אֲפִיצָם לִפְנֵי אוֹיְבֵיהֶם[d] אֶרְאֵם יוֹם
   אֶרְאֵם בְּיוֹם אֵידָם אָבְדָם
18 מַחְשָׁבוֹת מַחֲשָׁבָה
   וּנַכֵּהוּ בַלָּשׁוֹן וְאַל־נַקְשִׁיבָה אֶל־ וּנַכֵּהוּ בִּלְשׁוֹן וְנַקְשִׁיבָה אֶל־כָּל־
   כָּל־דְּבָרָיו דְּבָרָיו
19 הַקְשִׁיבָה יְהֹוָה אֵלַי וּשְׁמַע לְקוֹל הַקְשִׁיבָה אֵלַי יְהֹוָה וּשְׁמַע לְקוֹל
   יְרִיבַי רִיבִי[c]
20 כִּי־כָרוּ שׁוּחָה לְנַפְשִׁי כִּי־קָרְאוּ (הַדְּבָרִים) שִׂיחָה לְנַפְשִׁי
      וּמִכְשׁוֹלָם טָמְנוּ לִי
21 וְהַגְּרֵם עַל־יְדֵי־חֶרֶב וְתִהְיֶינָה וְתַגְּרֵם (וְהַאֲסֹף) עַל־יְדֵי־חֶרֶב
   נְשֵׁיהֶם תִּהְיֶינָה נְשֵׁיהֶם
   בַּחוּרֵיהֶם מֻכֵּי־חֶרֶב וּבַחוּרִים נְפָלֵי־חֶרֶב

---

[a] Targ. דְּרָכַי. [b] Targ. וּלְיִצְרֵי. [c] τὰ ἀρεστά. [d] Targ. דְּבָבֵיהוֹן. בְּצֶלֶם דְּבָבֵיהוֹן.
[e] at 20:12.—Targ. עוּלְבָּנִי.

22 תִּשָּׁמַע זְעָקָה מִבָּתֵּיהֶם כִּי־תָבִיא תָּהִי זְעָקָה בְּבָתֵּיהֶם תָּבִיא עֲלֵיהֶם
עֲלֵיהֶם גְּדוּד גְּדוּדִים[a] (שׂוֹדְדִים)
כִּי כָרוּ שׁוּחָה לְלָכְדֵנִי כִּי עָרְכוּ[b] (כרו) שִׁיחָה לְלָכְדֵנִי
טָמְנוּ לְרַגְלָי טָמְנוּ לִי
23 עֲוֹנָם וְחַטָּאתָם עֲוֹנוֹתֵיהֶם וְחַטֹּאותֵיהֶם[c]
וְ֯הָיוּ מֻכְשָׁלִים לְפָנֶיךָ יְהִי מִכְשֹׁלָם לְפָנֶיךָ

CAPUT XIX.

1 כֹּה אָמַר יהוה אָז אָמַר יהוה אֵלָ֯י[d]
יוֹצֵר חֶרֶשׂ וּמִזִּקְנֵי הָעָם וּמִזִּקְנֵי יוֹצֵר חֶרֶשׂ וְלָקַחְתָּ (וַהֲבֵאתָ) מִזִּקְנֵי
הַכֹּהֲנִים הָעָם וּמִן־הַכֹּהֲנִים
2 בֶּן־הִנֹּם בְּנֵי בְנֵיהֶם (בְּנֵי נִינָם)
שַׁעַר הַחַרְסוּת שַׁעַר הַחַרְסִית[f]
אֶת־הַדְּבָרִים אֶת־כָּל־הַדְּבָרִים הָאֵלֶּה
3 וְאָמַרְתָּ שִׁמְעוּ דְבַר־יהוה וְאָמַרְתָּ אֲלֵיהֶם שִׁמְעוּ דִּבְרֵי־יהוה
מַלְכֵי יְהוּדָה וְיֹשְׁבֵי מַלְכֵי יְהוּדָה וְאַנְשֵׁי יְהוּדָה
יְרוּשָׁלַ͏ִם וְהַיֹּשְׁבִים בִּירוּשָׁלַ͏ִם וְהַבָּאִים
בַּשְּׁעָרִים הָאֵלֶּה[g]
יהוה צְבָאוֹת יהוה
הִנְנִי מֵבִיא רָעָה עַל־הַמָּקוֹם הַזֶּה הִנְנִי מֵבִיא עַל־הַמָּקוֹם הַזֶּה רָעָה
4 אֲשֶׁר לֹא־יְדָעוּם אֲשֶׁר לֹא־יְרָאוּ
וּמָלְאוּ אֶת־הַמָּקוֹם הַזֶּה מָלְאוּ אֶת־הַמָּקוֹם הַזֶּה
דַּם נְקִים דְּמֵי נְקִים
5 אֶת־בָּמוֹת הַבַּעַל בָּמוֹת לַבַּעַל
עֹלוֹת לַבָּעַל Deest
וְלֹא דִבַּרְתִּי וְלֹא עָלְתָה עַל־לִבִּי וְלֹא הָשַׁבְתִּי בְּלִבִּי
7 וּבַקֹּתִי אֶת־עֲצַת יְהוּדָה וּבְקַעְתִּי(?) אֶת־עֲצַת יְהוּדָה וַעֲצַת
וִירוּשָׁלָ͏ִם יְרוּשָׁלַ͏ִם
וּבְיָד מְבַקְשֵׁי נַפְשָׁם וְנָתַתִּי אֶת־ וּבִידֵי מְבַקְשֵׁי נַפְשִׁי וְנָתַתִּי אֶת־

---

[a] Targ. בָּזִיזִין. [b] ἐνεχείρησαν. [c] Vid. 16:18; 31:34; 36:3—Targ. חוֹבֵיהוֹן וְחַטָּאֵיהוֹן. [d] Targ. אֲמַר יְיָ לִי. [e] Targ. יְדַבֵּר. [f] τῆς χαρσίθ.
[g] ut 7:2; 17:20; 22:2.

נבלתם למאכל לעופות השמים	נִבְלָתָם לְמַאֲכָל לְעוֹף הַשָּׁמַיִם
ולבהמת הארץ	וּלְבֶהֱמַת הָאָרֶץ
על־כל־מפתחה	עַל־כָּל־מִפְתָּחָה 8
ואכלו	וְהַאֲכַלְתִּים 9
במצור ובמצוק	בְּמָצוֹר וּבְמָצוֹק
Deest	וּמְבַקְשֵׁי נַפְשָׁם
ואמרת	וְאָמַרְתָּ אֲלֵיהֶם 11
יהוה	יהוה צְבָאוֹת
כאשר ישבר כלי־חרט	כַּאֲשֶׁר יִשְׁבֹּר אֶת־כְּלִי הַיּוֹצֵר
Deest	וּבְתֹפֶת יִקְבְּרוּ מֵאֵין מָקוֹם לִקְבּוֹר
כן־אעשה נאם־יהוה למקום הזה	כֵּן־אֶעֱשֶׂה לַמָּקוֹם הַזֶּה נְאֻם־ 12
ולישבים בו לתת את־העיר	יהוה וּלְיוֹשְׁבָיו וְלָתֵת אֶת־
הזאת כתפת	הָעִיר הַזֹּאת כְּתֹפֶת
מלכי ובתי ירושלם בתי	וְהָיוּ בָּתֵּי יְרוּשָׁלִַם וּבָתֵּי מַלְכֵי 13
התפת כמקום יהיו יהודה	יְהוּדָה כִּמְקוֹם הַתֹּפֶת
אשר הבתים בכל מטמאותיהם	הַטְּמֵאִים לְכֹל הַבָּתִּים אֲשֶׁר
קטרו בהם	קִטְּרוּ
וַיַּסִּיכוּ (וַיִּסְּכוּ) נסכיםa	וְהַסֵּךְ נְסָכִים
	יהוה צְבָאוֹת אֱלֹהֵי יִשְׂרָאֵל 15
על־העירb הזאת ועל־כל־	אֶל־הָעִיר הַזֹּאת וְעַל־כָּל־
עָרֶיהָ (שְׂדוֹתֶיהָ, מִגְרָשֶׁיהָ)	עָרֶיהָ
לבלתי שמוע אל־מצותי (?)	לְבִלְתִּי שְׁמוֹעַ אֶת־דְּבָרָי

CAPUT XX.

והוא היה פקיד נגיד בית יהוה	וְהוּא־פָקִיד נָגִיד בְּבֵית יהוה 1
ויכה פשחור את ירמיהו הנביא	וַיִּשְׁלַח אֹתוֹ אֶל־הַמַּהְפֶּכֶתc 2
אשר היתה בשער הבית העליון	וַיִּתֵּן אֹתוֹ עַל־הַמַּהְפֶּכֶת אֲשֶׁר
לבית העליון (בנין מטה?)	בְּשַׁעַר בִּנְיָמִן הָעֶלְיוֹן
Deest	וַיְהִי מִמָּחֳרָת 3
קרא	קָרָא יהוה
כי אם־מגור	כִּי אִם־מָגוֹר מִסָּבִיב

---

a Targ. יִנְסְכוּן נִדְבָּךְ. b Targ. עַל קַרְתָּא. c Targ. לְבֵי פָתָא.

[20:4-12] THE CONSPECTUS OF THE VARIATIONS.

לָכֵן אָמַר	4 כִּי־כֹה אָמַר
לְמָגוֹר עִם־כָּל־אֹהֲבֶיךָ	לְמָגוֹר לָךְ וּלְכָל־אֹהֲבֶיךָ
וְאוֹתְךָ וְאֶת־כָּל־יְהוּדָה אֶתֵּן בִּידֵי	וְאֶת־כָּל־יְהוּדָה אֶתֵּן בְּיַד־ מֶלֶךְ־
מֶלֶךְ־בָּבֶל וְהִגְלָם וְהִכָּם בַּחֲרָבוֹת	בָּבֶל וְהִגְלָם בָּבֶלָה וְהִכָּם בֶּחָרֶב
וְאֶת־כָּל־יְגִיעָהּ וְאֵת כָּל־אוֹצְרוֹת	5 וְאֶת־כָּל־יְגִיעָהּ וְאֶת־כָּל־יְקָרָהּ
מֶלֶךְ יְהוּדָה בִּידֵי אֹיְבָיו וְהֵבִיאוּם	וְאֵת כָּל־אוֹצְרוֹת מַלְכֵי־יְהוּדָה
בָּבֶלָה	אֶתֵּן בְּיַד אֹיְבֵיהֶם וּבְזָזוּם
	וּלְקָחוּם וֶהֱבִיאוּם בָּבֶלָה
וְאַתָּה וְכָל הַיֹּשְׁבִים בְּבֵיתֶךָ	6 וְאַתָּה פַּשְׁחוּר וְכָל יֹשְׁבֵי בֵיתֶךָ
וּבְבָבֶל תָּמוּת	וּבָבֶל תָּבוֹא וְשָׁם תָּמוּת
שְׁקָרִים	בַּשֶּׁקֶר
חֲזַקְתָּ וַתּוּכַל	7 חִזַּקְתַּנִי וָאוּכָל
כָּל־הַיּוֹם כֻּלֹּה (הָ)נִלְעָג‎	כָּל־הַיּוֹם כֻּלֹּה לַעַג לִי
כִּי־בְמָרֵי הַדָּבָר (בְּמָרֵי דְבָרַי)	8 כִּי־מִדֵּי אֲדַבֵּר אֶזְעָק
אֶצְחָק (אֶשְׂחָק)	
לְחֶרְפָּה לִי	לִי לְחֶרְפָּה
כָּל־יוֹמַי	כָּל־הַיּוֹם
לֹא־אֶזְכֹּר שֵׁם יְהֹוָה וְלֹא־אֲדַבֵּר עוֹד	9 לֹא־אֶזְכְּרֶנּוּ וְלֹא־אֲדַבֵּר עוֹד בִּשְׁמוֹ
עַל־שְׁמוֹ וְהָיָה כְּאֵשׁ בַּעֲרַת יָקוֹד	וְהָיָה בְלִבִּי כְּאֵשׁ בֹּעֶרֶת עָצֻר
בַּעֲצָמַי וְנִלְאֵיתִי כָּלִיל (כַּל כֹּל)	בַּעֲצְמֹתַי וְנִלְאֵיתִי כַּלְכֵל וְלֹא
וְלֹא אוּכַל נְשׂוֹא (שְׂאֵת)	אוּכָל
מְגוּרִים מִסָּבִיב‎ גּוּדוּ וְנַגִּידֶנּוּ	10 מָגוֹר מִסָּבִיב הַגִּידוּ וְנַגִּידֶנּוּ
(גֹּדוּ וְנַגִּידָה עָלָיו?) כָּל אַנְשֵׁי	כֹּל אֱנוֹשׁ שְׁלוֹמִי שֹׁמְרֵי
(שְׁלֹמוֹ) מֵרֵעָיו שָׁמְרוּ עֶצְתוֹ	צַלְעִי
(מַחֲשַׁבְתּוֹ)	
רֹדְפַי וְהִשָּׁכֵל לֹא יָכֹלוּ	11 רֹדְפַי יִכָּשְׁלוּ וְלֹא יָכֹלוּ
כִּי־לֹא יָדְעוּ כְּלִמּוֹתֵיהֶם עוֹלָם לֹא	כִּי־לֹא הִשְׂכִּילוּ כְּלִמַּת עוֹלָם לֹא
תִּשָּׁכַחְנָה	תִשָּׁכֵחַ
וַיהֹוָה צְבָאוֹת בֹּחֵן צֶדֶק (צְדָקוֹת) רֹאֶה	12 וַיהֹוָה צְבָאוֹת בֹּחֵן צַדִּיק רֹאֶה
כְּלָיוֹת וּלְבָבוֹת אֶרְאֶה נִקְמָתְךָ	כְלָיוֹת וָלֵב אֶרְאֶה נִקְמָתְךָ
בָּהֶם	מֵהֶם
אֶת־רִיבַי (רִיבוֹתַי)	אֶת־רִיבִי

---

[a] μυκτηριζόμενος.   [b] Targ. כְּהָבַּנְשִׁין נְסָחוֹר סָתוֹר.

X

13 הַלְלוּ אֶת־יְהוָה	הַלְלוּהוּ (הַלְלוּ אוֹתוֹ)
15 אֲשֶׁר בִּשַּׂר אֶת־אָבִי לֵאמֹר יֻלַּד־לְךָ בֵּן זָכָר שַׂמֵּחַ שִׂמֳּחָהוּ:	הַמְבַשֵּׂר אֶת־אָבִי לֵאמֹר יֻלַּד־לְךָ זָכָר שָׂמֵחַ:
16 וְהָיָה הָאִישׁ	יִהְיֶה[a] הָאִישׁ
אֲשֶׁר־הָפַךְ יְהוָה	אֲשֶׁר־הָפַךְ יְהוָה בְּאַף[b]
וְשָׁמַע זְעָקָה	יִשְׁמַע[c] זְעָקָה
בְּעֵת צָהֳרָיִם	בַּצָּהֳרַיִם
17 אֲשֶׁר לֹא־מוֹתְתַנִי מֵרָחֶם וַתְּהִי־לִי אִמִּי קִבְרִי וְרַחְמָה הָרַת עוֹלָם	אֲשֶׁר לַאֲמוֹתְתַנִי בָּרֶחֶם וַתְּהִי־לִי רַחְמֵי קִבְרִי וְהָרְחֵם הָרַת עוֹלָם
18 לָמָּה זֶּה מֵרֶחֶם יָצָאתִי	לָמָה זֶה יָצָאתִי מֵרֶחֶם

CAPUT XXI.

1 אֶל־יִרְמְיָהוּ מֵאֵת יְהוָה מַעֲשֵׂיָה	מֵאֵת יְהוָה אֶל־יִרְמְיָהוּ בְּעַשָׂיָה[d]
2 דְּרָשׁ־נָא בַעֲדֵנוּ אֶת־יְהוָה כִּי נְבוּכַדְרֶאצַּר מֶלֶךְ־בָּבֶל נִלְחָם עָלֵינוּ	דְּרֹשׁ בַּעֲדֵנוּ אֶת־יְהוָה כִּי מֶלֶךְ־בָּבֶל קָם עָלֵינוּ
אוֹתָנוּ	Deest
3 וַיֹּאמֶר יִרְמְיָהוּ אֲלֵיהֶם אֶל־צִדְקִיָּהוּ	וַיֹּאמֶר אֲלֵיהֶם יִרְמִיָּהוּ אֶל־צִדְקִיָּהוּ מֶלֶךְ יְהוּדָה
4 כֹּה־אָמַר יְהוָה אֱלֹהֵי יִשְׂרָאֵל	כֹּה־אָמַר יְהוָה
אֲשֶׁר בְּיֶדְכֶם	Deest
אֶת־מֶלֶךְ בָּבֶל וְאֶת־הַכַּשְׂדִּים	אֶת־הַכַּשְׂדִּים
5 וּבְאַף וּבְחֵמָה וּבְקֶצֶף גָּדוֹל	בְּאַף וּבְחֵמָה גְדוֹלָה
6 יוֹשְׁבֵי הָעִיר הַזֹּאת וְאֶת־הָאָדָם וְאֶת־הַבְּהֵמָה בְּדֶבֶר גָּדוֹל יָמֻתוּ	כָּל־הַיּוֹשְׁבִים בָּעִיר הַזֹּאת אֶת־הָאֲנָשִׁים וְאֶת־הַבְּהֵמוֹת בְּדֶבֶר גָּדוֹל יָמֻתוּ (וְיָמֻתוּ)
7 נְאֻם־יְהוָה	כֹּה־אָמַר יְהוָה
וְאֶת־הַנִּשְׁאָרִים בָּעִיר הַזֹּאת מִן־הַדֶּבֶר מִן־הַחֶרֶב וּמִן־הָרָעָב	הַנִּשְׁאָרִים בָּעִיר הַזֹּאת מִן־הַדֶּבֶר וּמִן־הֶחָרֶב וּמִן־הָהָרָב[e]

[a] Inc. vs. 16. [b] Cf. Deut. 29:22.—Targ. הֲפָכָהּ רָגֶז בְּרוּגְזֵהּ. [c] Targ. וְכֵן חַרְבָּא.
[d] ut I. Chron. 6:25. [e] Targ. יְשֵׁיצֵי.

[21:8-22:4] THE CONSPECTUS OF THE VARIATIONS. 323

Deest	בְּיַד נְבוּכַדְרֶאצַּר מֶלֶךְ־בָּבֶל
בִּידֵי איביהם מבקשׁי נפשׁוֹתֵיהֶם	וּבְיַד איביהם וּבְיַד מבקשׁי נפשׁם
והכם לפי־חרב לא־אחוס עליהם	והכם לפי־חרב לא־יחוס
ולא אֲרַחֲמֵםᵃ	עליהם ולא יחמל ולא ירחם
8 ואל־העם הזה	ואל־העם הזה
הנני נָתַתִּי	הנני נֹתֵן
9 וּבַדֶּבֶר	Deest
נָפֹל על־הכשׂדים	וְנָפַל על־הכשׂדים
יִחְיֶה והיתה נפשׁוֹᵇ לשׁלל וְהָיָה	חָיָה והיתה־לּוֹ נפשׁו לשׁלל
כי־שׂמתי פני על־הָעִיר הזאת	10 כי־שׂמתי פני בָּעיר הזאת
בִּידֵי מלך־בבל	נְאֻם־יְהוָה בְּיַד מלך־בבל
11 בית מלך יהודה	וּלְבית מלך יהודה
12 וְאַשֵּׁרוּ והצילו גזול מיד עָשְׁקוֹᶜ	והצילו גזול מיד עֹשֵׁק פֶּן־
פֶּן־תֵּצֵאᵈ כאשׁ	תֵּצֵא כאשׁ
Deest	מִפְּנֵי רֹעַ מַעַלְלֵיהֶם
13 צוּרᵉ המישׁר	צוּר המישׁר
Deest	נְאֻם־יְהוָה
ומי יבוא במעונוֹתֵינוּ	ומי יבוא במעונוֹתֵינוּ
Desunt {	14 וּפָקַדְתִּי עליכם כִּפְרִי מַעַלְלֵיכֶם נְאֻם־יְהוָה

CAPUT XXII.

1 רד	לֵךְ וָרַדᵉ
2 וַעֲבָדֶיךָ ועמך הבאים	וּבֵיתְךָ ועמך וְהַבָּאִים
3 מיד עָשׁוֹק	מיד עֹשְׁקוֹᵍ
יתום	ויתום
4 ישׁבים לדוד על־כסאוֹ רכבים	ישׁבים על־כסֵּא דודʰ ורכבים על־
בָּרֶכֶב ובסוסים הוא וַעֲבָדוֹ	מַרְכָּבוֹתⁱ ובסוסים הֵמָּה
וְעַמוֹ	וְעֲבָדֵיהֶם ועם

ᵃ Cf. 13:14.   ᵇ Vid. 38:2; 39:17.   ᶜ Vid. 22:3.—Targ. לְ״ה הָאָנֵס.
ᵈ Targ. הִלָּבָא יְדָלֵק.   ᵉ Σόρ.   ᶠ ut Exod. 19:24; 32:7.   ᵍ Vid. 21:12.—
Targ. לְ״ה הָאָנֵס.   ʰ ut vs. 2; 17:25.   ⁱ Targ. בִּרְכִּדִין.

[22:5-18]

ואם לא תעשׂו	5 ואם לא תשמעו
לא נושבה	6 לא נושבה
והבאתי (וּפְקַדְתִּי) עליך משחית איש וכליו (רְכֵילְפּוֹ)	7 וקדשתי עליך משחתים איש וכליו
אל־האשׁ[a]	על־האש
(בָּעִיר) ועברו גוים בתוך העיר רבים גוים	8 ועברו גוים רבים על־העיר
הזאת ואמר	הזאת ואמרו
לעיר הזאת הגדולה	לעיר הגדולה הזאת
ואל־תִּקוֹנְנוּ לו	10 ואל־תנדו לו
על־שלם[b]	אל־שלם
Deest	11 מלך יהודה
כי אם־בַּמקום הַזֶּה אשר־הגליתי	12 כי במקום אשר־הגלו
הוי בנה ביתו בלא־צדק ועליותיו לא במשפט	13 הוי בנה ביתו בלא־צדק ועליותיו בלא משפט
בנית לך	14 האמר אבנה־לי
עליות	ועליות
וקרע לו חלוני וספונים בארז ומשוחים בששר	קרעים חלוני וספונים בארז ומשוֹח בששר
כי אתה מתחרה בָּאָחָז[c] אביד	15 כי אתה מתחרה בארז אביד
לא יאכלו ולא יִשתוּ לך	הלוא אכל ושתה ועשה משפט
עשׂה משפט וצדקה	וצדקה אז טוב לו
לא ידעו לא דן די עני ולא־אדין אביון	16 הן דין־עני ואביון
Deest	אז טוב
הלא־ידעתך אתי	הלא־היא הדעת אתי
הִנֵּה אין עיניך וְאין לבד כי טוב כי אם־אל־בצעך ואל־דם־הנקי לשפט ואל־מעשקות ואל־רצח[f] לעשותם	17 כי אין עיניך ולבך כי אם־על־בצעך ועל־דם־הנקי לשפוך ועל־העשק ועל־המרוצה לעשות
על[g]־יהויקים	18 אל־יהויקים
מלך יהודה ועל־האישׁ הזה	מלך יהודה
הוי אחי והוי אחות הוי אה ולא־יספדו לו אוי לי אדון	הוי אחי והוי אחות לא־יספדו לו הוי אדון והוי הדה

[a] Targ. לִוְיָא. [b] Targ. עַל שָׁלְוִם. [c] Targ. אֱלָהֵן. [d] Targ. הַבְנֵי.
[e] Targ. בְּבַלְדָּא קַדְמָאָה. [f] εἰς ἐμφανῆ. [g] Targ. עַל.

22:19-30] THE CONSPECTUS OF THE VARIATIONS. 325

קבורת חמור יקבר סחוב וְהַשְׁלֵךְ מהלאה לשער ירושלם	19 קבורת חמור יקבר סחוב והשלך מהלאה לשַׁעֲרֵי ירושלם
עלי אֶל־הלבנון וּצעקי וְאֶל־הַבָּשָׁן תני קולך	20 עלי הלבנון וצעקי וּבבשן תני קולך
מֵעֲבָרִים (לְעֶבֶר־הַיָּם)	מֵעֲבָרִים
דברתי אליך בְּשָׁלוֹתֵךְ וְאמרת לא־שמעת	21 דברתי אליך בשלותיך אמרת כי לא־שמעת
בשבי יצאו	22 בשבי ילכו
מכל רֵעֲתָיִךְ (רֵעַיִךְ)	מכל רָעָתֵךְ
נֶאֱנַחְתְּ (תֵּאָנְחִי)	23 מַה־נֶּחֱנְתִּי
חבלים כיולדה	חבלים חיל כיולדה
אבי־הֹלָה יהיה וכניהו	24 כי אם־יהיה כניהו
משה אתקנ־ך	כי משם אתקך
ונתתיך בידי מבקשי נפשך אשר אתה יגור מפניהם Deest בידי הכשדים	25 ונתתיך בְּיַד מבקשי נפשך וּבְיַד אשר אתה יגור מפניהם וּבְיַד נבכדראצר מלך־בבל וּבְיַד הכשדים
אֶל־אָרֶץ[a] אשר לא־ילדת שם	26 על הארץ אחרת אשר לא־ ילדתם שם
וְאֶל־הארץ[b] לבל ישובו	27 וְעַל־הארץ לשוב שם שמה לא ישובו
נבזה יכניהו ככלי[c] אין חפץ בו כי הוטל והשלך אל־ארץ אשר לא־ידע	28 הַעֶצֶב נבזה נפוץ האיש הזה כניהו אם־כלי אין חפץ בו מדוע הוטלו הוא וזרעו והשלכו על־הארץ אשר לא־ ידעו
ארץ ארץ	29 ארץ ארץ ארץ
כתב	30 כה אמר יהוה כתבו
Deest	לא־יצלח בימיו
כי לא יצמח מזרעו מושל	לא יצלח מזרעו איש ומושל

[a] Targ. לְאַרְעָא. [b] Targ. וּלְאַרְעָא. [c] Targ. כְּמָנָא.

CAPUT XXIII.

1 מאבדים ומפצים את־צאן המאבדים וְהַמְפִצִים᪼ אֶת־צֹאן	
מַרְעִיתִי נְאֻם־יְהוָֹה	מַרְעִיתָם᪽
2 יהוה אֱלֹהֵי יִשְׂרָאֵל	יהוה
עַל־הָרֹעִים הָרֹעִים אֶת־עַמִּי	עַל־הרעים את־עמי
אַתְּדַע מַעַלְלֵיכֶם נְאֻם־יְהוָה	כְּרֹעַ מעלליכם
3 אֶת־שְׁאֵרִית צֹאנִי	אֶת־שְׁאֵרִית עַמִּי᪼
מִכֹּל הָאֲרָצוֹת	עַל־כָּל־הָאָרֶץ
עַל־נְוֵיהֶן	אֶל־נְוֵיהֶן᪻
4 והקמתי עליהם רעים ורעום והקמתי להם רעים אשר ירעום	
וְלֹא יִפָּקֵדוּ	Deest
6 הוֹשַׁע יהודה	וְתוֹשַׁע יהודה
צִדְקֵנוּ	יְהֹוָה צִדְקֵךְ
7 אֶת־בְּנֵי יִשְׂרָאֵל	אֶת־בֵּית יִשְׂרָאֵל
8 אֲשֶׁר הֶעֱלָה וַאֲשֶׁר הֵבִיא אֶת־ אשר העלה אשר קבץ כל־זרע ישראל	
זֶרַע בֵּית יִשְׂרָאֵל	
אֲשֶׁר הִדַּחְתִּים שָׁם וְיָשְׁבוּ עַל־ אֲשֶׁר הִדִּיחָם שָׁם וְהֵשִׁיבָם אֶל־	
אַדְמָתָם	אדמתם
9 לַנְּבִאִים	בַּנְּבִיאִים
כְּאִישׁ שָׁבוּר וּכְגֶבֶר עָבְרוֹ יָיִן כאיש שבור וכגבר עצור (עכור?) יין	
וּמִפְּנֵי דִבְרֵי קָדְשׁוֹ	וּמִפְּנֵי הֲדַר כְּבוֹדוֹ
10 כִּי מְנָאֲפִים מָלְאָה הָאָרֶץ	Deest
כִּי־מִפְּנֵי אָלָה	כי־מפני אלה
נְאוֹת מִדְבָּר	נאות המדבר
וּגְבוּרָתָם לֹא־כֵן	וגבורתם כן
11 כִּי־גַם־נָבִיא גַם־כֹּהֵן	כי־כהן ונביא
מָצָאתִי רָעָתָם נְאֻם־יְהוָה	רָאִיתִי רֹעוֹתֵיהֶם᪼ (רעתם)
12 כַּחֲלַקְלַקּוֹת	לַחֲלַקְלַקּוֹת
יִדַּחוּ	וְיִדַּחוּ
שְׁנַת פְּקֻדָּתָם נְאֻם־יְהוָה	בִּשְׁנַת᪾ פְּקֻדָּתָם

---

a Targ. הְקָאָבְדִין וּמְבַדְּרִין. b ut 10:21. c Targ. יַת שְׁאָרָא דְעַמִּי. d Targ. לְאַתְרְיהוֹן. e συνέλευσις. f Targ. עָלַן קֳדָמַי בִּישָׁתְהוֹן. g Vid. 11:23; 48:44.

[23:14-26] THE CONSPECTUS OF THE VARIATIONS. 327

14	נָאֹ֑ף וְהָלֹ֣ךְ בַּשֶּׁ֔קֶר וְחִזְּק֖וּ מְנַאֲפִ֑ים וְהֹלְכִ֤ים בַּשֶּׁ֙קֶר֙ וּמְחַזְּקִ֔ים	
	יְדֵ֣י מְרֵעִ֔ים לְבִלְתִּי־שָׁ֖בוּ אִ֣ישׁ	יְדֵ֣י רָעִ֔ים לְבִלְתִּי־שׁ֥וּב אִ֖ישׁ
	מֵרָעָת֑וֹ	מִדַּרְכּ֖וֹ הָרָעָ֑ה
15	יְהוָ֤ה צְבָאוֹת֙ עַל־הַנְּבִאִ֔ים	יְהוָ֑ה
	לָכֵ֗ן	עָנִ֖יb
	לְכָל־הָאָֽרֶץ	בְּכָל־הָאָֽרֶץ
16	אַל־תִּשְׁמְע֞וּ עַל־דִּבְרֵ֣י הַנְּבִאִ֗ים	אַל־תִּשְׁמְע֥וּ לְדִבְרֵיc הַנְּבִאִ֖ים
	הַנִּבְּאִ֤ים לָכֶם֙	Deest
	מַהְבִּלִ֥ים הֵ֖מָּה אֶתְכֶ֑ם חֲז֤וֹן לִבָּם֙ יְדַבֵּ֔רוּ	כִּ֤י מַהְבִּלִים֙ לָהֶ֣ם הָזֹ֔ון מִלִּבָּ֖ם יְדַבֵּ֑רוּ
	לֹ֖א מִפִּ֥י יְהוָֽה	וְלֹ֖א מִפִּ֥י יְהוָֽה
17	אֹמְרִ֤ים אָמוֹר֙ לִֽמְנַאֲצַ֔י דִּבֶּ֖ר יְהוָ֑ה	אֹמְרִיםd לִמְנַאֲצַ֖י דְּבַ֣ר יְהוָ֑ה
	וְכֹ֞ל הֹלֵ֗ךְ בִּשְׁרִר֣וּת לִבּ֔וֹ	וּלְכֹ֤ל הַהֹלְכִים֙ בְּחַפְצֵיהֶ֔ם וּלְכֹ֤ל הֹלֵ֗ךְ
		בִּתְאֹ֥ות לִבּ֖וֹ
	לֹֽא־תָב֥וֹא עֲלֵיכֶֽם	לֹֽא־תָב֥וֹא עָלֶֽיךָ
18	וְיֵ֥רֶא וְיִשְׁמַ֖ע אֶת־דְּבָר֑וֹ מִֽי־	וַיַּ֥רְא אֶת־דְּבָר֑וֹ מִֽי־הִקְשִׁ֖יב
	הִקְשִׁ֥יב דְּבָרִ֖י וַיִּשְׁמָֽע	וַיִּשְׁמָֽע
19	סַעֲרַ֤ת יְהוָה֙ חֵמָ֣ה יָצְאָ֔ה וְסַ֖עַר	סְעָרָ֞ה מֵאֵ֤ת יְהוָה֙e וְחֵמָ֣ה
	מִתְחוֹלֵ֔ל עַל־רֹ֥אשׁ רְשָׁעִ֖ים	יָצְאָ֔ה וּלְסַ֣עַר מִתְחוֹלֵ֔ל עַל־הָרְשָׁעִ֖ים
	יָחֽוּל	יָבֽוֹא
20	לֹ֤א יָשׁוּב֙	וְלֹ֤א ע֤וֹד יָשׁוּב֙ (יָשׁ֥וּב עֽוֹד)
	מְזִמּ֣וֹת לִבּ֑וֹ	מְזִמַּת֖f לִבּ֑וֹ
	תִּתְבּ֥וֹנְנוּ בָ֖הּ בִּינָֽה	יִתְבּ֥וֹנְנוּ בָֽהּ
22	וַיַּשְׁמִ֤יעוּ דְבָרַי֙ אֶת־עַמִּ֔י וִישִׁבוּם֙	וְאִ֤ם יַשְׁמִ֙יעוּ֙ (וְשָׁמְעִי֙) דְּבָרַי֙ וְאֶת־עַמִּ֔י
	מִדַּרְכָּ֣ם הָרָ֔ע וּמֵרֹ֖עַ מַעַלְלֵיהֶֽם	וִישִׁבוּם֙ מֵרַ֖ע מַעַלְלֵיהֶֽם
23	הַאֱלֹהֵ֤י מִקָּרֹב֙ אָ֔נִי	אֱלֹהִ֖ים קָר֣וֹב אֲנִ֑יg
	וְלֹ֥א אֱלֹהֵ֖י מֵרָחֹֽק	וְלֹ֥א אֱלֹהִ֖ים מַרְחִֽיק
24	נְאֻם־יְהוָֽה	Deest
25	אֵ֤ת אֲשֶׁר־אָֽמְרוּ֙ הַנְּבִאִ֔ים הַֽנִּבְּאִ֥ים	אֵ֤ת אֲשֶׁ֙ר אֹֽמְרִים֙h הַנְּבִאִ֔ים אֲשֶׁר־נִבְּא֥וּ
	חֲלַ֥מְתִּי חָלָֽמְתִּי	חֲלַמְתִּ֖י חֲלוֹםi
26	עַד־מָתַ֖י הֲיֵ֑שׁ	עַד־מָתַ֥י יֵ֖שׁk (וְהָיָ֣ה)

a Targ. נָאֲצִ֑ין וּבְחוֹבִ֔ין בְּשִׁקְרָ֥א וּבִכְפִירְפִּ֖ין . . . בְּדִ֣יל דְּלָ֥א לְבֵיתַ֖ב. b Vid.
9:14. c Targ. לְפִתְגָּמֵ֑י. d Targ. אָמְרִ֑ין. e Targ. רְ֥וּחַ קֳדָ֣ם יְ֝הוָ֗ה. f Targ. בְּחֻשְׁבָּ֑הּ.
g Targ. יָ֣ת דָּאֳדָרִ֔ין. h Targ. אֲנָ֤א אֱלָהָא֙ בְּרִ֔יָא עַלָּמָ֤א בְּבָרְאשִׁ֑ית. i Targ.
עַ֣ד אֶרְכָּרִ֖י אִ֑ית. k Targ. בְּהַב־נְבוּאָ֣ה בְּחֶלְמָ֑א בְּחֶלְמָ֖א אֲהַוָיָּ֥א לִֽי.

נְבִאֵי הַשֶּׁקֶר וּנְבִאֵי תַּרְמִת נבאי שקר בְּנָבְאָםᵃ הַפַצֵּי (תַּרְמִתᵇ?)	
לבם	לבם
לְשַׁכֵּחַ אֶת־תּוֹרָתִי	לְהַשְׁבִּיחַ אֶת־עַמִּי שְׁמִי 27
אֲשֶׁר־אִתּוֹ הַחֲלוֹם יְסַפֵּר חֲלוֹמוֹ	אֲשֶׁר־אִתּוֹ חֲלוֹם יְסַפֵּר חֲלוֹם 28
יְסַפֵּר דְּבָרִי	יְדַבֵּר דְּבָרִי
Deest	נְאֻם־יְהֹוָה
כֹּה דְבָרַיᶜ נְאֻם־יְהֹוָה הֲלֹא הִנֵּה	הֲלוֹא כֹה דְבָרִי כָּאֵשׁ נְאֻם־ 29
דְּבָרַי כָּאֵשׁ נְאֻם־יְהֹוָה	יְהֹוָה
הִנְנִי עַל־הַנְּבִיאִים נְאֻם־אֲדֹנָי	לָכֵן הִנְנִי עַל־הַנְּבִיאִים נְאֻם־ 30
יְהֹוָה	יְהֹוָה
הִנְנִי אֶל־הַנְּבִיאִים הַשֹּׁלְחִים לְשׁוֹן	הִנְנִי עַל־הַנְּבִיאִים נְאָם־יְהֹוָה 31
נְבוּאָהᵈ (נְבוּאוֹת לָשׁוֹן) וְיִנְאֲמוּ נְיֻם	הַלֹּקְחִים לְשׁוֹנָם וַיִּנְאֲמוּ נְאֻם
לָכֵן הִנְנִי אֶל־הַנִּבָּאִים הַמְנַבְּאִים	הִנְנִי עַל־נִבְּאֵי חֲלֹמוֹת שֶׁקֶר 32
חֲלֹמוֹת שֶׁקֶר וְלֹא יְסַפְּרוּם	נְאֻם־יְהֹוָה וַיְסַפְּרוּם
Deest	נְאֻם־יְהֹוָה
וְכִי יִשְׁאָלוּ	וְכִי־יִשְׁאָלְךָ 33
אוֹ־הַכֹּהֵן אוֹ־נָבִיא	אוֹ־הַנָּבִיא אוֹ־כֹהֵן לֵאמֹר
אַתֶּםᵉ הַמַּשָּׂא	אֶת־מַה־מַשָּׂא
הַנָּבִיא וְהַכֹּהֲנִים	וְהַנָּבִיא וְהַכֹּהֵן 34
אֲשֶׁר יֹאמְרוּ	אֲשֶׁר יֹאמַר
וּפָקַדְתִּי אֶת־הָאִישׁ הַהִיא	וּפָקַדְתִּי עַל־הָאִישׁ הַהוּא וְעַל־
וּבֵיתוֹ	בֵּיתוֹ
אִישׁ אֶל־רֵעֵהוּᶠ	אִישׁ עַל־רֵעֵהוּ 35
הַמַּשָּׂא לָאִישׁ יִהְיֶה דְּבָרוֹ	הַמַּשָּׂא יְהֹוָה לְאִישׁ דְּבָרוֹ 36
Desunt {	וַהֲפַכְתֶּם אֶת־דִּבְרֵי אֱלֹהִים חַיִּים יְהֹוָה צְבָאוֹת אֱלֹהֵינוּ:
	כֹּה תֹאמַר אֶל־הַנָּבִיא מֶה־עָנָךְ 37
	יְהֹוָה
וְעַל־מָה דִּבֶּר יְהֹוָה אֱלֹהֵינוּ	וּמַה־דִּבֶּר יְהֹוָה
וְאִם־מַשָּׂא יְהֹוָה תֹּאמֵרוּ לָכֵן כֹּה אָמַר יְהֹוָה אֱלֹהֵינוּ	לָכֵן כֹּה אָמַר יְהֹוָה 38
	אָמַר יְהֹוָה

ᵃ Targ. דְּכִזְנַבָּן. ᵇ Vid. 14:14. ᶜ Targ. פִּתְגָּמַי. ᵈ Targ. דְּבִרְחָנַן.
ᵉ Raschi: איברים לבם כה הבשא, אתם לבשא להקב"ה וכו'. ᶠ Targ. גְבַר לְחַבְרֵיהּ.

[23:39-24:10] THE CONSPECTUS OF THE VARIATIONS. 329

39 הִנְנִי וְנָשִׁיתִי אֶתְכֶם נָשֹׁא וְנִטַּשְׁתִּי הִנְנִי נֹשֶׁא (לָקַח) וְנִטַּשְׁתִּי
                             Deest   מֵעַל־פָּנָי

CAPUT XXIV.

1 הִרְאַנִי יהוה וְהִנֵּה שְׁנֵי   הִרְאַנִי יהוה שְׁנֵי
   וְאֶת־שָׂרֵי יְהוּדָה וְאֶת־הֶחָרָשׁ   וְאֶת־שָׂרֶיהָ וְאֶת־הֶחָרָשִׁים וְאֶת־
   וְאֶת־הַמַּסְגֵּר   הַמַּסְגְּרִים[a] וְאֶת־הָעֲשִׁירִים
2 הַדּוּד אֶחָד   הַדּוּד הָאֶחָד
   וְהַדּוּד אֶחָד   וְהַדּוּד הָאַחֵר
   אֲשֶׁר לֹא־תֵאָכַלְנָה מֵרֹעַ   אֲשֶׁר לֹא־תֵאָכַלְנָה מֵרֹעָן
3 אֲשֶׁר לֹא־תֵאָכַלְנָה מֵרֹעַ   אֲשֶׁר לֹא־תֵאָכַלְנָה מֵרֹעָן
6 וְשַׂמְתִּי עֵינִי עֲלֵיהֶם   וְשַׂמְתִּי עֵינַי עֲלֵיהֶם
   עַל־הָאָרֶץ הַזֹּאת   אֶל־הָאָרֶץ[c] הַזֹּאת לְטוֹבָה
   וְלֹא אֶהֱרֹס   וְלֹא אֶהֶרְסֵם
7 לָדַעַת אֹתִי   לְדַעְתָּם אֹתִי
8 אֲשֶׁר לֹא־תֵאָכַלְנָה מֵרֹעַ כִּי־כֹה   אֲשֶׁר לֹא־תֵאָכַלְנָה מֵרֹעָן כֹּה אָמַר
   אָמַר יהוה   יהוה
   וְאֶת־שָׂרָיו   וְאֶת־גְּדוֹלָיו[c]
   בְּאֶרֶץ מִצְרַיִם   בְּמִצְרַיִם
9 וּנְתַתִּים לְזַוֲעָה לְרָעָה   וּנְתַתִּים לְזַוְעָה[d] (לְזִיעַ)
   לְחֶרְפָּה   וְיִהְיוּ לְחֶרְפָּה
   לִשְׁנִינָה   לְשָׂנֵאָה
   בְּכָל־הַמְּקֹמוֹת אֲשֶׁר־אַדִּיחֵם שָׁם   בְּכָל־הַמְּקוֹם אֲשֶׁר־הִדַּחְתִּים[e] שָׁם
10 אֶת־הַחֶרֶב אֶת־הָרָעָב וְאֶת־   אֶת־הָרָעָב וְאֶת־הַדֶּבֶר וְאֶת־
    הַדָּבֶר   הַחֶרֶב
   אֲשֶׁר־נָתַתִּי לָהֶם וְלַאֲבוֹתֵיהֶם   אֲשֶׁר־נָתַתִּי לָהֶם

---

[a] Targ. יָתֵי אִיצָנָא וְיָת תְּרָעַיָּא. [b] Targ. לְאַרְעָא. [c] Targ. רַבְרְבוֹהִי.
[d] Vid. 34:17. [e] ut 8:3.

CAPUT XXV.

אֶל־יִרְמְיָהוּ Desunt {	1 עַל־יִרְמְיָהוּ הִיא הַשָּׁנָה הָרִאשֹׁנִית לִנְבוּכַדְרֶאצַּר מֶלֶךְ בָּבֶל
אשר דבר ירמיהו הנביא על־כל־עם יהודה ואל־ישבי ירושלם	2 אֲשֶׁר דִּבֶּר יִרְמְיָהוּ הַנָּבִיא עַל כל־עם יהודה ואל כל־ישבי ירושלם
בשלש עשרה שנה בן־אמֹץ" (אמון) שלש ועשרים שנה Deest הַשְׁכִּים וְדַבֵּר	3 מִן־שְׁלֹשׁ עֶשְׂרֵה שָׁנָה בֶּן־אָמוֹן זֶה שָׁלֹשׁ וְעֶשְׂרִים שָׁנָה הָיָה דְבַר־יְהֹוָה אֵלַי אַשְׁכִּים וְדַבֵּר וְלֹא שְׁמַעְתֶּם
וָאֶשְׁלַח יְהֹוָה אֲלֵיכֶם אֶת־כָּל־עֲבָדָיו הַנְּבִיאִים ᵇ הנבאים השכם שלח ולא־הקשבתם באזניכם	4 וְשָׁלַח יְהֹוָה אֲלֵיכֶם אֶת־עֲבָדָיו הנבאים השכם ושלח ולא־הטיתם את־אזנכם לשמֹע
שבו איש מדרכו וְתֵשְׁבוּ עַל־הָאֲדָמָה נָתַתִּי לָכֶם	5 שׁוּבוּ־נָא אִישׁ מדרכו וּשְׁבוּ עַל־הָאֲדָמָה נתן יהוה לכם
אל־תלכו במעשי ידיכם להרע לכם Desunt {	6 וְאַל־תֵּלְכוּ במעשה ידיכם ולא ארע לכם 7 נְאֻם־יְהֹוָה לְמַעַן הַכְעִסֵנִי בְּמַעֲשֵׂה יְדֵיכֶם לְרַע לָכֶם
יהוה לא־האמנתם לדברי את־כל־משפחות צפון (משפחה מעפון) Deest כל־הגוים סביב לה וְלָחֳרָפַת עוֹלָם ᶜ	8 יהוה צבאות לא־שמעתם את־דברי 9 אֶת־כָּל־מִשְׁפְּחוֹת צפון נְאֻם־יְהֹוָה וְאֶל־נְבוּכַדְרֶאצַּר מֶלֶךְ־בָּבֶל עַבְדִּי כל־הגוים האלה סביב ולחרבות עולם
קול שמחה וקול ששון רֵיחַ מֹר	10 קוֹל שָׂשׂוֹן וְקוֹל שִׂמְחָה קוֹל רֵחַיִם
הארץ לשמה	11 הָאָרֶץ הַזֹּאת לְחָרְבָּה לְשַׁמָּה ועבדו הגוים האלה את־מלך בבל עבדו גוים

ᵃ Vid. 1:2. ᵇ Cf. 35:15. ᶜ Cf. 23:40.

25:12-25] THE CONSPECTUS OF THE VARIATIONS. 331

12 וְהָיָה כִמְלֹאות שִׁבְעִים שָׁנָה אֶפְקֹד עַל־מֶלֶךְ־בָּבֶל וְעַל־הַגּוֹי הַהוּא	שבעים (וּבִמְלֹאות) וּבִמְלֹאות אֶפְקֹד אֶת־הַגּוֹי הַשָּׁנָה הַהוּא
וְאֶת־יִהְיָה אֶת־עֲוֹנָם וְעַל־אֶרֶץ כַּשְׂדִּים	Deest
וְשִׂמְתִּי אֹתִי לְשִׁמְמוֹת עוֹלָם	וְשִׂמְתִּי אֹתָם לְשִׁמַּמְתִּי עוֹלָם
13 עַל־כָּל־הַגּוֹיִם	עַל־הַגּוֹיִם
14 כִּי עָבְדוּ־בָם גַּם־הֵמָּה גּוֹיִם רַבִּים וּמְלָכִים גְּדוֹלִים וְשִׁלַּמְתִּי לָהֶם כְּפָעֳלָם וּכְמַעֲשֵׂה יְדֵיהֶם	Desunt
15 כִּי כֹה אָמַר יְהוָה אֱלֹהֵי יִשְׂרָאֵל אֵלַי קַח אֶת־כּוֹס הַיַּיִן הַחֵמָה הַזֹּאת מִיָּדִי וְהִשְׁקִיתָה אוֹתוֹ אֶת־כָּל־הַגּוֹיִם	כֹּה אָמַר יְהוָה אֱלֹהֵי יִשְׂרָאֵל קַח אֶת־כּוֹס הַיַּיִן חֵמָר הַזֶּה[b] מִיָּדִי וְהִשְׁקִיתָה אֶת־כָּל־הַגּוֹיִם
16 וְהִתְגֹּעֲשׁוּ	וְקָעוּ[c]
17 אֶת־כָּל־הַגּוֹיִם	אֶת־הַגּוֹיִם
18 וְאֶת־מְלָכֶיהָ אֶת־שָׂרֶיהָ לִשְׁמָה לִשְׁרֵקָה וְלִקְלָלָה כַּיּוֹם הַזֶּה	וְאֶת־מַלְכֵיָה יְהוּדָה וְאֶת־שָׂרֶיהָ לְשַׁמָּה וְלִשְׁרֵקָה
19 אֶת־פַּרְעֹה	וְאֶת־פַּרְעֹה
וְאֶת־עֲבָדָיו וְאֶת־כָּל־עַמּוֹ	וְאֶת־גְּדוֹלָיו: וְאֶת[d]־כָּל־עַמּוֹ
20 וְאֵת כָּל־מַלְכֵי אֶרֶץ הָעֵץ	Deest
כָּל־מַלְכֵי אֶרֶץ פְּלִשְׁתִּים	כָּל־מַלְכֵי פְּלִשְׁתִּים
21 אֶת־אֱדוֹם	
22 וְאֵת כָּל־מַלְכֵי צֹר וְאֵת כָּל־מַלְכֵי צִידוֹן וְאֵת מַלְכֵי הָאִי אֲשֶׁר בְּעֵבֶר הַיָּם	וְאֵת מַלְכֵי צֹר וְאֵת מַלְכֵי צִידוֹן וְאֵת הַמְּלָכִים אֲשֶׁר בְּעֵבֶר הַיָּם
23 אֶת־דְּדָן	וְאֶת־דְּדָן
וְאֶת־בּוּז	וְאֶת־רוֹז[e]
24 וְאֵת כָּל־מַלְכֵי עֲרָב וְאֵת כָּל־מַלְכֵי הָעֶרֶב	וְאֵת כָּל־מַלְכֵי עֲרָב וְאֵת כָּל־הָעֶרֶב
25 וְאֵת כָּל־מַלְכֵי זִמְרִי	Deest
וְאֵת כָּל־מַלְכֵי מָדַי	וְאֵת כָּל־מַלְכֵי פָרָס

[a] Targ. לְצָדִית. [b] ut Ps. 75:9 (Gk. & Heb.). [c] Cf. vs. 27. [d] Inc. vs. 20. [e] 'Pas.—Cf. Judges 5:23.

הָרְחֹקִים הַקֶּדֶם כָּל־מַלְכֵי הַקְּרֹבִים הַצָּפוֹן כָּל־מַלְכֵי 26	
וְהַקְּרֹבִים*	וְהָרְחֹקִים
וְאֵת כָּל־הַמַּמְלְכוֹת	וְאֵת כָּל־הַמַּמְלָכוֹת הָאָרֶץ
Deest	וּמֶלֶךְ שֵׁשַׁךְ יִשְׁתֶּה אַחֲרֵיהֶם
כֹּה־אָמַר יְהוָה צְבָאוֹת תִּשְׁתּוּ תִּשְׁכָּרוּ	כֹּה־אָמַר יְהוָה צְבָאוֹת אֱלֹהֵי 27
וְתָקִיאוּ וְתִפֹּלוּ	יִשְׂרָאֵל שְׁתוּ וְשִׁכְרוּ וּקְיוּ וְנִפְלוּ
וְאָמַרְתָּ	וְאָמַרְתָּ אֲלֵיהֶם 28
יְהוָה	יְהוָה צְבָאוֹת
כִּי הִנֵּה בָּעִיר אֲשֶׁר־נִקְרָא שְׁמִי עָלֶיהָ	כִּי הִנֵּה בָּעִיר אֲשֶׁר־נִקְרָא שְׁמִי 29
אָנֹכִי מַחֵל לְהָרַע וְאַתֶּם חִנָּקֵה	עָלֶיהָ אָנֹכִי מֵחֵל לְהָרַע וְאַתֶּם
לֹא תִנָּקוּ	הִנָּקֵה תִנָּקוּ לֹא תִנָּקוּ
עַל־כָּל־הַיֹּשְׁבִים עַל־הָאָרֶץ	עַל־כָּל־יֹשְׁבֵי הָאָרֶץ
Deest	נְאֻם יְהוָה צְבָאוֹת
וְאַתָּה תִנָּבֵא עֲלֵיהֶם אֶת־הַדְּבָרִים	וְאַתָּה תִנָּבֵא אֲלֵיהֶם אֵת כָּל־ 30
הָאֵלֶּה וְאָמַרְתָּ יְהוָה מִמָּרוֹם	הַדְּבָרִים הָאֵלֶּה וְאָמַרְתָּ אֲלֵיהֶם
יְדַבֵּר מִקְדָּשׁוֹ (מִמִּקְדָּשׁוֹ) יִתֵּן	יְהוָה מִמָּרוֹם יִשְׁאָג וּמִמְּעוֹן
קוֹלוֹ דָּבָר יְדַבֵּר עַל־מְקוֹמוֹ	קָדְשׁוֹ יִתֵּן קוֹלוֹ שָׁאֹג יִשְׁאַג
וְהָמָה (הֵידָד) כְּדֹרְכִים יַעֲנֵי	עַל־נָוֵהוּ הֵידָד כְּדֹרְכִים יַעֲנֶה
וְעַל־יֹשְׁבֵי הָאָרֶץ יָבֹא שָׁאוֹן:	אֶל כָּל־יֹשְׁבֵי הָאָרֶץ:
עַל[b] קְצֵה הָאָרֶץ	בָּא שָׁאוֹן עַד־קְצֵה הָאָרֶץ 31
שֹׁפֵט הוּא לְכָל־בָּשָׂר וְהָרְשָׁעִים נָתְנֵי	נִשְׁפָּט הוּא לְכָל־בָּשָׂר הָרְשָׁעִים
לַחֶרֶב	נְתָנָם לַחֶרֶב
יְהוָה	יְהוָה צְבָאוֹת 32
רָעָה יֹצֵאת מִגּוֹי עַל־גּוֹי וְסַעַר גָּדוֹל	רָעָה יֹצֵאת מִגּוֹי אֶל־גּוֹי וְסַעַר
יֹצֵא[a]	גָּדוֹל יֵעוֹר
וְהָיוּ חַלְלֵי יְהוָה בַּיּוֹם יְהוָה 33	וְהָיוּ חַלְלֵי יְהוָה בַּיּוֹם הַהוּא
מִקְצוֹת[d] הָאָרֶץ	מִקְצֵה הָאָרֶץ
לֹא יִסָּפְדוּ וְלֹא יֵאָסְפוּ וְלֹא יִקָּבֵרוּ	לֹא יִסָּפְדוּ וְלֹא יֵאָסְפוּ לֹא יִקָּבֵרוּ
הֵילִילוּ רֹעִים	הֵילִילוּ הָרֹעִים 34
וְהִתְגֹּדְדוּ	וְהִתְפַּלָּשׁוּ
Deest	וּתְפוֹצוֹתִיכֶם
כָּרֵי (כְּאֵילֵי) חֶמְדָּה	כִּכְלִי חֶמְדָּה

---

[a] Cf. 48:24. [b] Inc. vs. 31. [c] ἐκπορεύεται. [d] Targ. בְּסָפַּי.

הַצֹּאן וְהָאַדִּירִים	36 מֵאַדִּירֵי הַצֹּאן
כִּי־שֹׁדֵד יהוה	כִּי־שֹׁדֵד יהוה
וְנָדַמּוּ שְׁאֵרִית (יֶתֶר) הַשָּׁלוֹם מִפְּנֵי חָרוֹן אַפִּי	37 וְנָדַמּוּ נְאוֹת הַשָּׁלוֹם מִפְּנֵי חֲרוֹן אַף־יְהוָה
יִתְרוֹ (שְׁאֵרִיתוֹ, סֹפוֹ)	38 סָפוּ
מִפְּנֵי חֲרוֹן הַיּוֹנָה וּמִפְּנֵי חֲרוֹן אַפּוֹ מִפְּנֵי הַחֶרֶבᵃ הַגְּדוֹלָהᵇ	

CAPUT XXVI.

מֶלֶךְ (מְלֹךְ?) יְהוֹיָקִים	1 מַמְלְכוּת יְהוֹיָקִים
Deest	מֶלֶךְ יְהוּדָה
מֵאֵת יהוה	מֵאֵת יהוה לֵאמֹר
וְדִבַּרְתָּ אֶל־כָּל־הַיְּהוּדִים (עַב־יְהוּדָה?) וּלְכָל־הַבָּאִים לְהִשְׁתַּחֲוֺת בְּבֵית־יהוה	2 וְדִבַּרְתָּ עַל־כָּל־עָרֵי יְהוּדָה הַבָּאִים לְהִשְׁתַּחֲוֺת בֵּית־ יהוה
וְחָדַלְתִּי מִן־הָרָעָהᵈ	3 וְנִחַמְתִּי אֶל־הָרָעָה
וְאָמַרְתָּ	4 וְאָמַרְתָּ אֲלֵיהֶם
לָלֶכֶת בְּתוֹרָתִי	לָלֶכֶת בְּתוֹרָתִי
לִטְמֹעַ אֶל־דְּבָרֵיᵉ	5 לִשְׁמֹעַ עַל־דִּבְרֵי
הַשְׁכֵּםᶠ וְאֶשְׁלַח וְלֹא שְׁמַעְתֶּם אֵלָי	וְהַשְׁכֵּם וְשָׁלוֹחַ וְלֹא שְׁמַעְתֶּם
Deest	6 הַזֹּאת
גּוֹיֵי כָּל־הָאָרֶץ	גּוֹיֵי הָאָרֶץ
וּנְבִיאֵי הַשֶּׁקֶר	7 וְהַנְּבִיאִים
כָּל־אֲשֶׁר־צִוָּה יהוה אוֹתוֹ	8 כָּל־אֲשֶׁר־צִוָּה יהוה
וּנְבִיאֵי הַשֶּׁקֶר	וְהַנְּבִיאִים
כִּי נְבִיא	9 מַדּוּעַ נִבֵּיתָ
מְיוּשָּׁבִים (מְיוּטָּב)	מֵאֵין יוֹשֵׁב
עַל־יִרְמְיָהוּᵍ	אֶל־יִרְמְיָהוּ
הַדָּבָר הַזֶּה	10 הַדְּבָרִים הָאֵלֶּה
בְּפִתְחֵי שַׁעַר הֶחָדָשׁ	בְּפֶתַח שַׁעַר־יְהוָה הֶחָדָשׁ
וּנְבִיאֵי הַשֶּׁקֶר	11 וְהַנְּבִיאִים

ᵃ Targ. בֶּן קֳדָם חָרֵב. ᵇ Vid. 46:16; 50:16. Cf. Isa. 27:1. ᶜ Targ. בְּרִית.
ᵈ Targ. יַאֲהֵד בֶּן בִּישָׁתָא. ᵉ Targ. לְפִתְגָּמֵי. ᶠ Targ. בַּקְדַּם. ᵍ Targ. יִרְמְיָהוּ.

Deest	לֵאמֹֽר
כִּי נִבָּא עַל־הָעִיר^a הַזֹּאת	כִּי נִבָּא אֶל־הָעִיר הַזֹּאת 12
אֶל־עָל־הֶשָׁרִים	
עַל^b־הַבַּיִת הַזֶּה וְעַל־הָעִיר הַזֹּאת	אֶל־הַבַּיִת הַזֶּה וְאֶל־הָעִיר הַזֹּאת
Deest	אֱלֹהֵיכֶם 13
וַיִּנָּחֶל יהוה מִן־הָרָעָה^d	וַיִּנָּחֶם יהוה אֶל־הָרָעָה
וְהִנְנִי בְּיֶדְכֶם	וַאֲנִי הִנְנִי בְיֶדְכֶם 14
כִּישָׁר וְכַטּוֹב לָכֶם	כַּטּוֹב וְכַיָּשָׁר בְּעֵינֵיכֶם
דַּם נָקִי	כִּי־דָם נָקִי 15
וְעַל־הָעִיר הַזֹּאת וְעַל־הַיּוֹשְׁבִים בָּהּ	וְאֶל־הָעִיר הַזֹּאת וְאֶל־יֹשְׁבֶיהָ
שְׁלָחַנִי יהוה אֲלֵיכֶם	שְׁלָחַנִי יהוה עֲלֵיכֶם
וְאֶל־נְבִיאֵי הַשָּׁקֶר	וְאֶל־הַנְּבִאִים 16
Deest	לֵאמֹֽר 17
הָיָה בִּימֵי חִזְקִיָּהוּ	הָיָה נִבָּא בִּימֵי חִזְקִיָּהוּ 18
Deest	לֵאמֹֽר
כֹּה־אָמַר יהוה צְבָאוֹת צִיּוֹן כַּשָּׂדֶה תֵחָרֵשׁ וִירוּשָׁלִַם לְשַׁמָּה תִהְיֶה	כֹּה־אָמַר יהוה צְבָאוֹת צִיּוֹן שָׂדֶה תֵחָרֵשׁ וִירוּשָׁלִַם עִיִּים תִּהְיֶה
הֶהָמֵת הֱמִתָהוּ	הֶהָמֵת הֱמִתָהוּ 19
Deest	מֶלֶךְ־יְהוּדָה
הֲכִי לֹא יָרְאוּ אֶת־יהוה וְכִי־לֹא חָ֫לּוּ^e	הֲלֹא יָרֵא אֶת־יהוה וַיְחַל
וַיִּנָּחֶל יהוה מִן־הָרָעָה^f	וַיִּנָּחֶם יהוה אֶל־הָרָעָה
וַאֲנַחְנוּ עֹשִׂינוּ	וַאֲנַחְנוּ עֹשִׂים
וְאִישׁ הָיָה	וְגַם־אִישׁ הָיָה 20
עַל־הָעִיר הַזֹּאת וְעַל־הָאָרֶץ הַזֹּאת	עַל־הָעִיר הַזֹּאת וְעַל־הָאָרֶץ הַזֹּאת
Deest	וְכָל־גִּבּוֹרָיו 21
אֶת־כָּל־דְּבָרָיו וַיְבַקְשׁוּ הֲמִיתוֹ^h	אֶת־דְּבָרָיו וַיְבַקֵּשׁ הַמֶּלֶךְ הֲמִיתוֹ
וַיָּבֹא אֶל־מִצְרָיִם	וַיִּרָא וַיִּבְרַח וַיָּבֹא מִצְרָיִם
וַיִּשְׁלַח הַמֶּלֶךְ אֲנָשִׁים אֶל־מִצְרָיִםⁱ	וַיִּשְׁלַח הַמֶּלֶךְ יְהוֹיָקִים אֲנָשִׁים מִצְרָיִם 22

---

^a Targ. עַל קַרְיְתָא. ^b Targ. עַל. ^c Targ. וְעַל. ^d Targ. וְיִתִיב יְיָ בְּכֵן. ^e Targ. בְּדַחְלְתָא. ^f Targ. וְעַל. ^g Targ. יְתִיב יְיָ בְּכֵן בְּדַחְלְתָא. ^h Targ. לְקַטָּלֵיהּ. ⁱ Targ. לְמִצְרָיִם.

Desunt { אֶת־אֶלְנָתָן בֶּן־עַכְבּוֹר וַאֲנָשִׁים אִתּוֹ אֶל־מִצְרָיִם	
23 וַיּוֹצִיאוּ אֶת־אוּרִיָּהוּ מִמִּצְרַיִם וַיְבִאֻהוּ אֶל־הַמֶּלֶךְ יְהוֹיָקִים	וַיּוֹצִיאוּ אוֹתוֹ מִשָּׁם אֶל־הַמֶּלֶךְ
וַיַּכֵּהוּ אֶת־נִבְלָתוֹ אֶל־קִבְרֵי בְּנֵי הָעָם	וַיַּשְׁלֵךְ אוֹתוֹ אֶל־קֶבֶרa בְּנֵי עַמּוֹ
24 בְּיַד־הֶם	בִּידֵיהֶם

CAPUT XXVII.

1 בְּרֵאשִׁית מַמְלֶכֶת יְהוֹיָקִם בֶּן־יֹאושִׁיָּהוּ מֶלֶךְ יְהוּדָה הָיָה הַדָּבָר הַזֶּה אֶל־יִרְמְיָה מֵאֵת יְהוָה לֵאמֹר׃	Desunt
2 כֹּה־אָמַר יְהוָה אֵלַי וּנְתַתָּם עַל־צַוָּארֶךָ	כה־אמר יהוה ונתת על־צוארך
3 בְּיַד מַלְאָכִים הַבָּאִים יְרוּשָׁלִָם	בְּיָדֵי מַלְאֲכֵיהֶם הבאים לקראתם ירושלם
4 כֹּה־אָמַר יְהוָה צְבָאוֹת	כה־אמר יהוה
5 אָנֹכִי עָשִׂיתִי	כי אנכי עשיתי
אֶת־הָאָדָם וְאֶת־הַבְּהֵמָה אֲשֶׁר עַל־פְּנֵי הָאָרֶץ	Desunt
6 וְעַתָּה אָנֹכִי נָתַתִּי אֶת־כָּל־הָאֲרָצוֹת הָאֵלֶּה בְּיַד נְבוּכַדְנֶאצַּר מֶלֶךְ בָּבֶל עַבְדִּי וְגַם אֶת־חַיַּת הַשָּׂדֶה נְתַתִּי לוֹ לְעָבְדוֹ׃	וְעַתָּה אָנֹכִי נתתי את־הָאָרֶץ לנבוכדנאצר מלך בבל לְעָבְדוֹ וְאֶת־חַיַּת השדה לעבדו׃
7 וְעָבְדוּ אֹתוֹ כָּל־הַגּוֹיִם וְאֶת־בְּנוֹ וְאֶת־בֶּן־בְּנוֹ עַד בֹּא־עֵת אַרְצוֹ גַּם־הוּא וְעָבְדוּ בוֹ גּוֹיִם רַבִּים וּמְלָכִים גְּדֹלִים׃	Desunt
8 וְהָיָה הַגּוֹי וְהַמַּמְלָכָה אֲשֶׁר לֹא־	וְהַגּוֹי וְהַמַּמְלָכָה אֲשֶׁר לֹא־

---

a εἰς ὃ μνῆμα.

יַעֲבְדוּ אֹתוֹ אֶת־נְבוּכַדְנֶאצַּר	יִתְּנוּ אֶת־צַוָּארָם בְּעֹל מֶלֶךְ
מֶלֶךְ־בָּבֶל וְאֵת אֲשֶׁר לֹא־יִתֵּן	בָּבֶל
אֶת־צַוָּארוֹ בְּעֹל מֶלֶךְ בָּבֶל	
וּבַדֶּבֶר	Deest
עַל־הַגּוֹי הַהוּא	עֲלֵיהֶם
עַד־תֻּמִּי אֹתָם[a]	עַד־תֻּמָּם[a]
9 וְאַתֶּם אַל־תִּשְׁמְעוּ אֶל־	נְבִיאֵיכֶם וְאֶל־הַקֹּסְמִים לָכֶם[b]
נְבִיאֵיכֶם וְאֶל־קֹסְמֵיכֶם וְאֶל־	וְאֶל־הַחֲלֹמִים לָכֶם וְאֶל־מְנַחֲשֵׁיכֶם[c]
חֲלֹמֹתֵיכֶם וְאֶל־עֹנְנֵיכֶם	
אֲשֶׁר־הֵם אֹמְרִים אֲלֵיכֶם לֵאמֹר	הָאֹמְרִים
וְהִדַּחְתִּי אֶתְכֶם וַאֲבַדְתֶּם	Deest
11 נְאֻם־יְהוָה וַעֲבָדָהּ	וַעֲבָדוּ (וַעֲבָדָהּ)
12 הָבִיאוּ אֶת־צַוְּארֵיכֶם בְּעֹל מֶלֶךְ	הָבִיאוּ אֶת־צַוְּארְכֶם וְעִבְדוּ אֶת־מֶלֶךְ
בָּבֶל וְעִבְדוּ אֹתוֹ וְעַמּוֹ וִחְיוּ	בָּבֶל
13 לָמָּה תָמוּתוּ אַתָּה וְעַמֶּךָ בַּחֶרֶב	
בָּרָעָב וּבַדָּבֶר כַּאֲשֶׁר דִּבֶּר יְהוָה	
אֶל־הַגּוֹי אֲשֶׁר לֹא־יַעֲבֹד אֶת־	Desunt
14 מֶלֶךְ בָּבֶל: וְאַל־תִּשְׁמְעוּ אֶל־	
דִּבְרֵי הַנְּבִאִים הָאֹמְרִים אֲלֵיכֶם	
לֵאמֹר לֹא תַעַבְדוּ אֶת־מֶלֶךְ בָּבֶל	
15 וְהֵם נִבְּאִים בִּשְׁמִי לַשֶּׁקֶר לְמַעַן	וְהֵם נִבָּאִים בִּשְׁמִי עַל־שֶׁקֶר לְמַעַן
הַדִּיחִי	הַדִּיחִי[d]
וְהַנְּבִיאִים הַנִּבְּאִים לָכֶם	וּנְבִיאֵיכֶם הַנִּבָּאִים לָכֶם עַל־שֶׁקֶר פְּזָרִים
16 וְאֶל־הַכֹּהֲנִים וְאֶל־כָּל־הָעָם הַזֶּה	לָכֶם וְאֶל־כָּל־הָעָם הַזֶּה וְאֶל־הַכֹּהֲנִים
אֶל־דִּבְרֵי נְבִיאֵיכֶם	אֶל־דִּבְרֵי הַנְּבִיאִים
עַתָּה מְהֵרָה	Deest
17 אַל־תִּשְׁמְעוּ אֲלֵיהֶם עִבְדוּ אֶת־	לֹא שְׁלַחְתִּים
מֶלֶךְ בָּבֶל וִחְיוּ לָמָּה תִהְיֶה	
הָעִיר הַזֹּאת חָרְבָּה:	
18 יִפְגְּעוּ־נָא בַּיהוָה צְבָאוֹת לְבִלְתִּי	יִפְגְּעוּ־בִי[e]
בֹאוּ הַכֵּלִים הַנּוֹתָרִים בְּבֵית־	
יְהוָה וּבֵית מֶלֶךְ יְהוּדָה	
וּבִירוּשָׁלִַם בָּבֶלָה:	

[a] ut 24:10. [b] Targ. נְבִיֵּיכוֹן דְּשִׁקְרָא. [c] Cf. Gen. 44:5. [d] Cf. vs. 10.
[e] ut 28:15.

19 כִּי כֹה אָמַר יְהוָה צְבָאוֹת אֶל־ כִּי כֹה אָמַר יהוה וְעַל יֶתֶר
הָעַמֻּדִים וְעַל־הַיָּם וְעַל־ הכלים
הַמְּכֹנוֹת וְעַל יֶתֶר הַכֵּלִים
הַנּוֹתָרִים בָּעִיר הַזֹּאת:
20 אֲשֶׁר לֹא־לְקָחָם נְבוּכַדְנֶאצַּר מֶלֶךְ אשר לא־לקח מלך בבל בגלות את־
בָּבֶל בַּגְלוֹתוֹ אֶת־יְכָנְיָה בֶן־ יכניה מירושלם
יְהוֹיָקִים מֶלֶךְ־יְהוּדָה
מִירוּשָׁלִַם בָּבֶלָה וְאֵת כָּל־חֹרֵי
יְהוּדָה וִירוּשָׁלִָם:
21 כִּי כֹה־אָמַר יְהוָה צְבָאוֹת אֱלֹהֵי ⎧
יִשְׂרָאֵל עַל־הַכֵּלִים הַנּוֹתָרִים ⎪
בֵּית יְהוָה וּבֵית מֶלֶךְ־יְהוּדָה ⎪
וִירוּשָׁלִָם: ⎪
Desunt ⎨
22 וְשָׁמָּה יִהְיוּ עַד יוֹם פָּקְדִי ⎪
אֹתָם ⎪
וְהַעֲלִיתִים וַהֲשִׁיבֹתִים אֶל־ ⎪
הַמָּקוֹם הַזֶּה ⎩

CAPUT XXVIII.

1 וַיְהִי בַּשָּׁנָה הַהִיא בְּרֵאשִׁית וַיהִי בשנה הרביעית לצדקיה מלך־
מַמְלֶכֶת צִדְקִיָּה מֶלֶךְ־יְהוּדָה יהודה
בַּשְּׁנָת הָרְבִיעִית
הַנָּבִיא אֲשֶׁר מִגִּבְעוֹן הנביא הַשֶּׁקֶרᵃ מגבעון
2 יְהוָה צְבָאוֹת אֱלֹהֵי יִשְׂרָאֵל לֵאמֹר יהוה
3 אֲנִי מֵשִׁיב ואני משיב
אֶת־כָּל־כְּלֵי בֵית יְהוָה את־כלי בית יהוה
אֲשֶׁר לָקַח נְבוּכַדְנֶאצַּר מֶלֶךְ־בָּבֶל ⎧
מִן־הַמָּקוֹם הַזֶּה וַיְבִיאֵם Desunt ⎨
בָּבֶל ⎩
4 וְאֶת־יְכָנְיָה בֶן־יְהוֹיָקִים מֶלֶךְ־ ואת־יכניה ואת־גלות יהודה
יְהוּדָה וְאֶת־כָּל־גָּלוּת יְהוּדָה

ᵃ Targ. נְבִיָּא שִׁקְרָא.

Y

Desunt { הַבָּאִים בְּבֶלָה אֲנִי מֵשִׁיב אֶל־	
הַמָּקוֹם הַזֶּה נְאֻם־יְהוָה	
5 וַיֹּאמֶר יִרְמְיָה הַנָּבִיא אֶל־חֲנַנְיָה לְעֵינֵי	ויאמר ירמיהו אל־חנניה לעיני כל־
הַכֹּהֲנִים וּלְעֵינֵי כָּל־הָעָם	העם ולעיני הכהנים
6 וַיֹּאמֶר יִרְמְיָה הַנָּבִיא	ויאמר ירמיה
יָקֵם יְהוָה אֶת־דְּבָרֶיךָ	יקם את־דברך[a]
7 שְׁמַע־נָא הַדָּבָר הַזֶּה	שמעו דברי־יהוה
בְּאָזְנֶיךָ	באזניכם
8 וּלְפָנֶיךָ	ולפניכם
אֶל־אֲרָצוֹת רַבּוֹת	על־ארץ[b] רכה
לְמִלְחָמָה וּלְרָעָה וּלְדָבֶר	למלחמה
9 הַנָּבִיא אֲשֶׁר יִנָּבֵא לְשָׁלוֹם בְּבֹא	הנביא המנבא לשלום בבא הדבר
דְּבַר הַנָּבִיא יִוָּדַע הַנָּבִיא	וידעו הנביא אשר שלח אליהם
אֲשֶׁר־שְׁלָחוֹ יְהוָה בֶּאֱמֶת	יהוה באמת
10 וַיִּקַּח חֲנַנְיָה הַנָּבִיא אֶת־הַמּוֹטָה	ויקח חנניה בעיני כל־העם
מֵעַל צַוַּאר יִרְמְיָה הַנָּבִיא	את־המוטות מעל צואר ירמיה
וַיִּשְׁבְּרֵהוּ:	וישברן
11 נְבֻכַדְנֶאצַּר	Desunt {
בְּעוֹד שְׁנָתַיִם יָמִים	
מֵעַל צַוַּאר כָּל־הַגּוֹיִם	מעל צוארי כל־הגוים
יִרְמְיָה הַנָּבִיא	ירמיה
12 אַחֲרֵי שְׁבוֹר חֲנַנְיָה הַנָּבִיא אֶת־	אחרי שבור חניה את־המוטות מעל
הַמּוֹטָה מֵעַל צַוַּאר יִרְמְיָה	צוארו
הַנָּבִיא	
13 וְעָשִׂיתָ	ועשיתי (ואעשה)
14 יְהוָה צְבָאוֹת אֱלֹהֵי יִשְׂרָאֵל	יהוה
נָתַתִּי עַל־צַוַּאר כָּל־הַגּוֹיִם הָאֵלֶּה	נתתי על־צואר כל־הגוים לעבד
לַעֲבֹד אֶת־נְבֻכַדְנֶאצַּר מֶלֶךְ־בָּבֶל	את־מלך בבל
וַעֲבָדֻהוּ וְגַם אֶת־חַיַּת הַשָּׂדֶה	Desunt {
נָתַתִּי לוֹ	
15 וַיֹּאמֶר יִרְמְיָה הַנָּבִיא אֶל־חֲנַנְיָה	ויאמר ירמיה אל־חנניה
הַנָּבִיא	

---

[a] Targ. פִּתְגָּמָךְ. [b] Targ. עַל.

	Deest
שְׁמַֽע־נָ֣א חֲנַנְיָ֔ה	
וְאַתָּ֖ה הִבְטַ֥חְתָּ אֶת־הָעָ֥ם הַזֶּ֖ה	וְהִבְטַחַתּ את־העם הזה
16 הַשָּׁנָ֣ה אַתָּ֣ה מֵ֑ת	בַּשָּׁנָה הַזֹּאת^a אתה מת
כִּֽי־סָרָ֥ה דִבַּ֖רְתָּ אֶל־יְהוָֽה	Deest
17 וַיָּ֛מָת חֲנַנְיָ֥ה הַנָּבִ֖יא בַּשָּׁנָ֣ה הַהִ֑יא וַיָּ֖מָת בחדש השביעי	בחדש השביעי

CAPUT XXIX.

1 יִרְמְיָ֣ה הַנָּבִ֗יא	ירמיה
אֶל־יֶ֙תֶר֙ זִקְנֵ֣י הַגּוֹלָ֔ה	אל־זקני הגולה
וְאֶל־הַנְּבִיאִים֙	וְאֶל־נְבִיאֵ֥י הַשֶּׁ֖קֶר סֵ֥פֶר בְּבָבֶ֖לָה אֶל־הַגּוֹלָֽה
אֲשֶׁ֤ר הֶגְלָה֙ נְבֽוּכַדְנֶאצַּ֣ר מִירוּשָׁלִַ֔ם בָּבֶֽלָה	Desunt
2 שָׂרֵ֥י יְהוּדָ֖ה וִירוּשָׁלִַ֑ם וְהֶחָרָ֖שׁ (הֶחָרִ֑ים)^b וְהַמַּסְגֵּֽר	(הַחוֹרִים) וְהַמַּסְגֵּר והחרש
3 אֶל־נְבוּכַדְנֶאצַּ֥ר מֶ֥לֶךְ בָּבֶ֖ל	אל־מלך בבל
4 יְהוָ֣ה צְבָא֔וֹת	יהוה
לְכָל־הַ֨גּוֹלָ֔ה	על־הגולה
מִירוּשָׁלִַ֖ם בָּבֶֽלָה	מירושלם
6 קְח֣וּ נָשִׁ֗ים	וקחו נשים
וְתֵלַ֣דְנָה בָּנִ֣ים וּבָנ֑וֹת וּרְב֖וּ־שָׁ֑ם	ורבו
7 וְדִרְשׁ֞וּ אֶת־שְׁל֣וֹם הָעִ֗יר	ודרשו לשלום הארץ
וְהִתְפַּלְל֥וּ בַעֲדָ֖הּ	והתפללו בעדם
יִהְיֶ֥ה לָכֶ֖ם שָׁלֽוֹם	שלום לכם
8 כִּי֩ כֹ֨ה אָמַ֜ר יְהוָ֧ה צְבָא֛וֹת אֱלֹהֵ֥י יִשְׂרָאֵ֖ל אַל־יַשִּׁ֥יאוּ לָכֶ֛ם נְבִיאֵיכֶ֥ם אֲשֶׁר־בְּקִרְבְּכֶ֖ם וְקֹֽסְמֵיכֶ֑ם	כי כה אמר יהוה אל־ישיאו לכם נביאי השקר אשר בקרבכם ואל־נשיאו^c לָכֶם קסמיכם
9 כִּ֣י בְשֶׁ֔קֶר	כי שקר (שְׁקָרִים)

---

^{a} Targ. בְּשַׁתָּא הָדָא. ^{b} ἐλευθέρου. ^{c} Targ. דְּשִׁקְרָא.

לֹא שְׁלַחְתִּים נְאֻם־יְהוָֹה	וְלֹא שלחתים
10 כִּי לְפִי מְלֹאת	כי במלאת (למלאת)
וְהֲקִמֹתִי עֲלֵיכֶם אֶת־דְּבָרִי הַטּוֹב לְהָשִׁיב אֶתְכֶם	והקמתי את־דברי עליכם להשיב עמכם
11 כִּי אָנֹכִי יָדַעְתִּי אֶת־הַמַּחֲשָׁבֹת אֲשֶׁר אָנֹכִי חֹשֵׁב עֲלֵיכֶם נְאֻם־יְהוָֹה מַחְשְׁבוֹת שָׁלוֹם וְלֹא לְרָעָה לָתֵת לָכֶם אַחֲרִית וְתִקְוָה	וְאֶחְשֹׁב עֲלֵיכֶם מַחְשֶׁבֶת שָׁלוֹםª וְלֹא רָעוֹת לָתֵת לָכֶם אֵלֶּה
12 וּקְרָאתֶם אֹתִי וַהֲלַכְתֶּם	Deest
13 וּמְצָאתֶם	וּמְצָאתֶם אֹתִי
14 וְנִמְצֵאתִי לָכֶם	וְנִגְלֵיתִי (וְנִרְאֵיתִי) לָכֶם
נְאֻם־יְהוָֹה וְשַׁבְתִּי אֶת־שְׁבִיתְכֶם וְקִבַּצְתִּי אֶתְכֶם מִכָּל־הַגּוֹיִם וּמִכָּל־הַמְּקוֹמוֹת אֲשֶׁר הִדַּחְתִּי אֶתְכֶם שָׁם נְאֻם־יְהוָֹה וַהֲשִׁבֹתִי אֶתְכֶם אֶל־הַמָּקוֹם אֲשֶׁר־הִגְלֵיתִי אֶתְכֶם מִשָּׁם:	
16 כִּי־כֹה אָמַר יְהוָֹה אֶל־הַמֶּלֶךְ הַיּוֹשֵׁב אֶל־כִּסֵּא דָוִד וְאֶל־כָּל־הָעָם הַיּוֹשֵׁב בָּעִיר הַזֹּאת אֲחֵיכֶם אֲשֶׁר לֹא־יָצְאוּ אִתְּכֶם בַּגּוֹלָה:	Desunt
17 כֹּה אָמַר יְהוָֹה צְבָאוֹת הִנְנִי מְשַׁלֵּחַ בָּם אֶת־הַחֶרֶב אֶת־הָרָעָב וְאֶת־הַדָּבֶר וְנָתַתִּי אוֹתָם כַּתְּאֵנִים הַשֹּׁעָרִים אֲשֶׁר לֹא־תֵאָכַלְנָה מֵרֹעַ:	
18 וְרָדַפְתִּי אַחֲרֵיהֶם בַּחֶרֶב בָּרָעָב וּבַדָּבֶר וּנְתַתִּים לְזַוֲעָה לְכֹל מַמְלְכוֹת הָאָרֶץ לְאָלָה וּלְשַׁמָּה וְלִשְׁרֵקָה וּלְחֶרְפָּה בְּכָל־הַגּוֹיִם	
19 אֲשֶׁר־הִדַּחְתִּים שָׁם: תַּחַת אֲשֶׁר לֹא־שָׁמְעוּ אֶל־דְּבָרַי נְאֻם־יְהוָֹה אֲשֶׁר שָׁלַחְתִּי אֲלֵיהֶם אֶת־עֲבָדַי	

ª Targ. בְּהִשְׁבָּת שָׁלָבָּא.

[29:20-31] THE CONSPECTUS OF THE VARIATIONS.   341

	20 הַנְּבִיאִים הַשֶּׁבֶם וְשָׁלֹחַ וְלֹא
Desunt	שְׁמַעְתֶּם נְאֻם־יְהוָֹה: וְאַתֶּם
	שִׁמְעוּ דְבַר־יְהוָֹה כָּל־הַגּוֹלָה
	אֲשֶׁר־שִׁלַּחְתִּי מִירוּשָׁלַםִ בָּבֶלָה:
	21 צְבָאוֹת אֱלֹהֵי יִשְׂרָאֵל אֶל־אַחְאָב עַל־אַחְאָב וְעַל־צִדְקִיָּהוּ
	בֶן־קוֹלָיָה וְאֶל־צִדְקִיָּהוּ בֶן־
	מַעֲשֵׂיָה הַנִּבְּאִים לָכֶם בִּשְׁמִי
	שָׁקֶר
בִּידֵי מֶלֶךְ־בָּבֶל	בְּיַד נְבוּכַדְרֶאצַּר מֶלֶךְ־בָּבֶל
22 וְלֻקַּח מֵהֶם קְלָלָה בְּכָל גָּלוּת יְהוּדָה	גָלוּת לְכָל קְלָלָה מֵהֶם וִיקְחוּ
בְּבָבֶל	יְהוּדָה אֲשֶׁר בְּבָבֶל
כַּאֲשֶׁר עָשָׂה לְצִדְקִיָּהוּ וְכְאַחְאָב אֲשֶׁר	כְּצִדְקִיָּהוּ וּכְאַחְאָב אֲשֶׁר־קְלָם מֶלֶךְ־
מֶלֶךְ־בָּבֶל קָלָה בָאֵשׁ	בָּבֶל בָּאֵשׁ
וְדִבֶּר דְּבָרוֹ בִשְׁמִי	23 וַיְדַבְּרוּ דָבָר בִּשְׁמִי שֶׁקֶר
וְאָנֹכִי עֵד	וְאָנֹכִי הוּיֹדֵעַ וָעֵד
Deest	24 לֵאמֹר
לֹא שְׁלַחְתִּיךָ בָּשְׁמִי וְאֶל־צְפַנְיָה בֶן־	25 כֹּה־אָמַר יְהוָֹה צְבָאוֹת אֱלֹהֵי
מַעֲשֵׂיָה הַכֹּהֵן אָמַר	יִשְׂרָאֵל לֵאמֹר יַעַן אֲשֶׁר אַתָּה
	שָׁלַחְתָּ בְשִׁמְכָה סְפָרִים אֶל־כָּל־
	הָעָם אֲשֶׁר בִּירוּשָׁלַםִ וְאֶל־
	צְפַנְיָה בֶן־מַעֲשֵׂיָה הַכֹּהֵן
	וְאֶל־כָּל־הַכֹּהֲנִים לֵאמֹר:
לִהְיוֹת פָּקִיד[c] בְּבֵית יְהוָֹה לְכָל־אִישׁ	26 לִהְיֹת פְּקִדִים בֵּית יְהוָֹה לְכֹל
מִתְנַבֵּא וּלְכָל־אִישׁ מְשֻׁגָּע	אִישׁ מְשֻׁגָּע וּמִתְנַבֵּא
וְאֶל־הַצִּנּוּר[d]	וְאֶל־הַצִּינֹק
לָמָה גָעַרְתָּם	27 לָמָה לֹא גָעַרְתָּ
הֲלֹא עַל־כֵּן שָׁלַח עַל־כֵּן כִּי בְחֹדֶשׁ הַזֶּה	28 כִּי עַל־כֵּן שָׁלַח אֵלֵינוּ בָּבֶל
שָׁלַח אֲלֵיכֶם בְּבָבֶל[e] לֵאמֹר	לֵאמֹר
צְפַנְיָה	29 צְפַנְיָה הַכֹּהֵן
אֶת־הַסֵּפֶר	אֶת־הַסֵּפֶר הַזֶּה
יִרְמְיָהוּ	יִרְמְיָהוּ הַנָּבִיא
שְׁלַח אֶל־הַגּוֹלָה	31 שְׁלַח עַל־כָּל־הַגּוֹלָה

---

[a] Targ. עַל.   [b] Targ. וְצַל.   [c] Targ. בְּצַנָּא סָגַן כַּהֲנַיָּא.   [d] καταράκτῃ.
[e] Targ. לְבָבֶל.   [f] Targ. לָנַח.

	אֶל־שְׁמַעְיָה עַל־שְׁמַעְיָה
32	עַל־שְׁמַעְיָה הַנֶּחֱלָמִי עַל־שְׁמַעְיָה
אִישׁ (מֵהֶם) לָהֶם וְלֹא־יִהְיֶה	לָכֵן־כֹּה־אָמַר יְהוָה הִנְנִי פֹקֵד עַל־שְׁמַעְיָה הַנֶּחֱלָמִי וְעַל־זַרְעוֹ לֹא־יִהְיֶה לוֹ אִישׁ יוֹשֵׁב בְּתוֹךְ־
אֲשֶׁר־ הַטּוֹב לִרְאוֹת בְּתוֹכֲכֶם	הָעָם הַזֶּה וְלֹא־יִרְאֶה בַטּוֹב
לֹא לָכֶם עֹשֶׂה אֲנִי	אֲשֶׁר־אֲנִי עֹשֶׂה־לְעַמִּי נְאֻם־
יִרְאוּ	יְהוָה כִּי־סָרָה דִבֶּר עַל־יְהוָה

CAPUT XXX.

כְּתָב	2 כְּתָב־לְךָ
עַל‎ᵃ־סֵפֶר	אֶל־סֵפֶר
עַל־יִשְׂרָאֵל וִיהוּדָהᶜ	4 אֶל־יִשְׂרָאֵל וְאֶל־יְהוּדָה
אֵימָה קוֹל חֲרָדָה יְהוָה אָמַר כֹּה	5 כִּי־כֹה אָמַר יְהוָה קוֹל חֲרָדָה
תִּשְׁמָעוּ	שָׁמָעְנוּ
הַחֲרָדָה וְעַל־ זָכָר אִם־יָלַד וּרְאוּ שַׁאֲלוּ	6 שַׁאֲלוּ־נָא וּרְאוּ אִם־יֹלֵד
וָיֶשַׁע מָתְנַיִם יֹאחֲזוּ בָּהּ אֲשֶׁר	זָכָר
פָּנִים נֶהֶפְכוּ חֲלָצָיו עַל־ וִידֵיו כַּיּוֹלֵדָה חֲלָצָיו עַל־	מַדּוּעַ רָאִיתִי כָל־גֶּבֶר יָדָיו עַל־חֲלָצָיו
לְיֵרָקוֹן	כַּיּוֹלֵדָה וְנֶהֶפְכוּ כָל־פָּנִים לְיֵרָקוֹן
גָּדוֹל הָיָה כִּי	7 הוֹי כִּי גָדוֹל
כָּמֹהוּ וְאַיִן‎ᵈ	מֵאַיִן כָּמֹהוּ
אֶשְׁבֹּר יְהוָה נְאֻם הַהוּא בַּיּוֹם	8 וְהָיָה בַיּוֹם הַהוּא נְאֻם יְהוָה
וּמוֹסְרוֹתֵיהֶם צַוְּארָם מֵעַל הַעֵל	צְבָאוֹת אֶשְׁבֹּר עֻלּוֹ מֵעַל
עוֹד יַעַבְדוּ וְלֹא אַנְתֵּק	צַוָּארֶךָ וּמוֹסְרוֹתֶיךָ אֲנַתֵּק
לְזָרִים	וְלֹא־יַעַבְדוּ־בוֹ עוֹד זָרִים
אָקִים לָהֶם	9 אֲשֶׁר אָקִים לָהֶם
10	וְאַתָּה אַל־תִּירָא עַבְדִּי יַעֲקֹב
	נְאֻם־יְהֹוָה וְאַל־תֵּחַת יִשְׂרָאֵל כִּי
Desunt	הִנְנִי מוֹשִׁיעֲךָ מֵרָחוֹק וְאֶת־זַרְעֲךָ
	מֵאֶרֶץ שִׁבְיָם וְשָׁב יַעֲקֹב וְשָׁקַט
11	וְשַׁאֲנַן וְאֵין מַחֲרִיד: כִּי־אִתְּךָ
	אֲנִי נְאֻם־יְהוָה לְהוֹשִׁיעֶךָ כִּי

ᵃ Targ. עַל.   ᵇ Targ. עַל.   ᶜ Targ. עַל יִשְׂרָאֵל וִיהוּדָה.   ᵈ Targ. לֵיהּ.

[30:12-22]   THE CONSPECTUS OF THE VARIATIONS.   343

Desunt	אֶעֱשֶׂה כָלָה בְּכָל־הַגּוֹיִם אֲשֶׁר הֲפִצוֹתִיךָ שָּׁם אַךְ אֹתְךָ לֹא אֶעֱשֶׂה כָלָה וְיִסַּרְתִּיךָ לַמִּשְׁפָּט וְנַקֵּה לֹא אֲנַקֶּךָ:
כֹּה אָמַר יהוה נָשְׂאתִי שֶׁבֶר	12 כִּי כֹה אָמַר יהוה אָנוּשׁ לְשִׁבְרֵךְ
אֵין דָּן דִּינֵךְ לְמִזוֹר^a רָפָּאת (נִרְפֵּאת) תּוֹעֶלֶת אֵין לָךְ	13 אֵין דָּן דִּינֵךְ לְמָזוֹר רְפֻאוֹת תְּעָלָה אֵין לָךְ
לֹא יִדְרְשׁוּ עַל כָּל עֲוֹנֵךְ	14 אוֹתָךְ לֹא יִדְרְשׁוּ עַל רֹב עֲוֹנֵךְ
Desunt	15 מַה־תִּזְעַק עַל־שִׁבְרֵךְ אָנוּשׁ מַכְאֹבֵךְ עַל רֹב עֲוֹנֵךְ עָצְמוּ חַטֹּאתַיִךְ עָשִׂיתִי אֵלֶּה לָךְ
כָּל־בְּשֹׂרָם יְלַחֲכוּ (יֹאכֵלוּ) עַל רֹב עֲוֹנֵךְ עָצְמוּ חַטֹּאתַיִךְ עָשׂוּ אֵלֶּה לָךְ	16 כָּל־בַּבְּכִי יֵלֵכוּ
כִּי אֵלֶּה אַרְכַּתָךְ וּמַמְפָּה נָחֲלָה אַרְפָּאךְ	17 כִּי אַעֲלֶה אֲרֻכָה לָךְ וּמִמַּכּוֹתַיִךְ אֶרְפָּאֵךְ^{b}
כִּי נִדְחָה נִקְרֵאת צִידְכֶם הִיא כִּי דֹרֵשׁ אֵין לָהּ	כִּי נִדָּחָה קָרְאוּ לָךְ צִיּוֹן הִיא דֹּרֵשׁ אֵין לָהּ
הַנְּגִי־שָׁב שָׁבוּת יַעֲקֹב וְשִׁבְיוֹ (וּשְׁבוּתוֹ) אֲרַחֵם וְהָמוֹן (וְהָעָם)	הִנְנִי־שָׁב שְׁבוּת אָהֳלֵי יַעֲקוֹב וּמִשְׁכְּנֹתָיו אֲרַחֵם וְאַרְמוֹן
וַיֵּצְאוּ מֵהֶם מְשׁוֹרְרִים^c (תּוֹדוֹת) קוֹל מְשַׂחֲקִים Deest	19 וְיָצָא מֵהֶם תּוֹדָה וְקוֹל מְשַׂחֲקִים וְהִכְבַּדְתִּים וְלֹא יִצְעָרוּ
וּבָאוּ (וְיָהָלְכוּ) בְּנֵיהֶם וְעֵדָתָם עַל־לֹחֲצֵיהֶם^d	20 וְהָיוּ בָנָיו וַעֲדָתוֹ עַל כָּל־לֹחֲצָיו
וְהָיוּ אַדִּירָו (אַבִּירָו) עֲלֵיהֶם וּמֹשְׁלוֹ מֵהֶם יֵצֵא וְקִפַּצְתִּים וְיָשׁוּבוּ^{e} אֵלִי נָתַן אֶת־לִבּוֹ לָשׁוּב אֵלִי	21 וְהָיָה אַדִּירוֹ מִמֶּנּוּ וּמֹשְׁלוֹ מִקִּרְבּוֹ יֵצֵא וְהִקְרַבְתִּיו וְנִגַּשׁ אֵלַי עָרַב אֶת־לִבּוֹ לָגֶשֶׁת אֵלַי
Desunt	22 וִהְיִיתֶם לִי לְעָם וְאָנֹכִי אֶהְיֶה לָכֶם לֵאלֹהִים:

^{a} εἰς ἄλγηρόν. ^{b} Cf. vs. 12. ^{c} Targ. בְּחֶדְוֵי תּוּשְׁבְּחָתָא. ^{d} Targ. דְּחָקֵיהוֹן.
^{e} Targ. יְאָקְרְבִנּוּן וִיתֻנְהוֹן.

23 הִנֵּה סַעֲרַת יהוה חֵמָה יָצְאָה כִּי סַעֲרַת יהוה יָצְאָה בְחֵמָה*
    סַעַר מִתְגּוֹרֵר עַל־רֹאשׁ רְשָׁעִים   רָצָא סַעַר מִתְגּוֹרֵר עַל־רְשָׁעִים
    יָחוּל   יָבוֹא

CAPUT XXXI.

1 לְכֹל מִשְׁפְּחוֹת יִשְׂרָאֵל   לְמִשְׁפַּחַת יִשְׂרָאֵל
2 מָצָא חֵן בַּמִּדְבָּר עַם שְׂרִידֵי חָרֶב   מָצָא חֵן בַּמִּדְבָּר עַם־שְׂדוּדֵי
    הָלוֹךְ לְהַרְגִּיעוֹ יִשְׂרָאֵל   חֶרֶב הָלְכוּ וְלֹא הָרְגוּ יִשְׂרָאֵל
3 מֵרָחוֹק יהוה נִרְאָה לִי וְאַהֲבַת   יהוה מֵרָחוֹק נִרְאָה לוֹ אַהֲבַת
    עוֹלָם אֲהַבְתִּיךְ עַל־כֵּן מְשַׁכְתִּיךְ   עוֹלָם אֲהַבְתִּיךְ עַל־כֵּן מְשַׁכְתִּיךְ
    חָסֶד   לְחֶסֶד
4 עוֹד אֶבְנֵךְ   כִּי אֶבְנֵךְ
    תַּעְדִּי תֻפַּיִךְ   תִּקְחִי תֻפַּיִךְ[b]
    בִּמְחוֹל מְשַׂחֲקִים   בִּקְהַל[c] מְשַׂחֲקִים
5 עוֹד תִּטְּעִי כְרָמִים   כִּי תִטְּעוּ כְרָמִים
    נָטְעוּ נֹטְעִים וְחִלֵּלוּ   נָטְעוּ וְחִלֵּלוּ
6 קָרְאוּ נֹצְרִים בְּהַר אֶפְרַיִם קוּמוּ   קְרִיאַת נֹצְרִים בְּהָרֵי אֶפְרַיִם קוּמוּ
    וְנַעֲלֶה צִיּוֹן אֶל־יהוה אֱלֹהֵינוּ   וַעֲלוּ צִיּוֹן אֶל־יְהוָה אֱלֹהֵיכֶם
7 כִּי־כֹה אָמַר יהוה רָנּוּ לְיַעֲקֹב   כִּדְכָה אָמַר יהוה לְיַעֲקֹב שִׂמְחִי
    שִׂמְחָה וְצַהֲלִי   וְצַהֲלִי (וְדַבְּרִי)
    הַלְלוּ וְאִמְרוּ הוֹשַׁע יהוה אֶת־   וְהַלְלוּ אִמְרוּ הוֹשִׁיעַ יהוה אֶת־
    עַמְּךָ   עַמּוֹ[d]
8 מֵאֶרֶץ צָפוֹן   מִצָּפוֹן
    בָּם עִוֵּר וּפִסֵּחַ הָרָה וְיֹלֶדֶת יַחְדָּו   בְּמוֹעֵד (חַ)פֶּסַח וְיָלְדָה
    יָשׁוּבוּ הֵנָּה   וְיָשׁוּבוּ הֵנָּה
9 בִּבְכִי יָבֹאוּ   בִּבְכִי יָצְאוּ[e]
    אוֹלִיכֵם אֶל־נַחֲלֵי מַיִם   מְתַלְּנָן (אוּלְיָנַם) עַל־נַחֲלֵי מַיִם
    לֹא יִכָּשְׁלוּ בָהּ   וְלֹא יִתְעוּ בָהּ
10 דְּבַר־יהוה   דִּבְרֵי־יהוה
    וְאִמְרוּ   אִמְרוּ

---

[a] Targ. בְּרִגְזֵי נָפְקָא. [b] Cf. Exod. 15:20. [c] Targ. בְּסִיעָה. [d] Targ. יָת עַמֵּהּ. [e] Targ. בִּבְגִלְוָתְהוֹן כַּד הֲווֹ בָּכַן. [f] Targ. עַל.

31:11-20] THE CONSPECTUS OF THE VARIATIONS.

וִיקַבְּצֶנּוּ	יְקַבְּצֶנּוּ
11 וּגְאָלוּ מִיד חָזָק מִמֶּנּוּ	גָּאֲלוּ מִיד חֲזָקִים[a] מִמֶּנּוּ
12 וּבָאוּ וְרִנְּנוּ בִּמְרוֹם־צִיּוֹן וְנָהֲרוּ אֶל־טוּב יהוה עַל־דָּגָן וְעַל־תִּירֹשׁ וְעַל־יִצְהָר וְעַל־בְּנֵי־צֹאן וּבָקָר וְהָיְתָה נַפְשָׁם כְּגַן רָוֶה וְלֹא־יוֹסִיפוּ לְדַאֲבָה עוֹד	וּבָאוּ וְרִנְּנוּ בְּהַר־צִיּוֹן וּבְאֵר (וּמַהֵרוּ) אֶל־טוּב יהוה עַל־אֶרֶץ דָּגָן וְתִירֹשׁ[c] וּפְרִי וּבָקָר וָצֹאן וְהָיְתָה נַפְשָׁם כְּעֵץ פְּרִי וְלֹא־יִרְעָבוּ (לְרָעָבָה?) עוֹד[d]
13 אָז תִּשְׂמַח בְּתוּלָה בְמָחוֹל וּבַחוּרִים וּזְקֵנִים יַחְדָּו וְנִחַמְתִּים וְשִׂמַּחְתִּים מִיגוֹנָם	אָז תִּשְׂמַחְנָה בְּתוּלוֹת בִּקְהַל בַּחוּרִים וּזְקֵנִים יַחְדּוּ וְשִׂמַּחְתִּים
14 וְרִוֵּיתִי נֶפֶשׁ הַכֹּהֲנִים דָּשֶׁן	רִבִּיתִי (הִגְדַּלְתִּי) וְרִוֵּיתִי נֶפֶשׁ הַכֹּהֲנִים בְּנֵי לֵוִי[e]
נְאֻם־יְהוָה	Deest
15 בְּכִי תַמְרוּרִים רָחֵל מְבַכָּה עַל־בָּנֶיהָ מֵאֲנָה לְהִנָּחֵם עַל־בָּנֶיהָ כִּי אֵינֶנּוּ	וּבְכִי וְתַמְרוּרִים רָחֵל מְבַכָּה מֵאֲנָה לָנוּחַ עַל־בָּנֶיהָ כִּי אֵינָם[f]
16 מִנְעִי קוֹלֵךְ מִבֶּכִי וְעֵינַיִךְ מִדִּמְעָה כִּי יֵשׁ שָׂכָר לִפְעֻלָּתֵךְ נְאֻם־יְהוָה וְשָׁבוּ מֵאֶרֶץ אוֹיֵב	יִמָּנַע קוֹלֵךְ מִבֶּכִי וְעֵינַיִךְ מִדִּמְעוֹתָיִךְ כִּי יֵשׁ שָׂכָר לִפְעֻלָּתָיִךְ[g] מֵאֶרֶץ אוֹיְבִים[h]
17 וְיֵשׁ־תִּקְוָה לְאַחֲרִיתֵךְ נְאֻם־יְהוָה וְשָׁבוּ בָנִים לִגְבוּלָם	תִּקְוָה לְאַחֲרִיתֵךְ (זִכָּרוֹן לְבָנָיִךְ)
18 שָׁמוֹעַ שָׁמַעְתִּי כְּעֵגֶל לֹא לֻמָּד	שְׁמוּעָה שָׁמַעְתִּי אָנֹכִי (אֲנִי) כְּעֵגֶל לֹא לֻמַּדְתִּי[i]
19 כִּי־אַחֲרֵי שׁוּבִי	כִּי־אַחֲרֵי שְׁבִי
סָפַקְתִּי עַל־יָרֵךְ וְגַם־בֹּשְׁתִּי נִכְלַמְתִּי כִּי נָשָׂאתִי חֶרְפַּת נְעוּרָי	נֶאֱנַחְתִּי (סָפַדְתִּי) עַל־הַיּוֹם בֹּשֶׁת וְהָרְאֵיתִיךָ כִּי נָשָׂאתִי חֶרְפָּה מִנְּעוּרָי[k]
20 הֲבֵן יַקִּיר לִי אֶפְרַיִם אִם יֶלֶד שַׁעֲשׁוּעִים כִּי־מִדֵּי דַבְּרִי בּוֹ זָכֹר אֶזְכְּרֶנּוּ עוֹד חָמוּ מֵעַי לוֹ	בֵּן יָקִיר לִי אֶפְרַיִם לִי יֶלֶד שַׁעֲשׁוּעִים כִּי־מִדֵּי דְבָרַי[l] בּוֹ זָכֹר אֲזַכְּרֶנּוּ מֵהַרְתִּי אֵלָיו (לוֹ)

[a] Targ. בְּיָד דְּתַקִּיפִין. [b] Targ. בְּטוּר. [c] Cf. Deut. 33:28. [d] Vid. vs. 25.
[e] Cf. 33:18. [f] Targ. אֲרֵי גְלוֹ. [g] Targ. לִטְבָדָךְ. [h] Targ. בְּאַרְעָא בַעֲלֵי דְּבָבֵיחוֹן.
[i] Targ. לָא אֻלְפְנָא. [k] Cf. Ps. 129:1. [l] Targ. פִּתְגָמַי אֱיָרְתֵיהּ.

הַצִּיבִי לָךְ צִיֻּנִים שִׂמִי לָךְ 21	הִתְיַצְּבִי צִיּוֹן שִׂמִי תַּמְרוּרִים(?)ᵃ
תַּמְרוּרִים שִׁתִי לִבֵּךְ לַמְסִלָּה	שִׁתִי לִבֵּךְ לִפְתָחֵךְ(?)
שׁוּבִי אַל־עָרַיִךְ אֵלֶּה	שׁוּבִי אַל־עָרַיִךְ אֲבֵלָהᵇ
22 כִּי־בָרָא יהוה חֲדָשָׁה בָּאָרֶץ	כִּי־בָרָא יהוה תְּשׁוּעָה (וֶשַׁ?) לְמָטָ־
נְקֵבָה תְּסוֹבֵב גָּבֶר	חָדָשׁ פְּתְשׁוּעָה יְסוֹבֵב גְּבָרִים
23 כֹּה־אָמַר יהוה צְבָאוֹת אֱלֹהֵי	כִּי כֹּה־אָמַר יהוה
יִשְׂרָאֵל	
בְּשׁוּבִי אֶת־שְׁבוּתָם יְבָרֶכְךָ יהוה	בְּשׁוּבִי אֶת־שְׁבוּתוֹ יְבָרֵךְ(בָּרוּךְ)יהוה
נְוֵה־צֶדֶק הַר הַקֹּדֶשׁ	עַל־צֶדֶק הַר קָדְשׁוֹ
24 וְיָשְׁבוּ בָהּ יהוּדָה וְכָל־עָרָיו	וְיֹשְׁבִים בְּעָרֵי יְהוּדָה וּבְכָל־אַרְצוֹ
יַחְדָּו אִכָּרִים וְנָסְעוּ בַּעֵדֶר	יַחְדָּו עֲבָאכָר וְנָשָׂאוּ בַּעֵדֶר
25 כִּי הִרְוֵיתִי נֶפֶשׁ עֲיֵפָה וְכָל־נֶפֶשׁ	כִּי הִרְוֵיתִי כָּל־נֶפֶשׁ צְמֵאָה וְכָל־נֶפֶשׁ
דָּאֲבָה מִלֵּאתִי	רְעֵבָה מִלֵּאתִי
26 וּשְׁנָתִי עָרְבָה לִי	וּשְׁנָתִי עָרְבָה לִי הָיְתָה
27 הִנֵּה יָמִים בָּאִים	לָכֵן הִנֵּה יָמִים בָּאִים
אֶת־בֵּית יִשְׂרָאֵל וְאֶת־בֵּית יְהוּדָה	אֶת־יִשְׂרָאֵל וְאֶת־יְהוּדָה
28 וְלִנְתוֹץ וְלַהֲרֹס וּלְהַאֲבִיד	Deest
לֹא־יֹאמְרוּ עוֹד אָבוֹת אָכְלוּ בֹסֶר	לֹא־יֹאמְרוּ עוֹד אָבוֹת אָכְלוּ בֹסֶר וְשִׁנֵּי
וְשִׁנֵּי בָנִים תִּקְהֶינָה	הַבָּנִים תִּקְהֶינָה
30 כָּל־הָאָדָם הָאֹכֵל	וְהָאֹכֵל
32 אֲשֶׁר־הֵמָּה הֵפֵרוּ אֶת־בְּרִיתִי	כִּי הֵמָּה לֹא עָמְדוּ (הֵקִימוּ אֶת־)
וְאָנֹכִי בָּעַלְתִּי בָם	(בְּ)בְרִיתִי וַאֲנֹכִי בָּחַלְתִּי בָםᶜ
33 כִּי זֹאת הַבְּרִית	כִּי זֹאת בְּרִיתִי
נָתַתִּי אֶת־תּוֹרָתִי	נָתוֹן אֶתֵּן אֶת־תּוֹרָתִי
וְעַל־לִבָּם אֶכְתֳּבֶנָּה	וְעַל־לִבּוֹתֵיהֶם אֶכְתְּבֵן
34 וְלֹא יְלַמְּדוּ עוֹד	וְלֹא יְלַמְּדוּ
דְּעוּ אֶת־יהוה	דַּע אֶת־יהוה
לֵאמֹר	Deest
לְעֲוֹנָם וּלְחַטָּאתָם	לְעֲוֹנוֹתֵיהֶם וּלְחַטֹּאותֵיהֶםᵈ
35 נֹתֵן שֶׁמֶשׁ לְאוֹר יוֹמָם	נָתַן הַשֶּׁמֶשׁ לְאוֹר הַיּוֹם
חֻקֹּת	Deest
לְאוֹר לָיְלָה	לְאוֹר הַלַּיְלָה

ᵃ עמ׳ὄψις τιμωρίαν. ᵇ Aram. אֱלָיָה(?). ᶜ Cf. 14:19. ᵈ Vid. 16:18; 18:23; 36:3.—Targ. לְהֵבְיחוֹן נַשָׁאֲרוֹן.

37 כֹּה אָמַר יהוה אִם־יִמַּדּוּ שָׁמַיִם　　אָם־יֵרֹלּוּ (יָרֹמּוּ) שָׁמַיִם לְמַעְלָה
מִלְמַעְלָה וְיֵחָקְרוּ מוֹסְדֵי־אָרֶץ　　אָמַר יהוה וְאִם יִרְחַק (וְיִשָּׁפֵל)
לְמָטָּה גַּם־אֲנִי אֶמְאַס בְּכָל־　　יְסוֹד־אָרֶץ לְמַטָּה גַּם־אֲנִי לֹא
זֶרַע יִשְׂרָאֵל עַל־כָּל־אֲשֶׁר　　אֶמְאַס בְּזֶרַע יִשְׂרָאֵל נְאֻם־יהוה
עָשׂוּ נְאֻם־יהוה　　עַל־כָּל־אֲשֶׁר עָשׂוּ
38 ־ בָּאִים　　יָמִים בָּאִים
וְנִבְנְתָה הָעִיר　　וְנִבְנְתָה עִיר
מִמִּגְדַּל חֲנַנְאֵל　　מִמִּגְדַּל חֲנַמְאֵל
39 וְיָצָא עוֹד קָוֵה הַמִּדָּה נֶגְדּוֹ　　וְיָצָא קָו מִדָּתָהּ נֶגְדָּם עַד גִּבְעוֹת גָּרֵב
עַל גִּבְעַת גָּרֵב וְנָסַב　　וְנָסַב סָבִיב בָּאֲבָנִים יְקָרוֹת
גֹּעָתָה　　(בְּאַבְנֵי־חֵפֶץ)
40 וְכָל־הָעֵמֶק הַפְּגָרִים וְהַדֶּשֶׁן　　Deest
וְכָל־הַשְּׁרֵמוֹת　　וְכָל־הַשְּׁרֵמוֹת
לֹא־יִנָּתֵשׁ וְלֹא־יֵהָרֵס עוֹד לְעוֹלָם　　וְלֹא עוֹד יִנָּתֵשׁ וְלֹא־יֵהָרֵס עַד־עוֹלָם

CAPUT XXXII.

1 אֶל־יִרְמְיָהוּ מֵאֵת יהוה　　מֵאֵת יהוה אֶל־יִרְמְיָהוּ
לְצִדְקִיָּהוּ מֶלֶךְ יְהוּדָה הִיא　　לַמֶּלֶךְ צִדְקִיָּהוּ הִיא הַשָּׁנָה שְׁמֹנֶה־
הַשָּׁנָה שְׁמֹנֶה־עֶשְׂרֵה שָׁנָה　　עֶשְׂרֵה לַמֶּלֶךְ נְבוּכַדְרֶאצַר מֶלֶךְ
לִנְבוּכַדְרֶאצַר　　בָּבֶל
2 וְאָז חֵיל מֶלֶךְ בָּבֶל　　וְחֵיל מֶלֶךְ בָּבֶל
וְיִרְמְיָהוּ הַנָּבִיא הָיָה כְּלוּא　　וְיִרְמְיָהוּ כְּלוּא (שָׁמוּר)
אֲשֶׁר בֵּית־מֶלֶךְ יְהוּדָה　　אֲשֶׁר בְּבֵית־מֶלֶךְ
3 אֲשֶׁר כְּלָאוֹ צִדְקִיָּהוּ מֶלֶךְ־יְהוּדָה　　בַּאֲשֶׁר כְּלָאוֹ הַמֶּלֶךְ צִדְקִיָּהוּ
בְּיַד מֶלֶךְ־בָּבֶל　　בִּידֵי מֶלֶךְ־בָּבֶל
4 וְצִדְקִיָּהוּ מֶלֶךְ יְהוּדָה　　וְצִדְקִיָּהוּ
בְּיַד מֶלֶךְ־בָּבֶל　　בִּידֵי מֶלֶךְ־בָּבֶל
וְדִבֶּר פִּיו עִם־פִּיו　　וּדְבַר פִּיו אֶל־פִּיו
5 וּבָבֶל יוֹלִיךְ אֶת־צִדְקִיָּהוּ וְשָׁם יִהְיֶה　　וַיֵּלֶךְ צִדְקִיָּהוּ בָּבֶל (בְּבָלָה) וְשָׁם יָשַׁב

[a] ut 32:9. [b] καὶ πάντες 'Ασαρημώθ. [c] Vid. vs. 3; 34:6. [d] Targ. דִּי בְּבֵית. [e] Cf. Num. 12:8.

עַד־פָּקְדִי אֹתוֹ נְאֻם־יְהוָה כִּי Desunt תִּלָּחֲמוּ אֶת־הַכַּשְׂדִּים לֹא תַצְלִיחוּ	
6 וַיֹּאמֶר יִרְמְיָהוּ הָיָה דְבַר־יְהוָה אֵלַי לֵאמֹר	וּדְבַר־יהוה היה אֶל־יִרְמִיהוּ לאמר
7 מִשְׁפַּט הַגְּאֻלָּה לִקְנוֹת	משפט לקחת למקנה
8 בֶּן־דֹּדִי כִּדְבַר יְהוָה	בנ־שלם דדי
וַיֹּאמֶר אֵלַי קְנֵה נָא	ויאמר קנה לך
אֲשֶׁר־בַּעֲנָתוֹת אֲשֶׁר בְּאֶרֶץ בִּנְיָמִין	אשר בארץ בנימין אשר־בענתות
כִּי לְךָ מִשְׁפַּט הַיְרֻשָּׁה וּלְךָ הַגְּאֻלָּה קְנֵה־לָךְ	כי לך משפט לקנותו ואתה הגדול (ולך הגדלה)
9 וָאֶקְנֶה אֶת־הַשָּׂדֶה מֵאֵת חֲנַמְאֵל אֲשֶׁר בַּעֲנָתוֹת	ואקנה את־שדה הנמאל Deest
וָאֶשְׁקֲלָה־לּוֹ אֶת־הַכֶּסֶף שִׁבְעָה	ואשקלהלו שבעה שקלים ושרה שקלים ועשרה הכסך	כסך
10 וָאֶכְתֹּב בַּסֵּפֶר	ואכתב אל־ספר
11 הַמִּצְוָה וְהַחֻקִּים וְאֶת־הַגָּלוּי Deest	
12 וָאֶתֵּן אֶת־הַסֵּפֶר הַמִּקְנָה	ואתן אתו (ואתנהו)
לְעֵינֵי חֲנַמְאֵל בֶּן־דֹּדִי וּלְעֵינֵי הָעֵדִים הַכֹּתְבִים	לעיני חנמאל דדי ולעיני האנשים הלמדים והכתבים
לְעֵינֵי כָּל־הַיְּהוּדִים הַיֹּשְׁבִים בַּחֲצַר הַמַּטָּרָה	ולעיני היהודים אשר בחצר המטרה
14 יְהוָה צְבָאוֹת אֱלֹהֵי יִשְׂרָאֵל אֶת־הַסְּפָרִים הָאֵלֶּה	יהוה צבאות Deest
וְאֵת הֶחָתוּם וְאֵת סֵפֶר הַגָּלוּי הַזֶּה וּנְתַתָּם בִּכְלִי־חָרֶשׂ לְמַעַן יַעַמְדוּ	ואת ספר הקרוא ונתתו בכלי־ חרש למען יעמד
15 יְהוָה צְבָאוֹת אֱלֹהֵי יִשְׂרָאֵל	יהוה
בָּתִּים וְשָׂדוֹת	שדות ובתים
17 אֲהָהּ אֲדֹנָי יְהוִה הִנֵּה	אַתָּה יְהוָה[b]
בְּזְרֹעֲךָ הַנְּטוּיָה לֹא־יִפָּלֵא מִמְּךָ כָּל־דָּבָר	ובזרעך הנטויה והרמה[c] לא־יפלא[d] (יסתר) ממך כל־דבר

[a] ut vs. 7. [b] Cf. 1:6; 4:10; 14:13. [c] Targ. בִּדְרָעָא. [d] Vid. vs. 27. [e] Targ. לָא יְהַפַּשׁ.

32:18-32] THE CONSPECTUS OF THE VARIATIONS. 349

18 עון אבות	עֲוֹנוֹתᵃ אבות
יְהוָה צְבָאוֹת שְׁמוֹ	Deest
19 גְדל העצה ורב העליליה אֲשֶׁר	יְהוָה גדל העצה ורב העליליה הָאֵל
עֵינֶיךָ פְקֻחוֹת עַל־כָּל־דַרְכֵי בְנֵי	הַגָדוֹל צְבָאוֹת וגדל שם יְהוָה
אדם לתת לאיש כִּדְרָכָיו	עיניך אֶל־דרכי בני הָאדם לתת
וְכִפְרִי מַעֲלָלָיו	לאיש כְדַרְכּוֹ
20 וּבָאדם	וּבְבְנֵי אדם (וּבִילִידֵי הָאֲדָמָה)
21 וּבְיָד חזקה	בְיד חזקה
וּבְמוֹרָא גָדוֹל	וּבְמַרְאִיםᵇ גְדוֹלִיםᶜ
22 לָתֵת לָהֶם	Deest
23 וַיִּרְשׁוּ אתה	וַיִקְחוּ אתה
וּבְתֹרוֹתְךָ	וּבְתֹרוֹתֶיךָ
אֶת כָּל־אֲשֶׁר צִוִּיתָה לָהֶם לַעֲשׂוֹת	את כל־אשר צויתי להם
וַתִּקְרָא אֹתָם אֵת כל־הרעה הַזֹּאת	וַיַקְרִיאוּ לָהֶם אֵת כל־הרעות הָאֵלֶּה
24 הִנֵּה הַסֹּלְלוֹת בָּאוּ	הנה הֶהָמוֹן (הַחַיִל) בא
בְּיַד הכשדים	בִּידֵי הכשדים
וְהַדָּבֵר	Deest
	כַּאֲשֶׁר דִּבַּרְתָּ כֵּן היה
25 וְאַתָּה אמרת אלי אֲדֹנָי יְהוִה	וְאַתָּה אָמַרְתָּ אֵלִי
וְהָעֵד עדים	
בְּיַד הכשדים	וָאֶכְתֹּב סֵפֶר וָאֶחְתֹּם וָאָעֵד עֵדִים בִּידֵי הכשדים
אֱלֵי־יִרְמְיָהוּ לאמר	אֵלַי לאמר
27 הִנֵּה אני יהוה	אני יהוה
הֲמִמֶּנִּי יִפָּלֵא כל־דבר	הֲמִמֶּנִּי יִבָּלֵאᵈ (יִסָּתֵר) כל־דבר
28 לכן כה אמר יהוה הִנְנִי נֹתֵן	לכן כה אמר יהוה אֱלֹהֵי יִשְׂרָאֵל
אֶת־הָעִיר הַזֹּאת בְּיַד הַכַּשְׂדִּים	הִנָּתֹן תִּנָּתֵןᵉ העיר ההיא בִּידֵי
וּבְיַד נְבוּכַדְרֶאצַּר מלך־בבל	מלך־בבל
29 וּשְׂרָפוּהָ וְאֵת הבתים	וְשָׂרְפוּ אֶת־הבתים
30 כִּי בְנֵי־יִשְׂרָאֵל אַךְ מַכְעִסִים אֹתִי בְּמַעֲשֵׂה יְדֵיהֶם נְאֻם־יְהוָה	Desunt
31 הָיְתָה לִּי הָעִיר הַזֹּאת	היתה העיר הזאת
32 עַל כָּל־רָעַת בְּנֵי־יִשְׂרָאֵל וּבְנֵי־יְהוּדָה	על כל־רעת בני־ישראל ויהודה

ᵃ Targ. חוֹבֵי.   ᵇ Targ. וּבְחֶזְוָנָא.   ᶜ Cf. Exod. 3:3.   ᵈ Vid. vs. 17.
ᵉ Vid. 34:2.

וְשָׂרֵיהֶם וּמַלְכֵיהֶם כֹּהֲנֵיהֶם שָׂרֵיהֶם מַלְכֵיהֶם וְכֹהֲנֵיהֶם	
וּנְבִיאֵיהֶם וְאִישׁ יְהוּדָה וְיֹשְׁבֵי וּנְבִיאֵיהֶם אַנְשֵׁי יְהוּדָה	
יְרוּשָׁלָ͏ִם וְהַיֹּשְׁבִים בִּירוּשָׁלָ͏ִם	
33 וְלַמֵּד אֹתָם הַשְׁכֵּם וְלַמֵּד וְאֵינָם וְלִמַּדְתִּי אֹתָם הַשְׁכֵּם וְלֹא שָׁמְעוּ	
שֹׁמְעִים לָקַחַת מוּסָר עוֹד לָקַחַת מוּסָר	
34 לְטַמְּאוֹ בְּטֻמְאוֹתָם^{a}	
35 לְהַעֲבִיר אֶת־בְּנֵיהֶם וְאֶת־ לְהַקְרִיב אֶת־בְּנֵיהֶם וְאֶת־בְּנוֹתֵיהֶם	
בְּנוֹתֵיהֶם לַמֹּלֶךְ לַמֹּלֶךְ הַמֶּלֶךְ	
36 וְעַתָּה לָכֵן כֹּה־אָמַר יְהֹוָה אֱלֹהֵי וְעַתָּה כֹּה־אָמַר יְהֹוָה אֱלֹהֵי יִשְׂרָאֵל	
יִשְׂרָאֵל אֶל־הָעִיר הַזֹּאת אֲשֶׁר עַל־הָעִיר הַזֹּאת אֲשֶׁר אַתָּה	
אַתֶּם אֹמְרִים נִתְּנָה בְּיַד מֶלֶךְ־בָּבֶל אֹמֵר^{c} תִּנָּתֵן בְּיַד מֶלֶךְ־בָּבֶל	
וּבַדֶּבֶר וּבַשֶּׁבִי^{f} (וּבַמִּשְׁלַחַת)	
37 מִכָּל־הָאֲרָצוֹת מִכָּל הָאָרֶץ	
וְהִשְׁבַּתִּים לָבֶטַח וְהִשְׁבַּתִּים בֹּטְחִים	
39 לֵב אֶחָד וְדֶרֶךְ אֶחָד דֶּרֶךְ אַחֵר וְלֵב אַחֵר	
לְטוֹב לָהֶם וּלְטוֹב לָהֶם	
40 לַהֲטִיבִי אוֹתָם Deest	
לְבִלְתִּי סוּר מֵעָלַי לְבִלְתִּי סוּרָם מֵעָלַי	
41 וְשַׂשְׂתִּי עֲלֵיהֶם וּפְקַדְתִּי	
בְּכָל־לִבִּי וּבְכָל־נַפְשִׁי וּבְכָל־לִבִּי וּבְכָל־נָפֶשׁ	
42 כַּאֲשֶׁר הֵבֵאתִי אֶל־הָעָם הַזֶּה כַּאֲשֶׁר הֲבִאֹתִי עַל־הָעָם הַזֶּה אֵת	
אֵת כָּל־הָרָעָה הַגְּדוֹלָה הַזֹּאת כָּל־הָרָעוֹת הַגְּדוֹלוֹת הָאֵלֶּה	
אֶת־כָּל־הַטּוֹבָה אֶת־כָּל־הַטֹּבוֹת	
43 וְנִקְנָה הַשָּׂדֶה וְיִקְנוּ עוֹד שָׂדוֹת^{f}	
אַתֶּם אֹמְרִים אַתָּה אֹמֵר^{e}	
נִתְּנָה בְּיַד הַכַּשְׂדִּים וְנִתְּנוּ בִּידֵי הַכַּשְׂדִּים	
44 שָׂדוֹת בַּכֶּסֶף יִקְנוּ וְכָתוֹב בַּסֵּפֶר וְיִקְנוּ שָׂדוֹת בַּכֶּסֶף וְתִכְתּוֹב בַּסֵּפֶר	
וְחָתוֹם וְהָעֵד עֵדִים וְתַחְתּוֹם וְתָעִיד עֵדִים	
וּבִסְבִיבֵי יְרוּשָׁלַ͏ִם וּבִסְבִיב יְרוּשָׁלָ͏ִם	
וּבְעָרֵי הַשְּׁפֵלָה וּבְעָרֵי הַנֶּגֶב וּבְעָרֵי הַשְּׁפֵלָה וּבְעָרֵי הַנֶּגֶב^{h}	
נְאֻם־יְהֹוָה Deest	

^{a} Cf. Lev. 16:16. ^{b} Targ. עַל. ^{c} Vid. vs. 43. ^{d} ἐν ἀποστολῇ. ^{e} Targ.
עַל. ^{f} Targ. יְזַדַּבְּנוּן חַקְלִין. ^{g} Vid. vs. 36. ^{h} ἐν πόλεσι τῆς Σεφηλά
καὶ ἐν πόλεσι τῆς ναγέβ.

CAPUT XXXIII.

2 עֹשֵׂה יְהוָֹה יוֹצֵר אוֹתָהּ	עֹשֵׂה אֶרֶץ וְיוֹצֵר אוֹתָהּ[a]
3 וּבְצֻרוֹת לֹא יְדַעְתָּם	וּבְצֻרוֹת אֲשֶׁר לֹא יְדַעְתָּם[b] (וּנְצֻרוֹת?[c])
4 יהוה אֱלֹהֵי יִשְׂרָאֵל	יהוה
מַלְכֵי יְהוּדָה	מֶלֶךְ יְהוּדָה
אֶל־הַסֹּלְלוֹת וְאֶל־הֶחָרֶב	אֶל־הַסֹּלְלוֹת וְהַדָּיֵק
5 בָּאִים	Deest
וּלְמַלְאָם	וּלְמַלְאָה
וַאֲשֶׁר הִסְתַּרְתִּי פָנַי מֵהָעִיר הַזֹּאת	וְהִסְתַּרְתִּי פָּנַי מֵהֶם
6 וּרְפָאתָם וְגִלֵּיתִי לָהֶם עֲתֶרֶת שָׁלוֹם וֶאֱמֶת	וְגִלֵּיתִי לָהֶם וּרְפֵאתִיהָ וְעָשִׂיתִי גַב־שָׁלוֹם גַּם־אֱמֶת
8 מִכָּל־עֲוֹנָם	מִכָּל־עֲוֹנוֹתֵיהֶם[d]
וְסָלַחְתִּי לְכָול־עֲוֹנוֹתֵיהֶם	וְלֹא־אֶזְכֹּר לַעֲוֹנוֹתֵיהֶם[e]
וַאֲשֶׁר פָּשְׁעוּ בִי	וּפִשְׁעוּ בִי
9 וְהָיְתָה לִּי לְשֵׁם שָׂשׂוֹן	וְהָיְתָה לְשָׂשׂוֹן
גּוֹיֵי הָאָרֶץ	גּוֹיֵי הָאָרֶץ
אֵת כָּל־הַטּוֹבָה אֲשֶׁר אָנֹכִי עֹשֶׂה לָהּ	אֶת־כָּל־הַטּוֹבוֹת אֲשֶׁר אָנֹכִי עֹשֶׂה
אֲשֶׁר אָנֹכִי עֹשֶׂה לָהּ	אֲשֶׁר אָנֹכִי עֹשֶׂה לָהֶם[f]
10 מֵאֵין אָדָם וּמֵאֵין בְּהֵמָה	מֵאֵין אָדָם וּבְהֵמָה[g]
וּבְחֻצוֹת יְרוּשָׁלִַם	וּמִחוּץ יְרוּשָׁלִָם
מֵאֵין אָדָם וּמֵאֵין יוֹשֵׁב וּמֵאֵין בְּהֵמָה	מֵאֵין אָדָם וּבְהֵמָה
11 מְבִאִים תּוֹדָה בֵּית יהוה	וְיָבִיאוּ מִנְחוֹת (מַתָּנוֹת) לְבֵית[h] יהוה
אֶת־שְׁבוּת־הָאָרֶץ	אֶת־עַל־שְׁבוּת־הָאָרֶץ הַהִיא
מֵאֵין־אָדָם וְעַד־בְּהֵמָה וּבְכָל־עָרָיו	מֵאֵין אָדָם וּבְהֵמָה[i] בְּכָל־עָרָיו
נְוֵה רֹעִים	נְוֹת רֹעִים
13 בְּעָרֵי הַשְּׁפֵלָה וּבְעָרֵי הַנֶּגֶב	וּבְעָרֵי הַשְּׁפֵלָה וּבְעָרֵי הַנֶּגֶב[k]
עַל־יְדֵי מוֹנֶה	עַל־יַד־מוֹנֶה

---

[a] Cf. Isa. 45:18. [b] Targ. הֲלָא יְדַעְתְּנָן. [c] Targ. וּנְצִירָתָא=וּנְצֻרוֹת.
[d] Targ. חוֹבֵיהוֹן. [e] Targ. חוֹבֵיהוֹן. [f] Targ. דַּאֲנָא עָבֵיד לְהוֹן. [g] ut 32:43.
[h] Targ. לְבֵית. [i] ut 32:43. [k] Vid. 32:44.

14 הִנֵּ֨ה יָמִ֤ים בָּאִים֙ נְאֻם־יְהוָ֔ה וַהֲקִֽמֹתִי֙ אֶת־הַדָּבָ֣ר הַטּ֔וֹב אֲשֶׁ֥ר דִּבַּ֛רְתִּי אֶל־בֵּ֥ית יִשְׂרָאֵ֖ל וְעַל־בֵּ֥ית
15 יְהוּדָֽה׃ בַּיָּמִ֤ים הָהֵם֙ וּבָעֵ֣ת הַהִ֔יא אַצְמִ֥יחַ לְדָוִ֖ד צֶ֣מַח צְדָקָ֑ה וְעָשָׂ֛ה
16 מִשְׁפָּ֥ט וּצְדָקָ֖ה בָּאָֽרֶץ׃ בַּיָּמִ֤ים הָהֵם֙ תִּוָּשַׁ֣ע יְהוּדָ֔ה וִירוּשָׁלַ֖͏ִם תִּשְׁכּ֣וֹן לָבֶ֑טַח וְזֶ֥ה אֲשֶׁר־יִקְרָא־לָ֖הּ
17 יְהוָ֥ה ׀ צִדְקֵֽנוּ׃ כִּי־כֹ֖ה אָמַ֣ר יְהוָ֑ה לֹֽא־יִכָּרֵ֣ת לְדָוִ֔ד אִ֕ישׁ יֹשֵׁ֖ב עַל־
18 כִּסֵּ֥א בֵית־יִשְׂרָאֵֽל׃ וְלַכֹּהֲנִ֣ים הַלְוִיִּ֗ם לֹֽא־יִכָּרֵ֥ת אִ֖ישׁ מִלְּפָנָ֑י מַעֲלֶ֤ה עוֹלָה֙ וּמַקְטִ֣יר מִנְחָ֔ה
19 וְעֹ֥שֶׂה זֶ֖בַח כָּל־הַיָּמִֽים׃ וַֽיְהִי֙ דְּבַר־יְהוָ֔ה אֶֽל־יִרְמְיָ֖הוּ לֵאמֹֽר׃
20 כֹּ֚ה אָמַ֣ר יְהוָ֔ה אִם־תָּפֵ֙רוּ֙ אֶת־בְּרִיתִ֣י הַיּ֔וֹם וְאֶת־בְּרִיתִ֖י הַלָּ֑יְלָה וּלְבִלְתִּ֛י הֱי֥וֹת יֽוֹמָם־וָלַ֖יְלָה בְּעִתָּֽם׃
21 גַּם־בְּרִיתִ֤י תֻפַר֙ אֶת־דָּוִ֣ד עַבְדִּ֔י מִֽהְיֽוֹת־ל֥וֹ בֵ֖ן מֹלֵ֣ךְ עַל־כִּסְא֑וֹ וְאֶת־
22 הַלְוִיִּ֥ם הַכֹּהֲנִ֖ים מְשָׁרְתָֽי׃ אֲשֶׁ֤ר לֹֽא־יִסָּפֵר֙ צְבָ֣א הַשָּׁמַ֔יִם וְלֹ֥א יִמַּ֖ד ח֣וֹל הַיָּ֑ם כֵּ֣ן אַרְבֶּ֗ה אֶת־זֶ֙רַע֙ דָּוִ֣ד עַבְדִּ֔י וְאֶת־הַלְוִיִּ֖ם מְשָׁרְתֵ֥י אֹתִֽי׃
23 וַיְהִי֙ דְּבַר־יְהוָ֔ה אֶֽל־יִרְמְיָ֖הוּ
24 לֵאמֹֽר׃ הֲל֣וֹא רָאִ֗יתָ מָֽה־הָעָ֤ם הַזֶּה֙ דִּבְּר֣וּ לֵאמֹ֔ר שְׁתֵּ֣י הַמִּשְׁפָּח֗וֹת אֲשֶׁ֨ר בָּחַ֧ר יְהוָ֛ה בָּהֶ֖ם וַיִּמְאָסֵ֑ם וְאֶת־עַמִּי֙ יִנְאָצ֔וּן מִֽהְי֥וֹת ע֖וֹד גּ֥וֹי
25 לִפְנֵיהֶֽם׃ כֹּ֚ה אָמַ֣ר יְהוָ֔ה אִם־לֹ֥א בְרִיתִ֖י יוֹמָ֣ם וָלָ֑יְלָה חֻקּ֛וֹת שָׁמַ֥יִם
26 וָאָ֖רֶץ לֹא־שָֽׂמְתִּי׃ גַּם־זֶ֣רַע יַעֲק֣וֹב וְדָוִד֩ עַבְדִּ֨י אֶמְאַ֜ס מִקַּ֣חַת מִזַּרְע֗וֹ מֹשְׁלִים֙ אֶל־זֶ֙רַע֙ אַבְרָהָ֔ם

Desunt

CAPUT XXXIV.

1 וְכָל־מַמְלְכוֹת אֶרֶץ מֶמְשֶׁלֶת יָדוֹ וְכָל־אָרֶץ מִמְשַׁלְתּוֹ נִלְחָמוּ עַל־
וְעַל־כָּל־עָרֵי יְהוּדָה יְרוּשָׁלִַם נִלְחָמִים עַל־
יְרוּשָׁלִַם וְעַל־כָּל־עָרֶיהָ לֵאמֹר   לֵאמֹר

2 כֹּה־אָמַר יְהוָה אֱלֹהֵי יִשְׂרָאֵל כֹּה־אָמַר יְהוָה הָלֹךְ אֶל־
הָלֹךְ וְאָמַרְתָּ אֶל־צִדְקִיָּהוּ   צִדְקִיָּהוּ
הִנְנִי נֹתֵן אֶת־הָעִיר הַזֹּאת בְּיַד הִנְנִי נֹתָן* תִּפָּתֵן* הָעִיר הַזֹּאת בְּיָדֵי מֶלֶךְ־
מֶלֶךְ־בָּבֶל   בָּבֶל וּלְכָדָהּ

3 כִּי תָפֹשׂ תִּתָּפֵשׂ וּבְיָדוֹ תִנָּתֵן וְתֹפֵשׂ תִּתָּפֵשׂ וּבְיָדָיו תִּנָּתֵן
וְעֵינֶיךָ אֶת־עֵינֵי מֶלֶךְ־בָּבֶל וְעֵינֶיךָ אֶת־עֵינָיו תִּרְאֶינָה וּבָבֶל
תִרְאֶינָה וּפִיהוּ אֶת־פִּיךָ יְדַבֵּר   תָּבוֹא
וּבָבֶל תָּבוֹא

4 עָלֶיךָ לֹא־תָמוּת בֶּחָרֶב   Deest

5 וּבְמִשְׂרְפוֹת אֲבוֹתֶיךָ הַמְּלָכִים וְכַאֲשֶׁר סָפְדוּ (וּכְמִשְׂפְּדוֹת) אֶת־
הָרִאשֹׁנִים אֲשֶׁר־הָיוּ לְפָנֶיךָ כֵּן אֲבוֹתֶיךָ אֲשֶׁר־מָלְכוּ לְפָנֶיךָ
יִשְׂרְפוּ־לָךְ וְהוֹי אָדוֹן (בְּרֵאשֹׁנָה) יִסְפְּדוּ גַּם־לְךָ הוֹי*
יִסְפְּדוּ־לָךְ   אָדוֹן וְעַד־שְׁאוֹל יִסְפְּדוּ־לָךְ

6 וַיְדַבֵּר יִרְמְיָהוּ הַנָּבִיא אֶל־ וַיְדַבֵּר יִרְמִיָּהוּ אֶל־הַמֶּלֶךְ צִדְקִיָּהוּ*
צִדְקִיָּהוּ מֶלֶךְ יְהוּדָה

7 נִלְחָמִים עַל־יְרוּשָׁלִַם וְעַל כָּל־ נִלְחָם עַל־יְרוּשָׁלִַם וְעַל־עָרֵי יְהוּדָה
עָרֵי יְהוּדָה הַנּוֹתָרוֹת אֶל־ וְעַל־לָכִישׁ וְעַל־עֲזֵקָה
לָכִישׁ וְאֶל־עֲזֵקָה

8 אֶת־כָּל־הָעָם אֲשֶׁר בִּירוּשָׁלִַם אֶת־הָעָם לִקְרֹא דְּרוֹר
לִקְרֹא לָהֶם דְּרוֹר

9 לְבִלְתִּי עֲבָד־בָּם בִּיהוּדִי אָחִיהוּ לְבִלְתִּי עֲבֹד אִישׁ מִיהוּדָה
אִישׁ

10 וַיִּשְׁמְעוּ כָל־הַשָּׂרִים וְכָל־הָעָם וַיָּשֻׁבוּ כָל־הַשָּׂרִים וְכָל־הַבָּאִים בַּבְּרִית

---

[a] Vid. 32:28. [b] Targ. יְיָ. [c] Vid. 32:1, 3. [d] Targ. כָּל. [e] Targ. יְעַל.

אֲשֶׁר־בָּאוּ בַבְרִית לְשַׁלַּח אִישׁ	לשלח איש את־עבדו ואיש את־
אֶת־עַבְדּוֹ וְאִישׁ אֶת־שִׁפְחָתוֹ	שפחתו וישלחו
הָֽפְשִׁים לְבִלְתִּי עֲבָד־בָּם עוֹד	
וַיִּשְׁמְעוּ וַיְשַׁלֵּחוּ	
11 וַיָּשׁוּבוּ אַחֲרֵי־כֵן וַיָּשִׁיבוּ אֶת־ אוֹתָם^a לַעֲבָדִים וְלִשְׁפָחוֹת	
הָעֲבָדִים וְאֶת־הַשְּׁפָחוֹת אֲשֶׁר	
שִׁלְּחוּ חָפְשִׁים וַיִּכְבְּשׁוּם	
לַעֲבָדִים וְלִשְׁפָחוֹת	
12 מֵאֵת יְהוָה	Deest
13 יהוה אֱלֹהֵי יִשְׂרָאֵל	יהוה
14 מִקֵּץ שֶׁבַע שָׁנִים תְּשַׁלְּחוּ אִישׁ כִּמְלֹאת שֵׁשׁ שָׁנִים תְּשַׁלַּח אֶת־	
אֶת־אָחִיו	אחיך
וְשִׁלַּחְתּוֹ חָפְשִׁי מֵעִמָּךְ וְלֹא־ וְשִׁלַּחְתּוֹ חפשי ולא־שמעו אלי	
שָׁמְעוּ אֲבוֹתֵיכֶם אֵלָי	
15 וַתָּשֻׁבוּ אַתֶּם הַיּוֹם וַתַּעֲשׂוּ	וישבו היום לעשות
וַתִּכְרְתוּ בְרִית	ויכרתו ברית
16 וַתָּשֻׁבוּ אִישׁ אֶת־עַבְדּוֹ	להשב איש את־עבדו
וַתִּכְבְּשׁוּ אֹתָם	Deest
17 לִקְרֹא דְרוֹר אִישׁ לְאָחִיו וְאִישׁ לקרא דרור איש לרעהו הנני קרא	
לְרֵעֵהוּ הִנְנִי קֹרֵא לָכֶם דְּרוֹר	דרור לכם
נְאֻם־יְהוָה	Deest
אֶל־הַדֶּבֶר	וְאֶל־הַדֶּבֶר^b
לְזַעֲוָה לְכֹל מַמְלְכוֹת הָאָרֶץ	לזרעה^c בכל ממלכות הארץ
18 אֶת־דִּבְרֵי הַבְּרִית	את־בריתי
הָעֵגֶל אֲשֶׁר כָּרְתוּ לִשְׁנַיִם וַיַּעַבְרוּ העגל אשר עשו לעבד־לו	
בֵּין בְּתָרָיו	
19 שָׂרֵי יְהוּדָה וְשָׂרֵי יְרוּשָׁלַ͏ִם שרי יהודה והאדירים^d (והסרסים)	
הַסָּרִסִים וְהַכֹּהֲנִים וְכֹל עַם	והכהנים והעם
הָאָרֶץ הָעֹבְרִים בֵּין בִּתְרֵי	
הָעֵגֶל	
20 וְנָתַתִּי אוֹתָם בְּיַד אֹיְבֵיהֶם וּבְיַד וּנתתי אותם לאיביהם והיתה	

^{a} Inc. vs. 11. ^{b} Targ. וּבְן בּוֹתָא. ^{c} εἰς διασπορἀν. Vid. 24:9. ^{d} Targ. יְרַבְרְבַיָּא.

נְבָלָתָם מֵאֹכֶל	מְבַקְשֵׁי נַפְשָׁם וְהָיְתָה נִבְלָתָם לְמַאֲכָל
וְאֶת־שָׂרֵיהֶם אֶתֵּן בִּידֵי אֹיְבֵיהֶם וְבְיַד֙ מֶ֣לֶךְ בָּבֶ֔ל לְהַעֲלִים מֵעֲלֵיהֶם	21 וְאֶת־שָׂרָיו אֶתֵּן בְּיַד אֹיְבֵיהֶם וּבְיַד מְבַקְשֵׁי נַפְשָׁם וּבְיַד חֵיל מֶלֶךְ בָּבֶל הָעֹלִים מֵעֲלֵיכֶם
וַהֲשִׁבֹתִים אֶל־הָאָרֶץ הַזֹּאת וְאֶתֵּן אוֹתָן (וְאֶתְּנֵן) שׁוֹמֵמוֹת	22 וַהֲשִׁבֹתִים אֶל־הָעִיר הַזֹּאת אֶתֵּן שְׁמָמָה

CAPUT XXXV.

בִּימֵי יְהוֹיָקִים	1 בִּימֵי יְהוֹיָקִים בֶּן־יֹאשִׁיָּהוּ
הָלוֹךְ אֶל־בֵּית הָרֵכָבִים[a] וַהֲבֵאוֹתָם אֹתָם וַהֲבִאוֹתָם בֵּית יְהוָה אֶל־אַחַת הַלְּשָׁכוֹת	2 חֲלוֹךְ אֶל־בֵּית הָרֵכָבִים וְדִבַּרְתָּ אֶל־בֵּית יְהוָה אֶל־אַחַת הַחֲצֵרוֹת
וָאֶקַּח אֶת־יַאֲזַנְיָה וְאֶת־עַל־בָּנָיו	3 וָאוֹלִיךְ (וָאָבִיא) אֶת־יְכָנְיָה וְאֶת־בָּנָיו
בֵּית יְהוָה	4 אֶל־בֵּית[b] יְהוָה
בְּנֵי חָנָן בֶּן־יִגְדַּלְיָהוּ	בְּנֵי חָנָן בֶּן־חֲנַנְיָה בֶּן־יִגְדַּלְיָהוּ
לִשְׁכַּת הַשָּׂרִים	בֵּית הַשָּׂרִים
לִשְׁכַּת מַעֲשֵׂיהוּ	לְבֵית מַעֲשֵׂיהוּ
שֹׁמֵר הַסַּף	שֹׁמֵר הֶחָצֵר
5 לִפְנֵי בְּנֵי בֵית־הָרֵכָבִים גְּבִעִים לִפְנֵיהֶם גְּבִיעַ יַיִן מְלֵאִים יָיִן	
וָאֹמַר אֲלֵיהֶם	וָאֹמַר
7 וּבַיִת לֹא־תִבְנוּ	וּבָתִּים לֹא־תִבְנוּ
וְכֶרֶם לֹא־תִטָּעוּ וְלֹא יִהְיֶה לָכֶם עַל־פְּנֵי הָאֲדָמָה אֲשֶׁר אַתֶּם גָּרִים שָׁם.	וְכֶרֶם לֹא יִהְיֶה לָכֶם עַל־הָאֲדָמָה אֲשֶׁר אַתֶּם גָּרִים עָלֶיהָ (בָּהּ)
8 יְהוֹנָדָב בֶּן־רֵכָב	יְהוֹנָדָב
לְכֹל אֲשֶׁר צִוָּנוּ	Deest
נַחְנוּ בָּנֵינוּ	וְנָשֵׁינוּ וּבָנֵינוּ

---

[a] Ἀρχαβείν. Vid. vs. 3. [b] Targ. לְבֵית.

356   THE TEXT OF JEREMIAH.   [35:9-18

לְשִׁבְתֵּנוּ	לְשִׁבְתָּ־שָׁם
לֹא יִהְיֶה־לָּנוּ	לֹא הָיָה לָנוּ
11 בַּעֲלוֹת נְבוּכַדְרֶאצַּר מֶלֶךְ־בָּבֶל אֶל־הָאָרֶץ	בעלות נבוכדראצר על־הארץ[a]
בֹּאִי וְנָבוֹא יְרוּשָׁלִָם	לבא ונבוא אל־ירושלם[b]
וּמִפְּנֵי חֵיל אֲרָם וַנֵּשֶׁב בִּירוּשָׁלִָם	ומפני חיל אשור (אשורים) ונשב שם
12 אֱלַי־יִרְמְיָהוּ לֵאמֹר	אלי לאמר
13 יְהוָה צְבָאוֹת אֱלֹהֵי יִשְׂרָאֵל	יהוה
נְאֻם־יְהוָה	Deest
14 הוּקַם אֶת־דִּבְרֵי יְהוֹנָדָב	הקימו דבר בני יהונדב[c]
עַד־הַיּוֹם הַזֶּה כִּי שָׁמְעוּ אֶת מִצְוַת אֲבִיהֶם	Desunt
הַשְׁכֵּם וְדַבֵּר וְלֹא שְׁמַעְתֶּם אֵלָי	השכם ולא שמעתם
15 אֶת־כָּל־עֲבָדַי הַנְּבִיאִים הַשְׁכֵּם וְשָׁלֹחַ לֵאמֹר שֻׁבוּ־נָא אִישׁ מִדַּרְכּוֹ הָרָעָה	את־כל־עבדי הנביאים לאמר שבו איש מדרכו הרעה
וּשְׁבוּ אֶל־הָאֲדָמָה	וְתֵשְׁבוּ עַל־הָאֲדָמָה[d]
אֶת־אָזְנְכֶם וְלֹא שְׁמַעְתֶּם אֵלָי	את־אזניכם ולא שמעתם
16 כִּי הֵקִימוּ	וְהֵקִימוּ
אֲשֶׁר צִוָּם	Deest
לֹא שָׁמְעוּ אֵלָי	לא שמע אלי
17 יְהוָה אֱלֹהֵי צְבָאוֹת אֱלֹהֵי יִשְׂרָאֵל	יהוה
אֶל־יְהוּדָה וְאֶל־כָּל־יוֹשְׁבֵי יְרוּשָׁלִָם	על־יהודה ועל־יושבי ירושלם
יַעַן דִּבַּרְתִּי אֲלֵיהֶם וְלֹא שָׁמֵעוּ וָאֶקְרָא לָהֶם וְלֹא עָנוּ	Desunt
18 וּלְבֵית הָרֵכָבִים אָמַר יִרְמְיָהוּ כֹּה־אָמַר יְהוָה צְבָאוֹת אֱלֹהֵי יִשְׂרָאֵל יַעַן אֲשֶׁר שְׁמַעְתֶּם עַל־מִצְוַת יְהוֹנָדָב אֲבִיכֶם וַתִּשְׁמְרוּ אֶת־כָּל־מִצְוֹתָיו וַתַּעֲשׂוּ כְּכֹל אֲשֶׁר־צִוָּה אֶתְכֶם	לָכֵן כה־אמר יהוה יען אשר שמעו בני יהונדב בן־רכב (על) מצות אביהם לעשות כאשר צום אביהם

[a] Targ. עַל אַרְעָא.   [b] Targ. לִירוּשְׁלֵם.   [c] Cf. vs. 16.   [d] Vid. 25:5.—
Targ. עַל אַרְעָא.   [e] Targ. כָּל.   [f] Targ. יְעַל.

19 לָכֵן כֹּה אָמַר יְהוָה צְבָאוֹת } Desunt
אֱלֹהֵי יִשְׂרָאֵל
לְיוֹנָדָב   מִבְּנֵי יוֹנדב
כל־הימים   כל־ימי הארץ

CAPUT XXXVI.

1 וַיְהִי בַּשָּׁנָה הָרְבִיעִת   בשנה הרביעת
הָיָה הַדָּבָר הַזֶּה אֶל־יִרְמְיָהוּ   היה דְבַר יהוה אלי לאמר
מֵאֵת יהוה לֵאמֹר

2 וּכְתָבְתָּ אֵלֶיהָ   וכתבת עליה[b]
עַל־יִשְׂרָאֵל   על־ירושׁלם
מִימֵי יֹאשִׁיָּהוּ   מימי יאשיהו מֶלֶךְ יְהוּדָה

3 אוּלַי יִשְׁמְעוּ בֵּית יְהוּדָה   אולי ישמע בית יהודה
לְמַעַן יָשׁוּבוּ אִישׁ מִדַּרְכּוֹ הָרָעָה   למען ישובו מדרכם[c] הרעה וסלחתי
וְסָלַחְתִּי לַעֲוֹנָם וּלְחַטָּאתָם   לעונותיהם ולחטאתיהם[d]

4 וַיִּכְתֹּב בָּרוּךְ   ויכתב
עַל־מְגִלַּת־סֵפֶר   אל־מגלת־ספר

5 אֲנִי עָצוּר   אני נצור
בֵּית יהוה   אל־בית[e] יהוה

6 וּבָאתָ אַתָּה וְקָרָאתָ בַמְּגִלָּה   וקראת במגלה הזאת
אֲשֶׁר־כָּתַבְתָּ מִפִּי אֶת־דִּבְרֵי יְהוָה   Deest
בֵּית יהוה   בְּבֵית[f] יהוה
וְגַם בְּאָזְנֵי כָל־יְהוּדָה   ובאזני כל־יהודה
תִּקְרָאֵם   תקרא להם

7 וְיָשׁוּבוּ אִישׁ מִדַּרְכּוֹ הָרָעָה כִּי־   וישובו מדרכם[g] הרעה כי־גדול
גָדוֹל הָאַף וְהַחֵמָה אֲשֶׁר־   האף וחמת יהוה אשר־דבר על־[h]
דִּבֶּר יהוה אֶל־הָעָם הַזֶּה   העם הזה

8 וַיַּעַשׂ בָּרוּךְ בֶּן־נֵרִיָּה   ויעש ברוך
יִרְמְיָהוּ הַנָּבִיא   ירמיהו

---

[a] ut Gen. 8:22. [b] Targ. עֲלָהּ. [c] Vid. vs. 7. [d] Vid. 16:18; 18:23; 31:34.—Targ. לְחוֹבֵיהוֹן וּלְחַטָּאֵיהוֹן. [e] Targ. לְבֵית. [f] Targ. בְּבֵית. [g] Vid. vs. 3. [h] Targ. עַל.

	בְּבֵית יהוה	בֵּית יהוה
9	בִּשָׁנָה הַחֲמִשִׁית לִיהוֹיָקִים בֶּן־	בַּשָׁנָה הַשְּׁמִינִית לַמֶּלֶךְ יְהוֹיָקִים
	יֹאשִׁיָּהוּ מֶלֶךְ־יְהוּדָה	
	וְכָל־הָעָם הַבָּאִים מֵעָרֵי יְהוּדָה וּבֵית יְהוּדָה	
	בִּירוּשָׁלָ͏ִם	
10	בֵּית יהוה בְּלִשְׁכַּת גְּמַרְיָהוּ	בְּבֵית יהוה בְּבֵית גְּמַרְיָהוּ
	פֶּתַח שַׁעַר	בְּפִתְחֵי שַׁעַר
	בְּאָזְנֵי כָל־הָעָם	וּבְאָזְנֵי כָל־הָעָם
12	וַיֵּרֶד בֵּית־הַמֶּלֶךְ עַל־לִשְׁכַּת הַסֹּפֵר	וַיֵּרֶד אֶל־בֵּיתᵃ־הַמֶּלֶךְ אֶלᵇ־בֵּית הַסֵּפֶר
	כָּל־הַשָּׂרִים יוֹשְׁבִים	כָּל־שָׂרִים יָשְׁבוּ
	בֶּן־שְׁמַעְיָהוּ וְאֶלְנָתָן	בֶּן־שְׁלֶמְיָהוּ וִיהוֹנָתָן
13	בַּסֵּפֶר	Deest
11	אֶל־בָּרוּךְ	אֶל־בָּרוּךְ בֶּן־נֵרִיָּה
	רָץ	וּבָאᶜ
	בָּרוּךְ בֶּן־נֵרִיָּהוּ	בָּרוּךְ
	בְּיָדוֹ וּבֹא אֲלֵיהֶם	וַיֵּרֶד אֲלֵיהֶם
15	שֵׁב נָא וּקְרָאֶנָּה	שֵׁב (שׁוּב)ᵈ קְרָא
	וַיִּקְרָא בָרוּךְ בְּאָזְנֵיהֶם	וַיִּקְרָא בָרוּךְ
16	פָּחֲדוּ	הִתְרַגְּזוּ (נֹעֲצוּ)
	וַיֹּאמְרוּ אֶל־בָּרוּךְ	וַיֹּאמְרוּ
17	הַגֶּד־נָא לָנוּ אֵיךְ כָּתַבְתָּ	אֵיךְ (אָן) כְּתָבַת
	מִפִּיו	Deest
18	וַיֹּאמֶר לָהֶם בָּרוּךְ	וַיֹּאמֶר בָּרוּךְ
	יִקְרָא אֵלָי	קְרָא אֵלַי יִרְמְיָהוּ
	וַאֲנִי כֹּתֵב עַל־הַסֵּפֶר בַּדְּיוֹ	וַאֲנִי כָּתַבְתִּי בְּסֵפֶר
19	וַיֹּאמְרוּ הַשָּׂרִים	וַיֹּאמְרוּ
	לֵךְ הִסָּתֵר	לֵךְ וְהִסָּתֵר
	וְאִישׁ אַל־יֵדָע	אִישׁ אַל־יֵדַע
20	בְּלִשְׁכַּת אֱלִישָׁמָע הַסֹּפֵר	בְּבֵית אֱלִישָׁמָע
	בְּאָזְנֵי הַמֶּלֶךְ אֵת כָּל־הַדְּבָרִים	לַמֶּלֶךְ אֵת כָּל־הַדְּבָרִים הָאֵלֶּה
21	וַיִּקָּחֶהָ מִלִּשְׁכַּת אֱלִישָׁמָע הַסֹּפֵר וַיִּקְרָאֶהָ	וַיִּקָּחָהּ מִבֵּית אֱלִישָׁמָע וַיִּקְרָא

ᵃ Targ. לְבֵית.   ᵇ Targ. לְלִשְׁכַּת.   ᶜ Targ. יְאָתָא.   ᵈ ut vs. 28.—Targ. תּוּב.

36:22-32]   THE CONSPECTUS OF THE VARIATIONS.   359

22 וְהַמֶּלֶךְ יוֹשֵׁב בֵּית הַחֹרֶף	וְהַמֶלֶךְ יָשַׁב בְּבֵית הַחֹרֶף
בַּחֹדֶשׁ הַתְּשִׁיעִי	Deest
וְאֶת־הָאָח לְפָנָיו מְבֹעָרֶת	וְאֵח אֵשׁ (יְאֵשׁ הָאָח) לְפָנָיו
23 יְקָרָעֶהָ בְּתַעַר הַסֹּפֵר וְהַשְׁלֵךְ	יְקוֹרְעֶן בִּיתַר הַסֵפֶר וְיַשְׁלֵךְ בָּאֵשׁ
אֶל־הָאֵשׁ אֲשֶׁר אֶל־הָאָח	אֲשֶׁר עַל־הָאָח
עַד־תֹּם כָּל־הַמְּגִלָּה עַל־הָאֵשׁ אֲשֶׁר עַל־הָאָח	בָּאֵשׁ אֲשֶׁר עַל־הָאָח
24 וְלֹא פָחֲדוּ	וְלֹא־פָקְדוּ (דָרְשׁוּ)
וְכָל־עֲבָדָיו	וַעֲבָדָיו
25 וְגַם אֶלְנָתָן וּדְלָיָהוּ וּגְמַרְיָהוּ	וְאֶלְנָתָן וְדַלָּיָתָן וּגְדַלְיָהוּ וְיָבֹאוּ לַמֶּלֶךְ
הִפְגִּעוּ בַמֶּלֶךְ לְבִלְתִּי שְׂרֹף	לִשְׂרֹף
וְלֹא שָׁמַע אֲלֵיהֶם	Desunt
26 וְאֶת־שֶׁלֶמְיָהוּ בֶן־עַבְדְּאֵל	
אֶת־בָּרוּךְ הַסֹּפֵר וְאֵת יִרְמְיָהוּ	אֶת־בָּרוּךְ וְאֵת יִרְמְיָהוּ וְיִסְתָּרוּ
הַנָּבִיא וַיַּסְתִּרֵם יְהוָֹה	
27 וְאֶת־הַדְּבָרִים	כָּל־הַדְּבָרִים
28 וּכְתֹב עָלֶיהָ	וּכְתֹב
כָּל־הַדְּבָרִים הָרִאשֹׁנִים	כָּל־הַדְּבָרִים
עַל־הַמְּגִלָּה הָרִאשֹׁנָה	עַל־הַמְּגִלָּה
יְהוֹיָקִים מֶלֶךְ־יְהוּדָה	הַמֶּלֶךְ יְהוֹיָקִים
29 וְעַל־יְהוֹיָקִים מֶלֶךְ־יְהוּדָה תֹּאמַר	וְאָמַרְתָּ
וְהִשְׁבִּית	וְשָׁבַת (וְיִשְׁבַּת)
30 לִהְיוֹת בַּיּוֹם וְלַקֶּרַח בַּלָּיְלָה	לַחֹרֶב חָיוּב וְלַקֶּרַח הַלָּיְלָה
31 אֲדֹנָם	Deest
וְהֵבֵאתִי עֲלֵיהֶם	וְהֵבֵאתִי קְלָו
וְאֶל־אִישׁ יְהוּדָה	וְאֶל־אֶרֶץ יְהוּדָה
32 וְיִרְמְיָהוּ לָקַח מְגִלָּה אַחֶרֶת וַיִּתְּנָהּ	וַיִּקַּח בָּרוּךְ מְגִלָּה אַחֶרֶת
אֶל־בָּרוּךְ בֶּן־נֵרִיָּה הַסֹּפֵר	
מֶלֶךְ־יְהוּדָה בָּאֵשׁ	Deest
וְעוֹד נוֹסַף עֲלֵיהֶם דְּבָרִים רַבִּים	וְעוֹד נִסְפּוּ[a] עָלֶיהָ דְּבָרִים רַבִּים
כָּהֵמָּה	מֵהֵמָּה

---

[a] Targ. אֲתוֹסָפוּ.

CAPUT XXXVII.

וימלך צדקיהו	1 וַיִּמְלָךְ־מֶלֶךְ צִדְקִיָּהוּ
יהויקים	פָּנְיָהוּ בֶּן־יְהוֹיָקִים
למלך ביהודה	מֶלֶךְ־בָּבֶל בְּאֶרֶץ יְהוּדָה
ולא שמעו	2 וְלֹא שָׁמַע
ביד ירמיהו	בְּיַד יִרְמְיָהוּ הַנָּבִיא
אל־ירמיהו	אֶל־יִרְמְיָהוּ הַנָּבִיא
אל־יהוה	אֶל־יְהוָה אֱלֹהֵינוּ
בא ויצא בתוך חתיו	4 בָּא וְיֹצֵא בְּתוֹךְ הָעָם
אל־בית^a הכלוא	בֵּית הַכְּלִיא
Deest	5 הַצָּרִים עַל־יְרוּשָׁלִָם
ויעלו על־ירושלם	וַיֵּעָלוּ מֵעַל יְרוּשָׁלִָם
אל־ירמיהו^b לאמר	6 אֶל־יִרְמְיָהוּ הַנָּבִיא לֵאמֹר
יהוה	7 יְהוָה אֱלֹהֵי יִשְׂרָאֵל
כה תאמר	כֹּה תֹאמְרוּ
השלח אליך	הַשֹּׁלֵחַ אֶתְכֶם אֵלַי
ישבו לארץ מצרים	שָׁב לְאַרְצוֹ מִצְרָיִם
ושבו המה הכשדים	8 וְשָׁבוּ הַכַּשְׂדִּים
אל־תשאו כי כה אמר יהוה אל־תשׂאוּ	9 כֹּה אָמַר יְהוָה אַל־תַּשִּׁאוּ
(תנשאו) בנפשׁתיכם^c	נַפְשֹׁתֵיכֶם
ואם־הכיתם	10 כִּי אִם־הִכִּיתֶם
ונשארו	וְנִשְׁאֲרוּ־בָם
איש במקומו המה יקומו	אִישׁ בְּאָהֳלוֹ יָקוּמוּ
בעלות חיל הכשדים	11 בְּהֵעָלוֹת חֵיל הַכַּשְׂדִּים
יצא ירמיהו	12 וַיֵּצֵא יִרְמְיָהוּ
לקחת (ללקח?)	לַחֲלֹק
ושמו איש אשר שכן אצלו (צמו)	13 וְשָׁם בַּעַל פְּקִדֻת
שריה (צרויה)	יִרְאִיָּיה
את־ירמיהו	אֶת־יִרְמְיָהוּ הַנָּבִיא
ויאמר ירמיהו שקר ויאמר נפל לא אל־הכשׂדים^d אני נפל	14 וַיֹּאמֶר יִרְמְיָהוּ שֶׁקֶר אֵינֶנִּי נֹפֵל אֶל־הַכַּשְׂדִּים

^{a} ut vs. 18.—Targ. בְּבֵית. ^{b} Targ. יָב יְרִדְיָה לְבָרֵךְ. ^{c} Vid. 44:7.
^{d} ut vs. 13.—Targ. לְבַסְדָּאֵי.

37:15–38:1] THE CONSPECTUS OF THE VARIATIONS.

יִרְאִיָּיה	שְׂרָיָה (צְרוּיָה)
15 וְנָתְנוּ אוֹתוֹ בֵּית הָאָסוּר בֵּית	וְשָׁלְחוּ אוֹתוֹ אֶל־בֵּית יְהוֹנָתָן
יְהוֹנָתָן	
עָשׂוּ לְבֵית הַכֶּלֶא	עָשׂוּ לְבֵית כֶּלֶאa
16 כִּי בָא יִרְמְיָהוּ	וַיָּבֹא יִרְמְיָהוּ
וְאֶל־הַחֲנֻיּוֹת וַיֵּשֶׁב־שָׁם יִרְמְיָהוּ	וְאֶל־הַחֶרֶתb וַיֵּשֶׁב־שָׁם
17 וַיִּשְׁלַח הַמֶּלֶךְ צִדְקִיָּהוּ וַיִּקָּחֵהוּ	וַיִּשְׁלַח צִדְקִיָּהוּ וַיִּקְרָאֵהוּ וַיִּשְׁאָלֵהוּ
וַיִּשְׁאָלֵהוּ הַמֶּלֶךְ בְּבֵיתוֹ בַּסֵּתֶר	הַמֶּלֶךְ בַּסֵּתֶר לֵאמֹר הֲיֵשׁ הַדָּבָר
וַיֹּאמֶר הֲיֵשׁ דָּבָר מֵאֵת יְהוָה	מֵאֵת יְהוָה וַיֹּאמֶר יֵשׁ בְּיָדֵי
וַיֹּאמֶר יִרְמְיָהוּ יֵשׁ וַיֹּאמֶר	מֶלֶךְ בָּבֶל תִּנָּתֵן
בְּיַד־מֶלֶךְ בָּבֶל תִּנָּתֵן	
18 אֶל־הַמֶּלֶךְ צִדְקִיָּהוּ	אֶל־הַמֶּלֶךְ
כִּי־נְתַתֶּם אוֹתִי אֶל־בֵּית הַכֶּלֶא	כִּי־נָתַתָּ אוֹתִי אֶל־בֵּית כֶּלֶאc
19 וְאַיֵּה	וְאַיֵּה
לֹא־יָבוֹא מֶלֶךְ־בָּבֶל עֲלֵיכֶם וְעַל־	כִּי לֹא־יָבוֹא מֶלֶךְ בָּבֶל עַל־הָאָרֶץ
הָאָרֶץ הַזֹּאת	הַזֹּאת
20 שְׁמַע־נָא	Deest
תְּפָל־נָא תְחִנָּתִי	תְּפֹל תְּחִנָּתִי
וְאַל־תְּשִׁבֵנִי בֵּית יְהוֹנָתָן הַסֹּפֵר	וּלְמָה תְשִׁיבֵנִי אֶל־בֵּיתd יְהוֹנָתָן הַסֹּפֵר
וְלֹא אָמוּת שָׁם	וּמַתִּי שָׁם
21 הַמֶּלֶךְ צִדְקִיָּהוּ	הַמֶּלֶךְ
וַיַּפְקִדוּ אֶת־יִרְמְיָהוּ בַּחֲצַר	וַיִּשְׁלִיכוּ אוֹתוֹ אֶל־בֵּית הַמַּטָּרָה
הַמַּטָּרָה וְנָתֹן לוֹ כִכַּר־לֶחֶם	וַיִּתְּנוּe לוֹ לֶחֶם אֶחָד לַיּוֹם
לַיּוֹם	
עַד־תֹּם כָּל־הַלֶּחֶם מִן־הָעִיר	עַד־תֹּם הַלֶּחֶם מִן־הָעִיר

CAPUT XXXVIII.

1 שְׁפַטְיָה בֶן־מַתָּן	צְפַנְיָה (שְׁפַנְיָה) בֶן־נָתָן
וּפַשְׁחוּר בֶּן־מַלְכִּיָּה	Deest
מְדַבֵּר אֶל־כָּל־הָעָם לֵאמֹר	דְּבַר עֲלֵיהֶם לֵאמֹר

---

a Vid. vs. 18.   b καὶ εἰς τὴν χερςϑ.   c Vid. vs. 15.   d Targ. לְבֵי.
e Targ. וִיהָבִין.

בְּחֶרֶב בָּרָעָב	2 בַּחֶרֶב בָּרָעָב וּבַדָּבֶר
יִהְיָה וְהָיְתָה נַפְשׁוֹ לְשָׁלָל[a]	יִהְיָה וְהָיְתָה־לּוֹ נַפְשׁוֹ לְשָׁלָל
כִּי כֹה אָמַר יְהוָה	3 כֹּה אָמַר יְהוָה
בִּידֵי חֵיל מֶלֶךְ־בָּבֶל	בְּיַד חֵיל מֶלֶךְ־בָּבֶל
וַיֹּאמְרוּ הַשָּׂרִים אֶל־הַמֶּלֶךְ יוּמַת נָא	4 וַיֹּאמְרוּ הַשָּׂרִים אֶל־הַמֶּלֶךְ יוּמַת
אֶת־הָאִישׁ הַהוּא כִּי הוּא מְרַפֵּא	נָא אֶת־הָאִישׁ הַזֶּה כִּי עַל־כֵּן הוּא מְרַפֵּא
הַנִּשְׁאָרִים בָּעִיר	הַנִּשְׁאָרִים בָּעִיר הַזֹּאת
לְדַבֵּר אֲלֵיהֶם	לְדַבֵּר אֲלֵיהֶם
אֵינֶנּוּ נֹבֵא שָׁלוֹם	אֵינֶנּוּ דֹרֵשׁ לְשָׁלוֹם
וַיֹּאמֶר הַמֶּלֶךְ הִנֵּה־הוּא בְּיֶדְכֶם	5 וַיֹּאמֶר הַמֶּלֶךְ צִדְקִיָּהוּ הִנֵּה־הוּא
כִּי לֹא־יוּכַל הַמֶּלֶךְ לָהֶם	בְּיֶדְכֶם כִּי־אֵין הַמֶּלֶךְ יוּכַל אֶתְכֶם דָּבָר
Deest	6 וַיִּקְחוּ אֶת־יִרְמְיָהוּ
אֶל־בּוֹר מַלְכִּיָּהוּ[b]	אֶל־הַבּוֹר׀ מַלְכִּיָּהוּ
וַיְשַׁלְּחוּ אוֹתוֹ בַבּוֹר	וַיְשַׁלְּחוּ אֶת־יִרְמְיָהוּ בַּחֲבָלִים
וַיְהִי בַטִּיט	וַיִּטְבַּע יִרְמְיָהוּ בַּטִּיט
Deest	7 אִישׁ סָרִיס
וְהַמֶּלֶךְ חָיָה	וְהַמֶּלֶךְ יוֹשֵׁב
וַיֵּצֵא אֵלָיו וַיֹּאמַר	8 וַיֵּצֵא עֶבֶד־מֶלֶךְ מִבֵּית הַמֶּלֶךְ לֵאמֹר
הֲרֵעֹתָ אֵת אֲשֶׁר עָשִׂיתָ לְהָמִית	9 אֲדֹנִי הַמֶּלֶךְ הֵרֵעוּ הָאֲנָשִׁים הָאֵלֶּה
אֶת־הָאִישׁ הַזֶּה מִפְּנֵי הָרָעָב	אֵת כָּל־אֲשֶׁר עָשׂוּ לְיִרְמְיָהוּ הַנָּבִיא
כִּי אֵין עוֹד לֶחֶם בָּעִיר	אֵת אֲשֶׁר־הִשְׁלִיכוּ אֶל־הַבּוֹר וַיָּמָת תַּחְתָּיו מִפְּנֵי הָרָעָב כִּי אֵין הַלֶּחֶם עוֹד בָּעִיר
אֶת־עֶבֶד־מֶלֶךְ[c]	10 אֶת־עֶבֶד־מֶלֶךְ הַכּוּשִׁי
קַח בְּיָדְךָ	קַח בְּיָדְךָ
וְהַעֲלִיתָ אוֹתוֹ מִן־חַבּוּר וְלֹא (פֶּן) יָמוּת	וְהַעֲלִיתָ אֶת־יִרְמְיָהוּ הַנָּבִיא מִן־הַבּוֹר בְּטֶרֶם יָמוּת
Deest	11 בְּיָדוֹ
תַּחַת (הָ)אָרֶץ	אֶל־תַּחַת הָאוֹצָר

[a] Vid. 21:9; 39:18.   [b] Targ. לְגוּבָּא דְמַלְכִּיָּא.   [c] Targ. יַת עַבְדָּא דְמַלְכָּא. צִדְקִיָּה.

בְּלֵי הַסְּחָבוֹת וּבְלֹוי מְלָחִים בְּלוֹי	סְחָבוֹת	וּבְלוֹי	הֲבָלִים
וְיֻשְׁלְחֵם		וְיֻשְׁלְכֶם	
בְּהֲבָלִים	Deest		

12 וַיֹּאמֶר עֶבֶד־מֶלֶךְ הַכּוּשִׁי אֶל־ וַיֹּאמֶר אַלֶּה (תָּ)שִׂים מתחת
יִרְמְיָהוּ שִׂים נָא בְּלוֹאֵי לחבלים
הַסְּחָבוֹת וְהַמְּלָחִים תַּחַת
אַצִּלוֹת יָדֶיךָ מִתַּחַת לַחֲבָלִים

13 וַיִּמְשְׁכוּ אֶת־יִרְמְיָהוּ וַיִּמְשְׁכוּ אֹתוֹ

14 וַיִּשְׁלַח הַמֶּלֶךְ צִדְקִיָּהוּ וַיִּשְׁלַח הַמֶּלֶךְ
וַיִּקַּח אֶת־יִרְמְיָהוּ הַנָּבִיא אֵלָיו וַיִּקְרָאֵהוּ אֵלָיו אֶל־בֵּית הַשְּׁלִישִׁיa
אֶל־מָבוֹא הַשְּׁלִישִׁי
וַיֹּאמֶר הַמֶּלֶךְ אֶל־יִרְמְיָהוּ יֹאמֶר אֵלָיו הַמֶּלֶךְ
אֲלִי־תְכַחֵד מִמֶּנִּי דָּבָר וְאַל־תְּכַחֵד נָא מִמֶּנִּי דבר

15 אֶל־צִדְקִיָּהוּ אֶל־הַמֶּלֶךְ

16 וַיִּשָּׁבַע הַמֶּלֶךְ צִדְקִיָּהוּ אֶל־ וַיִּשָּׁבַע לוֹ הַמֶּלֶךְ
יִרְמְיָהוּ בַּסֵּתֶר
אֵת אֲשֶׁר עָשָׂה־לָנוּ אֲשֶׁר עשה־לנו
וְאִם־אֶתֶּנְךָ בְּיַד וְאִם־אֶתֶּנְךָ בִּידֵי
אֲשֶׁר מְבַקְשִׁים אֶת־נַפְשֶׁךָ Deest

17 וַיֹּאמֶר יִרְמְיָהוּ אֶל־צִדְקִיָּהוּ וַיֹּאמֶר אֵלָיו יִרְמְיָהוּ
יְהוָה אֱלֹהֵי צְבָאוֹת אֱלֹהֵי יִשְׂרָאֵל יהוה

18 וְאִם לֹא־תֵצֵא אֶל־שָׂרֵי מֶלֶךְ־בָּבֶל וְאִם לֹא־תֵצֵא תִּנָּתֵן הָעִיר הַזֹּאת
וְנִתְּנָה הָעִיר הַזֹּאת בְּיַד בִּידֵי הַכַּשְׂדִּים
הַכַּשְׂדִּים

וְאַתָּה לֹא־תִמָּלֵט מִיָּדָם וְאַתָּה לֹא־תִמָּלֵט

19 וַיֹּאמֶר הַמֶּלֶךְ צִדְקִיָּהוּ וַיֹּאמֶר הַמֶּלֶךְ
פְּנֵיתָנוּ אֹתִי בְּיָדָם פְּנֵיתָנוּ אֹתִי בִּידֵיהֶםb

20 לֹא יִתֵּנוּ שְׁמַע־נָא בְּקוֹל יְהוָה לֹא יִתְּנוּךָ שְׁמַע דְּבַרc יְהוָה אֲשֶׁר
לַאֲשֶׁר אֲנִי דֹבֵר אֵלֶיךָ אֲנִי דֹבֵר אֵלֶיךָ

22 הִסִּיתוּךָ בְּצֵעַ רַגְלֶךָ נִשְׂגוּ הִכְשִׁילוּ בַּחֲלַקּוֹת(בַּחֲלַקְלַקּוֹת)רַגְלֶיךָ
אָחוֹר נִסֹּגוּ מָקֹף

23 וְאֶת־כָּל־נָשֶׁיךָ וְאֶת־נָשֶׁיךָ

---

a 'Ασελεισίλ.   b Targ. בִּידֵיהֹן.   c Targ. דְּבַר.   לְבֵירְכָא דַךְ.

	Deest
וְאֶת־הָעִיר הַזֹּאת תִּשְׂרֹף בָּאֵשׁ	מִיָּדָם
וַיֹּאמֶר אֵלָיו הַמֶּלֶךְ אִישׁ אַל־יֵדַע מִדְּבָרִים־ (מִן־הַדְּבָרִים) הָאֵלֶּה	24 וַיֹּאמֶר צִדְקִיָּהוּ אֶל־יִרְמְיָהוּ אִישׁ אַל־יֵדַע בַּדְּבָרִים־ הָאֵלֶּה
וְכִי הַשָּׂרִים יִשְׁמְעוּ	25 וְכִי־יִשְׁמְעוּ הַשָּׂרִים
הַגִּידָה לָּנוּ מַה־דִּבֶּר אֵלֶיךָ הַמֶּלֶךְ	חֲגִידָה־נָּא לָנוּ מַה־דִּבַּרְתָּ אֶל־הַמֶּלֶךְ
וּמַה־דִּבֶּר עָלֶיךָ	וּמַה־דִּבֶּר אֵלֶיךָ
לְעֵינֵי הַמֶּלֶךְ	26 לִפְנֵי הַמֶּלֶךְ
אֶל־בֵּית יְהוֹנָתָן לַהֲמִיתֵנִי שָׁם	בֵּית יְהוֹנָתָן לָמוּת שָׁם
27 אֲשֶׁר צִוָּה הַמֶּלֶךְ וַיַּחֲרִשׁוּ מִמֶּנּוּ אֲשֶׁר צִוָּהוּ הַמֶּלֶךְ וַיַּחֲרִשׁוּ כִּי לֹא־
כִּי לֹא־נִשְׁמַע הַדָּבָר	נִשְׁמַע דְּבַר־יְהוָה
28 עַד־יוֹם	
Deest	וְהָיָה כַּאֲשֶׁר נִלְכְּדָה יְרוּשָׁלָםִ

CAPUT XXXIX.

1 בַּשָּׁנָה הַתְּשִׁעִית... בַּחֹדֶשׁ	וַיְהִי בֶּעָשֹׂרִי וַיְהִי בַּחֹדֶשׁ הַתְּשִׁעִי
אֶל־יְרוּשָׁלָםִ	עַל־יְרוּשָׁלָםִ
2 בְּעַשְׁתֵּי־עֶשְׂרֵה שָׁנָה	וּבְעַשְׁתֵּי־עֶשְׂרֵה שָׁנָה
3 נֵרְגַל שַׂרְאֶצֶר סַמְגַּר־נְבוּ שַׂר־סְכִים מַרְגְּנַאצָר וְסַמְגָּת וּנְבוּ־שָׁכָר וּנְבוּ־
רַב־סָרִיס נֵרְגַל שַׂרְאֶצֶר רַב־ סָרִיס נַגַּרְגָּס נַאצַרְבָּמוֹתa וּשְׁאֵרִית
מָג וְכָל־שְׁאֵרִית שָׂרֵי מֶלֶךְ־ שָׂרֵי מֶלֶךְ־בָּבֶל
בָּבֶל	

	4 וַיְהִי כַּאֲשֶׁר רָאָם צִדְקִיָּהוּ מֶלֶךְ־
	יְהוּדָה וְכֹל אַנְשֵׁי הַמִּלְחָמָה
Desunt {	וַיִּבְרְחוּ וַיֵּצְאוּ לַיְלָה מִן־הָעִיר
	דֶּרֶךְ גַּן הַמֶּלֶךְ בְּשַׁעַר בֵּין
	הַחֹמֹתָיִם וַיֵּצֵא דֶּרֶךְ הָעֲרָבָה:

---

[a] Μαργανασὰρ καὶ Σαμαγὼθ καὶ Ναβουσάχαρ καὶ Ναβουσαρείς, Ναγαργὰς, Νασερραβαμάθ.

	5 וַיִּרְדְּפוּ חֵיל־כַּשְׂדִּים אַחֲרֵיהֶם וַיַּשִּׂגוּ אֶת־צִדְקִיָּהוּ בְּעַרְבוֹת יְרֵחוֹ וַיִּקְחוּ אֹתוֹ וַיַּעֲלֻהוּ אֶל־נְבוּכַדְרֶאצַּר מֶלֶךְ־בָּבֶל רִבְלָתָה בְּאֶרֶץ חֲמָת וַיְדַבֵּר אִתּוֹ
	6 מִשְׁפָּטִים: וַיִּשְׁחַט מֶלֶךְ בָּבֶל אֶת־בְּנֵי צִדְקִיָּהוּ בְּרִבְלָה לְעֵינָיו וְאֵת כָּל־חֹרֵי יְהוּדָה שָׁחַט מֶלֶךְ
	7 בָּבֶל: וְאֶת־עֵינֵי צִדְקִיָּהוּ עִוֵּר וַיַּאַסְרֵהוּ בַּנְחֻשְׁתַּיִם לָבִיא אֹתוֹ
	8 בָּבֶלָה: וְאֶת־בֵּית הַמֶּלֶךְ וְאֶת־בֵּית הָעָם שָׂרְפוּ הַכַּשְׂדִּים בָּאֵשׁ
Desunt {	9 וְאֶת־חֹמוֹת יְרוּשָׁלִַם נָתָצוּ: וְאֵת יֶתֶר הָעָם הַנִּשְׁאָרִים בָּעִיר וְאֶת־הַנֹּפְלִים אֲשֶׁר נָפְלוּ עָלָיו וְאֵת יֶתֶר הָעָם הַנִּשְׁאָרִים הֶגְלָה נְבוּזַרְאֲדָן רַב־טַבָּחִים בָּבֶל:
	10 וּמִן־הָעָם הַדַּלִּים אֲשֶׁר אֵין־לָהֶם מְאוּמָה הִשְׁאִיר נְבוּזַרְאֲדָן רַב־טַבָּחִים בְּאֶרֶץ יְהוּדָה וַיִּתֵּן לָהֶם כְּרָמִים וִיגֵבִים בַּיּוֹם הַהוּא:
	11 וַיְצַו נְבוּכַדְרֶאצַּר מֶלֶךְ־בָּבֶל עַל־יִרְמְיָהוּ בְּיַד נְבוּזַרְאֲדָן רַב־
	12 טַבָּחִים לֵאמֹר: קָחֶנּוּ וְעֵינֶיךָ שִׂים עָלָיו וְאַל־תַּעַשׂ לוֹ מְאוּמָה רָע כִּי אִם כַּאֲשֶׁר יְדַבֵּר אֵלֶיךָ כֵּן עֲשֵׂה
	13 עִמּוֹ: וַיִּשְׁלַח נְבוּזַרְאֲדָן רַב־טַבָּחִים וּנְבוּשַׁזְבָּן רַב־סָרִיס וְנֵרְגַל שַׂרְאֶצֶר רַב־מָג וְכֹל רַבֵּי מֶלֶךְ־בָּבֶל:
וַיּוֹצִאֻהוּ	14 לְהוֹצִאֻהוּ אֶל־הַבַּיִת
Desunt {	15 בְּהִיוֹתוֹ עָצוּר
	16 לֵאמֹר
כֹּה־אָמַר יְהוָה	כֹּה־אָמַר יְהוָה צְבָאוֹת

עַל־הָעִיר[a] הַזֹּאת	אֶל־הָעִיר הַזֹּאת
Deest	וְהָיוּ לְפָנֶיךָ בַּיּוֹם הַהוּא
	17 נְאֻם־יְהֹוָה וְלֹא תִנָּתֵן בְּיַד וְלֹא אֶתֶּנְךָ בִּידֵי הָאֲנָשִׁים הָאֲנָשִׁים
וְהָיְתָה נַפְשְׁךָ לְשָׁלָל[b]	18 וְהָיְתָה לְךָ נַפְשְׁךָ לְשָׁלָל

CAPUT XL.

מֵאֵת יְהוָה אֶל־יִרְמְיָהוּ	1 אֶל־יִרְמְיָהוּ מֵאֵת יְהוָה
אֲשֶׁר מִן־הָרָמָה בְּקַחְתּוֹ אֹתוֹ בָּאזִקִּים בְּתוֹךְ גָּלוּת יְהוּדָה	מִן־הָרָמָה בְּקַחְתּוֹ אֹתוֹ וְהוּא אָסוּר בָּאזִקִּים בְּתוֹךְ כָּל־גָּלוּת יְרוּשָׁלִַם וִיהוּדָה
וַיִּקָּחֵהוּ (וַיִּקַּח אוֹתוֹ) רַב־טַבָּחִים עַל־הַמָּקוֹם[c] הַזֶּה	2 וַיִּקַּח רַב־טַבָּחִים לְיִרְמְיָהוּ אֶל־הַמָּקוֹם הַזֶּה
	3 וַיָּבֵא וַיַּעַשׂ יְהוָה כַּאֲשֶׁר דִּבֵּר וַיַּעַשׂ יְהוָה כִּי־חֲטָאתֶם לוֹ כִּי־חֲטָאתֶם לַיהוָה
Deest	וְהָיָה לָכֶם דָּבָר הַזֶּה
הִנֵּה פְּתַחְתִּיךָ מִן־הָאזִקִּים אֲשֶׁר עַל־יָדֶיךָ	4 וְעַתָּה הִנֵּה פִתַּחְתִּיךָ הַיּוֹם מִן־הָאזִקִּים אֲשֶׁר עַל־יָדֶךָ
וְאָשִׂים אֶת־עֵינַי עָלֶיךָ	בֹּא וְאָשִׂים אֶת־עֵינִי עָלֶיךָ
Desunt	וְאִם־רַע בְּעֵינֶיךָ לָבוֹא־אִתִּי בָּבֶל חֲדָל רְאֵה כָּל־הָאָרֶץ לְפָנֶיךָ אֶל־הַטּוֹב וְאֶל־הַיָּשָׁר בְּעֵינֶיךָ לָלֶכֶת שָׁמָּה לֵךְ:
וְשׁוּבוּ לִירוּשָׁלִַם וְשֻׁבָה אֶל־ וְאִם־לֹא[d] לֵךְ שׁוּב אֶל־גְּדַלְיָה גְּדַלְיָה	5
בְּאֶרֶץ יְהוּדָה בְּתוֹךְ וְשֵׁב אִתּוֹ בְּתוֹךְ הָעָם	בְּעָרֵי יְהוּדָה וְשֵׁב אִתּוֹ בְּתוֹךְ הָעָם אוֹ אֶל־כָּל־הַיָּשָׁר בְּעֵינֶיךָ
בְּאֶרֶץ יְהוּדָה אֶל־כָּל־הַטּוֹב בְּעֵינֶיךָ לָלֶכֶת שָׁמָּה וָלֵךְ מַשֵּׂאת[e]	לָלֶכֶת לֵךְ אֲרֻחָה וּמַשְׂאֵת

---

[a] Targ. עַל אַתְרָא הָדֵין. [b] Vid. 21:9; 38:2. [c] Targ. עַל אַתְרָא הָדֵין.
[d] Targ. וְאִם לֵית אַתְּ צָבֵי. [e] Targ. נְבִזְבֵּי.

40:6-15] THE CONSPECTUS OF THE VARIATIONS. 367

		6 וַיָּבֹא יִרְמְיָהוּ אֶל־גְּדַלְיָה בֶּן־ וַיָּבֹא אֶל־גְּדַלְיָה אֲחִיקָם
הַנִּשְׁאַר בָּאָרֶץ	עִמּוֹ בְּתוֹךְ	וַיֵּשֶׁב אִתּוֹ בְּתוֹךְ הָעָם הַנִּשְׁאָרִים וַיֵּשֶׁב בָּאָרֶץ
	כָּל־שָׂרֵי הַחַיִל Deest	7 כָּל־שָׂרֵי הַחֲיָלִים בֶּן־אֲחִיקָם
וּנְשֵׁיהֶם אֲשֶׁר לֹא־הָגְלוּ בָבֶל	וַיַּפְקִידוּ אִתּוֹ אֲנָשִׁים וְנָשִׁים וְטַף וּמִדַּלַּת הָאָרֶץ מֵאֲשֶׁר לֹא־ הָגְלוּ בָבֶל	
	וַיָּבֹאוּ יִשְׁמָעֵאל בֶּן־קָרֵחַ[a] Deest	8 וַיָּבֹאוּ יִשְׁמָעֵאל וְיוֹנָתָן בְּנֵי־קָרֵחַ 9 בֶּן־אֲחִיקָם בֶּן־שָׁפָן
	מִפְּנֵי עַבְדֵי הַכַּשְׂדִּים וְהִנֵּה אֲנִי יֹשֵׁב לִפְנֵיכֶם בַּמִּצְפָּה אֲשֶׁר בָּאוּ אֲלֵיכֶם (עֲלֵיכֶם) וְשִׁבוּ בֶּעָרִים אֲשֶׁר־תְּפַשְׂתֶּם וְכָל־הַיְּהוּדִים וַאֲשֶׁר בֶּאֱדוֹם וַאֲשֶׁר בְּכָל־הָאָרֶץ Deest	מֵעֲבוֹד הַכַּשְׂדִּים 10 וַאֲנִי הִנְנִי יֹשֵׁב בַּמִּצְפָּה אֲשֶׁר יָבֹאוּ אֵלֵינוּ וְשִׁבוּ בְּעָרֵיכֶם אֲשֶׁר־תְּפַשְׂתֶּם 11 וְגַם כָּל־הַיְּהוּדִים וּבֶאֱדוֹם וַאֲשֶׁר בְּכָל־הָאֲרָצוֹת בֶּן־שָׁפָן
	וַיָּבֹאוּ אֶל־גְּדַלְיָהוּ אֶרֶץ־יְהוּדָה	12 וַיָּשֻׁבוּ כָל־הַיְּהוּדִים מִכָּל־ הַמְּקֹמוֹת אֲשֶׁר נִדְּחוּ־שָׁם וַיָּבֹאוּ אֶרֶץ־יְהוּדָה אֶל־ גְּדַלְיָהוּ
	הַרְבֵּה מְאֹד וָשָׁמֶן[b] וְכָל־שָׂרֵי הַחַיִל אֲשֶׁר בַּשָּׂדוֹת	הַרְבֵּה מְאֹד 13 וְכָל־שָׂרֵי הַחֲיָלִים אֲשֶׁר בַּשָּׂדֶה
אֶת־ יִשְׁמָעֵאל לְהַכֹּת (אֹת־) נָפְשֶׁךָ	מֶלֶךְ בְּנֵי־עַמּוֹן שָׁלַח אֵלֶיךָ Deest	14 מֶלֶךְ בְּנֵי־עַמּוֹן שָׁלַח אֶת־יִשְׁמָעֵאל בֶּן־נְתַנְיָה לְהַכֹּתְךָ נָפֶשׁ בֶּן־אֲחִיקָם
	וַיֹּאמֶר יוֹחָנָן Desunt {	15 וְיוֹחָנָן בֶּן־קָרֵחַ אָמַר לֵאמֹר בֶּן־נְתַנְיָה

---

[a] Targ. בַּר־קָרֵחַ.   [b] Cf. vs. 10.

למה יכה (את־) נַפְשֶׁךָ	לָמָה יֻכֶּה נֶפֶשׁ 16
Desunt	בֶּן־אֲחִיקָם
	בֶּן־קָרֵחַ
אל־תעשה הדבר	אַל־תַּעַשׂ אֶת־הַדָּבָר הַזֶּה
אתה דבר על־ישמעאל	אַתָּה דֹבֵר אֶל־יִשְׁמָעֵאל

CAPUT XLI.

בן־אלישע מזרע הַמֶּלֶךְ	בֶּן־אֱלִישָׁמָע מִזֶּרַע הַמְּלוּכָה 1
	וְרַבֵּי הַמֶּלֶךְ
	בֶּן־אֲחִיקָם
Desunt	בַּמִּצְפָּה
	בֶּן־נְתַנְיָה 2
	בֶּן־אֲחִיקָם בֶּן־שָׁפָן בַּחֶרֶב וַיָּמֶת אֹתוֹ
עַל־הָאָרֶץ	בָּאָרֶץ
Deest	אֶת־גְּדַלְיָהוּ 3
ואת־על־הכשדים	וְאֵת־הַכַּשְׂדִּים
Desunt	אֵת אַנְשֵׁי הַמִּלְחָמָה הִכָּה יִשְׁמָעֵאל
לַהֲמִיתוֹ (לַהֲפִתוֹ) אֶת־גְּדַלְיָהוּ	לְהָמִית אֶת־גְּדַלְיָהוּ 4
וּמִשָּׁלֵם	מִשִּׁלֹה 5
שמנים אנשים	שְׁמֹנִים אִישׁ
ולבונה בִּידֵיהֶם[b]	וּלְבוֹנָה בְּיָדָם
ויצא לקראתם ישמעאל הֵמָּה הלכו ובכו ויאמר אליהם	וַיֵּצֵא יִשְׁמָעֵאל בֶּן־נְתַנְיָה 6 לִקְרָאתָם מִן־הַמִּצְפָּה הֹלֵךְ הָלֹךְ וּבֹכֶה וַיְהִי כִּפְגֹשׁ אֹתָם וַיֹּאמֶר אֲלֵיהֶם
Deest	בֶּן־אֲחִיקָם
וישחטם אל־הבור	וַיִּשְׁחָטֵם יִשְׁמָעֵאל בֶּן־נְתַנְיָה אֶל־ 7 תּוֹךְ הַבּוֹר הוּא וְהָאֲנָשִׁים אֲשֶׁר־אִתּוֹ

[a] Targ. עַל. [b] Targ. בִּידֵיהוֹן.

8 :נִמְצְאוּ־בָם	נמצאו־שָׁם
וְשֶׁמֶן וּדְבָשׁ	דְּבַשׁ וָשֶׁמֶן
9 פְּנֵי הָאֲנָשִׁים	Deest
וַיּ֯ר־גְּדַלְיָהוּ הוּא	בּוֹר גָּדֹל הוּא (הָיָה)
בֶּן־אֲחִיקָם	Deest
10 וַיִּשְׁבְּ יִשְׁמָעֵאל אֶת־כָּל־שְׁאֵרִית הָעָם אֲשֶׁר בַּמִּצְפָּה אֶת־בְּנוֹת הַמֶּלֶךְ וְאֶת־כָּל־הָעָם הַנִּשְׁאָרִים בַּמִּצְפָּה אֲשֶׁר הִפְקִיד נְבוּזַרְאֲדָן רַב־טַבָּחִים	וַיֵּשֶׁב יִשְׁמָעֵאל אֶת־כָּל־הָעָם הַנִּשְׁאָרִים בְּמִצְפָּה וְאֶת־בְּנוֹת הַמֶּלֶךְ אֲשֶׁר הִפְקִיד רַב־טַבָּחִים
וַיִּשְׁבֵּם יִשְׁמָעֵאל בֶּן־נְתַנְיָה	Deest
וַיֵּלֶךְ לַעֲבֹר אֶל־בְּנֵי עַמּוֹן	וילך לעבר בני עמון
11 וְכָל־שָׂרֵי הַחֲיָלִים	וכל־שרי החיל
בֶּן־נְתַנְיָה	Deest
12 וַיִּקְחוּ אֶת־כָּל־הָאֲנָשִׁים וַיֵּלְכוּ לְהִלָּחֵם עִם־יִשְׁמָעֵאל בֶּן־נְתַנְיָה אֶל־מַיִם רַבִּים אֲשֶׁר בְּגִבְעוֹן	ויקחו את־כל־מחנהם וילכו להלחם עמו על־מים רבים בגבעון
13 בֶּן־קָרֵחַ	Deest
כָּל־שָׂרֵי הַחֲיָלִים	כל־שרי החיל
וַיִּשְׂמָחוּ	Deest
14 וַיָּסֹבּוּ כָּל־הָעָם אֲשֶׁר־שָׁבָה יִשְׁמָעֵאל מִן־הַמִּצְפָּה וַיָּשֻׁבוּ וַיֵּלְכוּ אֶל־יוֹחָנָן בֶּן־קָרֵחַ	וישבו אל־יוחנן
15 בֶּן־נְתַנְיָה מִפְּנֵי יוֹחָנָן	} Desunt
16 יוֹחָנָן בֶּן־קָרֵחַ וְכָל־שָׂרֵי הַחֲיָלִים בֶּן־נְתַנְיָה מִן־הַמִּצְפָּה אַחַר הִכָּה אֶת־גְּדַלְיָה בֶּן־אֲחִיקָם	יוחנן וכל־שרי החיל } Desunt
גְּבָרִים אַנְשֵׁי הַמִּלְחָמָה וְנָשִׁים וְטַף וְסָרִיסִים אֲשֶׁר הֵשִׁיב מִגִּבְעוֹן	גְּבָרִיםᵃ בַּמִּלְחָמָה וְהַנָּשִׁים וְהַשְּׁאֵרִית וְהַסָּרִיסִים אֲשֶׁר הֵשִׁיבוּ מִגִּבְעוֹן
17 בְּנֵרוֹת כְּמוֹהֶםᶜ	בנברות(?) כמההᵇ

ᵃ Targ. כָּל. ᵇ Vid. 43:6. ᶜ ἐν Γαβηρωχαμάα.

[two-column Hebrew biblical text]

ללכת מצרים	ללכת לבוא מצרים
Desunt	18 בן־נתניה
	בן־אחיקם

CAPUT XLII.

ויגשו כל־שרי החיל וְיוֹחָנָן נְאֲזַרְיָה בן־מַעֲשֵׂיָה[a]	1 ויגשו כל־שרי החילים ויוחנן בן־קרח ויזניה בן־הושעיה
אל־ירמיהו הנביא ויאמרו אליו והתפלל	2 ויאמרו אל־ירמיהו הנביא והתפלל בעדנו
בעד הנשארים האלה	בעד כל־השארית הזאת
כאשר עיניך ראות	כאשר עיניך ראות אתנו
ירמיהו	4 ירמיהו הנביא
הנני מתפלל (אֶתְפַּלֵּל) בַּעֲדְכֶם אֶל־יהוה אלהינו	הנני מתפלל אל־יהוה אלהיכם
הדבר	כל־הדבר
יהוה אֱלֹהִים	יהוה אתכם
לא־אַסְתִּיר מכם דבר	לא־אמנע מכם דבר
לעד צדק ונאמן	5 לעד אמת ונאמן
אשר שָׁלַח יהוה אלינו	אשר ישלחך יהוה אלהיך אלינו
וְאִם־טוב ואם־רע אֶת־קוֹל יהוה	6 אם־טוב ואם־רע בקול יהוה
הָיָה דבר־יהוה	7 ויהי דבר־יהוה
Deest	8 בן־קרח
שרי החיל מקטון[b] ועד־גדול	כל־שרי החילים אשר אתו למקטון ועד־גדול
Desunt	9 אלהי ישראל אשר שלחתם אתי אליו להפיל תחנתכם לפניו
אֶבְנֶה אתכם	10 ובניתי אתכם
כי חָדַלְתִּי מן־הרעה[c]	כי נחמתי אל־הרעה
אל־תראו	11 אל־תראו מפניו
להושיע אתכם ולהציל אתכם מידם	להושיע אתכם ולהציל אתכם מידו

[a] Vid. 43:2. [b] ut vs. 1. [c] Targ. אֲרֵי תָבְרִית בִּן בִּישְׁתָּא.

12 וְרִחַם אֶתְכֶם וְהֵשִׁיב אֶתְכֶם אֶל־	ורחם אתכם והשיב אתכם אל־ ורחמתי אתכם ואשיב אתכם אל־
אַדְמַתְכֶם	אדמתכם
13 בְּקוֹל יְהוָה אֱלֹהֵיכֶם	בקול יהוה
14 לֵאמֹר לֹא כִּי אֶרֶץ מִצְרַיִם נָבוֹא	לאמר לא כי ארץ מצרים נבוא ולא־נראה
אֲשֶׁר לֹא־נִרְאֶה מִלְחָמָה	מלחמה
וְלַלֶּחֶם לֹא־נִרְעָב	ובלחם לא־נרעב
15 וְעַתָּה לָכֵן שִׁמְעוּ דְבַר־יְהוָה	לכן שמעו דבר־יהוה
שְׁאֵרִית יְהוּדָה	Deest
יְהוָה צְבָאוֹת אֱלֹהֵי יִשְׂרָאֵל	יהוה
שֹׂם תְּשִׂמוּן פְּנֵיכֶם לָבֹא מִצְרַיִם	תשמון פניכם למצרים° ובאתם
וּבָאתֶם לָגוּר שָׁם	שם לגור
16 אֲשֶׁר אַתֶּם יְרֵאִים מִמֶּנָּה שָׁם	אשר אתם יראים מפניה תשיג
תַּשִּׂיג אֶתְכֶם	אתכם
אֲשֶׁר־אַתֶּם דֹּאֲגִים מִמֶּנּוּ שָׁם	אשר־אתם דאגים מפניו ידבק
יִדְבַּק אַחֲרֵיכֶם מִצְרָיִם	אתכם אחריכם במצרים
17 כָל־הָאֲנָשִׁים אֲשֶׁר־שָׂמוּ אֶת־	כל־האנשים וכל־הזכרים (הזרים)
פְּנֵיהֶם לָבוֹא מִצְרַיִם לָגוּר שָׁם	השמים את־פניהם לארץ מצרים
יָמוּתוּ בַּחֶרֶב בָּרָעָב וּבַדָּבֶר	לגור שם יתמו° בחרב וברעב
וְלֹא־יִהְיֶה לָהֶם שָׂרִיד וּפָלִיט	ולא־יהיה להם פליט מן־
מִפְּנֵי הָרָעָה	הרעה
18 יְהוָה צְבָאוֹת אֱלֹהֵי יִשְׂרָאֵל	יהוה
כַּאֲשֶׁר נִתַּךְ אַפִּי וַחֲמָתִי	כאשר נתכה חמתי
לְאָלָה וּלְשַׁמָּה	לשמה ולעבדים°
19 דְּבַר יְהוָה	אֲשֶׁר דבר יהוה
יָדֹעַ תֵּדְעוּ כִּי־הַעִידֹתִי בָּכֶם	ועתה ידע תדעו^d
הַיּוֹם	
20 כִּי הִתְעֵיתֶם בְּנַפְשׁוֹתֵיכֶם כִּי־אַתֶּם	כי הרעותים בנפשותיכם שלחים אתי
שְׁלַחְתֶּם אֹתִי אֶל־יְהוָה אֱלֹהֵיכֶם	לאמר התפלל עלינו° אל־יהוה
לֵאמֹר הִתְפַּלֵּל בַּעֲדֵנוּ אֶל־יְהוָה	אלהינו וככל אשר יאמר אליך יהוה
אֱלֹהֵינוּ וּכְכֹל אֲשֶׁר יֹאמַר יְהוָה	נעשה
אֱלֹהֵינוּ כֵּן הַגֶּד־לָנוּ וְעָשִׂינוּ	

---

^a Targ. לְמִצְרַיִם. ^b Cf. 14:15; 44:12. ^c ὑποχείριοι. ^d ut vs. 22.
^e Targ. צְלִי כְעַנָּא.

אֲשֶׁר־שְׁלָחַנִי אֲלֵיכֶם	21 וָאַגִּד לָכֶם הַיּוֹם וְלֹא שְׁמַעְתֶּם וְלֹא שְׁמַעְתֶּם בְּקוֹל יְהוָה אֲשֶׁר־ בְּקוֹל יְהוָה אֱלֹהֵיכֶם וּלְכֹל שְׁלָחַנִי אֲלֵיכֶם
	22 וְעַתָּה יָדֹעַ תֵּדְעוּ כִּי בַחֶרֶב בָּרָעָב וְעַתָּה בַּחֶרֶב וּבָרָעָב תָּמוּתוּ[ᵃ] וּבַדֶּבֶר תָּמוּתוּ

CAPUT XLIII.

לְדַבֵּר אֶל־כָּל־הָעָם אֶת־כָּל־דִּבְרֵי יְהוָה אֲשֶׁר שְׁלָחוֹ יְהוָה	1 לְדַבֵּר אֶל־כָּל־הָעָם אֶת־כָּל־דִּבְרֵי יְהוָה אֱלֹהֵיהֶם אֲשֶׁר שְׁלָחוֹ יְהוָה אֱלֹהֵיהֶם
בֶּן־מַעֲשֵׂיָה[ᵇ]	2 בֶּן־הוֹשַׁעְיָה
Deest	הַזֵּדִים
אֹמְרִים אֶל־יִרְמְיָהוּ לֵאמֹר שֶׁקֶר לֹא־ שְׁלָחֲךָ יְהוָה אֵלֵינוּ	הָאֹמְרִים אֶל־יִרְמְיָהוּ שֶׁקֶר אַתָּה מְדַבֵּר לֹא שְׁלָחֲךָ יְהוָה אֱלֹהֵינוּ
	3 כִּי אִם
בְּיַד־הַכַּשְׂדִּים	בְּיַד־הַכַּשְׂדִּים
Deest	4 בֶּן־קָרֵחַ
וְכָל־שָׂרֵי הֶחָיִל	וְכָל־שָׂרֵי הַחֲיָלִים
Deest	5 בֶּן־קָרֵחַ
וְכָל־שָׂרֵי הֶחָיִל	וְכָל־שָׂרֵי הַחֲיָלִים
Deest	מִכָּל־הַגּוֹיִם אֲשֶׁר נִדְּחוּ־שָׁם
לָגוּר בָּאָרֶץ	לָגוּר בְּאֶרֶץ יְהוּדָה
אֶת־הַגְּבָרִים[ᶜ]	6 אֶת־הַגְּבָרִים
וְאֶת־הַטַּף הַנִּשְׁאָרִים	וְאֶת־הַטַּף
וְאֵת כָּל־הַנְּפָשׁוֹת[ᵈ] אֲשֶׁר הִנִּיחַ נְבוּזַרְאֲדָן	וְאֵת כָּל־הַנֶּפֶשׁ אֲשֶׁר הִנִּיחַ נְבוּזַרְאֲדָן רַב־טַבָּחִים
Deest	בֶּן־שָׁפָן
וַיָּבֹאוּ מִצְרַיִם	7 וַיָּבֹאוּ אֶרֶץ מִצְרַיִם
קַח־לְךָ[ᵉ]	9 קַח בְּיָדְךָ

[ᵃ] Cf. 14:15; 44:12. [ᵇ] Vid. 42:1. [ᶜ] Vid. 41:16. [ᵈ] Targ. כָּל נַפְשָׁתָא.
[ᵉ] Targ. סַב עִמָּךְ.

וטמנתם במלט במלבן אשר (ב)שַׁעַר בֵּית־ וטמנתם באלמים*ᵃ*	בְּפֶתַח בֵּית־פַּרְעֹה פרעה
אַנְשֵׁי יְהוּדָה	אֲנָשִׁים יהודים 10
וְאָמַרְתָּ	וְאָמַרְתָּ אֲלֵיהֶם
יהוה	יְהוָה צְבָאוֹת אֱלֹהֵי יִשְׂרָאֵל
וְהֵבֵאתִי אֶת־נְבוּכַדְרֶאצַּר מֶלֶךְ־בָּבֶל וְיָשֵׂם כִּסְאוֹ	לָקַחְתִּי אֶת־נְבוּכַדְרֶאצַּר מֶלֶךְ־ בָּבֶל עַבְדִּי וְשַׂמְתִּי כִסְאוֹ
אֲשֶׁר טָמַנְתָּ וְנָטָל (וְנָשָׂא) חַגֶּשֶׁק רָבָא	אֲשֶׁר טְמַנְתִּי וְנָטָה אֶת־שַׁפְרִירוֹ 11 וּבָאָ^b
וְהִצִּית אֵשׁ בְּבָתֵּי אֱלֹהֵיהֶם	וְהִצַּתִּי אֵשׁ בְּבָתֵּי אֱלֹהֵי מִצְרַיִם 12
וְעָדָה^c אֶת־אֶרֶץ מִצְרַיִם כַּאֲשֶׁר־ יַעְטֶה הָרֹעֶה אֶת־בִּגְדוֹ וְיָצָא מִשָּׁם בְּשָׁלוֹם	וְעָטָה אֶת־אֶרֶץ מִצְרַיִם כַּאֲשֶׁר־ יַעְטֶה הָרֹעֶה אֶת־בִּגְדוֹ וְיָצָא מִשָּׁם בְּשָׁלוֹם
עִיר שֶׁמֶשׁ אֲשֶׁר בְּאוֹן וְאֶת־ בָּתֵּיהֶם	בֵּית שֶׁמֶשׁ אֲשֶׁר בְּאֶרֶץ מִצְרַיִם 13 וְאֶת־בָּתֵּי אֱלֹהֵי־מִצְרַיִם

CAPUT XLIV.

וְהַיֹּשְׁבִים בְּמִגְדֹּל	הַיֹּשְׁבִים בְּמִגְדֹּל 1
Deest	וּבְנֹף
יהוה	יְהוָה צְבָאוֹת 2
וְעַל־עָרֵי יְהוּדָה וְהִנָּם חֳרָבוֹת מֵאֵין יוֹשֵׁב	וְעַל כָּל־עָרֵי יְהוּדָה וְהִנֵּם חָרְבָּה הַיּוֹם הַזֶּה וְאֵין בָּהֶם יוֹשֵׁב
Deest	לַעֲבֹד 3
אֲשֶׁר לֹא יְדָעוּם אַתֶּם אֲשֶׁר לֹא יְדַעְתָּם וַאֲבוֹתֵיכֶם	
אֶת־עֲבָדַי	אֶת־כָּל־עֲבָדַי 4
וָאֶשְׁלַח	וְשָׁלֹחַ
אַל־תַּעֲשׂוּ	אַל נָא תַעֲשׂוּ
וְלֹא שָׁמְעוּ אֵלַי	וְלֹא שָׁמֵעוּ 5
בְּשַׁעֲרֵי יְהוּדָה וּמִחוּץ^d יְרוּשָׁלִַם	בְּעָרֵי יְהוּדָה וּבְחֻצוֹת יְרוּשָׁלִָם 6

^a ἐν προθύροις. ^b καὶ φθειρεῖ.—Targ. וְיִדְּוֹכֵן. ^c ὥσπερ φθειρίζει.
^d יִשָּׁבֵעַ.—Vid. vss. 9, 17, 21.

לחרבות ולשממה	לחרבה לשממה
יהוה צבאות אֱלֹהֵי יִשְׂרָאֵל	7 יהוה אֱלֹהֵי צבאות אֱלֹהֵי יִשְׂרָאֵל
עַל‎ֹ‎[a]‎-(בְּ)נַפְשֹׁתְכֶם	אֶל-נַפְשֹׁתְכֶם
לבלתי הַוְתֵר לכם (מִכֶּם)[b] אִישׁ	לבלתי הוֹתִיר לכם שְׁאֵרִית
למען תִּכָּרֵתוּ	8 למען הַכְרִית לָכֶם
ואת רשות נְשׂוֹאֲכֶם (שָׂרֵיכֶם)	9 ואת רשות נָשָׁיו ואת רָלֵחֶיכֶם
וּמֵחוּץ[c] ירושלם	ובחצות ירושלם
לא חָדְלוּ[c]	10 לא דֻכְּאוּ
ולא‎-הֶחֱזִיקוּ (תָמְכוּ) בְּמִצְוֹתַי	ולא יָרְאוּ ולא‎-הָלְכוּ בתורתי
לפני אבותיהם	לְפָנֵיכֶם ולפני אבותיכם
לכן כה‎-אמר יהוה הנני שם פני	11 לכן כה‎-אמר יהוה צבאות אֱלֹהֵי
·	יִשְׂרָאֵל הנני שם פני בָּכֶם לְרָעָה
	וּלְהַכְרִית אֶת‎-כָּל‎-יְהוּדָה
לְאַבֵּד אֶת‎-כָּל‎-הַנִּשְׁאָרִים אשר	12 וְלָקַחְתִּי אֶת‎-שְׁאֵרִית יְהוּדָה
בְּמִצְרַיִם וְיִפְּלוּ בחרב וברעב	אשר‎-שָׂמוּ פְנֵיהֶם לָבוֹא אֶרֶץ‎-
וְיִתַּמּוּ מקטן עד‎-גדול	מצרים לָגוּר שָׁם וְתַמּוּ כֹל
	בְּאֶרֶץ מִצְרַיִם יִפְּלוּ בחרב
	ברעב יתמו מקטן וְעַד‎-גדול
Deest	בַּחֶרֶב וּבָרָעָב יָמֻתוּ
והיו לְאָלָה לשמה ולחרפה ולקללה	והיו לחרפה ולשמה ולקללה
	ולחרפה
Deest	13 וּבְדָבָר
ולא יהיה כָּל‎-פָּלִיט מָשָּׁאֲרִית	14 ולא יהיה פליט וְשָׂרִיד לִשְׁאֵרִית
יהודה הגָרִים בארץ מצרים	יהודה הַבָּאִים לָגוּר‎-שָׁם
לשוב ארץ יהודה אשר‎-	בארץ מצרים ולשוב ארץ
מנשאים המה בְּנַפְשׁוֹתֵיהֶם[d]	יהודה אשר‎-המה מנשאים
לשוב שם לא ישובו	אֶת‎-נַפְשָׁם לשוב לָשֶׁבֶת שם
	כי לא‎-ישובו
Desunt {	15 לֵאלֹהִים אֲחֵרִים
	הָעֹמְדוֹת
אֲשֶׁר‎-יָצָא מפינו	17 אֲשֶׁר יָצָא מפינו
וּמַלְכֵּינוּ	מַלְכֵּינוּ

[a] Targ. כָּל. [b] Vid. vss. 6, 17, 21. [c] Targ. לָא פְסָקוּ. [d] ἐλπίζουσι ταῖς ψυχαῖς αὐτῶν

וּבְחֻצוֹת יְרוּשָׁלִָם	וּמָחוּץ ירושלם[c]
18 וּמִן־אָז חָדַלְנוּ	וְכַאֲשֶׁר חדלנו
וְהַסֵּךְ לָהּ נְסָכִים	Deest
19 מְקַטְּרִים	תִקְטָרְנוּ
וּלְהַסֵּךְ לָהּ נְסָכִים	וּמְנַסְּכִים[b] לה נסכים
לְהַעֲצִבָה	Deest
וְהַסֵּךְ לה נסכים	וסכנו לה נסכים
20 עַל־הַגְּבָרִים וְעַל־הַנָּשִׁים וְעַל	עַל־הגברים ואל־הנשים[c] ואל־כל־
כָּל־הָעָם הָעֹנִים אֹתוֹ דָּבָר	העם הענים אתו דברים
21 וּבְחֻצוֹת יְרוּשָׁלִָם	וּמָחוּץ לירושלם
מַלְכֵיכֶם	וּמַלְכֵיכֶם
אֹתָם זָכַר יהוה	זכר יהוה
22 מִפְּנֵי הַתּוֹעֵבֹת	וּמֵהַתּוֹעֵבֹתֵיכֶם (וּמִן־הַתּוֹעֵבֹת)
וַתְּהִי אַרְצְכֶם לְחָרְבָּה	ותהי ארצכם לחרבות[d]
מֵאֵין יוֹשֵׁב	Deest
23 וּבְתוֹרָתוֹ וּבְחֻקֹּתָיו	ובחקתיו ובתרתו (וּבְעֵדֻתוֹ)
עַל־כֵּן קָרָאת אֶתְכֶם הָרָעָה הַזֹּאת	וַתִּקְרָאֶנָה אתכם הרעות האלה
כַּיּוֹם הַזֶּה	Deest
24 אֶל־כָּל־הָעָם וְאֶל כָּל־הַנָּשִׁים	אל־העם ואל־הנשים
כָּל־יְהוּדָה אֲשֶׁר בְּאֶרֶץ מִצְרָיִם	Deest
25 כֹּה־אָמַר יְהוָה־צְבָאוֹת אֱלֹהֵי	כה־אמר יהוה אלהי ישראל אתן
יִשְׂרָאֵל לֵאמֹר אַתֶּם וּנְשֵׁיכֶם	הַנָּשִׁים בפיכן דברתן ובידיכן
וַתְּדַבֵּרְנָה בְּפִיכֶם וּבִידֵיכֶם	מִלֵּאתֶן
מִלֵּאתֶם	
וַעֲשׂה תַעֲשֶׂינָה אֶת־נְדָרֵיכֶם	ועשה תעשינה
26 אִם־יִהְיֶה עוֹד שְׁמִי נִקְרָא בְּפִי	אם־יהיה עוד שמי בפי כל־יהודה
כָּל־אִישׁ יְהוּדָה אֹמֵר חַי־	אָמַר חַי־יְהוָה
אֲדֹנָי יְהוִה	
27 הִנְנִי שֹׁקֵד עֲלֵיהֶם לְרָעָה וְלֹא	כי אני שקד עליהם להרע להם
לְטוֹבָה וְתַמּוּ כָל־אִישׁ יְהוּדָה	ולא להיטיב ותמו כל־יהודה
אֲשֶׁר בְּאֶרֶץ מִצְרַיִם	הַיּוֹשְׁבִים בארץ מצרים
28 מֵאֶרֶץ מִצְרָיִם	Deest

[a] Vid. vss. 6, 9, 21.   [b] Targ. וּמְנַסְּכָן.   [c] Targ. לְגַבְרַיָּא וְלִנְשַׁיָּא.   [d] Vid. vs. 6.

וַיֵּדְעוּ כָּל־שְׁאֵרִית יְהוּדָה הַבָּאִים	וַיֵּדְעוּ שְׁאֵרִית יְהוּדָה הָעֹמְדִים
לְאֶרֶץ־מִצְרַיִם	בְּאֶרֶץ־מִצְרַיִם
מָשְׁעֵי וּמֵהֶם	Deest
29 וְזֹאת לָכֶם הָאוֹת נְאֻם־יְהֹוָה כִּי־	וְזֹאת הָאוֹת לָכֶם כִּי־פֹקֵד אֲנִי עֲלֵיכֶם
פֹקֵד אֲנִי עֲלֵיכֶם בַּמָּקוֹם הַזֶּה	לְרָעָה
לְמַעַן תֵּדְעוּ כִּי קוֹם יָקוּמוּ	
דְּבָרַי עֲלֵיכֶם לְרָעָה	
30 אֶת־פַּרְעֹה חָפְרַע	אֶת־חָפְרַע
בְּיַד אֹיְבָיו וּבְיַד מְבַקְשֵׁי נַפְשׁוֹ	בְּיַד אֹיְבוֹ וּבִידֵי מְבַקֵּשׁ נַפְשׁוֹ
בְּיַד נְבוּכַדְרֶאצַּר	בְּיָדֵי נְבוּכַדְרֶאצַּר

CAPUT XLV.

1 עַל־סֵפֶר	בַּסֵּפֶר
לֵאמֹר	Deest
2 כֹּה־אָמַר יְהוָה אֱלֹהֵי יִשְׂרָאֵל	כֹּה־אָמַר יהוה
3 אָמַרְתָּ אוֹי־נָא לִי כִּי־יָסַף יְהוָה	כִּי (יַעַן) אָמַרְתָּ אוֹי לִי אוֹי לִי כִּי־
יָגוֹן עַל־מַכְאֹבִי יָגַעְתִּי בְּאַנְחָתִי	יָסַף יהוה יָגוֹן מַכְאֹב לִי (?) יָגַעְתִּי
וּמְנוּחָה לֹא מָצָאתִי	(שָׁכַבְתִּי) בַּאֲנָחוֹת מְנוּחָה לֹא
	מָצָאתִי
4 כֹּה תֹּאמַר אֵלָיו	אָמֹר אֵלָיו
וְאֶת־כָּל־הָאָרֶץ הִיא	Deest
וְנָתַתִּי לְךָ אֶת־נַפְשְׁךָ לְשָׁלָל עַל	וְנָתַתִּ אֶת־נַפְשְׁךָ לְשָׁלָל בְּכָל־הַמָּקוֹם
כָּל־הַמְּקֹמוֹת אֲשֶׁר תֵּלֶךְ־שָׁם	אֲשֶׁר תֵּלֶךְ־שָׁם

CAPUT XLVI.

1 אֲשֶׁר הָיָה דְבַר־יְהוָה אֶל־	בְּרֵאשִׁית מַלְכוּת צִדְקִיָּהוּ מֶלֶךְ־יְהוּדָה
יִרְמְיָהוּ הַנָּבִיא עַל־הַגּוֹיִם	הָיָה הַדָּבָר הַזֶּה לְעֵילָם
2 בְּכַרְכְּמִשׁ	בכרמש[a]
נְבוּכַדְרֶאצַּר	נבוכדראצר[b]

---

[a] ἐν Χαρμείς. [b] Targ. נְבוּכַדְנֶצַּ֫ר.

46:3-14] THE CONSPECTUS OF THE VARIATIONS. 377

לִיהוֹיָקִים	לִיהוֹיָקִים בֶּן־יֹאשִׁיָּהוּ
הַחֲזִיקוּ (תִּפְשׂוּ) מגן (נֶשֶׁק) וְצִנּוֹת[a] וְאִסְרוּ הַסּוּסִים עָלוּ הַפָּרָשִׁים וְהִתְיַצְּבוּ בְּכוֹבָעֵיכֶם זִרְקוּ (הָרִיקוּ) הָרְמָחִים וְלִבְשׁוּ סְרִינוֹתֵיכֶם	3 עֶרְכוּ מגן וְצִנָּה אִסְרוּ הַסּוּסִים וַעֲלוּ הַפָּרָשִׁים וְהִתְיַצְּבוּ בְּכוֹבָעִים מִרְקוּ הָרְמָחִים לִבְשׁוּ הַסִּרְיֹנוֹת
מַדּוּעַ הֵמָּה הַתִּים וּנְסוֹגִים אָחוֹר כִּי גְּבוּרֵיהֶם יֻכַּתּוּ מָנוֹס נָסוּ	5 מַדּוּעַ רָאִיתִי הֵמָּה חַתִּים נְסֹגִים אָחוֹר וְגִבּוֹרֵיהֶם יֻכַּתּוּ וּמָנוֹס נָסוּ
עַל־צָפוֹן עַל־יַד פְּרָת כָּשְׁלוּ וְכִנְהָרוֹת יִתְגָּעֲשׁוּ מָיִם[b] מֵי מִצְרַיִם כַּיְאוֹר יַעֲלֶה Deest	6 צָפוֹנָה עַל־יַד נְהַר־פְּרָת כָּשְׁלוּ 7 כַּנָּהָר יַעֲלוּ מֵימָיו 8 מִצְרַיִם כַּיְאֹר יַעֲלֶה וְכַנְּהָרוֹת יִתְגֹּעֲשׁוּ מָיִם
אֶעֱלֶה וַאֲכַסֶּה־הָאָרֶץ וְאֲבִידָה יֹשְׁבֵי־בָהּ	אַעֲלֶה אֲכַסֶּה־אֶרֶץ אֲבִידָה עִיר וְיֹשְׁבֵי־בָהּ
עָלוּ עַל־הַסּוּסִים וְהִתְהַלְלוּ הַמֶּרְכָּבוֹת[c] צְאוּ גִּבּוֹרֵי־כּוּשִׁים[d] וְלוּבִים תֹּפְשֵׂי מגן וְלוּדִים עָלוּ דֹּרְכֵי קָשֶׁת	9 עֲלוּ הַסּוּסִים וְהִתְהֹלְלוּ הָרֶכֶב וְיֵצְאוּ הַגִּבּוֹרִים כּוּשׁ וּפוּט תֹּפְשֵׂי מגן וְלוּדִים תֹּפְשֵׂי דֹּרְכֵי קָשֶׁת
לַיהוָה אֱלֹהֵינוּ לְהִנָּקֵם מֵאוֹיְבָיו וַאֲכָלָה חֶרֶב יְהֹוָה[e] לַאדֹנָי מֵאֶרֶץ צָפוֹן עַל־נְהַר־פְּרָת	10 לַאדֹנָי יְהוִה צְבָאוֹת לְהִנָּקֵם מִצָּרָיו וְאָכְלָה חֶרֶב לַאדֹנָי יְהוִה צְבָאוֹת בְּאֶרֶץ צָפוֹן אֶל־נְהַר־פְּרָת
לִבְתוּלַת בַּת־מִצְרַיִם לַשָּׁוְא הִרְבִּיתִי רְפוּאוֹתַיִךְ תְּעָלָה אֵין בָּךְ	11 בְּתוּלַת בַּת־מִצְרַיִם לַשָּׁוְא הִרְבֵּיתִי רְפָאוֹת תְּעָלָה אֵין לָךְ
שִׁמְעוּ גּוֹיִם קוֹלֵךְ כָּשְׁלוּ יַחַד	12 שִׁמְעוּ גוֹיִם קְלוֹנֵךְ כָּשְׁלוּ יַחְדָּיו
אֲשֶׁר דְּבַר יְהוָה בְּיַד־יִרְמְיָהוּ בְּבוֹא מֶלֶךְ בָּבֶל	13 הַדָּבָר אֲשֶׁר דִּבֶּר יְהוָה אֶל־יִרְמְיָהוּ הַנָּבִיא לָבוֹא נְבוּכַדְרֶאצַּר מֶלֶךְ בָּבֶל
הַגִּידוּ לְ(ב)מִגְדּוֹל וְהַשְׁמִיעוּ אֶל־(ב)מֹף[g]	14 הַגִּידוּ בְמִצְרַיִם וְהַשְׁמִיעוּ בְמִגְדּוֹל וְהַשְׁמִיעוּ בְנֹף וּבְתַחְפַּנְחֵס

---

[a] Targ. גְּהָרְיָסָן. [b] ut vs. 8. [c] Targ. רְתִיכַיָּא. [d] Targ. כּוּשָׁאֵי.
[e] Cf. I. Chron. 21:12. [f] Targ. עַל. [g] Vid. vs. 19.—Targ. בְּפַּס.

כִּי־אָכְלָה חֶרֶב סְבָבֶיךָ	כִּי־אָכְלָה חֶרֶב סְבִיבֶיךָ
מַדּוּעַ נָס מָפָּה (‏=‏ מִן) אַפִּיס עַל בְּחִירֶךָ	15 מַדּוּעַ נִסְחַף אַבִּירֶיךָ
מַרְבִּיתָךְ (הָרַבָּה) כָּשַׁל גַּם־נָפַל וְאִישׁ אֶל־רֵעֵהוּ אָמַר נָקוּם מִפְּנֵי חֶרֶב הַיְוָנָה (הַיְוָנִית)	16 הִרְבָּה כּוֹשֵׁל גַּם־נָפַל אִישׁ אֶל־רֵעֵהוּ וַיֹּאמְרוּ קוּמָה מִפְּנֵי חֶרֶב הַיּוֹנָה
קִרְאוּ שָׁם פַּרְעֹה נָלָה מֶלֶךְ־מִצְרַיִם שָׁאוֹן הֶשְׁבִּי(ת) (הַ)מּוֹעֵד[a]	17 קָרְאוּ שָׁם פַּרְעֹה מֶלֶךְ־מִצְרַיִם שָׁאוֹן הֶעֱבִיר הַמּוֹעֵד
נְאֻם־אֲדֹנָי יְהוָה כִּי־טֹם[b]	18 נְאֻם־הַמֶּלֶךְ יְהוָה צְבָאוֹת שְׁמוֹ 19 כִּי־נֹף
וְנִצְתָה אוֹי מֵאֵין יוֹשֵׁב בָּהּ	וְנִצְּתָה מֵאֵין יוֹשֵׁב
קֶרֶץ מִצָּפוֹן בָּא בָהּ[c]	20 קֶרֶץ מִצָּפוֹן בָּא בָא
כְּעֶגְלֵי מַרְבֵּק מִגְדָּלִים בְּתוֹכָהּ וְנָסוּ יַחְדָּיו	21 כְּעֶגְלֵי מַרְבֵּק נָסוּ יַחְדָּו
כִּי יוֹם אֵיד בָּא עֲלֵיהֶם וְעֵת פְּקֻדָּתָם	כִּי יוֹם אֵידָם בָּא עֲלֵיהֶם עֵת פְּקֻדָּתָם
קוֹלָהּ כַּנָּחָשׁ יֵלֵךְ כִּי־בַחַיִל יֵלְכוּ בְּקַרְדֻּמּוֹת בָּאוּ עָלֶיהָ: כְּחֹטְבֵי[d] עֵצִים	22 קוֹלָהּ כַּנָּחָשׁ יֵלֵךְ כִּי־בַחַיִל יֵלֵכוּ וּבְקַרְדֻּמּוֹת בָּאוּ לָהּ כְּחֹטְבֵי עֵצִים:
כִּי לֹא יֵחָקֵר כִּי רַב מֵאַרְבֶּה	23 כִּי לֹא יֵחָקֵר כִּי רַבּוּ מֵאַרְבֶּה
נִתְּנָה בְּיַד עַם־צָפוֹן	24 נִתְּנָה בְּיַד עַם־צָפוֹן
הִנְנִי פוֹקֵד אֶת־אָמוֹן בְּנֹא עַל־פַּרְעֹה וְעַל הַבֹּטְחִים בּוֹ	25 אָמַר יְהוָה צְבָאוֹת אֱלֹהֵי יִשְׂרָאֵל הִנְנִי פוֹקֵד אֶל־אָמוֹן מִנֹּא וְעַל־פַּרְעֹה וְעַל־מִצְרַיִם וְעַל־אֱלֹהֶיהָ וְעַל־מְלָכֶיהָ וְעַל־פַּרְעֹה וְעַל הַבֹּטְחִים בּוֹ
Desunt	26 וּנְתַתִּים בְּיַד מְבַקְשֵׁי נַפְשָׁם וּבְיַד נְבוּכַדְרֶאצַּר מֶלֶךְ־בָּבֶל וּבְיַד עֲבָדָיו וְאַחֲרֵי־כֵן תִּשְׁכֹּן כִּימֵי־קֶדֶם נְאֻם־יְהוָה:
מְשֻׁבִים	27 מֵאֶרֶץ שִׁבְיָם

---

[a] Σαων Εσβει Μωηδ. [b] Vid. vs. 14. [c] Targ. יָיתֵי עֲלָהּ. [d] Inc. vs. 23.

[16:28-47:7] THE CONSPECTUS OF THE VARIATIONS.

וּשְׁאָנֵן וְאֵין מַחֲרִיד | וְיָשֵׁן וְאֵין מַחֲרִיד אוֹתוֹ
28 אַתָּה אַל־תִּירָא | אַתָּה אַל־תִּירָא
כִּי אִתְּךָ אָנִי כִּי אֶעֱשֶׂה כָלָה | כִּי אִתָּךְ אֲנִי הַבְטָחָה וְהָאֲדִינָה
בְּכָל־הַגּוֹיִם | (יָחַפְצָנָּה) סַנְּרָה כִּי אֶעֱשֶׂה
 | לְעַם כָּלָה בְּכָל־גּוֹי
וְיִסַּרְתִּיךָ לַמִּשְׁפָּט | וְיִסַּרְתִּיךָ לְמִשְׁפָּט

CAPUT XLVII.

1 אֲשֶׁר הָיָה דְבַר־יְהֹוָה אֶל־יִרְמְיָהוּ עַל־פְּלִשְׁתִּים
הַנָּבִיא אֶל־פְּלִשְׁתִּים בְּטֶרֶם
יַכֶּה פַרְעֹה אֶת־עַזָּה
2 וְזָעֲקוּ הָאָדָם וְהֵילִל כֹּל יוֹשֵׁב וְזָעֲקוּ הָאֲנָשִׁים[b] וְהֵילִלוּ כֹּל יוֹשְׁבֵי
הָאָרֶץ[c] הָאָרֶץ
3 מִקּוֹל שַׁעֲטַת פַּרְסוֹת אַבִּירָיו מִקּוֹל שַׁעֲטָתוֹ (שְׁאוֹנוֹ) מַפְרְסוֹת
מֵרַעַשׁ לְרִכְבּוֹ רַגְלָיו וּמֵרַעַשׁ לְרִכְבָּיו[d]
לֹא־הִפְנוּ אָבוֹת אֶל־בָּנִים מֵרִפְיוֹן לֹא־הִפְנוּ אָבוֹת אֶל־בְּנֵיהֶם מֵרִפְיוֹן
יָדָיִם יְדֵיהֶם
4 עַל־הַיּוֹם הַבָּא לִשְׁדוֹד אֶת־כָּל־ בַּיּוֹם הַבָּא לְאַבֵּד (לְכַלּוֹת) אֶת־כָּל־
פְּלִשְׁתִּים לְהַכְרִית לְצוֹר וּלְצִידוֹן פְּלִשְׁתִּים וְאַכְרִית (וְאֶכַלֶּה) צֹר
כֹּל שָׂרִיד עֹזֵר כִּי־שֹׁדֵד יְהֹוָה וְצִידוֹן וְכָל הַשְּׂרִידִים עֶזְרָם
אֶת־פְּלִשְׁתִּים שְׁאֵרִית אִי (מִדְיָנָם) כִּי־שֹׁדֵד יְהֹוָה אֶת
כַּפְתּוֹר שְׁאֵרִית הָאִיִּים
5 בָּאָה קָרְחָה אֶל־עַזָּה נִדְמְתָה בָּאָה קָרְחָה עַל־עַזָּה נִרְמְתָה
אַשְׁקְלוֹן שְׁאֵרִית עִמְקָם עַד־ אַשְׁקְלוֹן וּשְׁאֵרִית עֲנָקִים[f] עַד־
מָתַי תִּתְגּוֹדָדִי: מָתַי תְּגַדַּעִי[g]
6 הוֹי חֶרֶב לַיהֹוָה חֶרֶב יְהֹוָה
הַרְגְּעִי וְדֹמִּי הַרְגֵּעִי וְרֹמִי
7 אֵיךְ תִּשְׁקֹטִי אֵיךְ תִּשְׁקֹט

---

[a] Targ. עַל. [b] Targ. בְּנֵי אֱנָשָׁא. [c] Targ. כָּל יָתְבֵי אַרְעָא. יְיַלְלוּן. [d] Targ. לְרְתִיכוֹהִי. [e] Ἐνακίμ.—Targ. תּוּקְפְהוֹן. [f] Inc. vs. 6. [g] Aram. קָנַד.

אֶל־אַשְׁקְלוֹן וְאֶל־חוֹף הַיָּם שָׁם עַל־אַשְׁקְלוֹן וְעַל־חֹפֵי הַיָּם עַל־
יְעָדָהּ   שְׁאָר יְעָרָהּ

CAPUT XLVIII.

1 כֹּה־אָמַר יהוה צְבָאוֹת אֱלֹהֵי   כה־אמר יהוה הוי על־נבו כי
  יִשְׂרָאֵל הוֹי אֶל־נְבוֹ כִּי שֻׁדָּדָה   שדדה נלכדה קריתים הבישה
  הֹבִישָׁה נִלְכְּדָה קִרְיָתַיִם   חָמַת וָנָת (וְחַגָּת)ᵈ
  הֹבִישָׁה הַמִּשְׂגָּב וָחָתָּה

2 אֵין עוֹד תְּהִלַּת מוֹאָב בְּחֶשְׁבּוֹן   אין עוד תְּעָלַת מואב תהלה בחשבון
  חָשְׁבוּ עָלֶיהָ רָעָה לְכוּ וְנַכְרִיתֶנָּה   חשב עליה רעה נכריתנה מגוים
  מִגּוֹי גַּם־מַדְמֵן תִּדֹּמִּי   וְדֹם תדמי

3 קוֹל צְעָקָה   כי קול צעקים
4 הִשְׁמִיעוּ זְעָקָה צְעוֹרֶיהָ   השמיעו צוערהᶠ

5 כִּי מַעֲלֵה הַלֻּחוֹת בִּבְכִי יַעֲלֶה־   מָלְאָה הלחות בבכי יעלה־בֿכה
  בֶּכִי כִּי בְּמוֹרַד חוֹרֹנַיִם צָרֵי   בדרך חורנים צעקת־שבר
  צַעֲקַת־שֶׁבֶר שָׁמֵעוּ   שְׁמַעְתֶּם

6 נֻסוּ מַלְּטוּ נַפְשְׁכֶם וְתִהְיֶינָה   נסו מלטו נפשותיכם ותהיה
  כַּעֲרוֹעֵר בַּמִּדְבָּר   כְּעָרוֹד במדברᶠ

7 בְּמַעֲשַׂיִךְ וּבְאֹצְרוֹתַיִךְ   בְּמִבְצָרֵךְ
  כֹּהֲנָיו   וכהניו

8 וְיָבֹא שֹׁדֵד אֶל־כָּל־עִיר וָעִיר   ויבא שד על־כל־עיר
  אֲשֶׁר אָמַר יהוה   כאשר אמר יהוה

9 תְּנוּ־צִיץ לְמוֹאָב כִּי נָצֹא תֵּצֵא   תנו ציון למואב כי נצת תצת
  וְעָרֶיהָ לְשַׁמָּה תִהְיֶינָה מֵאֵין   וְכָל־עָרִיהָ לשמה תהיינה מאין
  יוֹשֵׁב בָּהֵן   יושב בה

10 וְאָרוּר   Deest
11 מִנְּעוּרָיו   מֹעַר
   וְשָׁקַט הוּא אֶל־שְׁמָרָיו   ושקט הוא על־כבודו (שמו?)
12 הִנֵּה־יָמִים בָּאִים   הנה־ימי באיםᵐ
   וְכֵלָיו יָרִיקוּ וּנְבְלֵיהֶם יְנַפֵּצוּ   וכליו ידיקו וקרניו יקצצו (יגדעו)ⁱ

ᵃ Targ. רְעַל. ᵇ Targ. עַל. ᶜ Cf. 50:27.—Targ. עַל. ᵈ Ἀμὰθ καὶ Ἀγάβ. ᵉ Cf.
Isa. 15:5.—Ζογόρα. ᶠ Cf. Job 39:5. ᵍ Targ. עַל. ʰ Cf. 50:27,31. ⁱ Cf. vs. 25.

48:13-31] THE CONSPECTUS OF THE VARIATIONS.

13 מבטחם	מבטחם בְּבִטְחָם (בְּבִטְחַ) בָּהֶם
14 וְאַנְשֵׁי חיל למלחמה	וְאִישׁ חיל למלחמות
15 וְעָרֶיהָ עָלָה	עָרָהּ (עִירוֹ)
נְאָם־הַמֶּלֶךְ יְהוָה צְבָאוֹת שְׁמוֹ	Deest
16 קרוב איד־מואב לבוא ורעתו מהרה מאד	קרוב עֵת־מואב לבוא ורעתו מְהֵרָה[a] מאד
17 וְכָל יֹדְעֵי שמו	כל הוֹדִיעוּ שמו
18 יֹשְׁבִי בַצָּמָא יֹשֶׁבֶת בַּת־דִּיבוֹן כי שֹׁדֵד מואב עלה בך שחת מבצריך	וּשְׁבִי בִּבְצָה ישבת דיבון בְּתָ(ה)[b] כי שָׁדַד מואב עלה בך מַשְׁחִית מבצרֶךָ
19 אל־דרך עמדי וצפי יושבת ערוער שאלי־נָס ונמלטה אמרי מה־נהיתה	עַל־דרך עמדי וצפי יושבת בָּערוער[d] וְשַׁאלי־נָס ונמלט וְאָמְרוּ מַה־נהיתה
20 הלילו וזעקו[c] הגידו בארנון	הלילי וזעקי הגידי בארנון
21 ומשפט בָּא אל־ארץ המישר אל־חלון ואל־יַהְצָה וְעַל־מוֹפָעַת	ומשפט יָבֹא אל־ארץ מישר[e] על־חלון וְרִיפַת ומופעת
22 ועל־בית דִּבְלָתִים	ועל־בית דְּלתים
24 ועל כל־ערי אֶרֶץ מואב	ועל כל־ערי מואב
25 נְאָם יְהוָה	Deest
26 וְסָפַק מואב בְּקיאו	וספק מואב בכפו[f]
27 ואם לוא הַשְּׂחוק היה לך ישראל אִם־בַּגַּנָּבִים נמצאה כִּי־מִדֵּי דְבָרֶיךָ בּוֹ תִּתְנוֹדָד	ואם לוא לשחק[g] היה לך ישראל וּבגנביך נמצא כי נִלְחַמְתָּ בו
28 עִזְבוּ ערים וְשִׁכְנוּ בַּסֶּלַע ישבי מואב וְהָיוּ כְּיוֹנָה תקנן בְּעֶבְרֵי פִי־פָחַת	עָזְבוּ הֶעָרִים וְשָׁכְנוּ בַסְּלָעִים ישבי מואב היו כיונים תקננה בסלעי (בצורי) פי־פחת
29 שמענו גאון־מואב גאה מאד גָּבְהוֹ וּגְאוֹנוֹ וגאותו וְרָם לבו	וְשָׁמַעְתִּי (וְאֶשְׁמַע)[?] גאון־מואב גָּאָה מאד גאונו וגאותו ורם לבו
30 אני ידעתי נְאֻם־יְהוָה עֶבְרָתוֹ וְלֹא־כֵן בַּדָּיו לֹא־כֵן עשׂוּ	וַאֲנִי ידעתי עֲבֹדָתוֹ[h] הֲלֹא בַדָּיו לא־כן עָשָׂה
31 על־כן על־מואב אֲיֵלִיל וּלְמוֹאָב כֻּלֹּה אֶזְעָק	על־כן למואב הֵילִילוּ[i] מַסְבִיב

---

[a] Targ. בּוֹחָרָא. [b] ἐκτριβήσεται. [c] Targ. עַל אוֹרְחָא. [d] Targ. בְּעֵרוֹעֵר.
[e] Μεισώρ. [f] καὶ ἐπικρούσει Μωὰβ ἐν χειρὶ αὐτοῦ. [g] ut vs. 26. [h] Targ.
דְּיִלְלִין. [i] Targ. שׁוּבְדֵי רַבְרְבָנֵיהוֹן.

כֹּה אֶזְעַק אֶל־אַנְשֵׁי קִיר־ (זַעֲקוּ) הַזְעִיקוּ עַל־אַנְשֵׁי קִיר־חָרָשׂ חֶרֶשׂ יֶהְגֶּה	
32 מִבְּכִי יַעְזֵר אֶבְכֶּה־לָּךְ הַגֶּפֶן שִׂבְמָה יִעְזֵר אֲבַכֶּה־לָּךְ הַגֶּפֶן כִּבְכִי עַזְרָמָה	
עַד יָם יַעְזֵר נָגָעוּ עַל־קֵיצֵךְ וְעַל־ בְּצִירֵךְ שֹׁדֵד נָפָל עִיר־יַעְזֵר (עָרֵי מֵיעָזֵר) נָגְעוּ עַל־קֵיצֵךְ עַל־בְּצִירֵךְ שַׂד נָפַל	
33 וְנֶאֶסְפָה שִׂמְחָה וָגִיל מִכַּרְמֶל וּמֵאֶרֶץ מוֹאָב וְיַיִן מִיקָבִים הִשְׁבַּתִּי לֹא־יִדְרֹךְ הֵידָד הֵידָד לֹא הֵידָד נֶאֶסְפָה שִׂמְחָה וָגִיל מִמּוֹאָב וְיַיִן הָיָה בִיקָבֶיהָ הַשְׁקֵם (הַשְׁדָּר) לֹא דָרְכוּ וּבְעֶרֶב לֹא עָשׂוּ הֵדָה (הֵידָד)	
34 מִזַּעֲקַת חֶשְׁבּוֹן עַד־אֶלְעָלֵה עַד־יַהַץ נָתְנוּ קוֹלָם עֶגְלַת שְׁלִשִׁיָּה כִּי גַּם־מֵי נִמְרִים לִמְשַׁמּוֹת יִהְיוּ עַד־אֶלְעָלֵה עַד־יַחַץ נָתְנוּ קוֹלָם וְעֶגְלֹת (?) שְׁלֹשִׁיָּה כִּי גַּם־מֵי נְבָרִים לִמְשׂוֹרָפוֹת יִהְיוּ	
35 וְהִשְׁבַּתִּי לְמוֹאָב מַעֲלֶה בָמָה וּמַקְטִיר לֵאלֹהָיו וְהִשְׁבַּתִּי אֶת־מוֹאָב מַעֲלִים בָּמָה וּמַקְטִירִים לֵאלֹהָיו	
36 עַל־כֵּן לִבִּי לְמוֹאָב כַּחֲלִילִים יֶהֱמֶה וְלִבִּי אֶל־אַנְשֵׁי קִיר־חֶרֶשׂ כַּחֲלִילִים יֶהֱמֶה עַל־כֵּן יִתְרַת עָשָׂה אָבָדוּ עַל־כֵּן לֵב מוֹאָב כַּחֲלָלִים יֶהֱמוּ לִבִּי עַל־אַנְשֵׁי קִיר־חָדָשׁ כְּחָלִיל יֶהֱמֶה עַל־כֵּן יִתְרַת עָשָׂה אָבְדוּ מֵאָדָם (מֵאֱנוֹשׁ)	
37 כִּי כָל־רֹאשׁ קָרְחָה וְכָל־זָקָן גְּרֻעָה עַל כָּל־יָדַיִם גְּדֻדֹת וְעַל־מָתְנַיִם שָׂק כָּל־רֹאשׁ בְּכָל־מָקוֹם יִקְרְחוּ וְכָל־יָדַיִם גְּדֻדֹת וְעַל־כָּל־מָתְנַיִם שָׂק	
38 עַל כָּל־גַּגּוֹת מוֹאָב וּבִרְחֹבֹתֶיהָ כֻּלֹּה מִסְפֵּד כִּי־שָׁבַרְתִּי אֶת־ מוֹאָב כִּכְלִי אֵין־חֵפֶץ בּוֹ נְאֻם־ יְהוָה וְעַל כָּל־גַּגּוֹת מוֹאָב וְעַל־רְחֹבוֹתֶיהָ כִּי־שָׁבַרְתִּי נְאֻם־יְהוָה כִּכְלִי אֵין־ חֵפֶץ בּוֹ	
39 הֵילִילוּ	Deest
40 כִּי־כֹה אָמַר יְהוָה הִנֵּה כַנֶּשֶׁר יִדְאֶה וּפָרַשׂ כְּנָפָיו אֶל־ מוֹאָב כִּי־כֹה אָמַר יְהוָה	

---

[a] Targ. בְּצִיצֵיהֶן. [b] Targ. עַל. [c] κειράδας αὐχμοῦ (=חָרֵס-חָרֵשׂ).— [d] Targ. . . . . . . כָּבָא. [e] Ἀσερημά. [f] αἴδε. [g] ἀγγελίαν Vid. vs. 36. Σελασία. [h] Targ. כָּל בֶּן בִּלְחוֹדוֹי מוֹאֲבָאֵי כִּבְצִינוֹרָא הָכֵן. [i] Targ. עַל. [k] Vid. vs. 31. [l] Cf. Deut. 32:26; Hos. 9:12.

[48:41-49:4] THE CONSPECTUS OF THE VARIATIONS. 383

41 וְהָיָה לֵב גִּבּוֹרֵי מוֹאָב בַּיּוֹם   Desunt
   הַהוּא כְּלֵב אִשָּׁה מְצֵרָה
43 פַּחַד וָפַחַת וָפָח   פַּח וּפַחַד וּפַחַת
   נְאֻם־יְהֹוָה   Deest
44 [הַ]נָּס מִפְּנֵי הַפַּחַד יִפֹּל אֶל־   וְיִלְכַּד בַּפַּח כִּי־אָבִיא אֵלֶה עַל־
   מוֹאָב שְׁנַת פְּקֻדָּתָם נְאֻם־יְהֹוָה   מוֹאָב בִּשְׁנַת פְקֻדָּתָם
45 בְּצֵל חֶשְׁבּוֹן עָמְדוּ מִכֹּחַ נָסִים
   כִּי־אֵשׁ יָצָא מֵחֶשְׁבּוֹן וְלֶהָבָה
   מִבֵּין סִיחֹן וַתֹּאכַל פְּאַת מוֹאָב
46 וְקָדְקֹד בְּנֵי שָׁאוֹן: אוֹי־לְךָ מוֹאָב   Desunt
   אָבַד עַם־כְּמוֹשׁ כִּי־לֻקְּחוּ בָנֶיךָ
47 בַּשְּׁבִי וּבְנֹתֶיךָ בַּשִּׁבְיָה: וְשַׁבְתִּי
   שְׁבוּת־מוֹאָב בְּאַחֲרִית הַיָּמִים
   נְאֻם־יְהֹוָה עַד־הֵנָּה מִשְׁפַּט
   מוֹאָב:

CAPUT XLIX.

1 הַבָּנִים אֵין לְיִשְׂרָאֵל אִם־יוֹרֵשׁ   הֲבָנִים אֵין בְּיִשְׂרָאֵל אִם־יוֹרֵשׁ אֵין
  אֵין לוֹ מַדּוּעַ יָרַשׁ מַלְכָּם אֶת־   לָהֶם מַדּוּעַ יָרַשׁ מְלָלֵל (מַלְכָּם)ᶜ
  גָּד וְעַמּוֹ בְּעָרָיו יָשֵׁב   אֶת־גִּלְעָד וְעַמָּם בְּעָרֵיהֶם יֵשֵׁב
2 וְהִשְׁמַעְתִּי אֶל־רַבַּת בְּנֵי־עַמּוֹן   וְהִשְׁמַעְתִּי עַל־רַבַּת תְּרוּעַת מִלְחָמוֹת
  תְּרוּעַת מִלְחָמָה וְהָיְתָה לְתֵל   וְהָיוּ לִשְׁמָמָה וּלְקָלָה וּבְמוֹתֶיהָ
  שְׁמָמָה וּבְנֹתֶיהָ בָּאֵשׁ תִּצַּתְנָה   בָּאֵשׁ תִּצַּתְנָה וְיָרַשׁ יִשְׂרָאֵל אֶת־
  וְיָרַשׁ יִשְׂרָאֵל אֶת־יֹרְשָׁיו אָמַר   רֹאשָׁיו (מְמַשַּׁלְתּוֹ)
  יְהֹוָה
3 הֵילִילִי חֶשְׁבּוֹן כִּי שֻׁדְּדָה־עַי   סִפְדָה וְהִתְחוֹטָטְנָה בַּגְּדֵרוֹת כִּי
  צְעַקְנָה בְּנוֹת רַבָּה חֲגֹרְנָה   וּסְפַדְנָה וְהִתְחוֹטַטְנָה כִּי מְלָלֵל (מַלְכָּם) יֵלֵךְ
  שַׂקִּים סְפֹדְנָה וְהִתְשׁוֹטַטְנָה   מַלְכָּם בַּגּוֹלָה יֵלֵךְ
  בַּגְּדֵרוֹת כִּי מַלְכָּם בַּגּוֹלָה יֵלֵךְ   בַּגּוֹלָהᵈ
4 מַה־תִּתְהַלְלִי בָּעֲמָקִים זָב עִמְקֵךְ   מַה־תִּתְהַלְלִי בְּעִמְקֵי עֲנָקִיםᵉ הַבַּת
  הַבַּת הַשּׁוֹבֵבָה הַבֹּטְחָה   הַשׁוֹבֵבָה הַבֹּטְחָה בְּאֹצְרוֹת
  בְּאֹצְרֹתֶיהָ מִי יָבוֹא אֵלָי   הָאֹמְרָה מִי יָבוֹא עָלָיᶠ

ᵃ Targ. עַל.   ᵇ Vid. 11:23; 23:12.   ᶜ Μελχόλ. Vid. vs. 3.   ᵈ Vid. vs. 1.   ᵉ Ἐνακείμ.—Targ. תּוּקְפָהּ.   ᶠ Targ. עֲלֵי יְעוּל בֵּן יַעֲרָהּ.

5 הִנְנִי מֵבִיא עָלַיִךְ פַּחַד נְאֻם־אֲדֹנָי יְהוִֹה צְבָאוֹת מִכָּל־סְבִיבָיִךְ וְנִדַּחְתֶּם אִישׁ לְפָנָיו וְאֵין מְקַבֵּץ לַנֹּדֵד	הִנְנִי מֵבִיא עָלַיִךְ פַּחַד נְאֻם־יְהוָֹה וְאֵין מְקַבֵּץ
6 וְאַחֲרֵי־כֵן אָשִׁיב אֶת־שְׁבוּת בְּנֵי־עַמּוֹן נְאֻם־יְהוָֹה	Desunt
7 כֹּה אָמַר יְהוָה צְבָאוֹת הַאֵין עוֹד חָכְמָה בְּתֵימָן	כֹּה אָמַר יהוה אֵין עוֹד הכמה בתימן
8 נֻסוּ הָפְנוּ הֶעְמִיקוּ לָשֶׁבֶת יֹשְׁבֵי דְּדָן כִּי אֵיד עֵשָׂו הֵבֵאתִי עָלָיו עֵת פְּקַדְתִּיו	נָשָׂא° מְקוֹמָם (הִנֵּה?) הֶעְמִקוּ לָשֶׁבֶת הַיֹשְׁבִים בְּדְדָן כִּי אֵיד עָשָׂה (עֵשָׂו) הֲבֵאתִי עָלָיו בְּעֵת פְּקַדְתִּיו
9 אִם־בֹּצְרִים בָּאוּ לָךְ לֹא יַשְׁאִרוּ עוֹלֵלוֹת אִם־גַּנָּבִים בַּלַּיְלָה הִשְׁחִיתוּ דַיָּם	כִּי־בֹצְרִים בָּאוּ לָךְ אֲשֶׁר לֹא יַשְׁאִרוּ לָךְ שָׁרִיד כְּגַנָּבִים בַּלַּיְלָה יָשִׁיתוּ (= שָׁתוּ) יָדָם^b
10 כִּי־אֲנִי חָשַׂפְתִּי אֶת־עֵשָׂו גִּלֵּיתִי אֶת־מִסְתָּרָיו וְנֶחְבָּה לֹא יוּכָל שֻׁדַּד זַרְעוֹ וְאֶחָיו וּשְׁכֵנָיו	כִּי־אֲנִי חָשַׂפְתִּי (סָתַבְתִּי) אֶת־עֵשָׂו גִּלֵּיתִי אֶת־מִסְתָּרֵיהֶם וְנֶחְבָּה לֹא יוּכְלוּ שָׁדְדוּ בְזַרְעֵי אָחִיו שְׁכֵנֵי
11 עָזְבָה יְתֹמֶיךָ אֲנִי אֲחַיֶּה	לַעֲזֹב יְתֹמָד לְמַעַן יִחְיֶה וְאֶהְיֶה
12 הִנֵּה	Deest
סְתֹה יִשְׁתּוּ וְאַתָּה הוּא נָקֹה תִּנָּקֶה לֹא תִנָּקֶה כִּי שָׁתֹה תִשְׁתֶּה	שָׁתוּ וְאַתָּה נָקֹה לֹא תִנָּקֶה
13 כִּי־לְשַׁמָּה לְחָרְפָּה לְחֹרֶב וְלִקְלָלָה תִּהְיֶה בָצְרָה וְכָל־עָרֶיהָ תִהְיֶינָה לְחָרְבוֹת עוֹלָם	כִּי־לְשַׁמָּה וּלְחֶרְפָּה וּלְקְלָלָה תִּהְיֶה בְּתוֹכָהּ (בְּקִרְבָּהּ) וְכָל־עָרֶיהָ תִּהְיֶינָה חֲרָבוֹת לְעוֹלָם°
14 וְצִיר בַּגּוֹיִם שָׁלוּחַ הִתְקַבְּצוּ וּבֹאוּ עָלֶיהָ וְקוּמוּ לַמִּלְחָמָה	וְצִירִים בַּגּוֹיִם שָׁלַח הִתְקַבְּצוּ וּבֹאוּ אֵלֶיהָ קוּמוּ לַמִּלְחָמָה
15 כִּי־הִנֵּה	Deest
16 זְדֹן לִבְּךָ שִׂבְכָךְ בְּחַגְוֵי הַסֶּלַע תֹּפְשִׂי מְרוֹם גִּבְעָה כִּי־תַגְבִּיהַּ כַּנֶּשֶׁר קִנֶּךָ מִשָּׁם אוֹרִידְךָ נְאֻם־יְהוָֹה	קָלוֹן לְבַדּ שָׁכֵן הַגּוֹי הַסְּלָעִים תָּפַשׂ מָעוֹז (מִבְצָר) גִּבְעַת מָרוֹם (מְרוֹם גִּבְעָה) כִּי הַגְבִּיהַּ כַּנֶּשֶׁר קִנּוֹ מִשָּׁם אוֹרִידְךָ

^a ἤπατη̣σεν.   ^b Cf. Exod. 23:1.   ^c Targ. (לְחֳלָם) לְעָלַם).

THE CONSPECTUS OF THE VARIATIONS.

כל עבר עליה ישם וישרק על־ כל עבר עליה ישרק 17	
כל־מכותה	
כמהפכת סדם ועמרה ושכניה כאשר נהפכה סדם ועמרה ושכניה 18	
אמר יהוה צבאות אמר יהוה	
ולא־יגור שם^a בן־אדם ולא־יגור בה בן־אדם	
מגאון הירדן אל־נוה איתן 19 מתוך הירדן אל־נוה איתם^b	
אריצם מעליה ומי בחור אליה אריצנו מעליה ובחורים עליה^c	
אפקד פקדו (תפקדו)	
ומי יועדני ומי יעמד נגדי (יעידני)	
20 אשר יעץ אל־אדום ומחשבותיו אשר יעץ על־אדום ומחשבתו^d	
אשר חשב אל־ישבי תימן אשר השב על־ישבי תימן	
21 מקול נפלם רעשה הארץ צעקה כי מקול נפלם רעשה הארץ וקול	
בים־סוף נשמע קולה (וצעקת) ים לא נשמע	
22 הנה כנשר יעלה וידאה ויפרש הנה כנשר יראה ויפרש כנפים	
כנפיו על־בצרה על־מבצריה (בצרה?)	
23 כי־שמעה רעה שמעו בים נמגו כי־שמע שמעה רעה נמוגו דאגו	
דאגה השקט לא יוכל השקט לא יוכלו^e	
24 ורטט החזיקה רטט החזיקה	
צרה וחבלים אחזתה כיולדה Deest	
25 איך לא־עזבה עיר תהלה קרית איך לא־עזב עירי קרית משושם	
משושי (קריה אהבו)	
26 לכן יפלו בחוריה ברחבתיה וכל־ לכן יפלו בהורים ברחבתך וכל־	
וכל־אנשי המלחמה ידמו אנשי מלחמתך יפלו (ירמו)	
ביום ההוא נאם יהוה נאם יהוה	
צבאות	
27 ואכלה ארמנות בן־הדד ואכלה ארמנות^h בן־הדר	
28 ולממלכות חצור למלכות חצר	
קומו עלו אל־קדר קומו ועלו על־קדר	
29 וקראו עליהם מגור מסביב וקראו עליהם כלה^k (מגור?) מסביב	
30 נסו נדו נסו	
ישבי חצור נאם־יהוה ישבים בחצר^l	

^{a} Vid. vs. 33; 50:40. ^{b} Αἰθαμ. ^{c} Targ. עֲלַהּ. ^{d} Targ. כָּל. ^{e} Targ. יִתְחַשְׁבְּתֵהּ. ^{f} Targ. כָּל. ^{g} Targ. לָא יָכְלִין לְדָנָח. ^{h} ἀμφοδα. ^{i} Targ. כָּל. ^{k} ἀπώλειαν. ^{l} Vid. vs. 33.

כִּי־יָעַץ עֲלֵיכֶם נְבוּכַדְרֶאצַּר מֶלֶךְ־ בָּבֶל עֵצָה וְחָשַׁב עֲלֵיהֶם מַחֲשָׁבָה	כי־יעץ עליכם נבוכדראצר מלך־ בבל עצה וחשב מחשבה
31 קוּמוּ עֲלוּ אֶל־גּוֹי שָׁלֵיו נְאֻם־יְהוָה לֹא־דְלָתַיִם וְלֹא־בְרִיחַ לוֹ	קומו ועלו על־גוי שליו Deest אֲשֶׁר לָהֶם לֹא־דְלָתַיִם לֹא־בְרִיחִים לֹא־בַדִּים[b]
32 לְשָׁלָל וּמִכָּל־עֲבָרָיו	לְכָלָה (לְשֶׁסַע) מִכָּל־עֲבָרָיו
33 וְהָיְתָה חָצוֹר לִמְעוֹן תַּנִּים שְׁמָמָה עַד־עוֹלָם לֹא־יֵשֵׁב בָּהּ בֶּן־אָדָם	והיתה חצר[c] מעון ינים ושממה עד־עולם ולא־יגור שם[d] בן־אדם
34 אֲשֶׁר הָיָה דְבַר־יְהוָה אֶל־יִרְמְיָהוּ הַנָּבִיא אֶל־עֵילָם בְּרֵאשִׁית מַלְכוּת צִדְקִיָּהוּ מֶלֶךְ־יְהוּדָה לֵאמֹר	אל־עילם
35 כֹּה אָמַר יְהוָה צְבָאוֹת הִנְנִי שֹׁבֵר אֶת־קֶשֶׁת עֵילָם	כה אמר יהוה ונשבר קשת עילם
36 וְהֵבֵאתִי אֶל־עֵילָם וְזֵרִתִים לְכֹל הָרוּחוֹת הָאֵלֶּה וְלֹא־ יִהְיֶה הַגּוֹי	והבאתי על־עילם וזרתים בכל הרחות האלה ולא־ יהיה גוי[e]
37 וְהַחְתַּתִּי אֶת־עֵילָם וְלִפְנֵי	והחתתי אותם Deest
וְהֵבֵאתִי עֲלֵיהֶם רָעָה אֶת־חֲרוֹן אַפִּי נְאֻם־יְהוָה וְשִׁלַּחְתִּי אַחֲרֵיהֶם אֶת־הַחֶרֶב עַד כַּלּוֹתִי אוֹתָם	והבאתי עליהם חרון אפי ושלחתי אחריהם חרבי עד כלתם
38 וְהַאֲבַדְתִּי מִשָּׁם מֶלֶךְ וְשָׂרִים נְאֻם־יְהוָה	והעברתי משם מלך ושרים
39 אָשׁוּב אֶת־שְׁבוּת עֵילָם	ואשיב את שבות עילם[f]

---

[a] Targ. כָּל בָּבֶל. [b] οἷς οὐκ εἰσὶ θύραι, οὐ βάλανοι, οὐ μοχλοί. [c] Vid. vs. 30. [d] Vid. vs. 18; 50:40. [e] Targ. עַם. [f] Targ. וְלָא יְהֵי עַם.

CAPUT L.

1 הַדָּבָר אֲשֶׁר דִּבֶּר יְהוָה אֶל־בָּבֶל דְּבַר־יְהוָה אֲשֶׁר דִּבֶּר עַל־בָּבֶל
אֶל־אֶרֶץ כַּשְׂדִּים בְּיַד יִרְמְיָהוּ
הַנָּבִיא

2 וּטְאוּ־נֵס הַשְׁמִיעוּ אַל־תְּכַחֵדוּ וְאַל־תְּכַחֵדוּ
הַת מְרֹדָךְ הֹבִישׁוּ עֲצַבֶּיהָ חַתּוּ בְּלִירֹחָת (חַתְבֹּשְׁתָּה) וְהַפְּעַנֶּגָה
גִּלּוּלֶיהָ (וְהָעֲדִינַה) סָגְרָה מְרֹדָךְ

3 נָדוּ הָלְכוּ   Desunt

4 נְאֻם־יְהוָה
יַחְדָּו הָלוֹךְ וּבוֹכִים יֵלְכוּ אֶת־יְהוָה   יַחַד הַהֹלְכִים וּבוֹכִים יֵלְכוּ אֱלֹהֵיהֶם מְבַקְשִׁים
יְהוָה אֱלֹהֵיהֶם יְבַקֵּשׁוּ

5 צִיּוֹן יִשְׁאָלוּ דֶּרֶךְ הֵנָּה פְנֵיהֶם   עַד־צִיּוֹן יִשְׁאָלוּ הַדֶּרֶךְ הִנֵּה פְּנֵיהֶם
בֹּאוּ וְנִלְווּ אֶל־יְהוָה בְּרִית   יִתְּנוּ (יָשִׂימוּ) וְיָבֹאוּ וְנִלְווּ אֶל־
עוֹלָם לֹא תִשָּׁכֵחַ   אֲדֹנָי יְהוָה כִּי בְרִית עוֹלָם לֹא תִשָּׁכֵחַ

6 צֹאן אֹבְדוֹת הָיָה עַמִּי רֹעֵיהֶם   צֹאן אֲבֵדוֹת הָיָה עַמִּי רֵעֵיהֶם
הִתְעוּם הָרִים שׁוֹבְבִים מֵהַר   הִתְעוּם עַל־הָרִים שׁוֹבְבָם מֵהַר
אֶל־גִּבְעָה הָלָכוּ   עַל־גִּבְעָה הָלָכוּ

7 וְצָרֵיהֶם אָמְרוּ לֹא נֶאְשָׁם   צָרֵיהֶם אָמְרוּ לֹא נִשְׁלַח (נָשָׁם)
וּמְקוֹה אֲבוֹתֵיהֶם יְהוָה   לִמְקוֹה אֲבוֹתֵיהֶם

8 וּמֵאֶרֶץ כַּשְׂדִּים יָצָאוּ וִהְיוּ   וּמֵאֶרֶץ כַּשְׂדִּים וְצֵאוּ וִהְיוּ כִּנְחָשִׁים
כְּעַתּוּדִים לִפְנֵי־צֹאן   (כְּתַנִּינִים) לִפְנֵי־צֹאן

9 כִּי הִנֵּה אָנֹכִי מֵעִיר וּמַעֲלֶה עַל־   כִּי הִנֵּה אָנֹכִי מֵעִיר עַל־בָּבֶל קְהִלּוֹת־
בָּבֶל קְהַל־גּוֹיִם גְּדֹלִים   גּוֹיִם
חִצָּיו כְּגִבּוֹר מַשְׂכִּיל   פְּחָץ גִּבּוֹר[d] מַשְׂכִּיל

10 נְאֻם־יְהוָה   Deest

11 כִּי תִשְׂמְחִי כִּי תַעֲלֹזִי   כִּי שְׂמַחְתֶּם וַתַּעַלְזוּ (וַתִּתְהַלְלוּ)
כִּי תָפוּשִׁי כְּעֶגְלָה דָשָׁה וְתִצְהֲלִי   כִּי תָפוּחוּ כַּעֲגָלָה בַּדֶּשֶׁא וַתִּתְנַגְּחוּ
כָּאַבִּירִים   כְּאַבִּירִים

12 הָפְרָה יוֹלַדְתְּכֶם   הָפְרָה אֵם יוֹלַדְתְּכֶם לְטוֹבָה

---

[a] Targ. כָּל. [b] Targ. לְצִיּוֹן. [c] Targ. רֵיקָן. [d] Cf. Ps. 120:4. [e] Targ אֲרֵי תְרִיצוּן.

הִנֵּה אַחֲרִית גּוֹיִם מִדְבָּר צִיָּה אחרית גוים מדבר
וַעֲרָבָה

13 וְהָיְתָה שְׁמָמָה כֻלָּה כֹּל עֹבֵר   והיתה לשממהᵃ כלה וכל עבר בבבל
עַל־בָּבֶל יִשֹּׁם וְיִשְׁרֹק עַל־כָּל־   (בְּתוֹךְ בבל) ישב וישרקוּ על־כל־
מַכּוֹתֶיהָ   מכתה

14 עִרְכוּ עַל־בָּבֶל ׀ סָבִיב כָּל־דֹּרְכֵי   ידו עליה אל־תחמלו על־
קֶשֶׁת יְדוּ אֵלֶיהָ אַל־תַּחְמְלוּ אֶל־חֵץ   חציכם
כִּי לַיהוָה חָטָאָה

15 הָרִיעוּ עָלֶיהָ סָבִיב נָתְנָה יָדָהּ   וְתִפְשׂוּתָהּ רָפוּ יְדֶיהָᵇ
נָפְלוּ אשויתיה נֶהֶרְסוּ חוֹמוֹתֶיהָ   וְנֶהֶרְסָה חוֹמָתָהּ
כִּי נִקְמַת יְהוָה הִיא הִנָּקְמוּ בָהּ   נקמת אלהים היא הנקמו עליה
כַּאֲשֶׁר עָשְׂתָה עֲשׂוּ־לָהּ

16 כִּרְתוּ זוֹרֵעַ מִבָּבֶל וְתֹפֵשׂ מַגָּל   כרתו זרע מבבל תפש מגל
מִפְּנֵי חֶרֶב הַיּוֹנָה   מפני חרב היונהᶜ (היינית)
אִישׁ אֶל־עַמּוֹ יִפְנוּ וְאִישׁ לְאַרְצוֹ יָנֻסוּ   ואיש לארצו ינוס

17 שֶׂה פְזוּרָה יִשְׂרָאֵל אֲרָיוֹת הִדִּיחוּ   אריות הדיחוᵈ (הדיחוהו)
הָרִאשׁוֹן אֲכָלוֹ מֶלֶךְ אַשּׁוּר וְזֶה הָאַחֲרוֹן   עָצְמוֹ מלך בבל
עִצְּמוֹ נְבוּכַדְרֶאצַּר מֶלֶךְ בָּבֶל   יהוה

18 לָכֵן כֹּה־אָמַר יְהוָה צְבָאוֹת אֱלֹהֵי יִשְׂרָאֵל
הִנְנִי פֹקֵד אֶל־מֶלֶךְ בָּבֶל וְאֶל־אַרְצוֹ   הנני פקד על־מלך בבל ועל־ארצו
כַּאֲשֶׁר פָּקַדְתִּי אֶל־מֶלֶךְ אַשּׁוּר   כאשר פקדתיᵉ על־מלך אשור

19 וְשֹׁבַבְתִּי אֶת־יִשְׂרָאֵל אֶל־נָוֵהוּ וְרָעָה הַכַּרְמֶל וְהַבָּשָׁן וּבְהַר   ורעה בכרמלᶠ ובגלעד ובהר אפרים
אֶפְרַיִם וְהַגִּלְעָד תִּשְׂבַּע נַפְשׁוֹ   ותשבע נפשו

20 בַּיָּמִים הָהֵם וּבָעֵת הַהִיא נְאֻם־יְהוָה יְבֻקַּשׁ אֶת־עֲוֹן יִשְׂרָאֵל   יבקשוּᵍ את־עון ישראל
וְאֵינֶנּוּ וְאֶת־חַטֹּאת יְהוּדָה וְלֹא תִמָּצֶאינָה כִּי אֶסְלַח לַאֲשֶׁר אַשְׁאִיר   כי אסלח לנשארים

21 עַל־הָאָרֶץ מְרָתַיִם עֲלֵה עָלֶיהָ   על־הארץ יהוהʰ מרירות עלה עליה
וְאֶל־יוֹשְׁבֵי פְּקוֹד חֲרֹב וְהַחֲרֵם   ועל־היושבים עליה פקוד חרב
אַחֲרֵיהֶם   והחרם

22 קוֹל מִלְחָמָה בָּאָרֶץ וְשֶׁבֶר גָּדוֹל   קול מלחמה ושבר גדול בְּאֶרֶץ כַּשְׂדִּים

24 יָקֹשְׁתִּי לָךְ וְגַם־נִלְכַּדְתְּ בָּבֶל וְאַתְּ   בָּאִי (עָלוּ) עָלַיִךְ ולא ידעת כבבל
לֹא יָדַעַתְּ   וגם־נלכדת

25 כִּי־מְלָאכָה הִיא לַאדֹנָי יְהוִה   כי־מלאכה לאדני יהוה
צְבָאוֹת

26 בֹּאוּ־לָהּ מִקֵּץ   כי באו קציהᵢ (עתותיה)

ᵃ Targ. לְצָדוּ.   ᵇ Cf. vs. 43; 6:24.   ᶜ Vid. 46:16.   ᵈ Targ. עַל.   ᵉ Targ.
יָעַל.   ᶠ Targ. עַל.   ᵍ Targ. בְּדַרְגָּלָא.   ʰ Targ. יִתְבַּשּׁוֹן.   ᵢ Targ. יָעַל.

50:27-37] THE CONSPECTUS OF THE VARIATIONS. 389

סָלּוּהָ כְּמוֹ־עֲרֵמִים	תָּרוּהָ (הֲקִרוּהָ) כְּמוֹ־מְעָרָה (מְעָרִים?)
27 חִרְבוּ כָּל־פָּרֶיהָ יֵרְדוּ לַטֶּבַח הוֹי עֲלֵיהֶם	חרבו כל־פריה וירדו לטבח הוי אליהםa
עֵת פְּקֻדָּתָם	וְעֵת פקדתם
28 קָמַת הֵיכָלוֹ	Deest
29 הַשְׁמִיעוּ אֶל־בָּבֶל רַבִּים כָּל־דֹּרְכֵי קֶשֶׁת	השמיעו על־בבל רבים כל־דרך קשת
אַל־יְהִיb־פְּלֵיטָה	שלמו־לה פליטה (אלי־יהי־לה פָלִיט) שלמו־לה כפעליה כְּפָעֳלָהּc
אֶל־קְדוֹשׁ יִשְׂרָאֵל	אל קדוש ישראל
30 וְדַמּוּ בַּיּוֹם הַהוּא נְאֻם־יְהֹוָה	ידמו נאם־יהוה
31 הִנְנִי אֵלֶיךָ זָדוֹן נְאֻם־אֲדֹנָי יֱהֹוִה צְבָאוֹת	הנני עליך הזדון נאם־יהוה
עֵת פְּקַדְתִּיךָ	ועת פקדתך
32 וְכָשַׁל זָדוֹן וְנָפַל וְאֵין לוֹ מֵקִים וְהִצַּתִּי אֵשׁ בְּעָרָיו	וכשל זדונה (הַזָּדוֹן) ונפל ואין מקים לו והצתי אש בְּיָעֳרוֹd
33 יְהֹוָה צְבָאוֹת	יהוה
יַחְדָּו וְכָל־שֹׁבֵיהֶם	יחדו כל־שביהם
מֵאֲנוּ שַׁלְּחָם	כי מאנו שלחם
34 גֹּאֲלָם	וגאלם (גַּם־גָאֲלָם)
רִיב יָרִיב אֶת־רִיבָם	ריב ירב ליריביו (לְמְרִיבָיו)
35 נְאֻם־יְהֹוָה	Deest
וְאֶל־יֹשְׁבֵי בָבֶל וְאֶל־שָׂרֶיהָ וְאֶל־חֲכָמֶיהָ	ועל־ישבי בבל ועל־שריה ועל־חכמיה
36 חֶרֶב אֶל־הַבַּדִּים וְנֹאָלוּ חֶרֶב אֶל־גִּבּוֹרֶיהָ וָחָתּוּ׃	Deest חרב על־גבוריה וחתו על־סוסיהם ועל־רכביהםe: חֶרֶבg
37 חֶרֶב אֶל־סוּסָיו וְאֶל־רִכְבּוֹ וְאֶל־כָּל־הָעֶרֶב אֲשֶׁר בְּתוֹכָהּ וְהָיוּ לְנָשִׁים חֶרֶב אֶל־אוֹצְרֹתֶיהָ וּבֻזָּזוּ	על־גבוריהם ועל־הערב אשר בתוכה והיו כנשיםf חרב על־האוצרות ופזרו (וּבָזְזוּ)

a Cf. 48:1. b Targ. כָּל. c Targ. כְּלָהּ. d Cf. 21:14. e Targ. וְגַם.
f Targ. כָּל. g Inc. vs. 37. h Targ. עַל סוּסְיָתְהוֹן וְעַל רְתִיכֵהוֹן. i Targ. וְגַם.
k Vid. 51:30.—Targ. כִּנְשַׁיָּא. l Targ. כָּל.

עַל־מֵימֶיהָ וְיָבֵשׁוּ	38 חֹרֶב אֶל־מֵימֶיהָ וְיָבֵשׁוּ
וּבָאִיִּים [אֲשֶׁר] יִתְהָלָלוּ	וּבָאֵימִים יִתְהֹלָלוּ
לָכֵן יֵשְׁבוּ צִיִּים (צִיָּרִים) בָּאִיִּים	39 לָכֵן יֵשְׁבוּ צִיִּים אֶת־אִיִּים וְיָשְׁבוּ
וְיֵשְׁבוּ בָהּ בְּנוֹת יִשּׁוּק(?) לֹא־	בָהּ בְּנוֹת יַעֲנָה וְלֹא־תֵשֵׁב עוֹד
תֵשֵׁב עוֹד לָנֶצַח	לָנֶצַח וְלֹא תִשְׁכֹּן עַד־דּוֹר וָדֹר
כַּהֲפוֹךְ אֱלֹהִים	40 כְּמַהְפֵּכַת אֱלֹהִים
וְלֹא־יָגוּר שָׁם בֶּן־אָדָם	וְלֹא־יָגוּר בָּהּ בֶּן־אָדָם
קֶשֶׁת וְכִידוֹן לָהֶם אַכְזָרִי הוּא וְלֹא יְרַחֵם	42 קֶשֶׁת וְכִידֹן יַחֲזִיקוּ אַכְזָרִי הֵמָּה וְלֹא יְרַחֵמוּ
עַל־סוּסִים יִרְכָּבוּ עָרוּךְ כְּאֵשׁ	וְעַל־סוּסִים יִרְכָּבוּ עָרוּךְ כְּאִישׁ
לַמִּלְחָמָה אֵלַיִךְ בַּת־בָּבֶל	לַמִּלְחָמָה עָלַיִךְ בַּת־בָּבֶל
יַעֲלֶה מִירְדֵּן אֶל־גֵּאַ אֵיתָן	44 יַעֲלֶה מִגְּאוֹן הַיַּרְדֵּן אֶל־נְוֵה אֵיתָן
וְכָל־בָּחוּר עָלֶיהָ אֶפְקֹד	וּמִי בָחוּר אֵלֶיהָ אֶפְקֹד
וּמִי יַעֲמֹד נֶגְדִּי (רְעִידַנִי)	וּמִי יוֹעִדֶנִּי
אֲשֶׁר יָעַץ עַל־בָּבֶל	45 אֲשֶׁר יָעַץ אֶל־בָּבֶל
עַל־יוֹשְׁבֵי כַשְׂדִּים	אֶל־אֶרֶץ כַּשְׂדִּים
אִם־לֹא יִסְחֲבוּ (נַשְׁחִיתוֹ) צְפִירֵי צֹאן	אִם־לֹא יִסְחָבוּם צְעִירֵי הַצֹּאן
אִם־לֹא יָשִׂים נְוֵה מֵעֲלֵיהֶם	אִם־לֹא יַשִּׁים עֲלֵיהֶם נָוֶה
כִּי מִקּוֹל תְּפִיסַת בָּבֶל תִּרְעַשׁ הָאָרֶץ	46 מִקּוֹל נִתְפְּשָׂה בָבֶל נִרְעֲשָׁה הָאָרֶץ
וּזְעָקָה בַּגּוֹיִם תִּשָּׁמֵעַ	וּזְעָקָה בַּגּוֹיִם נִשְׁמָע

CAPUT LI.

וְאֶל־יֹשְׁבֵי לֵב קָמָי רוּחַ מַשְׁחִית וְעַל־יֹשְׁבֵי כַּשְׂדִּים רוּחַ בֹּעֵר מַשְׁחִית	1
זָרִים וְזֵרוּהָ	2
כִּי־הָיוּ עָלֶיהָ מִסָּבִיב בְּיוֹם רָשָׁה הוֹי עַל־בָּבֶל מִסָּבִיב בְּיוֹם רָעָתָהּ	
אֶל־יִדְרֹךְ יִדְרֹךְ הַדֹּרֵךְ קַשְׁתּוֹ (יַעֲשֶׂה) יִתְעַלֶּה	3 אֶל־יִדְרֹךְ הַדֹּרֵךְ קַשְׁתּוֹ וְאֶל־
בְּסִירָיו וְאַל־תִּתַּחְמְלוּ עַל־בַּחוּרֶיהָ	יִתְעַל בְּסִרְיֹנוֹ וְאַל־תַּחְמְלוּ אֶל־
וְהַחֲרִימוּ כָּל־צְבָאָהּ	בַּחֻרֶיהָ הַחֲרִימוּ כָּל־צְבָאָהּ

---

[a] Targ. בְּשַׁבְּחִין. [b] σειρῆνα. [c] Targ. בָּבָא דְרָחֵק. [d] Vid. 49:18, 33. [e] Vid. 6:23. [f] Γαλάαν. [g] Targ. אֲבָנֵי בְלָה. [h] Targ. עַל. [i] Targ. בְּוֹדִין. [k] Targ. וְטַל יָתְהֵי אַרְעָא בְּסַדְּרֵי. [l] Cf. Isa. 4:4. [m] Targ. יְבָוּנָה. [n] Targ. עַל.

THE CONSPECTUS OF THE VARIATIONS.

מֵאֱלֹהֵיהֶםᵃ	5 מֵאלֹהָיו
מִקְדוּשֵׁי יִשְׂרָאֵל	מִקְדוֹשׁ יִשְׂרָאֵל
וּמַדְקְרִים מִחוּץ לָהּᵇ	4 וּמְדֻקָּרִים בְּחוּצוֹתֶיהָ
וְאַל־תֵּרָמוּ	6 אַל־תִּדַּמּוּ
עֵת נָקְמָתָהּ לַיהוה גְּמוּל הִיא	עֵת נְקָמָה הִיא לַיהוה גְּמוּל הוּא
יְגַמְלוּ לָהּ	מְשַׁלֵּם לָהּ
עַל־כֵּן יִתְנוֹדְדוּ (יִתְהַלָּלוּ)	7 עַל־כֵּן יִתְהֹלְלוּ גוֹיִם
וּפִתְאֹם	8 פִּתְאֹם
לִשְׁבְרָהּᶜ (לְמַכָּתָהּ)	לְמַכְאוֹבָהּ
נַעֲזָבְנָה	9 עֲזַבְנוּהָ
כִּי קָרַבᵈ	כִּי נָגַע
נִשָּׂא עַד־עֲרָבִים	וְנִשָּׂא עַד־שְׁחָקִים
אֶת־מִשְׁפָּטוֹ	10 אֶת־צִדְקֹתֵינוּ
אֶת־מַעֲשֵׂי יהוה	אֶת־מַעֲשֵׂה יהוה
הָכִינוּ הַחִצִּים מִלְאוּ הָאַשְׁפּוֹת	11 הָבֵרוּ הַחִצִּים מִלְאוּ הַשְּׁלָטִים
מֶלֶךְ מָדַי כִּי־אֶל־בָּבֶל זָמַם (הֵמָּה)	מַלְכֵי מָדַי כִּי־עַל־בָּבֶל מְזִמָּתוֹ
כִּי־נִקְמַת עַמּוֹ הִיא	כִּי־נִקְמַת הֵיכָלוֹ
עַל־חוֹמַת בָּבֶל	12 אֶל־חוֹמֹת בָּבֶל
הָקִימוּ הָאַשְׁפּוֹת הָקִיצוּ (הָעִירוּ)	הַחֲזִיקוּ הַמִּשְׁמָר הָקִימוּ שֹׁמְרִים
שֹׁמְרִים הֵכִינוּ הַחֲרָבִים (וֹת) כִּי	הֵכִינוּ הָאֹרְבִים כִּי גַם־זָמַם
זָמַם גַּם־עָשָׂה יהוה	יהוה גַּם־עָשָׂה
עַל־יֹשְׁבֵי בָבֶל	אֶל־יֹשְׁבֵי בָבֶל
טֹכְנִים (שֹׁכְנֵי)	13 שֹׁכַנְתִּי
וְעַל־רֹב אוֹצְרֹתֶיהָᶠ	רַבַּת אוֹצָרֹת
אֱמֶת אֶל־מֵעָיִךְ	אַמַּת בִּצְעֵךְ
כִּי נִשְׁבַּע יהוה בִּזְרֹעוֹᵍ	14 נִשְׁבַּע יהוה צְבָאוֹת בְּנַפְשׁוֹ
אֲנָשִׁים	אָדָם
וְעָנוּ עָלַיִךְ הַיָּרֵד (הַיֹּרְדִים)	וְעָנוּ עָלַיִךְ הֵידָד
יְהוָה עָשָׂה אֶרֶץʰ	15 עֹשֵׂה אֶרֶץ
בִּתְבוּנוֹהוּ	וּבִתְבוּנָתוֹ
לְקוֹל נָתַן	16 לְקוֹל תִּתּוֹ
מִקְצֵה הָאָרֶץ	מִקְצֵה־אָרֶץ

ᵃ Targ. בְּצַלְמָהוֹן. ᵇ אשבע αὐτῆς. ᶜ Targ. לְהַבְרָהּ. ᵈ Targ. אֲרֵי קְרֵיב. ᵉ Targ. כָּל. ᶠ Targ. בֵּית גִּנְזָהָא. ᵍ Cf. Isa. 62:8. ʰ Vid. 10:12.

THE TEXT OF JEREMIAH. [51:17-29]

וְיֵרְצָא אוֹרª	וְיֵרְצָא רוּחַ
17 מִפֶּסֶל כִּי שֶׁקֶר נָסְכּוֹᵇ לֹא־רוּחַ בָּם מְפַסִּילָיו כִּי שֶׁקֶר נָסְכּוּ	
18 הֲבָלִים הֵמָּה מַעֲשֵׂי תַעְתֻּעִים	הֶבֶל הֵמָּה מַעֲשֵׂה תַּעְתֻּעִים
19 וְשֵׁבֶט נַחֲלָתִי יְהוָה צְבָאוֹת שְׁמוֹ	נַחֲלָתוֹ יְהוָה שְׁמוֹ
20 מַפֵּץ־אַתָּה לִי.	מֵפִיץᶜ־אַתָּה לִי
וְנִפַּצְתִּי בְךָ גּוֹיִם וְהִשְׁחַתִּי בְךָ מַמְלָכוֹת	וְהִפַצְתִּיᵈ בְךָ גּוֹיִם וְהִשְׁחַתִּי מָעֹדᶜ (בְךָ) מְלָכִים
21 וְנִפַּצְתִּי בְךָ סוּס וְרֹכְבוֹ וְנִפַּצְתִּי רֶכֶב וְרֹכְבוֹ	וְהִפַצְתִּיᵈ בְךָ סוּס וְרֹכְבוֹ: וְהִפַצְתִּי בָךְ מַרְכָּבוֹת וְרֹכְבֵיהֶםᵉ
22 וְנִפַּצְתִּי בְךָ אִישׁ וְאִשָּׁה וְנִפַּצְתִּי בְךָ זָקֵן וָנָעַר וְנִפַּצְתִּי בְךָ בָּחוּר וּבְתוּלָה	וְהִפַצְתִּיᵈ בְךָ בָּחוּר וּבְתוּלָה וְהִפַצְתִּיᵈ בְךָ אִישׁ וְאִשָּׁהᶠ
23 וְנִפַּצְתִּי בְךָ רֹעֶה וְעֶדְרוֹ וְנִפַּצְתִּי בְךָ אִכָּר וְצִמְדּוֹ וְנִפַּצְתִּי בְךָ פַּחוֹת וּסְגָנִים	וְהִפַצְתִּיᵈ בְךָ רֹעֶה וְעֶדְרוֹ וְהִפַצְתִּיᵈ בְךָ אִכָּר וְצִמְדּוֹ וְהִפַצְתִּיᵈ בְךָ פַּחוֹת וּסְגָנֶיךָ
24 אֵת כָּל־רָעָתָם אֲשֶׁר עָשׂוּ בְצִיּוֹן	אֵת כָּל־רָעוֹתֵיהֶםᵍ אֲשֶׁר עָשׂוּ עַל־צִיּוֹן
25 נְאֻם־יְהוָה.	Deest
וְגִלְגַּלְתִּיךָ מִן־הַסְּלָעִים וּנְתַתִּיךָ לְהַר שְׂרֵפָה	וְגִלְגַּלְתִּיךָ עַל־הַסְּלָעִים וּנְתַתִּיךָ כְּהַר שְׂרֵפָה
26 וְאֶבֶן לְמוֹסָדוֹת כִּי־שִׁמְמוֹת עוֹלָם תִּהְיֶה	וְאֶבֶן לְמוּסָד כִּי־לְשַׁמָּה תִּהְיֶה לְעוֹלָם
27 שְׂאוּ־נֵס בָּאָרֶץ תִּקְעוּ שׁוֹפָר בַּגּוֹיִם	שְׂאוּ־נֵס עַל־הָאָרֶץ תִּקְעוּ בַגּוֹיִם שׁוֹפָר
מַמְלָכוֹת אֲרָרַט מִנִּי וְאַשְׁכְּנַז פִּקְדוּ עָלֶיהָ טִפְסָר	מַלְכִים הֲרֵמוּᴴ מִנִּי וְאַכְנַזִּיםᵍ פִּקְדוּ עָלֶיהָ כְּרָדִיםⁱ
הַעֲלוּ־סוּס כְּיֶלֶק סָמָר	הַעֲלוּ עָלֶיהָ סוּס כְּיֶלֶק כַּבִּיר
28 קַדְּשׁוּ עָלֶיהָ גוֹיִם אֶת־מַלְכֵי מָדַי אֶת־פַּחוֹתֶיהָ וְאֶת־כָּל־סְגָנֶיהָ וְאֵת כָּל־אֶרֶץ מֶמְשַׁלְתּוֹ	הַעֲלוּ עָלֶיהָ גּוֹיִם אֶת־מֶלֶךְ מָדַי וְאֶת־כָּל־הָאָרֶץ אֶת־פַּחֲווֹתָיו וְאֶת־כָּל־סְגָנָיו
29 וַתִּרְעַשׁ הָאָרֶץ מַחְשְׁבוֹת יְהוָה	**רָעֲשָׁה הָאָרֶץ** מַחְשֶׁבֶת יְהוָה

ª Vid. 10:13.   ᵇ Targ. אֲתָרְבִּגוּנָן.   ᶜ Targ. כְּבָדָר.   ᵈ Targ. יַאֲבַר.
ᵉ ἐκ σοῦ vel ἐν σοί.   ᶠ Inc. vs. 22.   ᵍ Targ. רְתִירְדֵן וְרִכְבֵיהוֹן.   ᴴ Ἀχαναζέοις.
ⁱ βελοστάσεις.

מֵאֵין יוֹשֵׁב	וְלֹא תוּשָׁב (וְאֵין יוֹשֵׁב בָּהּ)
30 חָדְלוּ גִבּוֹרֵי בָבֶל	חָדַל גִּבּוֹר בָּבֶל
יָשְׁבוּ בַּמְּצָדוֹת	יָשְׁבוּ שָׁם בַּמְּצָדָה
הָיוּ לְנָשִׁים הִצִּיתוּ מִשְׁכְּנֹתֶיהָ	הָיוּ כְנָשִׁים נָצְתוּ (הוּצְתוּ) מִשְׁכְּנֹתֶיהָ
31 כִּי־נִלְכְּדָה עִירוֹ מִקָּצֶה:	כִּי־נִלְכְּדָה עִירוֹ:
32 וְהַמַּעְבָּרוֹת נִתְפָּשׂוּ וְאֶת־הָאֲגַמִּים	מִקָּצֶה מַעְבְּרוֹתָיו נִתְפְּשׂוּ וְאֶת־
שָׂרְפוּ בָאֵשׁ וְאַנְשֵׁי הַמִּלְחָמָה	אֲגַמֵּיהֶם שָׂרְפוּ בָאֵשׁ וְאַנְשֵׁי
נִבְהָלוּ	הַלּוֹחֲמִים (וְאַנְשֵׁי מִלְחַמְתּוֹ) יָצְאוּ (הָלְכוּ)
33 כִּי כֹה אָמַר יְהוָה צְבָאוֹת אֱלֹהֵי	כִּי כֹה אָמַר יהוה בְּתֵי מֶלֶךְ־בָּבֶל
יִשְׂרָאֵל בַּת־בָּבֶל כְּגֹרֶן עֵת	כְּגֹרֶן עֵת יוּדָשׁוּ עוֹד מְעַט וּבָא
הִדְרִיכָהּ עוֹד מְעַט וּבָאָה עֵת	קְצִירָהּ
הַקָּצִיר לָהּ	
34 אֲכָלַנוּ הֲמָמַנוּ נְבוּכַדְרֶאצַּר מֶלֶךְ	אֲכָלָנִי חֲלָקָנִי (הֲדִיקָנִי) הִטְוַגְנִי אָצַל
בָּבֶל הִצִּיגָנוּ כְּלִי רִיק בְּלָעָנוּ	(כְּלָא) דַּק נְבוּכַדְרֶאצַּר מֶלֶךְ
כַּתַּנִּין מִלָּא כְרֵשׂוֹ מֵעֲדָנָי	בָּבֶל בִּלְעָנִי כְתַנִּין מִלָּא כְרֵשׂוֹ
הֱדִיחָנוּ:	מֵעֲדָנָי:
35 חֲמָסִי וּשְׁאֵרִי עַל־בָּבֶל	הֱדִיחוּנִי חֲמָסִי וְשַׁבְרִי (שֹׁדִי) אֶל־
	בָּבֶל
וְדָמִי אֶל־יֹשְׁבֵי כַשְׂדִּים	וְדָמִי עַל־יֹשְׁבֵי כַשְׂדִּים
36 הִנְנִי־רָב אֶת־רִיבֵךְ	הִנְנִי־רָב אֶת־יְרִיבֵךְ
37 וְהָיְתָה בָבֶל לְגַלִּים מְעוֹן תַּנִּים	וְהָיְתָה בָבֶל לְשַׁמָּה וְלֹא תוּשָׁב
שַׁמָּה וּשְׁרֵקָה מֵאֵין יוֹשֵׁב	
38 יַחְדָּו כַּכְּפִרִים יִשְׁאָגוּ נָעֲרוּ	כִּי יַחְדָּו כַּכְּפִירִים נָעֲרוּ וְכְגוֹרֵי
כְּגוֹרֵי אֲרָיוֹת	אֲרָיוֹת
39 אָשִׁית אֶת־מִשְׁתֵּיהֶם	אָתֵּן מִשְׁתֶּה לָהֶם
לְמַעַן יַעֲלֹזוּ	לְמַעַן יִרְדְּמוּ (יַעֲרֹלוּ, יִרְעָלוּ)
40 אוֹרִידֵם	וְהוֹרִידֵם
כְּאֵילִים	וּכְאֵילִים
41 שֵׁשַׁךְ	Deest
אֵיךְ הָיְתָה לְשַׁמָּה בָבֶל בַּגּוֹיִם	אֵיךְ הָיְתָה בָבֶל לְשַׁמָּה בַּגּוֹיִם
42 נִכְסְתָה	וְנִכְסְתָה

---

[a] Vid. 50:37.—Targ. כְּנִשְׁיָא. [b] Inc. vs. 32. [c] Targ. בְּטִיב אַרְעָא.
[d] Inc. vs. 35. [e] Targ. וּבִזִּי. [f] Targ. כָּל.

[51:43-55

43 הָיוּ עָרֶיהָ לְשַׁמָּה אֶרֶץ צִיָּה | הָיוּ עָרֶיהָ בְּאֶרֶץ צִיָּה וַעֲרָבָה לֹא־
וַעֲרָבָה אֶרֶץ לֹא־יֵשֵׁב בָּהֵן כָּל־ | יֵשֵׁב בָּהּ֯ גַּם־אֶחָד וְלֹא־יָלִין
אִישׁ וְלֹא־יַעֲבֹר בָּהֵן בֶּן־אָדָם | בָּהּ֯ בֶּן־אָדָם

44 וּפָקַדְתִּי עַל־בֵּל בְּבָבֶל | וּפָקַדְתִּי עַל־בָּבֶל
וְלֹא־יִנְהֲרוּ אֵלָיו עוֹד גּוֹיִם גַּם־ | וְלֹא יִנְהֲרוּ אֵלָיו עוֹד הַגּוֹיִם
חוֹמַת בָּבֶל נָפָלָה

45 צְאוּ מִתּוֹכָהּ עַמִּי וּמַלְּטוּ אִישׁ
אֶת־נַפְשׁוֹ מֵחֲרוֹן אַף־יְהוָֹה:

46 וּפֶן־יֵרַךְ לְבַבְכֶם וְתִירְאוּ בַּשְּׁמוּעָה
הַנִּשְׁמַעַת בָּאָרֶץ וּבָא בַשָּׁנָה
הַשְּׁמוּעָה וְאַחֲרָיו בַּשָּׁנָה
הַשְּׁמוּעָה וְחָמָס בָּאָרֶץ מֹשֵׁל

Desunt {

47 עַל־מֹשֵׁל: לָכֵן הִנֵּה יָמִים בָּאִים
וּפָקַדְתִּי עַל־פְּסִילֵי בָבֶל וְכָל־
אַרְצָהּ תֵּבוֹשׁ וְכָל־חֲלָלֶיהָ יִפְּלוּ

48 בְּתוֹכָהּ: וְרִנְּנוּ עַל־בָּבֶל שָׁמַיִם
וָאָרֶץ וְכֹל אֲשֶׁר בָּהֶם כִּי מִצָּפוֹן
יָבוֹא־לָהּ הַשּׁוֹדְדִים נְאֻם־יְהוָֹה:

49 גַּם־בָּבֶל לִנְפֹּל חַלְלֵי יִשְׂרָאֵל גַּם־ | גַּם־בְּבָבֶל יִפְּלוּ חַלְלֵי כָּל־
לְבָבֶל נָפְלוּ חַלְלֵי כָל־הָאָרֶץ | הָאָרֶץ

50 פְּלֵטִים מֵחֶרֶב הִלְכוּ אַל־תַּעֲמֹדוּ | פְּלֵטִים מֵחֶרֶב (מֵאָרֶץ) הִלְכוּ וְאַל־
זִכְרוּ מֵרָחוֹק אֶת־יְהוָֹה | תַּעַמְדוּ אֲשֶׁר מֵרָחוֹק (הָרְחוֹקִים)
זִכְרוּ אֶת־יְהוָֹה

51 כִּי־שָׁמַעְנוּ חֶרְפָּה | כִּי־שָׁמַעְנוּ חֶרְפָּתֵנוּ
כִּי בָאוּ זָרִים עַל־מִקְדְּשֵׁי בֵּית יְהוָֹה | בָּאוּ זָרִים אֶל־מִקְדָּשֵׁנוּ אֶל־בֵּית יְהוָֹה

52 יָאֱנֹק חָלָל | יִפְּלוּ חֲלָלִים֯

53 כִּי־תַעֲלֶה בָבֶל הַשָּׁמַיִם וְכִי | אָם־תַּעֲלֶה בָבֶל פַּסָּמִים וְכִי
תְבַצֵּר מְרוֹם עֻזָּהּ מֵאִתִּי יָבֹאוּ | אִם־תְּבַצֵּר הַחוֹמוֹת֯ בְּעֻזָּהּ מֵאִתִּי
שֹׁדְדִים לָהּ | יָבוֹאוּ שׁוֹדְדִים אוֹתָהּ

54 קוֹל זְעָקָה מִבָּבֶל וְשֶׁבֶר גָּדוֹל | קוֹל זְעָקָה בְּבָבֶל וְשֶׁבֶר גָּדוֹל בְּאֶרֶץ
מֵאֶרֶץ כַּשְׂדִּים | כַּשְׂדִּים

55 וְהָמוּ גַלֵּיהֶם כְּמַיִם רַבִּים הָמוּ כְּמַיִם רַבִּים נָתַן לִשְׁאִיָּה
שְׁאוֹן קוֹלָם | (שֹׁאָה) קוֹלָהּ

---
[a] Targ. בְּדֵן. [b] Targ. בַּהּ. [c] Targ. יִתְחֲזוֹן קֳדָמַיָּא. [d] Targ. יִתְקְטִלוּן. [e] Targ. בִּרְדִּין.

כִּי בָא עָלֶיהָ עַל־בָּבֶל שׁוֹדֵד כִּי בָא עַל־בָּבֶל שׁוֹד נִלְכְּדוּ גִבּוֹרֶיהָ	56
וְנִלְכְּדוּ גִּבּוֹרֶיהָ חִתְּתָה חִתְּתָה קַשְּׁתָם כִּי אֵל יִשַׁלֵּם	
קַשְּׁתוֹתָם כִּי אֵל גְּמֻלוֹת יְהוָה לָהֶםᵃ׃	
שַׁלֵּם יְשַׁלֵּם׃	
וְהִצַתִּי יְהוָה שָׂרֶיהָ וַחֲכָמֶיהָ שָׂרֶיהָ	57
פַּחוֹתֶיהָ וּסְגָנֶיהָ וְגִבּוֹרֶיהָ וְסַגָנֶיהָ פַּחוֹתֶיהָ וְשָׂרֶיהָ יַשְׁבִּיר שָׂרֶיהָ	
וְיָשְׁנוּ שְׁנַת־עוֹלָם וְלֹא יָקִיצוּ וַחֲכָמֶיהָ וּסְגָנֶיהָ	
כֹּה־אָמַר יְהוָה צְבָאוֹת חֹמוֹת כֹּה־אָמַר יְהוָה חֹמַת בָּבֶל	58
בָּבֶל הָרְחָבָה הָרְחָבָה	
וּשְׁעָרֶיהָ הַגְּבֹהִים בָּאֵשׁ יִצַּתּוּ וּשְׁעָרֶיהָ הַגְּבֹהִים יִצַּתּוּ וְלֹא יִגַּע	
וַיִגְעוּ עַמִּים בְּדֵי־רִיק וּלְאֻמִּים עַמִּים לָרִיק וּלְאֻמִּים בָּרֹאשׁ	
בְּדֵי־אֵשׁ וְיָעֵפוּ יִעֲפוּ (וְכָלוּ)	
הַדָּבָר אֲשֶׁר־צִוָּה יִרְמְיָה הַנָּבִיא הַדָּבָר אֲשֶׁר־צִוָּה יְהוָֹה אֶת־יִרְמְיָהוּ	59
אֶת־שְׂרָיָה הַנָּבִיא לֵאמֹר אֶל־שְׂרָיָה	
וּשְׂרָיָה שַׂר מְנוּחָה וּשְׂרָיָה שַׂר־מְנֻחָהᶜ	
אֲשֶׁר־תָּבוֹא אֶל־בָּבֶל אֶל־סֵפֶר אֶחָד אֲשֶׁר־תָּבוֹא עַל־בָּבֶל בְּסֵפֶר	60
הַכְּתֻבִים אֶל־בָּבֶל הַכְּתֻבִים עַל־בָּבֶלᵈ	
יְהוָה אַתָּה דִּבַּרְתָּ אֶל־הַמָּקוֹם יְהוָה יֱהוִה (אֲדֹנָי יֱהוִה) אַתָּה דִבַּרְתָּ	62
הַזֶּה לְהַכְרִיתוֹ לְבִלְתִּי הֱיוֹת־ עַל־הַמָּקוֹם הַזֶּה לְהַכְרִיתוֹ וּלְבִלְתִּי	
בּוֹ יוֹשֵׁב לְמֵאָדָם וְעַד־בְּהֵמָה הֱיוֹת־בּוֹ יוֹשְׁבִים מֵאָדָם וְעַד־	
כִּי־שְׁמָמוֹת עוֹלָם תִּהְיֶה בְּהֵמָה כִּי־שְׁמָמָה לְעוֹלָם תִּהְיֶה	
תִּקְשֹׁר וְתִקְשֹׁר	63
וְיָעֵפוּ עַד־הֵנָּה דִּבְרֵי יִרְמְיָהוּ Deest	

CAPUT LII.

בֶּן־עֶשְׂרִים וְאַחַת שָׁנָה הָיָה עֶשְׂרִים וְאַחַת שָׁנָה	1
וַיַּעַשׂ הָרַע בְּעֵינֵי יְהוָה כְּכֹל Desunt	2
אֲשֶׁר־עָשָׂה יְהוֹיָקִים׃ כִּי עַל־אַף	3

ᵃ Targ. לְהוֹן.   ᵇ Inc. vs. 57.   ᶜ Targ. תּוּקְרַבְתָּא.   ᵈ Targ. עַל.

Desunt {	יְהוָה הָיְתָה בִּירוּשָׁלַם וִיהוּדָה
	עַד־הִשְׁלִיכוֹ אוֹתָם מֵעַל־פָּנָיו
	וַיִּמְרֹד צִדְקִיָּהוּ בְּמֶלֶךְ בָּבֶל:
בחדש העשירי	4 בחדש הָעֲשִׂירִי
הוא וכל־חילו	
וכל־חילו	
ויבנו עליה דיק (?)ᵃ כביב	ויבנו עליה דיק סביב
בתשעה לחדש	6 בָּחֹדֶשׁ הָרְבִיעִי בתשעה לחדש
רצאו לילה	7 יִבָּרְחוּ וַיֵּצְאוּ מֵהָעִיר לילה
בין־החומה והחל	בין־החֹמֹתַיִם
וילכו דרך (אל־) ערבהᵇ	וילכו דרך הָעֲרָבָה
וירדפו חיל־כשדים	8 וַיִּרְדְּפוּ חֵיל־כַּשְׂדִּים
וישיגו אותו בעבר (בַּעֲבָרוֹת) ירחו	וַיַּשִּׂגוּ אֶת־צִדְקִיָּהוּ בְּעַרְבֹת יְרֵחוֹ
וכל־עבדיו נפצו מעליו	וכל־חילו נפצו מעליו
9 רבלתה בְּאֶרֶץ חֲמָת וידבר אתו דבלתה וידבר אליו במשפט	
	משפטים
10 וגם את־כל־שרי יהודה שחט ואת־כל־שרי יהודה שחט בדבלתה	
	ברבלתה
11 ויתנהו בבית־רחים	ויתנהו בבית־הַפְּקֻדֹּת
Desunt {	12 הִיא שְׁנַת תְּשַׁע־עֶשְׂרֵה שָׁנָה
	לַמֶּלֶךְ נְבוּכַדְרֶאצַּר מֶלֶךְ־בָּבֶל
עמד לפני מלך־בבל	עָמַד לִפְנֵי מֶלֶךְ־בָּבֶל
ואת־כל־בתי העיר	13 ואת־כל־בתי ירושלם
14 ואת־כל־חומת ירושלם סביב ואת־כל־חוֹמֹת ירושלם סביב נתץ	
נתצו כל־חיל כשדים	חיל כשדים
	15 וּמִדַּלּוֹת הָעָם וְאֶת־יֶתֶר הָעָם
	הַנִּשְׁאָרִים בָּעִיר וְאֶת־הַנֹּפְלִים
Desunt {	אֲשֶׁר נָפְלוּ אֶל־מֶלֶךְ בָּבֶל וְאֵת
	יֶתֶר הָאָמוֹן הֶגְלָה נְבוּזַרְאֲדָן
	רַב־טַבָּחִים:
16 וּמִדַּלּוֹת הָאָרֶץ השאיר נבוזראדן וְאֶת־יֶתֶר העם השאיר רב־	
רב־טבחים	טבחים
17 אשר לבית־יהוה	אשר בְּבֵיתᶜ־יהוה

ᵃ τετραπέδοις λίθοις. ᵇ εἰς Ἄραβα. ᶜ Targ. בְּבֵית.

52:18-27] THE CONSPECTUS OF THE VARIATIONS. 397

וִישְׂאוּ אֶת־כָּל־נְחֻשְׁתָּם בָּבֶלָה	וַיִּקְחוּ אֶת־נְחֻשְׁתָּם וַיִּשְׂאוּ (וַיְבִיאוּ) בָּבֶלָה
18 וְאֶת־הַסִּירוֹת וְאֶת־הַיָּעִים וְאֶת־הַמְזַמְּרוֹת וְאֶת־הַמִּזְרָקוֹת וְאֶת־הַכַּפּוֹת לָקֵחוּ	וְאֶת־הַסֵּתֶר וְאֶת־הַגְּבִיעִים וְאֶת־הַמְזִלָּגֹת[a] Deest
19 וְאֶת־הַסִּפִּים וְאֶת־הַמַּחְתּוֹת וְאֶת־הַמִּזְרָקוֹת וְאֶת־הַסִּירוֹת וְאֶת־הַמְּנֹרוֹת וְאֶת־הַכַּפּוֹת וְאֶת־הַמְּנַקִּיּוֹת	וְאֶת־הַסִּפּוֹת וְאֶת־מְזַמְּרוֹת וְאֶת־הַסִּירוֹת[b] וְאֶת־הַמְּנֹרוֹת וְאֶת־הַמַּחְתּוֹת (הַכַּפּוֹת) וְאֶת־הַמְּנַקִּיּוֹת
20 הָעַמּוּדִים שְׁנַיִם הַיָּם הָאֶחָד אֲשֶׁר תַּחַת הַמְּכֹנוֹת כָּל־הַכֵּלִים הָאֵלֶּה	וְהָעַמּוּדִים שְׁנַיִם וְהַיָּם אֶחָד תַּחַת הַיָּם Deest
21 שְׁמֹנֶה עֶשְׂרֵה נָבוּב	שְׁלֹשִׁים וְחָמֵשׁ סָבִיב
22 וְכֹתֶרֶת עָלָיו נְחֹשֶׁת וְקוֹמַת הַכֹּתֶרֶת הָאַחַת חָמֵשׁ אַמּוֹת לַעֲמוּד הַשֵּׁנִי וְרִמּוֹנִים	וְכֹתֶרֶת עָלָיו נְחֹשֶׁת וְכֹתֶרֶת עֲלֵיהֶם נְחֹשֶׁת וְחָמֵשׁ אַמּוֹת קוֹמָה גֹּבַהּ הַכֹּתֶרֶת הָאֶחָת לַעֲמוּד הַשֵּׁנִי שְׁמוֹנָה רִמּוֹנִים בָּאַמָּה לִשְׁתֵּים־עֶשְׂרֵה הָאַמָּה
23 רוּחָה כָּל־הָרִמּוֹנִים	רוּחַ (חֵלֶק) אֶחָת וַיִּהְיוּ כָל־הָרִמּוֹנִים
24 אֶת־שְׂרָיָה כֹהֵן הָרֹאשׁ וְאֶת־צְפַנְיָה כֹהֵן הַמִּשְׁנֶה שְׁלֹשֶׁת שֹׁמְרֵי הַסַּף	אֶת־כֹּהֵן הָרֹאשׁ וְאֶת־כֹּהֵן הַמִּשְׁנֶה וְאֶת־שְׁלֹשֶׁת שֹׁמְרֵי הַדֶּרֶךְ
25 וּמִן־הָעִיר לָקַח סָרִיס וְשִׁבְעָה אֲנָשִׁים מֵרֹאֵי פְנֵי־הַמֶּלֶךְ סֹפֵר שַׂר הַצָּבָא הַמַּצְבִּא אֶת־עַם הָאָרֶץ	וְסָרִיס וְשִׁבְעָה אֲנָשִׁים אֲשֶׁר שֵׁם בִּפְנֵי הַמֶּלֶךְ סֹפֵר הַצְּבָאוֹת הַשַּׂר לְעַם הָאָרֶץ
26 רַב־טַבָּחִים רִבְלָתָה	רַב־טַבָּחַי הַמֶּלֶךְ דְּבִלָּתָה
27 וַיַּמִּתֵם בְּרִבְלָה וַיִּגֶל יְהוּדָה מֵעַל אַדְמָתוֹ	בְּדִבְלָה Deest

---

[a] τὰς κρεάγρας. [b] καὶ τὰς ἀπφὼθ καὶ τὰς μασμαρὼθ καὶ τοὺς ὑποχυτῆρας καὶ τὰς λυχνίας καὶ τὰς θυΐσκας καὶ τοὺς κυάθους.

	28 זֶה הָעָם אֲשֶׁר הֶגְלָה נְבוּכַדְרֶאצַּר בִּשְׁנַת־שֶׁבַע יְהוּדִים שְׁלֹשֶׁת 29 אֲלָפִים וְעֶשְׂרִים וּשְׁלֹשָׁה: בִּשְׁנַת שְׁמוֹנֶה עֶשְׂרֵה לִנְבוּכַדְרֶאצַּר* מִירוּשָׁלַ͏ִם נֶפֶשׁ שְׁמֹנֶה מֵאוֹת
Desunt	30 שְׁלֹשִׁים וּשְׁנָיִם: בִּשְׁנַת שָׁלֹשׁ וְעֶשְׂרִים לִנְבוּכַדְרֶאצַּר הֶגְלָה נְבוּזַרְאֲדָן רַב־טַבָּחִים יְהוּדִים נֶפֶשׁ שְׁבַע מֵאוֹת אַרְבָּעִים וַחֲמִשָּׁה כָּל־נֶפֶשׁ אַרְבַּעַת אֲלָפִים וְשֵׁשׁ מֵאוֹת:

לגלות יהויקים	לגלות יהויכן	31
בעשרים וארבעה לחדש	בעשרים וחמשה לחדש	
אויל מדרך[b]	אויל מרדך	
את־ראש יהויקים מלך־יהודה	את־ראש יהויכן מלך־יהודה	
ויגלחהו[b] ויצא אתו מן־חבית	ויצא אתו מבית הכלא	
אשר היה כלוא בו (שמור בו)		
ממעל המלכים	32 ממעל לכסא °מלכים	
ושנה את בגד כלאו ואכל לחם	33 ושנה את בגדי כלאו ואכל לחם	
תמיד לפניו	לפניו תמיד	
וארחה לו נתנה תמיד	34 וארחתו ארחת תמיד נתנה־לו	
מדי יום ביום	דבר־יום ביומו	
Deest	כל ימי חייו	

[a] Οὐλαιμαδάχαρ. [b] Cf. Gen. 41:14.

T. and T. Clark's Publications.

In demy 8vo, Ninth Edition, price 7s. 6d.,

AN INTRODUCTORY HEBREW GRAMMAR:
With Progressive Exercises in Reading and Writing.

By A. B. DAVIDSON, M.A., LL.D.,
PROFESSOR OF HEBREW, ETC., IN THE NEW COLLEGE, EDINBURGH.

'Simple and elementary in form, while thoroughly scientific in principle, it is the production of a clear thinker and a sound scholar.'—*British Quarterly Review.*

BY THE SAME AUTHOR.

In Preparation,

A SYNTAX OF THE HEBREW LANGUAGE.

In demy 8vo, price 8s. 6d.,

SYNTAX OF THE HEBREW LANGUAGE OF THE OLD TESTAMENT.

By Professor HEINRICH EWALD.

Translated from the Eighth German Edition

By JAMES KENNEDY, B.D.

'The work stands unique as regards a patient investigation of facts, written with a profound analysis of the laws of thought, of which language is the reflection. Another striking feature of the work is the regularly progressive order which pervades the whole. The author proceeds by a natural gradation from the simplest elements to the most complex forms.'—*British Quarterly Review.*

In Two Vols., demy 8vo, price 18s.,

A NEW EASY AND COMPLETE HEBREW COURSE:

Containing a Hebrew Grammar, with Copious Hebrew and English Exercises, strictly graduated, with a Lexicon.

By Rev. T. BOWMAN, M.A.

WORKS BY PROFESSOR C. A. BRIGGS, D.D.

Just published, in One Volume, post 8vo, price 7s. 6d.,

MESSIANIC PROPHECY.

BY PROFESSOR C. A. BRIGGS, D.D.,

PROFESSOR OF HEBREW AND THE COGNATE LANGUAGES IN THE UNION THEOLOGICAL SEMINARY, NEW YORK;
AUTHOR OF 'BIBLICAL STUDY,' 'AMERICAN PRESBYTERIANISM,' ETC.

NOTE.—This Work discusses all the Messianic passages of the Old Testament in a fresh Translation, with critical notes, and aims to trace the development of the Messianic idea in the Old Testament.

'Professor Briggs' Messianic Prophecy is a most excellent book, in which I greatly rejoice.'—Prof. FRANZ DELITZSCH.

'All scholars will join in recognising its singular usefulness as a text-book. It has been much wanted.'—Rev. Canon CHEYNE.

'Prof. Briggs' new book on Messianic Prophecy is a worthy companion to his indispensable text-book on "Biblical Study." . . . He has produced the first English text-book on the subject of Messianic Prophecy which a modern teacher can use.'—*The Academy.*

Just published, Second Edition, in post 8vo, price 7s. 6d.,

BIBLICAL STUDY:

ITS PRINCIPLES, METHODS, AND HISTORY.

With Introduction by Professor A. B. BRUCE, D.D.

'We are sure that no student will regret sending for this book.'—*Academy.*

'Dr. Briggs' book is a model of masterly condensation and conciseness.'—*Freeman.*

'We have great pleasure in recommending Dr. Briggs' book to the notice of all Biblical students.'—*Nonconformist.*

'Written by one who has made himself a master of the subject, and who is able to write upon it, both with the learning of the scholar and the earnestness of sincere conviction.'—*Scotsman.*

In post 8vo, with Maps, price 7s. 6d.,

AMERICAN PRESBYTERIANISM:

ITS ORIGIN AND EARLY HISTORY.

Together with an Appendix of Letters and Documents, many of which have recently been discovered.

'We have no doubt this volume will be read with intense interest and gratitude by thousands.'—*Presbyterian Churchman.*

'This book travels over a great extent of ground. It is packed with information, and appears to be the fruit of protracted and enthusiastic study.'—*Aberdeen Free Press.*

'An honest and valuable contribution to ecclesiastical history.'—*Glasgow Herald.*

T. and T. Clark's Publications.

PROFESSOR GODET'S WORKS.
(Copyright, by arrangement with the Author.)

Just published, in Two Volumes, demy 8vo, price 21s.,

COMMENTARY ON ST. PAUL'S FIRST EPISTLE TO THE CORINTHIANS.
By F. GODET, D.D.,
PROFESSOR OF THEOLOGY, NEUCHATEL.

'A perfect masterpiece of theological toil and thought. . . . Scholarly, evangelical, exhaustive, and able.'—*Evangelical Review.*

'To say a word in praise of any of Professor Godet's productions is almost like "gilding refined gold." All who are familiar with his commentaries know how full they are of rich suggestion. . . . This volume fully sustains the high reputation Godet has made for himself as a Biblical scholar, and devout expositor of the will of God. Every page is radiant with light, and gives forth heat as well.'—*Methodist New Connexion Magazine.*

In Three Volumes, 8vo, price 31s. 6d.,

A COMMENTARY ON THE GOSPEL OF ST. JOHN.
A New Edition, Revised throughout by the Author.

'This work forms one of the battle-fields of modern inquiry, and is itself so rich in spiritual truth, that it is impossible to examine it too closely; and we welcome this treatise from the pen of Dr. Godet. We have no more competent exegete; and this new volume shows all the learning and vivacity for which the author is distinguished.'—*Freeman.*

In Two Volumes, 8vo, price 21s.,

A COMMENTARY ON THE GOSPEL OF ST. LUKE.

'Marked by clearness and good sense, it will be found to possess value and interest as one of the most recent and copious works specially designed to illustrate this Gospel.'—*Guardian.*

In Two Volumes, 8vo, price 21s.,

A COMMENTARY ON ST. PAUL'S EPISTLE TO THE ROMANS.

'We prefer this commentary to any other we have seen on the subject. . . . We have great pleasure in recommending it as not only rendering invaluable aid in the critical study of the text, but affording practical and deeply suggestive assistance in the exposition of the doctrine.'—*British and Foreign Evangelical Review.*

In crown 8vo, Second Edition, price 6s.,

DEFENCE OF THE CHRISTIAN FAITH.
TRANSLATED BY THE HON. AND REV. CANON LYTTELTON, M.A.,
RECTOR OF HAGLEY.

'There is trenchant argument and resistless logic in these lectures; but withal, there is cultured imagination and felicitous eloquence, which carry home the appeals to the heart as well as the head.'—*Sword and Trowel.*

T. and T. Clark's Publications.

CLARK'S FOREIGN THEOLOGICAL LIBRARY.

MESSRS. CLARK allow a SELECTION of EIGHT VOLUMES (*or more at the same ratio*) from the Volumes issued in this Series previous to 1884 (*see below*),

At the Subscription Price of Two Guineas
(*Duplicates cannot be supplied in such selections*).

NON-SUBSCRIPTION PRICES WITHIN BRACKETS.

Alexander (J. A., D.D.)—Commentary on Isaiah. Two Vols. (17s.)
Baumgarten (M., Ph.D.)—The Acts of the Apostles; or, The History of the Church in the Apostolic Age. Three Vols. (27s.)
Bleek (Professor)—Introduction to the New Testament. Two Vols. (21s.)
Christlieb (Theo., D.D.)—Modern Doubt and Christian Belief. One Vol. (10s. 6d.)
Delitzsch (Franz, D.D.)—Commentary on Job. Two Vols. (21s.)
—— Commentary on the Psalms. Three Vols. (31s. 6d.)
—— Commentary on the Proverbs of Solomon. Two Vols. (21s.)
—— Commentary on Song of Solomon and Ecclesiastes. One Vol. (10s. 6d.)
—— Commentary on the Prophecies of Isaiah. Two Vols. (21s.)
—— Commentary on Epistle to the Hebrews. Two Vols. (21s.)
—— A System of Biblical Psychology. One Vol. (12s.)
Döllinger (J. J. Ign. von, D.D.)—Hippolytus and Callistus; or, The Church of Rome in the First Half of the Third Century. One Vol. (7s. 6d.)
Dorner (I. A., D.D.)—A System of Christian Doctrine. Four Vols. (42s.)
—— History of the Development of the Doctrine of the Person of Christ. Five Vols. (52s. 6d.)
Ebrard (J. H. A., D.D.)—Commentary on the Epistles of St. John. One Vol. (10s. 6d.)
—— The Gospel History: A Compendium of Critical Investigations in support of the Historical Character of the Four Gospels. One Vol. (10s. 6d.)
Gebhardt (H.)—Doctrine of the Apocalypse. One Vol. (10s. 6d.)
Gerlach (Otto von)—Commentary on the Pentateuch. One Vol. (10s. 6d.)
Gieseler (J. C. L., D.D.)—Compendium of Ecclesiastical History. Four Vols. (42s.)
Godet (F., D.D.)—Commentary on St. Luke's Gospel. Two Vols. (21s.)
—— Commentary on St. John's Gospel. Three Vols. (31s. 6d.)
—— Commentary on the Epistle to the Romans. Two Vols. (21s.)
Goebel on the Parables. One Vol. (10s. 6d.)
Hagenbach (K. R., D.D.)—History of the Reformation. Two Vols. (21s.)
—— History of Christian Doctrines. Three Vols. (31s. 6d.)
Harless (G. C. A. von, D.D.)—A System of Christian Ethics. One Vol. (10s. 6d.)
Haupt (E.)—Commentary on the First Epistle of St. John. One Vol. (10s. 6d.)
Hävernick (Professor).—General Introduction to the Old Testament. One Vol. (10s. 6d.)
Hengstenberg (E. W., D.D.) Christology of the Old Testament, and a Commentary on the Messianic Predictions. Four Vols. (42s.)
—— Commentary on the Psalms. Three Vols. (33s.)
—— On the Book of Ecclesiastes. To which are appended: Treatises on the Song of Solomon; the Book of Job; the Prophet Isaiah; the Sacrifices of Holy Scripture; and on the Jews and the Christian Church. One Vol. (9s.)
—— Commentary on the Gospel of St. John. Two Vols. (21s.)
—— Commentary on Ezekiel. One Vol. (10s. 6d.)
—— Dissertations on the Genuineness of Daniel, etc. One Vol. (12s.)
—— The Kingdom of God under the Old Covenant. Two Vols. (21s.)

[*Continued on next page.*

T. and T. Clark's Publications.

CLARK'S FOREIGN THEOLOGICAL LIBRARY—*Continued.*

Keil (C. F., D.D.)—Introduction to the Old Testament. Two Vols. (21s.)
—— Commentary on the Pentateuch. Three Vols. (31s. 6d.)
—— Commentary on Joshua, Judges, and Ruth. One Vol. (10s. 6d.)
—— Commentary on the Books of Samuel. One Vol. (10s. 6d.)
—— Commentary on the Books of Kings. One Vol. (10s. 6d.)
—— Commentary on the Books of Chronicles. One Vol. (10s. 6d.)
—— Commentary on Ezra, Nehemiah, and Esther. One Vol. (10s. 6d.)
—— Commentary on Jeremiah and Lamentations. Two Vols. (21s.)
—— Commentary on Ezekiel. Two Vols. (21s.)
—— Commentary on the Book of Daniel. One Vol. (10s. 6d.)
—— Commentary on the Minor Prophets. Two Vols. (21s.)
Kurtz (J. H., D.D.)—History of the Old Covenant; or, Old Testament Dispensation. Three Vols. (31s. 6d.)
Lange (J. P., D.D.)—Commentary on the Gospels of St. Matthew and St. Mark. Three Vols. (31s. 6d.)
—— Commentary on the Gospel of St. Luke. Two Vols. (18s.)
—— Commentary on the Gospel of St. John. Two Vols. (21s.)
Luthardt (C. E., D.D.)—Commentary on the Gospel of St. John. Three Vols. (31s. 6d.)
Macdonald (D., M.A.)—Introduction to the Pentateuch. Two Vols. (21s.)
Martensen (Bishop)—Christian Dogmatics. One Vol. (10s. 6d.)
—— Christian Ethics. General—Social—Individual. Three Vols. (31s. 6d.)
Müller (Dr. Julius)—The Christian Doctrine of Sin. Two Vols. (21s.)
Murphy (Professor)—Commentary on the Psalms. To count as Two Volumes. One Vol. (12s.)
Neander (A., D.D.)—General History of the Christian Religion and Church. Nine Vols. (67s. 6d.)
Oehler (Professor)—Biblical Theology of the Old Testament. Two Vols. (21s.)
Olshausen (H., D.D.)—Commentary on the Gospels and Acts. Four Vols. (42s.)
—— Commentary on Epistle to the Romans. One Vol. (10s. 6d.)
—— Commentary on Epistles to the Corinthians. One Vol. (9s.)
—— Commentary on Philippians, Titus, and 1st Timothy. One Vol. (10s. 6d.)
Philippi (F. A., D.D.)—Commentary on Epistle to Romans. Two Vols. (21s.)
Ritter (Carl)—Comparative Geography of Palestine. Four Vols. (26s.)
Schmid (C. F., D.D.)—New Testament Theology. One Vol. (10s. 6d.)
Shedd (W. G. T., D.D.)—History of Christian Doctrine. Two Vols. (21s.)
Steinmeyer (F. L., D.D.)—History of the Passion and Resurrection of our Lord. One Vol. (10s. 6d.)
—— The Miracles of our Lord in relation to Modern Criticism. One Vol. (7s. 6d.)
Stier (Rudolf, D.D.)—The Words of the Lord Jesus. Eight Vols. (84s.)
—— The Words of the Risen Saviour, and Commentary on the Epistle of St. James. One Vol. (10s. 6d.)
—— The Words of the Apostles Expounded. One Vol. (10s. 6d.)
Tholuck (A., D.D.)—Commentary on the Gospel of St. John. One Vol. (9s.)
Ullmann (C., D D.)—Reformers before the Reformation, principally in Germany and the Netherlands. Two Vols. (21s.)
Weiss (B., D.D.)—Biblical Theology of the New Testament. Two Vols. (21s.)
—— The Life of Christ. Vols. I. and II. (10s. 6d. each.)
Winer (G. B., D.D.)—Collection of the Confessions of Christendom. One Vol. (10s. 6d.)

The Series forms an *Apparatus* without which it may be truly said *no Theological Library can be complete;* and the Publishers take the liberty of suggesting that no more appropriate gift could be presented to a Clergyman than the Series in whole or in part.

Subscribers' Names received by all Retail Booksellers.

LONDON: (*For Works at Non-subscription price only*) HAMILTON, ADAMS & Co.

WORKS BY PROFESSOR FRANZ DELITZSCH.

In Two Vols., demy 8vo.—Vol. I. now ready, price 10s. 6d.,
A NEW COMMENTARY
ON
GENESIS.

MESSRS. CLARK have pleasure in intimating, that by special arrangement with the author they are publishing a translation of the Fifth Edition, thoroughly revised, and in large part re-written, of this standard Commentary. The learned author, who has for a generation been one of the foremost biblical scholars of Germany, and who is revered alike for his learning and his piety, has here stated with evident care his latest and most matured opinions.

'Thirty-five years have elapsed since Prof. Delitzsch's Commentary on Genesis first appeared; fifteen years since the fourth edition was published in 1872. Ever in the van of historical and philological research, the venerable author now comes forward with another fresh edition in which he incorporates what fifteen years have achieved for illustration and criticism of the text of Genesis. . . . We congratulate Prof. Delitzsch on this new edition, and trust that it may appear before long in an English dress. By it, not less than by his other commentaries, he has earned the gratitude of every lover of biblical science, and we shall be surprised if, in the future, many do not acknowledge that they have found in it a welcome help and guide.'—Professor S. R. DRIVER, in *The Academy.*

In crown 8vo, price 4s. 6d.,
OLD TESTAMENT HISTORY OF REDEMPTION.

'Few who will take the trouble to look into it will not readily acknowledge that it is not only a masterly work, such as few men, if any, besides the Leipzig professor could give, but that there is nothing to be compared with it as a handbook for students.'—*Literary World.*

In One Volume, 8vo, price 12s.,
A SYSTEM OF BIBLICAL PSYCHOLOGY.

'This admirable volume ought to be carefully read by every thinking clergyman.'—*Literary Churchman.*

In Two Vols., 8vo, price 21s.,
COMMENTARY ON THE EPISTLE TO THE HEBREWS.

KEIL AND DELITZSCH'S
COMMENTARIES ON, AND INTRODUCTION TO, THE OLD TESTAMENT.

This Series (published in Clark's Foreign Theological Library) is now completed in Twenty-seven Volumes, price £7, 2s. nett. Any Eight Volumes are now supplied for £2, 2s., or more at same ratio.

Separate Volumes may be had, price 10s. 6d. each.

'Very high merit for thorough Hebrew scholarship, and for keen critical sagacity, belongs to these Old Testament Commentaries. No scholar will willingly dispense with them.'—*British Quarterly Review.*

PUBLICATIONS OF
T. & T. CLARK,
38 GEORGE STREET EDINBURGH.
LONDON: HAMILTON, ADAMS, & CO.

Adam (J., D.D.)—AN EXPOSITION OF THE EPISTLE OF JAMES. 8vo, 9s.

Ahlfeld (Dr.), etc.—THE VOICE FROM THE CROSS: Sermons on our Lord's Passion by Eminent Living Preachers of Germany. Cr. 8vo, price 5s.

Alexander (Prof. W. Lindsay)—SYSTEM OF BIBLICAL THEOLOGY. Two vols. 8vo, 21s.

Alexander (Dr. J. A.)—COMMENTARY ON ISAIAH. Two vols. 8vo, 17s.

Ante-Nicene Christian Library—A COLLECTION OF ALL THE WORKS OF THE FATHERS OF THE CHRISTIAN CHURCH PRIOR TO THE COUNCIL OF NICÆA. Twenty-four vols. 8vo, Subscription price, £6, 6s.

Augustine's Works—Edited by MARCUS DODS, D.D. Fifteen vols. 8vo, Subscription price, £3, 19s.

Bannerman (Prof.)—THE CHURCH OF CHRIST. Two vols. 8vo, 21s.

Bannerman (Rev. D.D.)—THE DOCTRINE OF THE CHURCH. 8vo, 12s.

Baumgarten (Professor)—APOSTOLIC HISTORY. Three vols. 8vo, 27s.

Beck (Dr.)—OUTLINES OF BIBLICAL PSYCHOLOGY. Crown 8vo, 4s.

—— PASTORAL THEOLOGY IN THE NEW TESTAMENT. Crown 8vo, 6s.

Bengel—GNOMON OF THE NEW TESTAMENT. With Original Notes, Explanatory and Illustrative. Five vols. 8vo, Subscription price, 31s. 6d. *Cheaper Edition, the five volumes bound in three,* 24s.

Besser's CHRIST THE LIFE OF THE WORLD. Price 6s.

Bible-Class Handbooks. Crown 8vo.
BINNIE (Prof.)—The Church, 1s. 6d.
BROWN (Principal)—The Epistle to the Romans, 2s.
CANDLISH (Prof.)—The Christian Sacraments, 1s. 6d.
—— The Work of the Holy Spirit, 1s. 6d.
—— Christian Doctrine of God. 1s. 6d.
DAVIDSON (Prof.)—The Epistle to the Hebrews, 2s. 6d.
DODS (MARCUS, D.D.)—Post-Exilian Prophets, 2s. Book of Genesis, 2s.
DOUGLAS (Principal)—Book of Joshua, 1s. 6d. Book of Judges, 1s. 3d.
HAMILTON (T., D.D.)—Irish Presbyterian Church History, 2s.
HENDERSON (ARCHIBALD, M.A.)—Palestine, with Maps. *The maps are by Captain Conder, R.E., of the Palestine Exploration Fund.* Price 2s. 6d.
KILPATRICK (T. B., B.D.)—Butler's Three Sermons on Human Nature. 1s. 6d.
LINDSAY (Prof.)—St. Mark's Gospel, 2s. 6d.
—— St. Luke's Gospel, Part I., 2s.; Part II., 1s. 3d.
—— The Reformation. 2s.
—— The Acts of the Apostles, Two vols., 1s. 6d. each.
MACGREGOR (Prof.)—The Epistle to the Galatians, 1s. 6d.
MACPHERSON (JOHN, M.A.)—Presbyterianism, 1s. 6d.
—— The Westminster Confession of Faith, 2s.
—— The Sum of Saving Knowledge, 1s. 6d.
MURPHY (Prof.)—The Books of Chronicles, 1s. 6d.
SCRYMGEOUR (WM.)—Lessons on the Life of Christ, 2s. 6d.
STALKER (JAMES, M.A.)—Life of Christ, 1s. 6d. Life of St. Paul, 1s. 6d.
SMITH (GEORGE, LL.D.)—A Short History of Missions, 2s. 6d.
THOMSON (W. D., M.A.)—Christian Miracles and Conclusions of Science. 2s.
WALKER (NORMAN L., M.A.)—Scottish Church History, 1s. 6d.
WHYTE (ALEXANDER, D.D.)—The Shorter Catechism, 2s. 6d.

Bible-Class Primers. Paper covers, 6d. each; free by post, 7d. In cloth, 8d. each; free by post, 9d.
CROSKERY (Prof.)—Joshua and the Conquest. GIVEN (Prof.)—The Kings of Judah.
GLOAG (PATON J., D.D.)—Life of Paul. IVERACH (JAMES, M.A.)—Life of Moses.
PATERSON (Prof. J. A.)—Period of the Judges.

T. and T. Clark's Publications.

Bible-Class Primers—*continued.*
   Robson (John, D.D.)—Outlines of Protestant Missions.
   Salmond (Prof.)—Life of Peter. The Shorter Catechism, 3 Parts. Life of Christ.
   Smith (H. W., D.D.)—Outlines of Early Church History.
   Thomson (P., M.A.)—Life of David.   Walker (W., M.A.)—The Kings of Israel.
   Winterbotham (Rayner, M.A.)—Life and Reign of Solomon.
   Witherow (Prof.)—The History of the Reformation.

Blaikie (Prof. W. G.)—The Preachers of Scotland from the 6th to the 19th Century. Post 8vo, 7s. 6d.

Bleek's Introduction to the New Testament. Two vols. 8vo, 21s.

Bowman (T., M.A.)—Easy and Complete Hebrew Course. 8vo. Part I., 7s. 6d.; Part II., 10s. 6d.

Briggs (Prof.)—Biblical Study: Its Principles, Methods, and History. Second Edition, post 8vo, 7s. 6d,
  ——— American Presbyterianism. Post 8vo, 7s. 6d.
  ——— Messianic Prophecy. Post 8vo, 7s. 6d.

Brown (David, D.D.)—Christ's Second Coming: Will it be Pre-Millennial? Seventh Edition, crown 8vo, 7s. 6d.

Bruce (A. B., D.D.)—The Training of the Twelve; exhibiting the Twelve Disciples under Discipline for the Apostleship. 3rd Ed., 8vo, 10s. 6d.
  ——— The Humiliation of Christ, in its Physical, Ethical, and Official Aspects. Second Edition, 8vo, 10s. 6d.

Buchanan (Professor)—The Doctrine of Justification. 8vo, 10s. 6d.
  ——— On Comfort in Affliction. Crown 8vo, 2s. 6d.
  ——— On Improvement of Affliction. Crown 8vo, 2s. 6d.

Bungener (Felix)—Rome and the Council in 19th Century. Cr. 8vo, 5s.

Calvin's Institutes of Christian Religion. (Translation.) 2 vols. 8vo, 14s.

Calvini Institutio Christianæ Religionis. Curavit A. Tholuck. Two vols. 8vo, Subscription price, 14s.

Candlish (Prof. J. S., D.D.)—The Kingdom of God, Biblically and Historically Considered. 8vo, 10s. 6d.

Caspari (C. E.)—A Chronological and Geographical Introduction to the Life of Christ. 8vo, 7s. 6d.

Caspers (A.)—The Footsteps of Christ. Crown 8vo, 7s. 6d.

Cassel (Prof.)—Commentary on Esther. 8vo, 10s. 6d.

Cave (Prof.)—The Scriptural Doctrine of Sacrifice. 8vo, 12s.
  ——— An Introduction to Theology: Its Principles, its Branches, its Results, and its Literature. 8vo, 12s.

Christlieb (Dr.)—Modern Doubt and Christian Belief. Apologetic Lectures addressed to Earnest Seekers after Truth. 8vo, 10s. 6d.

Cotterill—Peregrinus Proteus: Clement to the Corinthians, etc. 8vo, 12s.
  ——— Modern Criticism: Clement's Epistles to Virgins, etc. 8vo, 5s.

Cremer (Professor)—Biblico-Theological Lexicon of New Testament Greek. Third Edition, with Supplement, demy 4to, 38s. SUPPLEMENT, separately, 14s.

Crippen (Rev. T. G.)—A Popular Introduction to the History of Christian Doctrine. 8vo, 9s.

Cunningham (Principal)—Historical Theology. Review of the Principal Doctrinal Discussions since the Apostolic Age. Two vols. 8vo, 21s.
  ——— Discussions on Church Principles. 8vo, 10s. 6d.

Curtiss (Dr. S. I.)—The Levitical Priests. Crown 8vo, 5s.

Dabney (R. L., D.D.)—The Sensualistic Philosophy of the Nineteenth Century Considered. Crown 8vo, 6s.

Davidson (Professor)—An Introductory Hebrew Grammar. With Progressive Exercises in Reading and Writing. Ninth Edition, 8vo, 7s. 6d.

Delitzsch (Prof.)—A System of Biblical Psychology. 8vo, 12s.

T. and T. Clark's Publications.

Delitzsch (Prof.)—NEW COMMENTARY ON GENESIS. Two Vols., 8vo. Vol. I.
——— COMMENTARY ON JOB. Two vols. 8vo, 21s. [now ready, 10s. 6d.
——— COMMENTARY ON PSALMS. Three vols. 8vo, 31s. 6d.
——— ON THE PROVERBS OF SOLOMON. Two vols. 8vo, 21s.
——— ON THE SONG OF SOLOMON AND ECCLESIASTES. 8vo, 10s. 6d.
——— OLD TESTAMENT HISTORY OF REDEMPTION. Cr. 8vo, 4s. 6d.
——— COMMENTARY ON ISAIAH. Two vols. 8vo, 21s.
——— ON THE EPISTLE TO THE HEBREWS. Two vols. 8vo, 21s.
Doedes—MANUAL OF NEW TESTAMENT HERMENEUTICS. Cr. 8vo, 3s.
Döllinger (Dr.)—HIPPOLYTUS AND CALLISTUS; or, The Roman Church in the First Half of the Third Century. 8vo, 7s. 6d.
Dorner (Professor)—HISTORY OF THE DEVELOPMENT OF THE DOCTRINE OF THE PERSON OF CHRIST. Five vols. 8vo, £2, 12s. 6d.
——— SYSTEM OF CHRISTIAN DOCTRINE. Four vols. 8vo, £2, 2s.
——— SYSTEM OF CHRISTIAN ETHICS. 8vo, 14s.
Eadie (Professor)—COMMENTARIES ON ST. PAUL'S EPISTLES TO THE EPHESIANS, PHILIPPIANS, COLOSSIANS. New and Revised Editions, Edited by Rev. WM. YOUNG, M.A. Three vols. 8vo, 10s. 6d. each; or set, 18s. nett.
Ebrard (Dr. J. H. A.)—THE GOSPEL HISTORY. 8vo, 10s. 6d.
——— COMMENTARY ON THE EPISTLES OF ST. JOHN. 8vo, 10s. 6d.
——— APOLOGETICS. Three vols. 8vo, 31s. 6d.
Elliott—ON THE INSPIRATION OF THE HOLY SCRIPTURES. 8vo, 6s.
Ernesti—BIBLICAL INTERPRETATION OF NEW TESTAMENT. Two vols., 8s.
Ewald (Heinrich)—SYNTAX OF THE HEBREW LANGUAGE OF THE OLD TESTAMENT. 8vo, 8s. 6d.
——— REVELATION: ITS NATURE AND RECORD. 8vo, 10s. 6d.
——— OLD AND NEW TESTAMENT THEOLOGY. 8vo, 10s. 6d.
Fairbairn (Principal)—TYPOLOGY OF SCRIPTURE, viewed in connection with the series of Divine Dispensations. Sixth Edition, Two vols. 8vo, 21s.
——— THE REVELATION OF LAW IN SCRIPTURE, 8vo, 10s. 6d.
——— EZEKIEL AND THE BOOK OF HIS PROPHECY. 4th Ed., 8vo, 10s. 6d.
——— PROPHECY VIEWED IN ITS DISTINCTIVE NATURE, ITS SPECIAL FUNCTIONS, AND PROPER INTERPRETATIONS. Second Edition, 8vo, 10s. 6d.
——— NEW TESTAMENT HERMENEUTICAL MANUAL. 8vo, 10s. 6d.
——— THE PASTORAL EPISTLES. The Greek Text and Translation. With Introduction, Expository Notes, and Dissertations. 8vo, 7s. 6d.
——— PASTORAL THEOLOGY: A Treatise on the Office and Duties of the Christian Pastor. With a Memoir of the Author. Crown 8vo, 6s.
Forbes (Prof.)—SYMMETRICAL STRUCTURE OF SCRIPTURE. 8vo, 8s. 6d.
——— ANALYTICAL COMMENTARY ON THE ROMANS. 8vo, 10s. 6d.
——— STUDIES IN THE BOOK OF PSALMS. 8vo, 7s. 6d.
Frank (Prof. F. H.)—SYSTEM OF CHRISTIAN EVIDENCE. 8vo, 10s. 6d.
Gebhardt (H.)—THE DOCTRINE OF THE APOCALYPSE, AND ITS RELATION TO THE DOCTRINE OF THE GOSPEL AND EPISTLES OF JOHN. 8vo, 10s. 6d.
Gerlach—COMMENTARY ON THE PENTATEUCH. 8vo, 10s. 6d.
Gieseler (Dr. J. C. L.)—ECCLESIASTICAL HISTORY. Four vols. 8vo, £2, 2s.
Gifford (Canon)—VOICES OF THE PROPHETS. Crown 8vo, 3s. 6d.
Given (Rev. Prof. J. J.)—THE TRUTHS OF SCRIPTURE IN CONNECTION WITH REVELATION, INSPIRATION, AND THE CANON. 8vo, 6s.
Glasgow (Prof.)—APOCALYPSE TRANSLATED AND EXPOUNDED. 8vo, 10s. 6d.
Gloag (Paton J., D.D.)—A CRITICAL AND EXEGETICAL COMMENTARY ON THE ACTS OF THE APOSTLES. Two vols. 8vo, 21s.
——— THE MESSIANIC PROPHECIES. Crown 8vo, price 7s. 6d.

T. and T. Clark's Publications.

Gloag (P. J., D.D.)—INTRODUCTION TO THE PAULINE EPISTLES. 8vo, 12s.
——— INTRODUCTION TO THE CATHOLIC EPISTLES. 8vo, 10s. 6d.
——— EXEGETICAL STUDIES. Crown 8vo, 5s.
Godet (Prof.)—COMMENTARY ON ST. LUKE'S GOSPEL. Two vols. 8vo, 21s.
——— COMMENTARY ON ST. JOHN'S GOSPEL. Three vols. 8vo, 31s. 6d.
——— COMMENTARY ON EPISTLE TO THE ROMANS. Two vols. 8vo, 21s.
——— COMMENTARY ON 1ST EPISTLE TO CORINTHIANS. 2 vols. 8vo, 21s.
——— LECTURES IN DEFENCE OF THE CHRISTIAN FAITH. Cr. 8vo, 6s.
Goebel (Siegfried)—THE PARABLES OF JESUS. 8vo, 10s. 6d.
Gotthold's Emblems; or, INVISIBLE THINGS UNDERSTOOD BY THINGS THAT ARE MADE. Crown 8vo, 5s.
Grimm's GREEK-ENGLISH LEXICON OF THE NEW TESTAMENT. Translated, Revised, and Enlarged by JOSEPH H. THAYER, D.D. Demy 4to, 36s.
Guyot (Arnold, LL.D.)—CREATION; or, The Biblical Cosmogony in the Light of Modern Science. With Illustrations. Crown 8vo, 5s. 6d.
Hagenbach (Dr. K. R.)—HISTORY OF DOCTRINES. Three vols. 8vo, 31s. 6d.
——— HISTORY OF THE REFORMATION. Two vols. 8vo, 21s.
Hall (Rev. Newman, LL.B.)—THE LORD'S PRAYER. 8vo, 10s. 6d.
Hamilton (T., D.D.)—BEYOND THE STARS; or, Heaven, its Inhabitants, Occupations, and Life. Crown 8vo, 5s.
Harless (Dr. C. A.)—SYSTEM OF CHRISTIAN ETHICS. 8vo, 10s. 6d.
Harris (Rev. S., D.D.)—THE PHILOSOPHICAL BASIS OF THEISM. 8vo, 12s.
——— THE SELF-REVELATION OF GOD. 8vo, 12s.
Haupt (Erich)—THE FIRST EPISTLE OF ST. JOHN. 8vo, 10s. 6d.
Hävernick (H. A. Ch.)—INTRODUCTION TO OLD TESTAMENT. 10s. 6d.
Heard (Rev. J. B., M.A.)—THE TRIPARTITE NATURE OF MAN—SPIRIT, SOUL, AND BODY. Fifth Edition, crown 8vo, 6s.
——— OLD AND NEW THEOLOGY. A Constructive Critique. Cr. 8vo, 6s.
Hefele (Bishop)—A HISTORY OF THE COUNCILS OF THE CHURCH. Vol. I., to A.D. 325; Vol. II., A.D. 326 to 429. Vol. III., A.D. 431 to the close of the Council of Chalcedon, 451. 8vo, 12s. each.
Hengstenberg (Professor)—COMMENTARY ON PSALMS. 3 vols. 8vo, 33s.
——— COMMENTARY ON THE BOOK OF ECCLESIASTES. Treatises on the Song of Solomon, Job, and on Isaiah, etc. 8vo, 9s.
——— THE PROPHECIES OF EZEKIEL ELUCIDATED. 8vo, 10s. 6d.
——— THE GENUINENESS OF DANIEL, etc. 8vo, 12s.
——— HISTORY OF THE KINGDOM OF GOD. Two vols. 8vo, 21s.
——— CHRISTOLOGY OF THE OLD TESTAMENT. Four vols. 8vo, £2, 2s.
——— ON THE GOSPEL OF ST. JOHN. Two vols. 8vo, 21s.
Herzog—ENCYCLOPÆDIA OF BIBLICAL, HISTORICAL, DOCTRINAL, AND PRACTICAL THEOLOGY. Based on the Real-Encyklopädie of Herzog, Plitt, and Hauck. Edited by Prof. SCHAFF, D.D. In Three vols., price 24s. each.
——— ENCYCLOPÆDIA OF LIVING DIVINES, ETC., OF ALL DENOMINATIONS IN EUROPE AND AMERICA. (Supplement to Herzog's Encyclopædia.) Imp. 8vo, 8s,
Hutchison (John, D.D.)—COMMENTARY ON THESSALONIANS. 8vo, 9s.
——— COMMENTARY ON PHILIPPIANS. 8vo, 7s. 6d.
Janet (Paul)—FINAL CAUSES. By PAUL JANET, Member of the Institute. Translated from the French. Second Edition, demy 8vo, 12s.
——— THE THEORY OF MORALS. Demy 8vo, 10s. 6d.
Johnstone (Prof. R., D.D.)—COMMENTARY ON FIRST PETER. 8vo, 10s. 6d.
Jouffroy—PHILOSOPHICAL ESSAYS. Fcap. 8vo, 5s.
Kant—THE METAPHYSIC OF ETHICS. Crown 8vo, 6s.
——— PHILOSOPHY OF LAW. Trans. by W. HASTIE, B.D. Cr. 8vo, 5s.

T. and T. Clark's Publications.

Keil (Prof.)—COMMENTARY ON THE PENTATEUCH. 3 vols. 8vo, 31s. 6d.
—— COMMENTARY ON JOSHUA, JUDGES, AND RUTH. 8vo, 10s. 6d.
—— COMMENTARY ON THE BOOKS OF SAMUEL. 8vo, 10s. 6d.
—— COMMENTARY ON THE BOOKS OF KINGS. 8vo, 10s. 6d.
—— COMMENTARY ON CHRONICLES. 8vo, 10s. 6d.
—— COMMENTARY ON EZRA, NEHEMIAH, ESTHER. 8vo, 10s. 6d.
—— COMMENTARY ON JEREMIAH. Two vols. 8vo, 21s.
—— COMMENTARY ON EZEKIEL. Two vols. 8vo, 21s.
—— COMMENTARY ON DANIEL. 8vo, 10s. 6d.
—— ON THE BOOKS OF THE MINOR PROPHETS. Two vols. 8vo, 21s.
—— MANUAL OF HISTORICO-CRITICAL INTRODUCTION TO THE CANONICAL SCRIPTURES OF THE OLD TESTAMENT. Two vols. 8vo, 21s.
—— HANDBOOK OF BIBLICAL ARCHÆOLOGY. Two vols. 8vo, 21s.
Keymer (Rev. N., M.A.)—NOTES ON GENESIS. Crown 8vo, 1s. 6d.
Killen (Prof.)—THE OLD CATHOLIC CHURCH; or, The History, Doctrine, Worship, and Polity of the Christians, traced to A.D. 755. 8vo, 9s.
—— THE IGNATIAN EPISTLES ENTIRELY SPURIOUS. Cr. 8vo, 2s. 6d.
König (Dr. F. E.)—THE RELIGIOUS HISTORY OF ISRAEL. A Discussion of the Chief Problems in Old Testament History as opposed to the Development Theorists. Crown 8vo, 3s. 6d.
Krummacher (Dr. F. W.)—THE SUFFERING SAVIOUR; or, Meditations on the Last Days of the Sufferings of Christ. Eighth Edition, crown 8vo, 6s.
—— DAVID, THE KING OF ISRAEL: A Portrait drawn from Bible History and the Book of Psalms. Second Edition, crown 8vo, 6s.
—— AUTOBIOGRAPHY. Crown 8vo, 6s.
Kurtz (Prof.)—HANDBOOK OF CHURCH HISTORY. Two vols. 8vo, 15s.
—— HISTORY OF THE OLD COVENANT. Three vols. 8vo, 31s. 6d.
Ladd (Prof. G. T.)—THE DOCTRINE OF SACRED SCRIPTURE: A Critical, Historical, and Dogmatic Inquiry into the Origin and Nature of the Old and New Testaments. Two vols. 8vo, 1600 pp., 24s.
Laidlaw (Prof.)—THE BIBLE DOCTRINE OF MAN. 8vo, 10s. 6d.
Lange (J. P., D.D.)—THE LIFE OF OUR LORD JESUS CHRIST. Edited, with additional Notes, by MARCUS DODS, D.D. Second Edition, in Four vols. 8vo, Subscription price 28s.
—— COMMENTARIES ON THE OLD AND NEW TESTAMENTS. Edited by PHILIP SCHAFF, D.D. OLD TESTAMENT, 14 vols.; NEW TESTAMENT, 10 vols.; APOCRYPHA, 1 vol. Subscription price, nett, 15s. each.
—— ON ST. MATTHEW AND ST. MARK. Three vols. 8vo, 31s. 6d.
—— ON THE GOSPEL OF ST. LUKE. Two vols. 8vo, 18s.
—— ON THE GOSPEL OF ST. JOHN. Two vols. 8vo, 21s.
Lechler (Prof. G. V., D.D.)—THE APOSTOLIC AND POST-APOSTOLIC TIMES. Their Diversity and Unity in Life and Doctrine. 2 vols. cr. 8vo, 16s.
Lehmann (Pastor)—SCENES FROM THE LIFE OF JESUS. Cr. 8vo, 3s. 6d.
Lewis (Tayler, LL.D.)—THE SIX DAYS OF CREATION. Cr. 8vo, 7s. 6d.
Lisco (F. G.)—PARABLES OF JESUS EXPLAINED. Fcap. 8vo, 5s.
Lotze (Hermann)—MICROCOSMUS; An Essay concerning Man and his relation to the World. Second Edition, two vols. 8vo (1450 pages), 36s.
Luthardt, Kahnis, and Brückner—THE CHURCH. Crown 8vo, 5s.
Luthardt (Prof.)—ST. JOHN THE AUTHOR OF THE FOURTH GOSPEL. 7s. 6d.
—— ST. JOHN'S GOSPEL DESCRIBED AND EXPLAINED ACCORDING TO ITS PECULIAR CHARACTER. Three vols. 8vo, 31s. 6d.
—— APOLOGETIC LECTURES ON THE FUNDAMENTAL (*Sixth Edition*), SAVING (*Fifth Edition*), MORAL TRUTHS OF CHRISTIANITY (*Third Edition*). Three vols. crown 8vo, 6s. each.

Macdonald—Introduction to Pentateuch. Two vols. 8vo, 21s.
—— The Creation and Fall. 8vo, 12s.
M'Lauchlan (T., D.D., LL.D.)—The Early Scottish Church. To the Middle of the Twelfth Century. 8vo, 10s. 6d.
Mair (A., D.D.)—Studies in the Christian Evidences. Cr. 8vo, 6s.
Martensen (Bishop)—Christian Dogmatics: A Compendium of the Doctrines of Christianity. 8vo, 10s. 6d.
—— Christian Ethics. (General Ethics.) 8vo, 10s. 6d.
—— Christian Ethics. (Individual Ethics.) 8vo, 10s. 6d.
—— Christian Ethics. (Social Ethics.) 8vo, 10s. 6d.
Matheson (Geo., D.D.)—Growth of the Spirit of Christianity, from the First Century to the Dawn of the Lutheran Era. Two vols. 8vo, 21s.
—— Aids to the Study of German Theology. 3rd Edition, 4s. 6d.
Meyer (Dr.)—Critical and Exegetical Commentary on St. Matthew's Gospel. Two vols. 8vo, 21s.
—— On Mark and Luke. Two vols. 8vo, 21s.
—— On St. John's Gospel. Two vols. 8vo, 21s.
—— On Acts of the Apostles. Two vols. 8vo, 21s.
—— On the Epistle to the Romans. Two vols. 8vo, 21s.
—— On Corinthians. Two vols. 8vo, 21s.
—— On Galatians. 8vo, 10s. 6d.
—— On Ephesians and Philemon. One vol. 8vo, 10s. 6d.
—— On Philippians and Colossians. One vol. 8vo, 10s. 6d.
—— On Thessalonians. (*Dr. Lünemann.*) One vol. 8vo, 10s. 6d.
—— The Pastoral Epistles. (*Dr. Huther.*) 8vo, 10s. 6d.
—— The Epistle to the Hebrews. (*Dr. Lünemann.*) 8vo, 10s. 6d.
—— St. James' and St. John's Epistles. (*Huther.*) 8vo, 10s. 6d.
—— Peter and Jude. (*Dr. Huther.*) One vol. 8vo, 10s. 6d.
Michie (Charles, M.A.)—Bible Words and Phrases. 18mo, 1s.
Monrad (Dr. D. G.)—The World of Prayer. Crown 8vo, 4s. 6d.
Morgan (J., D.D.)—Scripture Testimony to the Holy Spirit. 7s. 6d.
—— Exposition of the First Epistle of John. 8vo, 7s. 6d.
Müller (Dr. Julius)—The Christian Doctrine of Sin. An entirely New Translation from the Fifth German Edition. Two vols. 8vo, 21s.
Murphy (Professor)—Commentary on the Psalms. 8vo, 12s.
—— A Critical and Exegetical Commentary on Exodus. 9s.
Naville (Ernest)—The Problem of Evil. Crown 8vo, 4s. 6d.
—— The Christ. Translated by Rev. T. J. Després. Cr. 8vo, 4s. 6d.
—— Modern Physics: Studies Historical and Philosophical. Translated by Rev. Henry Downton, M.A. Crown 8vo, 5s.
Nicoll (W. R., M.A.)—The Incarnate Saviour: A Life of Jesus Christ. Crown 8vo, 6s.
Neander (Dr.)—General History of the Christian Religion and Church. Nine vols. 8vo, £3, 7s. 6d.
Novalis—Hymns and Thoughts on Religion. Crown 8vo, 4s.
Oehler (Prof.)—Theology of the Old Testament. 2 vols. 8vo, 21s.
Oosterzee (Dr. Van)—The Year of Salvation. Words of Life for Every Day. A Book of Household Devotion. Two vols. 8vo, 6s. each.
—— Moses: A Biblical Study. Crown 8vo, 6s.
Olshausen (Dr. H.)—Biblical Commentary on the Gospels and Acts. Four vols. 8vo, £2, 2s. *Cheaper Edition,* four vols. crown 8vo, 24s.
—— Romans. One vol. 8vo, 10s. 6d.

Olshausen (Dr. H.)—CORINTHIANS. One vol. 8vo, 9s.
— PHILIPPIANS, TITUS, AND FIRST TIMOTHY. One vol. 8vo, 10s. 6d.
Orelli—OLD TESTAMENT PROPHECY REGARDING THE CONSUMMATION OF THE KINGDOM OF GOD. 8vo, 10s. 6d.
Owen (Dr. John)—WORKS. *Best and only Complete Edition.* Edited by Rev. Dr. GOOLD. Twenty-four vols. 8vo, Subscription price, £4, 4s.
The '*Hebrews*' may be had separately, in Seven vols., £2, 2s. nett.
Philippi (F. A.)—COMMENTARY ON THE EPISTLE TO THE ROMANS. From the Third Improved Edition, by Rev. Professor BANKS. Two vols. 8vo, 21s.
Piper—LIVES OF LEADERS OF CHURCH UNIVERSAL. Two vols. 8vo, 21s.
Popular Commentary on the New Testament. Edited by PHILIP SCHAFF, D.D. With Illustrations and Maps. Vol. I.—THE SYNOPTICAL GOSPELS. Vol. II.—ST. JOHN'S GOSPEL, AND THE ACTS OF THE APOSTLES. Vol. III.—ROMANS TO PHILEMON. Vol. IV.—HEBREWS TO REVELATION. In Four vols. imperial 8vo, 12s. 6d. each.
Pressensé (Edward de)—THE REDEEMER: Discourses. Crown 8vo, 6s.
Pünjer (Bernhard)—HISTORY OF THE CHRISTIAN PHILOSOPHY OF RELIGION FROM THE REFORMATION TO KANT. 8vo, 16s.
Räbiger (Prof.)—ENCYCLOPÆDIA OF THEOLOGY. Two vols. 8vo, 21s.
Rainy (Principal)—DELIVERY AND DEVELOPMENT OF CHRISTIAN DOCTRINE. (*The Fifth Series of the Cunningham Lectures.*) 8vo, 10s. 6d.
Reusch (Prof.)—NATURE AND THE BIBLE: Lectures on the Mosaic History of Creation in Relation to Natural Science. Two vols. 8vo, 21s.
Reuss (Professor)—HISTORY OF THE SACRED SCRIPTURES OF THE NEW TESTAMENT. 640 pp. 8vo, 15s.
Riehm (Dr. E.)—MESSIANIC PROPHECY: Its Origin, Historical Character, and Relation to New Testament Fulfilment. Crown 8vo, 5s.
Ritter (Carl)—THE COMPARATIVE GEOGRAPHY OF PALESTINE AND THE SINAITIC PENINSULA. Four vols. 8vo, 26s.
Robinson (Rev. S., D.D.)—DISCOURSES ON REDEMPTION. 8vo, 7s. 6d.
Robinson (Edward, D.D.)—GREEK AND ENGLISH LEXICON OF THE NEW TESTAMENT. 8vo, 9s.
Rothe (Prof.)—SERMONS FOR THE CHRISTIAN YEAR. Cr. 8vo, 4s. 6d.
Saisset—MANUAL OF MODERN PANTHEISM. Two vols. 8vo, 10s. 6d.
Sartorius (Dr. E.)—DOCTRINE OF DIVINE LOVE. 8vo, 10s. 6d.
Schaff (Professor)—HISTORY OF THE CHRISTIAN CHURCH. (New Edition, thoroughly Revised and Enlarged.)
— APOSTOLIC CHRISTIANITY, A.D. 1–100. 2 vols. Ex. 8vo, 21s.
— ANTE-NICENE CHRISTIANITY, A.D. 100–325. 2 vols. Ex. 8vo, 21s.
— POST-NICENE CHRISTIANITY, A.D. 325–600. 2 vols. Ex. 8vo, 21s.
— MEDIÆVAL CHRISTIANITY, A.D. 590–1073. 2 vols. Ex. 8vo, 21s.
(*Completion of this Period*, 1073–1517, *in preparation*).
— MODERN CHRISTIANITY, A.D. 1517–1530. 2 vols. Ex. 8vo, 21s.
— THE TEACHING OF THE TWELVE APOSTLES. The Didachè and Kindred Documents in the Original. Second Edition, ex. 8vo, 9s.
Schmid's BIBLICAL THEOLOGY OF THE NEW TESTAMENT. 8vo, 10s. 6d.
Schürer (Prof.)—HISTORY OF THE NEW TESTAMENT TIMES. Div. II. Three vols. 8vo, 31s. 6d.
Scott (Jas., M.A., D.D.)—PRINCIPLES OF NEW TESTAMENT QUOTATION ESTABLISHED AND APPLIED TO BIBLICAL CRITICISM. Cr. 8vo, 2nd Edit., 4s.
Shedd—HISTORY OF CHRISTIAN DOCTRINE. Two vols. 8vo, 21s.
— SERMONS TO THE NATURAL MAN. 8vo, 7s. 6d.
— SERMONS TO THE SPIRITUAL MAN. 8vo, 7s. 6d.
Simon (Rev. Prof. D. W.)—THE BIBLE; An Outgrowth of Theocratic Life. Crown 8vo, 4s. 6d.

T. and T. Clark's Publications.

Smeaton (Professor)—THE DOCTRINE OF THE ATONEMENT AS TAUGHT BY CHRIST HIMSELF. Second Edition, 8vo, 10s. 6d.
—— ON THE DOCTRINE OF THE HOLY SPIRIT. 8vo, 9s.
Smith (Professor Thos., D.D.)—MEDIÆVAL MISSIONS. Cr. 8vo, 4s. 6d.
Stalker (Rev. Jas., M.A.)—THE LIFE OF JESUS CHRIST. New Edition, in larger Type. Crown 8vo, 3s. 6d.
—— LIFE OF ST. PAUL. Large Type Edition. Crown 8vo, 3s. 6d.
Stanton (V. H., M.A.).—THE JEWISH AND THE CHRISTIAN MESSIAH. A Study in the Earliest History of Christianity. 8vo, 10s. 6d.
Steinmeyer (Dr. F. L.)—THE MIRACLES OF OUR LORD: Examined in their relation to Modern Criticism. 8vo, 7s. 6d.
—— THE HISTORY OF THE PASSION AND RESURRECTION OF OUR LORD, considered in the Light of Modern Criticism. 8vo, 10s. 6d.
Stevenson (Mrs.)—THE SYMBOLIC PARABLES: The Predictions of the Apocalypse in relation to the General Truths of Scripture. Cr. 8vo, 3s. 6d.
Steward (Rev. G.)—MEDIATORIAL SOVEREIGNTY: The Mystery of Christ and the Revelation of the Old and New Testaments. Two vols. 8vo, 21s.
—— THE ARGUMENT OF THE EPISTLE TO THE HEBREWS. 8vo, 10s. 6d.
Stier (Dr. Rudolph)—ON THE WORDS OF THE LORD JESUS. Eight vols. 8vo, Subscription price of £2, 2s. Separate volumes, price 10s. 6d.
—— THE WORDS OF THE RISEN SAVIOUR, AND COMMENTARY ON THE EPISTLE OF ST. JAMES. 8vo, 10s. 6d.
—— THE WORDS OF THE APOSTLES EXPOUNDED. 8vo, 10s. 6d.
Tholuck (Prof.)—THE EPISTLE TO THE ROMANS. Two vols. fcap. 8vo, 8s.
—— LIGHT FROM THE CROSS. Third Edition, crown 8vo, 5s.
Tophel (Pastor G.)—THE WORK OF THE HOLY SPIRIT. Cr. 8vo, 2s. 6d.
Uhlhorn (G.)—CHRISTIAN CHARITY IN THE ANCIENT CHURCH. Cr. 8vo, 6s.
Ullmann (Dr. Carl)—REFORMERS BEFORE THE REFORMATION, principally in Germany and the Netherlands. Two vols. 8vo, 21s.
—— THE SINLESSNESS OF JESUS: An Evidence for Christianity. Fourth Edition, crown 8vo, 6s.
Urwick (W., M.A.)—THE SERVANT OF JEHOVAH: A Commentary upon Isaiah lii. 13-liii. 12; with Dissertations upon Isaiah xl.-lxvi. 8vo, 6s.
Vinet (Professor)—STUDIES ON BLAISE PASCAL. Crown 8vo, 5s.
—— PASTORAL THEOLOGY. Second Edition, post 8vo, 3s. 6d.
Walker (J., D.D.)—THEOLOGY AND THEOLOGIANS OF SCOTLAND. New Edition, crown 8vo, 3s. 6d.
Watts (Professor)—THE NEWER CRITICISM AND THE ANALOGY OF THE FAITH. Third Edition, crown 8vo, 5s.
—— THE REIGN OF CAUSALITY: A Vindication of the Scientific Principle of Telic Causal Efficiency. Crown 8vo, 6s.
Weiss (Prof.)—BIBLICAL THEOLOGY OF NEW TESTAMENT. 2 vols. 8vo, 21s.
—— LIFE OF CHRIST. Three vols. 8vo, 31s. 6d.
White (Rev. M.)—SYMBOLICAL NUMBERS OF SCRIPTURE. Cr. 8vo, 4s.
Williams—SELECT VOCABULARY OF LATIN ETYMOLOGY. Fcap. 8vo, 1s. 6d.
Winer (Dr. G. B.)—A TREATISE ON THE GRAMMAR OF NEW TESTAMENT GREEK, regarded as the Basis of New Testament Exegesis. Third Edition, edited by W. F. Moulton, D.D. Ninth English Edition, 8vo, 15s.
—— THE DOCTRINES AND CONFESSIONS OF CHRISTENDOM. 8vo, 10s. 6d.
Witherow (Prof. T., D.D.)—THE FORM OF THE CHRISTIAN TEMPLE. 8vo, 10/6.
Workman (Prof. G. C.)—THE TEXT OF JEREMIAH; or, A Critical Investigation of the Greek and Hebrew with the Variations in the LXX Retranslated into the Original, and Explained. Post 8vo, 9s.
Wright (C. H., D.D.)—BIBLICAL ESSAYS. Crown 8vo, 5s.
Wuttke (Professor)—CHRISTIAN ETHICS. Two vols. 8vo, 12s. 6d.

www.ingramcontent.com/pod-product-compliance
Lightning Source LLC
Chambersburg PA
CBHW022135300426
44115CB00006B/198